Warman's FURNITURE

Edited by
HARRY L. RINKER

BRANCH COLLECTION
Wallace-Homestead Book Company
Radnor, Pennsylvania

Volumes in the Encyclopedia of Antiques and Collectibles

Harry L. Rinker, Series Editor

Warman's Americana & Collectibles, 5th Edition,
  edited by Harry L. Rinker

Warman's Country Antiques & Collectibles,
  by Dana Gehman Morykan and Harry L. Rinker

Warman's English & Continental Pottery & Porcelain, 2nd Edition,
  by Susan and Al Bagdade

Warman's Furniture,
  edited by Harry L. Rinker

Warman's Glass,
  by Ellen Tischbein Schroy

Warman's Oriental Antiques,
  by Gloria and Robert Mascarelli

Copyright © 1993 by Rinker Enterprises, Inc.

Published in Radnor, Pennsylvania 19089, by Wallace-Homestead, a division of Chilton Book Company

Manufactured in the United States of America

Library of Congress Cataloging-in-Publication Data
Warman's furniture / edited by Harry L. Rinker.
    p.   cm.—(Encyclopedia of antiques and collectibles)
    Includes index.
    ISBN 0-87069-626-2
    1. Furniture—History—19th century—Catalogs.   2. Furniture—
History—20th century—Catalogs.
    I. Rinker, Harry L.   II. Series.
    NK2385.W37   1993
    749.2'048'075—dc20   92-50191
                                                   CIP

1 2 3 4 5 6 7 8 9 0   2 1 0 8 7 6 5 4 3

Contents

Part I   American Furniture   1

Part II   American Vernacular Furniture   149

Part III   American Regional Furniture   213

Part IV   European Furniture   229

Introduction

Welcome to *Warman's Furniture*, the sixth volume to be published in the Warman Encyclopedia of Antiques and Collectibles. Those who regularly use *Warman's Antiques and Their Prices* and the other volumes in the Warman's Encyclopedia series are already familiar with the Warman format—category introductions featuring history, references, periodicals, collecting hints, and reproduction and copycat information complemented by detailed, accurate listings and values. You will find all these features and more in this book.

Warman's Furniture is a pioneering effort. It is the first general furniture price guide to include American, English, and Continental furniture in a single volume. Second, it covers a wide range of furniture, from high–style design period pieces to vernacular furniture built in the barn or basement. Third, its category introductions provide an important summary of historical information about furniture design periods. For many, it will serve as a textbook, a first point of reference, especially for furniture with which they are not familiar. If it accomplishes no other end, it will be successful.

Finally, *Warman's Furniture* is attempting to do what no other furniture price guide has done before—use words instead of pictures to provide information about the majority of the pieces. Hopefully these *word pictures* will be successful, allowing you to imagine the piece being described.

What is critical to understand is that a guide such as *Warman's Furniture* is a **general** price guide. Great care has been taken to ensure that category listings contain descriptions of pieces you are most likely to encounter in the field. However, it is possible that the piece you are researching will not exactly match one of these descriptions. This is to be expected. There is no way *Warman's Furniture* can list or picture every piece of furniture. What you will find is something that is comparable to what you have.

More than any other volume in the Warman Encyclopedia, this book requires you to interpret, use your imagination, and rely on field experience. You can do it. It will be difficult at first and you will make mistakes—everyone does. However, you will be surprised at how well you do with just a little practice.

Warman could have taken the easy road and not included a furniture volume in its Encyclopedia of Antiques and Collectibles series. Other publishers of antiques and collectibles price guides have chosen this safer path. But, this is not Warman's style—never has been, never will be. *Warman's Furniture* leads the way. Let the others follow. Catch us if you can.

CRITICAL FURNITURE TERMS

Confused by furniture vocabulary? So are most individuals. What do words like *original* or *old* mean? Isn't everything original, even if it was made yesterday? When you were twenty, didn't people past forty seem old? Once you reach fifty, people who are less than forty will seem, to borrow a phrase from Gabby Hayes, an old western side kick, like "young whipper snappers."

It is time to end some of the confusion. Toss out *original* and *old*. They are so misused that they are meaningless. It is time to introduce and properly use: *period, reproduction, copycat, style, design, fantasy,* and *fake*.

A *period* piece is a piece of furniture that was manufactured during the time period when a design style was first created or introduced into another country. The latter point is important because in the eighteenth and first half of the nineteenth centuries it often took several years for a design style to move from country to country. The English Chippendale period dates at least fifteen years earlier than its American counterpart.

Once a major design style evolves, it never truly goes out of style. There are always a few individuals who remain attracted to it and want pieces made which follow its principles. Major revivals occur and reoccur.

It is for this reason that attempting to date a piece of furniture simply by characteristics of its design style is dangerous. Instead, one must look at construction techniques and for the appropriate signs of age. If a piece is over two hundred years old, it should look like it is over two hundred years old and not like it was made yesterday.

Likewise, it is critical to understand how the period design was initially interpreted. Viewing eighteenth century pieces through a twentieth century mind set can be very dangerous and costly. It is the quickest way to make a mistake. Furniture size and interpretation have differed significantly through the years. These differences are critical to identifying a true period piece.

A *reproduction* is an exact copy of a period piece. It is made of the same wood, follows the exact same dimensions, employs the same details, and often is made using the same tools. If liberties are taken, they are taken inside the piece—never on the visible surfaces.

Reproductions do exist. Copies were often made of major family heirlooms so that each side of the family could have "great grandfather's highboy." A reproduction often hid the fact that one had to sell a family heirloom in a moment of financial crisis.

Reproductions are not something that have arrived upon the scene recently. Reproductions of colonial period pieces were made as early as the first quarter of the nineteenth century. Many reproductions are now over a hundred years old and show many of the same aging characteristics as the period pieces from which they were copied.

Most of the pieces that are called reproductions are actually *copycats*, stylistic copies of period pieces. Copycats are found in a wide variety of quality. Some are close to being exact copies of period pieces, e.g., a change in wood or subtle design enhancement. Others are a stretch, e.g., much of the Depression era "colonial" furniture.

The key concept is that they feature period design characteristics which allow them to be identified with the earlier period design. Often, as in many of the Victorian revivals and the 1920s Colonial Revival, they mix and match elements from different period designs. In such cases, the pieces are identified by the most prominent period design element.

The major auction houses use *Style* in their catalog descriptions to identify pieces that are "an intentional reproduction of an earlier style." As a result, the appearance of *Style* in any furniture description should set off an alarm bell—check and double check.

Some individuals in the field have suggested that using a small "s" rather than a capital "S" in style is enough to avoid confusion. A lower case "s" would designate the initial design period. Therefore, Chippendale *Style* is a later reproduction or copycat while Chippendale *style* represents a period piece. Given the way many dealers write, it is often difficult to tell whether or not a capital or lower case "s" was meant. The only way to avoid confusion is to use *period* to describe pieces made during the initial design period.

Design is a key concept used to differentiate pieces based on period designs from vernacular (generic) furniture. Vernacular pertains to common household furniture constructed in basic traditional forms, often spanning centuries, which are considered outside the mainstream of furniture design. High–style is concerned with design furniture. *Warman's Furniture* includes both.

Editor's Note: I have tried to be careful to follow the proper use of *Style* as outlined above in preparing the category introductions and listings. I fear that occasionally I slipped, especially when the phrase "period design style" seemed more appropriate than "initial design period." Read the words precisely. The exact meaning should be clear.

A *fantasy* piece is a form that never existed during the initial design period but which was later manufactured during a revival and featured design characteristics of the initial design period. A good example is a Chippendale coffee table. There were no Chippendale coffee tables in the eighteenth century. The form did not exist. However, Chippendale coffee tables, dating from the 1920s onward, abound. There is nothing wrong with a fantasy piece, just recognize it for what it is.

A *fake* is a piece that is deliberately meant to deceive. Furniture faking is a long established tradition, one with strong nineteenth century roots. There never has been enough antique furniture to meet the demand. Fakes help fill the need.

The problem with fakes is that there is a gray area. Older pieces that have been altered to make them appear even older and pieces made up from old parts are not viewed by many as fakes. These pieces, just as reproductions and copycats, were created primarily for the "look."

The intent to deceive is the key. If a reproduction, copycat, altered piece, piece made up of old parts, or a fake is properly presented for what it is, there is no problem. Unfortunately, far too many of these pieces are offered for sale as period originals.

For this reason, it is critical, when buying a piece of furniture, to have the dealer indicate the time span during which he believes the piece was made. Do not accept a spread of greater than twenty–five years. If you have any doubts, have the piece authenticated by an independent researcher, e.g., museum curator. Do not use another dealer. There is an unwritten code to protect the initial dealer whenever possible. If the authentication process establishes that the piece has been misdated, take it back and demand a refund. If the seller refuses, you have grounds for a law-suit based on fraud.

The above terms all assume the piece remains initially as made. What about repairs, restorations, and reconstruction? How do these affect the integrity of a piece? There is little agreement between collectors and dealers in this area. Smart individuals follow a conservative approach.

A repair to the visible surface of a piece of furniture detracts from its value—the more noticeable, the more it detracts. Repairs in non–visible areas are acceptable. All antique furniture should show signs of repair, e.g., regluing of joints and repairing every day wear and tear. When you find no signs of repair on furniture over fifty years old, be suspicious.

Restoration is another matter. If you replace one of four legs on a table, is it a major restoration? If you lost one of your four limbs, wouldn't you consider it major? Of course you would. The loss of a leg, replacement of a top or drawer, and reveneering of a surface are all major repairs. Collectors and dealers have been far too willing to downgrade major restoration to minor status. Major restoration lowers the value of a piece twenty–five to fifty percent.

A piece made from old parts is just that—*a piece made from old parts*. It was made for the designer, not collector, market. Yet, because of the scarcity of authenticated period pieces, these reconstructed pieces enjoy great popularity in key segments of the antiques market. While these pieces should sell for twenty to thirty percent on the dollar compared to the value of a period piece, they often realize better than fifty cents on the dollar. The tragedy is that they are often purchased by novice collectors who fail to realize (1) exactly what they are buying and (2) that such pieces have always proved to be poor investments.

ORGANIZATION OF THE BOOK

General Approach: *Warman's Furniture* is organized into four sections—American, American Vernacular, American Regional, and European (English and Continental). These represent the categories by which American collectors and dealers buy furniture.

The American and European sections follow a chronological, period design approach. Major periods, especially when they involve a number of designs occurring simultaneously, have an introduction that shows how these independent designs relate to one another and give the overall period a sense of unity.

The organization challenges some of the traditional notions of furniture design periods. One example is the contention that *Federal* is a term that describes a period of time, not a furniture design style. Another is the assertion that Art Nouveau and Art Deco are fringe, rather than mainstream furniture design developments.

The European section reflects how American collectors and dealers view English and Continental furniture. It is clearly understood that European scholars use a much more sophisticated design chronology. Note that the European categories and listings end around 1920. This is due to the lack of reliable sale and price information for later pieces. Because *Warman's Furniture* is designed to reflect what is happening in the American, not world, marketplace, the use of European sales information was considered inappropriate.

There are some obvious weaknesses in this first edition of *Warman's Furniture*. They deserve to be pointed out, if for no other reason than they offer opportunities for growth in future editions of this book. First, the categories in American regional furniture merely scratch the surface. One of the key developments of the 1990s in the furniture sector is the premium paid for regional pieces within the region in which they were created. Unfortunately, many of these pieces change hands at small auction houses and shows where it is very difficult to document sales. Second, the European section concentrates exclusively on English, French, and German furniture. Spanish, Italian, and other European period furniture is sold and collected in the United States, but buyers and pieces are few. Third, entire geographic regions are ignored—South America, Africa, and Asia. Those seeking information about Asian furniture pieces should consult Gloria and Robert Mascarelli's *Warman's Oriental Antiques*, another volume in the Warman Encyclopedia series.

History: The principal purpose of the history is to provide information on the historical evolution of a period design, identify the design elements that are characteristic of that period, note favored woods, introduce the leading designers and manufacturers, and, where applicable, discuss regional variations. Where appropriate, collecting hints have been added. They range from clues for spotting reproductions and copycats to understanding how collectors view the desirability of a specific design period.

Since this book is a general price guide, users are advised to read one or more books dealing with the historical evolution of architecture to become familiar with design characteristics of Baroque and Rococo, two design periods which influenced a large number of later furniture designs. *This book has been prepared with the assumption that its users have a basic knowledge of design periods and forms.*

Reading the category histories each time you are researching a piece is a habit worth establishing. Learning to properly identify design periods requires continuous study. In most cases, you will reinforce what you already know. Hopefully, what you think you know will be challenged occasionally.

Style Books: Many of the major furniture design periods were documented in style books. These books were eagerly bought by cabinetmakers and manufacturers around the world. Until the twentieth century, they were the major vehicle for the dissemination of furniture design.

Many of these furniture design books have been reprinted and are well worth the investment. The key is to not look at them once and then place them on a shelf, but to examine them at least twice a year.

Major Craftsmen or Manufacturers: Furniture value is increased if a piece can be attributed to a major craftsman or manufacturer. While the major craftsmen of the eighteenth and nineteenth centuries are known to most collectors, the major manufacturers of the late nineteenth and twentieth centuries are not. This needs to be changed. An American collector who is unfamiliar with Berkey and Gay, Kittinger, Herman Miller, or Knoll is at a distinct disadvantage.

These names are but a starting point. The next step is to seek out books and catalogs that identify pieces by these manufacturers so that you know the products and quality levels at which they worked. This is not easy. The literature is spare. Hopefully, this will change significantly in the next decade.

References: A few general references are listed which include author, title, most recent edition, publisher (if published by a small firm or individual, "published by author" is used), and a date of publication.

General references are found in the introductions to the four sections and in each introduction within these sections. The number of specific references are few. Far too often, they are catalog resumes of the holdings of a specific museum collection. Articles on specific design periods have appeared in specialized journals. Because of the general inavailability of these later volumes, they are not listed. The best bibliography to American furniture is found in Milo Naeve's *Identifying American Furniture: A Pictorial Guide to Styles and Terms, Colonial to Contemporary, Second Edition,* (American Association for State and Local History: 1989).

Finding the books listed may present a problem. The antiques and collectibles field is blessed with a dedicated core of book dealers who stock these specialized publications. You will find them at flea markets, malls, antiques shows, and through their advertisements in leading publications in the field. Many dealers publish annual or semi–annual catalogs. Ask to be put on their mailing lists. Books go out–of–print quickly. Some have been reprinted. Do not forget to haunt the used book dealers in your area for these critical reference sources.

Periodicals: There are no general periodicals devoted exclusively to antique or collectible furniture. The major trade papers report regularly on auctions and shows where furniture is sold. They are a good source of pricing information, although their descriptions of the pieces leave a great deal to be desired. Two papers that deserve special mention are:

Antique Week, P. O. Box 90, Knightstown, IN 46148.
Maine Antique Digest, P. O. Box 358, Waldoboro, ME 04572.

The best sources for documenting the sale of antique and collectible furniture in the American market are the auction catalogs from America's leading auction houses. Find the houses that sell the types of furniture in which you are interested and invest the money in their catalogs. Make sure the catalogs include the sale price of the items, otherwise they are worthless.

Transferring the prices from the "prices realized" sheet to the catalog forces you to concentrate on the pieces that sold, how much they sold for, and the pieces that did not sell. Learn to analyze the results. Ask yourself what each price means. Mentally compare these prices to those you have seen elsewhere.

Finally, do not ignore the catalog once your initial review is completed. Refer back to it occasionally. This will allow you to keep a historical perspective on market development.

Listings: We have attempted to make the listings descriptive enough so the specific object can be identified. Most guides limit their descriptions to one line, but not those with the name *Warman's* in the title. We have placed emphasis on those items which are actively being sold in the marketplace. Nevertheless, some harder–to–find objects are included in order to demonstrate the market spread.

Several of the listings are divided into more than one section. In most cases, this is to separate period pieces from other pieces such as those that are heavily restored, made up from old parts, or stylistic copies. A heavily restored Chippendale desk, a Hepplewhite sideboard made from the parts of other sideboards, or a stylistic copy of an Empire sofa serve as important pricing and collecting comparisons when they appear in the period design category. Pay close attention to these subdivisions with a category so that you fully understand why a piece that may sound great is not priced as high as you might have thought.

Warman's Furniture is not the only Warman title in which you will find furniture listed, and every effort has been made to avoid duplication of pieces. As a result, your furniture data base will be greatly expanded if you include other Warman titles in your library.

Illustrations: You will note that the illustrations which appear in *Warman's Furniture* are larger in size than those in other Warman titles. This has been done to allow you to study furniture details which are important to understanding design period characteristics.

Likewise, the captions contain much more information. Normally, Warman captions do not describe what you can see with your eyes—that would be redundant. The expanded descriptions will assist you in learning how to describe a piece of furniture. Read each caption carefully as you examine the illustration. In almost every case, the piece is described from top to bottom.

Reading and re–reading the illustration captions will strengthen your furniture vocabulary. However, like any foreign language, perfection only comes from practice. As you examine your own collection, visit a museum, attend a flea market, mall, shop, or show, prepare a mental description of the pieces you see. Check labels and tags to see how you did. Do not always assume that the person who made the label or tag is correct. They may know less than you. When in doubt, ask questions.

PRICE NOTES

Most prices within furniture are relatively stable, which is why this book has a "one price" system. When necessary, ranges are employed. But, as you will see, this is a rarity.

Pricing is based on an object being in very good condition. If otherwise, this is noted in the description. There are a large number of such notations in this book. This is as it should be. Furniture was designed to be used. Very little was purely decorative. It would be unrealistic to suggest that mint or unused furniture survived in quantity. Furthermore, do not forget the simple process of aging. Aging changes a piece, often causing damage such as cracking.

Prices ignore normal wear and tear. This is a given when dealing with furniture. However, an assumption is made that the pieces received regular care and maintenance thus minimizing the visual effect of such wear and tear. Beware when regular wear is too readily apparent on a piece. This is a favorite trick of the fakers.

The prices in this book are collector prices, not decorator prices. Furniture sold to decorators for their clients is often sold at a premium price significantly above the fair market price. While there may be a willing buyer and seller in such sales, there is rarely equal knowledge on both sides. The person most in the dark is the one paying the decorator for their services and advice.

Some furniture holds regional interest. However, a national price consensus has formed as a result of the publication of specialized price guides, collectors' club newsletters, and magazines and newspapers. Regional pricing is discounted in favor of the more general national consensus.

RESEARCH

Few collectors and dealers engage in furniture research. The principal reason is that much of the furniture sold in the antiques and collectibles market is actually sold for reuse. Furniture is frequently bought more for its appearance than its investment value. It is for this reason that those few individuals engaged in researching the history of furniture design and manufacture deserve the highest praise for their efforts.

Prices come from many key sources—dealers, publications, auctions, collectors, and field work. The generosity with which auction houses and furniture dealers have given advice is a credit to the field. Everyone recognizes the need for a guide that is specific and has accurate prices. Many of the listings resulted from coverage found in magazines, newsletters, and other publications in the collectibles and antiques field ranging from auction and show reviews to advertisements.

The staff of Rinker Enterprises, Inc., is constantly in the field—from Massachusetts to Florida, Pennsylvania to California. We utilize a Board of Advisors that provides regional as well as specialized information. Each *Warman's* title incorporates information from hundreds of auction catalogs generously furnished by the firms listed in the *Auction House* section. Finally, private collectors have worked closely with us, sharing their knowledge of price trends and developments unique to their specialties.

BUYER'S GUIDE, NOT SELLER'S GUIDE

Warman's Furniture is designed to be a buyer's guide, a guide to what you would have to pay to purchase an object on the open market from a dealer or collector. **It is not a seller's guide to prices.** People frequently make this mistake and are deceiving themselves by doing so.

If you have an object which is listed in this book and you wish to sell it, you should expect to receive approximately 35% to 40% of the value listed. If the object cannot be resold quickly, expect to receive even less. The truth is simple. Knowing to whom to sell an object is worth 50% or more of its value. Buyers are very specialized; dealers work for years to assemble a list of collectors who will pay top dollar for an item.

Examine your piece as objectively as possible. If it is something from your childhood, try to step back from the personal memories in evaluating its condition. As an antiques appraiser, I spend a great deal of my time telling people their treasures are not "gold," but items readily available in the marketplace.

In respect to buying and selling, a simple philosophy is that a good purchase occurs when both the buyer and seller are happy with the price. Don't look back. Hindsight has little value in the antiques and collectibles field. Given time, things tend to balance out.

COMMENTS INVITED

Warman's Furniture is a major effort to deal with a complex field. Our readers are encouraged to send their comments and suggestions to Rinker Enterprises, Inc., 5093 Vera Cruz Road, Emmaus, PA 18049.

Auction Houses

The following auction houses cooperate with Rinker Enterprises, Inc., by providing catalogs of their auctions and price lists. This information is used to prepare *Warman's Antiques and Their Prices*, volumes in the Warman's Encyclopedia of Antiques and Collectibles, such as *Warman's Furniture*, and Wallace–Homestead Book Company publications. This support is most appreciated.

Sanford Alderfer Auction
 Company
501 Fairgrounds Rd.
Hatfield, PA 19440
(215) 368-5477

Andre Ammelounx
P. O. Box 136
Palatine, IL 60078
(708) 991-5927

Al Anderson
P. O. Box 644
Troy, OH 45373
(513) 339-0850

Biders Antiques, Inc.
241 South Union St.
Lawrence, MA 01843
(508) 688-4347

Richard A. Bourne Co.,
 Inc.
Corporation St.
P. O. Box 141
Hyannis Port, MA 02647
(508) 775-0797

Butterfield & Butterfield
220 San Bruno Ave.
San Francisco, CA 94103
(415) 861-7500

W. E. Channing & Co.
53 Old Santa Fe Trail
Santa Fe, NM 87501
(505) 988-1078

Christie's
502 Park Ave.
New York, NY 10022
(212) 546-1000

Christie's East
219 E. 67th St.
New York, NY 10021
(212) 606-0400

Marvin Cohen Auctions
Box 425, Routes 20 & 22
New Lebanon, NY 12125
(518) 794-9333

Collector's Auction
 Services
P. O. Box 13732
Seneca, PA 16346
(814) 677-6070

Marlin G. Denlinger
R. R. 3, Box 3775
Morrisville, VT 05661
(802) 888-2774

William Doyle Galleries,
 Inc.
175 E. 87th St.
New York, NY 10128
(212) 427-2730

Early Auction Co.
123 Main St.
Milford, OH 45150
(513) 831-4833

Ken Farmer Realty &
 Auction Co.
1122 Norwood St.
Radford, VA 24141
(703) 639-0939

Fine Arts Co. of
 Philadelphia, Inc.
1808 Chestnut St.
Philadelphia, PA 19103
(215) 563-9275

William A. Fox Auctions,
 Inc.
676 Morris Ave.
Springfield, NJ 07081
(201)467-2366

Garth's Auction, Inc.
2690 Stratford Rd.
P. O. Box 369
Delaware, OH 43015
(614) 362-4771 or
 369-5085

Morton M. Goldberg
 Auction Galleries, Inc.
547 Baronne St.
New Orleans, LA 70113
(504) 592-2300

Grandma's Trunk
The Millards
P. O. Box 404
Northport, NI 49670
(616) 386-5351

Guerney's
136 East 73rd St.
New York, NY 10021
(212) 794-2280

Hart Galleries
2311 Westheimer
Houston, TX 77098
(713) 524-2979 or
 523-7389

Norman C. Heckler &
  Company
Bradford Corner Rd.
Woodstock Valley, CT
  06282
(203) 974-1634

Leslie Hindman, Inc.
215 West Ohio St.
Chicago, IL 60610
(312) 670-0010

Michael Ivankovich
  Antiques
P. O. Box 2458
Doylestown, PA 18901
(215) 345-6094

James D. Julia, Inc.
P. O. Box 830
Fairfield, ME 04937
(207) 453-7904

Charles E. Kirtley
P. O. Box 2273
Elizabeth City, NC 27906
(919) 335-1262

Howard Lowery
3818 W. Magnolia Blvd.
Burbank, CA 91505
(818) 972-9080

Martin Auctioneers, Inc.
Larry L. Martin
P. O. Box 477
Intercourse, PA 17534
(717) 768-8108

Robert Merry Auction
  Company
5501 Milburn Rd.
St. Louis, MO 63129
(314) 487-3992

Mid-Hudson Auction
  Galleries
One Idlewild Ave.
Cornwall-On-Hudson, NY
  12520
(214) 534-7828

Milwaukee Auction
  Galleries
318 N. Water
Milwaukee, WI 53202
(414) 271-1105

Neal Alford Company
4139 Magazine St.
New Orleans, LA 70115
(504) 899-5329

Richard Opfer
  Auctioneering, Inc.
1919 Greenspring Dr.
Timonium, MD 21093
(410) 252-5035

Pettigrew Auction
  Company
1645 South Tejon St.
Colorado Springs, CO
  80906
(719) 633-7963

David Rago Arts & Crafts
P. O. Box 3592, Station E
Trenton, NJ 08629
(609) 585-2546

Renzel's Auction Service
P. O. Box 222
Emigsville, PA 17318
(717) 764-6412

Roan Bros. Auction Gallery
R.D. 3, Box 118
Cogan Station, PA 17728
(717) 494-0170

Stanton's Auctioneers &
  Realtors
144 South Main St.
Vermontville, MI 49096
(517) 726-0181

Robert W. Skinner, Inc.
Bolton Gallery
357 Main St.
Bolton, MA 01740
(508) 779-6241

Sotheby's
1334 York Ave.
New York, NY 10021
(212) 606-7000

Winter Associates
21 Cooke St., Box 823
Plainville, CT 06062
(203) 793-0288

Wolf's Auction Gallery
13015 Larchmere Blvd.
Shaker Heights, OH 44120
(216) 231-3888

Woody Auction
Douglass, KS 67039
(316) 746-2694

State of the Market

The furniture market is complex and highly personalized. Few individuals actually collect furniture. Most buy it to use, often developing one or more room settings focused on a specific design period and, in a few specialized cases, a specific regional design period.

Furniture by the very nature of its form and size limits collectibility. Few individuals have space in their home or apartment for a Federal Neo–Classical dining room table that seats twenty or more. There is a limit to how many chest on chests can fit into a living or dining room. One tends not to have more bedroom suites than one has bedrooms.

Finally, furniture collecting is very much influenced by the current interior design trends. When Country is "in," rural vernacular furniture does well. At the moment, no one design style dominates interior decorating. Eclecticism reigns supreme. The fact that everything is collectible does not strengthen the market, it dilutes it. There is simply too much furniture for the market to be consistently strong across the board. The market is much better when a few segments are running hot and the rest of the market is stable.

AMERICAN FURNITURE

The early 1990s have witnessed a period of redefinition of what American furniture design styles are worth collecting and how value is assigned. As Queen Anne, Chippendale, and Federal period pieces escalated in price in the 1980s, those collectors interested in affordable formal pieces shifted their focus to American Colonial Revival examples. In the late 1980s Arts and Crafts replaced Art Deco as the trendy contemporary collectible furniture design style. As the 1990s progress, Post–World War II modernism designs are challenging Arts and Crafts furniture for dominance.

The recession of the early 1990s ended the upward spiral of record prices for the best pieces of early American furniture. Million dollar plus pieces are now a rarity, not because the quality of furniture offered for sale has slipped, but because buyers are simply unwilling to pay the price. Now when high prices are paid, the seller is more likely to be a major New England, New York, or big city antiques furniture dealer rather than an auction house.

One positive effect of the tight dollar is an increasing demand on the part of buyers for maximum quality for their money. Tough, new criteria are being applied in respect to authenticity and deductions assigned to repairs, replacements, restoration, and refinishing. The value of questionable and highly restored pieces has dropped significantly from their 1980s highs. Further, recent scholarship has shown that reproductions and copycats of early American furniture were being made as early as the first quarter of the nineteenth century. This fact alone has caused a careful re–examination of many previously identified "period" pieces.

Despite the strong Victorian trend in decorating styles, only modest price increases have been noted in most design styles and forms manufactured during the Victorian era. A few "museum quality" pieces have jumped significantly in value, but most prices have barely kept up with inflation

The strongest American furniture category is Colonial Revival, especially the quality pieces from the 1920 to 1940 period. Fifteen years ago, these pieces were nothing more than second hand furniture. Today they are found in antiques shops and shows throughout the country. A ten percent price increase per year for most of this furniture is not uncommon. Suites command premium prices.

Virtually ignored at the moment is post–World War II Colonial Revival furniture. Some of the 1950s Colonial Revival furniture exceeds the quality of its pre–war counterparts, yet sells for half the price because it simply is not "old" enough. It will be eventually. Buy quality, not date when acquiring Colonial Revival furniture. You will not regret this decision in the long run.

Arts and Crafts furniture hit its peak in 1990–91. Although prices are still rising for the rarer pieces, common pieces are experiencing modest declines in value. Many dealers are attempting to prop up the market and maintain the 1990 highs, although their efforts are proving largely unsuccessful.

The decline in popularity of Art Deco has paved the way for furniture from the Modernism and International Modernism eras. At the moment, a clear collecting methodology has not been established. As a result, collectors are not certain what is good and what is bad or what they should collect or not collect. The hot area is the 1950s and early 1960s with emphasis on pieces associated with famous designers and manufacturers. Chrome pieces, especially dinette sets, have attracted attention. This is an area that will see increased activity in the 1990s as writers and scholars provide the criteria by which to collect this furniture.

AMERICAN VERNACULAR FURNITURE

A number of significant changes are occurring in the field of American vernacular furniture as the 1990s progress. First, the decline of Country has significantly influenced the sale of pine and oak pieces. Primitive pieces have been especially hard hit. Do not interpret this to mean that primitive, pine, and oak pieces are not selling. They are—slowly and within a narrowly defined price structure. Oak continues to remain strong in the Midwest and scattered sections throughout the rest of the country.

In the late 1980s and early 1990s an attempt was made to instill new life into Country by touting formal English rural furniture, vernacular English furniture (Welsh cupboards), and bleached pine pieces from southern France and elsewhere throughout the Mediterranean area. The attempt was successful for a brief period, but has currently fizzled due to too many reproduction pieces being passed as period.

Second, a growing interest is being expressed among buyers in the better quality upholstered furniture living room suites made between 1930 and 1960. Prices in California are double and triple those seen in the rest of the country. While there is a strong resistance on the part of dealers to carry this furniture, a few "modernism" dealers are finding that there is a small, but viable market for it.

Third, garden furniture, driven by numerous articles in architectural and interior decorating magazines, received a great deal of attention in the late 1980s and early 1990s. The craze appears to be ending, although prices are still strong. One of the problems is the large number of cast iron garden furniture reproductions from the 1920–40 period that are being passed as late nineteenth century examples. The garden furniture is a very upscale market and restricted to large metropolitan areas.

Fourth, the speculation in Windsor, ladder, and slat back chairs that was popular in the 1980s has ended. Prices have stabilized. The high prices for period pieces have opened the way for a wealth of contemporary Windsor chair makers, craftspersons whose products are as well made as their period counterparts. Collectors who simply want the Windsor "look" are turning to these craftspersons or Colonial Revival Windsors.

Finally, while wicker furniture continues to appeal to a select group of collectors, it also has fallen out of favor with the masses. The principal reason is that wicker became very pricey in the 1980s. In the current tight monetary market, collectors are simply spending their dollars elsewhere.

AMERICAN REGIONAL FURNITURE

American regional furniture is closely tied to the folk art market. As such, it has suffered significantly as a result of the growing distrust of the folk art field in general among buyers. Prices are down twenty to fifty percent over the highs of the mid–1980s.

This is especially true for Shaker furniture. Several 1992 sales brought very disappointing results. A number of media stars who were propping up the market stopped buying. Leading dealers became nervous and bid very conservatively at auction.

A regional Pennsylvania auction house sold a Pennsylvania German painted schrank (*kas* or wardrobe) for over $130,000.00. However, one piece does not make a market. Overall, the price for formal and painted Pennsylvania German furniture is down. One factor is that collecting interest in this furniture remains focused in Pennsylvania and the surrounding states. Pennsylvania German furniture continues to fail to attract a national collecting audience.

Perhaps the biggest decline in prices has occurred in Adirondack furniture. This furniture was the darling of the folk art crowd in the late 1980s. A fickle bunch, they dropped Adirondack furniture like a hot potato the minute the market softened. Be careful how broadly you interpret this trend. Other forms of cottage and rustic furniture are holding their prices and, in fact, are increasing slightly in value.

While the broad categories of regional furniture are in decline, surprising strength has been noted in some "state" related furniture. One example is the record prices being paid at auction in Kentucky for locally made rural pieces. One explanation is increased knowledge of furniture makers and furniture making outside the large metropolitan areas. Look for even more increases in regional "state" furniture in the immediate future.

EUROPEAN FURNITURE

This is a complex market due to the lack of ability among buyers and sellers to differentiate period pieces from late nineteenth revival pieces and twentieth century mass production pieces. Except for a few sophisticated collectors, this furniture is sold more for its look than its investment quality.

One of the most important developments in this area is the number of European dealers who are buying back the European period pieces that were brought to America by collectors from the late nineteenth century through the 1960s. American buyers simply are not prepared to match the prices the European pickers are willing to pay.

The American market is no longer being flooded with container loads of second, third, and fourth rate English and French furniture. Do not imply from this that the flow has stopped. Far from it. These highly altered (often completely faked) refinished goods can still be seen at shows, often sold to novices more interested in look than quality.

Painted European folk furniture is entering the American market in large quantities. Much of it comes from various sections of former East Germany and Slavic countries. Similar in form and decorative design to some American painted regional furniture, it is often passed as American. Be extremely careful. It remains modestly priced, a definite clue that a piece is probably not American.

IN SUMMARY

Furniture collecting in America is experiencing change, more change than has been seen in decades. The recent presidential election is likely to further this trend. During Republican administrations the furniture market enjoys a formal approach. When the Democrats control the White House, an informal approach. Does this mean a return to Country? There is a strong possibility

American buyers still control the American furniture market. How much longer this will last is open to speculation. At the moment, European buyers are focused primarily on buying back their own pieces. However, there already is some indication that foreign buyers are becoming interested in acquiring premier quality American period pieces.

Finally, like it or not, twentieth century furniture, especially that made before 1940, has become a viable part of the "antiques" market. Several key furniture books now use 1945 as the dividing line between antique and collectible furniture. This continues to be a hard pill for the more traditional dealers and auction houses to swallow. For the middle and low range dealers and regional and local auction houses, it remains welcome news.

ACKNOWLEDGMENTS

A book such as this is never the result of one person's efforts. My name appears on the cover and title page, but the final product is a result of a team effort. Credit where credit is due.

First, I want to thank the research staff at Rinker Enterprises, Inc. Ellen T. Schroy, Director of Publications and Research, Terese J. Oswald, Research Associate, Dana G. Morykan, Assistant Research Associate, and Nancy M. Butt, Librarian, contributed significantly, especially in respect to the price descriptions and listings and references cited. You will recognize the names of these individuals from other Warman titles.

Second, this book would not have been possible without a tremendous cooperation from auction houses, show promoters, and individual dealers from across the country who willingly shared information with me. The list is extensive and, inevitably, I would miss someone if I tried to list everyone. As a result, please accept this general thanks from me and my staff for all that you have done.

Third, the photographs are one of the most important elements in this book. Among those who helped supply photographs were: *Antique Week*, Butterfield & Butterfield, William Doyle Galleries, Freeman Fine Arts of Philadelphia, Garth's, Greenup Estate & Auction Company, Leslie Hindman Auctioneers, Neal Auction Company, Pettigrew Auction Company, Gary Richardson, Skinner, Inc. and Sotheby's. *Warman's Furniture* is the first Warman title to note photographic sources as part of the caption information. These credits clearly indicate source so that users can recognize regional pricing trends.

Fourth, Harry L. Rinker, Jr., did the line drawings for the chair back style identification section. Further editions of *Warman's Furniture* will include more of his work.

Fifth, Troy Vozzella, developmental editor at Chilton, drew the assignment of shepherding this first edition of *Warman's Furniture* through the production process. His pleadings and cajoling were met with a "when I get to it" response far more often than he would have liked. His patience is appreciated.

I acknowledge the fact that learning to use a book about furniture that relies heavily on a listing rather than a picture format requires time. You have to learn to convert the written descriptions into mental pictures. You can do it. I have faith in you. Just stick to it.

Any praise for this book should be directed to those individuals mentioned above. Any problems, disagreements, or other forms of disgruntlement should be addressed to me. I alone am responsible for the organization, listing methodology, and the opinions expressed throughout. I have a reputation in the field for saying what I think. However, I always am willing to listen to argument. Since it is highly likely that there will be a second edition of this book, if you have a criticism, constructive or otherwise, send it to me. It will be considered. Send to: Rinker Enterprises, Inc., 5093 Vera Cruz Road, Emmaus (Vera Cruz), PA 18049.

Harry L. Rinker
December 1992

CHAIR DESIGN STYLE IDENTIFICATION GUIDE

The following drawings will assist you in identifying the design style for American side and arm chairs. They serve equally well for period and revival pieces. The number of variations is endless. Yet, within these variations is always the basic design vocabulary. Look for these design elements in other furniture forms as well.

William and Mary

Queen Anne

Chippendale

Sheraton

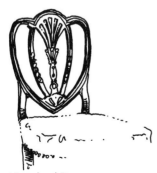

Hepplewhite

Sheraton Fancy Chair

Restauration

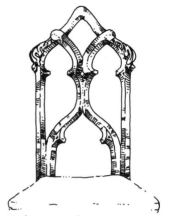

Gothic Revival

Elizabethan Revival

Renaissance Revival

Rococo Revival

Naturalistic Revival

Eastlake

Arts and Crafts

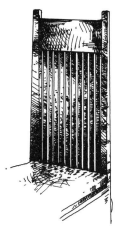

Prairie School

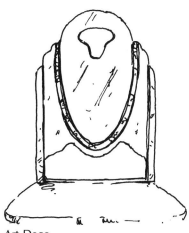

Art Deco

Colonial Revival (Queen Anne)

Colonial Revival (Federal)

Post War Modernism

Windsor

Bentwood

Wicker

George III

Biedermeier

Part I
American Furniture

WHAT MAKES A PIECE of furniture "American?" This is not an easy question to answer. Consider for a moment the situation of an eighteenth–century English master who immigrated to America after serving his apprenticeship, working as a journeyman, and eventually operating his own cabinetmaker's shop for several years. He opens a shop upon arrival in America and starts producing furniture. Is the furniture he makes American or English?

For many American collectors, the fact that a piece of furniture was made in America is enough to qualify it as American. It is time to question this assumption. First, almost all major furniture design styles originated outside America. American furniture craftspeople and manufacturers are responders, not innovators. It was not until well into the twentieth century that American design began to influence the rest of the world. How much can America claim the innovative genius of an Eliel Saarinen, founder of the Cranbrook Academy?

Second, English and Continental designers had a heavy impact on the American scene. Throughout the eighteenth, nineteenth, and early twentieth centuries, Americans looked to Europe for leadership in furniture design. Despite a growing trend toward American jingoism, Americans continued to believe that European goods were superior in design and craftsmanship. In the first half of the twentieth century, many American manufacturers hired the most famous of European designers to develop furniture lines.

Third, Americans did not produce exact copies of European design styles. Instead they altered, changed, and adapted these design styles to create products made "to the American taste." Yet, in every American piece is a design vocabulary and construction methodology that heavily bespeaks European ancestry.

A critical question that needs to be asked is whether these alterations, changes, and adaptations reflect an advance within the basic design vocabulary? The stock American answer is "yes." As long as it is American, it must be better. Sorely lacking in American museums and American furniture literature is a side-by-side comparison of the best American, English, and Irish examples. If done, the results would startle most American collectors and dealers. More often than not, the European examples would be the winners in respect to aesthetics and workmanship.

Throughout the eighteenth, nineteenth, and early twentieth centuries, American furniture design focused on home furnishings. The one major exception was furniture designed for eighteenth and early nineteenth century governmental buildings. Emphasis shifted in the mid–twentieth century. The 1990s American home is filled with contemporary reproductions and copycats of older styles or stock vernacular furniture. The innovative design pieces are now found in offices and public buildings. This institutional furniture is not well understood by collectors. Tremendous collecting opportunities exist.

Collectors and dealers are extremely comfortable with the furniture design styles of the eighteenth, nineteenth, and early twentieth centuries. The furniture literature discusses these styles in detail. These "traditional" categories are well established in the trade and seen regularly.

This is not to say that confusion does not exist. One of the biggest problems among Southern collectors and dealers is their inclusion of a wide range of styles within the Empire label. The bulk of Southern Empire is French Restauration and its later revivals. Likewise, many American auction houses and some literature treat Federal as a major design style. Actually, it is a catchall phrase to pull together a variety of styles, e.g., Hepplewhite, Sheraton, Neo-Classical, etc., that were prominent during the 1790 to 1820 period.

This section of *Warman's Furniture* introduces you to the major formal design styles that influenced American-made furniture. Federal and Victorian furniture have been broken down into their component parts. It is time that American collectors and dealers added a bit of sophistication to their furniture vocabulary.

However, the book's major contribution rests in its categorization of American furniture styles from 1920 through the present. Far too often, furniture surveys end in the late 1930s. Yet, furniture from the post–World War II era is playing a larger and larger role in the 1990s market. It is time to realize that 1950s kidney–shaped coffee tables, womb chairs, and blown–up plastic furniture are every bit as collectible as a Chippendale highboy.

REFERENCES: Joseph T. Butler, *Field Guide to American Furniture,* Facts on File, 1985; Philippe Garner, *Twentieth–Century Furniture* Van Nostrand Reinhold Company, 1980; William C. Ketchum, *Chests, Cupboards, Desks & Other Pieces* (Volume 2 of Knopf Collectors' Guide to American Antiques), Alfred A. Knopf, 1982; Milo M. Naeve, *Identifying American Furniture: A Pictorial Guide to Styles and Terms, Colonial to Contemporary, Second Edition, Revised and Expanded,* American Association for State and Local History, 1989; Marvin D. Schwartz. *Chairs, Tables, Sofas & Beds* (Volume 1 of Knopf Collectors' Guide to American Antiques), Alfred A. Knopf, 1982.

WILLIAM AND MARY (1690–1730)

History: A link between England and the Continent was created through the ascension of William III of Orange and Mary II, his wife, to the English throne in 1689. The dominant stylistic influence of the era was the court of Louis XIV of France, much of whose furnishings incorporated the design elements of Italian Baroque. The designs of Daniel Marot, a Huguenot craftsman in the employ of William and Mary, were copied throughout England and America.

William and Mary furniture features elaborate baluster–shaped turnings, high relief carvings, and color contrasting, often achieved through grained maple and walnut veneers surrounded by inlaid bands. Round or oval feet are most commonly found, albeit the Spanish (actually Portuguese paintbrush) foot was often used as a design element.

The rapidly increasing trade with China introduced an Oriental influence. Japanning, an attempt to simulate Oriental lacquer, was introduced. The use of Japanning continues into the Queen Anne and Chippendale design periods. Baluster turnings and carvings occasionally included an element that resembled the shape of an Oriental vase. Cane imported from the Orient was worked into chair design.

In case furniture, lines were simplified into crisp planes. Case pieces featured flat tops. Architectural trim, such as molding, often was exaggerated. American examples tend to follow simpler lines than their English counterparts.

The cabinetmaker replaced the joiner as the major furniture maker, as evidenced by the elaborate carvings found on the crests and front stretchers of William and Mary chairs. The Baroque influence is readily seen in these carvings.

The favorite American wood of the period was walnut, both in solid form for carving and in burl form for veneering. Maple also was popular as were ebonized finishes. Much of the hardware, e.g., teardrop pulls, was imported.

An emphasis was placed on comfort. Chairs had shaped backs and often were upholstered or caned. The *Boston chair*, featuring an upholstered center backsplat and seat, was popular along the Eastern seaboard. The wing (a.k.a. easy), chair was introduced.

Other popular furniture forms of the period included the daybed, settee or bench, and gateleg table (featuring turned supports and drop leaves), and divided box chests. The highboy (a chest of drawers on a stand), desk (evolving from the bureau–cabinet), tea table, and tall case clock were important innovations, albeit the latter two forms are difficult to find.

Although cabinetmaking centers in America extended from Maine to South Carolina, little period William and Mary furniture has survived. Much of what does survive is heavily restored.

Reference: Phillip M. Johnston, "The William and Mary Style in America," *Courts and Colonies: The William and Mary Style in Holland, England, and America*, University of Washington Press, 1988.

Period: Chest on stand, walnut and marquetry, rectangular molded top, two short drawers over three long drawers, raised on turned legs, joined by scrolled stretchers, 36¼" w, 22" d, 44½" h, $2,500.00. Photograph courtesy of Skinner, Inc.

PERIOD

Blanket Chest, New England, early 18th C, pine and turned maple, hinged molded lift top, two faux drawers over two molded working drawers, turned feet, 39¾" w, 18½" d, 37½" h	**1,760**
Chair	
Arm	
Connecticut River Valley, 1700–20, maple, painted, shaped crest rail with carved incised flowerhead and stylized leafage and finials, back with four split banister uprights, shaped arms, splint seat, turned legs joined by stretchers, one finial restored	**1,980**
Pennsylvania, early 18th C, walnut, shaped crest rail, three molded vertical slats, shaped arms, baluster turned arm supports, plank seat, block and cylinder turned	

legs joined by box stretcher, rear feet pieced, restored seat, 42½" h **58,500**

Unknown, late 17th C, walnut, arched back with caned panels, scrolled arms, caned seat, cabriole legs joined by turned stretchers, distressed caning, 43½" h **200**

Hall, c1710–30, pair, volute leaf carved, and scroll crest rail, turned stiles, turkey work upholstered splat, seats with remnants of turkey work upholstery, turned and scroll shaped legs joined by volute, leaf carved, and scroll front stretcher, turned stretchers, painted, unrestored condition, price for pair ... **3,500**

Side

American, 1690–1710, pair, oak, scroll carved crest rail flanked by turned stiles, baluster finials, three vertical molded slats, recessed plank seat, short baluster turned and block legs joined by turned stretchers, 43½" h, price for pair **6,600**

American, 1690–1710, shaped molded crest rail, molded stiles, upholstered back and seat, baluster and block turned legs, baluster and block turned medial stretcher, H–form baluster and block turned stretcher, Spanish feet **2,500**

American, early 18th C, pair, scroll carved crest rail, lozenge shaped caned back, turned stiles, caned seat, block and vase turned legs, bulbous medial stretcher, block and ring turned H–shape stretcher, price for pair **1,500**

Massachusetts, Boston area, 1690–1720, maple, square back, turned front legs joined by turned stretcher, square back legs, rectangular back and side stretchers, turned front feet, painted black, leather upholstery on back and seat **5,000**

Massachusetts, early 18th C, arched molded crest rail, leather upholstered back and seat, vase and block turned legs, bulbous turned medial stretcher, Spanish feet **5,500**

Pennsylvania, 1710–30, oak, shaped crest rail, three molded vertical slats, rectangular tapering stiles, plank seat, block and short baluster turned legs, baluster and ring turned medial stretcher, two balusters replaced, 38¼" h **8,900**

Pennsylvania, c1710–30, walnut, shaped crest rail, three vertical molded slats, rectangular tapering stiles, plank seat, block and ball turned legs, baluster turned medial stretcher, restored seat, 40" h **650**

Wing, Massachusetts, 1715–30, maple, arched back, out scrolled wings, rolled arm and support, loose cushion, shaped skirt, turned legs, double ball and ring turned medial stretcher, Spanish feet, velvet upholstery **7,250**

Chest of Drawers

American, late 17th C, oak, flat top, two paneled frieze drawers, geometrically molded cushion double fronted drawer, paneled sides, restored turnip feet, 38" w, 34½" h . **3,300**

American, early 18th C, oak, rectangular top with molded edge, two short and three long graduated cockbeaded drawers, bracket feet, restorations and veneer loss, 37" l, 36½" h **1,980**

New England, early 18th C, child's, maple, rectangular top with applied molded edge, molded base with beaded surrounds, two small drawers and two long drawers, turned legs, original brass handles and escutcheons, 25½" w, 15" d, 23½" h **45,100**

New York, 1690–1725, walnut and walnut veneer, two sections: upper section: rectangular top with cavetta molding, three short drawers, three long graduated drawers, brass hand pulls and lock plates; lower section: projected top cyma reversa molding, three drawers with brass hand pulls and lock plates; shaped skirt with side drop pendants, turned legs joined by shaped stretcher, ball turned feet **21,400**

Pennsylvania, 1720–40, walnut, rectangular top with applied cove molding, two short drawers, three graduated long drawers, molded base, compressed ball turned feet, 39⅝" w, 21¾" d, 40" h **38,700**

Chest on Chest, Philadelphia, 1710–20, walnut, two sections: upper section: flat top with molded cornice, two short drawers, three graduated long drawers; lower section: mid–molding above long drawer, arched apron, baluster and trumpet turned legs joined by shaped stretcher, ball feet, ink inscription on top board of lower section "Robert Pascall, Philadelphia, PA," repairs to four legs, two restored legs, 42" w, 22½" d, 61" h **12,650**

Chest on Frame, Pennsylvania, 1730–60, walnut, two sections: upper section: rectangular lift top, deep compartment; lower section: case with two horizontal fielded panels over two thumb molded short drawers, inverted baluster turned legs, ball turned feet joined by molded box stretcher, 48⅞" w, 24¾" d, 40½" h . **5,000**

Clock, tall case, late 17th, early 18th C, walnut, spiral turned columnar supports on hood, molded cornice, putto head spandrels, brass dial with Roman hours and Arabic numerals, waisted case, marquetry inlay, molded base, 12" w, 8" d, 67" h . . . **18,000**

Desk

Massachusetts, probably Boston, 1690–1720, walnut and white pine, walnut veneer facade slant front lid with compass inlay opens to fitted interior, lid supports, three short over two long drawers with herringbone banding, brass hand pulls and lock plates, cyma reversa molding, ball shaped feet **15,250**

New York, 1710–30, gumwood, slant front, rectangular hinged lid, fitted interior with valanced pigeonholes over concave small drawers, split baluster facings, and well with retractable lid, molded base, two short and two long graduated drawers with beaded surrounds, turned ball feet, 34" w, 19½" d, 41½" h . **14,300**

Highboy

Philadelphia, 1715–30, cedar, two sections: upper section: flat top with elaborate molded cornice, projected molded frieze drawer, three short drawers, three graduated long drawers, double beaded molded dividers; lower section: mid–molding over short central drawer flanked by two short deep drawers, ogival arched apron, short baluster and ring turned legs, molded arched stretcher, stained, 42" w, 23" d, 67¼" h **54,250**

New York, 1720, maple, carved decorations, two sections: upper, flat top with molded cornice, two short drawers, three long drawers; lower section: mid–molding, three short drawers, shaped skirt, turned legs, shaped stretcher, ball feet, minor repairs to base, 38½" w, 20½" d, 77" h **10,000**

Kas, Hudson River Valley, 1730–60, gumwood, two sections: upper section: elaborately molded projecting cornice, two hinged paneled doors open to removable shelf interior; lower section: one long drawer faced to simulate two short drawers with diamond molded reserves, ebonized ball feet, replaced feet, 72" w, 28½" d, 80" h **6,875**

Lowboy

American, curly maple, two board top with thumb molded edge, three dovetailed drawers, scrolled apron with drop pendants, applied molding, turned legs, X–form stretcher with center finial, ball feet, two apron drops missing, period replaced brass handles and engraved escutcheons, 30¾" w, 21¾" d, 27¾" h **16,200**

Boston, Massachusetts, 1680–1720, walnut veneer, two sections: upper section: flat rectangular top with molded flaring cornice, two feather banded short drawers, three graduated long drawers within double beaded surrounds; lower section: applied mid–molding, two short deep drawers, one shallow short drawer, deep arched skirt with beaded edge, trumpet turned legs, shaped serpentine flat stretchers, bun feet, 41" w, 22½" d, 66¼" h . **60,500**

Stool, foot, late 17th C, ebonized wood, rectangular top with upholstered wool creelwork, turned feet, H–form stretcher, 20" w, 15½" d, 16" h **1,100**

Table

Dining

Massachusetts, 1710–30, oblong top with cyma molding and two hinged D–shape leaves, frieze drawer with knob handle, block and double baluster turned legs and gate legs, block and baluster turned stretchers, Spanish feet . . **5,525**

Pennsylvania, early 18th C, walnut, oblong top with two hinged D–shape leaves, molded frieze fitted with a drawer on each end, vase and reel turned legs and gate legs, vase and reel turned stretchers, flattened ball feet, restored, 48¾" w, 56" l extended, 29" h . **4,400**

Dressing, Massachusetts, 1710–30, walnut veneer, two deep drawers, small center drawer, X–form stretcher with finial, replaced brass handles, reveneered top, minor imperfections, 33⅜" w, 23" d, 30" h **4,150**

Drop Leaf, walnut, oval top, scalloped apron, block and baluster turned legs, two block and baluster turned gate legs, block and baluster turned stretchers, turned feet, 46" w, 60" l extended, 29" h **3,900**

Side, walnut, oblong molded and calamander crossbanded top with outset corners, rectangular frieze with herringbone crossbanded drawer, cup and trumpet legs, X–form stretcher, compressed ball feet, 26" w, 17" d, 27½" h **1,000**

Writing, late 17th C, walnut, hinged rectangular top opens to writing surface and fitted interior, ends with fitted drawers, gate leg, spiral supports joined with plain stretcher, ball feet, restored, 36¾" w, 14¼" d, 31" h **2,970**

Style: Lowboy, walnut, rectangular molded top, three drawers, turned legs joined by scrolled stretchers, $2,300.00. Photograph courtesy of William Doyle Galleries.

STYLE

Bench, late 19th C, walnut, needlepoint upholstered top, 49" l, 21" d, 16" h . **1,045**

Chair, arm, late 19th C, pair, walnut, high rectangular back, out scrolled arms, pierced and carved stretcher, scrolled feet, 49" h, price for pair .. **1,760**

Chest of Drawers, maple, rectangular molded top, conforming case, two thumb molded short drawers, four graduated long drawers, molded base, turned bun feet, 27" w, 19" d, 41" h **1,200**

Highboy, walnut, straight front, two small over two long cockbeaded

drawers, brass bail handles, escutcheons and lock plates, trumpet form legs, box shape stretcher, bun feet, 30¾" w, 17" d, 47" h **660**

Lowboy, faced walnut, three drawers, turned legs, serpentine X–form stretcher, 33¼" w, 21" d, 29" h **550**

Stool, walnut, square green velvet upholstered seat, turned legs joined by X–form stretcher, bun feet, 18" w, 20" h **357**

Table

Dining, oak, rectangular top, two demilune drop leaves, frieze drawer, ring and baluster turned legs, 84" l, 30" h **1,650**

Tavern, country, 19th C, pine and maple, rectangular top, breadboard ends, recessed frieze, turned legs, box stretcher, 33" w, 22" d, 25" h **1,300**

QUEEN ANNE (1725–1730)

History: The Queen Anne design style revolutionized American furniture. Fluid, curving lines, the Queen Anne hallmark, first appeared in the early 1720s. By 1725 the design style was dominant. Look for curving lines in cresting, vase–shaped splats, and shell carving.

The major design element was the cabriole leg, a Baroque element introduced in England during Queen Anne's reign (1702–1714). Note the lag time, long after Queen Anne's death, in the arrival of the style to America. American Queen Anne furniture actually incorporates design styles from three English monarchs: Queen Anne, George I (1714–1727) and George II (1727–1760). A Queen Anne cabriole leg is somewhat straighter and less delicate than its Chippendale descendent.

Case furniture followed strict mathematical proportions. The overall concept was one of balance. Pediments and moldings were boldly done.

Although the pad and hoof foot was favored during much of the period, the claw and ball foot also gained acceptance. Many individuals make the mistake of associating the claw and ball foot only with the Chippendale period. It was an important design element of Queen Anne furniture as well.

New England's contribution to furniture construction was blocking, using a single piece of wood to form the raised and depressed areas of a case piece.

During the Queen Anne period, the number of desks, dressing tables, gateleg tables, high chests, rectangular tea tables, and side (easy) chairs increased. The slipper chair and circular tilting top table were introduced. Although armchairs, desks with bookcases, settees, sofas, and tall case clocks were manufactured, their numbers were small.

During the early part of the period, cherry, maple, and walnut were the most popular woods. The use of mahogany began around mid–century. Wood preference was somewhat regional in nature with New England favoring cherry, maple, and walnut while Middle Atlantic craftsmen favored mahogany and walnut. Queen Anne japanned furniture usually favors a blue–green ground.

Strong regional characteristics developed during the Queen Anne period. Stretchers survived well into the Queen Anne period in New England. Massachusetts pieces have a strong vertical feel and are delicate in appearance. Newport was known for its carving and blockfront pieces. Philadelphia craftsmen favored the trifid foot. Chair rails tend to be mortised through the back legs. Chair legs are often doweled into the front seat support.

Style Books: Batty and Thomas Langley, *The City and Country Builder's and Workman's Treasury of Designs,* 1740; Matthis Lock and M. A. Copland, *New Book of Ornaments,* 1746. Lock published several design books beginning as early as 1740.

Major Craftsmen: John Goddard (Newport), Thomas Johnston (Boston), Job Townsend (Newport).

References: Joseph Downs, *American Furniture: Queen Anne and Chippendale Periods in the Henry Francis duPont Winterthur Museum,* The Macmillan Co., 1952; Morrison H. Heckscher, *American Furniture in the Metropolitan Museum of Art: Late Colonial Period, The Queen Anne and Chippendale Periods,* The Museum and Random House, 1985.

PERIOD

Bed
    Pennsylvania, early 19th C, low poster, turned and painted pine, head and foot posts with flattened ball finials, shaped headboard and footboard, tapered feet, original rope rails, original green paint, 48½" w, 73¼" h **3,500**
    Rhode Island or Massachusetts, 1740–60, mahogany and maple, tester top, tapered head and foot posts, shaped headboard, cabriole legs, pad feet **5,525**
Candlestand, Pennsylvania, 1750–60, walnut, circular dished tilt top, revolving circular bird cage and compressed ball standard, cabriole legs, snake feet, patches to top, 19½" d, 29½" h **3,575**

Chair, Philadelphia, c1740, walnut, shaped crest rail with volutes, vasiform back splat, flaring arms ending with carved knuckles, balloon shaped slip seat, cabriole legs terminating in web feet, $38,500.00. Photograph courtesy of Freeman/Fine Arts of Philadelphia.

Chair
  Arm
    Connecticut River Valley, 18th C, maple, shaped crest rail, shaped carved splat with cutout heart, arm supports with carved handhold, rush seat, square legs joined with square stretchers, old refinish, 16½" h seat, 36" h overall **4,950**
    Hudson River Valley, 1750–1800, maple and ash, shaped crest rail, solid vasiform splat, shaped arms, rush seat, turned tapering legs, bead and reel stretchers, pad feet **1,760**
    New England, 1730–50, maple and tiger maple, shaped crest rail, vasiform splat, rush seat, turned front legs joined by turned stretcher, lion paw feet, straight back legs joined by straight stretchers, old refinish, 17½" h seat, 42" h overall **2,200**
    Philadelphia, 1730–50, walnut, molded and scrolled carved crest

rail, vasiform splat, cyma curved rounded stiles, scooped arms with knuckle terminals, shaped arm supports, cyma curved upholstered seat, cabriole legs with carved shells and C–scrolls on knees, shaped pad feet, repaired arms and arm supports, rear legs pieced **22,000**

Philadelphia, 1730–50, walnut, shaped crest rail with volutes, solid vasiform splat, flaring arms with carved knuckles, balloon shape slip seat, cabriole legs, webbed pad feet **38,500**

Philadelphia, 1745–55, walnut, serpentine crest rail with flared terminals, vasiform splat, serpentine arms with scrolled handholds, down curved arm supports, removable slip seat, arched skirt, cabriole legs, stockinged trifid feet, slight repair to front left leg and arms **13,200**

Commode, Pennsylvania, 18th C, corner, walnut and mahogany, old refinish, imperfections, 19½″ h seat, 32″ h, $1,650.00. Photograph courtesy of Skinner, Inc.

Corner
   Massachusetts, 1745–60, walnut, U–shaped back, shaped backrest, out scrolled handholds, two vasiform splats, turned uprights, overupholstered seat, one cabriole leg with pad foot, vase and

block turned X–shape stretcher, minor repair to one splat, three rear legs extended **1,980**

Pennsylvania, 18th C, walnut and mahogany, shaped crest rail, three turned stiles, two vasiform splats, upholstered seat, two large rounded drop aprons, cabriole legs, pad feet, old refinish, 19½″ h seat, 32″ h overall **1,650**

Unknown, 1725–50, tiger maple, yoked crest rail, vasiform splat, tapered back stiles, shaped arms with turned supports, legs with vase and ring design, front stretcher, Spanish feet, 41¼″ h . **4,000**

Side
   American, early 18th C, crest rail with rabbit ears, ladder back, rush seat, Spanish feet, 19th C repaint **650**

   American, country, hard and soft wood, yoke crest rail, vasiform splat, worn rush seat, turned legs, bulbous turned front stretcher, duck feet, dark brown refinishing **600**

   Massachusetts, 1745–55, walnut, slightly shaped crest rail, vasiform solid splat, leather upholstered seat, scalloped seat rail, cabriole legs, turned stretchers, pad feet, refinished, 18″ h seat, 40½″ h overall **4,675**

   New England, 1730–60, pair, maple, shaped crest rail, vasiform splat, rush seat, vase and block turned front legs joined by turned stretchers, front Spanish feet, painted black, gilt highlights, price for pair **1,760**

   New England, late 18th C, maple, shaped crest rail, vasiform splat, replaced rush seat, clock and baluster turned legs, carved Spanish feet, dark stain finish, minor imperfections, 17″ h seat, 42″ h overall **825**

   Newport, Rhode Island, 1750–60, walnut, shaped crest rail with center carved shell, vasiform splat, cabriole legs with shell carved knees, turned stretchers, pad feet, refinished, 18″ h seat, 38″ h overall **7,150**

   Pennsylvania, 1745–55, walnut, shaped crest rail with carved shell center, vasiform splat, balloon shaped seat rail with slip seat, volute carved cabriole legs, paneled pad feet, repaired crest rail, restored seat rail, branded on upper edge of seat rail "E McNeely" **3,300**

Philadelphia, 1730–50, pair, walnut, shaped crest rail with center carved shell, pierced vasiform splat, cyma curved stiles, balloon shaped seat rail, slip seat, shell and bell flower carved cabriole legs, trifid feet, restorations to front feet, repaired crest stile on one, price for pair **27,500**

Philadelphia, 1745–55, walnut, shaped crest rail with flared terminals and incised edges, vasiform splat, shaped seat rail, cabriole legs, stockinged trifid feet **8,800**

Philadelphia, 1740–60, pair, walnut, incise molded shaped and arched crest rail, center carved shell, solid spooned vasiform splat flanked by curved flat stiles, balloon shaped slip seat, shell carved cabriole legs, tongued slipper feet, repairs to stiles, 42" h, price for pair **44,000**

Philadelphia, 1740–60, attributed to Savery School, tiger maple, yoke crest rail, vasiform splat, drop in seat, cabriole legs, flat shaped stretchers, trifid feet **27,500**

Wing

Massachusetts, 1740–60, walnut, arched back flanked with ogival wings, out scrolled arms, bowed seat with loose cushion, cabriole legs joined by turned stretchers, pad feet, upholstered **30,250**

Pennsylvania, 1740–60, walnut, out curved wings and arms, cabriole front legs with shell carved knees, square slanted back legs, carved pad feet, 20th C upholstery, old refinish, 15" h seat, 41" h overall **53,900**

Rhode Island or Southeastern Connecticut, 1750–60, walnut, shaped back, out curved wings and arms, patterned upholstery, cabriole legs, turned stretchers, pad feet, old refinish, 16" h seat, 45½" h overall **11,000**

Chest of Drawers

New England, 1740–60, maple and pine, double arch molded case, two short drawers above three long graduated drawers, bracket feet, old refinish, replaced brass handles, escutcheons, and lock plates, 36½" w, 19" d, 37" h **1,650**

Chest on Frame

American, country, walnut, dovetailed case, seven dovetailed overlapping drawers, inlaid initials "M. E." on top drawer, replaced base with scalloped apron, cabriole legs, duck feet, repairs to drawers, replaced cornice, replaced brass handles and escutcheons, refinished, 39" w, 58½" h **1,150**

New Hampshire, 1750–60, flat top with molded cornice, five long graduated drawers, shaped apron, cabriole legs, pad feet, brass handles, escutcheons, and lock plates, missing drop pendants, 38" w, 20" d, 55" h **7,700**

Pennsylvania, 1750–60, walnut, two sections: upper section: flat top with molded cornice, five short and four long graduated molded drawers; lower section: projected molding, shaped skirt, short angular cabriole legs, stylized trifid feet, 43½" w, 24¾" d, 70" h **4,950**

Clock, tall case

Boston, Massachusetts, Robert Peaslee, 1730–40, inlaid walnut, coffered bonnet hood, coved molding, paneled pediment, arched glazed door, cylindrical colonettes, brass dial with Roman and Arabic chapter rings, circular engraved convex disk inscribed "Rob Peaslee, Boston," waisted line inlaid case, arched line inlaid box, line inlaid applied base molding, sweep seconds ring and calendar day aperture, some repairs to case molding, 18" w, 9¾" d, 91½" h **9,900**

Pennsylvania, Joseph Ellicott, 1740–60, mahogany, stepped and molded flat hood, flanking colonettes, arched and glazed door, brass dial with silvered Roman and Arabic chapter rings, inscribed day of month, C–scroll foliate spandrels, polychrome painted scene, waisted case, astragal bead molded cupboard door, bracket feet, side pane of hood cracked, 19¼" w, 87¾" h **24,200**

Corner Cupboard, Pennsylvania, 1745–55, hanging, cherry, flat molded cornice, hinged arched paneled door opens to white painted interior with scalloped shelves, molding on bottom, restorations to moldings, 29" w, 17¼" d, 37¼" h **3,190**

Desk

Boston, Massachusetts, 1740–60, mahogany, rectangular slant hinged lid opens to fitted interior with valanced pigeonholes and small drawers, block front, four graduated long drawers with cockbeading, molded base with shaped pendants, blocked bracket feet, 42" w, 21" d, 43½" h **27,500**

Unknown, early 18th C, walnut, rectangular top over slant lid, fitted interior with compartments and writing area, frieze with sham drawers above two short and two long graduated drawers, bracket feet, 35¾" w, 21" d, 20½" h **4,400**

Highboy, 18th C, carved mahogany, two sections. Upper section: Bonnet top, spiral finials, ornate fan carvings, three short over four graduated long thumb molded drawers. Lower section: One long over three short thumb molded drawers, shaped skirt with turned acorn drops, cabriole legs ending in pad feet, 39½" w, 86" h, $35,000.00.

Highboy
American, maple, flat top, six short drawers, five long drawers, fan carved upper and lower drawer, shaped apron, cabriole legs with

duck feet, refinished, replaced hardware, 32" w, 20¼" d, 73½" h **14,500**

Connecticut, coastal, 1745–55, tiger maple, two sections: upper section: flat top with molded cornice above convex secret drawer, two short drawers, three molded graduated long drawers, projected molding below; lower section: three short molded drawers, scroll cut shaped skirt, cabriole legs, pad feet, minor repair to front leg, 39¼" w, 21½" d, 78¼" h **37,400**

Connecticut, coastal, 1740–60, cherry, two sections: upper section: flat top with projecting molded cornice, five molded graduated long drawers; lower section: one long drawer above three short molded drawers, fan carved center drawer, shaped skirt with center scrolled pendant, cabriole legs, pad feet, repair to rear leg and molding, 43¾" w, 19¼" d, 73½" h **6,600**

Connecticut, 1750–60, carved cherry, two sections: upper section: molded scrolled pediment with pinwheel carved rosettes, center flame and urn finial and pendant shell, three short drawers with center drawer carved with convex shell above four thumb molded and graduated long drawers, flanked by fluted pilasters; lower section: single thumb molded long drawer over three short drawers, center short drawer with carved convex shell, triple flat arched apron with two urn turned drops, cabriole legs, pad feet, several small drawer lip repairs, rear left leg restored, 39" w, 20¼" d, 86¼" h **38,500**

Country, walnut front, pine sides, molded cornice, dovetailed case, seven molded edge dovetailed drawers, scalloped apron, maple cabriole legs, duck feet, original base, refinished, replaced cornice, 34" w, 19½" d, 56" h **4,500**

Massachusetts, 1740–60, maple, two sections: upper section: flat top with molded cornice, four long graduated cockbeaded drawers; lower section: one long drawer over three short drawers, scalloped apron with two drop pendants, cabriole legs, pad feet, replaced brass handles and escutcheons, old dark surface, 39¾" w, 21¼" d, 68½" h **9,350**

Massachusetts, 1740–60, mahogany, two sections: upper section: bonnet top with molded swan's neck cresting center ball turned finial, two spiral turned finials flanking three small drawers below, center drawer with carved fan, four graduated long drawers; lower section: applied molding above frieze drawer, three small drawers, center drawer with carved fan, shaped skirt with carved diamond motif center flanking pinwheels, cabriole legs, pad feet, 39" w, 20¾" d, 84" h **247,500**

Massachusetts, 1745–55, maple, two sections: upper section: flat top with molded cornice, two short and three long molded graduated drawers; lower section: one long and three short molded drawers, shaped and diamond pierced skirt, cabriole legs, pad feet, right foot repair, 38½" w, 22" d, 69" h **15,400**

Massachusetts, early 18th C, maple, two sections: upper section: flat top with molded cornice, five short and three long molded graduated drawers, center short drawer with fan carving; lower section: one long and three short molded drawers, center short drawer with fan carving, cyma shaped skirt, cabriole legs, pad feet, minor patches to drawer lips, 39" w, 20¼" d, 72" h **20,900**

Massachusetts, North Shore, 1740–60, maple, grained, two sections: upper section: flat top with molded cornice, five thumb molded long graduated drawers, top drawer faced to simulate two short drawers; lower section: projected base, two long thumb molded drawers, bottom drawer faced to simulate three short drawers with center fan carved drawer, shaped apron, cabriole legs, pad feet, five knee returns missing, minor wear, 40¼" w, 74½" h **25,300**

New England, curly maple, flat top with projected molding cornice, five short and four long drawers, shaped apron, original supports extend from bottom to top section on back, 35⅝" w, 19¾" d, 68¼" h .. **11,000**

New England, 1740–60, tiger maple, molded flat top, four long and five short walnut drawers, shaped apron, 38¼" w, 21" d, 68⅛" h ... **13,500**

New England, 1730–50, maple, two sections: upper section: flat top with molded stepped cornice, four wide graduated thumb molded drawers; lower section: one wide and three small drawers, brass bail handles, escutcheons, and lock

plates, shaped apron, cabriole legs, pad feet, 39" w, 17¾" d, 63¼" h . **6,600**

New England, 1735–45, maple and pine, two sections: upper section: flat top with cornice molding, two small drawers above three long graduated drawers; lower section: projected base, five small drawers, shaped apron, cabriole legs, pad feet, replaced brass handles and escutcheons, refinished, 39½" w, 20½" d, 68½" h **10,500**

New England, mid 18th C, maple, two sections: upper section: flat top with cornice molding, five long graduated drawers; lower section: projected base, one long drawer above three short drawers, center small drawer with fan carving, skirt with two drop pendants, cabriole legs, pad feet, refinished, traces of early paint, replaced brass handles and escutcheons, 39½" w, 21¼" d, 76½" h **6,600**

Newport, Rhode Island, 1750–60, maple, two sections: upper section: flat top with projected cornice molding, two small drawers above four long graduated drawers, fluted canted corners; lower section: projected base, one long drawer above three small drawers, shaped apron with two drop pendants, cabriole legs, slipper feet, brass handles and escutcheons, refinished, 38½" w, 19¼" d, 71½" h **18,700**

Newport, Rhode Island, 1750–60, attributed to Christopher Townsend, mahogany, two sections: upper section: flat top with projecting molded cornice, three short fitted drawers with wood spring locks, three long molded drawers, three short drawers, projecting mid-molding; lower section: one long and three short drawers, shaped skirt, removable angular cabriole legs, pointed slipper feet, two minor patches to lower case, brass handles and escutcheons appear original, 38" w, 19¾" d, 71½" h . **71,500**

Newport, Rhode Island, Goddard–Townsend School, 1740–60, mahogany, two sections: upper section: flat top with molded cornice, three short and three long graduated drawers, penciled inscription in bottom drawer "Mary P. Murry," inside upper case inscribed "Christopher Townsend, made 1748"; lower section: projected mid-molding, one long drawer above three short molded drawers, center drawer support with incised initials "T B," scalloped apron, removable angular cabriole legs, pointed slipper feet, brass handles and escutcheons appear original, 38¾" w, 20½" d, 71½" h **34,100**

Rhode Island or Connecticut, 1750–60, two sections: upper section: flat top with molded cornice, three short drawers above three long graduated drawers; lower section: projected edge, one long drawer above three small drawers, shaped apron, cabriole legs, pad feet, brass handles, escutcheons, and lock plates appear original, refinished, 46" w, 21" d, 72½" h **8,800**

Lowboy, PA, 1750–70, walnut, molded top, notched front corners, conforming case, thumb molded drawers, scrolled skirts, cabriole legs, tongued trifid feet, old refinish, replaced brasses, 33¾" w, 21¾" d, 28½" h, $13,200.00. Photograph courtesy of Skinner, Inc.

Lowboy
American, maple, rectangular top with molded edge, two short drawers and one long drawer, fan carved central drawer, scalloped apron, cabriole legs, pad feet, 31½" w, 36½" h **1,760**

American, walnut, satinwood inlay, rectangular top with molded edge, three drawers, scalloped apron, round tapered legs, pad feet, 32" w, 19½" d, 28¾" h **2,400**

Massachusetts, 1725–50, walnut, rectangular top with molded edge, three drawers with molded surrounds, shaped beaded skirt with turned pendants, circular tapering legs, pad feet, 33¾" w, 20½" d, 30" h **6,200**

New England, 1730–50, walnut, rectangular top, straight front, one wide thumb–molded drawer over fan carved center drawer and two small drawers, brass bail handles, escutcheons, and lock plates, acorn pendants, cabriole legs, pad feet, 35⅜" w, 20½" d, 31⅜" h **9,020**

Pennsylvania, walnut, top with molded edge and notched corners, four overlapping dovetailed drawers, scalloped front and side aprons, cabriole legs, trifid feet, good old dark alligatored finish, replaced bottom drawer, reset top, 33¾" w, 21¾" d, 28⅝" h **13,500**

Pennsylvania, 1730–50, cherry, rectangular thumb molded top with notched front corners, one long drawer faced to simulate three short drawers above two short molded drawers, fluted quarter columns on sides, pierced and scroll cut apron, scroll cut cabriole legs, paneled trifid feet, brass handles and escutcheons appear original, 40¼" w, 25½" d, 29⅛" h **38,500**

Pennsylvania, 1750–60, walnut, rectangular molded top with notched front corners, one thumb molded long drawer over three thumb molded short drawers, scrolled skirt, cabriole legs, tongued trifid feet, replaced brass handles and escutcheons, old refinish, 33¾" w, 21¾" d, 28½" h **13,200**

Pennsylvania, 1740–60, walnut, rectangular thumb molded top, one long and three short molded drawers, shaped skirt, cabriole legs, trifid feet, slight drawer and two leg brackets replaced, right rear leg repaired, 34" w, 18¼" d, 28½" h . .   **4,400**

Rhode Island, 1740–60, cherry, rectangular top with thumb molded edge, one long and three short molded drawers, center short drawer blocked and fan carved, blocked skirt with shaped lower edge, acorn pendants, removable angular cabriole legs, raised pad feet, 35½" w, 20⅜" d, 28¾" h . . .   **17,600**

Salem, Massachusetts, 1745–55, walnut and figured maple, rectangular molded top with cleated ends, one long and three short molded drawers, shaped skirt with acorn pendants, cabriole legs, pad feet, 33½" w, 20¾" d, 29" h **16,500**

Salem, Massachusetts, late 18th C, mahogany, rectangular thumb molded top with front notched corners, one long and three short molded drawers, center short drawer with carved fan, shaped skirt with turned pendants, cabriole legs, pad feet, 35¼" w, 21½" d, 32" h **50,600**

Unknown, walnut, oblong thumb molded top with notched corners, three molded drawers, center drawer with carved shell and leaf decoration, fluted canted corners, shaped volute, carved skirt, cabriole legs with shell carved knees, stockinged trifid feet, 33" w, 20½" d, 30½" h **4,950**

Mirror

American, gilted convex panel on crest, replaced glass, restorations, 32⅛" h **800**

Country, 18th C, painted black, shaped crest with white, red, and black floral sprigs and flourishes, rectangular mirror plate with matching decoration, slight imperfections, 9" w, 17⅜" h **10,450**

Secretary, Boston, Massachusetts, 1735–50, mahogany, oak and white pine secondary wood, two sections: upper section: scrolled broken arch pediment, three urn shape finials, inlaid band, two arched hinged doors with mirror panels, pilasters on sides, two candlestick slides, brass handles on each side; lower section: slant front hinged lid opens to fitted interior above block front fitted with four graduated drawers and lid supports, brass handles on side, bracket feet, restorations **15,375**

Table

Center

Boston, Massachusetts, 1730–50, walnut, rectangular marble top with shaped corners above projecting molding, apron with pendant on front and back rail, cabriole legs, platform pad feet, marble top with two repairs, restored bracket returns, two piece rear molding construction, 50" w, 26¼" d, 31½" h **52,250**

Pennsylvania, 1740–60, walnut, rectangular top overhangs apron with three short thumb molded drawers, turned tapering legs, pad feet, 62¼" w, 38" d, 29½" h **6,150**

Dining

New England, 1740–60, cherry, drop leaf, oblong top, two rectangular hinged leaves, molded frieze, cabriole legs, pad feet, 41" w extended, 27½" h **2,200**

Rhode Island, 1750–60, maple, rectangular top, two rectangular drop leaves, cabriole legs, pad feet, old refinish, restored, 46¼" x 47¼" extended, 26½" h **3,025**

Dressing

Connecticut, mid 18th C, cherry, rectangular projected top, one long drawer over three small drawers, center small drawer with fan carving, scalloped apron and sides, cabriole legs, pad feet, replaced brass handles and lock plates, old refinish, 33" w, 21¼" d, 32¼" h **17,600**

Essex County, Massachusetts, 1750–60, mahogany and white pine, rectangular top with cyma reversa molding, one long drawer with two brass handles and lock plate above three short drawers, fan carved center drawer with ring handle, shaped front and side skirt, cabriole legs, pad feet with disk below **18,350**

Unknown, oak and elm, rectangular top with molded edge, three drawers, scalloped apron, square cabriole legs with square molded block feet, 29" l, 28" h **3,025**

Drop Leaf

American, cherry and maple, swing legs, pad feet, refinished, 47" l, 27½" h **3,500**

New England, 1740–60, cherry, rectangular top, scalloped apron, cabriole legs, pad feet, 42¼" l, 39⅜" w, 27⅜" h **935**

Pennsylvania, late 18th C, walnut, rectangular top, two drop leaves, cabriole legs, refinished, repairs to top, 48½" w, 19" d, 28" h ... **1,500**

Unknown, mid 18th C, walnut, rectangular top with demilune drop leaves, shaped apron, cabriole legs, slipper feet, 29½" l, 32¾" l extended length, 27" h . **2,035**

Tavern

American, cherry, shaped sides, triangular pad feet, old refinishing, replaced glue blocks, 28¾" l, 27" h **2,500**

New England, mid 18th C, maple, oval green painted top, natural finish legs, duck feet, three new braces under top, 34¼" l, 27½" w, 26¼" h **3,500**

Tea

Boston, Massachusetts, 1745–55, walnut, rectangular tray top, cyma shape projected skirt, cabriole legs, pad feet, old repair

to one leg, 27¾" w, 18¾" d, 27"
h **22,100**
New England, tiger maple and maple, round top, plain frieze with
squared corners forming to tapered legs, pad feet, refinished,
reset top, 30½" w, 24⅝" d, 25¼"
h **3,080**
New England, 1745–55, cherry
and tiger maple, rectangular tray
top, shaped apron with acorn
shape pendants, cabriole legs,
paw feet, 24¾" w, 17¾" d,
28³⁄₁₆" h **27,500**
Philadelphia, 1740–60, mahogany,
rectangular tray top, cabriole legs
with shell carved knees, webbed
pad feet, 31⅛" w, 21⅜" d, 27½"
h **8,250**
Rhode Island, 1740–60, mahogany, rectangular tray top with applied molding, straight skirt with
drop pendants on each side, cabriole legs with collarino midway
down leg, pointed slipper feet . **12,500**

STYLE

Bed, Pennsylvania, early 19th C, pine,
low poster, turned head and foot posts
with flattened ball finials, shaped
headboard and footboard, tapered
feet, painted green, original rope rails
and paint, 48½" w, 73¼" l **3,300**
Chair
Arm, 18th C, fruitwood, crest rail with
molded ears, pierced splat, scrolled
arms, rush seat, bulb and wheel
front stretcher, Spanish feet, replaced rush seat, refinished **2,600**
Set of Six, yoke shaped crest rail, urn

shape splat, shaped stiles, balloon
shape seat rail with slip seat, cabriole legs, claw and ball feet, price
for set **1,800**
Side
Country, 19th C, yoke shaped crest
rail, vasiform splat, turned posts,
replaced rush seat, turned legs,
duck feet, turned front stretcher,
dark finish **175**
Highboy, maple, two sections: upper
section: molded cornice with hidden
drawer, five long drawers; lower section: four overlapping dovetailed
drawers, scrolled apron, cabriole
legs, duck feet, old repairs, replaced
legs and hardware, refinished, 36" w,
68" h **3,400**
Lowboy
Mahogany, late 19th C, rectangular
lip molded drawers, fan carved
center drawer, cabriole legs, pad
feet, 34" w **1,075**
Walnut, carved shell in skirt, drake
feet **1,300**
Night Stand, walnut, rectangular top,
open shelf over one drawer, cabriole
legs, pad feet, 20" w, 26" h **220**
Table
Banquet, Eldred Wheeler, maple,
double pedestal, two additional
leaves, 48" w, 124" l extended,
29½" h **1,600**
Tea, cherry, circular tilt top, vasiform
standard fitted with bird cage, cabriole legs, pad feet, 31" d, 28" h . **330**
Vanity, polychromed, serpentine form,
ivory, red, and blue fleur–de–lis decoration, five drawers with brass handles, cabriole legs, pad feet, 45" w,
20" d, 29" h **525**

**Table, Rhode Island,
c1760, maple, old refin-
ish, restoration, 46¼ x
47¼" open, 26½" h,
$3,025.00. Photograph
courtesy of Skinner, Inc.**

CHIPPENDALE (1755–1790)

History: The golden age of American Chippendale spans from the 1760s and 1770s. Chippendale incorporated three major design components: (1) French Rococo, a refinement of the Queen Anne Baroque, (2) Chinese, and (3) Gothic. From the Queen Anne period came the broken pediment, classical entablature, and pilaster. From the French Rococo came lighter forms, often featuring a fanciful shell or rockwork pattern. The Chinese influence was evident through form and interpretation. Gothic arches dominated chair backs and large case pieces.

This blending of stylistic design components meant that a Chippendale piece might feature a combination of C– and S– shaped scrolls; ribbons, flowers, and scallop shells; Gothic arches and quatrefoils; gadrooning; Chinese frets; acanthus leaves; and a host of other elements from Roman architecture. In addition, the ogee bracket and Marlborough foot appear; japanning continues.

Although mahogany was the favored wood, cherry, maple, and walnut pieces are not uncommon, especially in Queen Anne transitional forms requiring carving. Connecticut craftsmen continued to work primarily in cherry; Newport craftsmen favored Santo Domingo mahogany.

Some furniture forms, e.g., chairs and sofas, continued to follow the Queen Anne design style; others underwent transition: the chest of drawers continued to evolve; claw and ball feet replaced the pad foot found on tester beds; daybeds vanished; and firescreens and looking glasses became fashionable.

New furniture forms included the candlestand, fret–top table with a Chinese motif, kettle stand, Pembroke table, and piecrust top table. The secretary bookcase remained dominant in America, while in England the breakfront was the favored form. Some case pieces featured the *Bombe* front.

Regional characteristics are extremely pronounced. Massachusetts continued in a conservative vein, albeit developing a slender, highly refined cabriole leg. The buttress–top or turreted table is a Massachusetts form. Newport craftsman continued their tradition of bold, high relief carving, often on block front pieces. Connecticut furniture was a blend of the Boston, Newport, and Philadelphia schools with some original characteristics, (e.g. carved sunbursts and pinwheels) added for good measure. The Dutch Baroque continued to temper New York designs.

Philadelphia, with one hundred plus joiners and cabinetmakers, was the center for American Chippendale furniture, producing some of the most elaborate pieces made. Many of the pieces were in the London taste, copied directly from available style books. Philadelphia carving exhibited rich Rococo details. Cartouches often contained a central asymmetrical element. The claw and ball foot was almost sculptural.

Style Books: Thomas Chippendale, *Gentleman and Cabinet–Maker's Director*, 1754 (Revised editions published in 1755 and 1762); William Ince (partner in the firm of Ince and Mayhew), *Universal System of Household Furniture*, 1759–1763; Robert Manwaring, *The Cabinet and Chair Maker's Real Friend and Companion*, 1765.

Major Craftsmen: Thomas Affleck (Philadelphia), Gilbert Ash (New York), Thomas Burling (New York), Chapin family (Connecticut), John Cogwell (Boston), Thomas Elfe (Charleston), John Folwell (Philadelphia), James Gillingham (Philadelphia), Benjamin Frothingham (Boston), Goddard and Townsend family (Newport), Ephraim Haines (Philadelphia), Adam Hains (Philadelphia), Benjamin Randolph (Philadelphia), William Savery (Philadelphia), Daniel Trotter (Philadelphia).

References: Joseph Downs, *American Furniture: Queen Anne and Chippendale Periods in the Henry Francis duPont Winterthur Museum*, The Macmillan Co., 1952; Christopher Gilbert, *The Life and Works of Thomas Chippendale*, 2 volumes, London, Studio Vita in association with Christie, Manson & Woods, Ltd., 1978; Morrison H. Heckscher, *American Funiture in the Metropolitan Museum of Art: Late Colonial Period, The Queen Anne and Chippendale Periods*, The Museum and Random House, 1985; William Macpherson Hornor, *Blue Book, Philadelphia Furniture: William Penn to George Washington with Special Reference to the Philadelphia Chippendale School*, reprint by Highland House Publishers, 1977; Charles F. Hummel, *A Winterthur Guide to American Chippendale Furniture: Middle Atlantic and Southern Colonies*, Crown Publishers, Inc., for Rutledge Books, 1976.

PERIOD

Bed, tall post, curly maple, turned posts, scrolled headboard with poplar panel, original side rails, old mellow refinishing, minor repairs to posts, 60" w, 72" l, 80" h **3,000**

Bench, Philadelphia, settle, slat back, scrolled arms, worn original rush seat, turned legs, original red and black graining, yellow and green striping and floral decoration, 48" l **900**

Blanket Chest

American, 1770–80, curly maple, lift top, two drawers, refinished, replaced hardware, 39" l, 19¼" d, 41" h **250**

American, 1770–90, walnut, pine and poplar secondary wood, dovetailed case, two board top, wrought iron hinges, till, three dovetailed drawers, apron with drop pendant, ogee feet, old finish, replaced brass handles and escutcheons, minor damage, top with minor warp and separation at seam, 50¾" w, 22½" d, 35½" h **2,900**

New England, late 18th C, tall, hinged top opens to well, three drawers, replaced brass handles and escutheons, ogee bracket feet, old dark red paint, imperfections, 37½" w, 18¾" d, 57½" h **3,025**

Bookcase

Maryland or Philadelphia, 1765–85, mahogany, three sections: upper section: dentil molded triangular pediment, plinth with contemporary bust of William Shakespeare, plain veneered frieze; middle: bookcase with double glazed cupboard doors, astragal mullions, Chinoisere pattern, molded base; lower section: chest with short thumb molded central drawer flanked by two similar box drawers, two graduated long drawers flanked by fluted quarter columns, ogee bracket feet, 44¾" w, 25¼" d, 106¼" h **16,500**

New England, 1770–90, cherry, two sections: upper section: bookcase with ogival molded cornice, double diamond lattice pattern glazed doors, eight adjustable interior shelves; lower section: double paneled cupboard doors, fitted interior with compartments and shelves, two sliding drawers, molded base, minor restoration, 65½" w, 18½" d, 98¾" h **8,800**

Cabinet

New York, 1770–90, mahogany, rectangular thumb molded top, two hinged doors faced to simulate four drawers, shelved interior with cutout bottle recess, gadrooned skirt, claw and ball feet, 38" w, 21" d, 35½" h **10,450**

Virginia, 1770–90 walnut, two sections: upper section: removable molded cornice, pair hinged glazed doors, shelved interior; lower section: projected base, two cockbeaded drawers and two hinged cupboard doors, ogee bracket feet, 48" w, 21½" d, 97" h **9,075**

Candlestand

Pennsylvania, 1765–75, walnut, circular tilt top and revolving dished top, bird cage support, tapered compressed ball standard, cabriole legs, snake feet, minor standard repair, 21¾" d, 26¾" h **3,575**

Pennsylvania or Southern, 1770–90, mahogany, circular tilting and revolving dished top, bird cage support, vasiform standard, cabriole legs, claw and ball feet, lower part of standard repaired, 23¾" d, 29¼" h **2,090**

Philadelphia, 1755–65 mahogany, tilting and revolving circular dished top, bird cage support, ring turned and compressed ball standard, cabriole legs, claw and ball feet, 24¼" d, 27¾" h **7,700**

Philadelphia, 1760–70, mahogany, tilting and revolving circular top, bird cage support, compressed ball standard, cabriole legs, snake feet, 22½" d, 28½" h **17,600**

Philadelphia, 1755–65, mahogany, circular dish top, bird cage support, ball and ring turned round standard, cabriole legs, claw and ball feet, 21" d, 27" h **12,000**

Salem, Massachusetts, 1770–80, mahogany, serpentine shape edge tilt top, ring turned tapering standard, arched tripod, molded snake feet, 18" w, 17½" d, 27¾" h **6,050**

Unknown, 1765–75, walnut, octagonal tilt top, ring turned vasiform standard, cabriole legs, molded snake feet, 18" d, 29" h **4,950**

Chair

Arm

Pennsylvania, 1755–65, mahogany, shaped crest rail with central acanthus and volute carved shell, scrolled terminals, vasiform splat, serpentine arms with scrolled handholds, incurvate arm supports, shaped seat rail, slip seat, cabriole legs, claw and ball feet, reshaped seat rail, right arm repair **6,600**

Philadelphia, 1775–85, mahogany, four strapwork slats, shaped arms with scrolled handholds, molded seat rail, slip seat, square legs joined by stretchers **1,375**

Set of four, Pennsylvania, 1755–75, walnut, shaped crest rail with carved shell center and shell carved ears, pierced vasiform splat, shaped skirt, slip seat, cabriole legs, claw and ball feet, price for set **44,000**

Set of six, Massachusetts, 1760–80, mahogany, shaped crest rail with central leaf carved arched reserve, molded ears, pierced volute carved baluster form splat with cutout heart center, upholstered seat, angular cabriole legs, claw and ball feet, price for set   **66,000**

Side

American, 1755–75, mahogany, shaped crest rail with flowerhead and leaf carved terminals centering a carved shell, pierced lattice and volute carved vasiform splat, molded stiles, balloon shape seat rail, slip seat, acanthus and volute carved cabriole legs, pad feet, rear legs with square pad feet **10,450**

Hartford Area, Connecticut, 1775–90, cherry, shaped crest rail, pierced splat, square legs joined by square stretchers, old refinish, 16" h seat, 38½" h overall **1,320**

Hartford County, Connecticut, 1770–90, pair, cherrywood, arched crest rail, pierced vasiform Gothic style splat, molded seat rail, slip seat, square molded legs, H–form stretcher, price for pair **3,575**

Massachusetts, 1750–90, mahogany, crest rail with carved Masonic symbol terminals, pierced splat with carved square and compasses over raised incised rectangular panel of stars, cabriole legs with carved acanthus leaves joined with stretchers, claw and ball feet, repair, old refinish, 16" h seat, 37" h overall   **8,250**

Massachusetts, 1760–80, walnut, crest rail with raked molded ears, volute carved splat, compass seat, cabriole legs, pad feet, refinished, 17½" h seat, 38½" h overall **2,750**

Massachusetts, 1760–80, walnut, raked molded ears and carved volutes, entwined scrolls and pierced splat, compass seat, cabriole legs, pad feet, refinished, restored, 17½" h seat, 38½" h overall **1,100**

Massachusetts, 1760–90, pair, mahogany, crest rail with molded raked ears flanking lobed shell, pierced splat with C–scrolls, molded slip seat, cabriole legs with carved leaf knees, turned stretchers, claw and ball feet, refinished, 16½" h seat, 37¾" h overall, price for pair **11,000**

Massachusetts, 1755–75, mahogany, shaped crest rail with acanthus carved ears, pierced flowerhead and leaf carved splat, molded seat rail, front cabriole legs with carved knees, hairy paw feet, slanted back legs **33,500**

Massachusetts, 1755–65, pair, walnut, shaped crest rail, pierced volute carved baluster form splat with center pierced heart motif, drop–in seat, angular cabriole legs, pad feet, price for pair ...   **16,500**

Massachusetts, 1760–80, mahogany, shaped crest rail with central arched acanthus carved reserve,

Dining Chairs, 1760–80, pair (one arm, one side), carved mahogany, shaped crest rail with central fan carved arched reserve, molded ears, pierced baluster form splat, upholstered slip seat, shaped skirt, cabriole legs with shell carved knees, claw and ball feet, armchair has serpentine arms with scrolled handholds, price for the pair, $15,000.00.

molded ears, pierced volute carved baluster form splat, upholstered seat, angular cabriole legs, claw and ball feet **8,250**

Massachusetts, Coastal Essex County, 1760–80, pair, mahogany, shaped crest rail with leaf carved fan center and molded ears, pierced beaker form splat with diamond motif, upholstered seat, angular cabriole legs, claw and ball feet, price for pair **1,430**

Middle Atlantic States, late 18th C, pair, mahogany, three horizontal shaped splats, upholstered seat, square legs joined by square stretchers, old refinish, 17" h seat, 38½" h overall, price for pair **770**

New York, 1760–95, pair mahogany, shaped crest rail with central carved fan, pierced splat, cabriole legs, claw and ball feet, 17¼" h seat, 38" h overall, price for pair **5,500**

New York, 1760–80, pair, mahogany, shell and acanthus carved crest rail, scrolled ears, pierced and volute carved baluster form splat, molded seat rail with slip seat, shell and bellflower carved cabriole legs, claw and ball feet, price for pair **19,800**

North Carolina, 1765–75, pair, mahogany, shaped crest rail, pierced vasiform splat with stylized quatrefoil design, molded seat rail encloses slip seat, square molded legs joined by H–form stretcher, price for pair **4,675**

Pennsylvania, 1755–65, pair, walnut, shaped leaf carved crest rail with center carved shell, pierced vasiform splat, molded and shell carved seat rail, slip seat, shell carved cabriole legs, claw and ball feet, price for pair **7,150**

Pennsylvania or Delaware River Valley, 1745–60, mahogany, shaped crest rail and splat, upholstered seat, front cabriole legs with paw feet, square slanted back legs, refinished **1,870**

Philadelphia, 1755–65, walnut, incised shaped crest rail with center volute carved shell, volute carved terminals, vasiform splat, molded seat rail with shell carved pendant, slip seat, shell and volute carved cabriole legs, claw and ball feet **9,625**

Philadelphia, 1755–65, walnut,

shaped crest rail, acanthus and volute carved reserve above pierced and volute carved vasiform splat, molded shell carved seat rail, shell and volute carved cabriole legs, stocking paneled pad feet, one front leg return replaced **6,050**

Philadelphia, 1755–85, mahogany, shaped crest rail, pierced splat, upholstered seat, cabriole front legs, square back legs, 17½" h seat, 39¼" h overall **1,870**

Philadelphia, 1760–80, mahogany, shaped crest rail with carved design, shaped pierced splat, molded seat rail with upholstered seat, straight legs joined by straight stretchers, old refinish, 17" h seat, 37" h overall **2,090**

Portsmouth, New Hampshire, 1770–90, mahogany, shaped crest rail with incised edge, pierced vasiform splat with Gothic arch, upholstered seat, square molded legs joined by stretchers **3,300**

Wing

Connecticut, East Windsor Area, 1770–90, mahogany and cherrywood, arched back with ogival wings, out scrolled arms with

Wing Chair, attributed to PA, 1770–90, upholstered, molded front legs, refinished, restoration, 17½" h seat, 48" h overall, $2,550.00. Photograph courtesy of Skinner, Inc.

conical supports, serpentine seat rail with upholstered seat, cabriole legs, claw and ball feet joined by stretchers, needs reupholstering **38,500**

Massachusetts, 1770–90, mahogany, serpentine crest back, shaped scrolled wings, upright outward scrolling arms, front cabriole legs with claw and ball feet, straight back legs, joined by rectangular stretchers, orange upholstery **19,800**

New England, 1760–90, mahogany and walnut, out scrolled arms, front cabriole legs with claw and ball feet and square slanted back legs joined by stretchers, old refinish, 17" h, seat, 45" h overall **12,100**

New England, 1770–90, mahogany, upholstered arched crest back, ogival wings, out scrolled arms, upholstered seat, molded square legs, H–form stretcher, slightly reduced height, side stretcher restored **8,250**

Pennsylvania, 1770–90, mahogany, shaped back, shaped wings, out scrolled arms, upholstered with brass tack trim around bottom, molded front legs, straight stretchers, refinished, restored, 17½" h seat, 48" h overall **2,550**

Philadelphia, 1750–80, mahogany, molded straight legs joined by stretchers, 20th C upholstery, old refinish, 17" h seat, 48½" h overall **3,300**

Chest of Drawers

Boston, Massachusetts, 1755–75, mahogany, oblong thumb molded top, block front with four graduated long drawers, brass carrying handles on sides, molded base, scroll cut bracket feet, 35" w, 19½" d, 31½" h **52,250**

Boston, Massachusetts, 1755–75, mahogany, oblong top with thumb molded edge, block front, four graduated drawers with cockbeading, molded base, blocked bracket feet, 36" w, 20½" d, 30¼" h **19,800**

Boston, Massachusetts, 1755–75, mahogany, oblong top, thumb molded edge, reverse serpentine front with four graduated long drawers, apron with fan carved pendant, claw and ball feet, original brass handles and escutcheons, 40" w, 22½" d, 33½" h **14,300**

Boston/Salem Area, Massachusetts, 1770–90, mahogany, molded top

Chest of Drawers, Philadelphia, 1770–80, carved mahogany, molded rectangular top, reeded quarter columns flanking two short drawers over three graduated long drawers, ogee bracket feet, pierced back plates, $2,500.00.

with shaped front, serpentine front, four long drawers with blocked ends within beaded surrounds, molded base, central fan carved pendant, cabriole legs, claw and ball feet, 39" w, 22½" d, 31½" h . **148,500**

Massachusetts, 1770–90, mahogany and birchwood, oblong thumb molded top, reverse serpentine front shaped case, four graduated long drawers with incised edges, short cabriole legs, claw and ball feet, 38½" w, 20¼" d, 33⅓" h ... **9,900**

Massachusetts, mahogany, rectangular top, block front with four large drawers, brass handles and escutcheons, scalloped apron, ogee bracket feet, refinished, 34¾" w, 18½" d, 30½" h **36,300**

Massachusetts, 1770–90, inlaid shaped top with leading edge, four graduated long drawers with cockbeaded surrounds, original brass handles and escutcheons, short cabriole legs, claw and ball feet, refinished, 38⅜" w, 19¾" d, 34" h **9,625**

Massachusetts, 1760–80, mahogany, rectangular top, reverse serpentine front, four graduated long drawers with cockbeaded surrounds, short cabriole legs, claw and ball feet, old refinish, replaced brass handles and escutcheons, 39¼" w, 22" d, 33¾" h **13,200**

Massachusetts, 1760–80, rectangular molded top, block front with four molded graduated long drawers, molded base, volute carved ogee feet, 43¼" w, 23½" d, 37½" h ...   **10,450**

Massachusetts, 1775–85, oblong bowed top with thumb molded edge, bow front with four graduated cockbeaded drawers, ogee bracket feet, 42" w, 22¾" d, 34" h   **2,750**

Massachusetts, 1770–90, mahogany, rectangular top, bow front with four large drawers, handles on sides, brass handles and escutcheons, claw and ball feet, 39½" w, 24½" d, 32¼" h **5,500**

Middle Atlantic States, 1775–85, mahogany, molded edge on top, serpentine front with four cockbeaded and graduated long drawers, inlaid canted corners, canted blocked feet, 48¼" w, 25¼" d, 36¾" h ...   **13,200**

Newburyport, late 18th C, birchwood, rectangular top with molded edge, four graduated long drawers with beaded surrounds, original brass handles and escutcheons, molded base, bracket feet, maker's label on inside top drawer "Warranted/Cabinet Work/of all Kinds, Made and sold by Joseph Short/at his shop . . . Market SllNew T" ..   **25,300**

New England, 1770–80, maple, molded cornice, six graduated long drawers with incised edges, bracket feet, repair to feet, 39" w, 20" d, 56¼" h **3,300**

New England, late 18th C, maple, rectangular top with molded edge, four graduated long drawers, pull-out dressing slide, ogee bracket feet, 37½" w, 17½" d, 34¼" h ...   **3,190**

New England, late 18th C, tall, curly maple, molded cornice, seven thumb molded long drawers, bracket feet, 40½" w, 17½" d, 65½" h **8,250**

New England, 1770–90, birch, rectangular top, reverse serpentine front with four graduated drawers, replaced brass handles and escutcheons, ogee bracket feet, refinished, 36" w, 19" d, 33" h **4,675**

New England, late 18th C, birch, rectangular top with molding, straight front with five drawers, bracket feet, replaced brass handles and escutcheons, old surface, replaced rear foot, 38¾" w, 19¼" d, 41¼" h   **1,180**

New England, late 18th C, maple, rectangular, top, pullout dressing slide, four graduated long drawers,

bracket feet, refinished, 37½" w, 17½" d, 34¼" h **3,190**

New England, 1770–90, tiger maple, rectangular top, four small drawers, three large drawers, ogee bracket feet, replaced brass handles and escutcheons, refinished, 37½" w, 19⅝" d, 54" h **4,400**

New England, late 18th C, tall, maple, cavetta molding on rectangular top, six graduated drawers, scalloped apron, bracket feet, replaced brass handles and escutcheons, refinished, 38½" w, 20" d, 52½" h .   **3,390**

Pennsylvania, 1770–90, mahogany, rectangular top, straight front with four large drawers, fluted corners on front, ogee bracket feet, replaced brass handles and escutcheons, 38¾" w, 19¾" d, 35½" h ..   **2,475**

Pennsylvania, 1770–90, walnut, rectangular top, straight front with two small and three wide graduated thumb molded drawers, brass bail handles, escutcheons and lock plates, quarter reeded column sides, ogee bracket feet, 37½" w, 22" d, 36½" h **1,700**

Philadelphia, 1770–90, mahogany veneer, rectangular top, serpentine front with chamfered and fluted corners, four graduated long drawers, ogee bracket feet, old refinish, replaced brass handles and escutcheons, 48" w, 25" d, 37½" h .   **23,100**

Unknown, 1760–80, walnut, rectangular top, straight front with two small drawers over three wide graduated thumb molded drawers, brass bail handles, escutcheons, and lock plates, ogee bracket feet, 39½" w, 23" d, 34" h **1,925**

Chest on Chest

Boston, Massachusetts, 1760–80, birchwood, two sections: upper section: bonnet top with molded swan's neck crest with carved pinwheel terminals, three turned urn form finials, three short drawers shaped to top molding above four long graduated drawers; lower section: four graduated reverse serpentine long drawers with cockbeaded surrounds, scroll cut bracket feet, brass handles and escutcheons, 42½" w, 19½" d, 84¼" h **24,200**

Connecticut, 1760–80, cherrywood, two sections: upper section: bonnet top with molded swan's neck crest surmounted with three carved urn form finials, three short molded drawers, center drawer with carved fan, four molded graduated long drawers, stop fluted pilasters on sides; lower section: four molded and graduated long drawers, molded base, scroll cut bracket feet, 39″ w, 20½″ d, 87½″ h **31,900**

Connecticut, 1770–90, cherrywood, two sections: upper section: flat top with molded dentil carved cornice, two short and four long graduated drawers, fluted quarter columns along sides; lower section: molded base with four molded graduated long drawers, scrolled pendants and rope carved molding, ogee bracket feet, 41½″ w, 21½″ d, 77¾″ h **15,400**

Connecticut, New London County, 1760–80, mahogany, two sections: upper section: broken–arch pediment surmounted with three flame finials, central carved fan flanked by two short drawers above four graduated long drawers with cockbeaded surrounds, stop fluted engaged quarter columns along sides; lower section: serpentine front, stop fluted engaged quarter columns on sides, four graduated long drawers, shaped bracket feet, old refinish, replaced brass handles and escutcheons, 44¼″ w, 20¾″ d, 84½″ h **30,800**

Connecticut, 1770–90, cherrywood, two sections: upper section: bonnet top with molded swan's neck pediment centering spiral carved finial, fluted and mounted finial support with turned colonnettes, tympanum with shaped molded panels, four short and three long molded drawers, center short drawer with carved fan; lower section: four graduated long drawers, ogee bracket feet, 41¾″ w, 19½″ d, 86½″ h **8,800**

Conway, Massachusetts, late 18th C, attributed to Jonathon Smith or Elisha DeWolf Jr, cherrywood, three sections: upper section: enclosed serpentine bonnet top with original fluted drum form finials above molded keystone appliques centering shaped circular fan carved drawer, three short drawers below with fan carved center, four graduated long drawers, spiral carved quarter columns; middle section: three graduated long drawers, stop fluted quarter columns along sides; lower section: scalloped projected molding, short an-

gular cabriole legs, pad feet, 37½″ w, 23¼″ d, 83½″ h **110,000**

New England, 1760–80, walnut, two sections: upper section: bonnet top with broken–arch pediment centering flame cartouche, fan carved center drawer flanked by two small drawers, four graduated long drawers; lower section: four long graduated drawers with brass bail handles, escutcheons, and lock plates, replaced ogival bracket feet, 42½″ w, 23″ d, 84½″ h **30,800**

New England, 1760–80, maple, two sections: upper section: rectangular flat top with cornice shell carved center flanked by two small drawers on each side, three larger drawers; lower section: four graduated drawers, ogee bracket feet, brass handles and escutcheons, old refinish, 38¾″ w, 19½″ d, 78″ h **13,200**

Philadelphia, 1755–75, mahogany, two sections: upper section: bonnet top with molded swan's neck crest, three urn and flame finials on fluted plinths, central short cockbeaded drawer with carved concave shell and applied leafage above five short cockbeaded drawers and four cockbeaded graduated long drawers, fluted canted corners; lower section: two short cockbeaded drawers and two long graduated cockbeaded drawers, fluted canted corners, canted ogee bracket feet, 46″ w, 24″ d, 101¾″ h **41,800**

Clock, tall case

Pennsylvania, walnut, molded swan's neck hood pediment, pinwheel rosettes, three brass ball turned and spire finials on fluted plinths, floral fretwork frieze, brass dial, arched glazed door, tapering columns, waisted case, shaped cupboard door flanking quarter columns, cove molding applied to purple panel, quarter columns, ogee bracket feet, seconds and calendar register, signed: C Warner, 21″ w, 11″ d, 91″ h **4,500**

Connecticut, 1770–90, inlaid cherrywood, pierced crest hood, three brass ball and steeple finials, white painted dial with moon phases, arched glazed door, waisted case, scalloped oval inlaid door, fluted quarter columns, patarae inlaid base, ogee bracket feet, minute and date register, 84½″ h **14,300**

Corner Cupboard, late 18th C, two sections: upper section: molded cornice above arched double glazed cupboard doors, three shaped interior shelves, arched chip carved molding with center cartouche, doors flanked by molded pilasters; lower section: molded base with two molded edge panel doors, grain painted, losses to glass, minor restoration, 58½" w, 98½" h **3,775**

Day Bed, New England, 1760–80, mahogany, shaped crest with molded ears, pierced baluster splat, molded seat frame, cabriole legs, turned stretchers, pad feet, 74" l **5,775**

Desk, New England, 1770–80, mahogany, slant front, valanced fitted interior, three graduated drawers, refinished, restoration to base, 41" w, 21¼" d, 42½" h, $3,080.00. Photograph courtesy of Skinner, Inc.

Desk
  Boston, Massachusetts, 1760–80, slant lid opens to fitted interior with three end blocked concave drawers topped with fan carving, central door with carved colonnettes, and compartments with serpentine valances, replaced brass handles and escutcheons, old refinish, 40" w, 22" d, 44" h **9,900**
  Boston, Massachusetts, 1765–85, mahogany, rectangular molded lid opens to fitted interior with drawers and valanced pigeonholes, oxbow front with four graduated reverse serpentine drawers with cockbeaded surround, molded base, fan and volute carved pendant, ogee bracket feet, 42" w, 21½" d, 43¾" h **10,450**
  Chester County, Pennsylvania, late

18th C, walnut, carved slant lid opens to fitted interior with valanced compartments and drawers, three long drawers, fluted corners, scalloped bracket feet, refinished, replaced brass handles and escutcheons, restored base, 38" w, 22" d, 42¾" h **13,200**
  Connecticut, 1770–90, cherrywood, rectangular slant hinged molded lid opens to fitted interior with valanced pigeonholes and small drawers, four long graduated drawers flanked by fluted quarter columns, stylized gadrooned base, ogee bracket feet, some restorations, 35¾" w, 18¾" d, 41" h **4,400**
  Connecticut, New London County, late 18th C, cherry, slant lid opens to fitted interior with small drawers and valanced compartments, four thumb molded drawers, fluted quarter columns, ogee bracket feet, replaced brass handles and escutcheons, refinished, 37¾" w, 18½" d, 42¼" h **4,950**
  Massachusetts, Boston area, 1760–80, mahogany, rectangular hinged lid opens to fitted interior with valanced pigeonholes, small drawers, and center document drawers, serpentine front, four blocked and serpentine drawers, original brass handles and escutcheons, molded base with pendant, blocked ogee bracket feet, 41" w, 21½" d, 42½" h **18,700**
  Massachusetts, 1750–80, cherry, slant lid opens to fitted interior, four drawers in base, ogee bracket feet, replaced brass handles and escutcheons, refinished with mahogany stain, 35¾" w, 18⅞" d, 44" h   **3,025**
  Massachusetts or Rhode Island, 1765–85, mahogany, rectangular top with thumb molded edge, hinged fall front with writing area opens to fitted interior, one long drawer in case with incised edges, molded skirt with pierced leg brackets, stop fluted square legs, 42½" w, 24¾" d, 41½" h **15,400**
  New England, maple, slant lid opens to fitted interior with drawers and valanced compartments, four drawers in base, scrolled apron, bracket feet, replaced brass handles and escutcheons, refinished, 39" w, 19¾" d, 43" h **7,260**
  New England, late 18th C, tiger maple, slant lid opens to fitted interior, three drawers in base, brass han-

dles and escutcheons, bracket feet, refinished, 40½" w, 17¼" d, 42½" h **5,500**

New England, late 18th C, birch, slant lid opens to fitted interior with divided pigeonholes and two tiers of four drawers, four long drawers in base, original brass handles and escutcheons, old refinish, interior blocks and casters added, 39" w, 18⅜" d, 44¼" h **3,000**

New England, late 18th C, curly maple, rectangular top, slant lid with molded edge opens to stepped arranged fitted interior with seven dovetailed drawers, pigeon holes, and center door, four overlapping graduated drawers in base, ogee feet, replaced brass handles and escutcheons, old finish, minor damage, 36" w, 18" d, 41⅜" h **10,000**

New Hampshire, late 18th C, tiger maple, slant lid with shell carved center opens to stepped fitted interior with small drawers and valanced compartments, four graduated drawers in base, scalloped extended apron, bracket feet, replaced brass handles and escutcheons, refinished, 37½" w, 17½" d, 41¾" h **9,900**

Rhode Island, late 18th C, maple, slant lid opens to fitted interior with small drawers and open valanced compartments, varnish stained surface, replaced brass handles and escutcheons, 38¾" w, 19¼" d, 42¾" h **3,930**

Footstool, mahogany, rectangular upholstered top, shaped skirt, cabriole legs, claw and ball feet, 19¼" l, 8¼" h **990**

Highboy

Connecticut, 1755–65, cherrywood, two sections: upper section: flat top with molded projecting cornice, two short and three long graduated molded drawers; lower section: five short molded drawers, fan carved shaped skirt, notched cabriole legs, claw and ball feet, 44" w, 21½" d, 71" h **9,900**

Connecticut, East Windsor, 1770–90, cherrywood, two sections: upper section: molded swan's neck crest with open pierced fretwork ending with carved terminals, asymmetrical pierced cartouche center, two turned finials, three short molded drawers, center drawer with applied scrolling vines, four molded graduated long drawers; lower sec-

tion: one long and three short molded drawers, center drawer with applied scrolled vines, scalloped skirt, cabriole legs, claw and ball feet, replaced cartouche, 38½" w, 18" d, 88" h **143,000**

New England, 1770–90, maple, two sections: upper section: flat top with molded cornice, top drawer faced to simulate five drawers with pinwheel carved center above three long graduated drawers; lower section: two long drawers and one drawer faced to simulate three short drawers, angular cabriole legs, claw and ball feet, 37½" w, 18½" d, 70" h **8,250**

New Hampshire, Antrim Area, 1775–85, maple, two sections: upper section: flat top with molded cornice, top molded drawer faced to simulate five small drawers with fan carved center panel above four long molded drawers; lower section: two graduated drawers above drawer with three applied panels, center panel with carved fan, one drawer with interior penciled inscription "W B Morrill, Manchester, NH," heart pierced scroll cut skirt, angular cabriole legs, pad feet, repaired, 40⅛" w, 20" d, 74½" h **12,100**

Pennsylvania, 1755–65, walnut, two sections: upper section: flat top with molded cornice, five short and three long graduated molded drawers, fluted quarter columns along sides; lower section: projected molding, three short molded drawers, center drawer with carved shell and volute, fluted quarter columns along sides, shaped skirt with center carved shell, scroll cut cabriole legs, claw and ball feet, 42¼" w, 24" d, 66½" h **14,850**

Unknown, mahogany, two sections: upper section: bonnet top with molded swan's neck cresting centering petal carved and spiral carved twisted finial, two short and four long graduated molded drawers, stop fluted quarter columns along sides, projected molding; lower section: one long and three short molded drawers, skirt carved with nine lobed shell, scroll carved angular cabriole legs, claw and ball feet with open talons, 38¾" w, 21¾" d, 85¼" h **5,225**

Lowboy, Pennsylvania, 1760–70, walnut, rectangular top, straight front, one long and two small thumb molded drawers, shaped apron, cabriole legs with shell carved knees, claw and ball feet, repaired corner to top, 35" w, 20¾" d, 28¾" h **24,200**

Mirror

15" w, 29½" h, American, 1770–90, mahogany and giltwood, pierced and scrolled pediment, center carved eagle flanked by shaped ears, rectangular mirror plate with gilt molded frame, shaped pendant flanked by shaped ears, minor repairs **2,200**

19¾" w, 39" h, 1760–80, mahogany, swan's neck crest surmounted with giltwood phoenix finial, rectangular mirror plate with gilt slip, shaped pendant, replaced finial .. **2,640**

20" w, 38" h, American, 1770–90, walnut and giltwood, shaped crest, pierced shell reserve, rectangular mirror plate, shaped pendant with center gilt convex shell **4,000**

21" w, 45" h, mahogany veneer, shaped giltwood crest surmounted by eagle, flower head and leaf fillets continuing down each side, shaped pendant below **2,860**

21" w, 46¼" h, late 18th C, mahogany veneer, scrolled volutes centering giltwood phoenix, shaped crest, rectangular mirror plate with gilt incised liner enclosed by molded frame, leaf and fruit fillets on sides, scrolled pendant **12,100**

22½" w, 43½" h, 1765–75, mahogany, shaped crest with pierced gilt leaf carved reserve, oblong mirror plate with undulating gilt slip, sides with fruit and flowerhead fillets, shaped pendant below **7,700**

22½" w, 44" h, 1775–85, mahogany, shaped crest, rectangular mirror plate with gilt slip decoration, shaped pendant below **1,540**

23¾" h, late 18th C, mahogany veneer, scrolled crest, molded frame with gilt liner enclosing pendant below, reglazed, repaired **660**

24¼" w, 45½" h, American, 1770–90, mahogany veneer, gilted phoenix and liner, refinished and regilted, repairs, reveneered ears ... **800**

25½" w, 53½" h, 1760–70, mahogany, giltwood swan's neck crest with phoenix finial, rectangular mirror plate with fruit and leaf filets on sides, shaped pendant **7,700**

31" w, 61" h, American, 1770–90, mahogany and parcel gilt, scrolled crest with flowerhead terminals with center spread winged eagle, mirror plate with leaf tip carved border within egg and dart border, suspended floral vines on sides, scrolled pendant on bottom **1,430**

33¼" w, 65" h, 1775–85, mahogany, shaped crest surmounted with gilt Prince of Wales feather finial, rectangular mirror plate with fruit and flowerhead gilt filets on sides, shaped pendant below, slight restoration **3,025**

39¼" h, late 18th C, mahogany veneer, swan's neck crest with carved phoenix center, rectangular mirror plate with gilt incised liner, feather carved side arms, scrolled pendant **1,210**

Secretary, Pennsylvania, 1765–75, walnut, two sections: upper section: bonnet top with swan's neck crest ending with carved rosettes, pair of arched hinged doors open to adjustable

Secretary, molded cornice, recessed paneled doors, slant front, fitted interior with valanced pigeonholes over small drawers flanking central prospect door, pullout slides, three thumb molded graduated long drawers, reeded quarter column, ogee bracket feet, $12,500.00.

shelves, small drawers, and pigeonholes; lower section: hinged molded
lid opens to fitted interior, four
molded graduated long drawers,
bracket feet, 37½" w, 21" d, 96" h . . **18,700**
Sofa, Philadelphia, 1760–70, mahog-
any, camel back, upholstered arched
back, out scrolled arms, upholstered
seat with loose cushion, square
molded legs joined by stretchers, 97"
l **2,200**
Table
Breakfast, mahogany, rectangular top
with bowed ends, half round drop
leaves, shaped skirt, angular cabriole legs, claw and ball feet, 31"
w, 35¼" w extended, 26½" h **6,050**
Card
Newport, Rhode Island, 1770–80,
Goddard–Townsend School, mahogany, rectangular top with
rounded edge, molded apron
with end fitted drawer, bracket
square stop fluted legs, 14½" w
closed, 29¾" w opened, 27½" h **23,000**
New York, 1760–70, mahogany,
serpentine top, hinged leaf open
to baize lined playing surface
with candle recesses, conforming
shaped frieze below projected
lower molding, drawer fitted in
back, angular cabriole legs, claw
and ball feet, replaced drawer,
crossbanding on top added later,
28½" w, 14¾" d, 27½" h **8,800**
Philadelphia, 1760–70, mahogany,
carving attributed to Garvan
Carver, oblong top with outset
front corners, hinged leaf opens
to burgundy baize lined playing
surface with carved circular inset
candle recesses and oval dished
counters, conformingly shaped
frieze fitted with single cockbeaded drawer, projecting molding below with central cabochon
carved pendant flanked with interlaced carved motifs, projected
side molding carved with acanthus leaves, C–scrolls, and ruffles, half round turrets with cross-
hatched cartouche, each turret
framed with C–scrolls, ruffles,
and acanthus leaves, cabriole
legs with acanthus leaves, C–
scroll, and ruffles terminating in
bellflower pendant, partial mirrored acanthus carving on knees,
claw and ball feet, 33¼" w
opened, 29" h **1,045,000**
Philadelphia, 1760–80, mahogany,
rectangular top with hinged leaf,

shaped skirt with acanthus leaves
and cabochon carved pendant
center, flowerhead and acanthus
carved cabriole legs, claw and
ball feet, repaired swing rail at
hinge, 32" w, 15⅝" d, 28¾" h . **75,000**
Philadelphia, 1760–70, mahogany,
oblong turret top with outset corners, conformingly shaped
hinged leaf opens to playing surface with carved playing counters, conformingly shaped apron
with fitted cockbeaded frieze
drawer, acanthus carved cabriole
legs, claw and ball feet, 33" w,
16" deep, 29" h **23,100**
China, Williamsburg, Virginia, 1765–
75, attributed to Anthony Hay
Shop, mahogany, rectangular top
with flower and leaf carved gallery
and pierced fretwork, paneled
frieze with blind fretwork center
flanked by scrolled leafage and
flower heads, pierced foliate leg
brackets, flower head, grape and
leaf carved square tapered legs,
flower head carved Marlborough
feet, brass casters, restored gallery
and pierced brackets, 34¼" l, 22"
d, 28½" h **110,000**
Dining
Massachusetts, 1765–75, oblong
top, two hinged D–shape leaves,
arched skirt, angular cabriole
legs, claw and ball feet, split top
with old repair, 27½" l, 44½" w
extended, 28" h **1,650**
Massachusetts, 1770–90, drop leaf,
rectangular top, two oblong
hinged leaves with rounded corners, projecting cyma cut skirt,
angular cabriole legs, claw and
ball feet, restored corners of
leaves, 47½" w extended, 27½"
h **3,850**
New England, 1770–90, drop
leaves with shaped corners,
scrolled skirt, cabriole legs, claw
and ball feet, refinished, 47½" w,
17¼" d, 28" h **4,125**
Dressing
New York, late 18th C, mahogany,
rectangular top, three drawers,
scalloped apron, cabriole legs,
claw and ball feet, replaced brass
handles and escutcheons, refin-
ished, 32" w, 16¾" d, 28" h . . . **19,800**
New York, 1760–70, mahogany,
kneehole, rectangular thumb
molded top with front notched
corners, one long cockbeaded
drawer, two tiers of three gradu-

ated cockbeaded drawers, recessed scalloped hinged cupboard door, acanthus carved
valance, claw and ball feet, replaced feet, 39″ w, 19⅝″ d, 32½″
h **2,475**
Pennsylvania, 1760–80, walnut,
molded top, one long and two
short drawers, shaped skirt with
carved shell, shell carved cabriole legs, trifid feet, refinished,
replaced brass handles and escutcheons, 35″ w, 21″ d, 32″ h . **4,125**

Drop Leaf
New England, 1770–80, cherry,
single drawer with beaded edges
and replaced brass handle,
square legs, refinished, 36″ w,
32″ d, 27″ h **550**
Philadelphia, 1760–70, walnut,
rectanuglar top with two rectangular hinged leaves, shaped skirt,
cabriole legs, claw and ball feet,
46½″ w extended, 42″ l **4,000**
Game, late 18th C, walnut, hinged
top, fitted single drawer frieze,
brass bail handles, square tapering
legs, 38″ w, 29″ h **880**
Pembroke, New England, 1760–80,
cherry, serpentine top, single
drawer, molded chamfered legs, refinished, 33″ w, 33″ d, 28″ h **665**
Side, Philadelphia, 1770–80, mahogany, rectangular top, single drawer
frieze with incised edges, original
brass handle and escutcheon, applied projecting molding below,
square legs, 26¾″ w, 18¼″ d, 28″
h **4,125**

Tea
Massachusetts, 1760–80, mahogany, serpentine top with molded
edge, ring and vase turned standard, arched tripod base, pointed
pad feet, 33½″ w, 33½″ d, 27¾″
h **5,000**
Pennsylvania, 1765–75, mahog-
any, circular tilting and revolving
dished top, bird cage support,
compressed ball standard, cabriole legs, claw and ball feet,
34½″ d, 28½″ h **12,100**
Pennsylvania, 1770–80, walnut,
tilting circular dished top, bird
cage support, ring turned round
standard, cabriole legs, snake
head feet, 32½″ d, 28″ h **6,830**
Philadelphia, 1765–75, mahogany,
circular tilting and revolving
dished top, bird cage support,
ring turned and compressed ball

Corner Cupboard, central Kentucky, c1800, walnut, top portion with strong cornice and two blind cupboard doors featuring four vertical panels (two over two) each with raised rectangular center, serving board separates top section from base featuring two cupboard doors in the same motif as the top, valance shaped apron, simple bracket feet, $7,750.00. Photograph courtesy of Green River Antiques Auctions and *Antique Week*.

standard, cabriole legs, claw and
ball feet, 35½″ d, 29¼″ h **9,350**
Unknown, mahogany, circular tilting and revolving piecrust top,
birdcage support, spiral fluted
standard, acanthus carved cabriole legs, claw and ball feet,
31¾″ d, 28¾″ h **1,320**
Wilmington, North Carolina,
1760–70, mahogany, circular
tilting and revolving top, bird
cage support, bulbous ring
turned standard, cabriole legs,
snake feet, 35″ d, 30½″ h **3,300**

STYLE

Bed, mahogany, carved, four posters,
Drexel, 65″ w, 86½″ l, 67½″ h **700**
Bench, vanity, walnut, needlepoint up-
holstered seat, refinished, 33″ l, 15″ h **450**

Chest of Drawers, mahogany, block front, four graduated drawers, brass bail handles, escutcheons, and lock plates, ogee bracket feet, 34" w, 30" h 550

Chair

Arm, mahogany, shaped crest rail, leaf carved pierced strapwork back splat, salmon upholstered seat, chamfered legs 325

Concierge, 1900–10, mahogany, blue damask tufted upholstered back, loose cushion seat, cabriole legs with leaf carved knees, claw and ball feet 400

Set of six, dining, mahogany, ribbon back, brown velvet slip seat, chamfered legs, price for set 1,100

Side

Mahogany, shaped crest rail, pierced gothic back splat, bird and floral needlepoint upholstered slip seat, cabriole legs with carved knees, claw and ball feet 165

Mahogany, Centennial, side chair, Chippendale style, shaped crest rail, pierced gothic back splat, floral needlepoint upholstered slip seat, shell carved apron, cabriole legs with carved knees, claw and ball feet 385

Cradle, birch, canted sides, scalloped headboard, turned posts and rails, refinished, 37½" l 300

Desk

Country, American, slant front, cherry, dovetailed case and four drawers, beaded frame, fitted interior, bracket feet, old refinishing, 38" w, 19" d, 42½" h 3,400

Lady's, late 19th C, mahogany, four small leaf carved drawers with brass gallery, shell carved hinged front with fitted interior, carved cabriole legs, claw and ball feet, 29" w, 18" d, 45" h 825

Mahogany, tooled leather top, seven fitted drawers, brass bail handles,

Corner Cupboard, Kentucky, 19th C, cherry, simple molded cornice, two blind cupboard doors each featuring a small square panel over a larger vertical panel each panel having a raised center with chamfered edges over two cupboard doors with raised rectangular panel, chamfered sides, simple bracket feet, $2,000.00. Photograph courtesy of Green River Antiques Auctions and *Antique Week*.

Lowboy, Delaware Valley, c1760, walnut, rectangular molded top over straight front fitted with one wide and three small thumb molded drawers, flanked by recessed reeded column sides, shaped apron, cabriole legs with shell carved knees terminating on claw and ball feet, 33½" w, 20¾" d, 28½" h, descended in family of Richard Stockton, a signer of the Declaration of Independence, $20,900.00. Photograph courtesy of Freeman/Fine Arts of Philadelphia.

double pedestal, cabriole legs,
claw and ball feet, 60" w, 36" d,
31" h 1,265
Partner's, mahogany, rectangular top
with gadrooned rim, two wide and
two small thumb molded drawers
on each side, cabriole legs with
carved knees, claw and ball feet,
53" w, 29" d, 30" h 1,650
Highboy, mahogany, two sections: upper section: swan's neck pediment,
straight front with shell carved center
drawer flanked with two small drawers, four long graduated drawers;
lower section: three drawers and shell
carved center drawer, shell carved
apron, cabriole legs, claw and ball
feet, 41" w, 22" d, 86" h 2,090
Mirror
17½" w, 28¾" h, 19th C, mahogany
veneer on pine, shaped crest with
gilded Phoenix and liner, rectangular mirror plate, shaped pendant,
repairs and age cracks 525
18" w, 34" h, mahogany veneer on
poplar, scrolled crest, rectangular
mirror plate with molded edges,
scrolled pendant, repaired 400
26½" w, 54" h, carved and gilt, spread
eagle phoenix cartouche on crest,
leaf and scroll decoration 550
Secretary
American, cherry, two sections: upper
section: projecting molded cornice,
recessed paneled doors, shelved
and three drawers interior; lower
section: fold out velvet inset writing
surface, three graduated drawers,
turned feet, 39" w, 20" d, 78" h .. 1,500
Handmade, fan carved lid, block
front, claw and ball feet, 35½" w,
20¼" d, 91¾" h 2,250
Settee, walnut, shaped crest rail, rolled
arms and seat, salmon upholstery,
chamfered legs joined by stretcher,
59" l 425
Sofa, mahogany, camel back, rolled
arms and seat, salmon damask upholstery, square legs joined by stretchers, 80" l 1,500

Chest, tall, Rhode Island, late 18th C, cherry, molded cornice, six graduated drawers, ogee bracket feet, $4,250.00. Photograph courtesy of Skinner, Inc.

Table
Dining
Mahogany, rectangular, glass top,
pierced fretwork apron, Marlborough legs joined by pierced fretwork X–form stretcher, 79¾" l .   800
Mahogany, oval, gadrooned rim,
two vasiform standard with
carved cabriole legs, claw and
ball feet, one leaf, 43" w, 96" l
extended, 30" h 1,210
Writing, mahogany, green tooled
leather inset top, two drawers,
chamfered legs, 32" w, 19½" d,
29½" h 495
Vitrine Cabinet, mahogany, fretwork
cornice, two glazed panel doors enclose mirror back and six glass
shelves, molded base 750

· FEDERAL

Throughout the eighteenth century, a single furniture design style dominated. This changed
dramatically with the arrival of the nineteenth century, popularly known as the Federal
period. At best, Federal furniture is an accumulation of several major design styles based
upon a neoclassic revival. At worst, the style simply does not exist as a unit. It is for this
reason that trying to lump all American furniture manufactured between 1790 and 1815
under the single label of "Federal" is fraught with danger.

Robert and John Adams, sons of a Scottish architect, followed in their father's footsteps. In the 1750s, Robert traveled to Italy and was struck first by the classic designs of the ancient Roman civilization and second by the desire to unify a structure and its furnishings in a single style. Robert and James Adams authored *The Works in Architecture of Robert and James Adams, Esquires* in 1773. It was a culmination of their design influences, which had become widely known and well respected by the mid–1760s. The classic revival designs of the Adams brothers directly challenged the Chinese, Gothic, and Rococo influences of the Chippendale period. The Adams heritage strongly affected Hepplewhite and Sheraton.

"Revival" is a key word that will appear over and over again when describing nineteenth century furniture. The entire century was one of revivals, and revivals of revivals, a concept which remained strong until the First World War.

Before discussing the neoclassic revival in America, two things must be pointed out. First, American craftsmen and manufacturers continued to make furniture based upon the eighteenth century design styles. Once a design style enters the furniture vocabulary, it never goes out of existence. This point is often lost as scholars and historians classify furniture forms into narrowly defined date categories. The only purpose these dates serve is to tell us when the design style originated, and when it was dominated. None of the dates indicates how long the design style survived.

Second, most collectors and dealers have too late a mental date for the arrival of mass production in America. The simple truth is that the concepts of mass production were in place by the beginning of the nineteenth century. Chippendale, Hepplewhite, Sheraton, and others did not make the pieces that are attributed to them. They merely did the designs; others crafted the product. Further, they rarely made only one. Ten of the same objects made at the same time is mass production, no matter how much the purists would like to deny it.

The neoclassic revival, which provides the basis for the styles of the Federal period, originated in Europe where archaeological discoveries at Herculaneum and Pompeii in Italy were widely reported. European intellectuals as well as ordinary people traveled to the Mediterranean to view the remains of the ancient civilizations.

At first neoclassic motifs appeared as surface decoration on architectural buildings and furniture forms. Two favorites were the Greek key and egg and dart molding.

As the neoclassic style developed in Europe, the shape of furniture began to change. The cabriole leg gave way to a tapered straight leg or a turned leg. Furniture became delicate and balanced.

Inlays of satinwood and other exotic woods appeared as decorative accents. Popular motifs included bellflower, patera, thunderbolt, sheaf of wheat, and vase of flowers. American patriotic symbols, especially the eagle, were included in the design vocabulary.

The Rococo influence, however, was not dismissed entirely. Hepplewhite and Sheraton forms featuring a round, flowing motif were designated as being in the *French style*, a tribute to the influence of the Louis XVI style in France.

The neoclassical design style was brought to America by a new wave of English, Irish, Scottish, and French immigrants at the end of the eighteenth and early part of the nineteenth centuries. They catered to a rising American middle class anxious to have pieces reflecting the latest European fashions.

The dressing table and high chest virtually disappeared as furniture forms. New Federal era furniture forms include the sideboard (huntboard in the South), work (sewing) table, sectional dining table, tambour desk, and fall front chest of drawers flanked by a column on each side.

Regional characteristics became less pronounced, albeit differences continued to exist: Newport lost some of the importance that it held in the eighteenth century; Baltimore rose in importance; Baltimore painted Federal furniture is considered the best of American design; cabinetmakers within each region continued to work in a variety of design styles.

The first third of the nineteenth century was influenced by the neoclassic revival. Empire (Archaeological Classicism) and French Restauration (Late Classicism) are part of the movement. In truth, American preference for the "Federal" look remains a major factor, even in twentieth century decorating.

For the purpose of this book, the Federal era is divided into its principal component parts: (1) Hepplewhite, (2) Sheraton, (3) Greco-Roman, (4) Duncan Phyfe and his copyists, and (5) Country Formal and Transitional. It is important to remember that all these design styles are occurring simultaneously; beginning with the nineteenth century, no design style exists in isolation.

Finally, we have no problem accepting America as a great melting pot. What we need to do is think of American furniture in much the same way. While some pieces were created in the pure design style, the vast majority are mix and match. As a result, we must use the dominant design style to classify a piece of furniture. The independence of American taste gave a level of individuality to furniture that in a few cases virtually denies classification.

Major Craftsmen: Nehemiah Adams (Salem), John Aitken (Philadelphia), Michael Allison (New York), Nathaniel Appleton (Salem), John Budd (New York), Silas Cheney (Connecticut), Henry Connelly (Philadelphia), Edmund Johnson (Salem), Ephraim Haines (Philadelphia), Charles–Honore Lannuier (New York), Samuel McIntire (Boston–Salem), Duncan Phyfe (New York), Seymour Family (Boston–Salem), and John Shaw (Annapolis).

References: Benjamin A. Hewitt, Patricia E. Kane, and Gerald W. Ward, *The Work of Many Hands: Card Tables in Federal America, 1790–1820*, Yale University Art Gallery, 1982; Charles F. Montgomery, *American Furniture: The Federal Period in the Henry Francis duPont Winterthur Museum*, Viking Press, 1966.

HEPPLEWHITE (1790–1810)

History: Hepplewhite was strongly influenced by the designs of Robert and James Adams. Among the design elements most associated with him are the shield and oval back chairs, splayed curved foot (French foot), square tapered legs, and inlaid decoration. Hepplewhite included designs for serpentine and bow front commodes, cellarettes, knife boxes, and sideboards in his book. He is one of the leaders in introducing the square chest of drawers with either bracket or splayed feet into the furniture form vocabulary.

In America, the chest of drawers and sideboard epitomize the best of Hepplewhite design. Carefully selected veneers, carefully patterned on the piece, provide a richness that is difficult to achieve otherwise. Inlay is used to accent, never dominate. Its use is restrained in Baltimore and throughout the South. The overall effect of a Hepplewhite piece is one of total unity.

American collectors tend to think of the Federal era in the Hepplewhite furniture vocabulary. It clearly is the most prevalent style, especially in urban areas along the eastern seacoast. It never garnered favor among the rural cabinet makers.

Style Book: Alice (George) Hepplewhite, *Cabinet–Maker and Upholster's Guide*, 1788, published posthumously.

PERIOD

Bedstead, New England, 1795–1805, mahogany, tall post, tester, square tapering head posts, peaked arched headboard, reeded tapering foot posts ending in spade feet, old dark finish, 55" w, 76" d, 85" h **2,310**

Bench, 1800–10, window, mahogany, upholstered seat and rolled arms, square tapering legs, H–stretchers, refinished, minor repair to one leg, 39½" w, 16" d, 29" h **1,050**

Candlestand, 1790–95, birch, circular top, turned pedestal, tapered spider legs, spade feet, refinished, minor repairs to legs, 27¾" h **950**

Cellarette, mahogany, inlaid, inlaid edge on domed lid, eight bottle compartments in fitted interior, two cupboard doors, brass carrying handles on sides, flaring bracket feet, 22" w, 14¾" d, 30" h **1,760**

Chair
  Arm
    Massachusetts, 1790–1800, mahogany, carved, shield back carved with bellflower and wheat sheaf sprigs, pierced splat,

scrolled arms, upholstered serpentine seat, square molded tapered legs, stretchers **1,320**

Pennsylvania, Philadelphia, 1790–1810, mahogany, carved, shield back, molded and upholstered back, short shaped arms with carved rosettes over down curving molded arm supports, over-upholstered seat, reeded apron, square tapering reeded legs with carved rosettes, several old repaired breaks, 35¾" h **12,000**

Lolling

Massachusetts, eastern shore, 1790–1800, mahogany, inlaid, serpentine upholstered back, shaped arms and line and bellflower inlaid down curving arm supports, serpentine upholstered seat, molded square tapering legs, minor repair to right arm at juncture with arm support **13,200**

Massachusetts, 1800–10, mahogany, upholstered serpentine back, shaped arms on molded down curving arm supports, upholstered seat, molded square tapering legs joined by H-stretcher, one stretcher replaced **7,150**

New England, 1790–1810, mahogany, serpentine upholstered back, shaped arms on down curving arm supports with beaded edges, upholstered seat, square tapering legs joined by stretchers, 17" h seat, 45½" h overall **3,520**

New England, early 19th C, mahogany, inlaid, serpentine upholstered back, shaped arms, outline stringing on down curving arm supports, upholstered seat, outline stringing on square tapering legs joined by stretchers, casters, yellow upholstery, refinished, restored, 18" h seat, 46" h overall **1,980**

New England, early 19th C, mahogany, serpentine upholstered back, reeded down curving arm supports, upholstered seat, molded and beaded square tapering legs joined by stretchers, 15¾" h seat, 45" h overall **4,950**

Set of Four, New York, 1800–10, side, mahogany, carved, stepped and molded rectangular back, center pierced urn form splat carved with drapery swag, surmounted by Prince of Wales carved plume, flanked by leaf carved vertical slats,

Dining Chairs, New England, 1790–1800, set of six, carved mahogany, arched crest rail, pierced splat with urn, upholstered serpentine seat, square tapered legs joined by stretchers, price for set, $6,000.00.

overupholstered bow front seat, square tapering molded legs, spade feet, 35¾" h, price for set **14,500**

Set of Eight, New England, 1790–1810, mahogany, inlaid, two arm chairs, six side chairs, shield shaped back above five tapered uprights with fan inlaid pendant, overupholstered bowed seat on square molded tapering legs joined by stretchers, some repairs and restorations, price for set **9,900**

Side

American, 1790–1800, mahogany, carved, inlaid, shield back, arched crest rail, carved foliate pendant above pierced and fluted splat, flared seat, square molded legs **975**

Maryland, 1800–1810, mahogany, carved, shield back, serpentine overupholstered seat on square tapering molded legs, H–stretcher, old finish, 17½" h seat, 37" h overall **385**

Massachusetts, 1790–1810, mahogany, shield back, serpentine seat rail, upholstered seat, square molded tapering legs with beaded edges and stretchers, old refinish, 17½" h seat, 36½" h overall **415**

Massachusetts, Salem, 1800–10, pair, mahogany, inlaid, molded and incised shield back, five

Chest of Drawers, New England, 1790–1810, reeded edge on rectangular top, four cockbeaded graduated long drawers, shaped apron, French feet, oval brasses, 39½" w, 21" d, 40" h, $3,800.00.

shaped ribs terminating in inlaid fan above trapezoidal overupholstered seat, serpentine seat rail, square tapered line inlaid legs, H–stretcher, minor loss to inlays, 37¼" h, price for pair .. **1,350**

Wing

New England, 1790–1800, mahogany, serpentine upholstered back flanked by shaped wings, out scrolled arms, upholstered seat cushion, molded square tapering legs joined by stretchers, 47" h . **4,510**

New England, 1790–1800, cherrywood, serpentine upholstered back flanked by ogival wings, out scrolled arms, upholstered seat, square tapering legs joined by stretchers, center stretcher restored **2,750**

New England, early 19th C, mahogany, serpentine upholstered back flanked by shaped wings, out scrolled arms, upholstered seat, square tapering legs joined by stretchers, refinished, pumpkin color 20th C upholstery, 17½" h seat, 46½" overall **1,100**

Chamber Stand, Massachusetts, early 19th C, mahogany, bird's eye maple veneer, corner stand, bowed front, small shelf on scrolled crest, round cutout in top above bird's eye maple veneered frieze, medial shelf, small drawer in bird's eye maple veneered frieze below medial shelf, scrolled front on lower shelf repeats shape of crest, three square legs, out curving front feet, oval brasses, refinished, 21" w, 13½" d, 29⅛" h **2,090**

Chest and Bookcase, New York, 1800–10, mahogany, inlaid, flat top, two sections: upper section: molded cornice above a pair of hinged glazed doors with arched mullions, interior fitted with three adjustable shelves; lower section: projecting base, one large over three graduated cockbeaded inlaid long drawers, shaped skirt continuing to bracket feet, feet slightly reduced in height, some patches to molding and veneers, 46½" w, 22" d, 92" h **4,400**

Chest of Drawers

American, 1790–1810, cherry, poplar secondary wood, inlaid edge on rectangular top, walnut and maple inlay on stiles and top drawer, four cockbeaded dovetailed graduated long drawers, scalloped apron, cutout feet, turned wood pulls, embossed brass escutcheons, 36⅜" h **3,500**

American, 1800–10, walnut, inlaid, rectangular top, four cockbeaded dovetailed graduated long drawers, scrolled apron, French feet, 36⅜" w, 40½" h **3,250**

American, 1815, cherrywood and curly maple, inlaid, rectangular top, four graduating cockbeaded drawers, shaped skirt ending in flared bracket feet, oval brasses, 46½" w, 20" d, 39½" h **3,970**

American, 1810, cherry, poplar secondary wood, walnut and maple inlaid top edge, stiles, and top drawer, four dovetailed long drawers with applied edge beading, solid ends, square tapered feet, dated inside case, old refinish, turned replacement knobs, back leg broken and reattached, 39" w, 20½" d, 40½" h **2,000**

American, early 19th C, mahogany, inlaid, rectangular line inlaid top, pullout slide, stringing on three graduated long drawers, shaped apron continuing to bracket feet, 29½" w, 19" d, 33" h **1,540**

American, 1810, mahogany, inlaid, bow front, reeded edge top, four graduated drawers with fan inlay at corners, French feet, 40" h, 46½" w, 23¾" d, 40" h **1,870**

Connecticut, 1790–1810, cherry, inlaid, rectangular top, four graduated cockbeaded long drawers outlined with mahogany crossbanded veneer and stringing, scalloped bracket feet, oval brasses, old refinish, 44" w, 20½" d, 35½" h **1,750**

Connecticut, 1800–10, cherry, veneered, serpentine front, oblong top, conforming case, line inlay and cockbeading on four conforming graduated long drawers, scrolled bracket feet, refinished, replaced oval brasses, 39" w, 18" d, 33⅛" h **2,750**

Massachusetts, 1790–1810, mahogany, inlaid, bow front, banded inlay on slightly overhanging bow front top, conforming case, four cockbeaded graduated long drawers, inlaid stringing on shaped apron, flaring French feet, oval brasses, restoration to feet, small repairs to inlay, 39" w, 38" h **2,750**

Massachusetts, 1800–10, cherrywood, inlaid, bow front, oblong top, center diamond shape and trefoil point inlay, conforming case with four cockbeaded graduated long drawers, inlaid rectangular line panel with trefoil leaf motifs at each corner, molded base, bracket feet, 37" w, 18¾" d, 33½" h **7,250**

Massachusetts, 1800–10, mahogany and branch satinwood, inlaid, bow front, inlaid edge on bowed front oblong top, conforming case with four beaded and bowed long drawers inlaid with oval feathered birch panels and fitted with ivory knobs, central square inlaid pendant on shaped skirt which continues to flaring bracket feet, 39½" w, 20¾" d, 38¼" h **6,050**

Middle Atlantic States, 1810, mahogany and cherrywood, rectangular top above three short and three long cockbeaded drawers, shaped skirt continuing to flared bracket feet, minor repairs to veneer, 43¼" w, 19" d, 37¼" h **1,650**

New England, 1790–1810, curly maple and mahogany, inlaid, bow front, line inlaid edge on oblong top, conforming case, four cockbeaded graduated long drawers, shaped skirt, slightly splayed bracket feet, 41¼" w, 20½" d, 37½" h **7,250**

New England, 1790–1810, mahogany, inlaid, bow front, oblong top, conforming case, patterned inlaid stringing, maple banding and stringing on four graduated long drawers, shaped apron, French feet, 38¾" w, 20½" d, 34" h **6,250**

New England, eastern shore, 1810, mahogany, bird's eye maple inlaid, bow front, checkerboard inlaid edge on oblong top, bowed case with four crossbanded and graduated long drawers, shaped skirt continuing to flared bracket feet, some patches to top, 42½" w, 22½" d, 36¼" h **3,740**

New England, early 19th C, mahogany veneer, inlaid, stringing on edge of rectangular overhanging top, line inlaid cockbeaded long drawers, stringing on shaped skirt, French feet, oval brasses, rear foot repaired, 41¼" w, 18⅜" d, 38¼" h **1,875**

New Hampshire or Vermont, 1800–15, cherrywood, rectangular top, four fan and line inlaid graduated long drawers, shaped apron centering a patera inlay, French feet, losses to front right foot, 42" w, 40¾" h **1,425**

Pennsylvania, western, 1810, mahogany, inlaid, bow front, oblong top, conforming case, contrasting crossbanded veneer surrounds, four graduated long drawers, 43¼" w, 23" d, 38¼" h **1,750**

Ohio, Adena, Chillicothe, walnut, rectangular overhanging top, four cockbeaded graduated long drawers, invected corners in line inlay on curly walnut veneered drawer fronts, inlaid escutcheons, line inlaid stiles, shaped apron continuing to French feet, replaced oval brasses, 39¾" w, 18" d, 40½" h .. **4,000**

Clock, tall case

American, 1800–10, unknown maker, walnut, inlaid, molded swan's neck pediment, arched glazed door, white painted dial with moon phases, waisted case with crossbanded hinged door, line inlaid quarter columns, fan inlaid base, shaped skirt, bracket feet, 103" h, 20" w, 10" d **4,550**

Maryland, Fredericktown, 1800–10, John Fessler, walnut, inlaid, molded swan's neck pediment hood, fan inlaid terminals, three urn finials, arched hinged door, white painted dial with moon phases, minute and date registers, waisted case with hinged door, canted corners, paneled base with inlaid canted corners, splayed bracket feet, inscribed "John Fessler Fredericktown," 99¾" h **8,250**

New England, 1800–10, unknown maker, cherrywood, pierced crest, two ball finials, white painted dial with calendar date and minute register, columns with brass caps, waisted case, oval inlaid door, quarter columns with brass caps, oval inlaid base, splayed bracket feet, 90¾" h, 18" w, 9" d **5,500**

Commode, Massachusetts, Salem, 1800–10, mahogany, demilune top, conforming case, central cockbeaded molded drawer flanked by similar hinged compartment drawers, double cupboard doors with molded panels, three sliding trays flanked by similar cupboard doors, shelved interior, scalloped apron, French feet, 55" w, 32" d, 40" h **46,500**

Desk

Butler's, 1790–1810, walnut, inlaid, rectangular top, three dovetailed long drawers, fitted interior, scalloped apron, straight feet, some repairs, 43" w, 42" h **1,500**

Lady's, mahogany, pine secondary wood, inlaid, two sections: upper section: molded cornice, geometric

mullions on double doors over pair of short drawers, line inlay and beaded edge on drawers, interior shelf, pigeonholes, and single drawer; lower section: fold down writing surface, line inlay and beaded edge on three dovetailed long drawers, scalloped apron, French feet, old worn finish, top shows signs of reconstruction, 35" w, 18" d, 57" h **2,100**

Mid Atlantic, 1800–10, mahogany, inlaid, rectangular top above pull-out writing section, hinged front flap faced to simulate two working drawers, fitted interior with small drawers over pigeonholes centering a prospect drawer, four cockbeaded drawers below, line inlaid square tapering legs ending in crossbanded cuffs, brass caps, left front leg repaired, 43¾" w, 18¼" d, 36½" h **4,400**

Slant Front

American, walnut, inlaid, rectangular fall front writing surface, interior drawers centering prospect door, reeded document slides, two aligned over three graduated cockbeaded drawers, scalloped skirt, bracket feet reduced in height, 43" w, 20½" d, 44" h .. **2,475**

Connecticut, 1795–1810, cherry, inlaid, thumb molded slant lid with line inlay border and quarter fans, fitted interior with central prospect and document drawers, two banks of short drawers over longer drawer above three valanced pigeonholes, case of four cockbeaded line and quarter fan inlaid graduated long drawers, chamfered and fluted corners, modified French feet, some veneer chips, 40" w, 21" d, 42¼" h **4,750**

Pennsylvania, early 19th C, walnut, inlaid, rectangular top, thumb molded edge and string and quarter fan inlays on hinged slant front, fitted interior with six small string inlaid drawers above eight valanced pigeonholes, centering a string and quarter fan inlaid prospect door opening to single small string inlaid drawer above a valanced pigeonhole, pullout slides, four line inlaid graduated long drawers, oval brasses, banded inlay on shaped skirt, French feet, small pieces of lid molding missing, 42" w, 45" h . **2,200**

Tambour

American, early 19th C, mahogany, inlaid, two sections: upper section: stringing on edge of rectangular top, two tambour shutters flanked by reeded pilasters, fitted interior with ten small drawers above nine valanced pigeonholes; lower section: hinged line inlaid fold down writing surface, pullout slides, three graduated drawers with invected corners on line inlay, oval brasses, bellflower and line inlaid stiles, band inlaid edge on straight apron, square tapering legs with band cuff inlay ending in brass casters, 42″ w, 44″ h **1,650**

Massachusetts, Boston, 1800–10, curly maple and mahogany, ivory inlaid, two sections: upper section: two short drawers above two tambour slides flanking central oval inlaid prospect door, interior drawers and pigeonholes painted blue; lower section: hinged writing flap above four graduated cockbeaded long drawers, shaped skirt continuing to bracket feet, 30½″ w, 19″ d, 40¾″ h **3,850**

Massachusetts, north shore, 1800–10, mahogany, inlaid, two sections: upper section: line inlaid rectangular top, crossbanding above hinged line inlaid rectangular door, interior with stack of two short drawers over valanced compartment flanked by tambour sliding doors, flanked by crossbanded and line inlaid pilasters; lower section: line inlaid and crossbanded hinged writing flap above two line inlaid long drawers, flanked by line inlaid pilasters, square tapering line and bellflower inlaid legs, 37″ w, 20″ d, 44¼″ h **8,950**

Massachusetts, Salem, 1800–10, 46″ h, 38″ w, 20″ d, mahogany, satinwood inlay, two sections: upper section: molded cornice above line and diamond lined frieze and tambour slides opening to two drawers and three valanced pigeonholes flanking central inlaid prospect door enclosing two small drawers; lower section: hinged baize lined writing flap above three graduated cockbeaded drawers,

slightly flared bracket feet, 38″ w, 20″ d, 46″ h **1,980**

Hunt Board, mahogany, poplar secondary wood, line inlaid edge on overhanging rectangular top, figured veneer, crossbanding, line inlay, and fan inlaid corners on three deep aligned dovetailed drawers, embossed brass pulls, inlaid vines and outline stringing on shaped apron, inlaid stringing and bellflowers on square tapering legs, crossbanded cuffs, refinished, age cracks in replaced top, repairs and restoration, 42½″ w, 21¾″ d, 41″ h **5,000**

Linen Press, 1790–1800, mahogany, arched projecting cornice with three urn finials, pair of paneled doors enclosing pullout shelves, leather inset linen slide above two aligned drawers over two graduated cockbeaded drawers, shaped skirt, French feet, 52″ w, 23″ d, 114½″ h **7,975**

Mirror, shaving, bow front, pine, mahogany veneered, line edge inlay, turned posts, beveled frame, rectangular mirror panel, single dovetailed drawer, turned feet, 15½″ w, 19″ h . **135**

Secretary

Massachusetts, 1790–1810, mahogany, inlaid, blind door, two sections: upper section: molded paneled cupboard doors enclosing interior drawers and compartments and hinged baize lined writing surface with inlaid oval medallion; lower section: three graduated long drawers flanked by inlaid dies, square double tapering legs ending in crossbanded cuffs, 35¾″ w, 21¾″ d, 45¾″ h **1,870**

New England, late 18th C, mahogany, inlaid, two sections: upper section: cupboard top, three shelves; lower section: butler style drawer and two long drawers in base, 40¾″ w, 67¼″ h **3,150**

Secretary Bookcase

American, 1810, mahogany, inlaid, two part, upper section: three urn finials, shaped crest, pair of arched mullion glazed doors, shelved interior, prospect door flanked by pigeonholes; lower section: hinged fold out writing surface, three long drawers, French feet, 42″ w, 20″ d, 88″ h **2,500**

Massachusetts, eastern shore, 1810, flat top, mahogany, two sections: upper section: molded cornice, pair of glazed hinged doors enclosing shelves, valanced pigeonholes, and three small drawers; lower section: hinged flap opening to a leather lined writing surface above three graduated drawers, pullout slides, and square double tapering legs ending in crossbanded cuffs, 40″ w, 20½″ d, 60″ h **5,500**

Settee, early 19th C, mahogany, carved, triple shield back, carved and pierced urn shaped splats, outstretched shaped arms on S–form supports, upholstered slip seat, square fluted tapering legs, 54″ l **3,025**

Sideboard

Maine, York, signed by Thomas Chandler, 1810, mahogany, flame birch inlaid, bow front, oblong top with bowed front above conforming case with three convex drawers above two pair of hinged cupboard doors centering bottle drawers, rectangular inlaid dies, intersecting line, bellflower, and dot inlaid square double tapering legs ending in crossbanded cuffs, brass knobs, sides and bottom of upper center drawer replaced, 69″ w, 26″ d, 41½″ h **38,500**

Maryland, Baltimore, 1790–1810, bow front, mahogany, inlaid, inlaid edge on rectangular top, frieze drawer above a pair of cupboard doors, flanked by cupboard doors faced to simulate small drawers, inlaid apron continuing to square tapering legs ending in crossbanded cuffs, oval brasses, 70¾″ w, 25½″ d, 40″ h **6,600**

Maryland, Baltimore, 1790–1810, serpentine front, mahogany, inlaid, oblong top with serpentine front and canted corners, conforming case, sliding plate shelf, bowed drawer over two bowed cupboard doors flanked by two concave drawers and doors, centering line inlaid dies on line inlaid square tapering legs ending in crossbanded cuffs, oval brasses, minor patches to veneers, 67¾″ w, 25¾″ d, 40¼″ h **22,000**

Massachusetts, 1790–1810, mahogany, inlaid, bow front, shaped top, conforming case, central long drawer over pair of bottle drawers centering cupboard doors, flanked by short drawer over cupboard door each side, line inlaid doors and drawer fronts, line inlaid rectangular dies, line inlaid square double tapering legs, old refinish, replaced brasses, 72″ w, 25″ d, 42½″ h **2,750**

Mid Atlantic, 1790–1810, mahogany, inlaid, serpentine front, oblong top, three concave drawers, one fitted

Sideboard, 1790–1810, mahogany, line inlaid, bow front, oblong top, conforming case with two short drawers over two cupboard doors flanking a single long drawer over a pair of recessed cupboard doors, square tapered legs ending in brass caps and casters, oval brasses, 72″ w, 26½″ d, 39″ h, $7,500.00.

with bottle dividers, centering a convex drawer above a pair of hinged cupboard doors, centering paterae inlaid dies on line inlaid square tapering legs ending in crossbanded cuffs, restorations and repairs to inlay, 70" w, 28" d, 39½" h **4,950**

Mid Atlantic, 1795–1810, mahogany, inlaid, oblong top, two hinged convex doors centering a concave drawer and a pair of hinged cupboard doors, centering rectangular inlaid dies, line inlaid square tapering legs ending in crossbanded cuffs, octagonal brasses stamped with wingspread eagle, repairs to one rear leg and veneers, 67" w, 24" d, 41¾" h **5,500**

New York, 1790–1810, mahogany, inlaid, serpentine front, slightly overhanging serpentine shaped oblong top, conforming case with three band inlaid short drawers over a recessed central pair of hinged band inlaid cupboard doors flanked by a band inlaid deep drawer on one side and a band inlaid cupboard door on the other, inverted corners in band inlaid designs on lower drawer and doors, line inlay on square tapered and canted legs with band cuff inlay, restorations to inlay and interior, 74" w, 40" h **3,575**

New York, 1790–1810, mahogany, inlaid, serpentine front, line inlaid edge on oblong top, serpentine case with two concave line inlaid drawers centering a bowed line inlaid frieze drawer above two pairs of fan and line inlaid doors, centering rectangular inlaid dies, line inlaid tapering legs ending in crossbanded cuffs, some veneer loss, 69¾" w, 26" d, 39¾" h **19,250**

New York, 1790–1810, mahogany, inlaid, serpentine front above two concave and one convex drawer, two fan inlaid bottle drawers below centering a recessed section with fan inlaid convex hinged doors, bookend and diamond inlaid dies, on line and dot inlaid tapering legs ending in crossbanded cuffs, oval brasses, minor veneer repair, 72" w, 29¼" d, 42" h **9,350**

New York, 1800–10, mahogany, inlaid, D–shaped top above a conforming case, three line inlaid short drawers centering tombstone shaped inlaid dies, four line inlaid

cupboard doors centering tombstone shaped inlaid dies, center cupboard doors flanked by two line inlaid tall bottle drawers, corn husk inlays on square line inlaid tapering legs, restoration to interior and legs, veneer missing, 72" w, 41¾" h . . .   **4,400**

New York, 1800–10, mahogany, inlaid, oblong top, central drawer flanked by two convex drawers, pair of hinged doors flanked by pair of convex doors, oval and carrot inlaid dies, line and bellflower inlaid square tapering legs, crossbanded cuffs, 71½" w, 27½" d, 39" h **38,500**

Southern, 1790–1810, mahogany, inlaid, line inlaid edge on oblong top, two oval inlaid convex hinged doors centering an oval inlaid frieze drawer above a pair of recessed hinged cupboard doors, all centering paterae and bookend inlaid dies, intersecting line and bellflower inlaid square tapering legs ending in crossbanded cuffs, minor veneer repairs, top back patched where once fitted with later brass gallery, 72¾" w, 27¾" d, 42" h . .   **7,700**

Sofa

Massachusetts, Salem, 1790–1810, mahogany, carved and inlaid, molded serpentine exposed crest rail centering a carved basket of flowers and fruit, upholstered arms flanking with acanthus carved front panels, serpentine overupholstered seat raised on line inlaid square tapering legs ending in crossbanded cuffs, feet extended, repair to back and front left legs, 89" l **16,500**

New England, 1790–1810, mahogany, cabriole, arched upholstered back, molded and shaped down curving arms, molded and shaped down curving arm supports, upholstered arms and bowed seat, molded square tapering legs, 82" l   **4,400**

Stand

Night, New England, coastal, 1810, cherry, inlaid, rectangular top and single drawer outlined with stringing and quarter fan inlays, stringing on skirt and square tapered legs, refinished, replaced glass pull, 18⅛" w, 17" d, 26¾" h **1,900**

Work, New England, 1810, cherry, inlaid, square top with outline stringing and quarter fan inlays on ovolo corners, line inlaid drawer and skirt, line inlaid square tapering legs, crossbanded cuffs, brass drawer pull, refinished, 19" w, 19" d, 27" h **2,420**

Sugar Chest, North Carolina, cherry, inlaid, lift off lid, dovetailed case, large well, inlaid stars, lines, and circles, single dovetailed long drawer in base, square tapered legs, cutout leg brackets, old repairs, replaced moldings, 31¼" w, 15¾" d, 36" h **11,250**

Card Table, New York, 1800–10, mahogany, line inlaid, oblong top with ovolo corners, conforming frieze with oval reserves, square tapered legs with crossbanded cuffs, 36" w, 18" d, 29½" h, $3,750.00.

Table
  Card
    American, 1790–1810, mahogany, folding top, demilune, circular molded edge baize lined top, swing leg concealing drawer, molded square tapering, reticulated brackets, 35" d open top, 28" h **2,250**
    Massachusetts, 1800–10, mahogany, birch inlaid, band inlaid edge on D–shaped top and hinged leaf, conform frieze with an oval birch panel flanked by oval birch dies above a banded lower edge, square double tapering legs with inlaid cuffs, repair to swing leg, 36" w, 29½" h . . . **3,850**
    Massachusetts, 1800–10, mahogany, birch inlaid, bow front, hinged top above conforming string inlaid frieze, string inlaid square tapering legs surmounted by rectangular birch inlaid dies, small chips to veneer, inlays missing, 35" w, 29" h **4,675**

New England, 1800–10, inlaid birch and mahogany, molded edge on D–shaped hinged top above conforming frieze with astragal line inlaid panels centering a birch inlaid die, square tapering line inlaid legs surmounted by rectangular birch inlaid dies, repairs to veneer and interior frame, 36" w, 29" h **1,320**

New England, 1810, curly maple and mahogany, oblong top, serpentine sides, hinged leaf above conforming shaped crossbanded frieze, square tapering legs ending in crossbanded cuffs, 35" w, 17" d, 29" h **3,575**

New Hampshire, Concord, mahogany, inlaid, demilune, hinged leaf, top edges and skirt banded with stringing, outline stringing and bellflower inlays above ebonized teardrops on square tapered legs, refinished, 36" w, 17½" d, 28½" h **2,530**

New Hampshire, 1810, maple, demilune, oblong top with hinged leaf above rectangular inlaid frieze on line inlaid square tapering legs ending in crossbanded cuffs, top and leaf juxtaposed, some alteration to swing leg, 36¼" w, 17½" d, 30¾" h **1,980**

Rhode Island, Newport or Providence, 1790–1800, mahogany, inlaid, demilune, hinged leaf above conforming bookend inlaid frieze, line inlaid edges, inlaid pendants on square tapered legs ending in crossbanded cuffs, 36" w, 18¼" d, 28" h **2,750**

Rhode Island, 1790–1810, mahogany, veneered, oblong top, shaped corners, line inlaid edges, hinged leaf above conforming frieze, line inlaid geometric shapes, oval veneered patera with ebony surround and ebony cuff inlays, square double tapering legs, old refinish, two minor veneer patches on top, 36" w, 17" d, 29¼" h **1,980**

Dining
  New England, 1790–1810, mahogany, veneer, inlaid, two part, rectangular hinged leaves on D–shaped end sections, line inlaid frieze, square double tapering legs, old finish, 41¾" l, 72¾" extended length, 20⅝" w, 29" h . . **2,750**

New England, probably Rhode Island, 1800–10, mahogany, inlaid, three part, center section with rectangular top and two rectangular leaves flanked by two D–shaped end sections, each section with line inlaid frieze centering bookend inlaid dies, line inlaid square tapering legs ending in crossbanded cuffs, repair to top of two legs, minor repairs to inlay, 87″ l, 45″ w, 28¾″ h **17,600**

Pembroke

Connecticut, 1800–10, cherrywood, inlaid, oblong top centering an inlaid paterae, flanked by two D–shaped hinged leaves similarly inlaid, frieze with line inlaid drawer at each end, flanked by bookend inlaid dies, line and icicle inlaid square tapering legs ending in crossbanded cuffs, 35¼″ l, 40½″ extended length, 28½″ h **3,850**

New York, 1800–10, mahogany, rectangular top with two shaped and line inlaid leaves above single drawer frieze, reverse faced to simulate a working drawer, line inlaid square tapering legs ending in crossbanded cuffs, repairs to inlay, 40¼″ extended length, 32″ w, 28¼″ h **2,475**

Sofa, Massachusetts, Salem, 1790–1810, mahogany, satinwood inlaid, rectangular top flanked by D–shaped drop leaves, skirt fitted with two cockbeaded inlaid working and two mock drawers, drawers flanked by diamond inlaid dies, stringing on lower skirt edge, two upright rectangular columns each continuing to two line inlaid tapering–down curving legs, brass animal paw casters, ring turned transverse stretcher, repairs to legs and uprights, 53¾″ extended length, 27¼″ w, 28½″ h **82,500**

Wardrobe, Maryland, attributed to John Shaw, Annapolis, 1790–1800, mahogany, five sections, breakfront molded cornice with plain frieze above case with double cupboard doors with applied astragal bead molded panels and hollow corners, five sliding tray shelves, lower case of single long drawer with fold down writing surface flanked by compartments and sliding covers, two bead molded short drawers, two bead molded graduated long drawers, straight bracket feet, two flanking full length sections with bead molded

panels and cupboard doors, 70″ w, 21½″ d, 92″ h **17,500**

STYLE

Blanket Chest

American, pine, edge molding on lid, dovetailed case, walnut till, French feet, iron strap hinges, brown paint graining, old repaint, lock removed, crack in bottom filled with white caulking, 53½″ w, 22″ d, 24¾″ h **425**

Pennsylvania, pine, original red paint, traces of grain painting, three dovetailed drawers and case, original locks, wrought iron strap hinges, brass escutcheons, stenciled initials, "W H G," French feet, 50″ w, 23″ d, 29¼″ h **2,200**

Candlestand

American, birch, tilt top, rectangular one board top, cut corners, well turned column, spider legs, high feet, old varnish finish, dark varnish stain on base, 14½″ w, 21¼″ d, 28″ h **700**

American, maple, shaped top and column, spider legs, spade feet, refinished **400**

Chair, dining

Set of Eight

American, mahogany, two arm chairs, six side chairs, shield shaped back, three tasseled splats, upholstered bowed seat, molded square tapering legs joined by stretchers **1,200**

American, walnut, carved, two arm chairs, six side chairs, shield shaped back, pierced plume carved splat, slip seat, square tapering legs ending in spade feet **1,300**

Set of Ten, two arm chairs, eight side chairs, satinwood, inlaid, square back, inlaid drapery on tablet and seat rail, leaf carving at top of pierced double X–form splat above scalloped shoe, down curving continuous arms on arm chairs, pink shell pattern on upholstered slip seat, inlaid patera at top of front square tapered legs terminating in spade feet, H–stretcher **5,775**

Desk

Lift Lid, figured walnut, yellow pine and poplar secondary woods, molded edge on rectangular hinged paneled lid, interior well, paneled ends, single dovetailed overlapping long drawer, square tapering legs,

Desk and Bookcase, Eastern Massachusetts, c1815, mahogany and mahogany veneer, valanced cornice featuring central plinth with reeded accent and fan finial, urn finials on all four corners; bookcase section top with two doors each featuring twelve glass panes in a diamond motif; bookcase bottom with two blind cupboard doors that open to reveal desk interior; bottom with three graduated drawers, tapered feet in the Sheraton tradition featuring ring and spool turning at top, reeded sides, and ending in a squat ball resting on a short tapered piece, $2,750.00. Photograph courtesy of Skinner, Inc.

old varnish finish, 24¾" w, 21½" d, 33" h **425**

Tambour, late 19th/early 20th C, mahogany, inlaid, rectangular top above frieze drawer over prospect door flanked by sliding tambour doors, interior drawers and balanced pigeonholes, fold out baize lined writing surface, three gradu-

ated long drawers, square tapering legs, 29½" w, 18¾" d, 45½" h . . .   **1,430**

Dough Box, poplar, decorated case and base, yellow and white striping, invected corner rectangles, corner fans on two tone red ground, rectangular one board lid, dovetailed box, splayed base, square tapering legs, age cracks, some shrinkage, repainted over earlier red paint, 38" w, 17¾" d, 30¼" h **575**

Secretary Bookcase, mahogany, inlaid, breakfront, inlaid urn on arched and blocked cornice, crossbanded frieze, four mullioned glazed doors enclosing shelves, central secretary drawer above three drawers flanked by two drawers over urn inlaid cupboard doors, all drawers crossbanded and cockbeaded, shaped aprons, French feet, 59¾" w, 17½" d, 83" h **225**

Sideboard, southern, hunt board, poplar, ash, and birch, molded top edge, applied beading, two nailed drawers, high square tapered legs, handmade, brownish stain repaint, 49¾" w, 21½" d, 48¾" h **450**

Table
Tavern
American, maple and cherry, breadboard ends on pine one board top, single dovetailed drawer, mortised and pinned apron, square tapering legs, reattached top, drawer pull missing, 43" w, 28½" d, 27½" h **500**

American, maple and pine, scrubbed pine breadboard top, pine mortised and pinned apron, maple square tapering legs, traces of old red paint on base, 37½" w, 26½" h **750**

American, pine, one board rectangular breadboard top, splayed hardwood base, square tapering legs, old red repaint, 38½" w, 24" d, 26¼" h **450**

Work
American, pine, single dovetailed drawer, square tapered legs, worn patina on top, old brown finish on base, 36" w, 29¾" d, 28¾" h **650**

American, pine and hardwood, cut out ovolo corners on two board top, single dovetailed drawer, square tapered legs, brown grain painting, warped top, 22¼" w, 23" d, 27½" h **200**

Washstand, poplar and pine, shaped gallery, cutouts for bowls and accessories, square tapering legs, base shelf, embossed brass pulls on nailed drawer, black blocking and linear decoration on yellow ground, 18½" w, 15½" d, 37¼" h **400**

SHERATON (1795–1815)

History: Thomas Sheraton, again strongly influenced by the Adams', was a publisher, not a cabinet maker. His principal design component is the square form: chair backs became almost square in design; his tapered turned legs, often reeded in American furniture, often contained square block sections; although occasionally using inlay, Sheraton furniture relied on large boldly contrasting veneers or painting. Kidney shaped tables, cylinder and tambour desks, and washstands were popular furniture forms.

The card and side tables, work table, and chest of drawers are the most common Sheraton forms in America. Sheraton designs provided a greater sense of movement, albeit highly restrained, to pieces than did the box–like Hepplewhite forms. Accents were bold and visual, not delicate.

While the Sheraton design style enjoyed a high degree of popularity in the urban areas, it was dominant in middle size and small town America where it was perceived as a sturdy, long lasting design form. The use of decorative painting also added to its popularity. Many Sheraton design elements worked their way into vernacular furniture with decorative motifs of the period.

Style Books: Thomas Shearer, *Designs for Household Furniture*, 1788; Thomas Sheraton, *Cabinet Maker's and Upholsterer's Drawing Book*, published in parts between 1791 and 1794.

PERIOD

Bedstead
New England, 1805–15, mahogany, four post, tester, turned head posts centering shaped mahogany headboard, reeded and ring turned foot posts raised on ring turned feet, 81" l, 57" w **3,025**
New England, 1810–15, mahogany, four post, turned and reeded head posts centering a shaped mahogany headboard, turned and reeded foot posts raised on baluster turned feet, restorations to headboard and foot posts, 81½" l, 56" w **1,100**
Chair
Set of Ten, Philadelphia, Pennsylvania or Baltimore, Maryland, 1800–10, mahogany, carved, two arm, eight side, serpentine shaped molded crest above three pierced and feather carved arrow splats flanked by molded stiles over a

Bedstead, carved mahogany, tester, fluted tapered head posts, shaped headboard, fluted tapered foot posts with leaf carving, turned tapered legs, $5,000.00.

trapezoidal upholstered slip seat, square tapering legs joined by H–stretchers, two arm chairs have shaped arms on molded down curving arm supports, repairs to stretchers, price for set **8,800**
Side
Connecticut, pair, Hitchcock style, turtle back slats, cane seat, turned legs and front stretcher, simulated rosewood graining, black and gold stenciled and freehand decoration, painted landscape on center oval slat, one has minor age crack in turtle slats, both have touch up repairs to paint, 35" h, price for pair . .   **1,400**
New York or Philadelphia, Pennsylvania, 1800–15, mahogany, carved, square back centering a pierced and scrolled wheat stalk decorated urn shaped splat, trapezoidal upholstered slip seat, square tapering legs joined by H–stretcher, repair to back of splat center **385**
Wing, Pennsylvania, Philadelphia, 1795, mahogany, serpentine upholstered back flanked by ogival wings, out scrolled arms, upholstered serpentine seat fitted with loose cushion, fluted square taper-

Armchair, Philadelphia, 1795–1805, attributed to Henry Connolly, mahogany, carved, openwork splat decorated with ribbons, rosettes, and a central urn, down-curving arms, upholstered seat, reeded round tapered legs, $750.00.

ing legs ending in spade feet joined by H–stretcher, brass casters **23,100**

Chest of Drawers

American, mahogany, carved, bow front, oblong top, conforming case, four graduated long drawers, reeded stiles and upper and lower bands, circular carved motifs, inset panel sides, bracket feet, 42½" w, 37¼" h **1,875**

American, maple and cherry, bow front, curly and bird's eye maple veneer, applied edge beading on four dovetailed long drawers, paneled ends, scalloped apron, turned feet, refinished, 39¾" w, 44" h **2,400**

Connecticut, 1815, cherry, carved, inlaid, serpentine front, outset rounded corners on crossbanded oblong cockbeaded top, conforming case, four cockbeaded graduated long drawers, reeded and fluted three–quarter columns con-

tinuing to reeded cone and tapering feet, shaped cockbeaded and crossbanded skirt, old refinish, replaced oval brasses, 40¼" w, 20" d, 37¾" h **2,090**

Massachusetts, 1805–15, mahogany, inlaid, bow front, outset rounded corners and bowed front on oblong top, conforming case with four graduated cockbeaded and crossbanded long drawers, reeded three–quarter round stiles ending in turned feet, 44" w, 21" d, 40" h . . **2,420**

New England, 1815, bird's eye maple and mahogany, veneered, bow front, outset rounded corners on oblong top, cockbeading on four bowed long drawers, mahogany banding and bird's eye maple veneered drawer fronts, reeded three–quarter columns ending in ring turned vasiform feet, shaped skirt, replaced brasses, 41¼" w, 21¾" d, 38½" h **1,045**

New England, 1815, cherry, mahogany veneer, outset rounded corners on oblong top, four cockbeaded long drawers, reeded three–quarter columns ending in ring turned vasiform feet, shaped skirt, refinished, replaced brasses, 40½" w, 18" d, 39½" h **1,320**

Rhode Island, Providence, 1805–15, mahogany, inlaid, four outset rounded corners on oblong top, lunette inlaid top edge, four crossbanded and cockbeaded long drawers, reeded and fluted three–quarter columns continuing to ring turned vasiform legs and tapered feet, checkered inlay at lower edge continuing around legs, refinished, replaced brasses, 41½" w, 20" d, 42" h **2,090**

Clock, tall case

Massachusetts, Boston, 1805–15, Aaron Willard Jr, mahogany, inlaid, pierced fretwork crest on hood, three brass ball and steeple finials, arched glazed door, white painted dial, polychrome basket of fruit decoration above inscription "Aaron Willar, Jun'r, Boston," minute and calendar date registers, waisted case with hinged molded door, fluted quarter columns with brass capitals, splayed bracket feet, 99½" h **20,000**

Massachusetts, Higham, 1810–15, Joshua Wilder, mahogany, dwarf, three brass urn finials, pierced fretwork, arched glazed door, white painted dial, Roman chapter ring, sweep seconds, calendar day and day of the week rings, lunar dial, arch inscribed, spandrels embellished with gilt scrolls flanked by turned colonettes, waisted case, rectangular crossbanded door, molded edge, crossbanded box base, shaped apron, bracket feet, chalk inscription on reverse with initials "JW" and "1820," 48½" h, 11" w, 6⅛" d **99,000**

Massachusetts, Roxbury, 1800–10, Simon Willard, mahogany, inlaid, pierced pediment hood, three ball and steeple finials, arched glazed door, white painted dial, minute and date registers, inscribed "S Willard," brass stop fluted colonettes, waisted case, crossbanded hinged door, brass stop fluted quarter columns, crossbanded base, ogee bracket feet **20,000**

New Jersey, Patterson, 1805–15, John Parke, mahogany, inlaid, molded hood with swan's neck pediment ending with flowerhead pressed gesso caps, brass ball and steeple finials, arched glazed door, white painted dial, minute and calendar date registers, rocking ship mechanism above inscription "John Parke Patterson," oval inlaid door below with fluted quarter columns, molded and cyma shaped skirt, bracket feet **29,700**

Cupboard, early 19th C, birch, carved, corner, two sections: upper section: swan's neck pediment centering three urn shaped finials on fluted plinths, hinged arched glazed door opening to four shelves flanking applied half baluster and rope turned columns; lower section: two hinged molded and raised panel doors opening to two shelves, molded base on bracket feet, restorations to glazed door, 45" w, 93" h **3,300**

Desk

Fall Front, New Hampshire, 1815, mahogany and mixed wood, two sections: upper section: shaped pediment flanked by urn finials, slightly overhanging rectangular top over two short drawers, alternating bird's eye maple and mahogany vertically striped fall front hinged writing flap, fitted interior; lower section: slightly overhanging rectangular top, long frieze drawer between panels of bird's eye maple above two graduated recessed long

Desk, lady's, New England, 1825–35, mahogany veneer, three drawers over two cupboard doors, interior compartments, foldout writing surface, four drawers, turned feet, some old brass, refinished, repairs, 40¼" w, 20" d, 55½" h, $1,210.00. Photograph courtesy of Skinner, Inc.

drawers flanked by acanthus leaf carved half columns, turned bulbous feet, 43½" w, 20" d, 62" h .. **1,750**

Tambour, Rhode Island, 1795–1805, mahogany veneer, rectangular top, four reeded columns, two tambour doors enclosing two pigeonholes and three small drawers, center prospect door, fold out writing surface, pullout slides, three graduated long drawers, old finish, replaced brasses, minor surface imperfections, 40" w, 21" d, 51" h **4,750**

Desk and Bookcase, Massachusetts, Boston area, 1815, mahogany, inlaid, cylinder front, two sections: upper section: flat top, molded cornice, pair of hinged double arched glazed doors opening to shelved interior; lower section: cylinder lid opening to interior with small drawers centering valanced pigeonholes and one long drawer and pullout writing surface, two short over one long cockbeaded drawers, ring turned reeded tapering legs, lion's head pulls, 35¼" w, 21¾" d, 74½" h **5,500**

Dressing Bureau, Massachusetts, Boston or north shore, 1805–15, mahogany, carved, inlaid, mirror with shaped crest, tiger maple and dart inlay framing rect mirror plate, supported by fluted posts with brass acorn finials and scrolled side arms, case with three small drawers on oblong top with reeded edge and outset rounded front corners, two short over two graduated long drawers in case, cockbeaded drawers, ring turned reeded and fluted three–quarter columns continuing to ring turned reeded and fluted legs ending in tapered feet, lunette inlay at lower edge continuing around legs, old refinish, replaced brasses, 38½" w, 21⅛" d, 70½" h .. **15,400**

Etagere, New England, 1805–15, mahogany, four tier, cyma shaped gallery, four ring and block turned uprights centering three rectangular shelves, crotch figured single drawer, turned legs ending in turned feet, small patch to one shelf support, 20" w, 19¾" d, 54¾" h **3,850**

Low Boy, walnut, dovetailed construction, interior divided into three sections, single drawer in base, turned legs, signed "Read Atlanta GA," old refinish, 29" w, 18¾" d, 39" h **3,000**

Mirror, hanging
American, 1800–10, pair, giltwood, carved, projecting cornice hung with spherules above frieze with applied lion's heads and angled molding over two rectangular mirror plates flanked by fluted columnar stiles with acanthus carved capitals on molded base, some regilding, some spherules missing, 34" w, 60" h, price for pair **7,700**

American, 1800–10, giltwood, molded cornice surmounted by an eagle standing on a rocky plinth flanked by two urn finials three spherules hung from chain held by eagle's bead and stretching to urns, beveled rectangular glass mirror panel flanked by half columns with acanthus leaf capitals on a molded base, small pieces of molding missing, chips off acanthus leaves, 21¼" w, 42" h **2,475**

Massachusetts, Salem, 1810, giltwood, outset corners on molded cornice hung with spherules, frieze with leaf molding, gilt classical figures on white eglomise panel flanked by molded columns, surface imperfections, 20¼" w, 28½" h **1,430**

Secretary
American, 1795–1805, lady's, ma-

hogany, two sections: upper section: scrolled crest with reeded posts and brass finials, applied molding on double doors, fitted interior; lower section: hinged writing shelf, three cockbeaded dovetailed long drawers, turned feet, 37½" w, 18" d, 65" h **2,000**

Ohio, attributed to East Liverpool, 1795–1805, cherry, two sections: upper section: bookcase top, molded cornice, paneled doors, adjustable interior shelves; lower section: fold down slant front, four pigeon holes and two dovetailed drawers in fitted interior, dovetailed case, three dovetailed long drawers, turned feet, old brown graining, replaced brasses, 34" w, 19¼" d, 76½" h **2,200**

Server, New England, 1815, mahogany, carved, outset circular corners on rectangular top, two short drawers over single long drawer, ring and rope turned legs surmounted by reeded three–quarter columns, serpentine shaped medial shelf, round tapering feet ending in brass casters, 36" w, 59" h **1,210**

Settee
American, 1815, mahogany, inlaid, upholstered back and arms, down curving reeded and vase turned arm supports, upholstered seat flanked by rectangular inlaid dies, ring turned legs ending in brass casters, 76" l **1,980**

American, mahogany, inlaid, straight upholstered back, exposed down curving arms continuing to ring turned and fluted arm supports, upholstered sides, inlaid swag design and line edging on exposed seat rail, upholstered seat, ring turned and fluted tapering legs ending in ring turned feet, ivory colored upholstery, 51" l **1,540**

American, painted white, black, red, and gold shell and vintage decoration on crest, pierced rail back, scrolled arms, turned arm supports, balloon shaped rush seat, turned legs, outward curved feet, repainted **2,300**

Massachusetts, north shore, 1800–15, mahogany, inlaid, slightly arched upholstered back flanked by molded down curving arms, reeded baluster turned arm supports, bowed upholstered seat, turned and reeded tapering legs surmounted by rectangular inlaid panels outlined with patterned stringing, old break and repair to one leg at frame juncture, 35¼" h, 71" w, 26" d, 35¼" h **16,500**

New England, 1815, mahogany, gadrooned crest, reeded scroll arms supported by ring turned posts, well reeded frame, ring turned legs terminating in brass cup casters, 75" w, 28" d, 33" h **1,325**

Pennsylvania, Philadelphia, 1805, mahogany, arched crest rail flanked by downward curving arms, molded handrests on ring and baluster turned uprights, plain seat on frontal ring turned and reeded tapering legs, unupholstered, 74" l . **4,675**

Sideboard

American, curly maple, poplar secondary wood, scalloped crest, three dovetailed drawers, base shelf, turned posts and feet, turned curly maple pulls, light natural refinishing, 36½" w, 36½" h **3,750**

Massachusetts, Boston, attributed to John and/or Thomas Seymour, 1805–15, mahogany, satinwood inlaid, oblong top with lunette inlaid edge, three crossbanded frieze drawers above a pair of cupboard doors, a pair of bottle drawers, and small silver drawers centering a pair of hinged cupboard doors and reeded half column pilasters, lunette inlaid molded skirt, acanthus

carved and reeded tapering legs, five legs extended below carving, some losses to veneers, 83½" w, 24½" d, 41½" h **3,960**

Massachusetts, Boston, attributed to John and/or Thomas Seymour, 1801–15, mahogany, inlaid, outset rounded corners and lunette inlaid edge on oblong top, five short drawers and two bottle drawers flanked by a pair of hinged cupboard doors, centered by reeded half round columns, lunette inlaid apron continuing to ring turned reeded tapering legs, tapered feet, lion's head pulls, 68½" w, 23" d, 40¾" h **20,900**

Massachusetts, Salem or eastern shore, 1815, mahogany, flamed birch inlaid, carved, oblong top, two cockbeaded small drawers centering a bowed frieze drawer, pair of bottle drawers and two pair of cupboard doors, leaf carved and punchwork decorated reeded pilasters, reeded tapering legs ending in tapered feet, some repair to legs, 73½" w, 22¾" d, 42" h **5,500**

New York or Philadelphia, Pennsylvania, 1810–15, mahogany, rectangular top above three cockbeaded short drawers over two hinged cockbeaded cupboard doors centering two recessed bowed cockbeaded doors, reeded

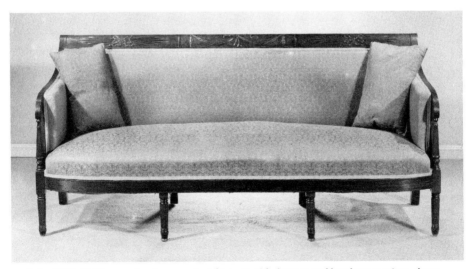

Sofa, 1795–1810, carved mahogany, straight crest with drapery and bowknot carvings, downcurving reeded arms, reeded tapered arm supports, upholstered back, sides, and seat, bowed reeded seat rail, round reeded legs, $1,200.00.

stiles, ring turned and reeded tapering legs ending in ball feet, minor repairs to veneer, 72" w, 42" h   **2,200**

Sofa

American, figured mahogany, inlaid, simple inlay on exposed crest, upholstered back, arms, and seat, line inlaid scrolled arms, scrolled legs terminating in brass paw feet, new silk brocade upholstery, repairs to frame and front legs, 71¼" l **1,000**

Massachusetts, Salem, early 19th C, mahogany, carved, straight crest, down curving scrolled arms, upholstered back, arms, and seat, exposed seat rail flanked by carved flowerhead dies, ring turned and reeded tapered legs terminating in tapered feet, 75¼" l, 15½" h seat, 33½" h overall **2,310**

New Hampshire, Portsmouth, mahogany and figured maple veneer, arched crest, down curving arms continuing to ring turned and reeded bulbous arm supports, upholstered back, arms, and seat, ring turned and reeded tapered legs ending in ring turned and tapered feet, refinished, 79" l, 17" h seat, 37" h overall **1,100**

New York, 1800–15, attributed to Slover and Taylor, mahogany, carved, molded crest centering a carved sunburst rectangular tablet, down curving molded arms with carved flowerheads at top and bottom, waterleaf carved and fluted tapering arm supports, upholstered back, arms, and seat, square tapering reeded legs ending in brass and wood wheel casters, white muslin upholstery, small patch to inside back leg, 78" l, 40½" h **14,300**

New York, 1800–10, mahogany, molded crest centering a fluted rectangular reserve, molded fluted arms, slightly bowed upholstered seat, flowerhead dies flanking, square reeded legs ending in brass spade feet, brass casters, some restoration, 73" l **9,900**

New York, 1805–15, mahogany, reeded crest, center tablet carved with thunderbolts tied with bow, upholstered back, reeded arm supports, reeded and waterleaf carved uprights, bowed upholstered seat, turned reeded legs, brass casters, legs reduced, repairs to two rear legs, 71¼" l **8,750**

Pennsylvania, Philadelphia, 1815, mahogany, carved, slightly arched

crest above upholstered back flanked by leaf carved terminals, semi–exposed seat rail below with flowerhead carved dies, reeded tapering legs, some restoration to legs and crest, 74¾" l **2,420**

Stand

Night, New York, 1790–1810, mahogany, thumb molded rectangular top, plain apron, incised cockbeaded drawer, four thin turned tapering legs, bulbous cuffs, 15" w, 21½" d, 27" h **1,800**

Work, New England, 1805–15, mahogany, veneered, outset rounded corners on shaped top, pullout suspended fabric bag below single drawer, ring turned and reeded round tapering legs ending in ring turned tapering vasiform feet, old refinish, 16½" w, 18½" d, 28¼" h   **3,300**

Card Table, 1805–15, carved mahogany, hinged serpentine leaf on conforming top, inlaid edges and frieze, reeded round tapered legs, 36" w, 29½" h, $3,500.00.

Table

Card

American, mahogany, flame veneer, oblong top with conforming hinged leaf, convoluted apron with flame veneer and conforming reeded edge top, turned and reeded legs, swing leg support, brass acanthus leaf caps and casters, old refinish, 37¾" w, 17" d, 30¼" h **1,300**

Massachusetts, 1795–1805, mahogany, tiger maple veneer, outset rounded corners on scrolled front and sides, conforming hinged leaf, line inlaid edges, outline stringing on tiger maple veneered frieze, ring turned and reeded tapering legs ending in tapering feet, refinished, 37¼" w, 18¼" d, 30½" h **3,410**

Massachusetts, 1795–1805, mahogany, tiger maple and flame birch veneers, oblong top, serpentine front and sides, conforming hinged leaf, inlaid edges, inlaid frieze, ring turned corner columns, ring turned and reeded tapering legs ending in tapering feet, refinished, 35¾" w, 19½" d, 29½" h **2,750**

Massachusetts, north shore, 1800–10, mahogany, flame birch inlaid, oblong top, serpentine front and sides, conforming hinged leaf above a crotch figured frieze with similarly inlaid dies, reeded tapering legs ending in elongated vasiform feet, minor repair to top of two legs, 37½" w, 18" d, 29¾" h **3,850**

Massachusetts, 1810–15, mahogany and birch, bow front, band inlaid edges on oblong top with bowed front and conforming hinged leaf, inlaid and flame birch veneered frieze flanked by rectangular inlaid and flame birch veneered dies, ring turned and reeded tapering legs, repairs to swing leg rail and knuckle section, feet slightly reduced in height, 42" w, 29" h **3,850**

Massachusetts, north shore, 1810–15, mahogany, carved, serpentine front, serpentine shaped hinged leaf with outset corners on conforming top and case, carved concentric rings on outset corners, ring turned and reeded tapering legs surmounted by flower carved panels, ball feet, 37½" w, 30½" h **2,200**

Massachusetts, Salem, 1815, mahogany, veneered, carved, serpentine front and sides, ovolo corners, conforming hinged leaf and frieze, leaf carving on star punched ground above ring turned and reeded round tapering legs ending in ring turned feet, casters, old refinish, 38¾" w, 18¼" d, 29¾" h **1,050**

New England, 1805–15, pair, mahogany, flame birch inlaid, serpentine top with outset rounded corners and hinged leaf, con-

forming frieze with rectangular inlaid panels, ring turned tapering legs ending in elongated vasiform feet, one with restoration to leaf, one with patches to top near hinges, both with repairs to inlay, 35" w, 17" d, 29¾" h, price for pair **4,950**

New Hampshire, early 19th C, cherry, oblong top, bowed front, conforming hinged leaf above cockbeaded drawer, mahogany veneered drawer front, ring turned and reeded tapering legs ending in tapering feet, brass pulls, 35¼" w, 16½" d, 30" h . .   **1,100**

Pennsylvania, Philadelphia, Haines–Connelly School, 1805–15, mahogany, carved, oblong top, serpentine front and conforming hinged leaf above cockbeaded frieze, acanthus carved reeded tapering legs ending in vasiform feet, repair to leaf near hinge, 35¾" w, 17¾" d, 29¼" h   **1,650**

Console, Massachusetts, Salem, 1795–1815, pair, mahogany, carved, inlaid, molded edge and crossbanded border on demilune top, conforming veneered apron, three astragal inlaid end panels, four waterleaf carved turned tapering stop fluted legs surmounted by astragal inlaid dies, waterleaf carved cuffs, tapering feet joined by open curved X–stretcher, central astragal shaped medial block, repairs to stretchers and one leg, price for pair **31,000**

Dining

American, 1815, mahogany, veneer, two part, two D–shaped end sections each with a hinged leaf, beaded edge on skirt, ring turned and reeded tapering legs ending in ring turned tapering feet on casters, refinished, some veneer replaced, 93" l, 48" w, 30" h **2,100**

American, 1815, drop leaf, gate leg, pair of rectangular leaves flanking rectangular top, straight apron, ring turned and reeded tapering legs terminating in turned tapering feet, 22" l, 66½" open length, 48" w, 29" h, ...   **715**

American, 1815, mahogany, three parts, center section with two hinged leaves, two D–shaped end sections each with a hinged leaf, beaded edge on skirt, reeded tapering legs ending in turned feet, center section now fitted with extension mechanism, 106½" l, 48" w, 29½" h **3,850**

American, 1815, mahogany, three parts, rectangular top, rounded corners on end sections, each section with ring turned pedestal and four splayed down curving reeded legs ending in cast bronze animal paw feet and casters, 112" l, 60" w, 28½" h **11,000**

Dressing

American, 1815, mahogany, inlaid, rectangular mirror panel flanked by columnar supports surmounted by urn finials, scrolled brackets, inlaid edge and rounded front corners on slightly overhanging rectangular top, similarly shaped case with single frieze drawer, tapering rope turned legs ending in ball feet, bail handles on solid backplates, top may be a later addition, 36" w, 18" d, 63½" h **875**

New York, 1815, cherry, painted red, scalloped back and conforming side panels, varnished rectangular top, square legs with ringed capitals changing to round tapering legs, ball feet, brass pulls, 30¾" w, 16¼" d, 32" h .. **850**

Pembroke

American, 1805–15, mahogany, inlaid, line inlaid border and reeded edge on rectangular top, pentagonal leaves, single drawer frieze, reverse faced to simulate a working drawer, flanked by rectangular inlaid dies on reeded tapered legs ending in vasiform feet, brass casters, oval brasses, some repair to inlay and top of one leg, 23½" l, 39½" extended length, 28¼" h **1,980**

New York, 1800–10, mahogany, inlaid, oblong top, two shaped hinged leaves above single cockbeaded drawer, reverse faced to simulate working drawer, tombstone inlaid dies flanking, reeded tapering legs ending in vasiform feet, brass casters, 36" l, 46" extended length, 29" h **1,760**

Sewing

Massachusetts, 1805–15, cherry, rectangular top, two cockbeaded drawers, outset rounded corners, leaf carved stiles form reeded cylindrical legs, turned feet, 22" w, 27½" h **1,450**

Mid Atlantic, probably Baltimore,

Maryland, 1815, mahogany, carved, rectangular top, two hinged shaped leaves above two cockbeaded drawers, upper drawer fitted with divided compartments, sewing bag slide below, reeded tapering legs ending in brass casters, 33¾" extended length, 18" w, 30" h **1,650**

Work

Massachusetts, 1805–15, mahogany, rectangular top with rounded outset corners, two cockbeaded drawers, ring and baluster turned tapering reeded legs ending in tapering feet, restoration to three legs, slightly reduced in height, some veneer missing, 18½" w, 29" h **875**

Massachusetts, Boston, possibly by Elijah Tucker, 1801–15, mahogany, bird's eye maple inlaid, outset rounded corners on oblong top, single drawer frieze, inlaid diamond escutcheon on drawer front, divided compartments in drawer, turned tapering legs, brass pulls, 20½" w, 15½" d, 28¾" h **9,350**

New England, 1805–15, bird's eye maple and mahogany, reeded edge and outset rounded corners on oblong top, two drawers, divided compartment in upper drawer, three–quarter round ring turned columns continuing to ring turned vasiform legs ending in tapered feet, 20½" w, 16" d, 28¼" h **4,400**

New York, 1800–10, mahogany, bow front, oblong top with bow front, two conforming drawers, reeded and ring turned legs terminating in casters, restoration to veneers, 16½" w, 31" h **1,120**

Writing, New York, 1795–1805, mahogany, inlaid, rectangular crossbanded top opening to interior well with covered compartments and ink and pen recesses, ratcheted writing flap, simulated drawer over single working drawer in case, ring turned and reeded tapering legs ending in brass casters, 22¼" w, 22¼" d, 32¾" h **3,080**

STYLE

Blanket Chest

American, pine and poplar, painted red, molded edge on hinged lift lid, paneled front and ends, square cor-

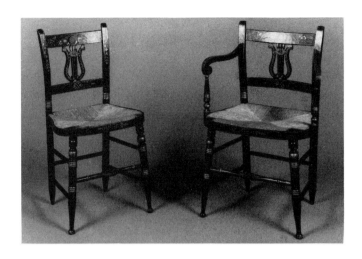

Chairs, set of eight (two armchairs and six side chairs), Sheraton Fancy Chairs, New England, early 19th C, rectangular crest above pierced lyre form splat flanked by chamfered round stiles above a balloon shaped rush seat on ring–turned tapering legs ending in button feet joined by a diamond shaped front stretcher, decorated with leafage, arrows, and fruit, $5,225.00. Photograph courtesy of Butterfield & Butterfield.

ner posts, mortised and pinned frame, scalloped apron, turned feet, 44" l, 19½" d, 25½" h   675

American, walnut, molded edge on hinged lift lid, interior molded till, paneled front and ends, square corner posts, turned feet, refinished, 37½" l, 17" d, 21½" h   400

Stand, wash

American, cherry, dovetailed gallery, rectangular top, turned posts, single dovetailed drawer, turned feet, refinished, 19½" w, 16½" d, 28" h .   300

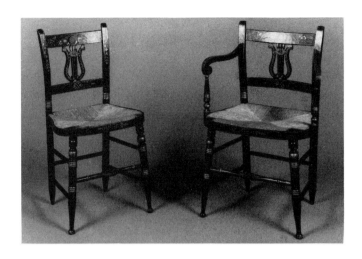

Card Table, probably Massachusetts, c1815, mahogany, lunette inlay, serpentine front and bowed sides, legs feature ring turning in section at apron, a bulb–ring–spool turning at top, reeded tapered sides ending in ring–tapered–ball–tapered foot, $2,350.00. Photograph courtesy Skinner, Inc.

American, cherry, scalloped edge on 8½" high dovetailed gallery, rectangular top, straight apron, slender turned vasiform posts, medial shelf above single dovetailed drawer, opalescent pulls, ring turned tapering legs ending in ring turned feet, old dark varnish stain finish, age crack in top, 19¾" w, 15" d, 37¾" h   525

American, pine, decorated, red and green striping on white ground, corner shelves on crest, rectangular top, cutout hole for bowl, single dovetailed drawer, white porcelain pulls, turned posts and legs, 20¾" w, 16¼" d, 32¾" h   225

Table

Breakfast, pine, dropleaf, two 11" rounded corner leaves, single dovetailed drawer, turned hardwood legs, red flame graining, warped leaves, 42" w, 17¾" d, 29¾" h . . .   450

Drop Leaf, upper New York state, cherry, rectangular leaves and top, six slender turned vasiform legs continuing to tapering feet on casters, refinished, repaired split in one corner of reattached top, one leaf replaced, leg turnings vary slightly, crack in one leg, 45" w, 19" d, 19¾" l leaves, 29" h   215

GRECO–ROMAN OR NEOCLASSIC (1790–1815)

History: As the eighteenth century ended, American furniture tastes favored a more literal borrowing from the forms of ancient Greek and Roman civilization. Although the influence came from both England and France, it is the French taste that appears the most dominant. The principal influence was the work of Charles Percier and Pierre Fontaine, Napoleon's architects.

Chair designs were heavier and followed more closely the ancient klismos model. The classical Grecian couch found popularity as a daybed. Sofa designs became simpler, featuring either a straight top or curved back.

Thomas Hope's *Household Furniture and Decoration* was one of the first furniture design style books to be published in America. Hope's formal classical designs incorporated zoological decorations and drew heavily on the designs of ancient civilizations.

Do not confuse these pieces with those of the Empire (Classic Style) of the first quarter of the nineteenth century. Empire pieces are much heavier in design form and contain decorative accents not found in Federal neoclassical pieces.

Style Books: Thomas Hope, *Household Furniture and Decoration*, 1807; Charles Percier and Pierre F. L. Fontaine, *Recuil de decorations interieures*, 1801, revised edition in 1812.

Bedstead
    Massachusetts, Salem, attributed to Samuel McIntire, 1800–10, birchwood, mahogany, and pine, carved, four post, tester, tapered birchwood head posts centering an arched pine headboard with cyma shaped cutouts, foot posts comprising baluster form reeded upper section above acanthus leaf and water leaf carved vasiform midsection with draped grapes and leaves tied with bowknots against a punch work ground, turned feet, tester is later addition, 79" l, 58" w **7,425**
    New York, c1805–15, mahogany, carved, four post, baluster turned and tapered head posts, ring turned foot posts, reeded, carved acanthus leafage and drapery swags, arched headboard, square tapering legs ending Marlborough feet, feet restored, 87½" h **3,575**
    New York, 1815, mahogany and pine, tester, four post, turned head posts, shaped pine headboard, reeded and acanthus carved foot posts ending in carved animal paw feet, top of foot posts cut and reattached, 78¼" l, 55½" w **5,225**
Chair
    Set of Eight, Maryland, one c1800, seven late 19th C, assembled, side, mahogany, carved, molded flowerhead carved crest above swag

Side Chair, Boston, c1825, mahogany, klysmos form, curved crest rail ending in fleur-de-lis carving, demilune drapery carving as center splat, bowed stiles extending along side seat and ending with a circular accent, front seat rail accented by rope carving with diamond shaped leaf in center, acanthus leaf carving at top of front legs, $6,250.00 Photograph courtesy of Skinner, Inc.

and tassel and bellflower carved splat, overupholstered serpentine seat on molded square tapering legs joined by stretchers, price for set . **6,600**
Side
    Connecticut or Rhode Island, pair, serpentine shaped crest rail, pierced splat with urn, upholstered slip seat, square legs joined by stretchers, old refinish, 17" h seat, 37" h overall, price for pair **1,100**
    Massachusetts, Boston, Samuel Gragg, 1800–1815, bentwood, painted and decorated, shaped monogrammed crest rail, five bentwood uprights, slatted seat, splayed legs joined by stretchers, hoof feet, painted black, yellow outline striping, stamped "Gragg Patent" on seat underside, paint restored **1,650**
    Rhode Island, Providence, 1790–1810, mahogany, carved,

molded back, pierced splat carved at center with a kylix and swags, serpentine shaped front on upholstered seat, molded square legs joined by H– stretcher, minor repair to shoe . **4,400**

Rhode Island, Providence, 1790– 1810, mahogany, shield shaped molded back centering a pierced splat carved with an urn, swags and flowerheads with a fan carved reserve below, trapezoidal seat rail enclosing a slip seat, tapered molded legs joined by stretchers **4,675**

Mirror, Salem, MA, 1809–10, giltwood, molded cornice with outset corners, leaf molding frieze, white eglomise panel with gilt classical figures, molded columns, surface imperfections, 20¼″ w, 38½″ h, $1,450.00. Photograph courtesy of Skinner, Inc.

Mirror, hanging
American, 1815, giltwood, projected molded cornice hung with spherules, eglomise tablet entitled "Harmony," over rectangular mirror plate flanked by carved and ring turned half columns, minor gilt loss, 26½″ w, 46″ h **3,300**
American, early 19th C, giltwood, projecting molded cornice hung with spherules above tablet with applied floral decoration over bi-

partite mirror plate flanked by columnar supports, upper mirror glass replaced, 45″ h **415**
American, 19th C, giltwood, surmounted by an eagle on a plinth above an arch with stars, scrolled leafage flanking, rectangular mirror plate below with a gilded slip, corner mounted with rosettes, 24½″ w, 61″ h **2,090**
New York, New York City or Albany, 1790–1810, giltwood, rosettes and urn finials on outset corners of molded cornice, castle and tree vignette decoration on black and gold eglomise panel above rectangular mirror plate flanked by molded columns ending in plinths with flowerhead decoration, 22¾″ w, 42″ h **715**
New York, 1790–1800, mahogany giltwood, inlaid, swan's neck crest centering a giltwood urn with spray of flowers, bookend inlaid tympanum and rectangular mirror plate below flanked by giltwood filets above a shaped pendant, finial and one scroll restored, minor repairs to crest, 56″ h **4,400**
New York, 1790–1810, pair, giltwood, eglomise, wingspread eagle perched on a patarae molded plinth with ball and wire in its beak continuing to flanking urns, gold and black vase of flowers on eglomise panel above rectangular mirror plate, fluted half columns flanking, 18¼″ w, 37½″ h, price for pair ... **35,200**
New York, 1790–1810, mahogany and giltwood, eglomise, surmounted by a giltwood urn finial with a spray of leaves above a tympanum inlaid with a conch shell, flanked by molded swan's neck crest, bucolic landscape with castle and birds depicted on eglomise panel above a rectangular mirror plate, flowerhead and leaf filets flanking, shaped pendant below, finial replaced, 23″ w, 59½″ h ... **9,350**
New York, 1800–15, giltwood, eglomise, projecting reeded broken cornice surmounted by an eagle raised on a tall fluted plinth applied with a crossed bow and arrow, suspending from his beak a chain punctuated with spherules linked to the flanking amphora form finials holding wheat stalks and flowers, eglomise panel reserved with a hexagonal view of a house in a landscape flanked by grape clusters

above a rectangular mirror panel, flanked by fluted columnar stiles with acanthus leaf capitals and flowerhead plinths, molded base, early regilding, replaced backboard, eglomise panel restored, 26" w, 61" h **1,100**

Secretary Bookcase, American, early 19th C, mahogany, shaped cornice, Gothic mullioned doors enclosing shelves, three aligned drawers, foldout baize lined writing surface, three reeded molded graduated drawers, tapered reeded legs, 36½" w, 22" d, 74" h **2,100**

Settee, New York, 1815, mahogany, carved, paneled crest, rectangular upholstered back and seat flanked by scrolled arms, carved flowerheads and leafage decoration on arms, inlaid brass stringing on apron, cornucopia carved legs ending in animal paw feet, 103" l **3,300**

Sideboard

New York, 1815, mahogany, carved, rectangular top with Palladian arched splashboard flanked by reeded columns with acorn finials, broken frieze with three short drawers over four hinged paneled cupboard doors centering two acanthus carved and reeded columns flanked by acanthus carved square tapering applied pilasters, shelved interior, turned tapering acanthus carved legs ending in lion's paw feet, lion's head drawer pulls, restoration to interior center drawer, repairs to veneer and feet, 52" h, 72½" w, 52" h **1,650**

New York, mahogany, painted and inlaid, bow front, oblong top with bowed front, conforming case with two convex cupboard doors centering two convex drawers above two recessed cupboard doors, bookend and line inlaid dies, reeded cones at top of line inlaid square tapering legs ending in crossbanded cuffs, polychrome painted griffins, bacchanalic figures, masks, and garlands, reeded cones and painted figures are later additions, 68" w, 27½" d, 39¼" h **4,125**

Rhode Island, 1800–10, band inlaid edge on D-shaped oblong top, conforming case with three band inlaid and cockbeaded short drawers above two band inlaid and cockbeaded cupboard doors centering two similarly banded and cockbeaded tall bottle drawers centering

a band inlaid cockbeaded drapery carved hinged door, square tapering line inlaid legs terminating in carved spade feet, restoration to veneer and legs, 70½" w, 41½" h . .   **4,500**

Sofa, Maryland, Baltimore, early 19th C, Pompeian, painted red, polychrome and gilt stenciled decoration, scrolled crest, scrolled arms, upholstered, brass lion's paw feet on casters, 95" l **6,500**

Table

Breakfast, New York, 1815, mahogany, rectangular top with two hinged shaped leaves, frieze with cockbeaded drawer, reverse faced to simulate a working drawer, reeded urn form standard, reeded down curving legs ending in brass animal paw feet on brass casters, lacks turned pendants on skirt, 45½" extended length, 36" w, 29" h **3,025**

Card

Massachusetts, Boston, attributed to Timothy Hunt, 1815, fold top, mahogany, carved, rectangular rounded corner top, fluted ball and ring turned standard, cabriole legs, acanthus leaf carvings on knees, brass lion's paw feet on casters **2,420**

Pennsylvania, 1815, cherrywood, curly maple inlaid, swivel top, shaped corners on oblong top, conforming hinged leaf swiveling to reveal marbleized paper lined well, crossbanded frieze with two pendants above lyre form support, reeded down curving legs ending in brass animal paw feet and casters, 36¾" w, 18¾" d, 30" h **3,850**

DUNCAN PHYFE AND PHYFE COPYISTS (1795–1840)

History: Duncan Phyfe (1768–1854) was trained as a cabinet maker in Scotland. After a brief sojourn in Albany, he was working in New York by 1792. Phyfe quickly evolved from cabinet maker to furniture executive. At its height, his firm, Duncan Phyfe & Sons, employed approximately 150 individuals—quite a contrast to the typical cabinet maker's shop consisting of three to nine workers.

Phyfe relied on a division of labor to produce his pieces. His factory consisted of master craftsmen, journeymen, apprentices, carvers, turners, and upholsterers—each performing a different operation. A single piece of furniture was the work of many hands.

Phyfe dominated American furniture style along the eastern seaboard. His pieces were noted for their design restraint and excellence in manufacture. Contemporary manufacturers went out of their way to identify their work as in the Phyfe manner. Mahogany from Cuba and Santo Domingo was the favored wood but by 1830, much of Phyfe's furniture was made of rosewood.

Phyfe was not a design innovator; he was an adapter and blender of existing English styles. During his early period, the Sheraton influence was strong. One of Phyfe's major design sources was the *London Chair–Maker's and Carver's Book of Prices for Workmanship*, first published in 1802 and reissued and updated in 1808. He later shifted design emphasis to the design styles of the French Directoire.

Among the motifs commonly found in Phyfe furniture are the acanthus leaf, cornucopia, drapery, harp, laurel, lyre, rosette, sheaf of wheat, and trumpet. Reeding is prevalent. Brass and ormolu feet are common. The more commonly found Phyfe forms include the settee with reeded back and seat, chairs, tripod footed card tables, work (sewing) tables, and extension dining tables.

Only a small amount of surviving furniture can be attributed to Phyfe's shop. It is impossible to use general design, carved motifs, and construction techniques for accurate indentification because many of his employees carried these traditions with them as they moved between shops.

Phyfe's adaptability did not end with a blending of neoclassical styles. The products of his shop kept pace with changing period tastes. At the end of his career, he was working actively in the French Restauration design style.

Bench, window
  American, early 19th C, mahogany, carved, X–form slats, reeded stiles, openwork armrests, upholstered rectangular seat raised on reeded saber legs ending in brass feet on casters, 38¾" l, 28¾" h **950**
  New York, c1835, mahogany and mahogany veneer, rectangular seat with linen and wool reupholstery, S–scrolled legs with concentric circle motifs at ends, each pair of legs mounted on a rectangular platform with molded ends, 45" l, 16" h ... **3,500**
Candlestand, New York, 19th C, mahogany, carved, tilt top, reeded edge on shaped oblong top, waterleaf carved urn form standard, reeded down curving legs ending in ball feet, 25½" l, 19" d, 28" h **3,850**
Chair
  Arm
    New York, New York City, 1800–10, mahogany, carved, scroll back, crest rail with carved motif of reeds tied with bowknot, double X–shaped slats with carved rosettes at centers, reeded posts and lower rail, reeded down curving scrolled arms, turned arm supports, upholstered

Sideboard, New York, 1810–30, carved mahogany, pineapple finials on stepped crest, rectangular top, three drawers, central concave section with tambour doors flanked by cupboard doors, tapered columns with scrolled capitals, animal paw feet, lion's head brasses, $7,500.00.

bowed seat, reeded saber legs, 32½" h **4,500**
New York, 1805–15, pair, mahogany, carved, scrolled crest centering a panel carved with sheaves of wheat tied with a bowknot above a double X–form splat centering carved rosettes, reeded down curving arms flanking on turned and leaf carved arm supports, balloon shaped overupholstered seat with reeded seat rail, reeded tapering legs ending in vasiform feet, one slightly reduced in height, both with repairs to crests and splats, 31½" h, price for pair **23,100**
Set of Five, assembled, New York, 1800–20, mahogany, comprising a pair and a set of three, each of klismos form with concave crest, pierced horizontal splat with central carved flowerhead held by upper and lower fans within scrolling rails, molded stiles continuing to enclose upholstered slip seat, sabre legs, brass stringing on crest of set of three, price for set of five **2,250**
Side
New York, 1795–1805, mahogany, carved, scroll back, curved rectangular crest rail with carved motif of reeds tied by bowknot, reeded stiles continue to vase shape below reeded lower rail, double X–shaped slats centering carved rosettes, curved and reeded seat rail, tapered and reeded round front legs continue to round tapered feet, flared square rear legs, 31½" h **5,000**
New York, New York City, 1810–20, mahogany, carved, scroll back, scrolled crest rail, lyre shaped splat, down curving reeded stiles form continuous sweep to sides of trapezoidal upholstered slip seat, saber legs, front legs with acanthus leaf carving terminating in carved lion's paw feet, 32" h **6,750**
New York, New York City, 1810–20, pair, chairs numbered XI and XII, mahogany, side, each of klismos form with convex paneled crest rail carved with intertwined overflowing cornucopias filled with fruit and wheat stalks, pierced lyre splat carved with acanthus leaves and with brass strings and an ebony yoke, reeded stiles and lower rail, up-

holstered drop–in set, molded sabre legs, price for pair **16,000**
Chest of Drawers, New York, New York City, 1810–20, mahogany, tulip, and white pine, carved, reeded edge on oblong top with rounded outset corners and elliptical front, conforming case with three long drawers divided by crossbanded inlays, three–quarter column stiles continuing to turned legs terminating in carved lion's paw feet, lion's head pulls **4,750**
Daybed, New York, New York City, 1835, mahogany veneered, asymmetrical back with wide veneered band above upholstery, scrolled upholstered arms with concentric circle motif on exposed mahogany veneered fascia and seat rail, square legs on variation bun feet, linen and wool reupholstery **1,250**
Settee, New York, New York City, 1810–20, mahogany, carved, convex crest rail with carved cornucopia flanked by swags, reeded outer stiles sweep to sides to brace arms, reeded scrolled arms with carved armrest panels, triple back, three caned panels separated by two reeded stiles, upholstered cushion on rectangular caned seat, reeded seat rail, acanthus leaf carved out curving legs surmounted by carved lion's faces, lion's paw feet **18,125**
Table
Breakfast, New York, 1810–30, mahogany, carved, molded edge on rectangular top and demilune drop leaves, beaded edge on frieze drawer, opposing faux drawer, ring turned pendants at corners, four leaf carved supports resting on fluted plinth issuing four leaf carved downswept legs terminating in brass paw feet, one leg repaired, 51" extended length, 39" w, 27½" h **2,300**
Card
Massachusetts, 1810–15, mahogany, bird's eye maple veneer, rectangular bow front top and conforming hinged leaf swivels to reveal interior well, three rectangular inlaid bird's eye maple panels flanked by lion's head brasses, lyre form support, down curving legs ending in square brass casters, restorations to base, 33½" w, 29½" h **3,300**
New York, 1810–15, mahogany, carved, rectangular top with canted corners and conforming

hinged leaf swivels to reveal interior well, acanthus carved pedestal above quadrupartite base with outward scrolling acanthus carved legs ending in lion paw casters, 36½" w, 29½" h **3,850**

New York, New York City, 1810–20, mahogany, triple elliptical fronted top and conforming hinged leaf, ring turned vasiform pedestal with acanthus leaf carving, tripod base with down curving reeded and acanthus leaf carved legs terminating in brass lion's paw feet and brass casters, rear legs rotate when top is opened **3,500**

New York, c1825, mahogany, rounded corners and banded border on hinged leaf and conforming top, top swivels to reveal storage well, brass inlaid edges on top and leaf, baize covered playing surface, rounded corners on recessed skirt with brass line inlays on lower edge, tapered columnar pedestal mounted on X–shaped base with rounded outset ends, brass inlaid decoration on edge of base, round tapered feet on brass casters, 29½" h **7,500**

Center, New York, 1800–10, mahogany, carved, drop leaf, rectangular top flanked by pair of triple elliptical shaped leaves hinged to long sides, swing out supports, single drawer, corners hung with turned pendants, double pedestal base with waterleaf carved vasiform pedestals conjoined by reeded vasiform stretcher, four down curving waterleaf carved legs ending in gilded bronze lion's paw feet on casters, 42" l extended length, 27" h **8,100**

Dining

American, mahogany, rectangular top with two drop leaves, frieze drawer, splayed legs, brass paw caster feet, 54" extended length, 47" w, 28½" h **1,100**

New York, mahogany, two part, two D–shaped end sections above a beaded frieze, reeded tapering legs ending in vasiform feet on brass casters, two leaves, 77½" extended length, 53½" w, 28¾" h **9,350**

Drop Leaf, New York, 1803, mahogany, carved, rectangular top flanked by drop leaves with rounded corners, rectangular veneered panels on straight aprons, corners hung with ring turned pendants, slightly tapering hexagonal pedestal on ring turned base, four down curving legs with incised outlining and concentric rings on knees, lion's paw feet on casters, 49¼" l, 41" w, 29⅜" h **1,980**

Pier, New York, New York City, 1830–40, mahogany, rounded corners and reeded edge on rectangular marble top, curviate frieze with crossbanded edge, square columnar back legs support mirrored back panel, shaped lower shelf with outset corners, front corners canted, concentric circle motif at top and bottom of S–scrolled front legs, block feet **2,500**

Work

American, 1815–35, highly figured mahogany veneer, rounded corners on slightly overhanging rectangular top, conforming case with three graduated drawers, ring turned and acanthus leaf carved pedestal base, acanthus leaf carvings on four fluted down curving legs, animal paw feet, casters, brass pulls **1,800**

New York, 1800–10, mahogany, carved, astragal shaped hinged top, interior fitted with adjustable baize lined writing surface flanked by two demilune divided removable wells, reeded tambour sliding door, acanthus leaf carving on reeded down curving legs, brass animal paw feet on brass casters, some restoration to one foot, 25½" w, 13" d, 31½" h **16,500**

New York, New York City, 1810–20, mahogany, tulip, and white pine, carved, brass banded edge on rectangular marble top with canted corners, conforming case with single drawer frieze and brass banding over tapering lower storage area with molded edge, four ring turned and swirled columns on single plinth forms pedestal type base, four down curving reeded legs terminating in carved lion's paw feet on casters **17,000**

Pennsylvania, Philadelphia, 1800–20, mahogany, curly maple inlaid, outset rounded corners on oblong top, two drawers, ring turned three–quarter round columns flanking drawers, double lyre base with brass strings, plinth base continuing to down curving legs ending in brass animal paw feet, casters, some restoration to applied turnings, repair to one leg, 20¾" w, 15¼" d, 30" h **17,600**

Pennsylvania, Philadelphia, 1800–20, mahogany, curly maple inlaid, outset rounded corners with applied metal flowerheads on oblong top, ring turned three–quarter round columns flanking two drawers, upper drawer fitted with removable divided compartments, pendants on corners, double lyre standard with brass strings, plinth base continuing to down curving legs ending in brass animal paw feet, restoration to two pendants on skirt, losses to appliques on base, 21" w, 16¼" d, 30½" h **12,100**

COUNTRY FORMAL AND TRANSITIONAL (1790–1830)

History: By the beginning of the nineteenth century, America was expanding westward. The dominance of the eastern seaboard was being challenged by towns along the Erie Canal, Ohio River, and Southern Piedmont. Cabinet makers from the large urban areas could not meet the demands of the country as a whole. As a result, in middle–size and small towns across America, cabinet makers attempted to copy their big city counterparts—some were successful; many were not.

Far too many collectors view furniture made in the countryside as lacking high–style design elements. Nothing could be further from the truth. This is found in formal country furniture. Small town and village cabinet makers were not isolated from their urban brethren, just as local residents were cognizant of the latest big city tastes and desired to emulate them.

Country formal often does compromise proportion, construction techniques, and design elements. While the trend is toward greater durability and simplicity, this shift should not be viewed as lessening a piece's design aspects. When a Country piece shows clear evidence of design form and elements, it must be placed in the "formal" category.

In the neoclassical period, the most popular design style in the countryside is Sheraton. Its popularity continued throughout the nineteenth century and well into the twentieth century. It was a form which traveled well.

The American willingness to blend elements from more than one design style into a single piece leads to a group of "transitional" pieces as

major design styles shift. As the neoclassicism of the Federal period evolved into its later stages, i.e., Empire and French Restauration, pieces that could easily be placed in either period were made.

In the countryside, Sheraton pieces from the 1820s and later often contained Gothic elements. These pieces represent a transition from the neoclassic design styles to the Victorian revivals. Because so many of the forms are utilitarian (e.g., chests of drawers, washstands, and work tables) collectors tend to look past their design components. Remember, if there are identifiable design elements, think formal rather than vernacular.

Desk, 1790–1800, transitional, slant front, fitted interior with valanced pigeonholes and small drawers flanking central prospect door, hinged writing surface, pullout slides, three graduated thumb molded drawers, reeded quarter columns, shaped apron continuing to French feet, eagle brasses, $2,500.00.

Bedstead
American, cherrywood, quarter tester, octagonal shaped head posts, shaped headboard, acorn finials on foot posts, baluster turned legs, 59½" l, 78" h **725**
New England, early 19th C, maple and cherry, child's tall post, canopy, urn finials continuing to matching turned and tapering head posts and foot posts, shaped headboard, turned feet, original side rails, restoration, 72¼" l, 38" w, 50" h **1,650**
Candlestand
Massachusetts, western, 1810–20, cherry, tilt top, scalloped top, ring turned standard, cabriole tripod

legs ending in snake feet, old refinish, 19¼" w, 19¾" d, 27" h **1,425**

New England, 1800–15, mahogany, tilt top, octagonal shaped top with banded inlay edge, ring turned baluster standard, spider legs, 28½" h **650**

New England, 1810–20, maple and birch, tilt top, line inlaid octagonal shaped top, ring and baluster turned standard, cabriole legs, pad feet, restoration to one pad foot, 20" w, 26" h **825**

Rhode Island, 1790–1800, mahogany, circular top, turned pedestal, cabriole tripod legs ending in pad feet, refinished, top reset, 19½" d, 26" h **775**

Cellarette on Stand, mid Atlantic, 1790–1815, walnut, two sections: upper section: molded edge on rectangular top, rectangular case, fitted interior; lower section: molded edge stand with one long pullout tray, square tapering legs, 21" w, 40½" h **6,100**

Chair

Set of Eight, New York, attributed to Slover and Taylor, 1800–10, assembled, two arm, six side, fluted crest above four tapered reeded uprights, slightly bowed upholstered seat on square reeded tapering legs ending in spade feet, some with repairs, armchairs with restoration to arm supports at juncture with arms, price for set **9,350**

Side, Pennsylvania, Philadelphia, 1810–20, pair, mahogany, reeded slightly bowed crest above three reeded split baluster uprights, bowed seat rail enclosing slip seat on ring turned and reeded tapering legs ending in vasiform feet, minor repair to one crest, price for pair . **5,225**

Chest of Drawers

American, Hepplewhite style, birch, red and black flame graining, yellow and green striping, four dovetailed long drawers, turned wood pulls, embossed brass escutcheons, beaded frame, scalloped apron, cutout feet, 36⅜" h **3,400**

Connecticut River Valley, 1790–1810, cherry, mahogany veneer, bow front, inlaid edge on overhanging bow front top, conforming case, four graduated cockbeaded long drawers, scrolled skirt continuing to French feet, refinished, replaced oval brasses, 41" w, 23" d, 38" h **2,310**

New England, 1790–1800, serpentine front, serpentine top, conforming case, stringing and cockbeading on four conforming long drawers, shaped bracket feet, refinished, replaced brasses, 41" w, 23½" d, 36½" h **1,650**

New England, 1790–1810, cherry and veneer, bow front, stringing on edge of slightly overhanging oblong top, four cockbeaded long drawers, shaped apron continuing to French feet, refinished, replaced glass pulls, 38½" w, 22½" d, 38" h **2,100**

New England, 1800–20, mahogany veneer, bow front, oblong top, conforming case, four cockbeaded long drawers, shaped bracket feet, oval brasses, refinished, 40½" h, 38¾" w, 19¾" d **1,875**

New England, 1810–20, birch, rectangular top, four cockbeaded long drawers, shaped apron continuing to French feet, oval brasses, restoration to back edge of top, 41" w, 41½" h **1,100**

New England, northern, 1820s, maple and bird's eye maple veneer, bow front, slightly overhanging oblong top, bird's eye maple veneer drawer fronts on four long drawers flanked by fluted three–quarter columns, scalloped skirt on front and sides, ring turned tapered legs ending in ball feet, refinished, replaced turned wood pulls, 44½" w, 18½" d, 43" h **1,320**

New Hampshire, 1790–1810, cherry and mahogany, rectangular top, four cockbeaded long drawers, shaped skirt continuing to French feet, old refinish, replaced oval brasses, 36" w, 18¾" d, 37¼" h .. **1,975**

New York or Pennsylvania, 1800–15, mahogany, rectangular molded edge top, four long graduated cockbeaded edge drawers, shaped bracket feet, repairs to feet, 44" w, 38" h **990**

Cupboard

Corner

Mid Atlantic, early 19th C, cherrywood, molded cornice above two hinged glazed doors, three interior shelves, molded waist, two hinged paneled cupboard doors opening to a shelved interior, molded bracket feet, restoration to cornice and base, 51" w, 86" h **2,750**

Pennsylvania, 1790–1800, cherrywood, inlaid, two sections: upper section: triglyph inlaid molded pitched pediment centering a turned urn finial above an arched glazed hinged door opening to a painted blue shelved interior; lower section: three cockbeaded line inlaid drawers, pair of hinged paneled line inlaid cupboard doors opening to a shelf, scrolled faceted bracket feet, 46" w, 27¼" d, 97⅝" h ... **19,800**

Linen Press, New England, 1800–10, mahogany, two sections: upper section: molded edge top above two paneled cupboard doors opening to three long sliding drawers; lower section: two beaded edge short drawers over three beaded edge long drawers, shaped skirt, flaring French feet, small chips missing to front feet and skirt, brasses replaced with turned wood pulls, 54" w, 89" h **4,000**

Straight Front, New Jersey, Bergen County, 1810–20, pine and curly maple, stained red, bonnet top, two sections: upper section: molded swan's neck crest ending in gilt metal flowerhead caps, reeded geometric tympanum, pair of hinged glazed doors opening to shaped shelves flanked by curly maple turned half columns; lower section: three molded drawers, pair of hinged cupboard doors opening to single shelf, flanked by turned half columns, turned feet, 51" w, 21" d, 98½" h **5,500**

Desk
  Lady's Writing
    New England, probably Massachusetts, 1790–1810, mahogany and bird's eye maple, two sections: upper section: slightly projecting cornice above a pair of hinged doors opening to pigeonholes and small drawers; lower section: lined hinged writing flap above single maple veneered drawer above a pair of bottle drawers, centering a pair of hinged cupboard doors, turned feet, some minor veneer repairs, 37¾" w, 22" d, 49½" h **1,550**
    New England, 1825–35, mahogany veneer, slightly overhanging rectangular top over three cockbeaded drawers above a pair of hinged doors, small interior drawers and compartments, hinged fold out writing surface supported by fluted pullout slides, four cockbeaded long drawers, ring turned tapered legs

Desk on Frame, Country Hepplewhite, refinished pin, square tapered legs, one dovetailed drawer, slant top desk compartment with wide early dovetailing, overlapping drop lid with fitted interior consisting of row of pigeon holes with arched top baffles, base has been skillfully reconstructed, lid replaced, 37¾" w, 19¾" d, 37¾" h, $412.50. Photograph courtesy of Garth's Auctions, Inc., and *Antique Week*.

and feet, brass pulls and escutcheons **1,210**

Slant Front
  American, early 19th C, pine, rectangular top above long drawer, fall front writing surface enclosing small drawers, three graduated long drawers, reeded stiles, three graduated long drawers, shaped apron continuing to bracket feet, 41½" w, 21" d, 52" h **1,550**

  American, early 19th C, tiger maple, hinged slant front opening to fitted interior with leather inset writing surface, pullout slides, four graduated overlapping drawers, molded base, bracket feet, 36½" w, 17½" d, 41" h ... **3,950**

New England, 1800–15, walnut, rectangular top, slant lid, fitted interior with six short drawers and six valanced pigeonholes centering two fluted document drawers and a paneled prospect door opening to three short drawers, four graduated long drawers, ogee bracket feet, feet replaced, 38½" w, 44½" h **1,100**

Medical cabinet, c1815, cherrywood, stepback maple line inlays, inlaid stars, diamonds, and spearpoints, segmental arch molded and vaulted top with central stylized keystone block, inlaid with concentric diamonds, whole case molded, Sandwich type opalescent pressed glass knobs, period finish, mounted on later casters, 42" w, 20¾" d, 84" h, $1,875.00. Photograph courtesy of Pettigrew Auction Company.

Pennsylvania, 1800–15, walnut, rectangular top, rectangular slant lid, compartmentalized interior with eight valanced pigeonholes above eight short drawers centering two document drawers and a hinged prospect door opening to two short drawers, four gradu-

ated long drawers, shaped apron, flaring French feet, restorations to feet, 40½" w, 39" h **2,200**

Pennsylvania, 19th C, cherrywood, rectangular top, thumb molded edge on slant lid, compartmentalized interior with eight small drawers centering a prospect door opening to five graduated small drawers, pullout slides, thumb molded edge on four graduated long drawers, shaped apron, flaring French feet, 39¾" w, 47" h **1,870**

Desk and Bookcase, southern New England, early 19th C, cherry, molded broken scroll pediment, cast brass ball finials, double raised panel doors open to shelved interior, hinged writing flap, interior small drawers flanking center prospect door, pullout slides, four graduated overlapping drawers, shaped skirt continues to French feet, refinished, replaced brasses, 41½" w, 20¼" d, 85½" h .. **3,300**

Mirror, hanging

American, 1815–35, giltwood, broken projecting cornice hung with acorn drops above a pediment centering a shell flanked by applied wheat sheaves, two part rectangular mirror plate with molded border flanked by ring and cylinder turned split balusters, base with drapery swag molding, backboard replaced, three acorn drops missing, 26½" w, 45" h **600**

American, bull's eye, giltwood, parcel ebonized, carved, circular, convex mirror plate, molded surround, foliate and shell crest, foliate pendant, 28" w, 48" h **1,750**

Pole Screen, Massachusetts, 1800–20, mahogany, inlaid, octagonal frame enclosing floral embroidered needlework panel, sliding on rod with removable finial, ring turned standard raised on three down curving line inlaid legs joined by shaped plinth, ebonized tapered feet, some repairs, 57¼" h **1,870**

Secretary, New England, 1820–40, mahogany, veneered, broken scroll pediment ending in reeded columns, central reeded block, molded cornice, pair of tombstone arched glazed panes in double doors, interior with four open compartments over four small drawers, cockbeading on two short drawers, foldout lined writing surface, pullout slides flanking cockbeaded long drawer over two recessed cockbeaded long drawers, rope turned columns on square plinths, straight skirt, ring turned vasiform feet, old refinish, 37½" w, 18½" d, 66" h **2,200**

Sideboard

American, curly maple, poplar secondary wood, scalloped crest, three dovetailed drawers, turned curly maple pulls, base shelf, turned legs and feet, light natural refinishing, 36½" w, 36½" h **3,750**

New York, 1790–1810, mahogany, veneered, rectangular top, single cockbeaded drawer over recessed central molded paneled cupboard doors, flanked by three cockbeaded drawers each side, compartmentalized bottle drawer, square tapering legs, bail handle brasses, refinished, age crack in side, 60¼" w, 25" d, 38¼" h **3,300**

Sofa, Massachusetts or New York, 1790–1810, mahogany, carved, cabriole, upholstered arched back and curving sides, upholstered seat cushion, molded square tapering legs, straight front legs, curving back legs, 80½" l **13,200**

Sugar Chest, attributed to North Carolina, cherry, lift off lid, inlaid stars, lines, and circles on dovetailed case, large till, single dovetailed long drawer in frame, square tapering legs, cutout leg brackets, old finish, old repairs, replaced moldings, 31¼" w, 15¾" d, 36" h **11,000**

Table

Breakfast

New England, 1790–1800, cherry, dropleaf, serpentine top, shaped leaves, cutout skirt, molded square tapering legs, old refinish, 34" extended length, 34" w, 27¾" h **2,250**

New England, 1810–20, cherry, dropleaf, rectangular top, rounded corners on leaves, single beaded drawer, square double tapered legs, inlaid cuffs, 18½" w, 36" d, 29" h **650**

Card

American, butternut, pine secondary wood, folding top, swing leg supports hinged rectangular leaf, rectangular overlapping top, single dovetailed drawer, turned wood pulls, square tapered legs, old dark finish over earlier red, edge strips added to leaf, reset hinges, one back foot chipped, 35½" w, 14" d, 28½" h **800**

Delaware Valley, 1815–35, mahogany, carved, hinged rectangular folding top with rounded corners, conforming apron with a stylized pineapple carved central panel, four ring turned and acanthus leaf carved legs terminating in ball feet, 36" l, 17½" d, 30" h **1,650**

Dining, New England, 1800–20, cherry and mahogany, veneer, two part, gate leg, hinged leaf on D–shaped ends, veneered frieze, square tapering legs on casters, refinished, 88⅝" l, 51¼" w, 28½" h **1,425**

Work

Massachusetts, 1810–20, curly maple, shaped corners on oblong top, octagonal frieze with molded edge and ring turned pilasters centering a single cockbeaded drawer, ring turned tapering legs ending in tapered feet, 19¼" w, 18¾" d, 26" h ... **7,150**

New England, 1810–30, mahogany veneer, rectangular top, pair of rectangular drop leaves, two drawers, ring turned and fluted tapered legs terminating in ring turned tapered feet on casters, refinished, replaced brasses, 18" w, 17¾" d, 27½" h **650**

New England, 1820–30, mahogany veneer, molded edge on rectangular top, rounded corners on pair of drop leaves, two drawers, ring and rope turned tapered legs ending in tapered feet, brass pulls, refinished, 18¼" w, 17¼" d, 29½" h **600**

New England, 1820–40, rectangular top, two drawers, ring turned pedestal on tripod base, scrolled cyma shaped legs, simulated mahogany graining, replaced brasses, 17¾" w, 15⅝" d, 30" h **325**

New York, 1800–20, mahogany, rectangular top above two drawer frieze, upper drawer fitted with divided compartments, ring and block turned legs joined by a shaped medial shelf, ring turned feet, slight restoration to shelf, 22½" w, 15½" d, 31½" h **1,975**

Pennsylvania, Philadelphia, 1810–20, mahogany, outset rounded and ring turned corners on rectangular top, columnar standard, rectangular base continuing to four out scrolling legs ending in carved animal paw feet, casters, 21¾" w, 15½" d, 28½" h **1,425**

EMPIRE, CLASSICISM SECOND PHASE (1805–1830)

History: The archaeological investigations of the late eighteenth and early nineteenth century resulted in the study of Roman and Greek furniture forms. What evolved was a desire to live and dress like the ancients.

New York was the American center for the Empire design style, introduced by Phyfe. Charles–Honore Lannuier provided the French influence and continued many stylistic elements of the Federal Greco–Roman revival.

The carved decoration is often gilded or painted black. Furniture is often embellished with anthemia, flat floral–form ornamentation. Ormolu, gold or gilded brass or bronze used for decorative purposes, is prevalent and is often imitated through gilt stenciling. Although veneer is subdued, it occurs as inlaid lines of ebony and strips of maple.

Egyptian motifs are introduced, especially after Napoleon's campaigns and Nelson's victories. The American eagle, often elaborately gilded, appears as a decorative motif. The beginnings of a Gothic revival are seen in pointed arches and quatrefoils.

The klismos chair remained the popular form. Phyfe introduced a curule base to some chairs and settees. Lion and dog feet, often rendered as brass castings, were common. New forms included parlor tables, sofa tables, and wardrobes. The sleigh bed, mirrored pier or console table, and window seat were also interpreted in Empire design motifs.

Period Empire was short–lived in America and mainly confined to a few large eastern seaboard cities. The French Restauration design style quickly replaced it and today lives in the mind of American collectors as "Empire."

An off–shoot of Empire was the stenciled decorated "fancy" chair incorporating Sheraton design styles. The best known examples are the famed Hitchcock chairs produced by Lambert Hitchcock at his factory in Hitchcockville, Connecticut. The chairs were mass produced and sold throughout America.

Style Books: Rudolph Ackermann's *Repository of Arts*, a monthly periodical; Pierre de la Mesangere, *Collections des muebles et objets de gout de decorations interieures*; George Smith, *A Collection of Designs for Household Furniture and Interior Decoration*, 1808.

PERIOD

Armoire, New York, 1830, carved mahogany, double doors, blind paneled finely figured veneered doors, separated by brass bead, interior fitted with belt of three drawers, foliate carved and turned legs, ball feet, 72" w, 31" d, 98" h **3,000**

Bed
High Poster
Birch, shaped headboard, rope and acanthus carved turned posts, original rope rails, arched canopy frame, 66¾" h, 55 x 72" mattress **1,500**
New York, 1820–25, carved maple, baluster and ring turned head posts, carved acanthus, leaves, and swag drapery, double paneled headboard surmounted by carved bowl of fruit, bow shaped scrolled footboard, carved paw feet, 55 x 77" **2,500**
Rope, 1830, cherry, bold turnings, pineapple carving, cannon ball finials, paneled headboard with scalloped detail, original rails, 56 x 71¼" **900**
Tester, 1820, tiger maple posts, bird's eye maple headboard, refinished, replaced tester, 83" h **2,400**

Bookcase, American
Mahogany, rectangular top, cushion molded frieze, three glazed doors enclosing shelves with three quarter columns, shaped feet, electrified, 78" w, 17½" d, 58½" h **525**
Mahogany, reeded top molding, three pairs of doors with Winthrop style glass dividers, rope twisted columns, paw feet **2,950**

Butler's Chest, early 19th C, rectangular top, pullout fall front writing drawer, fitted interior, three recessed graduated cockbeaded drawers, circular brass pulls, bun feet, 45" w, 24" d, 45½" h **660**

Candlestand, Portsmouth, New Hampshire, 1805–30, mahogany, satinwood, and tiger maple, elliptical shaped top, bird cage support, beehive pedestal, saber legs, original brass paw casters, 18" w, 12" d, 30" h **3,500**

Chair
Arm, mahogany, barrel back, green watered silk upholstery **675**
Piano, 1825, mahogany, plain paneled crest rail, open work scroll and leaf carved slat, reeded stiles continue into seat rail, upholstered swivel seat, turned shaft, four leaf carved legs, paw feet, 28½" h ... **1,100**
Set
Set of Six, dining, side, 1805–30, mahogany, gadrooned crest rail, stop reeded stiles, upholstered

slip seat, saber legs, minor repair
to rear legs, price for set **12,000**
Set of Eight, Philadelphia, 1825,
mahogany, rounded concave
crest rail with brass string inlay,
leaf and rondel carved slat,
molded stiles continue into seat
rail, gold silk upholstered slip
seat, saber legs, price for set ... **3,850**
Side, mahogany and mahogany ve-
neer, fiddleback, serpentine seat,
saber leg **250**

Chest of Drawers
Cherry, curly maple facade with
cherry drawer edge beading, seven
dovetailed drawers, paneled ends,
turned pilasters and feet, refinished,
41⅜" w, 21½" d, 49" h **950**
Curly maple, cherry, and figured walnut, seven dovetailed drawers and
three step back handkerchief drawers, original crest finials, turned feet
and pilasters, alligatored varnish,
45" w, 46¼" h **700**
Curly maple, poplar secondary wood,
four dovetailed drawers, cockbeading, turned quarter columns, solid
ends, turned feet, replaced brasses,
old refinishing, 41" w, 18" d, 35¾"
h **2,000**
Mahogany, 1825, rectangular top,
two small frieze drawers over three
wide drawers, turned pilasters on
sides, turned feet, 44" w, 43½" h . **715**
Mahogany, serpentine front, rectangular marble top with ovolo corners, four graduated drawers,
reeded three quarter columns,
turned feet, casters, 48" w, 43½" d,
24" h **900**
Mahogany, straight front, two small
over three wide graduated drawers,
circular wood pulls, half spiral column sides, ring turned round legs,
43½" w, 21" d, 45½" h **300**
Mahogany and mahogany veneer,
bow front, shaped top with ovolo
corners, spiral turned front columns, pineapple carved capitals,
four graduated drawers, turned
feet, 45" w, 22" d, 40" h **4,500**
Maple and cherry, attributed to New
England, 1825, wide frieze drawer
with banded border above three
matching wide drawers, turned pilasters on sides, reeded feet, 40" w,
44" h **2,530**
Rosewood, rectangular marble top,
three graduated drawers, top with
combed fluting, rosette type pulls,
bracket feet, signed by M Haynie,
Baltimore, March 4, 1851 .... **1,200**

Daybed
1805–30, mahogany, ormolu
mounted, rectangular back, rectangular splat applied with ribbon tied
wreath and winged eagle, bowed
padded seat, square tapering
splayed legs, gray cotton upholstery **700**
1830, mahogany, curved and carved
crest rail, rolled arms, fruit and
claw carved feet **1,430**
Dumb Waiter, 1830, mahogany, three
tier octagonal shelves, cylindrical
standard, scroll feet, brass caster, 52"
h **660**
Knife Box, Philadelphia, 1820, pair, mahogany, leaf carved, veneer paneled
square top, rectangular case, carved
front, 14½" w, price for pair **2,500**

Mirror
Architectural
American, giltwood, eglomise
panel of house in landscape, rectangular glass, turned half spindle frame with pataera on corner
blocks, 13¾" w, 29½" h **350**
Rhode Island, 1815–20, mahogany
frame, flat reeded and acorn decorated cresting above frieze with
applied fretwork motif, eglomise
panel of house in landscape, rectangular glass, flanked by reeded
pilasters, damaged, 18" w, 35" h **175**
Bull's Eye, attributed to Albany, 1830,
pair, giltwood, circular glass surrounded by ebonized slip and
spherule hung frame, surmounted
by elaborate carved fruit filled basket flanked by overflowing cornucopia, acanthus carved pendant be-
low, 32" w, 47" h, price for pair .. **20,000**
Ogee, mahogany, veneered, gilted
molding, 41" h **125**
Ormolu mounted, mahogany, rectangular inset plate, conforming
paneled frame, arched molded
cornice, classical bust in center of
foliate wreath, pataera corners, 30"
w, 57" h **900**
Pier
New England, 1820, mahogany,
rectangular top, triptych mirror
back, ormolu mounted cylindrical column supports, stretcher
shelf, ball feet, 54" w, 14" d, 37"
h **1,700**
New York, 1815, gilt and gesso
decorated wood frame, flat
molded cornice decorated with
row of balls projecting at sides
over leaf decorated scroll brackets, center black painted ground
eglomise panel with gilt classical

figures of music and art, octagonal medallion and flowers, rectangular glass flanked by pairs of colonettes, 27" w, 50" h **800**

New York, 1820–30, gilt gesso decorated wood frame, flat reeded cresting decorated with acorns above frieze centering three dimensional shell, over two part glass flanked by ring turned and floral decorated half spindles, matching base, regilded, mirror replaced, 30" w, 54" h **1,100**

Secretary

Cherry and mahogany, two sections: upper section: molded and peaked cornice with turned medallions, removable bookcase top with freestanding brass trimmed columns, double doors with brass edge strip; lower section: one dovetailed drawer with fitted interior, turned, acanthus carved legs, replaced clear blown glass drawer handles, 38¼" w, 23½" d, 81" h **1,200**

Mahogany, carved, projecting cornice, mullioned glazed doors, shelf interior, fall front drawer with fitted interior, carved rope turned half columns, front hairy paw carved feet, turned back feet, signed and dated "Edward West, 1829," 51¾" w, 22" d, 93¾" h **4,850**

Mahogany, rectangular projecting cornice above pair of doors enclosing shelves, fall front writing surface, fitted interior with pigeonholes and drawers, base with drawer above pair of recessed doors flanked by applied three quarter columns, turned feet, 43" w, 19" d, 84" h **1,000**

Sideboard, mahogany

1820, New York, rectangular top, frieze with three inlaid drawers, three hinged cupboard doors, shelves, carved flanking columns, carved animal paw feet, brass casters, 66½" w, 24" d, 43½" h **5,000**

1820–30, partially carved front posts, original finish, original brass hardware, 48" w, 21" d, 44¾" h **750**

1825, Baltimore, John Needles, shaped back with centered arched mirror section, flanked by pair of columns, center marble top drop well, lift top fan veneered door, flanked by pair of columns with Ionic capitals, pair of cabinet doors, acanthus carved ball feet, original maker's label, 79" l **8,500**

1825, figural veneered mahogany columns, ormolu capitals and bases, well proportioned, 60" l . . .   **1,600**

1825, top with three quarter gallery and triangular pediment shape, three small drawer frieze alternating with leaf carved pataera over four leaf carved and spiral turned colonettes and four paneled doors with plain rectangular panels, upper part of each side with sliding

Sofa, Middle Atlantic states, 1820–40, mahogany veneer, raked veneered crest flanked by carved volutes, veneered arms, leaf carved supports, veneered seat rail, four hairy paw feet, refinished, minor imperfections, 77" w, 15" h seat, 33¼" h overall, $725.00. Photograph courtesy of Skinner, Inc.

shelf pulls, plinth with leaf and paw carved feet, 73¼" w, 50¼" h **690**

1825–30, rectangular top with paneled splashboard, frieze with three small drawers, two paneled cupboard doors centering two small drawers, spiral turned engaged colonettes with leaf carved vase Ionic capitals, paw feet, 61" w, 53½" h **770**

1830, elaborate carved back splashboard, shaped rectangular top, two cushion molded drawers, three paneled doors, Corinthian columns, acanthus carved paw feet, 73" l, 22¾" d, 55½" h **900**

1830, top with gadrooned border, three small drawer frieze, four curved fronted doors, four round tapered colonettes, leaf and paw carved feet, 66" w, 43" h **600**

Sofa

1805–10, mahogany, bar form crest rail, acanthus carved rolled arms, gadrooned apron, winged paw feet, 78" l **1,155**

1805–30, mahogany and mahogany veneer, cornucopia carved arms, carved legs, hoof feet, some repair to splint veneer on arms, nicely reupholstered, 76" l, 20" d, 36" h **3,000**

1815–20, New York, box style, carved mahogany and rosewood, cherry and pine secondary woods, carved eagle brackets, brass inlay, paw feet, slightly reduced, original damaged brocade upholstery **1,800**

1820, mahogany, straight crest rail with carved pineapple and leaf panel, gold velvet upholstered seat, back, and rolled arms, straight apron, cornucopia carved legs, paw feet, 86" l **550**

1820–30, mahogany, scrolled back, cornucopia legs, paw feet, reupholstered, 88" l **700**

1820–40, Middle Atlantic states, mahogany veneer, raked crest rail flanked by carved volutes, out scrolled arms with leaf carving, leaf carving continues to veneered seat rail with brass tack decorations, hairy paw feet, refinished, minor imperfections, 77" l, 15" h seat, 33¼" h overall **725**

19th C, Philadelphia, carved mahogany, scroll reticulated crest rail, out scrolled dolphin arms, carved saber feet, original upholstered removed **1,200**

Stand

Dressing, walnut, rectangular top, frieze drawer, adjustable swing mirror with turned supports, ring turned standard on trefoil base, flat bun feet, 17" w, 13¾" d, 49" h ... **300**

Sewing, mid 19th C, rosewood, molded hinged top, fitted interior, two rounded full drawers, scrolled supports, carved anthemion, scrolled feet, 21" w, 16" d, 31" h . **1,000**

Wash

Cherry, mahogany and curly maple veneer, turned and rope carved legs with biscuit corners, two dovetailed drawers, refinished, 20¾" w, 29" h **750**

Hardwood and mahogany veneer, turned and rope carved legs, two dovetailed drawers with curved fronts, clear blown glass drawer pulls, dark varnish finish, 19¾" w, 15¾" d, 30" h **350**

Work

1820–25, Northeast coast, mahogany, rectangular banded top, rectangular case with outset leaf carved posts and two wide drawers, top drawer with fitted writing surface, pineapple carved pedestal, leaf carved dog legs, brass feet with casters, 23" w, 28¾" h **2,640**

1840, mahogany, two wide drawers Rectangular top, rectangular tapered standard, rectangular incurvate plinth, stylized scroll feet, 24" w, 26¾" h **575**

Rectangular top with rounded front corners, square tapered standard, rectangular incurvate plinth, stylized scroll feet, 21½" w, 27" h **360**

Stool

Foot

1805–30, Philadelphia, mahogany, turned trestle arms, saber leg, nicely reupholstered, repair to one leg **1,350**

1830, mahogany, needlepoint and burgundy velvet upholstery **125**

Ottoman, 1830, pair, mahogany, curule form, lotus leaf carving, reupholstered tasseled cushions, 18" w, 16" d, 18" h, price for pair **4,000**

Table

Breakfast, mahogany, rectangular top, two shaped drop leaves, single molded edge drawer, four turned drops at each corner, foliate carved pedestal, four down curving acanthus and lion paw carved legs, 38" l, 28" h **750**

Card

1805–30, attributed to Anthony Quervelle, Philadelphia, mahogany and mahogany veneer, column on pedestal, four paw feet, replaced hinges, 36" w, 18" d, 29" h **3,600**

1805–30, attributed to New York area, mahogany, applied brass band on skirt, gilded bronze mount, four turned and heavily carved columns on platform, hairy paw feet, 36" w, 18" d, 29" h **10,000**

1805–30, birch and inlaid burlwood, D–shaped leaves, trestle shaped feet, 35" h **450**

1815–20, mahogany, fold over top with canted corners, opens to ten sided playing surface, conforming frieze, four reeded and foliate carved colonettes, rectangular incurvate plinth, canted leaf and paw carved feet, 36¼" w, 29" h **935**

1820, New England, cherry and mahogany veneer, hinged top, scalloped frieze, baluster and spiral turned legs, old surface, 36" w, 17½" d, 30" h **825**

1820–30, mahogany, rectangular top with canted corners, ten sided playing surface, conforming cove molded frieze, leaf carved baluster standard, rectangular plinth, canted curved legs with leaf carved knees, brass paw feet with casters, 36" w, 29¾" h **1,100**

1830, probably Philadelphia, mahogany, rectangular top with canted front corners, conforming cove molded frieze, opens to ten sided playing surface, round tapered standard with ring of carved lotus leaves at base, rectangular incurvate plinth, carved wing and paw feet, 36" w, 29½" h **715**

Center

1805–30, mahogany, rectangular top, gadrooned edge, conforming frieze, turned acanthus carved standard, circular medial platform, molded downswept legs, acanthus carved returns, paw feet, casters, 45" w, 37" d, 30" h **900**

1805–35, marble, square molded green variegated marble top, rounded corners, conforming mahogany frieze, marble pedestal and tripod foot, 37" w, 37" d, 32" h **2,000**

1825–30, Philadelphia, mahogany, circular tilt top with inlaid sunburst pattern grain mahogany, to-

rus molded frieze with plain brass border, leaf carved and gadrooned basket standard, triangular incurvate plinth, carved and gilt leaf decorated paw feet, 48" d, 28½" h **4,400**

Console

1800, carved mahogany, circular tilt top, radiating crotch mahogany veneers, tapering triangular paneled pedestal, trefoil concave base, three winged eagle and lion paw feet, restoration to veneers, 47" d, 28½" h **2,750**

1805–10, mahogany, pair, rectangular gray flecked marble top, plain frieze, drawer with two stylized swans drinking from fountain, swan within berried laurel wreath mounted on corners, tapered columnar supports with gilt bronze mountings, rear pilasters support mirror, rectangular plinth, 40" l, 35¼" h, price for pair **6,600**

Game, Benjamin Myrick, Charlestown, Massachusetts, 1805–30, mahogany, modified serpentine D–shaped top, brass inlaid, carved star punched leg capital, spiral turned legs, original brass cap casters, signed by maker, 36" w, 19" d, 30" h **8,000**

Sewing, Boston, 1805–30

Mahogany and mahogany veneer, basket, column supports, trestle base, original casters, later brasses, 18" w, 16" d, 29" h ... **3,500**

Mahogany, three drawers, carved lyre shape supports, turned trestle, saber feet, lion paw casters, attributed to Rufus Pierce, 22" w, 18" d, 30" h **5,500**

Sofa, New York, 1805–30, mahogany, rectangular top, rounded drop leaves, straight skirt, two working drawers, two faux drawers, reeded, turned, down tapered pedestal, platform with four outswept legs, brass paw feet, minor repairs, 36" w, 27" d, 30" h **7,500**

Work

Early 19th C, New York

Mahogany and mahogany veneer, shaped lift top with concave corners, two drawers with brass inlay, heavily carved pedestal, hairy paw feet, 18" w, 18" d, 30" h **5,000**

Mahogany, rectangular top, two drawers, twisted scroll carved pedestal, four acanthus carved curved hairy lion paw feet, casters, repairs to side, veneer missing, repairs to two feet, 22½" w, 30½" h **600**

Second quarter 19th C

Cherry, two drawers, refinished, replaced knobs, 28¾" h **200**

Mahogany, flame veneer, turned biscuit corners, two dovetailed drawers, top with divided interior, rope turned posts, turned and acanthus carved columns on case, pullout work bag frame, carved acanthus and paw feet, old worn refinishing, minor edge damage and veneer repair, replaced brasses, 19" w, 22¼" l, 30" h **1,200**

Mahogany, square top, two drawers, turned legs, medial shelf, hairy paw caster feet, 32½" w, 30¼" h **750**

Wardrobe, New York state, 1815–30, tiger maple, pedimented top, central drawer above recessed panel door flanked by quarter columns with capitals and bases, refinished, feet missing, 46½" w, 12¼" d, 74" h **3,300**

STYLE

Candlestand, country, curly maple, two board tilt top, scrolled legs, turned column, refinished, repairs, 19" d, 26¾" h **600**

Chair, arm, mahogany, rectangular padded back, padded arms, ormolu mounted classical busts, bowed padded seat, square tapered legs with brass caps, white striped fabric upholstery **825**

Chest of Drawers, country

Cherry and walnut, four dovetailed drawers with applied edge beading, turned feet, refinished, 42" w, 44½" h **850**

Cherry, curly maple facade, four dovetailed drawers, applied edge beading, turned and rope carved pilasters and feet, opalescent glass swirled pulls, old dark finish, 41" w, 20½" d, 46½" h **500**

Cherry, walnut, and curly maple inlay, paneled ends, turned feet, turned and rope carved pilasters, scrolled apron, carved added detail on top edge, six dovetailed drawers with applied edge bead, turned wood pulls, refinished, 38¼" w, 47" h **2,500**

Mirror, mantel

American, early 19th C, giltwood, three parts, flat leaf carved molded cornice, half spindle decorated frieze and sides, 70" w, 30" h **575**

Eastern America, split baluster, giltwood, classical motifs including lion's head, leafage, and C–scrolls, imperfections, 63" w, 25" h **825**

Settee

Gilt metal mounted and mirrored wal-

Settee, mid-19th C, mahogany, eagle head terminals to crest, rectangular back and seat, rolled arms, acanthus and fruit carved lion paw feet, $750.00. Photograph courtesy of Leslie Hindman Auctioneers.

nut, reupholstered, columnar arm supports, 57¾" l **1,900**

Mahogany, ivory damask upholstery, carved, 56" l **550**

Stand

Plant, mahogany, rectangular form, green variegated marble top, two lion form supports, paw feet, platform base, 31" w, 11½" d, 37" h . **330**

Work, mahogany, rectangular top with drop leaf

Three drawers, gadrooned edge, acanthus column supports, platform base, paw feet, 16" w, 15½" d, 30" h **250**

Two drawers

Early 19th C, rectangular single pedestal, platform base, scroll feet, 34½" w extended, 18" d, 28½" h **220**

Early 20th C, round tapered standard, rectangular incurvate plinth, leaf and paw feet, 35" w extended, 29½" h **190**

Table, work, country, early 19th C, figured mahogany veneer, drop leaf top, two dovetailed drawers, four clear lacy glass pulls, tapered pedestal with edge beading, four legs, acanthus carved knees, brass paw feet with casters, minor repairs, two replaced pulls, old refinishing, 17" w, 20½" d, 8¾" l leaves, 29¼" h **450**

VICTORIAN

Queen Victoria assumed the English throne on June 20, 1837, was coronated on June 28, 1838, and died on January 22, 1901. She gave her name to an era. The influence of the Queen and her court on world taste continued long after her death.

In the United States the Victorian age lasted from 1840 through 1915, the beginning of the first World War. The impact of high style influences such as Arts and Crafts and English Edwardian was limited. Americans adopted the English revivals of the nineteenth century as their own and developed a comfort level that would not be broken until the 1920s.

American collectors and dealers have a tendency to lump anything made between 1840 and 1915 under the broad label of "Victorian." The simple truth is that they are too lazy to study the various Victorian design styles in order to label furniture correctly. Likewise, they prefer to see Art Nouveau, Art Furniture, and Arts and Crafts as part of twentieth

The Victorian era witnessed the introduction of the furniture suite as a major design element. Three piece Flemish Baroque Style carved mahogany suite, c1870, settee and pair of armchairs, arms carved with heads of maidens, backs with elaborate motifs of foliate scrollwork, female masks, arched crests surmounted by shells, settee: 57" l, 24" d, 52" h, price for set of three, $2,250.00. Photograph courtesy of Neal Auction Company.

Victorian furniture often contained elements from more than one design style. These chairs have the cartouche in the crest and saddle back associated with Renaissance Revival and the open fretwork associated with the Rococo Revival. J. & J. W. Meeks, parlor chairs, Stanton Hall pattern, laminated rosewood, "in a serious state of delamination and will require restorations," price for set of four, $1,485.00. Photograph courtesy of Pettigrew Auction Company.

century "modern" as opposed to the last of the major design styles of the Victorian era. Denial aside, these latter styles are as much Victorian as the Gothic Revival.

The Victorian age was an age of revivals, revivals of revivals, and reaction to revivals. In order to achieve some sense of order, scholars have assigned labels to major design styles. The problem with these labels is that they are deceptive. The Elizabethan Revival contains more design elements from Restoration and William and Mary England than it does from the reign of Queen Elizabeth I.

More than any other period, Victorian design styles were mix–and–match. Design influences came from far and wide—the Orient, Middle East, Far East, Middle Ages, Bourbon courts, and English history. Basic to all Victorian designs was a revival of one or more design elements from the past. With few exceptions, none of the pieces were exact copies of past forms and designs. Instead, they were a mixture of designs from a wide range of periods and countries. The end result was a furniture piece that could easily incorporate elements from two to six of the major Victorian design styles.

Sound confusing? It is. Classifying Victorian furniture correctly is work. Perhaps this is why so few individuals in the antiques and collectibles market try to do so. The key is to look for the most dominant stylistic element. This provides the basic label. Qualify the description with references to the piece's secondary design elements.

During the Victorian period factory production of furniture became dominant. By 1825 it was possible to make the entire frame of a piece of furniture by machine. Mass production became the order of the day.

Handwork continued, especially in the factory environment. Labor was inexpensive; not all tasks were mechanized. Some individual cabinet shops did survive, often producing pieces in early styles to special order.

Europe remained the stylistic leader. However, the Victorian era witnessed a more rapid assimilation of European design styles in America due to a more rapid exchange of ideas through trade magazines and newspapers. American manufacturers played an increasingly important role in world trade following the Civil War. These expanded horizons

The Renaissance Revival was one of the most popular design styles in the Victorian period. This typical rosewood and ebonized table has a marquetry inlaid top and is accented with gilt incising, top measures 49" x 31", $3,190.00. Photograph courtesy of Pettigrew Auction Company.

Occasionally the Renaissance Revival did produce a piece that had strong "Renaissance" design characteristics, albeit, once again, great interpretive liberties were taken. This walnut table features carvings throughout including relief carvings of maidens and babies on the trestle ends, label for B. Altman under top, 42" l, $525.00. Photograph courtesy Pettigrew Auction Company

enhanced the desire to be "fashionable." The nouveau riche had no qualms about buying their good taste. After all, couldn't money buy everything? The middle class joined the bandwagon as they "kept pace with the Joneses."

The Victorian era witnessed a tremendous geographic expansion in American furniture manufacturing. Few towns of any size failed to have a furniture factory. Many of the largest manufacturers moved to the forested areas of America to be near a primary wood source.

The marketing of furniture also changed. Large companies supplied a national market. Few individuals bought their furniture from the person or factory that made it. Furniture was purchased through local merchants or department stores, many of whom stocked only a limited quantity of merchandise but had a wealth of catalogs from which they could place orders.

In the final analysis, the Victorian age is hardly an age at all. The key is not unity, but

Rococo Revival rivaled Renaissance Revival in popularity. Premium prices are paid for pieces that can be attributed to famous makers. John Henry Belter designed this sofa in laminated rosewood. $25,300.00. Photograph courtesy of Pettigrew Auction Company.

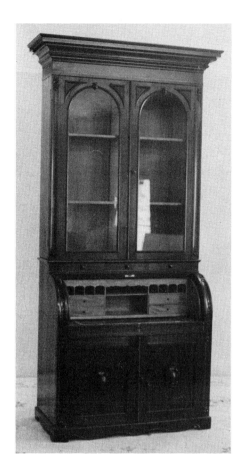

Eastlake was the last major design style to enjoy mass popularity during the Victorian era. The style stressed simplicity and a return to craftsmanship. Secretary, rosewood, cylinder roll top, well fitted maple interior, New York City origin, 45" wide in body, 53" wide in cornice, 23" d, 102½" h, $6,600.00. Photograph courtesy of Pettigrew Auction Company.

unbridled diversity. Victorian is nothing more than a catchall phrase used to describe the chronological time period from 1840 to 1915.

References: Eileen and Richard Dubrow, *American Furniture of the 19th Century*, Schiffer Publishing, 1983; Kathryn McNerney, *Victorian Furniture*, Collector Books, 1981, updated values 1988; Robert W. and Harriett Swedberg, *Victorian Furniture, Book I* (1976), *Victorian Furniture, Book II* (1983), and *Victorian Furniture, Book III* (1985), Wallace–Homestead.

FRENCH RESTAURATION (1830–1850)

History: French Restauration marks the end of the neoclassic revivals and is the transition to the formal revivals of the Victorian era. The style is associated with the Bourbon restoration to the French throne, 1814 to 1848.

The basic classical forms of Empire furniture continued. Undulating curves are introduced to offset the strict balanced proportions of the earlier period. What disappears is decorative ornamentation. When decoration, e.g., astragal or bead molding, ormolu, or Egyptian lotus, does appear, it is spare. The simplicity and practicality of French Restauration is best described as austere.

French Restauration furniture tends to be more massive in form than Empire pieces. A major design component is the elliptical curve supplemented with C– and S–scrolls. The pillar and scroll motif on furniture, especially mirrors, and clocks was popular. Comfort was important. Leather–covered library chairs of the period appear identical to their post–World War II counterparts, a tribute to the basic nature of French Restauration furniture design.

Much of French Restauration furniture was inexpensive, one of the reasons for its enormous popularity during the Victorian era. Tulip poplar and pine are the favored secondary woods. The surfaces of pieces are covered with richly grained mahogany. In many cases, the mahogany grain is the principal decorative element on the piece.

New York continued as the major design leader. Joseph Meeks' & Sons (1797–1868) was a major manufacturer. Meeks' gondola chair can be found in many variations. In the South, New Orleans supplanted Charleston as the major design center.

The French Restauration style enjoyed great popularity throughout the Midwest and South. In the minds of many collectors and dealers, it, rather than the classical styles of the 1805–1830 period, is real "Empire." Its longevity was such that during the 1920s it was one of the leading forms in the Colonial Revival movement although as a design style it arrived long after the American Revolution.

Style Books: John Hall, *The Cabinet Makers Assistant*, Baltimore, 1840; Pierre de la Mesangere, *Collection de meubles et objets de gout*, French periodical; George Smith, *Cabinet–Maker and Upholster's Guide*, London, 1826.

Armoire, 1840, carved mahogany, molded cornice, two doors with arched inset panels, Ionic columns, paw feet **2,200**
Bed
High Poster, 1835, mahogany, shaped headboard, acanthus, spiral, and pineapple carved posts, 77" l, 44½" w, 96" h **3,600**
Rope, 1830–45
Painted, red paint on poplar, bold deeply scrolled headboard, high cannonball posts, turned legs, original side rails, 60" w, 70" d, 51½" h **1,000**
Walnut, scrolled and rolled headboard, octagonal posters, original screw–in rails, worn finish, 65" w, 80" d, 89½" h **1,000**
Sleigh
Mahogany, carved, S–scrolled side rails, fan carving on headboard and footboard, queen size **2,500**
Tiger maple and mahogany, scrolling headboard and footboard . . **1,000**
Suite, Dauler, Close, and Johns, Pittsburgh, Pennsylvania, flamed mahogany veneer, book matched and end to end matched veneer drawer fronts and panels, gently scrolling headboard, swelled facade on top drawers, rectangular mirror with lyre side supports, glass knops,

Secretary, Boston, 1830s, mahogany veneer, pedimented top above doors, Gothic tracery mullions, three shelved interior, small drawers, foldout writing surface, blind convex drawer, two concave recessed panel doors flanked by columns, turned feet, imperfections, 44½" w, 24" d, 91" h, $3,300.00. Photograph courtesy of Skinner, Inc.

claw and ball feet, bedstead: 64" w, 51" h headboard; chest of drawers: 57" w, 25" d, 71" h; chiffonier: 41" w, 23" d, 72" h; matching dressing table, price for four piece suite **6,500**
Youth, 1850, half tester, carved walnut, shaped headboard, molded rectangular tester supported by tapering ring turned posts, scalloped angular supports, conforming footboard with central circular medallion, acorn posts and turned legs . **1,100**
Bookcase, New York, 1830, two sections: upper section: flat top with projected cornice, fruit and leaf stenciled tympanum, two glazed hinged doors

Drum table, octagonal top, c1840, four false drawers in frieze, circular pedestal, platform base, C-scroll feet, top 28" d, 27½" h, $605.00. Photograph courtesy of Neal Auction Company.

The French Restauration style enjoyed numerous revivals during the 19th and 20th centuries. This four drawer mahogany veneer chest of drawers with flat sides appears to date between 1840–1860, $330.00. Photograph courtesy of Pettigrew Auction Company.

with gilt mullions enclosing shelved interior; lower section: projected case, two small convex drawers over deep long drawer with gilt metal mounted decoration, two cupboard doors with gilt metal mounted decoration flanked by two gilt metal mounted columns, acanthus carved animal paw feet, 56½" w, 23" d, 100" h **8,800**

Chair, reclining, 1840, carved mahogany, scalloped side apron, curved side rails, striped tufted upholstery extending to footrest **750**

Mirror, petticoat, mahogany, apron with long drawer, short shaped back, scrolled sides terminating in scrolled feet, 45" w, 19" d, 35" h **700**

Mirror, 1835, mantel, gilt gesso decorated wood, three part mirror, flat molded cornice, half spindle decorated frieze and sides, three part mirror, 57" w, 22" h **375**

Rocker, oak, open shaped arms, gondola shaped stiles, brown velvet tufted upholstery **600**

Secretary
    Boston, 1830, mahogany veneer, pedimented top, flanking columns end in gently carved arch over two doors with Gothic tracery, three shelved interior, small drawers,

Chest of drawers, c1870–80, mahogany veneer, four drawers, mirror with strong Rococo Revival characteristics, $495.00. Photograph courtesy of Pettigrew Auction Company.

Linen Press, late 19th C, mahogany, offset central section consisting of top and bottom section each with two cupboard doors, separated from flanking full vertical units by full relief Corinthian column on base the length of bottom door section of the central unit, slight Gothic arch to recessed panels on side sections and top of central section, 91½" w, 23" d, 86" h, $4,125.00. Photograph courtesy of Skinner, Inc.

foldout writing surface, blind convex drawer, two concave recessed panel doors flanked by columns ending in turned feet, imperfections, 44½" d, 24" d, 91" h **3,300**

New York, 1835, mahogany veneer, cherry, and pine, two sections: upper section: beaded cornice, veneered band, glazed cupboard doors with off center mullions, two small drawers with brass escutcheons and wooden knops; lower section: foldout writing surface, three graduated drawers, outset top drawer with wooden knops, scrolled sides extending to scrolled feet, 41" w, 20" d, 77" h **3,000**

Sofa

1830, mahogany, carved cornucopias, acorns, oak leaves, and acanthus leaves, basket of flowers finial, refinished, gold brocade reupholstery, 83" l **1,750**

1830–45, carved mahogany and mahogany veneer, heavily carved claw feet, nicely reupholstered, back rail missing, feet reworked, 89" l, 28" d, 33" h **500**

1835, New York, mahogany, acanthus carved shaped crest rail continuing to carved scrolled arms, rounded base, acanthus carved hairy paw feet, gilt feather returns, 78" l **1,500**

Server, Kentucky, 19th C, cherry, strongly shaped splash board, large extended vertical drawer over two cupboard doors each with a recessed panel, applied turned half columns featuring ring and spool turnings, tapering turned feet, $1,250.00. Photograph courtesy of Green River Antiques Auctions and *Antique Week*.

This is an excellent example of a married piece. A blind two door cupboard was added to the top of mid-19th C French Restauration chest of drawers to create a "Kentucky linen press." The cherry chest of drawers features a single offset drawer over three graduated drawers flanked by a large bulbous and tapered turned column, squat tapered and flattened ball legs ending in a tapered foot. Married pieces do sell—this piece realized $3,900.00. Photograph courtesy of Greenup Estate & Auction Company and *Antique Week*.

1835–40, mahogany, scrolling back
extends to carved arms, original upholstery removed 1,200
Table
Banquet, New York, 1840, mahogany, highly figured, 62" l 3,000
Card, 1840, mahogany, rectangular
fold over top, molded frieze, serpentine U–shaped standard, rectangular molded base, bracket feet,
36" w, 29" h 500
Center
American, 1840, mahogany, rec-

tangular marble top, pillar and
scroll base 375
New York, 1830, mahogany, radiating circular veneered top, 38"
d 1,500
Dining, mahogany, pillar and scroll,
round leaves, extension with two
matching leaves, 48" d, 80" l extended 1,500
Pier, attributed to J & J W Meeks, New
York, 1835, figured mahogany, rectangular veined marble top with
canted front corners, pillar and
scroll base, shaped lower shelf,
large spade feet, 42" l, 36" h 2,000
Suite, New York, Philadelphia, or Baltimore, 1835, pair of console tables
and corner table, mahogany, gilt
stencil decoration, raised on ring
and baluster turned pedestal, down
curved legs ending in paw feet,
consoles: 38½" w, 19" d, 35" h;
corner: 28" w, 19½" d, 35" h 7,500

GOTHIC (1840–1865) AND ELIZABETHAN REVIVALS (1850–1915)

Nineteenth century furniture manufacturers liked to believe they were making exact copies of historic design forms; they were not. In most cases, a quick look will distinguish the nineteenth century example from an earlier period piece.

The Victorian era saw two major design styles evolve that had strong English roots: Gothic and Elizabethan. Gothic remained truer to form and enjoyed greater popularity in England than it did in America. Americans fell in love with the Elizabethan Revival. This love affair would resurface in the 1920s revival of English Tudor architecture.

GOTHIC REVIVAL

History: Chippendale and some neoclassic furniture contained Gothic elements. When Gothic features did occur, they were applied as ornamentation within the existing design rather than as actual imitations of Gothic furniture forms.

English architectural styles from the twelfth through the sixteenth centuries were the inspiration for the nineteenth century Gothic Revival. That is why the style is often referred to as *Medieval* or *Norman*. The primary reason earlier forms were not copies was that they were uncomfortable. It is not uncommon to find Gothic style elements mixed with those from the French Restauration and Rococo Revival.

The Gothic Revival in America is largely associated with church architecture and furnishings, an area where it remained dominant through the mid–twentieth century. Alexander Jackson Davis (1803–1892) was the main proponent of the style in America.

Among the principal design elements found in Gothic furniture are: pointed and lancet arches, clustered columns, crockets, finials, heraldic devices, Tudor roses, and trefoil and quatrefoil rosettes. Pieces usually have very bold silhouettes. Oak and walnut are common woods, albeit some pieces can be found in mahogany and rosewood.

Style Books: Robert Conner, *Cabinet Makers Assistant*, New York, 1842; A. W. Pugin, *Gothic Furniture in the Style of the Fifteenth Century*, London, 1838.

Major Craftsmen: Richard Byrne, John Jelliff, John Needles, Alexander and Frederick Roux, and Ambrose Wright.

ELIZABETHAN REVIVAL

History: The romantic novels written by Walter Scott in the 1820s drew attention to Elizabethan England. However, the Elizabethan Revival was inspired by the period of Charles I (1626–1649) and Charles II (1660–1685) rather than that of Elizabeth I (1558–1603). It was a lighter, more open style than the Gothic Revival.

Principal style elements include spiral and ball Baroque turnings and strapwork. The most commonly found form is the side chair, usually made from mahogany, rosewood, or walnut. It is quite common to find these elements included in a Rococo or Renaissance Revival piece.

In the United States, the Elizabethan Revival exercised a strong influence of the mass–produced cottage furniture of the middle and late nineteenth century. The spiral twist became a simple ball– or spoon–turned member. In order to keep this practical form inexpensive, it often was made from softwood and paint–decorated in a variety of colors and motifs, the latter favoring Rococo floral and scroll designs.

Style Books: Robert Bridgen, *Furniture with Candelabra and Interior Decoration*, London, 1838; Henry Shaw, *Specimens of Ancient Furniture*, London, 1836.

GOTHIC REVIVAL

Bed, double, carved mahogany and flame mahogany, crested headboard with applied carved leafage, beaded scrolling scalloped sides, 52" w, 85" l, 65" h **1,200**
Chair
  Arm, 1830–45, walnut, elaborate spire and quatrefoil back, plank seat, trefoil decorated skirt, spiral turned legs, 51" h **1,200**

Fireplace Screen, Elizabethan Revival, late 19th C, carved, urn finials, floral panel, rope turned posts and stretcher, trestle base with scroll feet, $500.00.

Side, New York City
  1845, rosewood, original stump work upholstery, seat cover decorated with applied multicolored birds and cherry tree bough, 46" h **550**
  1850, carved walnut, quatrefoil and trefoil arches with urn shaped finials, rope turned uprights, upholstered oval back, upholstered seat, pendant skirt, attributed to J & J W Meeks **300**
Desk, oak, drop front, pierced carved crest with Gothic arch motif, hinged slant front, applied conforming Gothic carvings, small drawers and pigeonholes interior, case with two short drawers, three slightly recessed long drawers flanked by columnar tiles **975**
Etagere, New York, 1850, corner, carved mahogany, three shelves with beaded edges, trefoil arches, urn shaped finial, beaded columns, base with glazed door with trefoil mullions, shelved interior, plinth base .. **2,400**
Rocker, child's, walnut, shaped solid bentwood seat, perforated Gothic designs **150**
Secretary, J & J W Meeks, mid 19th C, carved and laminated rosewood, two sections: upper section: rectangular top with rounded front corners above

Rocking Chairs, Elizabethan Revival, George Hunzinger, patented duplex spring. Left: Padded velvet upholstered back seat and arm rests, original paper label, $440.00. Right: Padded velvet upholstered back, seat, and head rests, original paper label, $550.00. Photograph courtesy of Pettigrew Auction Company.

Gothic carved band, pair of Gothic arched glazed cabinet doors, shelved interior; lower section: cylinder front, writing surface, pair of cabinet doors, molded base, bracket feet, original label 17,500

Table, library
   1840, attributed to John and Joseph Meeks, New York, carved rosewood, oblong top with drop leaves, apron with two mock and two working drawers, scrolled supports, 64" w, 24" d, 30" h 5,500
   1845, carved rosewood, rectangular yellow veined black marble top with rounded corners, molded edge, pierced carved quatrefoil frieze, scrolled legs joined by scrolled stretcher, mounted at intersections with turned finials, scrolled feet on rectangular pads and casters, executed by John and Joseph Meeks for Matthew Vassar, inscription in black on underside of marble: "M Vassar, Esq, Poughkeepsie," 41" l, 30¼" h 12,100

ELIZABETHAN REVIVAL

Bed, child's, spool turned headboard and footboard each with three spool turned splats, plain beaded side rails, spool turned legs 275
Chair
   Lady's, 1860, finger carved walnut frame, grape carved crest, fine upholstery 265

Lounging, 1855, bobbin turned frame, reupholstered 600
Side
   1850, walnut, elaborately pierced and carved back splat, rope turned stiles terminating in urn shaped finials, upholstered spring seat, rope turned front legs on casters 250
   1885, maple, wide crest rail with scalloped ends, turned spindles terminating in scalloped rail,

Table, combination of Gothic and Elizabethan Revival design elements, rosewood, top 27 x 15½", $1,155.00. Photograph courtesy of Pettigrew Auction Company.

Chest of Drawers, Elizabethan Revival with design elements from Hepplewhite and later French Restauration pieces, shaped splash board, two square drawers with false two drawer front slightly offset over three graduated drawers with four veneer panels, three-quarter spool turned columns aside three graduated drawers, two vertical recessed panels on each side, tapering spool turned feet ending in a slightly flattened ball foot, signed on back but obscured by refinishing, a perfect example of the blending of a number of styles in a single piece so typical of Victorian era furniture, $7,750.00. Photograph courtesy of Greenup Estate & Auction Company and *Antique Week*.

caned seat, turned legs and front
  stretcher 85
1900, Shaw Furniture Co, Cam-
  bridge, Massachusetts, walnut
  and laminated walnut, tall narrow back, open cut arched scroll
  cut crest, scroll and urn carved
  wide back, columnar turned
  stiles, upholstered seat, trumpet
  turned front legs, scrolled front
  stretcher, original label 365
Chest of Drawers, New York, 1850,
  mixed woods, painted, swivel mirror
  in shaped and crested frame, rectangular top, four long drawers, floral
  decoration on each drawer, spooled

columns, wooden pulls, scalloped
  apron 300
Rocker, 1890, platform, oak, scrolled
  line incised crest flanked by stiles,
  scrolled finials above shield shaped
  upholstered back, trimmed with open
  cut scrolls, topped with seven turned
  spindles radiating from top crest,
  shaped arms, spool arm supports, rectangular upholstered seat, turned rung
  at front 300
Table
  Side, pine, scrolling apron with
    arched cresting terminating in drop
    finials, conforming arched feet
    joined by turned stretcher 195
  Work, pine, two board top, wide
    overhang, apron with small drawer,
    turned wood pull, turned legs, ta-
    pering feet, dark brown painted fin-
    ish, 48" w, 29¾" d, 27¾" h 275

RENAISSANCE REVIVAL (1860–1885)

History: As the number of Victorian era revivals increased, designers vied with one another for attention. The principal way to achieve recognition was to create elaborate, showy pieces of furniture. The Renaissance Revival presented plenty of opportunity.

The first evidence of Renaissance Revival design elements dates to the early 1850s, combining Renaissance, Baroque, and Mannerist historic elements. The style achieved its golden age in the United States during the period immediately following the Civil War.

Renaissance Revival pieces are architectural in form (inspired by the Italinate villa), and often massive in size. The square and rectangle are the dominant design motifs. Pieces tend to have a vertical pull. A major design element is the applied cartouche or medallion. Other components include broken pediments, tapering baluster turned legs, and acorn trim.

The style underwent several changes during its long time span. Pieces from the 1850s are florid and curvilinear while pieces from the 1870s are severe and angular. Rococo cabriole legs seen on 1850s pieces were replaced by the straight legs of the Louis XVI style. The style borrowed floral, game, and fruit motifs from the neoclassical period. Occasionally Egyptian motifs, such as the cloven hoof foot, are found. Inscribed linear decoration is common in pieces from the 1870s forward.

Mahogany and walnut are the favored woods. Ash and pine appear in less expensive examples. The use of rosewood and ebony occasionally occurs. After 1870 applied burled walnut panels were common.

Popular forms include beds; upholstered chairs and sofas; pedestal, extension, and center tables; and stools. The choice of fabric and upholstery style is critical to the integrity of a piece. Reupholstery with a non–period fabric or style will change the aesthetics of a piece.

A major designer of the period was James Renwick of New York. Another designer, C. B. Sheldon, is credited with designing the adjustable folding chair in 1876. Grand Rapids, Michigan, is the principal mass production center.

Style Book: J. C. London, *Encyclopedia of Cottage, Farm and Villa Architecture*, 1833.

Major Craftsmen: Thomas Brooks (Brooklyn, NY), George Hunzinger (New York), John Jelliff (Newark), Daniel Pabst (Philadelphia), Thomas Palmer (New York).

Major Manufacturer: Berkey & Gay.

Armoire
    1860, rosewood, arched molded cornice, rectangular mirrored door, long drawer, flattened bun feet, 51" w, 23" d, 98" h **3,425**
    1865, pair, design attributed to Frank Furness, walnut, rectangular, flat reeded cornice flanked by pitched flower carved corner blocks, two long glazed cupboard doors flanked by side quarter columns ending in plinth base, 44" w, 82" h, price for pair **2,400**
Bedroom Suite, walnut, bed: arched walnut veneer panels, applied decoration, Jelliff influenced Columbia profile pediment; dresser: matching pediment, marble top, two drawer piers, center well section with marble top, long base drawer, canted carved corner with conforming pediment base; bed: 62" w x 88" h, dresser: 55" w, 22" d, 93" h, price for two pieces   **8,000**
Cabinet
    Corner, New York, 1855, mahogany, two tiered fretwork top over central drawer flanked by faux drawers, base fitted with two carved and glazed curved doors, bird's eye maple interior, 62" h **1,650**
    Music, New York, 1865, Gustave Herter, rosewood, 35" w, 21⅛" d, 47½" h **2,000**
    Parlor, New York, 1855, inlaid mahogany, ebonized, gilt decoration, 51" w, 21" d, 87¾" h **4,000**
Chair
    Arm
        1860, attributed to John Jelliff, Newark, New Jersey, walnut, surmounted by cartouche with medallion featuring bearded knight's profile, each arm carved with figural bearded knight's head, shaped seat, pendant decorations, turned short front legs with casters, tapered rear legs, upholstery removed **950**
        1876, George Hunzinger, New York, arched crest with spindles and inlay, cloth covered woven metal back and seat, original la-

Pair of Chairs, John Henry Belter, laminated rosewood, Rosalie pattern, price for pair, $8,910.00. Photograph courtesy Pettigrew Auction Company.

Chair, 1860–85, finger molded, nut carved crest, upholstered back and seat, cabriole legs, $475.00.

bel reads: Hunzinger N. Y. Pat March 20, 1868, Pat. April 18, 1876, 18" w, 17½" d, 38" h ...   1,200

Easy, carved walnut, upholstered back, scrolling arms and seat, arm rests with carved dog's heads, turned front legs, tapered rear legs   400

Folding, New York, George Hunzinger, 1865, original upholstery and seat fringe, shield shaped back and seat, surmounted by carved crest, turned arms and legs, braided arm rest, hoof feet, one arm braid missing   1,000

Chest of Drawers

1860, walnut, center cheval mirror surmounted by foliate carved shaped cartouche, flanked by two piers of four drawers, shaped rectangular white marble tops, burl veneer drawer fronts, three secret drawers in base, applied circular molding, 55" w, 19" d, 72" h   2,400

1875, walnut, rectangular mirror surmounted by shaped cartouche with carved rosettes, applied burl veneer panels to mirror frame, turned candle arms support dish shaped

shelves, rectangular white marble top with gently rounded edges and corners, applied burl veneer panels, applied decorations, three drawers, teardrop hardware, conforming skirt with applied molding, rectangular legs, casters, 30" w, 18" d, 91" h   800

Clock, tall case, Tiffany and Company, New York, 1900, carved oak case, glazed door enclosing brass and silvered dial, quarter striking Westminister chimes, 105" h   7,750

Commode, bedside, New York, Kingman & Murphy, walnut, rectangular marble top with rounded corners, single molded drawer over single beaded cupboard door, conforming plinth base, casters, original label reads: S. A. Kingman, Robert H. G. Murphy, Kingman & Murphy, Manufacturers of Cabinet Furniture, Warerooms, 93 Bleeker St, New York, 18½" d, 32" h   600

Console and Mirror, 1872, ebonized and inlaid maple, mirror with slightly arched crest centered by parcel–gilt and ebonized berry sprig, beveled mirror plate flanked by turned stiles,

Child's Crib, Renaissance Revival characteristics in crest, walnut, canopy, $880.00. Photograph courtesy of Pettigrew Auction Company.

Desk, Wooton, walnut and burl walnut, 42″ h, $4,400.00. Photograph courtesy of Pettigrew Auction Company.

console with Rouge Royale marble top over palmette inlaid frieze drawer flanked by corresponding inlaid panels, raised on gilt incised tapering cylindrical front legs, H–form stretcher centered by large carved rosette, marble repaired, bracing to stretcher, executed for third floor hallway, Thurlow Lodge, Menlo Park, by Herter Bros, New York, 53″ l, 70″ h ... **7,700**

Cupboard, hanging, walnut, molded frame, applied grapes and foliage decoration on door, 20″ w, 13″ d, 28″ h **300**

Desk, country style, 1870, walnut, two sections: upper section: coved cornice over three short drawers, foliate carved pulls, open central compartment flanked by paneled cupboard doors; lower section: slant front writing surface, hidden compartment, pair of short drawers, conforming pulls, turned legs and feet **875**

Hall Tree, walnut, Eastlake influence, scrolled carved pediment terminating in teardrop finials, gently arched mirror with applied molded frame, incised lines, applied decorations, rectangular molded white veined marble top over drawer, shaped lower shelf, side umbrella holders with shell shaped brass pans, 38″ w, 14″ d, 82″ h **1,200**

Mantel, 1872, parcel–gilt, ebonized, and inlaid rosewood, husk swags later

painted gold, firebox replaced, some wear to painted panels, executed for downstairs tower parlor, Thurlow Lodge, Menlo Park, by Herter Bros, New York, 86″ l, 30½″ d, 47¾″ h .. **6,600**

Mirror, cheval, 1875, walnut, burl walnut veneer panels, arched beveled mirror, conforming frame, center crest, flanked by columns, gilt bronze two arm candleholders, scrolled feet on casters, 44″ w, 82″ h **3,300**

Parlor Suite

Two pieces, 1870, settee and lady's arm chair, walnut and burl walnut frames, heavy carvings, turned roundels at stiles with pendants below, needlepoint upholstery, price for two piece set **1,250**

Three pieces, New York, 1865, carved walnut, settee, arm chair, side chair, carved owl motif, reupholstered, price for three piece set **2,000**

Rocker

New York, George Hunzinger, 1876, walnut, ring turned armrests and stretchers, cloth wrapped wire seat and back, dated April 10, 1876, 21″ w, 33″ h **375**

Southern, mahogany, open arm, gondola shaped stiles, leaf carved motif on crest and inside arm supports, concave front legs, burl veneer skirt, maroon velvet tufted upholstery **600**

Secretary

Rosewood, two sections: upper sec-

Desk, Wooton, burl walnut veneer, fitted interior with valanced pigeonholes, $9,500.00.

Hall Tree, 1860–85, walnut, beveled mirror, brown marble insert, 80″ h, $2,000.00.

tion: arched crest centering full relief carved bust of Shakespeare type gentleman flanked by scrolling open work leafage, bookcase with two arched and glazed cupboard doors, shelved interior, flanked by caryatid supports and drawers;

lower section: three graduated drawers flanked by caryatid supports, plinth base, original label reads: Thomas Brooks, New York, 1865, 52″ w, 109″ h   5,500

Walnut, two sections: upper section: bookcase section with S–curved pediment with center applied grapes and foliage carving, two arched and molded glazed doors, shelved interior, three small drawers with applied grapes and foliage carved pulls; lower section: foldout writing surface, two short drawers over two long drawers with oval molding and applied grapes and foliage carved pulls, matching ornamentation of skirt, 48″ w, 21″ d, 95″ h   3,600

Settee
  1860, carved
    Rosewood, shaped crest rail extends to foliate carved outset arm rails, upholstered back, seat, and arm rests, skirt with central carved pendant, fluted columnar legs, reupholstered   800
    Walnut, surmounted by cartouche with medallion featuring bearded knight's profile, foliate medallions and other carving separates back sections, each arm carved with figural bearded knight's head, shaped seat, pendant decorations, turned short front legs with casters, tapered rear legs, upholstery removed, attributed to John Jelliff, Newark, New Jersey   1,600
  1870, carved mahogany, scroll arm, paw foot, upholstery removed . . .   1,000

Sofa, carved rosewood, distinct three-unit design, cartouche centers in crest, 74″ l, $1,760.00. Photograph courtesy of Pettigrew Auction Company.

Library Table, Alexander Roux, New York, 1860–85, oak, rectangular leather inset top over a two drawer frieze, turned legs joined by a turned H-stretcher surmounted by a central urn form finial, 52″ w, 33¼″ d, 28½″ h, $1,200.00. Photograph courtesy of Skinner, Inc.

Sideboard
    Walnut, attributed to Mitchell and Rammelsberg, Cincinnati, Ohio, 1860, elaborately carved back board with shelf and three stands, shaped marble top, carved and applied hunting and grape motif on cupboard doors, 78½″ l, 102″ h .. **2,500**
    Walnut, foliate carved pediment over burl veneer panel, scrolled shelf supports, rectangular mirror plate above rectangular marble top with canted corners, burl veneer panels and decorations on conforming case, two drawers with foliate carved wooden pulls, two cupboard doors with applied carved decorations, 57″ w, 23″ d, 84″ h . **2,750**
    Walnut, two sections: upper section: broken arch crest with center baroque cartouche flanked by full carved fruit, open shelf, urn shaped supports, incised line carvings in backboard and carved medallion details; lower section: shaped oblong top with molded edge, conforming case with small drawers and cupboard doors, applied carvings and ornate trim, plinth base . **2,650**
Stool, piano
    1870, walnut, square upholstered seat, acanthus carved baluster supports, four outswept legs, hoof feet **275**
    1875, walnut, arched crest rail, flaring corners, carved and incised with palmette and scrolls above padded back panel, round padded upholstered seat, low skirt guards,

adjustable on ring turned pedestal, four scrolled and line incised legs, 38¼″ h **950**
Table
    Center, parlor
        1860, attributed to Leon Marcotte, New York, ebonized wood, shaped hexagonal top inset with rouge marble, gilt incised apron flanked by gilt bronze cherub masks, urn shaped tapering legs joined by stretcher with gilt incised trim, 47″ w, 30″ h **2,500**
        1865, walnut, inset marble top, oblong top, rounded corners, medallion carved apron, four shaped legs and cabriole supports at ends, urn capped stretcher, 42″ w, 32½″ h **800**
    Library, late 19th C, mahogany, oblong top, carved edge, gadroon carved apron, trestle base with caryatid supports at each side joined by flat stretcher shelf, acanthus carved wide scroll feet, 60″ l, 30″ h **3,300**

ROCOCO (1845–1900) AND NATURALISTIC (1850–1870) REVIVALS

The Rococo and Naturalistic revivals are so interlinked that they merit treatment as a single unit. Both were inspired by the same design forms; the principal difference appears to be a slightly more realistic carving on the Naturalistic pieces.

ROCOCO REVIVAL

History: Inspired by the court of Louis XV, the Rococo Revival, also known as French Antique, *Louis Quatorze*, or *Louis Quinze*, gained popularity in Europe in the early 1840s. The style quickly spread to the United States where it became the most popular style of the Victorian era.

The basic design elements are the C– and S–scrolls that dominate floral, leaf, scallop, and shell decorations. The cabriole leg reappears, often ending in scroll feet.

Much of what appears to be hand carving was done by machine, especially the "finger–rolled" carving that appears on inexpensive pieces. The premier pieces are those made in the factory of Henry Belter. Using laminated wood panels, some consisting of a dozen or more wood strips, he was able to do intricate carving that survived well.

It is not difficult to distinguish nineteenth century examples from earlier period pieces. Rococo Revival pieces have heavier lines, less delicate cabriole legs, and rear legs that are chamfered at the base. The overall feel is heavy.

Rococo Revival furniture was made at all price levels. Inexpensive pieces tended to be made of walnut; more expensive pieces of rosewood.

While furniture *en suite* was made in earlier periods, it became the standard during the Rococo Revival. Parlor and bedroom suites dominated. The etagere or whatnot was introduced. Side tables often featured shaped marble tops. The balloon–back chair in both a formal and vernacular form achieved widespread popularity.

Major Craftsmen/Manufacturers: Charles Baudouine (New York), John Henry Belter (New York), Ernest Hagen (New York), George Henkels (Philadelphia), Gustave Herter (New York), August Janson (New York), S. S. Johns (Cincinnati), Leon Marcotte (New York), the Meeks Brothers (New York), Purdent Mallard (New Orleans), Daniel Pabst (Philadelphia); Alexander Roux (New York), Francois Signouret (New Orleans), and Gottlieb Volmer (Philadelphia).

NATURALISTIC REVIVAL

History: The naturalistic revival added realistic carving to the form vocabulary of the Rococo Revival. In addition to the standard floral and fruit motifs, carvers focused on grape, oak, and rose leaves. Carvers used the lamination process developed by Belter to insure the longevity of their work.

Mahogany, rosewood, and walnut are the favored wood. The most elaborate pieces are center tables followed closely by bedstead head and footboards and sofa backs.

ROCOCO REVIVAL

Armoire, laminated rosewood, high scroll carved crest flanked by turned finials, rectangular top with deep cove molded cornice over large single door with mirror trimmed with arched lattice panel at top, single drawer with scroll carved decoration in base, molded base **5,000**

Pair of Chairs, attributed to J. & L. W. Meeks, New York, mid-nineteenth c, Rococo Revival, laminated rosewood, Stanton Hall pattern, part of a suite consisting of a settee, armchair, and two side chairs, price for suite $15,400.00. Photograph courtesy of Skinner, Inc.

Bed, John Henry Belter, laminated rose-
wood, double
  Carved cupids flanking flower bowl
    finial, branded mark, patent mark   **110,000**
  Carved mermaids flanking crest on
    both headboard and footboard ... **40,000**
Chair
  Arm, attributed to John Henry Belter,
    1845–55, laminated rosewood
    Fountain Elms pattern, tufted back,
      velvet upholstery **5,000**
    Henry Clay, velvet upholstery **3,250**
    Milwaukee pattern, open arms
      Damask upholstery on back and
        seat **22,000**
      Velvet, red, upholstery, tufted
        back, spring seat, four casters **15,000**
    Pierced floral and scroll carved
      crest rail, clusters of grapes at
      base, fully developed skirt with
      carved fruits and flowers **25,000**
    Rosalie pattern, open arms
      Gentleman's **6,600**

**Bed Suite, Rococo Revival. Bed, carved
walnut, tester, 102″ h; accompanied en
suite by dresser and commode, price for
suite, $4,125.00. Photograph courtesy of
Pettigrew Auction Company.**

      Lady's, smaller version **4,675**
    Rosalie without Grapes pattern,
      open arms
      Gentleman's **3,850**
      Lady's **4,675**
    Shell pattern, closed arms, applied
      crest rail, damask upholstery ... **4,950**
    Tuthill King, open arms, four cast-
      ers **20,000**
  Arm, attributed to J & J W Meeks,
    carved and laminated rosewood
    Hartford pattern, pair, open arms,
      price for pair **13,500**
    Hawkins pattern, open arms, velvet
      upholstery, c1860 .... **4,000**
    Henry Ford pattern **5,500**
    Stanton Hall pattern, open arms,
      damask upholstery **4,600**
  Set, arm chair and matching footstool,
    attributed to John Henry Belter,
    1845–55, laminated rosewood,
    scroll and cartouche shaped back,
    wide carved decorations, bold flo-
    ral carved arms and legs, price for
    two piece set **16,500**
  Side, attributed to John Henry Belter,
    carved and laminated rosewood
    Fountain Elms, damask upholstery,
      four casters **8,250**
    Henry Clay, damask upholstery,
      four casters **2,750**
    Patent Model, 1852, pair, original
      factory finish and damask uphol-
      stery, labeled and hand dated in
      ink, price for pair **32,000**
    Rosalie pattern, pair, spring seat,
      canted rear legs, velvet uphol-
      stery, tufted back, four casters,
      price for pair **3,500**
    Rosalie without Grapes pattern,
      pair, spring seat, velvet uphol-
      stery, four casters, price for pair **4,000**
    Tuthill King pattern, velvet uphol-
      stery, four casters **10,000**
  Side, attributed to J & J W Meeks,
    carved and laminated rosewood
    Hawkins pattern, c1860 .... **2,400**
    Henry Ford pattern, pair, tufted
      seat, red damask up-
      holstery, casters on front legs,
      price for pair **3,750**
    Stanton Hall pattern, pair, damask
      upholstery, casters on front legs,
      price for pair **2,800**
  Slipper, attributed to John Henry Bel-
    ter, pair, carved and laminated
    rosewood, arched wooden back
    pierced carved overall, fruit clus-
    ters, leafy scrolls and vines, low
    spring seat, damask upholstery, four
    casters, price for pair **8,000**

Bureau, Rococo Revival, John Henry Belter, laminated rosewood, marked "Patent," 48" w, 24" d, 82" h, $27,500.00. Photograph courtesy of Pettigrew Auction Company.

Chest of Drawers
American, 1850, walnut, etagere work around arched beveled mirror, surmounted by carved central cartouche, two shaped handkerchief boxes with hinged rectangular lids, rectangular marble top with ovolo corners, conforming case with four drawers with walnut veneer panels and applied molding, round wood escutcheons, 53" w, 25" d, 87" h **2,750**
Belter, John Henry, laminated rosewood, tall arched center panel with floral carved crest above mirror flanked by shorter side panels, scroll carved crests over small mirror shelves, two small handkerchief drawers, shaped white marble top, serpentine front, four graduated drawers, scroll carvings flanked by fruit carved front corner bands, original casters, branded name and patent mark **42,500**
New York, 1855, rosewood, highly carved, serpentine mirror, molded marble top, four graduated draw-

ers, rosette drawer pulls, scrolling apron, acanthus carved feet **2,500**
Etagere, attributed to Thomas Brooks, New York City, c1855, rosewood, well carved crest, split shelves supported by multiple turned posts, elaborate finials, rectangular molded mirrored back, shaped marble top, shelved base with two center arched mirrored panels, 95" h **4,250**
Meridiennes (fainting couch), 1855, attributed to John Henry Belter, pair, laminated rosewood
  Carved shaped crest rail, floral carving with center rose, tufted shaped back, velvet upholstery, cabriole legs, original casters, price for pair **9,000**
  Simple carved scrolls, velvet upholstery, cabriole legs, price for pair . **5,775**
Recamier, attributed to John Henry Belter, laminated rosewood pierced and carved frame, lacy vines, grapes and leaf design, looping and undulating arabesques, crest carved with roses, grapes, foliage, and cornucopia, rose carved apron and knees, tufted back, blue velvet upholstery, four new metal casters, 68" l, 43" h **10,000**
Settee
  Attributed to John Henry Belter, laminated rosewood
    Fountain Elms pattern, damask upholstery **32,000**
    Rosalie pattern, 1855, triple arched back, ornately carved floral and fruit crest rail continuing to downswept arms, cabriole legs, velvet upholstery, 63" l **6,500**
    Tuthill King, gold damask upholstery, four casters **40,000**
  Attributed to J & H W Meeks, carved and laminated rosewood
    Hartford pattern, tufted back, shaped seat, damask upholstery **6,500**
    Henry Ford pattern, mint restored condition **12,000**
    Stanton Hall pattern, damask upholstery **3,200**
Sofa
  Attributed to John Henry Belter, laminated rosewood
    Henry Clay pattern, damask upholstery **6,000**
    Rosalie pattern, tripled arched back with ornately carved floral and fruit crest rail flanked by downswept C–scroll armrests, cabriole legs, light blue damask upholstery, tufted back, four casters, 80" l **8,000**
    Shell pattern, 1850, applied crests, tufted back **15,000**

Meridiennes, matched pair, Rococo Revival, John Henry Belter, c1855, laminated rosewood, delicate and detailed crest carvings of flowers, foliage, fruit, and nuts, period finish, price for pair, $9,900.00. Photograph courtesy of Pettigrew Auction Company.

Tuthill King, damask upholstery, tufted back, four casters **35,000**

Suite

  Attributed to John Henry Belter

    Two pieces, sofa and arm chair, laminated rosewood, Cornucopia pattern, tufted back, red damask upholstery, price for two piece set **82,500**

    Three pieces, sofa and two side chairs, laminated rosewood, Rosalie pattern, tufted back, damask upholstery, price for three piece set **13,500**

  Attributed to J & J W Meeks

    Four pieces, sofa, arm chair, and two side chairs, laminated rosewood, Hawkins pattern, dark rose velvet upholstery, casters on all front legs, price for four piece set **22,000**

    Five pieces, sofa, two arm chairs, and two side chairs, Stanton Hall pattern, tufted backs, damask upholstery, casters on all front legs, price for five piece set **20,000**

Table

  Center, parlor

    Attributed to John Henry Belter, laminated rosewood, white marble turtle top

    Scroll carved apron, boldly carved C–scroll legs terminating in different animal heads, S–scroll stretcher feet joined in center by ornately carved fruit and flower basket, casters . . . **22,000**

    Turtle apron carved with fruiting vines centered on sides by large double blossoms, cabriole legs with carved knees joined by scroll carved X–stretcher centered by fruit and flower filled urn finial **12,500**

    Turtle apron carved with scrolls and cartouches at each corner, inwardly curving cabriole legs joined by arched stretchers centering urn form finial at center **10,000**

  Attributed by J & J W Meeks, laminated rosewood, white marble top

    Carved and pierced apron on stretchers, urn finial center . . **5,000**

    Turtle shaped top, pierced and scroll carved apron, rose carved cartouche, S–scroll legs, rose carved knees joined by arched and pierce carved stretchers joined by urn form finial **17,500**

Table, John Henry Belter, New York City, 1845–60, Rococo Revival, marble turtle-shaped top, laminated rosewood base, carved scrolls, leafage, flowers, and fruit, scroll feet on casters, $12,500.00.

Dressing, attributed to John Henry Belter, rosewood, tall arched back, ornate scroll carved crest, arched mirror flanked by small mirrored shelves above shaped marble top, conforming base, scroll carved apron, slender cabriole legs **4,500**

Sewing, carved rosewood, raised rectangular top, two drawers, scroll and flower carved knees and apron, cabriole legs, original label reads: Mitchell & Rammelsberg **1,500**

Side, attributed to John Henry Belter, laminated rosewood, round, white marble top, pierced and carved apron, paw feet **16,500**

NATURALISTIC REVIVAL

Bed, youth, laminated rosewood, carved fruit and flower cluster, simple curved sides **25,000**

Candle Shield, mahogany, ivy leaf and tendrils carving, needlepoint oval

Table, Naturalistic Revival, oak, round top, animal carved pedestal, $1,500.00.

Parlor Chairs, Naturalistic Revival, J. & J. W. Meeks, Hawkins pattern, laminated rosewood, price for pair, $4,400.00. Photograph courtesy of Pettigrew Auction Company.

Etagere, Naturalistic Revival, John Henry Belter, carved rosewood, marble top, 60" w, 16" d, 86" h, $27,500.00. Photograph courtesy of Pettigrew Auction Company.

center, turned pedestal, carved tripod base, 26" w, 58" h   400
Chair, arm, c1855, laminated rosewood, open arms, simply carved frame, gentle scrolls, four casters . . .   1,925
Chest of Drawers, 1860, rosewood, bow front, conforming marble top, egg shaped mirror, serpent carved

Table, parlor, Naturalistic Revival, John Henry Belter, 42 × 30" marble top, $30,800.00. Photograph courtesy of Pettigrew Auction Company.

Etagere, Rococo Revival, rosewood and laminated rosewood, marble top, music cabinet base, $4,070.00. Photograph courtesy Pettigrew Auction Company.

mirror supports and foliate carving, surmounted by plumes and scrolls, four graduated drawers, carved ivy drawer pulls, shaped escutchesons, signed William Denzenger, 89" h ... **2,750**

Daybed, Prudent Mallard, New Orleans, c1855, rosewood, headboard and footboard surmounted by urn and scrolled carving, scrolled finials, shaped sideboards with applied shell and acanthus carving, 88½" l, 49" w, 43" h **13,000**

Easel, walnut, carved leaf and grape finial, tripod base with twig carved legs, out curved feet, 19" d, 78" h **575**

Mirror

   Cheval, carved rosewood, high pierced scroll, flower, and bird carved arched crest, tall swiveling mirror between slender octagonal posts, turned finials, shaped post bases, shaped white marble shelf

above conforming platform, animal paw feet **16,500**

Over Mantel, 1850, carved wood and gilded gesso, ornate rectangular frame, central crest decorated with winged putti flanking cornucopia, 75" w, 97" h **1,250**

Wall, late 19th C, giltwood, shaped mirror plate, foliate decorated conforming frame, applied putto holding swag and putto mask, 59" h .. **6,875**

Stool, piano

   1855, attributed to John Henry Belter, laminated rosewood, upholstered back and seat, foliate carved frame and skirt, ornate standard and scrolling feet **5,500**

   1885, rosewood, upholstered spring seat, carved pedestal, tripod base **3,500**

LOUIS XVI REVIVAL (1850–1914)

History: Empress Eugenie of France, consort to Napoleon III, inspired the Louis XVI Revival when she restored her private apartments at the Tuileries and St. Cloud palaces. The style is also known as the Marie Antoinette Revival. Formal classicism was reintroduced through the design elements of oval backs and straight stiles and legs. Earlier forms were closely duplicated.

The style featured the introduction of inlay in classical motifs and the application of porcelain plaques and ormolu medallions. Furniture frames often were done in an ebonized fashion to contrast with gilt metal mounts, marquetry, or inlaid panels of lighter material such as ivory. French fabrics and Aubusson were used for upholstery.

Louis XVI Revival pieces generally are examples of extremely high quality workmanship, incorporating expensive materials as part of the construction. Rosewood was popular at the beginning of the period; walnut in the 1890s. Many cottage pieces imitated the more elaborate styling through paint.

Many variations of the style occurred. In the 1850s, carving was central, often in an exaggerated motif. By the end of the period, manufacturers adapted the style to a wider range of forms.

The style enjoyed its greatest popularity in the eastern United States. New York was the style center, as it was for much of the Victorian era furniture. Look for its elements, e.g., straight legs, to appear on pieces of Renaissance Revival and Neo–Greek Revival furniture.

Major Craftsmen/Manufacturers: Thomas Brooks (New York), Henkels (Philadelphia), Christian and Gustave Herter (New York), Jelliff (Newark), Leon Marcotte (New York), Alexander Roux (New York), and Szypher (New York).

Screen, three panel, gilt, $1,870.00. Chairs, Colonial Revival, Sheraton features, upholstered, $275.00. Photograph courtesy of Pettigrew Auction Company.

Armoire, late 19th C, rosewood and bird's eye maple, carved crest, mirrored door flanked by two side mirrors, cabriole legs, 62" w, 19" d, 101" h 1,200

Bed, walnut

Carved giltwood crest, headboard with arched and molded back, inlaid brass molding and decorations, center quartered panel, turned tapered legs, conforming footboard, 48" h headboard 400

Diamond shaped walnut burl veneer, shaped headboard and footboard, oval motif on footboard skirt and side rails 500

Cabinet

Display, bow front, mahogany, shaped incurved molded top, swag decoration, glazed sizes and door, pale lime green silk lined shelf interior, fluted tapered legs, 30¼" w, 17" d, 60" h 2,000

Vitrine, mahogany, projected molded cornice, gilt metal dentil frieze, two glazed doors, foliate gilt metal mounted apron, toupie feet, 48" w, 74½" h 4,125

Cabinets, pair, c1880–1915, $550.00. Photograph courtesy of Pettigrew Auction Company.

Center Table, 1875–1900, walnut, marquetry, and ebonized, rectangular molded top inset with a lithograph of the Sistine Chapel ceiling, inlaid frieze centered by a bronze medallion, raised on circular gilt incised legs joined by scrolled stretchers surmounted by a central ebonized and carved urn shaped finial, 49" w, 26¼" d, 30½" h, $2,250.00. Photograph courtesy of Skinner, Inc.

Chair
  Arm, slightly bowed sides, relief carving, green velvet upholstery **350**
  Pair
    Gentleman's with arms, matching lady's chair, shaped crest rail with carved fruits and foliage, original black horsehair uphol-

stery, button back, finger roll carving, cabriole legs; gentleman's: 25" w, 43" h; lady's: 23" w, 41" h, price for pair **1,250**
Gentleman's with arms, matching lady's chair with shaped hip brackets, finger roll oval reupholstered back, shaped reup-

Settee, c1870, carved, ebonized, and giltwood, period tapestry upholstery of floral and neoclassical motifs, 59" w, 26" d, 41" h, $800.00. Photograph courtesy Neal Auction Company.

holstered seat, cabriole legs, gentleman's: 25″ w, 40″ h; lady's: 22″ w, 38″ h, price for pair **950**

Side, Rococo influence

Rosewood, carved crest and splat, shaped upholstered seat, cabriole legs, 36″ h **500**

Walnut, balloon back, applied burl veneer panels on crest, shaped upholstered seat, shaped hip brackets, 36″ h **325**

Walnut, crest carved with morning glories, grapes, and leaves, tufted upholstered back, shaped upholstered seat, cabriole legs, 38″ h **600**

Rocker, walnut, upholstered oval back and shaped seat, finger roll carving, cabriole legs, 24″ w, 35″ h **500**

Settee, walnut

Curved foliate carved crest, upholstered double cartouche shaped back, curved acanthus carved arms, foliate apron, cabriole legs . **850**

Curved floral carved crest, medallion back, carved and finger molded frame, cabriole legs, pink velvet upholstery, 53¼″ w **600**

Table

Card, walnut, inlay, fitted with single drawer, square reeded tapering legs, 30″ w, 30″ d, 28″ h **525**

Center, parlor

Marquetry, 1900, shaped brass beaded top, four shaped drop leaves, floral satinwood inlay, band and string inlay, cabriole legs, 31″ w, 31″ d, 30″ h **500**

Walnut, white marble oval top, finger molded apron and shaped legs, central turned standard . . . **600**

Library, fruitwood, oblong top, pull-out draw leaves at each end, apron with single drawer, square tapering legs, 77½″ w, 32½″ d, 31″ h **1,875**

NEO–GREEK (1860–1885) AND EGYPTIAN (1870–1890) REVIVALS

A new wave of archaeological investigations coupled with the publication of a host of new books on the Middle East led to a revisiting of antiquity in the middle of the nineteenth century. The furniture response became known as the Neo–Greek and Egyptian revivals.

NEO–GREEK REVIVAL

History: The Neo–Greek Revival, also known as Victorian Renaissance, began in France in the 1850s, reaching the United States during the Civil War. Ringuet, LePrince & Marcotte, a Paris–

and New York–based firm, introduced the style. The Neo–Greek Revival enjoyed its greatest popularity in the 1870s and later.

This mid–nineteenth century Greek Revival differed from the neoclassicism of the early part of the century primarily in proportion and exaggeration of design motifs. Case pieces often have a bold plinth base. Curves and angles are strongly balanced. New combinations of design elements also identify later pieces.

Design elements include columns and pilasters from Greek architecture. Floral scrolls and the Greek key appear regularly. Carving is done in high relief. Strong contrasts between light and dark appear in inlay and gilding.

The cabinet (often as one of a pair), library or center table, and stand are the premier furniture forms. Highly ornate curule and klismos chairs were made. Look for Neo-Greek influences in pieces from the Louis XVI Revival and Renaissance Revival.

EGYPTIAN REVIVAL

History: The 1862 London exhibition of Egyptian antiquities, the completion of the Suez Canal in 1869, and increased British presence in the Middle East in the 1870s aroused a strong interest in things Egyptian. Egyptian monuments and tomb artifacts provided the motifs that fueled the Egyptian Revival movement.

Principal design motifs include lotus capitals, clustered columns, palmettes, and zigzag lines. Sphinx heads appeared in a variety of locations ranging from a leg knee to a drop finial. The key was contrast—light against dark. Some chairs featured cloven hoof or paw feet.

Exotic combinations of materials, e.g., gilt bronze, marble, and wood, were common. The popular furniture forms were chairs, tables, stools, and stands. Look for Egyptian Revival motifs throughout the Victorian revival styles.

Armoire, New York, mahogany, two sections: upper section: removable cornice with arched frieze centering stenciled fruit decorations; lower section: pair of hinged doors, interior fitted with two long drawers, flanked by free standing Ionic columns, eagle carved hairy paw feet, some restoration to gilding, 66″ w, 34″ d, 93″ h . **12,000**

Bedroom Suite, 1880, carved and burled walnut; bed: carved acanthus and foliate cornice with center carved pediment, central burled carved pendant on shallow tester type frame, arched panels on headboard with floral carving, ring turned columns, side rails with burled panels and molded trim, footboard with rounded top, conforming burled carved pendant

Bed, walnut, arched headboard with carved center pediment and carved raised panels over peaked recessed panel, shaped side rails, footboard with rounded top and similarly carved raised panels flanking a concentric ring decoration, 88″ h, $1,250.00

over four panels with floral carving; armoire: two arched mirrored doors, two small drawers in base; chest of drawers: rectangular mirror mounted between columns, flanked by small shelves and foliate carving, stepped veined marble top with elevated center section over small drawer, center drawer flanked by two small drawers over two long drawers; bed: 100″ h, 69″ w, armoire: 116″ h, 60″ d, chest of drawers: 111″ h, 21″ d **13,000**

Bench, mahogany and mahogany veneer, three chair back type, shaped crest rail, butterfly wings, and oval medallions, oval center splat with painted classical figures, carved Sphinx arm supports, old cane seat, wear and veneer damage, 59″ l **2,150**

Bookcase, Blake and Alden, Boston, Massachusetts, mid 19th C, walnut, carved crest, molded cornice over two arched glazed doors, applied burl decoration, carved pilasters, two molded drawers, stamped name, 54″ w, 20″ d, 91″ h **1,750**

Chair, side, carved walnut, shaped crest rail, carved back splat, incised seat rail, slip seat, straight tapering front legs **300**

Desk, ormolu mounted mahogany, pedestal, rectangular molded top, inset gilt tooled green leather writing surface, fitted side slides, frieze fitted

with central drawer flanked by two drawers over two pedestals containing three drawers, Egyptian terminals, conforming plinth, 59½″ w, 33½″ d, 30″ h **7,000**

Log Basket, walnut, gilt incised walnut U–shaped frame, wicker lining and handle, frame, needlework fringed trim, monogrammed SJRC **700**

Pedestal, 1865, ebonized and gilt incised decoration, rectangular top, vase shaped over ring turned swelled baluster standard, circular footed base, 38″ h **750**

Table

Occasional, 1860, carved walnut, well figured circular top inlaid with satinwood of St George slaying the dragon, ringed standard, tripod base with acanthus carving and paw feet **800**

Pier, attributed to J and J W Meeks, New York, stenciled and giltwood,

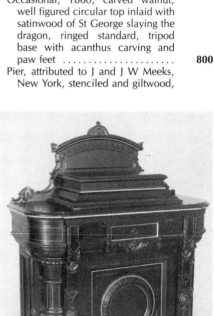

Cabinet, Neo-Greek with strong Renaissance Revival influences, c1875, pedimented top with acroteria above a raised superstructure resting on a case having a projecting drawer above a cupboard door centered by a raised circle and flanked with medallion decorated pilasters leading to quarter column corner and paneled sides, 44″ w, 21″ d, 60″ h, $1,650.00. Photograph courtesy of Neal Auction Company.

black and white veined marble top, convex frieze stenciled with fruit and foliate motifs in gold above pair of giltwood swans centering metal lyre strings, flanked by marble columns with Corinthian capitals, shaped and stenciled plinth with mirror, acanthus and fruit carved legs, painted and gilded animal paw feet, 44" w, 18" d, 37½" h .. **35,000**

EASTLAKE OR REFORMED GOTHIC (1870–1890)

History: By the third quarter of the nineteenth century, a number of critics called attention to what they felt was the deteriorating quality of furniture design and manufacture. Criticism began as early as the 1850s. Henry Cole and Owen Jones, a designer, both reacted negatively to the furniture exhibited at the 1851 London Crystal Palace exhibition. The battle cry was taken up by John Ruskin, an English art critic.

What developed was a desire to rid furniture of excessive ornamentation and return to a more "honest" use of materials. This was coupled with a hostile reaction to increased mechanization. The reformers felt that "handcrafted" pieces were superior in quality to factory–made examples.

William Morris, a trained architect, led the fight against the machine in England. He turned to thirteenth century English Gothic for inspiration, adapting, but not copying its basic lines, proportion, and structure. However, Morris quickly learned that his "handcrafted" furniture had to be priced above the means of the average consumer.

Charles Locke Eastlake, another English designer, took the Morris concepts and adapted them to mass produced products. Oak was his favorite wood. American Eastlake is a loose interpretation of Eastlake's concepts.

American Eastlake shapes are rectilinear with design motif ranging from the simple to elegant. Decorative motifs, often carved in low relief, tend toward geometric and floral designs. Machines produced much of the linear line decoration, covering a wide range of chamfering, grooving, and spindles. Inset panels on cupboard doors and sides were common. Occasionally a Middle East or Far East motif is seen.

Although Eastlake favored oak, American manufacturers produced Eastlake forms in cherry, maple, and walnut as well. Beds; chair sets (4 to 6); pedestal, side, and center tables; sofas; and stools are common furniture forms.

Mass produced Eastlake pieces combined a wide variety of Victorian revival styles. Renaissance Revival backs, Sheraton legs, Sheraton fancy period decoration, and Egyptian pyramid motifs are just a few of the design elements

found. Look to Eastlake's formal designs as the inspiration for Art Furniture and the Arts and Crafts Movement.

Style Book: Charles Locke Eastlake, *Hints on Household Taste,* London, 1868, American editions from 1872 through 1890.

Major Manufacturers: Gardner and Co. (New York), Grand Rapids, Michigan, manufacturers, Herter Brothers (New York), George Hunzinger and Sons (New York), William Holmes Co. (Boston), Issac E. Scott (Chicago), E. W. Vail (Worcester, MA), and W. S. Wooton (Indianapolis).

Reference: Mary Jean Smith Madigan, *Eastlake–Influenced American Furniture, 1870–1890,* The Hudson–River Museum, 1973.

Cylinder Desk, lady's type, fitted interior, $800.00.

Bed
    1870, walnut and burl walnut veneer, spoon carving, incised lines, applied roundels, 58" w, 83" l **1,500**
    1875, walnut, half tester, incised lines, applied burl veneer panels and decorations, 43½" w, 80" h, 10" crest on half tester **2,000**
Bedroom Suite, walnut, incised lines and fretwork; bed: high headboard surmounted by pediment with incised

carving, reeded upright columns, conforming footboard; chest of drawers: rectangular beveled adjustable mirror surmounted by carved pediment, flanked by two candle arms, galleried back, rectangular top, three graduated drawers with teardrop pulls, wood escutcheons, paneled skirt; commode washstand: back splashboard with conforming fretwork, towel bar ends, single long drawer with teardrop pulls over two paneled cupboard doors; bed: 44" w, 70" h headboard, 36" h footboard; chest: 43" w, 20" d, 76" h; washstand: 33" w, 19" d, 8" h splashboard, 32" h overall, price for three piece set **3,875**

Bookcase
  1870, carved walnut and burl walnut, three sections: upper section: broken pediment with architectural center ornament; middle section: pair of glazed doors; lower section: plinth base with drawers **1,800**
  1880, walnut, single door, spoon carving and incised lines, shelved interior, 31" w, 13" d, 59" h **900**

Cabinet
  Barber, walnut, rectangular marble top with curved front corners, incised lines, conforming outset top with two small drawers, burl walnut veneer panels on foldout drawer fronts, ebonized pulls, brass decorative escutcheons, 29" w, 19" d, 35" h **600**
  Dental, walnut, incised lines, spoon carving, two flanking cupboards with turned finials, two drawers over center recessed mirrored well, pullout section over long drawer, two lower cupboard drawers, side drawers, 32" w, 19" d, 65" h **1,250**

Chair
  Lady's, walnut, Minerva head carving on crest, incised lines, applied burl veneer panels and roundels decoration, shaped hip brackets with conforming decoration, shaped reupholstered back and seat, turned front legs, 36" h **400**
  Office, cane tilt back and seat, incised lines and burl veneer decorations, 23" w, 39" h **300**
  Side
    1875, F W Krause, Chicago, pair, walnut, crest rail with carved central trefoil, carved quatrefoil decoration on back splat and lower rail, cane seat, plain legs, H–stretcher base, price for pair **850**
    1880, walnut, shaped hip brackets,

cane seat, turned H–stretcher base **225**

Chest of Drawers, cherry, projection front, sidelock, incised lines, 4" h top brass rail, five graduated drawers, original embossed rectangular brass hardware, paneled sides, 38" w, 20" d, 53" h **1,000**

Cradle, platform
  1875, walnut, paneled headboard, footboard, and sides, scrolling crest above short turned spindles, swings

Cylinder Desk, burl walnut and mahogany, shaped cornice above pair of glazed cabinet doors and cylinder door enclosing writing surface over two doors, shaped base, 27″ w, 22″ d, 66″ h, $1,000.00. Photograph courtesy of Leslie Hindman Auctioneers.

on platform support, original finish, dated **475**

1890, walnut and burl walnut veneer, incised carving, crested pediment on headboard, cutout sides with central roundels, platform support with iron foot rocking pedal **600**

Desk, walnut

Davenport, lift top, incised lines, applied burl veneer panels, pair of molded panels on front, three side drawers, ring brass hardware, 30" w, 22" d, 43" h **1,400**

Parlor, drop front, rectangular marble top over carved well, fitted interior, applied burl veneer panels on drawer fronts and drop panel, paneled sides, 34" w, 18" d, 53" h **1,875**

Meridienne (fainting couch), walnut, machine carvings on frame, original upholstery, turned legs with casters . **250**

Magazine Rack, walnut, pierced sides, turned posts, machine carved, 13½" w, 26" l **195**

Mirror, walnut, carved and line incised sides, ebonized crest and applied decoration, rectangular beveled mirror, 24" w, 32" h **200**

Rocker

1875, platform, mahogany, incised and pierced cresting over center square back panel, padded reeded arms, upholstered velvet seat, reeded supports **225**

1880, platform, walnut, incised carved crest rail, stiles, arm supports, skirt, side rails, and platform, cutwork under arms, four metal casters, gold velvet reupholstery .. **300**

1885, walnut

Nursing, walnut burl panel on crest, keystone shaped back, shaped hip brackets, recaned seat and back, 19" w, 35" h ... **175**

Sewing, cutout crest panel, caned back panel and shaped seat, applied burl panels, incised carving on stiles and hip brackets **150**

1890, nursing, maple, gondola shaped sides, decorated plywood panel seat and back **110**

Secretary, walnut, two sections: upper section: carved corniced bookcase, two glazed doors, applied moldings, three interior shelves, cylinder front with applied burl veneer panel and ebonized pulls; lower section: single long drawer over pair of cupboard doors, incised columns extending to feet, 37" w, 22" d, 84" h **2,500**

Sideboard, walnut, incised lines and burl veneer panels, two glazed doors over mirrored splashback, rectangular marble top, base with two drawers over pier of three drawers and single cupboard door, decorative brass pulls and escutcheons, 42" w, 20" d, 76" h **1,200**

Sofa, walnut, carved crest, back splat with conforming carving, tufted double framed back, incised lines, applied burl veneer panels, reupholstered, 58" w, 38" h **400**

Stand

Music, late 19th C, ebonized, rectangular top over floral inlaid fall front, folio compartment, square legs, medial shelf above single drawer, 22½" w, 15½" d, 39" h **325**

Rockers, George Hunzinger, patented duplex spring. Left: Padded velvet upholstered back seat, and arm rests, original paper label, $880.00. Right: Padded velvet upholstered seat, original paper label, $880.00. Photograph courtesy of Pettigrew Auction Company.

Secretary, walnut, bookcase, fitted interior, cylinder roll top desk, 34" w, 22" d, 89" h, $1,540.00. Chair, Rococo Revival and Eastlake design style characteristics, walnut, $90.00. Photograph courtesy of Pettigrew Auction Company.

Pedestal, New York, Kimbel & Cabus, c1875, ebonized, gilt, and painted, circular top with narrow bead trim, cross shaped standard extending to tulip shape and medallion over conforming molded base, 40" h .. **1,600**

Table

Center, walnut, incised lines, drop corner finials, 36" w, 36" d, 30" h **400**

Library, walnut, rectangular top, satinwood inlay center, banded borders, four reeded supports extending to turned central support and continuing to outswept feet, 44" w **275**

Side, walnut, rectangular beige marble top with canted corners, conforming carved apron, pedestal base with incised lines, finials, and applied decoration, four bracket feet; label reads: Frank B Brown,

Hampton, New Hampshire, 1886, 20" w, 15" d, 30" h **325**

ART FURNITURE (1875–1914)

History: One of the responses to the excessive decoration and mass production of late Victorian furniture was to treat furniture as an "art" form. While the concept originated in England, it was quickly adapted by American designers such as George Grant Elmslie and William Purcell in Chicago and Louis Comfort Tiffany and Associates in New York.

Although art furniture has a box–like quality similar to Arts and Crafts furniture, its decorative ornamentation ranging from Near Eastern and Moorish to Japanese motifs easily distinguishes it from this former group. Overall the furniture has a light feel. Shallow carving, inlays of wood and metal, and marquetry were used to achieve ornamentation. Many of the designs exhibit an asymmetrical composition.

Classic Japanese furniture strongly influenced furniture forms, especially sideboards. Commissioned pieces frequently were done en suite. A variety of woods were used. In vernacular furniture, imported bamboo lead to heavy use of the bamboo motif on mass produced chairs.

Style Book: *Art Furniture Designed by Edward W. Godwin F.S.A. and Others, with Hints and Suggestions on Domestic Furniture and Decoration by William Watt*, London, 1887.

Major Manufacturers: Herter Brothers (New York), Kimbel & Cabus (New York), and Niedecken Walbridge Company (Milwaukee, WI).

Chest of Drawers, five drawers, center domed recess with carved floral motif on upper two drawers, $495.00. Photograph courtesy of Pettigrew Auction Company.

Bedroom Suite

1880, Aesthetic Movement, Herter Bros, dresser and bedstead with lunette panels inlaid in cherrywood and walnut, stylized rose sprigs above furled banner, dark stained ground, stiles incised with roundels and geometric motifs, matching nightstand, dresser stamped "Herter Bros," marble inscribed in blue "Store, N 2891," side rails stamped "Herter Bros," nightstand inscribed beneath marble "Flanagan;" bedstead: 64½" w, 65¾" h; dresser: 50½" w, 84" h; nightstand: 18" w, 30¾" h, price for three piece set **22,000**

1885, Aesthetic Movement, Gotlieb Vollmer, inlaid florals, brass inlay, carved walnut and burled walnut, bronze mounts, bedstead with high headboard surmounted by floral carved pediment with carved rib-

Umbrella Stand, carved wood, $385.00. Much too sophisticated to be classified as rustic vernacular furniture which was being made during the same period. Photograph courtesy of Pettigrew Auction Company.

Etagere, c1890–1915, strong Eastlake feel in overall form, shows Far East influences, $825.00. Photograph courtesy of Pettigrew Auction Company.

bons, ring banded columns over reeded pilasters, central burl panel, conforming footboard, chest of drawers with large rectangular mirror surmounted by floral carved pediment with carved ribbons, four graduated drawers flanked by ring banded columns over reeded pilasters, and dressing table with central full length mirror flanked by two piers of five graduated drawers, brass casters, price for three piece set **14,000**

1880–85, maple and bird's eye maple, faux bamboo, bed and chest of drawers, bed with faux bamboo crest over shaped headboard, conforming footboard, chest of drawers with mirrored superstructure swiveling within bamboo turned frame, spindled gallery, lower section with three long drawers; bed: 62" l, 60" w, 75½" h; chest of drawers: 48" w, 77" h, price for two piece set . **2,750**

Cabinet, music or portfolio, ebonized cherrywood, gilt incised, pedestal has revolving door (open and closed view), 39″ h, $715.00. Photographs courtesy of Pettigrew Auction Company.

Cabinet

Parlor, Aesthetic Movement, 1880, inlaid and ebonized cherry, superstructure with arrangement of shelves with floral pierced galleries on turned baluster supports, beveled rectangular mirror panel surrounded by floral embossed red velvet, pair of glazed doors below flanked by inlaid stylized floral sprigs over two cupboard doors carved with large flowerheads, flanked by inlaid sprigs single shelf interior, stylized bracket feet, 36″ w, 72½″ h **2,500**

Side, New York, c1875, breakfront outline, stepped rectangular top, raised central section incised and inlaid with stylized flowerheads, palmettos, fluting and Greek key scrolls, foliate and swag inlaid frieze, central cupboard door below incised and ebonized with central floral sprig medallion flanked by glazed doors, shelved interior, molded plinth base, 43½″ w, 72″ h   **1,000**

Wall, c1875, carved and ebonized, central cushioned rectangular door carved with stylized fruiting and blossoming cherry sprigs, stippled ground, rectangular shelf, turned baluster supports, spindled gallery, repairs, age crack in door, 11¼″ w, 25″ h **350**

Chair

Arm, 1880, parcel gilt and incised walnut, arched crest rail carved with stylized flowerheads and floral sprigs, gilt incised frieze decorated with rosettes, inlaid stiles leading to padded armrests over spindled galleries, flared seat, turned cylindrical legs, black leather upholstery . **650**

Set of Six, side, bird cage crest over seven bamboo turned uprights, saddle seat, bamboo turned legs joined by stretchers, original paint, price for set of six **15,400**

Side, 1912, Paul Follott, carved walnut, open rounded back set with wide I–form gridwork splat carved at top with flowers, buds, and foliage, curved supports, rounded rectangular seat, shallow groove apron, two tapering square front legs with acanthus terminals, flattened ball feet, two tapering rectangular back legs **4,000**

Desk, Wooten, single rotary, rosewood, slanted writing surface with gallery, rotary to right with brass pulls, patent dates **5,500**

Shelf, hanging, ebonized, two tiers, central mirrored back surrounding gilt and painted panel, top and bottom with corresponding medallions, 44" h   **750**

ART NOUVEAU (1896–1914)

History: Most dealers and collectors identify Art Nouveau with the twentieth century more than they do with the nineteenth century. However, it correctly belongs in a listing of furniture design styles of the Victorian era, because its principal influence was in Europe, not America.

Siegfried Bing, a Parisian art dealer, is credited with introducing the style in late 1895 at his shop, known as Maison de l'Art Nouveau. Bing's shop featured expensive handcrafted furniture pieces that incorporated the curving lines of the French Rococo and Japanese art. A 1900 exhibition in Paris drew international attention. Bing closed his shop in 1904.

The appeal of Art Nouveau was limited, especially in the United States. Charles Rohlfs of Buffalo, New York, designed a number of pieces with Art Nouveau elements. The sinuous curves and naturalistic design elements did not win favor with a public that was used to more sturdy furniture. American manufacturers of mass produced furniture utilized some of the design motifs between 1900 and 1905.

Major Manufacturers: George C. Flint and Company (Chicago), Larkin Manufacturing Co. (Buffalo), and Louis Comfort Tiffany and Associates (New York).

Armoire, Louis Majorelle, 1900, carved walnut and fruitwood, upright rectangular form, crested top, carved apron with clusters of lilac blossoms and foliage, central cupboard door set with beveled glass mirror plate, flanked by two smaller conforming cupboard doors, one long and two short drawers, gilt–bronze leaf molded handles, four lug feet, 74½" w, 96" h **8,500**

Bed, Louis Majorelle, fruitwood marquetry, headboard inlaid with pen-

Vitrine, gilted, c1885, two mirrored back, curved shelves each with a projecting gallery above a glass enclosed display cabinet, the whole raised on turned legs terminating in bulbous feet, locked signed "G. Bayer, N.Y., Patented 1881," 46" w, 18" d, 64" h, $660.00. Photograph courtesy of Neal Auction Company.

dant wisteria, footboard inlaid in floral motif, twisted fluted side columns, tapering fluted feet, 80" l, 48" w, 62" h **1,750**

Bedroom Suite, mahogany, double bed: headboard and footboard with inlaid trumpet creeper florals, crest rails with floral carving; dresser: marble top, carved mirror; pair of matching night tables, headboard 74" w, 56" h, price for five piece set **8,000**

Bookcase, 1900, Majorelle, carved walnut, molded crest, carved splayed leaves, glazed door mounted with central textured purple glass panel, silvered bronze branch form spandrels, pair of narrow cupboards, molded base, carved feet, 64¼" w, 79" h **3,500**

Cabinet, vitrine, 1900, Galle, marquetry, shaped rectangular top, chamfered corners, molded edge, rectangular cabinet, glazed door and sides, back and door inlaid with tall stalks of cow parsley and butterfly, reeded legs, 25¾" w, 18" d, 47¾" h **5,225**

Chair

Arm

Mahogany, attributed to Karpen Brothers, Chicago, reed and tendril carved frame, undulating crest rail carved in high relief with female heads emerging from a cluster of poppy blossoms, continuing to poppy carved scrolled armrests, seat rail carved to match, cabriole legs **1,045**

Walnut, intricate undercut carved foliage on arms, legs, and crest, olive–green crushed velvet upholstery **200**

Set

Set of two, carved walnut, crest rail over solid vertical splat, carved poppy sprigs, nail studded light brown simulated leather bow front seat, channeled cabriole legs, pointed toes, price for pair   **800**

Set of four, 1900, walnut, pressed leather seat and back, flowing iris design, price for set of four **350**

Side, New York, attributed to George C Flint, 1896, carved mahogany, relief carved flower buds on back splat, carved side rails, upholstered seat, carved shaped apron, French cabriole legs **800**

Clock, tall case, Walter Durfee, Providence, Rhode Island, retailed by Theodore B Starr, New York, 1900, oak, fully carved case, beveled glass doors, and case sides, eight tube, three train movement with moon phases, striking Westminister or chime on eight bells, three brass cased weights, mercury pendulum, 93½" h **5,000**

Desk, Carlo Bugatti, 1900, ebonized wood, carved, applied hammered copper and inlay in Moorish taste, rectangular top, inset leather writing surface, small superstructure holding six short drawers inlaid in pewter with birds and bamboo, arched cubbyhole, arched and outward flaring front

legs, trestle back supports, 24" w, 19½" d, 38" h **6,600**

Hall Tree, 1900, carved walnut, thumb molded cornice over shaped mirror plate, molded tendril border, serpentine projecting shelf, panel carved at sides with tendrils and leafy sprays, shaped feet, 50" w, 85" h **1,500**

Rocker, c1900

Parlor, oak, fumed finish, curved arms, saddle seat, three splats with floral type capitals **225**

Sewing, oak, carved and pierced back panel and front stretcher, incised line carving on stiles, carved and incised rockers mounted on outside legs, pink velvet upholstered seat .   **275**

Sideboard, Louis Majorelle, 1900, oak and mahogany, rectangular, bowed front, inset marble top, two long drawers, undulating brass pulls cast with sheaves of wheat, two cupboard doors with large applied brass sheaves of wheat and undulating leaves, molded apron, four lug feet, 65" w, 39⅜" h **5,000**

Sofa, Carlo Bugatti, 1900, ebonized wood, rectangular back and mechanical seat, slightly scrolling rectangular arms, parchment upholstery, painted swallows and leafy branches, hammered brass trim, four block form feet, 68⅜" l **1,750**

Table

Console, mahogany, shaped top, modified cabriole legs, curved brackets, hoof feet, 45" w, 19" d, 33" h **400**

Side

Emile Galle, marquetry, burlwood curved top, decorative stringing, inlaid columbine decoration, three slender fluted triangular legs, inlaid signature, 29" h **900**

Gustave Serruier–Bovy, 1900, walnut, shaped rectangular top, arched apron, four molded rectangular legs, stylized feather supports conjoined by straight stretchers, 35½" w, 30" h **2,250**

ARTS AND CRAFTS/PRAIRIE

History: Both the American Arts and Crafts and Prairie movements began while Queen Victoria reigned in England. If one extends the American Victorian period to 1915, then both movements began, developed, and ended during the American Victorian period. However, few American collectors and dealers are willing to associate these movements with the Victorian era.

American scholars proudly point to the Prairie school as one of the first design styles to evolve from the United States. In truth, it is as deeply indebted to European antecedents as other Victorian revival styles.

However, the clear transmission of design ideas becomes muddy once the twentieth century begins. A wealth of publications, photographs, and the ability to travel conveniently led to a rapid, almost instantaneous exchange of ideas. Furniture design had become international.

Until the 1970s, American collectors tended to lump Arts and Crafts and Prairie school furniture as "Mission," a label suggesting strong Southwest influences. Modern scholars now clearly recognize that two distinct but related design styles evolved. Likewise, although much of the furniture goes well with Southwestern architecture, the influence of the Southwest on design was minimal.

Finally, never look at Arts and Crafts and Prairie school furniture in isolation. These were total looks. All decorative accessories were coordinated. Furniture is just one component, albeit an important one.

References: David M. Cathers, *Furniture of the American Arts and Crafts Movement*, New Amsterdam Library, 1981; David Hanks, *The Decorative Arts of Frank Lloyd Wright*, E. P. Dutton, 1979; Malcolm Haslam, *Collector's Style Guide: Arts and Crafts*, Ballantine Books, 1988; Wendy Kaplan (ed.), *"The Art that is Life": The Arts & Crafts Movement in America, 1875–1920*, Boston Museum of Fine Arts, 1987; Bruce Johnson, *The Official Identification and Price Guide to Arts and Crafts*, House of Collectibles, 1988; Randell L. Makinson, *Greene & Greene: Furniture and Related Designs, Volume 2*, Gibbs M. Smith, Inc., 1979.

ARTS AND CRAFTS (1885–1915)

History: The Arts and Crafts movement is America's response to the concerns raised by Eastlake, Godwin, and Morris in England. Emphasis was placed on handcraftsmanship. Hubbard went so far as to create a community of craftsmen at his Roycroft community in East Aurora, New York. An individualistic approach was taken with each piece of furniture.

The basic style is rectilinear and stresses a relationship between function and form. It is more fluid than its Prairie School cousin and often contains subdued design elements from a wide range of sources ranging from Oriental to Gothic. Unlike Art Furniture, decoration was secondary to form. Look for shallow carving, marquetry, and some inlaid wood and metals. Complex decorated pieces are known.

Oak is the favored wood, especially for those pieces with a strong Medieval or Renaissance heritage. Other woods included maple and bamboo.

The concept of a workers guild comprised of designer, manufacturer, and decorator developed. The Art Workers Guild of Providence, Rhode Island, included John G. Aldrich (architect), Sydney Burleigh (cabinetmaker), and Charles W. Stetson (painter).

Critical to the style was a coordination between building design and furnishings. The Greenes and Wright were leaders in putting this concept into effect. Although each approach was individualistic, the movement quickly achieved national recognition.

Leading Designers: Charles and Henry Greene (California), Elbert Hubbard (East Aurora, NY), Lucia K. and Arthur F. Mathews (West Coast), George Niedecken (Midwest), Henry Hobson Richardson (Boston), Frank Lloyd Wright (Illinois).

Major Manufacturers: Ernest Hagen and J. Matthew Meier (New York), Peter and John Hall (Pasadena, CA), Limbert Arts and Crafts Furniture (Holland, MI), George and Leopold Stickley (Grand Rapids, MI), Gustav Stickley (Eastwood, NY), and Tobey Furniture Company (Chicago).

Bed
    Charles P Limbert Co, Grand Rapids, Michigan, 1910, oak, sloping sides form backrest, head panels pierced with heart form handles, branded label, 74½" l, 23" h **425**
    Gustav Stickley, double, Model No. 923, c1909, oak, tapered posts and five wide slats across headboard and footboard, red decal, 59" w, 78" l, 42½" h **5,000**
    L & J G Stickley
        Model No. 92, 1910, oak, canted end posts joining headboard and footboard panels of one wide and

six narrower slats, rails joined by large removable legs, white decal mark

Double, 58″ w, 79″ l, 44½″ h . . **14,300**

Single **3,000**

Model No. 738, crib, oak, thirteen slats across back, five slats on each end, sides canted inward, massive posts of quadruple laminate, curved molding under top rails, original black–brown finish, unmarked, new platform and cushion, 76″ l, 30″ d, 39″ h . . . **6,875**

Bench

Ali Baba, Roycroft, 1910, oak, slab seat, exposed bark underneath, plank ends joined by long center stretcher, exposed keyed tenons, signed with orb mark and carved initials, 42″ l, 15″ d, 17″ h **1,500**

Settle, Model No. 265, oak, sixteen vertical slat back, slat sides, leather upholstered seat cushion, white L & J G Stickley decal mark, 75½″ l, 31″ d, 34″ h **800**

Window

Charles P Limbert Co, Grand Rapids, Michigan, 1907, No. 243, oak, canted flat sides with four square cutouts each centering seat, leather cushion, branded mark, dark color, shellac finish, 24″ w, 18″ d, 24″ h **4,500**

Gustav Stickley, Model No. 178, 1903, oak, raised ends with posts joined by exposed tenons, rectangular leather seat, flat stretcher with exposed tenon keyed cross stretcher, 35½″ l, 26″ d, 18½″ h **2,850**

Bookcase

Charles P Limbert Co, Grand Rapids, Michigan, oak, rectangular top, caned inset splashboard back, two cabinet doors with glass panes, four straight legs, paper label, 35″ l, 60″ h **500**

Gustav Stickley, Model No. 716, 1905, oak, gallery top, two doors with eight panes, V swing pulls, red decal, 42½″ w, 13¼″ d, 56½″ h . **4,000**

L & J G Stickley

Model No. 645, oak, three interior shelves, glass paned doors, L & J G Stickley mark, 49″ w, 12″ d, 55″ h **3,200**

Model No. 647, c1906, oak, gallery top, exposed key tenons over three doors with twelve panes each, copper swing pulls, straight apron, stenciled number on back, splits in back, metal

brace under front, minor nicks, 69¼″ w, 12″ d, 55″ h **5,500**

Stickley Bros, 1910, oak, rectangular top, two glazed doors, interior with three adjustable shelves, square legs, impressed mark, 35″ w, 13″ d, 56″ h **550**

Box, Goody, Roycroft, c1910, mahogany, rectangular, impressed logo on lid, brass hinges, 22⅞″ l, 12¼″ w, 9½″ h **400**

Cabinet

China

Stickley, L & J G, Model No. 746, c1912, oak, overhanging top, two doors, six smaller panes above single glass panels, adjustable shelves, arched toe board, 44″ w, 16¼″ d, 62″ h **3,500**

Stickley Bros, Grand Rapids, Michigan, c1912, oak, rectangular top, two doors with gently arched divider, top interior fitted with mirror, branded mark, 46″ w, 14½″ d, 62¼″ h **850**

Smoking, Gustav Stickley, 1912, oak, one drawer above cabinet door, fitted interior, copper hardware, 20″ w, 15″ d, 29″ h **1,450**

Chair

Arm

Charles P Limbert, Grand Rapids, Michigan, Model No. 933, oak, three vertical back slats, open arms, corbels, wide stretchers, drop in spring seat, 27″ w, 28″ d, 43″ h . . **225**

Gustav Stickley

Oak, cube, Model No. 391, 1907, rectangular rails above series of slender square spindles, square seat, raised on shaped square posts **8,800**

Oak, five horizontal slat back, spindled sides, decal mark, 33″ w, 37½″ d, 39½″ h **10,450**

Oak, fixed back, Model No. 324, 1904, four horizontal back slats, flat arms over five vertical slats, reupholstered spring cushion seat, signed: Gustav Stickley, 29″ h **1,500**

Stickley Bros, early 20th C, oak, flat crest rail over five wide slats flanked by heavy square stiles, wide flat arms over wide slats in sides, exposed tenon construction, original deep reddish–brown finish, metal tag, 38″ w, 32″ d, 33″ h **3,300**

Child's, Model No. 342, oak, two horizontal slats, original leather seat, two side stretchers, dark finish, original paper label **300**

Hall, Charles P Limbert Co, Grand Rapids, Michigan, Model No. 79, 1910, oak, splayed vertical back support posts originally covered with leather for support, wooden bicycle type seat, 19½" d, 43" h . **600**

Morris

Child's, oak, adjustable back, original cushions **275**

Charles P Limbert Co, Grand Rapids, Michigan, c1910, oak, four horizontal back slats, slightly shaped arm over five vertical slats, spring cushion seat, branded, replaced pegs, 34" w, 41" d, 36" h **2,800**

Morris, William Co, Model No. 498, oak, four horizontal slat back, five vertical slat sides, 33½" w, 37" d, 35" h **1,540**

Gustav Stickley

Model No. 346, 1912–16, oak, curved rectangular back, five horizontal slats, slightly flared rectangular arms, square legs, later white muslin cushions, branded mark **1,875**

Model No. 2342, c1902, oak, flat arms, through tenons, five slats down each side, adjustable back, five horizontal slats, 31¼" w, 35½" d, 44½" h ... **6,400**

L & J G Stickley

Model No. 412, oak, four horizontal slat back, broad shaped arms, leather upholstered cushions, white L & J G Stickley decal mark, 35" w, 38¼" d, 38½" h **700**

Model No. 471, oak, four horizontal slat back, six slat sides, faux leather upholstered cushions, L & J Stickley red decal mark **1,870**

Office, Charles P Limbert Co, Grand Rapids, Michigan, 1910, oak, swivel, upholstered leather back and seat, shaped curving open arms, branded label, 29" w, 42" h **550**

Sets, dining

Set of six, four side chairs, two armchairs, Gustav Stickley, c1910, Model Nos. 353 and 353A, designed by Harvey Ellis, oak, three vertical back slats, arched apron, drop in seats with original red Fabricoid, 40" h, price for set of six **8,250**

Set of seven, Stickley Bros, c1907, Model No. 901 1/2, oak, crest rail bowed vertical back slats,

upholstered seats, double side stretchers, stenciled number, damage to seats, minor nicks and scratches, 19¾" w, 38¼" h, price for set of seven **1,100**

Set of twelve, Stickley, L & J G, c1910, Model No. 1340, oak, straight crest over three vertical slats, upholstered seats, double side stretchers, unsigned, varnish, nicks, restoration to seat, price for set of twelve **1,700**

Side

Charles P Limbert, Grand Rapids, Michigan, Model No. 851, oak, five vertical back slats, curved crest rail, double side and front stretchers, wrap around leather seat, 21" w, 18" d, 37" h **125**

Gustav Stickley

Model No. 308, 1912, oak, flat crest rail over wide H–splat suspended between square stiles, upholstered slip seat, square legs joined by flat stretchers, branded mark, 39¼" h **300**

Model No. 338, oak, designed by Harvey Ellis, c1904, three back slats with inlaid copper, pewter, and fruitwood sinuous organic forms, drop in rush seat, red Gustav Stickley decal, 39" h **3,850**

Model No. 358, oak, square back, nine vertical spindles, original leather seat and tacks, 39¾" h **900**

L & J G Stickley

Model No. 808, oak, five vertical slat back, leather upholstered seat, white L & J G Stickley decal mark, 38" h **265**

Model No. 1350, oak, three horizontal slats, original upholstered leather seat, two lower side stretchers, signed: The Work of L & J G Stickley, 34½" h, price for set of four **700**

Wing, arm, L & J G Stickley, 1910, oak, clamp decal mark **950**

Chests of Drawers, Gustav Stickley

Model No. 622, 1902, oak, four long graduated drawers, two short drawers, panel construction sides, large red Gustav Stickley decal with "Stickley" outlined, 41" w, 22½" d, 50" h **4,500**

Model No. 902, oak, arched back rail, two top drawers, four horizontal drawers, oval hammered pulls,

red decal in top right drawer, 39¾"
w, 22" d, 53½" h **4,200**
Model No. 909, oak, two short drawers over three graduated drawers,
panel construction sides, red Gustav Stickley decal in top right
drawer, paper label, 37¼" w, 19"
d, 42" h **2,450**
Desk
  Harvey Ellis design for Gustav Stickley, 1903, oak, oblong table type
  top above three drawers, flat legs,
  trestle base, flat floor stretcher,
  pewter and copper inlay at sides,
  41½" l **2,750**
  Charles P Limbert Co, oak, oblong
  table type top above apron, single

**Desk Chair, Quaint Furniture, c1910,
arched crest rail over two horizontal rails
and wide vertical slat with three inlaid
stylized tulips, arched side stretchers,
shaped front feet, branded mark, 16" w,
15" d, 38¼" h, $900.00. Photograph
courtesy of Skinner, Inc.**

drawer, square legs supporting two
tiers of shelves joined by flat central
stretcher, poor condition of original
finish **250**
Hall Tree, Gustav Stickley, oak, double,
original light finish, six black iron
hooks, small version of Stickley No.
53, from Cleveholm Manor, CO, 13"
w, 22" d, 66" h **1,870**
Magazine Stand
  Derby Co, Boston, oak, vertical double side stretchers, five shelves, rectangular legs, dark finish, remnants
  of paper label **140**
  Michigan Chair Co, 1910, oak,
  square over hanging top, four open
  shelves, sides with two vertical
  slats, lower shelf with keyed tenons, 33⅛" h **500**
  Roycroft, 1910, oak, carved emblem,
  37" h **450**
  L & J G Stickley, 1910, Model No.
  47, oak, trapezoidal sides, arched
  toe boards, four shelves, original
  color and finish, decal reads: The
  Work of L & J G Stickley, 20" w,
  15" d, 42" h **1,650**
  Tobey Furniture Co, oak, rectangular
  top, four shelves, canted plant
  sides, arched cutout base, 48" h .. **375**
Mirror, Boston Society of Arts and
Crafts, 1910, carved wood, rectangular, carved and gilded frame, ink
mark, initials, and original paper label, 11¼" w, 18½" h **550**
Rocker
  Harvey Ellis, 1900, lady's, curly maple, three vertical black slats inlaid
  with Arts & Crafts–Art Nouveau
  pewter and green wood design,
  curved skirt under front and sides,
  inset leather seat, designed by Ellis
  for Gustav Stickley, 17" w, 25¾" d,
  34" h **3,850**
  Harden & Co, oak, concave crest rail
  over four vertical slats, flat arms
  with corbels over three vertical
  slats, spring cushion seat, 38½" h **250**
  Charles P Limbert Co, Grand Rapids,
  Michigan, Model No. 518, 1910,
  oak, tall back, adjustable slats, flat
  arms over elongated corbels, original upholstered spring cushion
  seat, 36¾" h **1,250**
  Roycroft Shop, 1900, oak, armless,
  five vertical slats in back, new thick
  canvas seat, dark brown finish,
  branded orb trademark on front,
  18" w, 31" d, 35" h **300**
  Gustav Stickley
    1900
      Gentleman's, oak, high back

with eleven spindles, nine spindles under each seat, inset leather seat, original brown color, new lightly oiled finish, red decal mark, 27½" w, 22½" d, 45" h 9,000

Lady's, oak, armless, nine slender spindles on back, five below seat on each side, new black leather seat, new brown finish, red decal mark, 16" w, 14" d, 36" h 1,200

1912–13, Model No. 387, oak, armless, tall straight back, three flat slats, leather upholstered seat, three flat slats on each side under seat, branded signature, 41½" h 675

Sideboard

Charles P Limbert Co, Grand Rapids, Michigan, 1910, oak, oblong top, mirrored back above case with three short drawers flanked by paneled cupboard doors over long drawer, copper pulls and strap hinges, square legs, chamfered tenons, branded mark, 49½" w, 53½" h 600

L & J G Stickley, Model No. 738, 1912, oak, rectangular top over two center drawers flanked by cabinet doors with strap hinges, branded 1,900

Sofa, L & J G Stickley, 1910, oak, decal clamp mark, 72" l 1,400

L & J G Stickley, oak, oblong top, straight backboard supporting plate rail, four short drawers flanked by cupboard doors over long drawer, 54" l 1,200

Stool, foot

Gustav Stickley

1902, Model No. 725, oak, rectangular leather top, arched sides tacked down, four square legs, tapering feet joined by X–stretcher, unsigned, retail label of A A Gray Company, Detroit, Michigan, 19½" l, 17" d, 16½" h 1,320

1912, oak, rectangular, original leather seat and tack trim, four posts joined by offset lower stretchers, branded mark, worn leather, 18¾" w, 16" d, 15" h .. 715

L & J G Stickley, 1918, Model No. 397, oak, rectangular spring cushion seat, straight apron and side stretchers, decal mark, roughness at corners, 20" w, 14" d, 16" h 500

Table

Dining

Gustav Stickley, 1905, oak, oblong

Footstool, Roycroft, leather cover, square tapered legs, branded orb mark, 15" l, 10" w, $195.00.

top, trestle base joined by tenon and key stretcher, decal mark .. 1,450

L & J G Stickley, oak, square top, plain apron, square pedestal, four downswept supports, six extension leaves, 50" square top, 30" h 2,875

Library

Gustav Stickley, 1910, oak, oblong top, apron with two short drawers, hammered copper pulls, square legs joined by medial shelf, branded mark, 42" l, 30¾" h 1,875

Tobey Furniture Co, oak, cross lapped stretchers, key and tenon construction, 17¼" l, 23½" h 300

Occasional, Gustav Stickley, 1910, oak, round top, conforming stretcher, four square legs joined by flat cross stretchers, chamfered tenons, medial shelf, 24" d, 29" h ... 550

Tea, Gustav Stickley, 1904–12, oak, round top, plain apron, four legs joined by arched cross stretchers supporting medial shelf, 26" d, 29" h 600

Wardrobe, Gustav Stickley, 1905, oak, flat rectangular top, two long paneled doors, two interior compartments, eight narrow drawers over two shelves, lower arched toe board, red decal mark, remnants of original paper label, 33¼" w, 59¾" h 5,500

PRAIRIE (MISSION) SCHOOL (1900–1920)

History: The Prairie School is a subdivision of the Arts and Crafts movement. Its unadorned, severe rectilinear lines, often incorporating cantilevered elements, are distinctive enough to be designated as a "unique" design style. Frank Lloyd Wright and his Midwestern Prairie School disciples are the leading exponents of the style. In its more popular form, the style is known as "Mission."

As with the American Arts and Crafts movement, inspiration came from a variety of sources: the English Arts and Crafts movement played an important role; Charles Rennie Mackintosh, a Scottish designer, contributed the concept of tall back chairs; Koloman Moser of Austria stressed the importance of modular decoration.

In many cases, architect and manufacturer worked closely together. Further, the manufacturer often enjoyed a wide latitude in interpreting the architect's designs. As a result, assigning a specific piece to a single individual often is incorrect.

Most furniture features rows of vertical and/or horizontal splats. Tenons are exposed, often secured with wooden pegs or keys. Leather is the favored upholstery material.

The favored wood is stained or fumed oak. The most commonly found forms are benches, chairs, small and large tables, and settees.

Major Designers: George Grant Elmslie, George Feick, William Gray Purcell, and Frank Lloyd Wright.

Major Manufacturers: Charles Limbert (Grand Rapids, MI), Niedecken Walbridge Co. (Milwaukee, WI), George and Albert Stickley (Grand Rapids, MI), Gustav Stickley (Eastwood, NY), and L. & J. G. Stickley (Fayetteville, NY).

Bed, Frank Lloyd Wright, designed for Evans Residence, Chicago, 1909, oak, solid headboard and footboard, heavy crest rail, twin size **7,000**

Bench, hall, Gustav Stickley, Model No. 205, oak, five broad slats across back, one broad slat at each side, exposed tenons, red decal mark, some original finish, 55¾" w, 22" d, 30" h **2,500**
Bookcase
Lifetime, Grand Rapids, Michigan, c1912, oak, rectangular top, three doors each with eight panes, iron pulls, corner posts with through tenons, signed metal tag, 61⅜" w, 13" d, 49¼" h **4,000**
Skandia Furniture Co, Rockford, Illinois, oak, birch type varnish finish, sectional, four graduated sections, hinged glass front, Viking trademark **575**
Cabinet
China, Lifetime Co, 1912, oak, rectangular top cut around corner posts, two plain glass doors, and sides, adjustable shelves, 43" w, 14½" d, 57" h **650**
Liquor, Gustav Stickley, Model No. 86, oak, copper lined flip up top over single door, interior with small locking compartments, side shelves, and rotating bottle rack, red decal mark, original finish, repaired veneer on door, 24" w, 17" d, 42" h **3,850**
Smoking, square top, impressed for circular tray, single door, copper strap hinges and lock, fitted interior, four splayed legs, old finish, tray missing, 26" h **325**
Vitrine, K Hpanderez Hollandia, c1910, ebony inlaid oak, arched recessed backboard, central pair of beveled glass cupboard doors over

Suite, three piece, settee, armchair, and rocker, Plail Brothers, Wayland, New York, c1910, oak, (settee No. 64½, armchair No. 641), bowed crest rail, vertical slats, period spring cushion, flared rear feet, paper label, one of rockers repaired, some old refinish, edge roughness, chair 24½" w, 19" d, 33½" h, settee 46" w, $6,750.00. Photograph courtesy of Skinner, Inc.

Bookcase, revolving, oak, four sides, each fitted with four shelves, all within slatform divisions, four sided base on castors, 24¾" w, 69⅝"h, $1,250.00. Photograph courtesy of Leslie Hindman Auctioneers.

long door, interior shelves, open shelves, drawers, pair of leaded glass cupboard doors, square legs, stamped maker's mark, 42½" w, 72" h 2,475
Chair
Arm, oak
    Harden Co, Camden, New York, c1910, slat back, double crest rail over five vertical slats, curved arms over four vertical slats per side, spring cushion, original paper label, 30" w, 38¼" h 500
    Phoenix Furniture Co, Grand Rapids, Michigan, c1894–1920, designed by David Wolcott Kendall, caned back and seat, wide flat arms 1,500

Morris, Frank Lloyd Wright, designed for Little House, Peoria, Illinois, 1902, wide single back slat, wide seat, paneled sides, 32" w, 40" h . 80,000
Sets, set of four, dining, Indiana Hickory Furniture Co, hickory, log and twig construction, woven seats, branded manufacturer's mark, retailers metal tag "Paine Furniture Boston," price for set of four 800
Side
    Charles Rohlfs, 1900, oak, octagonal stiles, butterfly pierced single back splat, shaped skirt, 37½" h 1,500
    Unknown maker, fumed oak, slim, tall lines, cutout design in back panel, shaped wooden seat, 16" w, 38" h 200
Chest of Drawers
    George Washington Maher, Chicago, Illinois, 1912, poplar, painted ivory, four short drawers over four long drawers, trapezoidal splashback and sides, bronze pulls, 42" w, 22" d, 72" h 3,000
    Stickley Bros, quarter sawn oak, rectangular pivoting mirror mounted above rectangular overhanging top over two narrow short above two graduated long drawers, wooden knobs, arched skirt 800

Chair, side, quarter sawn oak, three slats, shaped seat, $175.00.

Morris Chair, slant arm, No. 369, Gustav Stickley, c1912, adjustable back with fine horizontal slats, slanted arms over corbels and five vertical side slats, bearing castors, brand mark, refinished, 32½" w, 41½" h, $4,750.00. Photograph courtesy of Skinner, Inc.

Clock, tall case, George Washington Maher, Chicago, Illinois, 1912, oak, stained light green, arched bonnet, circular glass door, trapezoidal case, lower shaped glass door, brass weights and pendulum, 31" w, 15" d, 80" h **27,000**

Daybed, Frank Lloyd Wright, designed for Little House, Peoria, Illinois, 1902, headboard and footboard connected by broad sideboards with applied moldings, 79" l, 25" w, 40" h . **17,500**

Desk
  Lifetime, Model No. 8548, c1910, oak, drop front, gallery fitted interior compartments, two long drawers, arched apron, round copper pulls, escutcheon plate missing, decal on lower side stretcher **600**
  Charles Rohlfs, 1930, oak, three legs, 30" h **1,150**
  Otto Wagner, executed by Gebruder Thonet, 1904–06, stained beechwood, rectangular top, beige felt inset writing surface, back mounted with shelf, two short drawers in apron, round straight legs and side stretchers, front legs with aluminum studs, back panel with row of aluminum studs, 42½" w, 26⅜" d, 43" h **22,000**

Hall Bench, attributed to Brooks or Imperial, oak, slightly canted ends with four square cutouts, triangular face boards face the long lift top seat, deep apron, recent medium brown finish, 84" l, 19½" d, 24" h **900**

Room Divider, leaded glass panels, stained glass grape pattern on trellis, contemporary oak frame, wrought iron hardware, 27" w, 46" h **1,400**

Shelf, wall, reticulated plank ends, D–shaped handles, four shelves, exposed keyed tenons, 27⅛" w, 6⅛" d, 36" h **125**

Stand, smoker's, Charles Rohlfs, 1900, oak, square top, paneled cupboard doors and paneled sides, plinth base, 30" h **800**

Stool, foot, 1910, oak, rectangular frame, spring cushion seat, legs with corbel supports, lower side stretcher, side tenoned median stretcher, 23" l, 17" d, 18" h **300**

Table
  Dining, Gustav Stickley, oak, round overhanging top, wide apron, five tapering legs, original medium brown color, recent shellac finish, 48" d, 30½" h **750**
  Library, George Washington Maher, Chicago, Illinois, 1906, mahogany,

massive square legs, molded feet, overhanging top, wide apron, lower shelf, 66" l, 30" d, 36" h . . .   **2,700**

ART DECO (1925–1940)

History: While Arts and Crafts and Prairie school writers like to tout their design styles as the beginning of the modern era, Art Deco is the rightful claimant to that title. The key reason is World War I; its scope coupled with the technological advances profoundly affected the generation that prepared for peace in 1920. The world made safe for democracy was a vastly different world.

Art Deco derives its name from the 1925 Paris exhibition "l'Exposition Internationale des Arts Decorative et Industriels Modernes." Elements of the design style were in place by 1920.

The essential design elements are bold, simplistic geometric shapes based on traditional forms. Ornamentation is greatly simplified, surfaces are smooth, angles are crisp, and curves, when used, are highly controlled.

Art Deco has a strong feminine quality, stressing luxury and refinement. It found a ready home in the bedroom (boudoir) and living room (parlor). The use of exotic materials, such as Macassar ebony and tortoiseshell or snakeskin for cabinet fronts or desk tops, was viewed as an attempt to achieve refinement.

Quality furniture featured excellent craftsmanship and materials. Lacquered or painted pine or maple was used for less expensive furniture. Veneers, often of boldly contrasting inlay, were lavish. Innovative designs, drawing upon the contemporary International style, introduced metal and glass into furniture composition.

Seated furniture tended to be overstuffed, whether armchair or ottoman. Furniture sets were the order of the day in the dining room and kitchen. Cocktail, coffee, side, and end tables entered the form vocabulary.

High style Art Deco failed to survive the stock market crash of 1929. Its link with luxury condemned it. A few exponents such as Donald Deskey kept the flame alive. Further, Modernism's functional principles, clean lines, and undecorated surfaces were rising to challenge it for pre–eminence. Because of its ability to blend with modernistic forms, Art Deco continued to influence mass production furniture through the 1930s.

Major Designers: Jules Bouy, Donald Deskey, Paul Frankel, Hammond Knoll, Harry Lippman, Samuel Marx, Eliel Saarinen, and Eugene Schoer.

Major Manufacturers: Heywood–Wakefield and Knoll.

References: Yvonne, Brunhammer, *The Art Deco Style*, London, Academy Editions, 1983; Karen Davies, *At Home in Manhattan: Modern Deco-rative Arts, 1925 to the Depression*, Yale University Art Gallery, 1983; Alastair Duncan, *American Art Deco*, Harry N. Abrams, Inc., 1986; Tony Fusco, *The Official Identification and Price Guide to Art Deco*, House of Collectibles, 1988; David Hanks with Jennifer Toher, *Donald Deskey: Decorative Design and Interiors*, E. P. Dutton, 1987.

Bar, attributed to Ray Hille, c1930, bleached burl walnut, upright rectangular center section, fluted doors, illuminated shelved interior, mirrored peach glass, sliding shelf fitted with peach glass, two cupboard doors, two lower rectangular sections set with cupboard door and shelved interior, scrolling H–form support, rectangular plinth base, 56¾" w, 59¾" h **1,600**

Bookcase
1925, polished aluminum, tin plate, pair of leaded glass doors, bird's eye maple back panels, 58" w, 17" d, 65" h **7,500**
1930, Emile–Jacques Ruhlman, corner style, mahogany, three sections, molded top and sides, stepped base   **12,000**

Cabinet, 1948, walnut veneer, center raised lift top section with three long drawers flanked by side cabinets with large cupboard doors, shaped platform base, bakelite handles **1,350**

Chest, cedar, Lane, 1930, waterfall veneer **175**

Arm Chair, tubular, attributed to Warren McArthur, vinyl upholstered seat, $1,875.00. Photograph courtesy of Leslie Hindman Auctioneers.

Chair

Arm

1925, Paul Frankl, matched pair, black lacquer, continuous low back and arms formed by square U–slat alternating with inset rectangular panels, upholstered square seat, four straight rectangular legs, pink brocade upholstery, relaquered, price for pair . **2,400**

1934, Kam Weber, airline style, cantilevered wood and leather . **18,000**

1935, tiger's eye maple, brown leather inserts, red lacquered fretwork **500**

1938, Russel Wright, bentwood frame, vinyl yellow upholstered seat and back, contrasting blue piping **750**

Club, pair, square back, scroll over arms, upholstered in quilted green and ivory floral chintz and fringed trim, designed by Michael Taylor, price for pair **2,500**

Set

Set of Two, designed by Eileen Gray, side, tubular, chromed steel and leather, price for pair . **8,800**

Set of Six, Ruhlman, silvered bronze sabots, drop in pumpkin velveteen upholstered seat, branded mark, 37″ h, price for set of four **15,400**

Side, 1940, walnut, black satin, shaped back, scrolled side rails, upholstered seat **350**

Chifforobe, 1935, herringbone design waterfall veneer, arched center mirror, dropped center section, four deep drawers flanked by tall cupboard doors, shaped apron **195**

Commode

1925, Clemènt Mëre, matched pair, rectangular inset top, rolled edges, one long drawer, center cupboard door opening to shelved interior, six short drawers, interior lined with burled sycamore, gently curving apron, four Chinese inspired rectangular legs, covered in pressed leather, dyed all over pattern of circular stylized buds and blossoms, shades of rust, dark amber, mustard, brown, and gold, painted ivory circular handles, 32⅞″ w, 37½″ h, price for pair **42,000**

Cabinet, wood, made by Secessions Ltd., Chicago, Illinois, rectangular top over facet carved cupboard doors revealing interior drawers and cubby holes over two aligned drawers set on block feet, together with the original design rendering, 51″ w, 19½″ d, 62″ h, $1,450.00. Photograph courtesy of Leslie Hindman Auctioneers.

1935, ivory inlaid and birch, front opening to reveal two cabinets, four fluted legs tapering to ivory sabots, 48" w, 15¾" d, 35" h **3,100**

Daybed, Jules Leleu, 1925, walnut, two high scrolling ends, rectangular plinth, tapering everted feet ending in scrolls, upholstered cushion and rolled pillows **4,000**

Desk

1928, birch and steel, matching stool, variation of Model BM 744 and MS 419 .... **88,000**

1935, painted, single pedestal, rectangular top, case of three drawers at one end, tall turned tapering leg **2,400**

Living Room Suite, 1933, arm chair and sofa, chair: barrel back, channeled bright pink velour upholstery, boldly carved arm fronts and apron; sofa: barrel back, serpentine front, three cushion seat, conforming upholstery, price for two piece set **2,500**

Rocker, Louis Sognot, c1930, chromed metal, upholstered back and seat, 36" h **1,200**

Secretary, Rene Drouet, c1925, two sections: parchment, fall front, upper section: oval inset door, leather lined writing surface, lighted shelved interior, two short drawers, lower section: single cupboard door, shelved interior, inset oval base, two ivory mounted keys, 29¼" w, 49½" h **8,000**

Sofa, Chesterfield, 105" l, straight back, scroll over arms, upholstered in quilted green floral ivory ground chintz with fringed valance and pillows, two seat cushions, designed by Michael Taylor, 1930s **3,500**

Stand, night, 1935, walnut, waterfall veneer, open shelf above single cupboard door **200**

Table

Architect's, 1935, white lacquer, painted black metal, and oak **4,400**

Dining, maple, ebony, blue rectangular mirror top, apron, three supports on plinth base, 72" l **1,500**

Telephone, 1937, alder, rectangular top, rounded end above case with open shelves, cutout support and small drawer **200**

Vanity, 1935, walnut, large round mirror, flanked by two three–drawer sections, dropped center well **250**

CENTENNIAL AND COLONIAL REVIVAL

History: Americans never fell out of love with colonial styles. Although not dominant during the first half of the Victorian period, some copies were made. Colonial era pieces were modernized (e.g., hardware changed) to keep them in fashion. In areas such as New England, the Middle Atlantic states, and the South, heirloom pieces linked modern generations to their historic past.

The handmade quality of colonial period pieces often made them simply too good to discard. Instead, they were moved to secondary settings, e.g., the guest bedroom. Many were passed on to newlyweds just setting up housekeeping. A large number were sent to the attics to await the time when "they might be needed."

In some instances, period pieces were enhanced: carving was added where it never existed before; plain surfaces were painted; often the piece's very character was changed. What did not change were the original construction techniques—the clue to spotting these pieces from identical late nineteenth and early twentieth century copies.

America's Centennial in 1876 reawakened interest in the period of American settlement. Museums were established; collectors developed. Period pieces were available, but hardly prevalent. Demand quickly exceeded supply, albeit this is a concept that modern collectors find hard to believe.

The February 15, 1890, *Scientific American* reported: "The rage for having furniture of the antique pattern has grown wonderfully during the last few years. Antique oak dining suites, bedroom suites, and hall furniture seem to be most popular, but anything of an antique character now sells rapidly. . . . There are not nearly enough of these precious relics to go around, so it is a blessing that provision is made for reproducing them indefinitely at comparatively cheap rates."

The statement is important for two reasons. First, notice the emphasis on suites. Colonial period furniture was rarely made in suites. Second, the mass–production manufacture of colonial period reproductions is well established by 1890. In fact, the trend began in the 1880s.

Centennial and Colonial Revival furniture comes in many different styles. Reproductions are exact copies of their period counterparts. They are often the work of craftspersons as opposed to manufacturers, albeit some manufacturers produced excellent reproductions. Copycats are stylistic copies, i.e., copies that differ in size, decorative motif, and/or form. There were no Chippendale coffee and end tables during the Chippendale period.

The demand for "antique" (period) furniture produced a number of craftspersons who built antique pieces using parts from period pieces or old wood. Most were never meant to deceive, albeit some were. Now, after almost a century, many have developed a patina, or oxidation, and other signs of wear and tear that make it difficult to distinguish them from their historic counterparts.

The faker complicates the picture. The goal is to deceive. The faker wants the buyer to believe the piece is period. The faking of period early American pieces is not of recent vintage. The process was well in place by the turn of the twentieth century. A 1902 article by Luke Vincent Lockwood discussing the problems associated with furniture collecting noted the following about New York auctions: "The majority of collections offered for sale are made up of the unsalable articles from the shops of antiques dealers, and perfectly new and badly made material, furnished by men whose business it is to supply furniture for this purpose. In several instances, new and poorly constructed furniture has been placed in old Southern houses, photographed in these surroundings, and brought to New York, to be sold at auction from an illustrated catalogue . . ."

Beginning with the Centennial revival of the 1880s, American colonial period furniture design styles became the most commonly purchased furniture by middle and working class America. It was traditional and safe. New design styles were viewed as trendy, expensive, and elitist. It is not by accident that the major design styles of the twentieth century have a big city/Hollywood flavor. Many failed to impact heavily on small town and rural America.

The revivals of early American styles are poorly understood by the modern collector and dealer. Rodris Roth's "The Colonial Revival and 'Centennial Furniture'" in Volume 27, Number 1 (1964) of *The Art Quarterly* is a must read. A number of revivals occurred, many producing a variety of quality levels.

There are five major colonial revival movements. The Centennial Revival (1880–1915) focuses on mass–produced pieces that are close copies of period pieces. The pieces were expensive, made largely for an upscale clientele. Exact copies were left to the Colonial Revival Craftsmen of the 1900 to 1940 period.

The patriotism of World War I and the events leading up to the American Sesquicentennial in 1926 renewed interest in colonial period styles. Demand was universal, ranging across the broad economic spectrum. Manufacturers obliged. Great liberties were taken in design and form. Some pieces were based on design elements from the nineteenth century.

Mass–produced post–World War I pieces that retain some degree of period integrity fall in the Colonial Revival movement. Pieces of questionable design and quality are grouped as "Confused Colonial," a much larger segment of the furniture market than is realized.

The principal question is what to do with furniture manufactured after 1945 in early American design styles. Much of the mass–production furniture is part of the secondhand furniture market. While this is fine for Ethan Allen and even pieces from firms such as Pennsylvania House, it is not the place one is likely to encounter examples from Kittinger or Henredon.

In fact, many of the "average" quality 1950s and early 1960s mass–produced colonial revival pieces have started to appear in antiques malls, shops, and shows. They have reached a point where their value is increasing, rather than declining. Forty years of age on a quality piece is more than a enough to attract the young buyer on a limited budget.

The American Bicentennial in 1976 reawakened an interest in handcrafted furniture in early American styles. Hundreds of small firms, ranging from one individual to several dozen employees, are manufacturing high quality pieces that either are direct copies (reproductions) or very close copies of colonial pieces. The works of some of these firms have been included here to acquaint readers with the wide range of forms and styles being offered by these firms and the prices charged. Knowledge of the latter has a direct effect on the value of older pieces.

CENTENNIAL (1880–1915)

History: The 1876 Philadelphia Centennial Exhibition featured a highly romanticized re-creation of a colonial, i.e., open hearth, kitchen, and a set of furniture made from one of the oldest trees in Philadelphia. America discovered its past; a call to action was sounded. In the decades that followed, state, county, and local museums were founded throughout the United States. Antique collecting became a popular pastime. In fact, it became the rage.

The 1876 experience, where most of the centennial celebrations and activities took place following July of 1876, provides an interesting contrast to the American Bicentennial period during which most of the activity associated with the celebration took place *before* July 1976. By the time the event arrived, many Americans were worn out.

The Bicentennial celebration lacked a central focus. It seemed that everyone did their own thing. As a result, the Bicentennial did not trigger a great renewal in early American material. If anything, it marked an end to the affordability of early American period pieces by the average collector.

Centennial is a Colonial revival. The trend began in the 1880s, reached its zenith in the 1890s, and hung on until the beginning of World War I. It primarily impacted on the wealthy, due in part to the high cost of most handcrafted Centennial pieces.

There are basically two types of Centennial furniture: The first group is made up of high quality, handcrafted reproductions. Although some liberties may occur in size, proper proportions were usually maintained. The second group consists of pieces whose forms are period but whose ornamentation is more in keeping with Victorian tastes. Carving tends to be more elaborate, often extending to areas that would be left plain on a period piece. Victorian inlay, e.g., the conch shell, replaces period designs on some Federal forms.

It is important not to forget that Centennial furniture actually is a Victorian revival. As such, Victorian conventions apply. Furniture is found in suites, living room and parlor as well as bedroom. Victorian forms are colonialized, one of the best examples being high style Chippendale and Empire telephone stands.

The Victorian took a much broader view of the "colonial" period than we do today. Colonial included pieces from the sixteenth through the early nineteenth century. Further, they did not like the "new" look. Wear was manufactured into the pieces. The artificial nature of much of this wear is one of the easiest methods to separate a Centennial from a period piece.

Much of this furniture is now over one hundred years old. Its patina, oxidation, shrinkage, and wear is often similar to period pieces. It takes a skilled eye and knowledgeable person to separate a Centennial reproduction from its period counterpart. If in doubt, assume Centennial.

Chair
Arm
    Chippendale Style, mahogany, shaped crest rail, shaped curving arms, pierced Gothic back splat, floral needlepoint upholstered slip seat, shell carved apron, cabriole legs with carved knees, claw and ball feet **425**
    Queen Anne Style, painted, cupid's bow crest rail over vase form splat, arms raised on baluster supports continuing to turned legs, bead and reel frontal stretcher, worn alligatored dark finish **175**
Set
    Set of Four, Chippendale Style, mahogany, hand carved pierced splat and crest, slip seat with blue satin upholstery, claw and ball feet, 41" h, price for set of four **1,300**
    Set of Six
    Chippendale Style, New York, 1876, mahogany, cupid's bow crest rail above pierce carved splat, plain seat rail, needlepoint covered slip seat, cabriole legs, carved knees, claw and ball feet, price for set of six **1,800**

Queen Anne Style, pair of arm chairs, four side chairs, worn original dark finish, minor damage to Spanish feet, two with replaced rush seats, price for set of six 1,950

Queen Anne Style, side chairs, mahogany, slip seats upholstered in pale green brocade, refinished, 40" h, price for set of six 1,800

Set of Eight, Federal Revival, c1900, dining, two arm chairs, six side chairs, mahogany, flat crest, lyre form splat, curving stiles, upholstered seats, saber form front legs, price for set of eight 3,850

Side, Chippendale style, mahogany, shaped crest rail, pierced Gothic back splat, floral needlepoint upholstered slip seat, shell carved apron, cabriole legs with carved knees, claw and ball feet 385

Desk

Chippendale Style

Partner's, walnut, gadrooned top edge, four dovetailed drawers on back, fluted quarter columns, cabriole legs, acanthus carved knees, claw and ball feet, old finish, some edge damage, 54" l, 30" d, 30" h 1,450

Slant front, mahogany, brass gallery over shell carved hinged lid opens to fitted interior, straight front with four graduated drawers, brass bail handles, gadrooned apron, claw and ball feet, 30" w, 17" d, 45" h 1,595

Library, walnut, rectangular top with inset brown leather with gadrooned rim, straight front, one wide thumb molded drawer flanked by four small drawers, brass bail handles, cabriole legs, claw and ball feet, 28½" w, 31½"d, 30½" h 770

Hall Tree, bronze, embossed tin, bust of Washington flanked by flags, locomotive, ship, and eagle, mirror in center, 25" h 125

Mirror, Queen Anne style, late 19th C, mahogany faced, scalloped, shell pediment, 32" h 200

Sideboard

Chippendale style, late 19th C, mahogany, block front with shell carving, four drawers, four cabinet doors, gadrooned apron, cabriole legs, claw and ball feet, 68" w, 24" d, 40" h 900

Hepplewhite Style, made by Mers-

man Bros Corp, Celina, Ohio, 1932, mahogany, figured veneer and inlay, shaped top, conforming case, center section with long drawer over pair of cupboard doors flanked by pair of cupboard doors, oval brasses, added iron braces, 72" w, 24½" d, 40¼" h 850

Sofa, Chippendale style, late 19th C, mahogany, shaped back, rolled arms, yellow velvet upholstered seat, gadrooned apron, cabriole legs with carved knees, claw and ball feet, 62" l 1,400

Stand, fern, Regency style, c1930, mahogany, three tiers, three legs, brass feet, 10½" d, 47" h, pr 250

Table, card, mahogany, rectangular folding top, reeded edge, conforming apron with central fretwork panel flanked by cross banded panels, ring turned and circular tapering reeded supports, 36" l, 30" h 660

COLONIAL REVIVAL (1915–1940)

History: The Colonial Revival of the 1920s and 30s reached all levels of society. Furniture was made in every grade; it could be purchased from the finest furniture store as well as the leading mail auction catalogs.

If we had to select one piece that best symbolized the period, it would be the Governor Winthrop Secretary, a Chippendale style slant–front desk with bookcase top. The bookcase top had two doors, each divided with wood frets into a pattern consisting of thirteen sections, one for each of the thirteen colonies, or so the story goes. Obviously Governor Winthrop of Massachusetts never owned such a desk, because the Chippendale design style developed long after his death. A collection of over a hundred examples can be made from this one form alone.

Several construction and design characteristics of Colonial Revival furniture differentiate it from period and Centennial pieces. It tends to be much more simplified in design; it looks right from a distance, but not upon close inspection. In addition, the carving lacks vigor; thinner wood was used on many pieces; proportions are narrower and more slender; heavy metal support braces are used; and many pieces have factory markings.

Colonial Revival furniture is primarily a stylistic copy, not an exact reproduction, of period pieces. In overall appearance, it retains a period feel. This is in sharp contrast to Confused Colonial pieces that have little link to a specific historical design style.

Colonial Revival furniture is well made. Although mass-produced, there is a high degree of quality control. Better pieces were not inexpensive. Less expensive pieces often featured veneered, rather than solid, surfaces.

Colonial Revival left no form untouched. Whether coffee table or coffee server, a Colonial Revival example exists in styles ranging from Chippendale to Federal. Hanging shelves and bookcases were manufactured in "period" designs.

Collectors and dealers are just beginning to identify manufacturers whose material should command premium prices. Be on the alert for pieces by Baker, Berkey & Gay, Charak, Grand Rapids Furniture Co., Henredon, Heywood-Wakefield, Kittinger, Kling, Margolis, and H. C. Valentine. Companies in and near Grand Rapids, Michigan, and High Point, North Carolina, also deserve attention.

References: Robert W. and Harriett Swedberg, *Furniture of the Depression Era: Furniture & Accessories of the 1920's, 1930's, & 1940's,* Collector Books, 1987; *Zone 3 Furniture Dealers' Reference Book, 1928–1929,* reprinted as *American Manufactured Furniture,* Schiffer Publishing, 1988.

Bed
  Empire Style, mahogany, removable pineapple finials, turned and reeded posts, acanthus carving, mi-

nor edge damage, 50¾" w, 74¼" l, 60¾" h **225**
  Regency Style, inlaid rosewood, upholstered headboard, conforming footboard, shaped framework, brass inlay and mounts, double mattress size, 56" h **600**
Bench, Chippendale Style, mahogany, cabriole legs, slip seat with ivory damask upholstery, claw and ball feet, 44" l, 19" w, 20" h **150**
Cabinet, china
  Chippendale Style, 1940, walnut veneer, breakfront, scrolled broken pediment, center urn finial, pair of glazed doors and panels, long drawer over two cupboard doors, 44" w, 15" d, 76" h **600**
  Hepplewhite Style, mahogany, inlay, three urn finials on shaped pediment, pair of glazed cupboard doors, two small drawers flank center drawer over one long drawer, tapering legs, some edge damage, slight damage to grill work, 38" w, 17" d, 81" h **350**
Chair
  Arm
    Chippendale style, Martha Washington, mahogany frame, worn finish, worn gold striped upholstery, 38" h **100**

Bed, Hepplewhite Style, satinwood inlay in mahogany, circa 1920–30, $250.00. Photograph courtesy of Pettigrew Auction Company.

Sheraton, matched pair, mahogany stained arms and legs, green striped upholstery, 34½" h, price for pair 170

Set of Six, two arm chairs, four side chairs, Adams style, mahogany, upholstered seat, worn finish, some damage, break in one arm, 37" h, price for set of six 600

Side, Queen Anne Style, 1920, Ohio, walnut veneer, vase splat, slip upholstered seat, modified cabriole legs 90

Desk, Bishop Furniture Co., Grand Rapids, Michigan, fall front, crossbanded mahogany, hinged lid, fitted interior, recessed center drawer flanked by four short drawers, turned wood knobs, columnar front legs, shaped base shelf, ball feet, 34" w, 40" h, $350.00.

Wingback Armchair, Queen Anne Style, Williamsburg reproduction by Kittinger, pink striped silk upholstery, 49" h, price for a pair, $2,255.00. Photograph courtesy of Garth's Auctions, Inc., and _Antique Week._

Wing, Chippendale Style, claw and ball feet, worn green upholstery, 40" h 95

Chest of Drawers, Hepplewhite Style, 1920, solid mahogany, inlay on drawers and back rail, two small drawers over two long drawers, eagle brasses, 42" w, 19" d, 38" h 350

Desk
Chippendale Style
Block Front, 1930, solid walnut case, walnut veneered slant front lid, block front, fitted interior with secret drawer, paw feet, 32" w, 18" d, 42" h 425

Slant Front
Colonial Desk Co, Rockford, Illinois, blister mahogany, fitted interior with valanced pigeonholes, two small drawers, flanking open center prospect, three drawers, shaked skirt, cabriole legs, eagle brasses, 37" w, 20" d, 43" h 300

Rockford Chair & Furniture Co, Rockford, Illinois, mahogany veneer and gumwood, floral decorated oval inlay on slant front, four graduated drawers, bracket feet, eagle brasses, 38" w, 38" h 475

Governor Winthrop Style, 1920, mahogany veneer, solid mahogany slant front, serpentine front, fitted interior with two document drawers, shell carved center door, four long drawers, brass pulls, and escutcheons 450

Hepplewhite Style, lady's, mahogany, inlay, tambour, fitted interior, oval brasses, 35" w, 19" d, 42½" h 475

Jacobean Style, oak, carved, nine dovetailed drawers, applied foliage scrolls and lion heads, pullout writing surface, worn blue felt covering, rope carved legs, old soft finish, 51″ w, 28½″ d, 40¾″ h **525**

Queen Anne Style, 1940, walnut veneer top, sides, and front, crotch walnut veneer on two side drawers, shell carved cabriole legs, 44″ w, 20″ d, 31″ h **475**

Spinet Style, 1920, solid mahogany, hinged front, fitted interior with drawers and pigeonholes, cylindrical reeded legs, 33″ w, 21″ h, 39″ h **300**

Hall Tree, Baroque Style, 1910, cherry, shell carved crest over cartouche and griffin carved panel back, lift seat, high arms, mask carved base, paw feet, 39½″ w, 21½″ d, 51″ h **500**

Rocker, Windsor Style, Colonial Furniture Co, Grand Rapids, Michigan, comb back, birch, mahogany finish, turned legs, 21″ w, 17″ d, 27½″ h from seat to top of back **175**

Secretary

Governor Winthrop

1928, unknown manufacturer, mahogany veneer, two sections: upper section: broken pediment, center urn finial, molded cornice, pair of glazed doors, shelved interior, lower section: slant front, fitted interior, three long drawers, oval brasses, ball feet, 33″ w, 80″ h **600**

1930, Colonial Desk Co, Rockford, Illinois, mahogany, broken arched pediment, center finial, pair of glazed mullioned doors, fluted columns, slant front, fitted interior with document sleeves, four small drawers, center prospect with acanthus carving flanked by columns, four graduated drawers, eagle brasses, carved claw and ball feet, 41″ w, 21″ d, 87″ h **750**

Sheraton Style, Luce Furniture, Grand Rapids, Michigan, veneered, broken pediment with fretwork, urn finial, pair of glazed arched mullioned doors, slant front with fitted interior, two small and two long drawers, tapered square legs and feet **475**

Settee

Chippendale Style, mahogany, Neo–classical details, maroon and gold silk upholstery, 50″ l **675**

William and Mary Style, loose cush-

Sideboard, Chippendale Style, c1920, mahogany, central bow front over two frieze drawers, over two deep drawers flanked by two wine drawers, central section flanked by two drawers over curved door cupboards, whole raised on ball and claw feet, 46″ w, 18″ d, 40½″ h, $1,045.00. Photograph courtesy of Neal Auction Company.

During the various colonial revivals, many "foreign" revivals also took place. Some of the pieces were highly imaginative. These pieces (part of a Chippendale/Rococo Revival walnut dining room suite) play foot loose and fancy free with the female form. Price for the eleven piece suite, $9,350.00. Photographs courtesy of Pettigrew Auction Company.

ions, turned baluster legs and
stretcher, 48" l 650
Sideboard
  Federal Style, Landstrom Furniture
  Co, mahogany, serpentine front,
  molded edge top, two drawers
  flanked by doors, square tapering
  legs, 66" w, 22" d, 37" h 500
  Queen Anne Style, 1920, striped mahogany veneer, two long drawers
  over pair of drawers flanked by
  cupboard doors, fiddleback veneer
  on oval panels, solid cabriole legs 300
Stand, sewing, Martha Washington
  Style, 1920, solid mahogany, three
  drawers, shaped ends, ring turned
  legs, 28" w, 14" d, 29" h 100
Table
  Card
    Duncan Phyfe Style, Imperial Fur-
    niture Co, Grand Rapids, Michi-
    gan, mahogany veneer top and
    rails, solid mahogany lyre shaped
    pedestal base, carved down-
    swept legs, carved feet 300
    Hepplewhite Style, mahogany, in-
    lay, D–shaped top, minor wear,
    19" w swings open to 38" w, 38"
    d, 31" h 625
  Dining
    Hepplewhite Style, mahogany, in-
    lay, D–shaped drop leaf ends,
    minor wear and damage, 78" l,
    46" w, 29½" h 100
    Queen Anne Style, mahogany, con-
    sole table shape, pullout frame,
    two shaped leaves, worn finish,
    66" l extended, 39" w, 30½" h . 550

Sheraton Style, cherry, six turned
  and rope carved legs, 49¼" l, 22"
  w, 23" l leaves, 26½" h 275
Drop Leaf, Hepplewhite Style, 1940,
  mottled mahogany veneer, rectangular top, hinged leaves, two drawers, 17" l, 15" d, 25" h 225
Game, Chippendale Style, 1936, figured mahogany veneer top and
  apron, hardwood pedestal base,
  three splayed legs, brass paw feet,
  32" w, 15" d, 29" h 175
Library, Empire Style, 1920, oak, pillar base, scrolled feet, 48" l, 28" d,
  28" h 400
Pembroke, Hepplewhite Style, Grand
  Rapids, 1940, plain cut mahogany
  veneer top and drop leaves, figured
  mahogany drawer front, solid base,
  medallion inlay, square tapering
  legs, 17" l, 15" d, 22" h 95
Tavern, William and Mary Style, oval
  top, recessed frieze, turned splayed
  legs joined by box stretcher, 34" l,
  25" d, 25" h 675

COLONIAL REVIVAL CRAFTSMEN (1900–1940)

History: This is a category where one name dominates—Wallace Nutting. The tragedy is that the
emphasis on Nutting has obscured the work of a
host of cabinet shops that made high quality reproductions of colonial era period pieces, often
using the same tools as their historic counterparts. Individuals such as John M. Bair of Ab-

bottstown, Pennsylvania, and the Margolis family deserve equal recognition.

Colonial Revival Craftsmen furniture is identified in two ways: by being either an exact or extremely close copy of a period piece; and by the high quality handcraftsmanship. It also helps that most of the furniture is marked, and that catalogs from these cabinet shops survive. Smart collectors know to pay a premium when they encounter these pieces.

The Colonial Revival Craftsmen worked throughout a wide range of colonial styles starting with "Pilgrim" furniture and extending through the Empire period. However, principal focus was on pieces from the Queen Anne, Chippendale, and Federal periods. They also are known for their superb Windsor furniture.

Wallace Nutting began actively collecting antiques sometime around 1912. In 1917 he published his first book on furniture, *American Windsor*. In 1928 the first two volumes of *The Furniture Treasury* appeared. Volume 3 followed in 1933.

In 1917–18 Wallace Nutting began offering for sale reproduction furniture made at his factory in Framingham, Massachusetts. During the early 1920s the business prospered. However, by 1927–28 the business was in decline. The Depression only made things worse. Nutting laid off employees, but refused to allow the business to fold. It was operating on a very limited basis at the time of his death in 1941.

During his lifetime Nutting had a close relationship with Berea College in Kentucky. Upon his wife's death, Berea was given the remains of the furniture business. After copying the blueprints and patterns at the Framingham factory for their records, Berea sold the business to the Drexel Furniture Company.

A thorough study of the Colonial Revival Craftsmen and their firms is badly needed. Hopefully, one will soon be forthcoming.

References: Michael Ivankovich, *The Guide To Wallace Nutting Furniture*, Diamond Press, 1990; *Wallace Nutting General Catalog, Supreme Edition* (reprint of 1930 Wallace Nutting catalog), Schiffer Publishing.

WALLACE NUTTING

Bed
Brewster, #811	675
Federal, tester, #832	1,800
Low urn post, #809	400
Sheraton, four poster, #846	2,400
Bench, #290, William and Mary 550
Blanket Chest, 1910–30, 17th century style, lift top, branded mark, oak with black ornamentation, single drawer, #909 in catalog, 48" w, 21" d, 31" h   1,250
Chair
#301, Windsor, side, bow back	350

#301 and #415, two arm, six side, Windsor, price for set of eight	16,000
#302, Windsor, side, bow back	425
#310, Windsor, side, bow back with brace	550
#326, Windsor, side, fan back with brace	725
#327, Windsor, side, fan back	550
#327, Windsor, side, swivel	625
#329, Windsor, side, swivel	650
#349, Windsor, side, slipper	525
#361, Queen Anne, maple, side, paper rush seat, old nut brown finish, branded label on bottom back rung, 41¼" h, price for pair	1,150
#374, ladderback, three slat	425
#380, Spanish foot, side	500
#390, ladderback, five slat	525
#392, ladderback, New England ...	725
#401, Windsor, continuous arm ...	875
#408, Windsor, knuckle arm	525
#411, Brewster, arm	1,800
#412, Windsor, comb back, arm, Pennsylvania style	1,500
#415, Windsor, comb back, arm, branded label on bottom of seat, worn original brown finish, repairs to one arm rail and one spindle, 45¼" h, price for pair	2,500
#430, corner	600
#438, Hepplewhite, arm	1,200
#466, Chippendale style, wing	1,650
#468, Chippendale style, wing	900
#490, ladderback, five slats	1,100
#492, ladderback, New England, four slats	600
#493, Pilgrim, arm	1,250
#495, office, arm	400
#451, Windsor, writing arm	2,500
Clock, tall case, copied from John Goddard case, Chippendale style, c1800, mahogany, broken arch hood with three flame finials, carved rosettes, fluted hood column, fluted quarter column, blocks and shells on waist, door, and base, movement, eight day brass time and strike movement with moon phases 7,250
Daybed, #828 2,600
Desk
#701, drop front	1,750
#729, Chippendale, slant front	3,600
Hat Rack, #40, spinning wheel type .. 450
Mirror
#755, walnut, picture	300
#764, Queen Anne, gilded bird	900
#764, Chippendale, gilded bird	1,250
#766, Chippendale	1,600
#769, Hepplewhite	2,750
#774, walnut	800

Tavern Table, Wallace Nutting, pine top, maple legs, block branded signature, $1,250.00.

Settee
  #502, Windsor, double bow back, six legs 3,000
  #589, Waincot 1,000
  #594, Windsor, comb back, ten legs 3,250
Sofa
  #525, Chippendale 750
  #539, Sheraton 1,200
Stand, wig, #1210, Chippendale 1,250
Stool
  #101 200
  #102 275
  #110 300
  #145, Windsor style 235
  #163, long 750
  #165, joined, 15" 475
  #166, William and Mary, 15" 425
  #169, William and Mary, 30" 500
  #292, Gothic 300
Table
  #601, Refractory 1,200
  #605, Windsor, three legs 325
  #613, tavern 825
  #615, trestle 1,200
  #621, gateleg 385
  #624, William and Mary, butterfly . 625
  #637, library 900
  #653, William and Mary 750
  #660, tavern 900

OTHER MAKERS

Candlestand, cherry stain, tilt top, splayed legs, 25½" w, 16½" d, 27¼" h 225
Chest of Drawers
  Chippendale Style, unknown maker, attributed to Ohio craftsman, refinished cherry, handmade reproduction crafted from old wood, 37" w, 18½" d, 35¾" h 450

Empire Style, Stickley, four graduated dovetailed drawers, turned feet, cherry, label reads: Stickley, Fayetteville, Syracuse, 40¾" w, 21" d, 37" h 200
Cupboard, unknown maker, attributed to Zoar, Ohio, chestnut, cherry, poplar, and walnut, paneled construction with wire nails, applied diamonds on door panels and drawer front, drawer dovetailed in front, nailed in back, wooden pull, brass thumb latch, old finish, 24" w, 28" h 600
Mirror, unknown maker, Chippendale style, curly maple, light natural finish, scroll work, attributed to Ohio area, 17" w, 27¾" h 110
Wash Stand, Wm Brown, Successor to Brown & Tate, Manufacturer, Lawrenceburgh, Ind, Warranted, poplar, old cherry colored refinishing, dovetailed gallery, single dovetailed drawer, base shelf, turned feet and posts, stenciled label, 24½" w, 16½" d, 27¾" h 350

CONFUSED COLONIAL (1920–1940)

History: Following World I, the demand for American colonial furniture was strong at all buying levels. Manufacturers did not hesitate to use the "colonial" label whenever they felt they could get away with it. After all, the majority of the buying public had virtually no knowledge of early American period design styles. If the seller said something was colonial, this was more than enough.

It requires a great deal of courage and insight for any colonial period traditionalist to admit that this furniture has a kinship with the past. In truth, many of the designs and forms have absolutely nothing to do with late seventeenth and eighteenth century America.

Confused Colonial is truly confused. Design elements can range from English Tudor and Jacobean to French Louis XV or Louis XVI. During this time period, every contemporary form was colonialized. A fair amount of colonial furniture bears a striking resemblance to French Restauration revivals.

Forget about purity of design. Confused colonial mixes and matches. There is no taste that cannot be satisfied. Further, many design elements are simplified to the point where we must stretch the imagination to see the historic design component at all. Pieces are called "Colonial" in many catalogs because no other label fits.

Some Confused Colonial pieces are well made. However, the vast majority lack quality. It was common to use inferior woods hidden by paper thin veneer and painted pieces to hide construction for a variety of wood types to reduce manufacturing costs.

It would be wrong on several counts to identify Confused Colonial as the furniture sold in mail order catalogs and rural department stores. In many cases, these catalogs and stores carried several varieties of furniture to appeal to individuals at all price levels. Some pieces of very poor design are very well made.

One final point must be made. Many collectors and dealers have tried to place this furniture in the vernacular tradition. It does not belong there. Although not a high design style, Confused Colonial *is* a design style. It evolved, was dominant for a brief period, and then disappeared. Post–World War II furniture designs do not copy it, preferring instead to remain truer to the period design styles.

In the 1990s, Confused Colonial continues to gain popularity among collectors. It is affordable, representing a fine starting point. It is associated more with one's grandparent's generation than with one's parents'. It is often in suite, a fact that appeals to young collectors. Finally, it now looks "old."

References: Robert W. and Harriett Swedberg, *Furniture of the Depression Era: Furniture & Accessories of the 1920's, 1930's, & 1940's*, Collector Books, 1987; *Zone 3 Furniture Dealers' Reference Book, 1928–1929*, reprinted as *American Manufactured Furniture*, Schiffer Publishing, 1988.

Bed
  Mahogany, 1920, veneer, incised lines, applied decorative medal-

lions, shell shaped crest, four turned high posts, 50" h **200**
Walnut, double, shaped solid headboard, footboard shaped as two Queen Anne chair backs, shell carving on short feet, 57" w, 36" h   **325**
Bedroom Suite, bed, dresser, dressing table, and bench, poster bed: burl walnut veneered headboard, oak broken arch pediment, center urn finial, burl walnut and oak panel on footboard; dresser: plain cut walnut veneer top and sides, two outside shaped mirrors, center arched and engraved mirror, arched and diamond molding on drawer fronts; dressing table with plain cut walnut veneer top and sides, burl walnut veneer drawer front, mirror shaped like dresser with larger proportions; bench: turned and scrolled hardwoods, velvet upholstered sides and seat, price for four piece suite **900**
Bookcase, mahogany and mahogany veneer, rectangular molded top, pair glazed doors with Gothic type mullions, adjustable shelved interior, French Restauration scrolling feet . . .   **400**

Vanity, walnut, swing mirror, reeded mirror supports, stiles, and legs, three drawers, two doors, applied molding, casters, 48" w, 20" d, $125.00.

Cabinet, china

1920

Figured walnut veneer panels and drawer front, solid walnut back rail, three curly maple overlay shield designs, selected hardwood frame, bulbous turned front legs, H–stretcher base, 38" w, 14" d, 65" h 130

Oak, bow front, shaped top with molded back, rectangular center glazed door, convex glass side panels flanked by scrolled upright columns, scroll bracket feet, 38" w, 58" h 600

1930, bird's eye maple veneer, zebrawood veneer, and marquetry on drawer front and cabinet facing, oval crest with inlay and scrolled foliate, doubled arched doors with intricate mullions, shelved interior, lower drawers, shaped shelf with carved center urn finial, turned reeded legs 250

Chair

Arm

Blistered maple veneer pierced splat, curved Oriental wood veneer top rail, down curving arms with carved handholds, upholstered slip seat, turned reeded legs, H–stretcher base 90

Overstuffed, matching overstuffed ottoman, carved mahogany frame, foliage carved apron, carved scrolling legs, animal paw front feet, new cut velvet floral upholstery, 36½" h, price for two pieces 50

Set

Set of Four, side, Duncan Phyfe style, 1940, mahogany stain, upholstered slip seat, mahogany veneered lyre back, 33" h, price for four piece set 200

Set of Six, dining, mahogany, cupid's bow crest, pierced splat, slip seat, cabriole legs joined by box stretcher, price for six piece set 720

Side

1910, oak

Plain crest rail, narrow rectangular back splat, pressed cane seat and back, rope carved front legs, H–stretcher type base, 37" h 100

Scalloped crest rail, fancy scrolled back splat with upholstered panel, upholstered seat, ring turned baluster side rails, heavy cabriole legs with

pressed carving at knees, spool carved leg rails, 45" h 170

1920, Queen Anne style, walnut veneer slat, walnut stained hardwood frame, pressed cane seat, French legs, 37" h 50

1940, maple stained, incised wide, flat seat, shaped Moravian type back splat with trefoil cutout, turned legs, 17" w, 29" h 35

Chifforobe, 1929, burl walnut, burl mahogany, bird's eye maple, and Macassar ebony veneers, shaped scalloped top with two shaped doors over two drawers, molded cornice, three smaller drawers over three long drawers, ring turned bulbous feet, 59" h . 195

Commode, maple, rectangular molded top, harp shaped towel rack, swing mirror with shell carved crest, ogee top drawer, serpentine base with single cupboard door, two small drawers, 36" w, 76" h 400

Desk

Oak, lady's, fall front with applied and carved designs, shaped mirrored back, two swelled drawers, cabriole legs, claw and ball feet, 29" w, 55" h 600

Satinwood veneer top, ebony, bird's eye maple veneer, and stumpwood walnut veneer drawer fronts, several small drawers in top, two pedestals with three graduated drawers, short tapered legs 100

Dressing Table

1920, walnut veneer, adjustable side mirrors, arched full length center mirror, pair of two drawer pedestals, fluted front legs, 48" w, 19" d, 69" h 200

1925, oak, adjustable side mirrors, arched center mirror, two small drawers, scalloped apron, long front cabriole legs, straight back legs 250

Meridiennes (fainting couch), oak, tufted upholstered back and seat, upholstered head rest and pillow on back, applied and incised decorations, carved bracket feet, 67" l, 36" h 400

Sideboard

Empire style, oak, rectangular molded top, two long drawers with glass knobs, center section with glass center door, bowed glass end panels, demilune carved side stiles, long swelled front base drawer with brass pulls, side rails continue to carved grotesque paw feet, 44" w, 38" h 400

Queen Anne style, striped mahogany veneer on rectangular top and sides, fiddleback mahogany veneer on drawers, doors, and shaped apron, burl mahogany veneer oval panels, long drawer over two center drawers, flanked by two cupboard doors, solid mahogany cabriole legs **250**

Night Stand, walnut, applied molding, reeded stiles and legs, 15″ square top, $45.00.

Stand
Plant, 1920, three tier, mahogany veneer, solid mahogany frame with acanthus and reeded carving, bottom tier with flower pot cutouts, out swept feet **85**
Sewing, Priscilla type, 1930, painted red, dark trim, floral decal, turned rod type handle, 13″ w, 11″ d, 25″ h **28**
Smoking, straight cut walnut veneer rectangular top, figured walnut veneer door, painted William and Mary style base, 18″ w, 11″ d, 30″ h **95**
Telephone, cherry and poplar, gently curved sides and front, single dovetailed drawer, high back, cutout sides, old worn finish, 23″ w, 14¾″ d, 36″ h **250**
Table
Coffee, 1935, turtle shaped top, four piece V–matched striped walnut veneer, center bleached striped walnut veneer, holly inlay border, four red dyed flower accents, cab-

riole legs with carved knees, 34″ w, 19″ d, 17″ h **180**
Dining
Chippendale style, Rockford Furniture Co, Rockford, IL, rectangular top, rounded corners, corner inlays, five pairs of Sheraton type legs, 66″ l **200**
Duncan Phyfe style, 1940, drop leaf, mahogany stained and veneered, 16″ l D–shaped leaves, brass casters on outswept reeded legs, 41″ l, 24″ d, 30″ h **225**
Extension, 1925, rectangular, walnut veneer top, molded apron, hardwood base, six heavy carved legs, pair of U–shaped stretchers, 60″ l, 31″ d, 41″ h **195**
Game, 1910, oak, rotating shaped top, four demilune troughs for game pieces with applied beading, S–scrolled legs with applied beading on shoulder, 36″ w, 29″ h **350**
Side, 1940, nesting, walnut veneer tops and aprons, solid walnut base, ring turned legs, animal paw feet, largest table with 6″ l drop leaves, 24″ w, 15″ d, 24″ h, price for set of three **275**

CONTEMPORARY CRAFTSPERSONS AND MANUFACTURERS (1990s)

History: The return to nature movements of the 1960s coupled with the American Bicentennial fostered two important developments in Colonial Revival furniture. The first was a renewed interest in making exact reproductions using the tools and implements of the colonial period. The second was the making of high quality mass-produced reproductions, a reaction to the growing decline in quality, especially in interiors, found in factory–made pieces.

One of the first furniture forms to attract significant attention was the Windsor chair. Most crafts festivals featured one or more Windsor chair makers by the early 1970s. Several appeared in juried shows. Their success attracted other craftspersons, many of whom found expression in the more formal styles.

By the 1980s, formal early American replaced Country informality as the favored design style of the masses. The high prices realized at auction for period American colonial pieces (a Chippendale secretary sold for over twelve million dollars) also drew attention to colonial design styles. High demand and a limited base drove pricing to a level where only the very rich could afford to collect quality period pieces.

Yet, the general public continued to favor the early American look. A number of small to medium size manufacturers began to produce high quality reproductions in response. Major museums licensed the reproduction of prime pieces in their collections.

Manufacturers and craftspersons exhibit at specialized furniture markets held throughout the United States, often in the company of other manufacturers of American collectibles, country accents, and contemporary folk art. Their products are found in specialized gift shops, museum shops, and furniture stores.

The following is a small sampling from a select group. The principal purpose is to show you the variety of reproductions that are available and the price ranges. Price is important. When a reproduction costs significantly less than the period piece from which it is copied, the incentive to purchase the period piece is seriously diminished for the person who is simply after a look.

Charles Shackleton Furniture, The Mill, Bridgewater, VT 05034

Bed, cherry, ball finials, headboard and footboard with beaded edge rail and four arched raised panels separated by columns with beaded capitals, square legs, 60 x 80" queen size **2,200**

Bench, teak, serpentine-shaped crest rail, square posts with rolled ears, nine flat slats in back, shaped down-curving arms, circular handholds with concentric ring design, five separated boards, serpentine shaped seat, shaped seat rail, square legs, ring and block turned side stretchers, mortise and tenon construction, 72" l, 16" h seat, 37½" h overall **1,400**

Chair

Arm, walnut, straight curved crest rail, five flat slats with chamfered corners in back, straight lower rail, shaped arms ending in scrolled handholds, down curving arm posts with beaded bottom edge, upholstered slip seat, square tapered legs, 24" w, 18" h seat, 36½" h overall **980**

Cottage, side, cherry, pyramid shaped tops and chamfered corners on square posts and front legs, chamfered corners on crest rail, four flat slats, and two lower rails, trapezoidal woven splint seat, chamfered corners on box stretchers, 19" w, 15½" d, 17½" h seat, 37½" h overall **320**

Chest of Drawers, cherry, thumb molded edge on slightly overhanging rectangular top, two banks of three drawers each, cockbeaded dovetailed drawers with turned wood pulls, ovolo molded front corners on case, molded base, 60" w, 19" d, 36" h **3,400**

Cupboard, step back, cherry, molded cornice over beaded decoration, ovolo molded front corners on top and base, cockbeaded edge on two open adjustable shelves, projected waist molding, three cockbeaded dovetailed short drawers over pair of cockbeaded raised panel cupboard doors separated by center stile, molded base, turned wood pulls, 51" w, 82" h **4,300**

Sideboard, cherry, molded edge on overhanging rectangular top, three cockbeaded dovetailed short drawers over two cockbeaded raised panel cupboard doors separated by center stile with similar cockbeaded raised panel, single interior shelf, molded base, 60" w, 20" d, 36" h **3,600**

Table, dining, cherry, molded edge on round top, straight apron with beaded lower edge, square tapered legs, three 20" w leaves, 48" d closed size, 108" l oval open size, 29¾" h **3,800**

David T Smith, 3600 Shawhan Rd, Morrow, OH 45152

Bed, low post, Queen Anne style, cherry, ball finials on turned posts, arched headboard, poplar rails, cabriole legs with padded Queen Anne feet, full mattress size, 32" h **1,885**

Bench

Bucket, poplar, three shelves, shaped ends with projecting lower shelves, cutout feet, 36" w, 12" d, 44" h **450**

Settee, Windsor, arrow back, shaped crest rail, back consists of thirteen arrow form spindles, down curving scrolled arms on turned canted arm posts, shaped plank seat, splayed base with turned legs joined by box stretchers, 60" l **620**

Cupboard, Ohio corner, two sections: upper section: curly maple, projected cornice over single glazed door with nine panes; lower section: small waist drawer over single cupboard door with pair of raised panels, shaped apron, bracket feet, 39" w, 16½" d, 80" h **2,665**

Durham Cabinet Shoppe, Box 119, Route 413, Gardenville, PA 18926

Cupboard, corner, pine, two sections: upper section: molded cornice, single triple arched glazed door flanked by molded recessed panels; lower section: molded waist, pair of cockbeaded recessed panel cupboard doors flanked by molded recessed panels, ogee bracket feet .. **2,500**

High Chest of Drawers, cherry, molded edge on rectangular top, inlaid stringing below, three short over two short over four graduated long drawers, oval brasses, inlaid stringing on upper edge of scalloped apron, French bracket feet . **4,000**

Huntboard, Southern, pine, slightly overhanging rectangular top, one over one short drawer flanked by doors, square tapered legs, brass bail handle hardware **1,100**

Eastman Woodworking, PO Box 41442, Baltimore, MD 21203–6442

Bed, pencil post, chamfered corners on tapered posts, shaped headboard, slightly tapering square legs **1,900**

Chair, lolling, Chippendale style, serpentine shaped upholstered high back, shaped arms ending in scrolled handholds, down curving arm supports, upholstered trapezoidal seat, cabriole legs ending in claw and ball feet **2,000**

Table
 Harvest, Hepplewhite style, tiger maple, rectangular drop leaves on rectangular top, square tapered legs, 6" l, 4" open width . **1,700**
 Tea, pie crust, scalloped edge on round cleated top, turned tapered fluted column surmounted by bird cage, tripod base, cabriole legs with carved knees, claw and half–ball feet **6,000**

Hershey's Wood Shop Inc, 6303 Hickory Rd, Oxford, PA 19363

Cupboard, corner, molded cornice, pair of glazed tombstone arched doors enclosing two butterfly shaped shelves below a fan carved hooded interior, molded waist, pair of raised panel cupboard doors, molded base, ogee bracket feet .. **2,200**

Highboy, Queen Anne style, bonnet top, molded broken pediment centering an urn finial on plinth, upper case has three short over two short over three graduated long drawers, base has single long over three short drawers, center top and bottom drawers with carved fan decorations, shaped apron, cabriole

legs ending in padded Queen Anne feet, brass bat's wing back plates . **2,500**

Settee, Windsor, double sack back, pair of hooped crest rails, rod spindles joined by U–shaped arm rail ending in knuckle handholds, canted baluster turned arm supports, shaped oblong seat, splayed base with baluster turned legs joined by two turned H–stretchers **675**

Howerton Antique Reproductions, PO Box 215, 120 Buffalo Rd, Clarksville, VA 23927

Bed, pencil post, mahogany, spire turned finials on tapered posts with chamfered corners, shaped headboard, square legs, mortise and tenon construction with old style bed bolts, 80" h, 60 x 80" queen size frame **895**

Bookcase, Chippendale style, mahogany, molded edge rectangular top, pair of nine paned glazed doors, bracket feet, 60" w, 16" d, 46" h . **995**

Breakfront, Chippendale style, mahogany, block front, two sections: upper section: molded cornice over dentil molding, three doors with thirteen geometric shaped glass panes each door, two interior shelves; lower section: ogee molded waist, central bank of four drawers flanked by a short drawer over a recessed paneled cupboard door, molded base, oval brasses, 60" w, 19" d, 84" h **2,995**

Cupboard, corner, Chippendale style, mahogany, molded cornice above dentil molding, pair of glazed doors enclosing three interior butterfly shaped shelves with plate grooves, molded waist, pair of raised panel cupboard doors, straight apron continuing to bracket feet, brass H–hinges, 44" w, 84" h **1,650**

Huntboard, Hepplewhite style, mahogany, boxwood line inlays, slightly overhanging rectangular top, pair of line inlaid cupboard doors centering two short line inlaid drawers, stringing along lower edges, square tapering line inlaid legs surmounted by bellflower inlays, 54" w, 18" d, 40" h **1,095**

Lowboy, Queen Anne style, mahogany, molded edge rectangular top, single long drawer over three short drawers, center short drawer with carved decoration, scrolled apron, cabriole legs, padded Queen Anne feet, brass bat's wing back plates and escutcheon, 40" w, 20" d, 32" h **695**

Secretary, Chippendale style, mahogany, molded cornice over dentil molding, pair of raised panel doors enclosing shelves, hinged slant front, fitted interior with central fan carved prospect door flanked by valanced pigeonholes over five small drawers, pullout slides, three overlapping long drawers with brass bat's wing back plates, ogee bracket feet, 40" w, 21" d, 84" h .   **2,665**

Settee, Chippendale style, mahogany, serpentine shaped crest rail, double chair back with open fret splats, shaped arm with scrolled handholds on down curving arm supports, upholstered slip seat, square legs joined by H–stretcher, double doweled construction, 47" w, 18" d, 39" h **665**

Table, hall, Hepplewhite style, mahogany, slightly overhanging rectangular top, two short drawers with brass bat's wing back plates, scalloped apron, square tapering legs, 36" w, 12" d, 36" h **295**

Irion Company Furniture Makers, 44 North Valley Rd, Paoli, PA 19301

Chair

Arm, Queen Anne style, mahogany, carved, shaped crest rail with central fan carved decoration, shaped splat, shaped arms with carved knuckle handholds, upholstered balloon shaped slip seat, cabriole legs with fan carved knees and trifid feet, striped upholstery **2,295**

Wing, Philadelphia, upholstered, high back flanked by wings continuing to rolled arms, loose seat cushion, mahogany cabriole legs with ornate scroll carved knees and claw and ball feet **1,995**

Chest, Newport, block front, molded edge on slightly overhanging rectangular top, four conforming cockbeaded long drawers, top drawer with triple carved fan decoration, molded base, ogee bracket feet, brass bail handles and escutcheons   **4,995**

Kas, Lancaster County, PA style, molded cornice, pair of doors with six raised panels each door, molded waist, three over two overlapping short drawers, molded base, ogee bracket feet **5,450**

Linen Press, tiger maple, molded cornice over pair of cupboard doors with raised panels, upper panels tombstone shaped, shelved interior, molded waist, two short over three long graduated overlapping drawers, molded base, ogee bracket feet   **4,365**

James D Redway Furniture Maker, 93 Porter Hill, Middlebury, CT 06762

Bench, Chippendale style, cherry, upholstered rectangular slip seat, mortise and tenon construction, beaded edge on rails, square legs with beaded chamfered corners, dovetailed H–stretcher, 42" l, 13½" w, 19½" h **300**

Blanket Chest, cherry, slightly overhanging rectangular lid, dovetailed case, molded base, straight apron continuing to dovetailed bracket feet, brass bat's wing back plate es-

Kenneth W. Heiser, Carlisle, PA, blanket chest, white pine and red oak, paint decorated, 49½" w, 22" d, 27½" h, $5,800.00.

cutcheon and side bale handles, 30" w, 15½" d, 19½" h **700**

Stand, night, cherry, Chippendale style, thumb molded edge on overhanging rectangular top, single drawer frieze, pine dovetailed drawer with cherry drawer front, square chamfered beaded legs, base shelf, brass bat's wing back plate, 17¼" w, 21½" d, 25" h **350**

Table, tea, Queen Anne style, cherry, ovolo corners on overhanging top, shaped apron, cabriole legs ending in padded Queen Anne feet, 23½" w, 18" d, 25" h **425**

J L Treharn & Co, 1024 Mahoning Ave, Youngstown, OH 44502

Bed, cannonball, maple, ball finials and chamfered corners on posts, shaped headboard, octagonal blanket rail, 43" h, full size frame **520**

Cupboard, chimney, poplar, slightly overhanging rectangular top, cupboard door with two raised panels over lower single raised panel door, shaped apron, 20½" w, 13" d, 75" h **455**

Highboy, Queen Anne style, cherry, molded edge flat top, upper case with five graduated overlapping drawers, lower case with single overlapping drawer over three short drawers, shaped apron with turned pendants, cabriole legs ending in padded Queen Anne feet, 39" w, 20½" d, 75½" h **1,825**

Table, sofa, Queen Anne style, tiger maple, molded edge on rectangular overhanging top, scalloped apron with central carved fan, cabriole legs with padded Queen Anne feet, 48" w, 16½" d, 30" h **490**

Kenneth W Heiser, 195 E Yellow Breeches Rd, Carlisle, PA 17013

Blanket Chest, Lebanon/Berks County, PA, white pine and red oak, molded edge and breadboard ends on hinged lift lid, interior well, dovetailed case with stepped construction, dentil molding at waist, three short drawers in base, brass bat's wing back plates, molded base, ogee bracket feet, paint decorated with stylized flowers in pillared panels, red and black, 49½" w, 22" d, 27½" h **5,800**

Table, Philadelphia, c1770, tilt top, revolving, walnut, circular dished top, ring turned column surmounted by bird cage, tripod base, cabriole legs with padded snake feet, 29" d, 29" h **1,995**

Longenecker Cabinetmakers, 313 E Bridge St, Covington, OH 45318

Candlestand, cherry, circular top, slender tapered soda bottle shaped column, tripod base, spider legs, natural finish, 18" d, 25" h **156**

Chest of Drawers, cherry, slightly overhanging rectangular top, five dovetailed graduated long drawers, turned wood pulls, dovetailed bracket feet, natural finish, 32" w, 20 d, 44 h **1,080**

Table, end, cherry, overhanging rectangular top, single drawer frieze, dovetailed drawer with turned wood pull, square tapered legs, natural finish, 24" w, 19" d, 26" h **312**

Michael Camp, 495 Amelia, Plymouth, MI 48170

Bed, hired man's, cherry, ball finials on square posts, shaped peaked headboard, beaded rails, square legs, twin size, 36" h **415**

Candlestand, octagonal top, slender turned column, tripod base, cabriole legs ending in padded slipper feet, 14" w, 24" h **150**

Chest, dower, decorated, molded edge on rectangular hinged lid, dovetailed case, molded waist, two thumb molded overlapping short drawers, molded base with straight apron and bracket feet, central heart enclosing pair of love birds flanked by arched panels with potted stylized flowers, brass bat's wing back plates on bail handles, 51" l, 21" d, 26" h **900**

Desk, Connecticut slant front, cherry, rectangular top, hinged writing surface enclosing central fan carved prospect drawer flanked by valanced pigeonholes over seven small drawers, pullout slides, three graduated thumb molded overlapping drawers, cabriole legs ending in padded Queen Anne feet, brass bail handles with bat's wing back plates and escutcheons, 34" w, 17" d, 41½" h **2,375**

Highboy, bonnet top, tiger maple, broken swan's neck pediment, three flame and urn turned finials on plinths, three short over four long graduated drawers, molded waist, base with two long graduated over three short drawers, center top and bottom drawers with carved fan decoration, shaped apron with pair of central S-scrolls flanked by fan carvings, cabriole legs ending in padded Queen Anne feet, 38½" w, 17" d, 81" h **3,250**

Table, tavern, breadboard ends on overhanging rectangular top, single dovetailed drawer, block and baluster turned legs joined by box stretchers, flattened ball feet, 35" w, 19" d, 26" h **225**

Mount Royal Reproductions, 141 Child St, Warren, RI 02885

Chair, Windsor, side, bow back, hooped back, nine tapered spindles, shaped saddle seat, splayed base with baluster turned legs ending in tapered feet, turned H–stretcher, 16" w seat, 17¼" d, 18¼" h seat, 39¼" h overall **279**

Settee, Windsor, continuous arm, bowed back continues to shaped arms, tapered spindle back, canted baluster turned arm supports, shaped seat, splayed base with baluster turned legs ending in tapered feet, two turned H–stretchers, 48" w seat, 17½" d, 18¼" h seat, 40½" h overall **500**

Oley Valley Reproductions, RD 1, Box 207A, Oley, PA 19547

Chest, apothecary, poplar, molded cornice over open two shelf top, vertical random board back, case with three rows of five small drawers over two rows of larger drawers, total of seventeen dovetailed drawers, cutout feet, painted blue, 35" w, 16" d, 77" h **1,200**

Pie Safe, Ohio style, poplar, paint grained, slightly overhanging rectangular top, single long drawer over pair of doors, two punched tin panels each door and side, turned tapered feet, turned wood pulls, 44" w, 18" d, 51" h **810**

Settee, Windsor, rod back, U–shaped arm rail ending in shaped handholds, thirty–three spindles, canted baluster turned arm supports, shaped seat, splayed base with baluster turned legs joined by two bulbous turned H–stretchers, 43" l   . .   **400**

R Trammell and Son, 8519½ Chestnut Ave, Historic Old Bowie, MD 20715

Chair, Windsor, fan back, cherry, shaped crest rail with carved ears, thirteen tapered spindles back joined by U–shaped arm rail, scrolled knuckle handholds, vase turned arm supports, shaped saddle seat, splayed base with vase turned legs joined by H–stretcher **435**

Chest of Drawers, cherry, slightly overhanging rectangular top, two

Warren Chair Works, Warren, RI, sack back armchair, U-shaped arm rail, shaped plank seat, bulbous turnings, 17½" h seat, 40½" h overall, $240.00.

short over four graduated long drawers, dovetailed drawers, turned wood pulls, bracket feet, 41½" w, 21" d, 49" h **1,240**

Stand, cherry, rectangular overhanging top, two long overlapping dovetailed drawers, square tapered legs, 28" w, 22" d, 28" h **480**

Strafford House, 43 Vansant Rd, New Hope, PA 18938

Blanket Chest, six-board, white pine and walnut, walnut rectangular lift lid, white pine decorated case with multicolored painted stylized potted flower design on antique white ground, bootjack ends, 36" w, 14" d, 23" h **325**

Cupboard, jelly, New England, white pine, decorated, slightly overhanging rectangular top, pair of cupboard doors with stylized potted flowers and bird decoration, three interior shelves, square tapered legs, painted blue, 29" w, 14" d, 46" h **500**

Fireboard, white pine, decorated,

three board, rectangular, painted floral decoration of potted stylized flowers, red, blue, mustard, green, and black on white ground, 34″ w, 28″ h **200**

Warren Chair Works, 79 Joyce St, Warren, RI 02885

Chair, Windsor, arm, Nantucket, fan back with brace, curved crest rail with carved ears, five tapered spindles, baluster turned posts, braced back, shaped arms with knuckle handholds, canted baluster turned arm supports, shaped oval seat, splayed base with baluster turned legs joined by bulbous turned H–stretcher, milk paint finish, 23″ w seat, 17½″ h seat, 45″ h overall .. **440**

High Chair, Windsor, continuous arm, hooped crest rail continues to shaped handholds, eleven tapered spindles, canted baluster turned arm supports, shaped saddle seat, splayed base with baluster turned legs ending in tapered feet, rectangular footrest, bulbous turned H–stretcher, 13″ w, 22″ h seat, 37″ h overall **240**

Settee, Windsor, camel back, serpentine shaped crest, twenty–three bamboo turned spindles, shaped scrolled arms with bamboo turned supports, shaped rectangular seat, splayed base with bamboo turned legs joined by tapered box stretchers, 54″ w seat, 17½″ h seat, 38″ h overall **600**

Stool, Windsor, bow back, nine bulbous turned spindles, shaped plank seat, splayed base with baluster turned legs ending in tapered feet, bulbous turned front rung and H–stretcher, antique milk paint finish, 16½″ w, 26″ h seat, 46½″ h overall **270**

MODERNISM

History: American collectors and dealers are comfortable with Art Deco. In their minds, it is a reasonably well defined and wonderful catchall term for design style furniture of the 1920s and 1930s. The problem is that Art Deco is at the periphery of the main evolutionary furniture design stream. As a movement it has identifiable starting and ending dates. Art Deco's influence on furniture manufacture was minimal and heavily focused toward a narrow segment of society.

Art Deco is one of the most misused attributions in the current antiques market for both furniture and the decorative arts. More than half the "Art Deco" pieces actually should be attributed to Modernism, a movement little understood by collectors and dealers alike.

Modernism continued and expanded upon the design style advances of the Arts and Crafts movement. Perhaps it is easier to understand Modernism by viewing it as Machine Modern, a design period when functionalism and carefully reasoned design were dominant. Architects provided the motivating force for much of the design.

Modernism's origins are Germanic, beginning with Hermann Muthesius. Vienna was the geographic center whose Wiener Werkstatte pieces are best known to American collectors and dealers. Legendary names include Josef Hoffmann and Koloman Moser. Charles Rennie Mackintosh, a Glasgow architect–designer, and Herbert McNair laid the ground work in Great Britain.

It is extremely helpful to understand that Modernism developed side by side with Art Deco during the 1920s. Gerrit Reitveld in the Netherlands and the Bauhaus movement in Germany were design pioneers. Functionalism and rationalism of design, the guiding principles of modernism, allowed for a wide variety of design interpretations. Do not forget the unity of the overall movement when concentrating on one of the specific parts.

As Modernism moved into the 1930s, design became even more diversified. It was a decade of eclecticism. Modernistic furniture of the 1920s rejected decoration and relied heavily on the use of glass and steel. The 1930s saw a return to wood and leather along with richly padded surfaces on seating furniture. Design continued to respond to architectural and artistic trends. Surrealist furniture enjoyed a brief vogue.

Modernism is international. Designers worked worldwide. Frances U.A.M. (Union des Artistes Modernes) designed the furniture for the palace of the Maharaja of Indore in 1931–33. Mies van der Rohe's "Barcelona" chair and Le Corbusier's "Chaise Lougune" designs were copied by manufacturers around the world. America's Cranbrook Academy blended the talents of Eliel Saarinen, Eero Saarinen, Charles Eames, and Harry Bertoia.

Part of the difficulty involved in understanding modernism is that the term is used to describe the movement as a whole as well as one of its major components. Establishing a mental decade chronology can help keep the sequence of events straight. International Modernism, the first period, covers the period of conception (1900s through World War I) and the period when the movement was centered in Germany (1920s). Modernism is the period when many of the German designers fled Germany and moved to England and America (1930s). Just as did World War I, World War II temporarily halted the movement's evolution. After World War II, Modernism reached its zenith in the Contemporary Style (1945 through 1960s) that enjoyed great popularity in the United States. The Neo–Modernism of the 1970s was a brief attempt to rechannel the movement.

Thoroughly confused? Hopefully, the introductions in this section and the one that follows will end the chaos. Also read the introductions to the English Post War I, French 3rd Empire, and German Jugendstil/Modernism categories. Remember from 1920 forward, furniture design is international—time to put national prejudices and pride aside and join the world community.

References: Philippe Garner, *Twentieth–Century Furniture*, Van Nostrand Reinhold Company, 1980; Penny Sparke, *Furniture: Twentieth–Century Design*, E. P. Dutton, 1986.

INTERNATIONAL ERA (1920s)

History: The principals of International Modernism were first put forward at the end of the nineteenth century and experimented with in the period leading up to World War I. When Modernism finally emerged in the mid–1920s it was a revolutionary force. The movement introduced rationalized, functional design into machine production. A marriage between designer and machine occurred.

Prior to World War I, three key groups laid the foundation for Modernism: (1) Netherland's *De Stijl* under the driving force of Gerrit Rietveld, (2) Germany's Deutscher Werkbund and the Weimar Kunstgewerbeschule, re–opened in 1919 at the Bauhaus, and (3) Austria's Weiner (Vienna) Werkstatte. Each movement witnessed a linkage created between architect, interior designer, and furniture designer. Buildings were viewed as a unified whole. A completeness was achieved only when all elements, from structure to decoration to furnishings, were in a balanced harmony.

Following World War I, the Bauhaus became the chief exponent of this new philosophy. One of the first tasks undertaken was to create newly designed furniture models that could be mass produced. Many of these forms became classics. Some examples include: Marcel Breuer's Wassily chair (1925) a box–like tubular steel chair with a canvas seat; Marcel Breuer's cantilever chair (1928) in tubular steel; Josef Albers' bentwood

chair (1928) with upside down "U" sides and an "L" seat that could be dismantled easily for packing and transport; Mies van der Rohe's Barcelona chair (1929) with its framework of flat steel and hide cushions; and, Mies van der Rohe's Brno chair (1930) in flat or tubular steel featuring a quarter curved arm ending in an "L" base.

In France, Le Corbusier outlined the Modernism philosophy in *L'Esprit Nouveau*, a journal published between 1920 and 1925. Basic design forms that emerged are: Le Corbusier and Charlotte Perriand's Chaise Lounge (1928–29) a tubular steel chair with a raised "V" section at the knees resting on a steel base; Le Corbusier and Charlotte Perriand's Grand Comfort armchair (1928–29) featuring leather covered cushions in an exposed steel frame; Le Corbusier and Charlotte Perriand's Basculant armchair (1928–29) a tubular steel frame with slanted "L" and arms; and Eilen Gray's Transant armchair in lacquered wood, chromium metal, and leather.

The second half of the 1920s saw Modernism firmly established in Europe and beginning to gain acceptance in the United States. The introduction of the use of metal as a key furniture frame component and the mass production of design quality pieces was firmly established. The individuals who would dominate furniture design in the period between the two world wars were internationally recognized.

American manufacturers were slow to produce these new designs. American collectors seeking 1920s International Modernism furniture must

purchase European examples, more recent reproductions, e.g., Cassina's 1970s Basculant armchair, or lesser quality copycats of later origin
based on the historic designs.

The forms are the key. It pays to learn them.
They establish the foundations upon which the
designs of the 1930s and post–World War II era
are based.

Chair
  Arm
    Marcel Breuer, adapted by Adrian
    Bloome as a variant of Marcel
    Breuer's B55, manufactured by
    Thonet, c1935, tubular steel
    frame in gold finish supporting
    brown leather backs and seats,
    flanked by black–painted
    wooden arm rests, period leather
    upholstery done as part of
    Bloome's commissioned design
    for Hotel Metrople, Brussels,
    changes made to Breuer's design
    include: lowered back, substi-
    tuted leather for canvas, modi-
    fied chromed finish to gold matte   **4,125**
  Josef Hoffmann for J. & J. Kohn,
    c1905, ebonized ash, arched up-
    holstered back continuing to
    arms and U–form seat enclosed
    by laminated surround, above
    two straight tapering front legs
    and two slightly cabriole back
    legs, conjoined by a U–form
    stretcher, brass sabots **8,800**

Side Chair, designed by Josef Hoffmann, first quarter 20th C, U-form back rail above three cross bars continuing to a shaped rectangular upholstered seat, four cylindrical legs on a U-form base, $1,250.00. Photograph courtesy of Leslie Hindman Auctioneers.

Soda Fountain Table and Matching Set of Four Chairs, note triangular shape of chair seats to fit properly with the "x" stretcher of the table, price for set $275.00. Photograph courtesy of Pettigrew Auction Company.

Side
  Eileen Gray, pair, tan leather rectangular back and seat between
  a framework formed of angular
  slender chromed–steel supports,
  price for pair **8,800**
  Josef Hoffmann for J. & J. Kohn,
  c1905, ebonized ash, arched upholstered back and U–form seat
  enclosed by laminated surround
  above two straight tapering front
  legs and two slightly cabriole
  back legs conjoined by a U–form
  stretcher, brass sabots **6,600**
Stacking Tables, set of four, bentwood,
  designed by Josef Hoffmann for J. &
  J. Kohn, c1910, rectangular top with
  rounded corners, multiple sphere
  handles, inset with a fabric panel beneath glass, raised on cylinder spindles continuing to U–form base, three
  graduated panels with laminated tops,
  width of tallest 24½", height of tallest
  29¼", price for set of four **4,125**

STREAMLINED MODERN
(1930s and Early 1940s)

History: Much of the furniture designed during
the International Modernism of the 1920s was
cubist in nature with a slight hint of controlled
motion. Although there were major advances in
form design, the real innovation occurred in the
materials sector. The results were indeed revolutionary. However, in the 1930s, these advances
were given wings and allowed to fly into a
boundless universe. Modernism of the 1930s and
early 1940s involved motion.

As the 1930s began, Modernism emphasized
minimalism. A stark, open interior design was in
vogue. As the 1930s drew to a close, an increased emphasis on large numbers of decorative
accessories once again enjoyed popularity. The
key is that many incorporated Modernism design
features.

Despite the Great Depression, America made
a major contribution to the evolution of Modernism. American Streamlined Modern blended the
symbolic representations of speed with the dy-
namism and aesthetics of the machine. Sleek,
streamlined contours appeared everywhere, from
furniture to railroad engines.

Four major American designers led the movement: Norman Bel Geddes, Henry Dreyfuss,
Walter Dorwin Teague, and Raymond Loewy.
Under their leadership American packaged its
lifestyle in Streamlined Modern designs.

The 1929 New York Metropolitan Museum of
Art's exhibit entitled "The Architect and the In-

dustrial Age," witnessed the first expressions of
Streamlined Modern. Many of the pieces exhibited were a cooperative effort between architects–turned–furniture designers and leading furniture manufacturers. The approach was
conservative.

A shift away from conservative ideals was
noted at the 1934 New York Metropolitan Museum of Art's exhibit that included Eliel Saarinen's "Room for a Lady," Raymond Loewy and
Lee Simonson's "Designer's Office and Studio,"
and William Lescaze's "Living Room." Other key
designers who exhibited were Donald Deskey,
Norman Bel Geddes, Arthur Loomis Harmon,
Gilbert Rohde, and Walter Dorwin Teague.

Streamlined Modern enjoyed its greatest popularity in the interiors of public buildings, ocean
liners, trains, and airplanes. Images were often
visionary, stressing a future of easy travel and
mechanized modern living. The movement cul-
minated in the "Building the World of Tomor-
row" building at the 1939–40 New York World's
Fair.

One special feature involving Streamlined
Modern interior design is worth noting. In many
cases antiques and reproduction and copycat Baroque furniture were selected as the furnishing
accessories for the highly stylized Modernism interior. This represented a major departure from
the concept of total design unity.

Streamlined Modern worked its way into the
homes of most Americans through decorative accessories. The dominant popular furniture styles
remained oak vernacular and Colonial Revival.
Collectors wishing to acquire examples of
Streamlined Modern furniture are best advised to
seek institutional, also known as contract, furniture.

First cousins to Streamlined Modern are the
Surrealism and Eclecticism movements of the late
1930s. The leading Surrealism exponent was
Jean–Michel Frank, a Parisian decorator/designer
who arrived on the scene in the 1920s. Frank
stressed the use of natural materials in his colors.
As the 1930s progressed Frank's work became
more fanciful; he enlisted the aid of a variety of
collaborators ranging from Albert and Diego Giacometti to Salvador Dali.

The Giacometti brothers developed a line of
bronze furniture inspired by antique furniture
forms. Their tables, chairs, and lamps featured
slender tubular elements with terminals in the
shape of animal or human heads. However,
Dali's designs—from his Mae West lips sofa
(1936) to his chair with a back support of full
relief hands raised in supplication—actually introduced the surreal into furniture design. The
movement's high point was the 1938 Paris Surrealist exhibition.

Surrealism was a fad that quickly faded. A
renewed interest in antique period styles and
forms, another 1930s development, enjoyed a

far different fate. Carlos de Bestegui introduced the neo–Baroque and stressed extravagant settings in rooms of Modernistic design. Although some new Baroque pieces were created, a major revival did not occur.

Instead, decorators turned to the antiques themselves and worked them into their decorating schemes. This juxtaposition of old with new remains a valid decorating approach today. Thus, a new buying force, the interior decorator, entered the antiques marketplace. In some market cycles, such as the 1980s, the interior decorator often plays a more significant role than the collector.

Chair
  Arm
    Andre Arbus, attributed to, set of eight, c1930, rectangular upholstered back flanked by shaped arms centering a D–form over upholstered seat, raised on tapering legs, upholstered in pale orange leather, price for set of eight **5,500**
    Marcel Breuer, adjustable, made by Kurt Adam, mid–20th C, separate scroll seat and backrest interlocking with an inverted double U–form base, arm portion extended outward from U–form frame, upholstered in knobby tweed fabric **2,000**
    Heywood–Wakefield and Lloyd Manufacturing, 1935, tubular metal, back rest and seat upholstered in brown vinyl **150**
    Ludwig Mies van der Rohe, "MR", manufactured by Berliner Metallgewerbe Joseph Muller, 1927, continuous tubular frame beginning with a flat shelf–like crest flowing into an L–shaped body extending into a half circle leg ending in an extended U–form foot, arm attached to back and bottom of leg portion consisting of flat back, right angle bend for arms running parallel to set and then swept down in a quarter circle, exploits spring capabilities of tubular metal, continuous band of caning forming seat back, canned arm rests **3,000**
    Unidentified designer or maker, c1940, upholstered, roll crest, L–shaped heavily padded back and seat, D–shaped solid sides, four lucite U–form feet **400**
  Club, attributed to Louis Süa and Andrea Maré, 1930, Ebené de Macas-

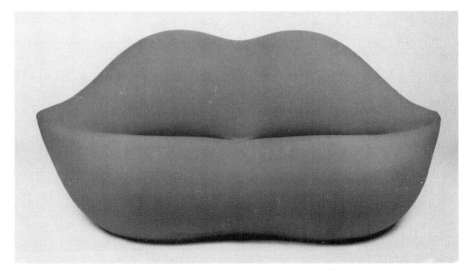

Marilyn Lips Sofa, c1975, based upon Salvidor Dali's mixed media "Faces of Mae West Which May Be Used As an ApArtment," period piece made by Jean-Michel Frank for Baron de L'Epee and Edward James, c1934, red nylon upholstery over foam rubber frame, unsigned, albeit in 1972 Studio 65 in Milan, Italy, resurrected the design renaming it the "Marilyn," some stains, 82″ w, 31″ d, 33½″ h, $2,350.00. Photograph courtesy Skinner, Inc.

Two Pairs of Chairs, laminated and bent walnut, two arm and two side chairs, price for four $250.00. Photograph courtesy of Pettigrew Auction Company.

sar, barrel back, straight sides and front, vertical concave fluting around sides and back, cut green velvet upholstery 650

Side, "MR", designed by Ludwig Mies van der Rohe and executed by the Berliner Metallgewerge Joseph Muller, 1927, continuous tubular frame beginning with a flat shelf–like crest flowing into an L–shaped body extending in a half circle leg ending in an extended U–form foot, exploits the spring capabilities of tubular frame, continuous caned seat and back (also found with leather seat and back) 2,500

Desk

Desk, Wolfgang Hoffmann for Howell Co., c1935, inverted tubular U–form frame, rectangular top, two drawers (one file) on right tubular frame that is extension of desk frame, each chromed pull conjoined asymmetrically to a metal drawer, remains of decal printed "Howell/ST. CHARLES, ILL./Exclusive/Design," 42" l, 30" h 1,500

George W. Neff, mid–20th C, trapezoidal top set on four drawers at left and a canted support at right, darked stained panels with black bands, 54" l, 28" h 1,750

Desk Set, desk and chair, designed by Russel Wright, c1935, maple, desk with rectangular top above three drawers with block form handles at left and a simple angular support at

right, chair with rectangular upholstered back, curved open arms and square upholstered seat, raised on four straight legs, desk branded "BUILT BY CONTANT–BALL CO./ DESIGNED BY RUSSEL WRIGHT/ AMERICAN MODERN/BC", chair branded "CB. H." 750

Stool, designed by Gilbert Rhode, manufactured by Troy Sunshade, Troy, OH, metal, round black cushion seat, chrome Z–form support, foot rest above circular base ring, 14" d, 23½" h 525

Table

Dining Room, designed by Andre Arbus, c1935, rectangular top edged with brass molding, raised on two pedestal supports framed in rosewood and enclosing red textured lacquer panels above rectangular brass base ending in scrolls, signed on both pedestals Andre Arbus, 96" w, 39¾" d, 29" 14,300

Dressing, designed by Gilbert Rhode, Herman Miller Furniture Company, 1935, lucite mounted walnut, three circular gilt mirrors, rectangular top with demilune cutout kneehole, demilune shaped glass shelf insert, two banks of three graduated drawers, demilune base, 48" w, 50" h . 2,750

Occasional, circular, designed by Russel Wright, c1935, two–tier, maple, circular top, two pairs of vertical supports centering a lower shelf, branded mark, 28" d 500

POST WORLD WAR II

History: The Second World War had a profound impact on furniture design and manufacture. First, production of domestic and office furniture virtually stopped. Many of the factories converted to wartime production. Second, tremendous advances were made in materials and construction technology. Once the war ended, these advances presented new opportunities and challenges to furniture designers.

One of the key technological advances was Chrysler Corporation's 1941 development of cycle welding. This technique allowed the secure binding of wood and rubber, glass, or metal. Metal composition that greatly increased strength allowed a growing minimalism in furniture structure support. This paved the way for chair designs by Charles Eames and Harry Bertoia.

Modernism dominated the first three decades of the post–war period. Organic Modernism, also known as the Contemporary Style in its more popularized form, experienced a Neo–Modernism period, largely based on a revival of International Modernism of the 1920s, before fading from the scene in the mid–1970s. Rivaling Modernism for popular favor was the Scandinavian Style, a highly resilient design form that still remains strong in the 1990s.

The post–war period was one of tremendous eclecticism. No one style dominated. In the suburban home, the Contemporary Style competed with Colonial Revival and the Mediterranean Style for influence. While the masses remained highly conservative, the trendy turned to Pop and Memphis as a means of expressing their contempt for tradition.

The chair, more than any other form, documents the infinite variety of furniture design forms of the post–war era. It was a period when seating furniture dominated. One of the reasons for this is the shift from the home to the office and public and private institutions as the major impetus for designer furniture. As the twentieth century ends, contract furniture dominates. Unfortunately, the mass has little contact with such furniture. As a result, one has to question this furniture's future collectibility.

The post–war period began with the United States at the center of the International design movement. Knoll International and Herman Miller, two leading American furniture manufacturers, aggressively promoted new designs. By the late 1960s, however, the U.S. no longer held center stage. The Neo–Modernism and Pop movements were based in England and on the Continent. The Memphis movement of the 1980s is headquartered in Italy.

One of the reasons for this shift was the growing conservatism in American tastes during the 1980s and 1990s. America felt more comfortable looking backward for its furniture inspiration than forward into the future. The United States does continue its historic role of adopting and adapting styles that originate aboard and giving them a unique "American" feel. However, acceptance of most 1990s contemporary styles is limited.

Understanding American collector's attitudes toward post–World War II designer furniture is difficult. American museums recognize its importance and have added it to their collection. European and Japanese collectors are attracted to it. Yet, the generation of Americans who grew up with it and are now in a position to buy back their childhood continue to ignore it. Instead, it is the twentysomething and thirtysomething crowd that leads the current collecting surge. Perhaps they are attracted to it because of its affordability, something that is rapidly vanishing for 1950s examples, or its non–conformity to mass contemporary tastes. Whatever the reason, the furniture from this era deserves to be documented and collected.

Note: It would have been very easy to end the American furniture section at 1940. This is the approach taken by most books dealing with antique and collectible furniture. Warman's has never been noted for taking the safe, sure road.

Warman's Furniture is a first attempt for the antiques trade to designate the key collecting periods for post–war furniture, provide information that allows collectors and dealers to distinguish one period from another, identify key forms, designers, and manufacturers, and provide a partial listing of pieces and prices. It is a start, not the final word. Ideas and collecting categories presented in this volume will be revised and redefined in subsequent editions.

The categories in this section are information heavy; illustration and listings are light. The primary reason for this is either that few pieces are selling actively on a documentable secondary market or that many of the prices being recorded appear to be highly speculative in nature. New collecting categories often enter the market as crazes. True market value is established only after the initial bubble bursts. Much of post–war furniture is still in its initial price run. This does not mean it should be ignored.

A few of the categories dealing with furniture still in production have no listings or illustrations. They are designed to alert you to what the future holds. Now is the time to learn about them.

References: Philippe Garner, *Twentieth–Century Furniture*, Van Nostrand Reinhold Company, 1980; Penny Sparke, *Furniture: Twentieth–Century Design*, E. P. Dutton, 1986.

CONTEMPORARY/POST WAR MODERNISM (Late 1940s through Early 1960s)

History: While World War II had a great impact on the availability of materials for furniture production, it did not slow the evolution of modern furniture design. American designers such as Harry Bertoia, Charles Eames, and Eero Saarinen created new furniture forms that softened the austere Bauhaus functionalism. The talents of these great designers came together at the Cranbrook Academy, founded in 1936 by Eliel Saarinen. As the war ended, America was on the cutting edge of furniture design.

New York's Museum of Modern Art was one of the leading forces encouraging innovative furniture design. In 1940 the museum, inspired by an idea from Bloomingdale's, sponsored a competition for "Organic Design in Home Furnishings." A 1941 exhibition of the winning designs introduced Charles Eames and Eero Saarinen to the American public. Other Museum of Modern Art competitions and events were: New Furniture Designed by Charles Ames (1946); One Hundred Objects of Fine Design (1947); and Competition for Low Cost Furniture Design (1948) which introduced Americans to British designers Robin Day and Clive Latimer.

Two strong influences on American Contemporary style were a trend toward the informal and the "California Style," a West Coast living style that stressed flexible open spaces, informal positioning of furniture, and a linkage between indoor and outdoor space. American furniture design of the 1950s and early 1960s easily met these criteria.

Dozens of classic forms emerged, many of which remain in production in the 1990s. Among them are: Charles Eames' low chair (1950) consisting of a molded polyester seat on a wire frame; Charles Eames' Lounge Chair 670 and Ottoman (1956), consisting of a leather upholstered seat, arm, and back units in a three–part cradle of rosewood ply on a cast aluminum base and flat supporting legs; Eero Saarinen's Tulip chairs and tables (1957) with a reinforced plastic seat and aluminum pedestal base; Isamu Noguchi's, and low table with a top of bowed triangular plate–glass on two sculptured walnut leg elements; Harry Bertoia's chicken wire chairs (1950); and George Nelson's Coconut chair (1956), and Marshmallow sofa (1956), consisting of a seat and back made up of eighteen padded cylinders on a slender metal base. Saarinen, Noguchi, and Bertoia designed for Hans and Florence Knoll, whose company was one of the most progressive furniture manufacturers. Charles Eames and George Nelson worked for Herman Miller, a firm which actively propagated new furniture styles.

Knoll International, which reissued Mies van der Rhoe's Barcelona chair in the 1950s, was just one of many manufacturers that turned to classic pre–war designs. When Knoll International acquired the Italian firm of Gavina, it received the rights to manufacture furniture based upon the designs of Marcel Breuer.

Post–War Modernism, also known as Organic Modernism, was popularized as the Contemporary Style of the 1950s and early 1960s. It blended America's Post–War Designer Modernism with Scandinavian influences. The Contemporary Style was quickly adopted by the prosperous American middle class and became a symbol of their success and good taste.

Contemporary furniture is fluid in design. The incorporation of storage space into furniture forms is evident in the increased use of modular wall, display, and/or free–standing units which allowed maximum flexibility in the design of one's living space. Architect and furniture designer worked closely together. Contemporary furniture is a direct response to new living spaces found in the suburban tract home.

The interpretations of the Contemporary Style are limitless. They range from the formica top, chromed skirt, and "v" legged kitchen table to a champagne finish wood TV table. One of the hottest segments of the 1990s market in 1950s furniture are the products from Heywood–Wakefield. Although currently most in vogue in large urban areas and on the West Coast, it has the potential to attract a nationwide following.

When buying popular interpretations of Contemporary Style, stress pieces that have strong design elements, are well constructed, period, and made by recognized manufacturers. Do not overstress the latter point. As more research is done, the list of "significant" manufactures will grow considerably.

DESIGNER FURNITURE

Chair
  Arm
    Charles Eames, 1950, molded orange Fiberglas, bent steel base with X–form design **250**

Chair, designed by Charles Eames, molded plywood, $525.00. Photograph courtesy of Leslie Hindman Auctioneers.

Lounge
  Charles Eames for Herman Miller, 1956, #67 lounge chair and matching #671 ottoman, curved laminated rosewood frames with

Side Chairs, designed by Charles Eames, manufactured by Herman Miller, molded plywood, painted, price for set of four, $800.00. Photograph courtesy of Leslie Hindman Auctioneers.

tufted black hide upholstery, swivel base, chair 31″ h, price for set **1,000**

Jens Risom, 1952, curvilinear seat frame, angular arm and leg supports, 26″ d, 30″ h **165**

Russel Wright, 1955, horizontal slatted back, deep seat, flat angular arm and leg supports, striped linen seat cushions, 32″ d, 29¾″ h **350**

Side

Charles Eames, c1946, pair, molded plywood, curved back, serpentine support, shaped seat resting on arched legs, price for pair **415**

Charles Eames, c1946, molded plywood, curved back, serpentine support, shaped seat resting on arched legs **175**

Charles Eames, c1946, molded black–stained plywood back and seat, raised on two inverted U–form chrome–plated supports, 29½″ h **150**

Charles Eames, c1946, molded plywood, curved back, serpentine support, shaped seat resting on arched ebony legs **360**

Charles Eames, c1950, arms and back in molded pumpkin orange Fiberglas, raised on a black wire cat's cradle support, 31″ h **250**

Charles Eames, c1951, black painted wire mesh, shaped white vinyl upholstery, splayed wire base with four legs, 32¾″ h ... **425**

Ray Komai, c1949, manufactured by J. G. Furniture Systems, molded plywood, shaped plywood shell back, seat on four chrome plated steel rods **165**

Jens Risom, c1952, manufactured by Knoll, rock maple frame, upholstered yellow back panel and seat, steel spring supported seat, splayed square tapered legs, period finish, 20″ w, 28¼″ d, 30″ h, seat height 16″ **225**

Set

Luigi Tagliabue, 1950, arm chair and matching side chair, light wood, vertical ebony stripes, black seats, 39″ h, price for two piece set **550**

Harry Bertoia, 1952, manufactured by Knoll, arm chair and matching foot stool, Diamond Chair Model 422 with formed steel wire and rod base and orange pad seat, Model 424 foot stool with rounded rectangular top on steel rod base, price for two piece set **450**

Dining Room Suite, Eero Saarinen, 1956–57, manufactured by Knoll International, table and six chairs, #151 Tulip chairs with Fiberglas–reinforced polyester molded back and seat on cast aluminum pedestal base,

Lounge Chair and Ottoman, designed by Harry Bertoia, manufactured by Knoll International, welded steel wire frame and legs, detachable fabric cover, 38½″ w, 39″ d, 39″ h, $500.00. Photograph courtesy of Leslie Hindman Auctioneers.

upholstered seat, matching circular table, table 53½" d, price for seven piece suite **1,500**

Sofa, Charles Eames, 1954, straight back comprised of two slightly angled horizontal rectangular sections, rectangular seat, gray vinyl upholstery, chrome steel trestle type base, 72" w **1,150**

Table, coffee
Noguchi, 1945, retailed by Herman Miller, glass and maple, kidney–shaped glass top raised on movable maple support, 15"h **3,000**

Eero Saarinen, 1956, circular mahogany top, cast metal pedestal base, white finish, top 42½" d, 15" high **325**

Side Table, designed by Eero Saarinen, manufactured by Knoll Associates, white plastic laminate top, cast metal base, top 18" d, 20" h, $125.00. Photograph courtesy of Leslie Hindman Auctioneers.

MASS PRODUCTION PIECES

Bar Seat, painted metal, foliate back, hide seat **75**

Bed, 1950, mahogany, cane inserts, double size, 57" w **125**

Chair
Arm
Thonet, c1955, laminated bentwood, rectangular high back, square seat, upholstered foam rubber cushions, bentwood arms continue to form legs, period paper label, period finish, 24½" w, 31½" d, 40¼" h, seat height 17½" **375**

Heywood–Wakefield, 1953, champagne oak finish, green uphol-

stered dog bone back, shaped tapered arms, bentwood seat frame, slightly bowed seat rail, green upholstered slip seat, elliptical tapered legs, color, maker's mark, and date of "August 23, 1953" stamped on underside of seat, period fabric and finish, 18" w, 19½" d, 33¾" h, seat height 18" **175**

Heywood–Wakefield, 1954, square back, tufted sides, and cushion upholstered in green fabric with gold and black speckles, champagne finish oak arm fronts, square tapered legs, period fabric, 34" w, 34" d, 32" h **750**

Heywood–Wakefield, attributed to, c1954, blond oak, curved upholstered back, round posts, shaped bentwood arms, overstuffed seat, splayed round tapered legs, 26" w, 22" d, 33¼" h, seat height 20", refinished frame, unbleached muslin covering ready for new fabric upholstery **275**

Club, unknown maker, c1950, box–like design, rectangular upholstered back and sides centering a rectangular seat, fabric in tones of green, black, and orange to simulate paint splashes, raised on ebonized U–form with triangular legs **750**

Lounge Chair, stainless steel and leather, rolled and pleated leather seat cushion, head roll supported by leather buckled straps, fitted X–shaped stainless steel frame, 25¾" w, 38" d, 29¼" h **600**

Side
Heywood–Wakefield, c1952, blond oak, dog bone back, striped velour upholstered slip seat, concave seat rail, bentwood seat frame, splayed base, elliptical tapered front legs, signed, refinished, 17¾" w, 20½" d, 31¾" h, seat height 18¼" **150**

Unknown maker, laminated wood, scrolling integral seat and back applied with yellow webbing raised on four outward–flaring tapering legs joined by stretchers, 36" h **750**

Desk, Heywood–Wakefield, c1955, knee hole, champagne oak finish, rectangular top, single central long drawer with divided interior, double pedestal, drawer fronts curved toward knee hole, divided file drawer on left, stamped with color and maker's

Settee, designed by Jon Cockerll, painted wood and upholstered, metallic pillows, rectangular back, purple painted shape supports, 75″ l, $975.00. Photograph courtesy of Leslie Hindman Auctioneers.

mark, period finish, 50″ wide, 24″ d, 30¼″ h   1,200

Kitchen Set, table and four chairs, c1955–60, Rachlin Furniture Company, table with rectangular top with rounded corners, gray marble Formica surface, aluminum apron, chromed tubular steel legs, one leaf extension, chairs with chromed handle on top of crest, butterfly shaped back rest in gray marbleized vinyl, slip seat in yellow vinyl, chromed tubular steel frame and legs, original paper label under seat, table measures 47¾″ w, 35¾″ d, 30″ h, chairs measure 15½″ w, 21″ d, 34¼″ h, seat height 17½″, price for five piece set   250

Lounge Set, 1955, matched pair of chairs, black wire frame seat and back, decorated wooden armrests, coiled spring seat support, four prong shaped splayed legs, 32½″ h, price for two piece set   1,000

Table

Coffee, c1960, circular mosaic top fitted with polychromed tiles in a radiating pattern, raised on Noguchi style walnut base, 15″ h   500

Corner, Heywood–Wakefield, c1958, champagne oak finish, serpentine shaped front on step shelf, square top base, slightly bowed square tapered legs, color stamped on bottom, top 32¼″ square, 20¾″ h . . .   250

Dining Room, Heywood–Wakefield, c1952, blond oak, drop leaf, two leaf extension, rounded corners on drop leaves, rectangular top, straight apron, triple wishbone (whalebone) base, refinished 27″ l, 40″ d, 29″ h, extended top 59¼″ l   1,250

End, pair, step shelf on square tapered pedestal sides, rectangular top base, canted incised apron, flat tapered legs, simulated blond oak Formica on shelf and top base, speckled painted sides, 15¾″ w, 29¾″ d, 22″ h, price for pair   100

Television Stand, Heywood–Wakefield, c1955, champagne oak finish, rectangular top, canted sides, medial shelf, bowed half–round tapered legs, color and maker's mark stamped on underside of shelf, 26″ w, 24½″ d, 26″ h, refinished   300

SCANDINAVIAN (1950s Onward)

History: During the 1930s, Scandinavian designers practiced a design style stressing a more humanistic approach to functionalism. They considered the tubular and other new materials furniture of the Bauhaus as hostile in appearance. The key word is tradition. Furniture forms more closely copied standard forms and emphasis was placed on furniture–making craftsmanship and wood. Leading designers during this period were Kaare Klint, a Dane; and Alvar Aalto, a Finn.

Immediately following World War II the Scandinavian governments encouraged close cooperation between designers and manufacturers, and engaged in consumer education focused on touting Scandinavian furniture designs. The Swedish Slojdforeningen, an official government body, published *Mobelad*, a consumer's guide outlining furniture design standards that would benefit public and industry alike.

Among the pioneers of post–World War II Scandinavian furniture are: the Swedes Carl Malmsten and Bruno Mathsson; the Danes Hans Wegner, Borge Mogensen, and Finn Juhl; and the Finn Alvar Aalto. Among the classic designs of the era are: Marianne Boman's "V" steel rod frame and bucket seat fabric chair; Arne Jacobsen's egg and swan chairs, both featuring a leather upholstered swivel seating surface on an aluminum base of four flat legs; and France & Daverkosen's armchairs and tables featuring frames that stressed wood grain and suggested just a hint of movement.

Scandinavian furniture designs received worldwide attention through a number of international exhibitions, including "Design in Scandinavia" which opened in the United States in 1954. In 1960–61 "The Arts of Denmark" exhibit toured America.

Scandinavian furniture designs complemented the Contemporary Style of Post–War Modernism. The airy, open quality of much of the furniture found favor among growing middle income groups. The solid earth tone colors of fabric and other upholstery accented the natural wood grains. When metal was used, it was subdued, rather than dominant in the form. The overall look was "natural."

Scandinavian furniture was made in a wide variety of quality levels. Collectors are advised to seek well–made pieces by recognized furniture manufacturers. Beware of replaced fabric and other coverings that do not preserve the period color tones associated with the pieces.

Chair

Egg–Shell, designed by Arne Jacobsen, c1960, plastic undulating shell upholstered in yellow (sometimes green) worsted wool, raised on an X–form chrome swivelling base ..   **500**

Armchair, attributed to Ralph Rapson, shaped and continuous back and seat side rails with leather webbing, on frame with shaped arms, unsigned, Knoll, some wear, 42" w, 20" d, 29½" h, $175.00. Photograph courtesy of Skinner, Inc.

Chair and Ottoman, Swan chair, designed by Arne Jacobsen, circa 1955, grey upholstery, $225.00. Photograph courtesy of Leslie Hindman Auctioneers.

Dining Room Set, table and chairs, Drexel, maple, table with rectangular top with rectangular drop leaves, L-form tapering legs, three leaves, six matching chairs with woven wood slat rectangular back, upholstered seat, square tapering legs, table 40″ w, 31″ d, 29″ h, $500.00. Photograph courtesy of Leslie Hindman Auctioneers.

Kubbestol, folk furniture, Terkel Landsverk, 1925, hollow log construction, round curved back, round wedged seat, concave circular base with center band flanked by carved acanthus leaf decoration, cut–out carrying handle in lower back, "T.L." and "1925" carved in back **650**

Set of six, designed by Finn Juhl for The Baker Furniture Company, wood and vinyl, concave wood crest rail, ovoid black vinyl back, oblong curved black vinyl seat, straight seat rail, shaped and turned legs, two slender stretchers, 32″ h, price for set of six **650**

Side, retailed by Knoll Associates, c1960, maple, worsted wood seat and back cushion **100**

Table, occasional

Blond wood, one frieze drawer, metal stretchers, branded "MADE IN SWEDEN/FACTORY NO. 4" **200**

Walnut, crossed legs adjusting to various heights, paper label printed "RUD. RASMUSSESNS/SNEDKER-IER/42 NORRE–BROCADE/KO-BENHAVEN", height ranges from 23″ to 27½″ **300**

NEO–MODERNISM (1960s)

History: The 1960s witnessed a rebirth of International Modernism. The furniture forms of the Contemporary Style's Organic Modernism were considered old fashioned by the mid–1960s. A new, younger, monied generation wanted to make its own fashion statement. London served as the movement's center.

The Neo–Modernism movement was fueled in part by the technological advances associated with the 1960s Space Race. Plastics and other synthetics were used in creative new ways. Tubular chromium–plated seating and table furniture associated with Bauhaus designs were revived.

Much of the creative design was done for the corporate office and public institution. Space was once again controlled. Two leading English design groups were Zeev Aram and Associates and the O.M.K. studio founded in 1966.

The chair, more than any other form, exhibits the wide variety of design practiced during the Neo–Modernism period. Classic forms include: Robin Day's stackable Polyprop chair (1963) for Hille featuring an inverted "V" tubular steel rod side leg and molded polypropylene single unit seat; Poul Kjaerholm's "Hammock Chair 24" (1965), Archizoom Associati's "Mies" (1969) consisting of an open wedge of steel, chromium–plated, and stretched rubber sheet seat; and Eero Aarnio's "Globe" or womb chair (1966) designed for Finn International. The later is an excellent example of Space Age furniture, especially with its emphasis of a shiny white surface.

Many of the 1960s furniture designs were passé by the late 1970s. Too many of the designs were trendy. The era's principle contribution was in its creative use of materials, plastic and synthetic upholstery. The ability to mold many of these new furniture designs created a new commercial furniture manufacturing industry. Designers such as Eero Aarnio and Helmut Batzner created chairs that could be made by this process.

The end of the Neo–Modernism period witnessed the growing supremacy of Italian designers and manufacturers. They produced a wide range of furniture, from sculptured forms to modular units that could be manufactured at low cost.

One of the most creative designers was Joe Colombo of Milan. His Additional System furniture premiered at the 1969 Milan Triennale. Key Italian manufacturers include: Kartell, who made the first injection molded plastic chair, and Cassina who manufactured furniture designed by Mario Bellini, Vico Magistretti, and Afra and Tobia Scarpa.

American collectors and dealers will not recognize many of the forms and names listed above. Much of this furniture is either still in use, in storage, or long since discarded. Although now being collected actively in Europe, it remains outside the mainstream of American collecting. However, just as Contemporary furniture is at long last enjoying a collecting vogue in the 1990s, Neo–Modernism is destined to enjoy a similar vogue in the first decades of the 21st century. Consider yourself forewarned.

Chair
    Globe, unknown manufacturer, based
        upon 1966 design by Eero Saarnio
        for Akso Finninternational, white
        Fiberglas shell, upholstered inside,
        stereo speakers, flared circular base   **250**
Side
    Helmut Batzner, BA1171 Chair,
        made by Whilhelm Bofinger of
        Stuttgart, 1966, stackable, injec-
        tion molded **50**
    Vernon Panton, cantilevered chair,
        designed in 1960, produced by
        Herman Miller after 1967, red Fi-
        berglas **75**

POP (1960s)

History: The Swinging Sixties witnessed the emergence of a strong youth market and brought under attack many social traditions and taboos. Furniture design responded. Although clever marketing has made American Pop artists better known worldwide, the center for Pop furniture design is the Independent Group at the Institute of Contemporary Arts in London.

Two major groups of Pop furniture evolved. The first stressed pieces that were fun and often disposable. Carla Scolari, Donato D'Urbino, Paolo Lomazzi, and Jonathan De Pas's inflatable P.V.C. chair (1967) is an excellent example. The second group featured pieces that were aesthetic in nature, yet challenged conventional standards. A set of card suite pouffes designed by Jon Weallans for Tommy Robert's Mr. Freedom, and Allen Jones' table, chair, and coat stand modeled in full relief in the form of a pin-up girl clad in fetishistic garb illustrate the lively, tongue–in–cheek furniture of this latter group.

Like Art Deco and similar furniture styles that were expensive, trendy, and selective in their appeal, Pop had far more impact on decorative accessories than it did on furniture design. One group of Pop furniture that enjoyed some popularity was "knock–down" forms. Two examples are John Wright and Jean Schofield's "Chair C.I." (1964) featuring painted flat plywood quarter circle arms and a loose fabric–covered cushion; and Max Clendenning's "take it home in a carton and assemble it yourself" chairs manufactured by Race Furniture. Bright primary colors were the favorite color scheme.

French and Italian designers also produced Pop furniture, especially in designs that rejected traditional forms through the creation of pieces designed to humor, surprise, and shock. Names worth remembering are Francois Lalanne and Cesar in France and Lomazzi, D'Urbino, and De Pas in Italy. Lalanne is best known for his animal seats, especially of sheep. Lomazzi, D'Urbino, and De Pas "Joe Sofa" in the shape of a baseball glove is well known to collectors.

A first cousin of pop is the "Hippie" furniture that evolved in the late 1960s. This look rejected almost all standard furniture forms in favor of floor cushions and floor level daybeds. Pierro Gatti, Cesare Paolini, and Franco Teodoro's Sacco seat (1968–69), or bean bag chair, is the movement's best known form.

Chair, soft, Robert Breslau, black leather
    with multicolored stitching and two
    bull's eyes, 60" w, 48" d, from the
    collection of Andy Warhol **2,000**
Sofa, Kim McConnell, signed and dated,
    stuffed, upholstered in spray painted
    fabric featuring large scalloped flow-
    ers among diagonally striped lines,
    72" w, 36" d, 28" h, from the collec-
    tion of Andy Warhol **3,500**

CRAFT REVIVAL (1970s)

History: America witnessed a craft revival in the 1970s. On the popular level, the chief motivating factor was the Bicentennial. In furniture design, the craft revival was a reaction to the extremely efficient designs of the Industrial Style.

The craft revivalist emphasizes hand craftsmanship. Designs are very intimate and often poetic. Function is stressed. Craft revival pieces are useful works of art. The movement has its philosophical roots in Ruskin and Morris.

Craft revival pieces are expensive. Designers and craftspersons accept the fact that their work is destined for the select few that can afford it. They rationalize their efforts by stressing the regeneration of traditional craft skills, preservation of standards lost through mass production, and creating a renewed sense of involvement between creativity and environment.

Wharton Esherick, who died in 1970, pioneered the movement. In 1913 he established a workshop outside of Philadelphia. Furniture historians view him as continuing the Shaker tradition.

Wendell Castle, who studied industrial design and sculpture in Kansas, is the recognized leader of the 1970s Craft Revival. His numerous one–man shows across America stress the pieces he carves out of a layered block of wood. Many of his pieces are characterized by sweeping contours.

Other leading American Craft Revival designers are Michael Coffey (Poultney, Vermont) and Paul Epp. A group of designers whose pieces show a strong linkage to the extravagant organic forms of Art Nouveau are Peter Danko, Sam Forest, Stephen Harris, Stephen Hogbin, and Roy Superior.

America is not the only country to experience a craft revival. In 1963 England's John Makepeace established his first shop and exhibition gallery. Makepeace's influence is strongly felt because in 1977 he founded his School for Craftsmen in Wood to train a new generation of wood handcrafters. A craft revival also occurred in Sweden.

Many leading American museums have purchased Craft Revival pieces for their permanent collections. The principle is to buy pieces while they are still affordable. However, the practice often establishes a market for a specific craftsperson and suggests long term investment potential, something which only time can determine.

Major New York and several regional auction houses have sold pieces from the Craft Revival. Initial results indicate a strong market. Collectors are advised to keep in mind that these prices are highly speculative. Until pieces are bought and resold several times, a clear market course cannot be charted.

Chairs, set of six, dining, designed by
    George Nakishima for Widdicomb
    Furniture, Grand Rapids, MI, 1955,
    turned wood, long narrow gently
    curved crest rail above nine spindle
    back, wide shaped seat, simple
    turned canted legs joined by high H–
    form stretcher, branded "George Nak-
    ishima 2771," 36" h, price for set of
    six **1,550**
Desk, checkerboard marquetry top,
    three drawer pedestal, long top
    drawer over kneehole opening,
    paneled sides, Lake Geneva, Wiscon-
    sin, Franciscan Monastery, signed
    "Brother B.A.," 1938, 34" l, 30" h .. **200**
Dining Room Suite, designed by George
    Nakishima, c1955, English walnut,
    eight pieces, comprising six seven
    spindle side chairs with shaped saddle
    seats and tapering legs joined by

stretchers, rectangular dining table with incurvate sides raised on trestle support, sideboard with incurvate ir-regularly–shaped rectangular top above two sliding doors set with slats against a straw matt back, opening to reveal an interior set with short and long shelves and a tray compartment, all inlaid with ribbon–form and cir-cular joints, table 72" l and 28¼" h, sideboard 71" l and 32" h, price for eight pieces **4,500**
Table and Armchair, George Nakishi-ma, c1957, table with free form top raised on trestle support, chair with slat back, table 95" l, price for two pieces **3,000**

INDUSTRIAL STYLE (1970s)

History: The 1970s was a period of consolidation. No new materials were introduced into furniture construction. Two design styles did emerge. The Industrial Style with its emphasis on contract furniture stands in marked contrast to the Craft Revival. Architecturally, the Industrial Style is best symbolized by Richard Rogers and Renzo Piano's Centre Pompidou in Paris.

America's Herman Miller and Knoll International, and England's Hille and Race Furniture are the four key firms that dominated Industrial Style contract furniture. Furniture designs by Charles Eames retained their strong influence in the Herman Miller line. Miller's Action Office stressed modular furniture. Bill Stumpf's Ergon chair (1976) was a major design contribution.

Knoll and Form International, its British counterpart, relied heavily on the classic designs that made the company famous. New designs by Gae Aulenti, Andrew Morrison and Bruce Hannah, Max Pearson, and Charles Pollock were added to the line to keep it fresh.

Robin Day designed the Polo chair (1979), a cubist tubular design with a molded plastic top, for Hille. Race Furniture introduced the "Molecula" range, a group of fully upholstered furniture pieces that can be placed in a straight line or circle.

Contract furniture of the Industrial Style enjoyed an international market. Cassina, an Italian firm, became a major factor in the market. Under the direction of Mario Bellini, it developed "Marcatre," office furniture capable of meeting made–to–measure requirements.

The Industrial Style is the furniture of the work station. A wide variety of quality levels were made. Collectors should focus on pieces from major international manufacturers and ignore all copycats.

Desk, Italian enameled–steel modular
    office desk and typing station, "Spa-

zio" series, Olivetti, c1959, rectangular, central component fitted with an olive baize top set at center with a leather band–form blotter, unit set at right with three graduated locking drawers, corners set with black composition recesses for addition of further modules, integral swivelling typing stand set at left, original key, 73½" l, 30½" h **1,500**

MEMPHIS (1980s)

History: In the 1980s, furniture design leadership shifted to Italy. As in any furniture design center, a multiplicity of design styles was being pursued. One movement, Memphis, began to question Modernism's spare, clean–lined, and neutral or primary color oriented designs. The reaction was a movement that stressed a highly decorative, architectural approach to furniture. By the 1970s, Italian furniture developed a reputation for its sleek allure, a marked contrast to America's involvement with the pre–1900 reproductions and adaptations, and its business community's love affair with 1920s International Modernism.

Ettore Sottsass, Jr., an industrial designer for Olivetti in the late 1950s, developed the design philosophies that set the stage for the Memphis movement. Sottsass created furniture that was fanciful, playful, and incorporated a wide range of materials from ceramics and jewelry to plastic and lighting. Sottsass' designs created a dissatisfaction with Modernism that found favor with a several Milanese designers. The status quo was under attack.

In the 1970s, Sottsass, Sandro Guerriero, and a group of architect/designers (Andrea Branzi, Michele de Lucchi, Alessandro Mendini, and Paola Navone) founded Studio Alchymia in Milan. Many new designs emerged. Design was arbitrary and exuberant; pieces stressed the un-

expected. Many of the pieces were handcrafted and produced in limited quantities.

In 1981 a number of Italian designers including Sottsass, Marco Zanini, and Aldo Cibic created Memphis. Floating in and out of the group are a number of internationally known architects and furniture designers. The name was inspired by a Bob Dylan song, "Stuck Outside of Mobile with the Memphis Blues Again." A level of appropriateness was sensed since the name alluded to both the ancient capital of Egypt and the birthplace of Elvis Presley, a juxtaposition of high and low cultures.

The first Memphis collection appeared at the fall 1981 Milan Furniture Fair. Many of the pieces were only prototypes. The pieces created an uproar. A number of manufacturers quickly backed Memphis, including Knoll International.

The Memphis collection consists of two main groups, one of sixty–four and one of sixty–five items. The designers view their pieces as political statements, visible poetry, and a challenge to traditional design styles. Viewed simply, Memphis means funky status.

Two Knoll International Memphis oriented furniture groupings are best known to American collectors. The first is the Robert Venturi chair collection. The second is Marco Zanini's "Dublin" sofa of wood and plastic laminate, four splayed metal legs, and strongly contrasting yellow and orange cushions.

Memphis has yet to enjoy a popular interpretation. Because it remains a trendy fad among a small, elite, wealthy group of individuals, we have not included listings in this edition. Only time will tell if its trendiness will fade just as did Pop's. Meanwhile, buy any designer furniture or decorative accessories that you can find, especially if they are cheap. There will always be a museum market.

Reference: Richard Horn, *Memphis: Objects, Furniture & Patterns*, Simon and Schuster Fireside Book, 1986.

Part II
American Vernacular Furniture

PERIOD DESIGN STYLE furniture rarely graced the homes of the middle and lower classes throughout the eighteenth, nineteenth, and much of the twentieth centuries. When it did, it often was a cheaper and less pure version of the style. Some pieces worked their way into these environments through the secondhand market, albeit only after they were long out of fashion.

The vast majority of furniture found in the home of the "common man" was highly functional and based on traditional designs often centuries old. The Windsor chair is an excellent example. The general term used by the trade to describe this furniture is "vernacular" or "generic."

Do not assume that vernacular implies primitive or crude. Nothing is further from the truth. Vernacular furniture is usually well constructed, whether handmade or mass–produced. It should be—it was made to last for generations. This was its strong selling point.

As a result, a typical lower or middle class household contained a wide variety of furniture styles and forms, depending on what could be afforded "new" through purchase and what was handed down from family, friends, and relatives. Pieces were repaired, refinished, and repainted to prolong their usefulness. Vernacular furniture was recycled, over and over again.

Perhaps this explains why so little vernacular furniture from the eighteenth and nineteenth centuries has survived. It was used and used hard. Eventually, it did wear out and was no longer repairable; another coat of paint did not solve the problem. It was burned for heat or simply junked. Some found its way into attics and barns. However, much of this has been lost as owners have sold off and moved or died and left the problem of disposal to their heirs.

Another reason for the poor survival of eighteenth and nineteenth century vernacular furniture is lack of collector interest until the 1970s. Early Windsors were saved because they were "colonial." Pennsylvania German and other painted furniture survived because it was "regional," but only if the painting was spectacular. By the time collectors and dealers did understand the importance of collecting and documenting vernacular furniture, the vast majority of what remained dated from the post–1875 period.

Vernacular furniture is common household furniture—the kitchen table and chairs and the bedroom suites. It is the furniture people use each and every day. When period design furniture is affordable or available, it is placed in the rooms where company is entertained: the front room or parlor, dining room, and guest bedroom. In far too many cases, period design furniture is for show.

It is amazing how much this tradition continues in the present. Collectors who own premier period design pieces often display them in a situation where visitors are allowed to admire, but not use, them. Perhaps this is why modern design styles are institutional and corporate in nature. Neither of these entities gets upset when a piece is used for the purpose for which it was designed.

Vernacular furniture is not devoid of style. A good Windsor chair sings to its owner. A large golden oak table with a complementary set of chairs is at home in a wide variety of settings. In other words, vernacular furniture can exhibit a strong aesthetic sense.

In fact, developing an understanding of aesthetics, i.e., proportion, and applying it is critical for anyone collecting vernacular furniture. A good vernacular piece has harmony and unity, whether a bench or ladderback chair. The piece flows together.

Much vernacular furniture fails to meet these aesthetic criteria, yet it is still collected. The fact that it has survived at all is one reason. America's love of things related to the "common man" is another. Finally, much of it is what one remembers seeing at one's grandparents' home.

For many, vernacular furniture implies handmade, an adherence to the "primitive" collecting mentality. Reality indicates that most vernacular furniture is mass–produced. The fact that a piece is mass–produced should not be a negative, however. The key is to look at the aesthetics first, and then look at the quality of construction.

The difficulty with mass–produced vernacular furniture is that it was made in a wide variety of quality levels. In many instances one is dealing with more than six quality grades for a single form. Most collectors and dealers neither understand nor appreciate these quality differences. As the 1990s progress and more and more attention is paid to vernacular furniture, a growing sophistication will occur. Those who are willing to invest their time and energy to learn the differences now will be a jump ahead of the pack.

Vernacular forms were copied over and over again; the designs were not copyrighted. Hundreds, and in some cases thousands, of manufacturers made the same basic form. As a result, vernacular furniture collectors and dealers do not tend to pay a premium for specific manufacturers. They will pay a small premium, i.e., a few percent, for a "marked" piece.

Be alert to marked pieces (often marked by stencil or brand) that were totally handmade. In this case, a premium is paid if the craftsperson is identified. Do not overestimate the value of a marked piece. The key lies in the piece's aesthetics, quality, and condition.

Vernacular furniture is collected by form (e.g., Windsor chairs), type of wood used for construction (e.g., oak or pine), surface decoration (e.g., grain painted or stenciled), and material used for construction (e.g., bentwood or wicker). Many individual pieces cross over into more than one category (e.g., a painted pine blanket chest).

Regional furniture, such as Pennsylvania German and Shaker, belong in this section. However, collectors and dealers have given regional furniture types special weight. As a result, they have been placed in a separate section in this book. The one exception is a stripped piece of painted furniture. In many cases, once the paint has been removed, the regional feature is lost. As a result, these stripped pieces have been placed in this section.

Almost all collector and dealer interest has focused on vernacular furniture made of wood, whether natural grain or painted. The listings in this section reflect that collecting preference. While this works well for pieces from the nineteenth and early twentieth centuries, it does not work well for some forms from the twentieth century, notably upholstered and metal furniture forms from the 1920s through the present. As a way of including this furniture, which is just beginning to become collectible, the category "Department Store Modern" has been created. The listing concentrates on pieces sold by the larger city department store, e.g., Macy's, Marshall Field, or Wanamakers. The present listing does not include material from the large discount chains, e.g., K–Mart. In time even this material will be collectible. The frightening thing is that this is going to happen in the short, rather than long–term future.

WINDSOR

History: The Windsor form originated in or near London in the early part of the eighteenth century. Pieces were designed for use on porches and in garden settings. The furniture's comfortable nature led to its indoor use as well. It was quickly adopted by English rural craftsmen and worked its way to America by the 1730s. Windsor's American golden age dates from the 1750s through the 1840s.

Windsor furniture relies on a variety of woods to accomplish specialized tasks. The hardness of oak was used for arms and crests. Maple was favored for legs. Supple birch and hickory became spindles and rails. Seats are found in ash, pine, and tulip. During the eighteenth century, Windsor chairs with design period elements were made in walnut.

Because of the wide variety of woods, most Windsor chairs began life painted. A dark blue–green paint was the favored eighteenth and nineteenth century color, albeit examples can be found painted in red, white, and yellow. Mid–nineteenth century Windsors are grain painted or assembled in such a fashion as to allow the natural grains to carry the piece.

The Windsor chair was one of the first mass–produced American furniture pieces. Craftsmen specialized, buying the parts that they did not make. Production moved into the factory environment by the second quarter of the nineteenth century. In the mid–twentieth century, and again in the 1970s and 1980s, revival craftspersons renewed the handmade Windsor tradition.

The traditional Windsor forms from the eighteenth century were adapted and modified throughout the nineteenth and twentieth century. The pressed back chair from the turn of the century is a Windsor derivative as is the bow back, three to six spindled, plank seat, splayed leg chair of the late nineteenth century.

When looking at a Windsor that appears to be early, check the legs. Eighteenth century Windsors had legs with strong baluster turnings. Bamboo legs and stiles were popular during the first third of the nineteenth century. By mid–century, concentric rings were the fashion. Plain legs are a hallmark of twentieth century mass–production pieces.

Windsor furniture is identified by form. In the area of chairs, scholars have developed a vocabulary that distinguishes key form variations: bow–back, continuous–arm, comb–back, fan–back, low–back, rod–back, sack–back, and writing arm. In addition to chairs, Windsor forms include baby tenders, baby walkers, candlestands, cradles, cribs, daybeds, highchairs, settees, stools, and tables.

Building on a tradition of scholarship dating back to Wallace Nuttings's *A Windsor Handbook* (1917) and Thomas H. Ormsbee's *The Windsor Chair* (1962), Charles Santore had done yeoman work in recording regional Windsor characteristics and identifying the principal Windsor manufacturers. The tragedy is that his work ends in 1840. The field badly needs a volume devoted to the Windsor form from 1840 to the present.

References: Bernard D. Cotton, *The English Regional Chair*, Antique Collectors' Club, 1990; Charles Santore, *The Windsor Style In America, 1730–1830*, Running Press, 1981; Charles Santore, *The Windsor Style in America, Volume II*, Running Press, 1987.

Set of Six Side Chairs, bowback, old worn black repaint with yellow striping, splayed base with "H" stretcher and bulbous bamboo turnings, shaped seat and seven spindle backs with molded crest rails, seats measure 17¾" w, 30¼" h, $5,280.00. Photograph courtesy of Garth's Auctions, Inc., and *Antique Week*.

Bench
   Kneeling, 36¾" l, 6¾" d, 6" h, splayed base, reeded edge top, bamboo turned legs, gray over olive green and red paint **325**
Settee
   25" l, 10¼" h seat, 24" h overall, New England, early 19th C, rod back, nine bamboo turned spindles, bamboo turned posts, arms, and arm supports, shaped incised seat, splayed base with bamboo turned legs joined by H–form stretcher with central tablet, refinished, repairs **3,500**

73½" l, flat crest, twenty–six arrow shaped spindles, splayed base, bamboo turned legs, double arrow shaped front stretchers, red and black striping, red, green, and black floral decoration, mustard ground **2,950**

78" l, rod back, flat crest, down curving scrolled arms, rod arm supports, shaped seat, splayed base with bamboo turned legs joined by stretchers, old refinish, repaired arms, plugged holes in seat front edge **1,150**

79½" l, low back, rounded crest rail curves around to sides, shaped knuckle arms, tapered spindle back, canted baluster turned arm supports, shaped seat, splayed base, turned legs and stretchers, tapered feet, refinished, repaired split in seat, iron reinforcement rods added, mismatched leg and arm support turnings **2,600**

Chair
  Bow Back
    16" h seat, arm, turned spindles, turned arm supports, oval shaped

Comb back armchair, shaped crest rail, carved ears, bulbous turnings, H-form stretcher, $750.00.

seat, splayed base, bulbous turnings, H–form stretcher, old worn black and green paint **2,100**

16½" h seat, arm, turned arm supports, wide flat arms, saddle seat, splayed base, bulbous turnings and H–form stretcher, old refinishing, repairs to seat **575**

16¾" h seat, 36¾" h overall, arm, hooped crest and U–shaped arm rail joined by seven rods, shaped arms, canted baluster turned arm posts, oval dished seat, splayed base, bamboo turned legs joined by bulbous turned H–form stretcher, old refinish, repaired breaks in seat and crest rail, mismatched arm posts and legs ... **225**

17" h seat, 36" h overall, reeded bowed crest, six bamboo turned spindles, shaped saddle seat, splayed base, bamboo turned legs joined by bulbous turned H–form stretcher, old dark refinishing, repaired split in seat **300**

17⅜" h seat, 37¼" h overall, Connecticut, c1800, side, beaded edge on hooped back with carved ears midway up back, seven turned tapered spindles, shaped saddle seat, splayed base with baluster turned legs joined by bulbous turned H–form stretcher, tapered feet, old black paint **2,475**

17¾" h seat, arm, hard and softwood, cherry arms, bamboo turnings, worn green paint **1,300**

18½" h seat, side, seven spindle back, bamboo turning, saddle seat, H–form stretcher, red repaint **350**

New England, 1805–15, pair, side, maple and pine, back supported by seven turned spindles, horseshoe shaped seat, bamboo turned legs joined by bamboo turned H–form stretcher, painted red over black, price for pair .. **495**

Rhode Island, late 18th C, bowed molded crest rail, seven baluster turned spindles, shaped outstretched arms raised on ring and baluster turned arm supports, horseshoe shaped seat, splayed base, ring and baluster turned legs joined by bulbous turned H–form stretcher, tapered feet, painted black with gilt decoration **1,325**

Brace Back
  34" h, Rhode Island, 1780–1805,

set of five, side, maple and pine, molded hoop back, seven spindles, supporting brace behind, incised edge on saddle seat, ring and baluster turned tapering legs, H–form stretcher, gold striping on black, price for set **23,100**

New York, New York City, Walter MacBride, 1785–1810, arm, maple and pine, molded bow over nine turned spindles, supporting brace behind, shaped arms, double ring and baluster turned uprights, incised edge on saddle seat, ring and baluster turned tapering legs, H–form stretcher, painted black over bottle green, gold striping, underside of seat branded "W–Macbride, N–York" **6,650**

Child's

13½" h seat, 29½" h overall, side, flat crest, rabbit ear posts, three arrow shaped spindles, shaped plank seat, bamboo turned splayed legs, stretchers, black and red striping, red–brown flame graining on crest and seat, yellow ground **175**

14¾" h seat, 29" h overall, pair, side, flat crest, rabbit ear posts, three bamboo turned spindles, shaped seat, bamboo turned legs and stretchers, splayed base, black and green striping, green stenciled floral decoration on crest, yellow ground, repainted over cream colored paint, price for pair **750**

15" h seat, 29" h overall, side, flat crest, rabbit ear posts, four turned spindles, shaped seat, bamboo turned splayed legs and stretchers, yellow–green ground, black striping, stenciled and freehand fruit and foliage decoration on crest, damage and repair ... **65**

Continuous Arm

18¼" h seat, 37¾" h overall, beaded edge on bowed back, shaped arms, nine tapered spindles, canted baluster turned arm posts, shaped saddle seat, splayed base, bulbous turned legs joined by similarly turned H–form stretcher, high tapered feet **3,500**

18½" h seat, 39½" h overall, bowed back, seven turned tapered spindles, shaped arms, turned tapered arm supports, canted baluster turned arm posts,

shaped saddle seat, splayed base, baluster turned legs joined by bulbous turned H–form stretcher, high tapered feet, old red repaint, arms replaced, one back spindle broken, minor age cracks in seat **850**

New York or Connecticut, late 18th C, maple and cherry, braced back, bowed molded crest rail, flaring arms, turned spindles, horseshoe shaped seat, splayed base, ring and baluster turned legs ending in tapered feet, bulbous turned H–form stretcher .. **1,200**

Doll Size, sack back, arm, bentwood crest, three ring and baluster turned spindles, U–shaped bentwood down curving arm rail, canted baluster turned arm supports, shaped seat, turned legs joined by box stretcher, worn dark paint with yellow striping, breaks in arm rail ... **350**

Fan Back

15¾" h seat, side, shaped crest, turned posts saddle seat, splayed base, bulbous turnings, H–form stretcher, refinished, well executed repairs **350**

17" h seat, 35¾" h overall, New England, 1780–1800, side, serpentine crest rail, seven turned spindles flanked by baluster turned stiles, saddle seat, splayed base with ring and baluster turned legs joined by bulbous turned H–form stretcher, painted black **325**

17¼" h seat, 37½" h overall, side, braced back, curved yoke crest, seven spindles, baluster turned posts, shaped saddle seat, splayed base, baluster turned legs joined by bulbous turned H–form stretcher, high tapered feet, later decoration, old black paint with gold leaf stenciled decoration **925**

17½" h seat, 42½" h overall, arm, curved yoke crest with carved ears, nine turned tapered spindles, U–shaped arm rail ending in shaped handholds, turned tapered arm supports, canted baluster turned arm posts, wide shaped saddle seat, splayed base with baluster turned legs ending in ball feet, bulbous turned H–form stretcher, repaired **850**

17½" h seat, 43½" h overall, arm, curved yoke crest with carved ears, seven tapered spindles, U–

shaped arm rail ending in scrolled knuckle handholds, baluster turned arm posts, oval shaped seat, splayed base, similarly turned legs joined by bulbous turned H–form stretcher, old mellow refinish, crisp carvings, underside of seat has traces of old paint and is stamped "P.S. Byrn 1708," repair to one knuckle arm **5,700**

18" h seat, 35" h overall, New England, 1830s, pair, side, straight crest, rabbit ear posts, four bamboo turned spindles, shaped plank seat, splayed base, bamboo turned legs and stretchers, green stenciling, striping, and freehand decoration on yellow ground, black accents, price for pair **715**

18" h seat, 35½" h overall, New Hampshire, side, scalloped crest, five spindles, bamboo turned posts, legs, and stretchers, shaped seat, red and black paint graining, yellow striping, gold stenciled eagle and flowers on crest, chalk initials and ink presentation inscription on seat underside **900**

18¼" h seat, 35½" h overall, side, shaped crest with carved ears, seven turned tapered spindles, baluster turned posts, shaped saddle seat, splayed base with baluster turned legs joined by bulbous turned H–form stretcher, refinished, one ear restored, possible replaced leg **300**

New England, late 18th C, pair, side, maple and pine, serpentine bowed crest with carved ears, seven turned spindles flanked by ring and baluster turned stiles, horseshoe shaped plank seat, splayed base, ring and baluster turned legs joined by H–form stretcher, price for pair **2,200**

Rhode Island, late 18th C, side, maple, pine, and ash, serpentine shaped crest rail, seven spindle back flanked by double baluster turned T–stiles, saddle seat, ring and baluster turned legs joined by ring and bulbous turned H–form stretcher **1,650**

Rod Back, 16¾" h seat, 23½" h overall, New Hampshire, early 19th C, pair, side, double rail crest joined by three short rods, seven bamboo turned spindles flanked by flaring

bamboo turned stiles, horseshoe shaped plank seat, splayed base with bamboo turned legs and box stretchers, painted black, price for pair **525**

Sack Back

16¼" h seat, 39¾" h overall, New Hampshire, 1790s, arm, hooped crest rail, six spindles joined by U–shaped arm rail, canted baluster turned arm supports, saddle seat, splayed base, ring and baluster turned legs joined by bulbous turned H–form stretcher, inscribed "Ebn Cressy Bradford, NH 1796," repainted **1,100**

17½" h seat, 37¼" h overall, arm, hooped crest, seven spindles, U–shaped arm rail ending in knuckle handholds, canted baluster turned arm supports, shaped seat, splayed base, baluster turned legs, bulbous turned H–form stretcher, black repaint, old red paint on underside of seat, age crack in seat, minor damage to knuckle arms **700**

Pennsylvania, c1780, arm, arched crest rail, spindle back, horizontal rail forms scrolled arms, canted baluster form supports, oval saddle seat, splayed base with baluster turned legs, H–form stretcher, painted dark green **1,430**

Spindle back side chair, bamboo turnings, shaped plank seat, refinished, $150.00.

Pennsylvania, late 18th C, arm, arched crest rail, seven tapering spindles joined by a U–shaped arm rail ending in knuckle handholds on ring and baluster turned uprights, saddle seat, splayed base with ring and baluster turned legs joined by ring and bulbous turned H–form stretcher, blunt arrow feet, two small repairs to crest rail, traces of old white paint over green **3,000**

Spindle Back

16" h seat, 33¾" h overall, pair, side, straight crest rail, four bamboo turned spindles, rabbit ear posts, shaped saddle seat, splayed base with bamboo turned legs joined by box stretchers, old refinishing, price for pair **150**

16¼" h seat, 35" h overall, side, step down crest rail, six bamboo turned spindles, bamboo turned posts, shaped plank seat, splayed base with bamboo turned legs joined by box stretchers, green repaint, one end of crest loose from post **325**

17" h seat, 34" h overall, side, slightly arched round crest rail, splayed back with bamboo turned posts and eight bamboo turned turned spindles, shaped seat, splayed base with bamboo turned legs joined by similarly turned box stretchers, old worn refinish **90**

17" h seat, 35½" h overall, assembled set of nine, side, curving stepped crest rail, seven turned tapered spindles, shaped saddle seat, splayed base, bamboo turned legs joined by box stretchers, old refinish, one has repaired split in seat, one has age crack in crest, price for set **2,250**

17½" h seat, 34½" h overall, pair, arm, double rail crest joined by central octagonal tablet flanked by rods, seven bamboo turned spindles, down curving shaped arms, shaped seat, splayed base, bamboo turned legs joined by similarly turned box stretchers, originally painted, refinished, price for pair **1,000**

Writing Arm

Comb Back, Pennsylvania, 19th C, maple, pine, and ash, serpentine shaped crest ending in scroll carved ears, nine spindles joined by U–shaped arm rail, shaped writing surface fitted with a sliding drawer, shaped plank seat, shaped apron, splayed base with ring and baluster turned legs ending in arrow feet, ring and bulbous turned H–form stretcher .. **1,500**

Fan Back, curved yoke crest with carved ears, seven turned tapered spindles, U–shaped arm rail with knuckle handhold one side, shaped writing surface other side, scrolled fronts on drawers under writing surface and seat, turned tapered arm supports, canted bulbous turned arm posts, shaped saddle seat, splayed base, bulbous turned legs joined by similarly turned H–form stretcher, high tapered feet, possibly a Nutting chair, old mellow refinishing **1,600**

Youth, 16¾" h seat, 31¼" h overall, sack back, bowed crest rail and U–shaped arm rail joined by six tapered spindles, canted baluster turned front posts, laminated saddle seat, splayed base with baluster turned legs joined by bulbous turned box stretchers, old dark finish, one broken spindle, some glued repairs **75**

Cradle

36" l, hardwood, hooped bentwood ends with three turned spindles, upper and lower flat rails on sides joined by ten short rods, pinned mortise construction, old green paint, nailed reinforcement to joints, some spindles are old replacements **250**

New England, 1800–20, bamboo turned spindles, worn finish **800**

Daybed, 84" w, 26" d, 19½" h seat, 36½" h overall, New England, 1820–30, triple seat back, three rails over eighteen half spindles, turned arms, baluster turned arm posts, upholstered seat cushion, foldout hinged sleeping area supported by four wooden pinned legs, 49½ x 80⅝" open size, original yellow paint with gold and black stenciled fruit and leaf decoration, seat replaced **1,750**

Footstool

13½" w, 8" d, 7" h, pine, oval top, turned splayed legs, underside of top branded "A.W.. Pratt.," old black paint with striping on legs, worn red overpaint on top, worn top **225**

14" w, 10" d, 7" h, oval upholstered top, splayed base with turned legs ending in tapered feet, bulbous turned H–form stretcher, old worn brown paint, reupholstered brown leather top **175**

Hat Rack, 33¾″ l, pine, bamboo turned, six knob like hooks, original yellow varnish, black striping **150**

High Chair

Comb Back, York, Pennsylvania, c1790, arched crest, volute carved terminals, six tapered spindles and shaped arms, elliptical seat, turned legs and stretchers, original worn red and black paint, yellow highlights **40,000**

Rod Back, early 19th C, straight crest rail, spindle back, open arm, saddle seat, splayed base with ring turned legs conjoined by stretcher, footrest replaced **225**

Spindle Back

20¾″ h seat, 31″ h overall, New England, 1810–20, slightly arched crest rail, three turned tapered spindles, shaped saddle seat, splayed base, bamboo turned legs, shaped footrest, box stretchers, old yellow paint, some paint loss **350**

23¾″ h, shaped crest rail, three turned tapered spindles, turned tapered arms and front posts, shaped seat, splayed base, shaped footrest, double tapered turned legs joined by box stretchers, decorated, worn original red and black grain painting with green striping and traces of floral design on crest, replaced footrest supports **225**

24″ h seat, 36½″ h overall, Pennsylvania or Ohio, flat crest, bamboo turned spindles, shaped plank seat with rolled rail, splayed base, shaped footrest, bamboo turned legs, original yellow paint with olive green stencil decoration and black striping .. **925**

Rocker

Bow Back, 34″ h, hooped crest rail, seven tapered rods, U–shaped arm rail with knuckle hand holds, baluster turned arm posts, oval dished seat, splayed base, baluster turned legs joined by similarly turned H–form stretcher, cheese cutter rockers, repaired split in seat, arms ended out, rockers are later addition **150**

Child's, 26¼″ h, curving arrow form crest rail, seven tapered spindles, dished oval seat, splayed base,

Side Chair, fan–back, New England, late 18th C, old black paint, gold leaf stenciled dec, paint and dec of later origin, 37½″ h, seat height 17¼″, $2,250.00. Photograph courtesy of Skinner, Inc.

bamboo turned legs joined by similarly turned H–form stretcher, old dark finish, rockers worn flat **200**

Comb Back, arrow form spindles, black repaint, gold striping, painted holly crest **150**

Stool, 14″ l, 10″ w, 10¾″ h, oval, splayed base, old green repaint **225**

Table, 18″ w, 11½″ d, 28″ h, cherry, oval one board top with chamfered bottom edge, chamfered edges on tapered posts joined by single similar stretcher, curved shoe feet, old refinish **700**

LADDER OR SLAT–BACK CHAIRS

History: The origin of the ladderback chair rests in the late seventeenth century. They appear to be an evolution from the famed Brewster chairs of the 1640–60 period. Early examples are from the shop of a turner, not a joiner.

Seventeenth century ladderback chairs have flat, shaped tops, and horizontal splats, usually three or four in number. Arms on armchairs are sloped. Strong baluster turnings appear on stiles and front legs. Stretchers usually were plain.

The ladderback quickly worked its way into the vernacular furniture vocabulary. Cabinetmakers throughout New England, the Middle Atlantic states, Midwest, and Southern Piedmont made ladderback chairs. It became the preferred form of the Shaker community.

Like the Windsor and Hitchcock chairs, the ladderback lent itself well to mass–production. Early cabinetmakers made hundreds or thousands at a time. Early ladderbacks were often painted, albeit many have been stripped over the years. By the middle of the nineteenth century, however, emphasis was placed on the natural wood; chairs were stained, shellacked, or varnished.

The ladderback's popularity never waned. Visit a modern furniture store; you will find several dozen varieties from which to choose. The key is to determine the date when a particular ladderback was made.

The shape of the stile is often a key to dating; the stiles mirror the design preferences of the period. However, the large number of reproductions make dating by this method alone very uncertain. Wear is helpful. However, most ladderbacks are heavily used. A late nineteenth century reproduction can easily exhibit the same wear of an example made half a century or more earlier.

Because so many different individuals made ladderbacks, value rests in pleasing proportions, age, and unusual features. In respect to the latter, look for elaborately shaped top slats and distinctive finials. Collectors generally pay a premium for examples with maker's marks and with period seats.

Chair
  Arm
    41¼" h, hardwood, turned button on flattened ball finials on back posts, five graduated serpentine shaped arched slats, scrolled arms, baluster turned arm supports, rush seat, ring and bulbous turned front stretcher, padded ball feet, side stretchers, refinished, replaced seat **3,000**
    44¼" h, maple, turned button and ball finials on sausage turned back posts, four slightly arched slats, down curving scrolled arms, rush seat, turned vasiform arm posts continuing to sausage turned front posts, padded ball feet, bulbous turned upper front stretcher, tapering lower front stretcher, refinished, replaced seat, repairs to one front post at

seat frame, one arm may be old replacement **625**
44¼" h, turned acorn finials on back posts, four slightly arched slats, turned arms on turned tapered front posts, woven splint seat, box stretchers, round tapered feet, refinished, replaced seat, feet ended out, small nailed repair to one back post, old hole in one arm above post **75**
46½" h, maple, acorn turned finials on round back posts, five graduated serpentine shaped arched slats, shaped down curving arms, scrolled handholds, paper rush seat, turned arm posts, padded ball feet, bulbous turned front stretcher, side stretchers, old nut brown finish, replaced seat **4,250**
46½" h, turned button and egg shaped finials on sausage turned back posts, four arched slats, shaped down curving arms, scrolled handholds, rush seat, sausage turned front posts, turned flattened ball feet, two bulbous and ball turned front stretchers, side stretchers, old red paint with traces of green, worn seat, repair to one arm at post . **550**
46¾" h, turned urn form finials on sausage turned back posts, four arched slats, shaped arms with scrolled handholds, rush seat, sausage turned arm posts ending in ball feet, two bulbous turned front stretchers, box stretchers, natural refinish, feet ended out, replaced finials **275**
50" h, attributed to Wallace Nutting, ball finials on sausage turned back posts, five wide graduated shaped slats with bowed upper edge, scrolled arms, ring and sausage turned front posts, flattened ball feet, rush seat, ring and bulbous turned front stretchers, worn black paint, tattered seat **350**
Shaker, turned bulbous finials, three graduated slightly arched slats, shaped arms on tapered arm posts, splint seat, box stretchers, purchased at Sabbath Day Lake, Maine, 1938, replaced seat **400**
Child's
  23½" h, arm, ball finials on rounded stiles, three arched slats, splint seat, rounded legs joined by box stretchers, old red re-

paint, feet worn down to bottom stretcher, replace set damaged . **95**

25¼" h, rabbit ear posts, two arched slats, paper rush seat, round legs, tapered feet, box stretchers, old dark finish, worn replaced seat **45**

Set of Four

38¼" h, side, turned ball finials on back posts, three graduated slats with serpentine shaped upper edges, rush seat, box stretchers, tapered feet, old brown patina, price for set **725**

39½" h, side, maple and other hardwoods, elongated turned finials, three slightly arched slats, woven splint seat, box stretchers, old red paint, purchased from the Shakers of Sabbath Day Lake, Maine, price for set **1,000**

Side

36" h, flared rabbit ear posts, three graduated straight slats, woven splint seat, ring turned front legs, box stretchers, tapered feet **75**

37½" h, lady's, turned inverted teardrop shaped finials on back posts, three slightly arched slats, rush seat, box stretchers, old dark brown paint, replaced seat **45**

41¾" h, turned acorn finials on back posts, four graduated arched slats, paper rush seat, round front legs, bulbous turned front stretcher, flattened ball feet, side stretchers, old dark finish, replaced seat **275**

High Chair, 38¾" h, splayed posts, turned urn shaped finial on back posts, three stepped slats, rod arms, woven splint seat, box stretchers, tapered feet, old red repaint, repaired break in one back post **650**

Rocker

24" h, child's, turned mushroom finials on sausage turned back posts, three wide graduated arched slats, rod arms, mushroom arm caps on sausage turned arm posts, rush seat, box stretchers, cheese cutter runners, old worn yellow and white repaint shows earlier blue beneath **325**

27¼" h, child's, turned acorn finials, three narrow stepped slats, rod arms, turned arm posts, blue and white tape seat, box stretchers, cheese cutter runners, old dark alligatored varnish, replaced seat . . **225**

38½" h, turned urn form finials on back posts, four slightly arched slats, turned arms, ball finials on

Rocker, turned finials, shawl rail, two arched slats, rush seat, shaped runners, $375.00.

turned vasiform arm posts, woven splint seat, box stretchers, shaped rockers, refinished, runners are later addition, damaged seat **175**

39" h, turned elongated acorn finials on back posts, four serpentine shaped arched slats, paper rush seat, ring and bulbous turned front stretchers, box stretchers, cheese cutter runners, old green repaint over earlier red, replaced seat **175**

41" h, late 18th C, pine, turned ball finials, four slightly arched slats, ring turned back posts, shaped half arms on tapered arm posts, rush seat, ring turned front legs and stretchers, box stretchers, shaped runners **300**

41¾" h, Shaker #6, arm, turned finials, four arched slats, mushroom arm caps, vasiform front posts, paper rush seat, box stretchers, cheese cutter runners, faint remains of "Mt. Lebanon, N.Y." label, light natural refinish, replaced seat **750**

42" h, Shaker #7, arm, shawl bar crest rail, four arched slats, mushroom arm caps, vasiform front posts, rush seat, box stretchers, cheese cutter runners, light natural refinish **400**

42¾" h, curly maple, ball finials on back posts, four slightly arched slats, down curving scrolled arms, woven splint seat, ring turned arm posts, flat rectangular upper front stretcher, box stretchers, shaped cheese cutter runners, old refinish, damaged seat, runners are old replacements or additions **200**

46¾" h, hardwood, turned onion shaped finial, five graduated serpentine shaped arched slats, shaped arms, bulbous turned arm supports, woven splint seat, scalloped curly maple apron on seat front, box stretchers, refinished, replaced seat **425**

47" h, Belmont County, Ohio, arm, turned acorn finials on ring and sausage turned back posts, four wide step down slats, scrolled arms with chip carved handholds, woven splint seat, bulbous and ring turned chip carved front posts, similarly turned upper front stretcher, lower front and side rod stretchers, shaped runners, worn black repaint over original blue, replaced seat painted to match chair, worn bottom stretcher and front of rockers . **2,700**

Wagon Seat, 33½" w, 32¼" h, double chair back, two slightly arched slats each seat, flattened center stile, woven splint seats, turned arm posts, box stretchers, old dark brown refinishing, replaced seat **550**

OAK

History: Oak was a popular furniture wood in England. It was heavily used in period furniture during the Jacobean period (seventeenth century) and was the wood of choice for English vernacular furniture throughout the eighteenth, nineteenth, and early twentieth centuries.

Oak also is an important secondary wood in furniture construction. Because of grain variations, it is possible to distinguish a piece of English oak from a piece of American oak. This difference, which can be detected under a microscope, is helpful in determining the origin of period pieces from the eighteenth and early nineteenth centuries.

Although it is possible to find early American pieces made of oak, this wood achieved a level of mass popularity in the 1870s—a trend that lasted into the 1920s. This is the period of the famed "golden oak," pieces finished to a rich golden tone. At the turn of the century, oak also gained favor as the wood of choice among craftsmen and manufacturers of Mission furniture.

Hardness, durability, and strength are among the characteristics of oak that appealed to furniture manufacturers. In addition, oak is very slow to rot. An oak piece placed in an environment subject to temperature and/or humidity extremes would survive well.

Virtually all furniture forms can be found in oak. Vernacular pieces focus on the kitchen (the round oak expansion table with thick standard and trifid paw feet), the bedroom (oak beds, chiffoniers, dressers, and washstands), and the living room (oak side by side desk and china cabinet). All forms were made in a number of quality levels. It is critical that one learns what constitutes a quality piece.

Oak veneer, rather than solid oak, was used on less expensive pieces. Check pieces carefully to determine if a veneer was used. Pieces of solid oak are much more desirable.

Four woods—ash, chestnut, elm, and hickory—have grains that are very similar to oak. Ash, with its gray to creamy tone, was a less expensive alternative to walnut in many Victorian furniture suites. Chestnut, with a grayish brown tone, lacks the large rays found in oak. Elm has a light brown tone and is the veneer found on many Victorian "oak" iceboxes. Hickory is identified by its tan tone.

Also be alert for oak grain painting. If in doubt, check the grain on both sides of a board. It should be identical. Look around hardware to check for painting wear.

Major Manufacturers: Baker Furniture Factories, Allegan MI; Berkey & Gay, Grand Rapids, MI; Empire Furniture Co., Rockford, IL; Grand Rapids Bookcase & Chair Co., Grand Rapids, MI; Grand Rapids Chair Co., Grand Rapids, MI; Grand Rapids Furniture Co., Grand Rapids, MI; William A. French Furniture Co., Minneapolis, MN; Knetchel Furniture Co., Hanover, Ontario, Canada; Chas. P. Limbert Co., Holland, MI; Ottawa Furniture Co., Holland, MI; Phoenix Furniture Co., Grand Rapids, MI; Saginaw Furniture Shops, Saginaw, MI; Henry C. Steul & Sons, Buffalo, NY; and Steinman & Meyer Furniture Co., Cincinnati, OH.

References: Conover Hill, *Antique Oak Furniture: An Illustrated Value Guide, Values Updated,* Collector Books, 1987; Robert and Harriett Swedberg, *American Oak Furniture, Styles and Prices, Book I, Third Edition* (1992); *Book II, Second Edition* (1991); *Book III, Second Edition* (1991), Wallace–Homestead; Robert and Harriett Swedberg, *Collector's Encyclopedia of American Furniture, Volume 2: Furniture of the Twentieth Century,* Collector Books, 1992.

Bed

76" l, 40" w, applied feather and fan decorations on shaped top of paneled headboard, flat rectangular

Armoire, curved pediment, pediment frieze featuring layered circles, two cupboard doors each with dome top and divided into two sections, bottom full-width drawer with wood leaf handles, shaped bottom apron on front and sides, $825.00. Photograph courtesy of Pettigrew Auction Company.

top on paneled footboard, square legs **300**

79" l, 59" w, 60" h, applied feather, C–scroll, and S–scroll decoration on paneled headboard with square stiles, paneled footboard, square legs **325**

Bench

Hall, 39" w, 17" d, 38" h, c1900, Mission style, straight crestrail and lower rail with exposed mortise and tenon construction, five flat arrow form spindles, square stiles with arched tops, shaped arms, flat arrow form arm supports, hinged lift lid seat, straight apron, square legs, 24" h, 36" w matching hanging wall mirror with arched crest, double hat hooks on each corner, exposed mortise and tenon construction, and beveled mirror plate **800**

Piano, 39" w, 19" d, 21" h, rounded corners on overhanging rectangular seat, straight aprons, square tapering legs, flared feet **125**

Settee

39" w, 17" d, 36" h, Windsor style, straight crest rail on splayed turned stiles, twenty–one slender turned tapered spindles, downswept scrolled arms, turned tapered arm supports, shaped seat, splayed base, ring and baluster turned legs conjoined by double H–form stretcher **450**

46" w, 18" d, 35" h, Mission style, double seat back with quarter sawn veneered straight crest rails, eight vertical slats, shaped armrests, shaped plank seat, square tapering legs conjoined by box stretchers .. **475**

Bookcase

34" w, 12" d, 47" h, quarter sawn, stacking, five sections, slightly projecting cornice, three graduated bookcases with retractable pull up glass doors, faux drawer in base, brass pulls, "Manufactured by the

Bookcase, molded cornice, two glazed doors, four adjustable shelves, two short drawers with brass bail handles, scrolled feet, golden oak finish, 41" w, 13" d, 60" h, $600.00.

Globe–Wernicke Co., Cincinnati, O'' paper label 525
34" w, 12" d, 66" h, quarter sawn, stacking, six sections, applied leafy decoration on shaped gallery, slightly projecting cornice, four graduated bookcases with retractable pull up glass doors, leaded glass in upper door, shaped base, "Gunn Sectional Bookcase, pat., Dec. 5, 1899; June 1, 1901, Grand Rapids" label 750
48" w, 13" d, 51" h, rectangular top, two glass doors, divided shelved interior, cabriole legs with center leg 750
90" w, 97" h, Victorian, c1870, three part, globe form finial over flat molded cornice fitted with four keystones, three arched glazed doors, three wide drawers, molded base . 2,600

Bookcase Desk
38" w, 14" d, 65" h, asymmetrical, shaped crest, full length bookcase with glass door, shelved interior, square beveled mirror, paneled fall front writing surface, three overlapping short drawers, shaped apron, bracket feet, bail handle drawer pulls 475
42" w, 14" d, 67" h, Larkin Company, bombe shaped cornice supported by beveled mirrored back panel and front columns surmounted by scrolled capitals, shape of top shelf conforms to bowed bookcase with convex glass door panel, recessed beveled mirror over fall front writing surface, three graduated short drawers with turned wood pulls, columns mounted on outset corners on scroll feet 1,500
46" w, 14" d, 73" h, left handed style, incised and applied decorations, central beveled swing mirror flanked by ornately shaped and scrolled mirror supports fronted by demilune etagere shelves on baluster turned pillars, cut corners on oblong top, single drawer over fall front writing surface, pair of paneled cupboard doors beside bookcase with glass door panel and shelved interior, reeded chamfered stiles, shaped apron continuing to French feet 1,000

Cabinet
China
40" w, 12" d, 63" h, quarter sawn veneer, rectangular cornice, two full length glass doors, interior shelves, molded base, cabriole legs on casters 500

40" w, 13" d, 60" h, slightly overhanging rectangular top, pair of glass doors with leaded glass panels at top, scroll feet 775
42" w, 15" d, 64" h, bow front, quarter sawn, applied decorations, demilune top, applied acanthus leaf decorations to half columns flanking central bowed full length glass door, interior mirror panel above four conforming shelves, molded base, paw feet 850
44" w, 14" d, 51" h, 1920s, quarter sawn, slightly overhanging oblong top, pair of glass doors, scroll pillars and feet 450
52" w, 14" d, 55" h, bow front, convex glass in side panels, straight glass full length door with muntins, square legs 750

Curio, 18" w, 5½" d, 38¼" h, hanging, flat molded cornice, single glazed cabinet door, six shelf interior, shaped apron 145

Filing
13" w, 16" d, 9" h, table top, dovetailed case, four drawers hold index cards, brass label holder pulls 150
20" w, 25" d, 53" h, locking, four drawers with brass handles and label frames, paneled ends 350

Kitchen
40" w, 25" d, 71" h, Ingram Richardson Manufacturing Company, Frankfort, Indiana, 1930s, Hoosier style, white factory finish, two sections: upper section: shaped crest, floral decoration on three paneled cupboard doors, lower paneled cupboard door beside pull down tambour door; lower section: porcelain pullout work surface, large paneled cupboard door beside bank of three graduated overlapping short drawers, paneled ends, square feet, casters 350
41" w, 27" d, 70" h, Sellers, Elwood, Indiana, Hoosier style, two sections: upper section: full length paneled door enclosing flour sifter, pair of double paneled cupboard doors over pull down tambour door, "Sellers The Better Kitchen Cabinet Kitchen Maid, Elwood, Ind., U.S.A. Trademark registered" metal label; lower section: porcelain pullout work surface, overlapping drawer over paneled

cupboard door beside bank of three graduated overlapping short drawers, paneled ends, square legs **750**

42" w, 24" d, 77" h, two sections: upper section: shaped crest on rectangular molded top, pair of glass doors enclosing interior shelves over central possum bellied flour drawer flanked by four spice drawers, shaped sides; lower section: overhanging rectangular work surface, paneled cupboard door, single overlapping short drawer, pull down paneled potato bin, paneled ends, square feet **1,200**

42" w, 25" d, 71" h, Hoosier, New Castle, Indiana, two sections: upper section: three paneled doors over pair of horizontally sliding tambour doors, oval zinc label at top reads "The Hoosier Saves Steps"; lower section: porcelain pullout work surface, large paneled cupboard door, pair of graduated overlapping short drawers, zinc lined lower drawer, square legs **650**

Medicine, 17" w, 6" d, 28" h, incised lines on straight crest, shaped ends, glass door, shelved interior, incised lines on lower rail **125**

Music, 18" w, 16" d, 34" h, rounded corners on rectangular top, single door with scalloped lower edge, cabriole legs **175**

Chair

Arm

22" w, 35" h, pair, bentwood, double hooped back, down curving hooped arms, round cane seat, round tapering cabriole legs with bentwood stretcher, price for pair **150**

25½" w, 42" h, carved floral design on double concave crest rail, ball finials on ring and baluster turned stiles, five tapered ring and baluster turned spindles, shaped arms with pressed lion's head decoration, ring and baluster turned arm supports, shaped seat with bowed front, ring and baluster turned legs ending in tapered feet, similarly turned H-form stretcher **375**

Desk

26" h, child's, curved crest rail, two curved slats, rounded corners on seat, straight apron, square tapered legs with rounded front corners, H-form stretchers **45**

Desk, lady's, slant front, quarter sawn, beveled mirror, applied molding on hinged lid, fitted interior, two swell fronted long drawers, shaped apron, 28" w, 13" d, 50" h, $300.00.

36" h, 21" w, swivel, quarter sawn, curved crest rail, seven square spindles, square stiles, shaped arms on square S-curved arm supports, shaped saddle seat, swivel pedestal on four down curving legs with casters **95**

42" h, 22" w, swivel, shaped crest with pressed foliage and beading design, baluster turned stiles, nine baluster turned spindles, pressed beaded lines on lower rail, shaped scrolling arms on baluster turned arm supports, caned trapezoidal seat, straight apron, swivel pedestal on four down curving legs ending in scroll feet on casters **250**

Set of Four

37" h, side, T-back, upholstered trapezoidal slip seat, square tapered legs, H-form stretcher, price for set **200**

41" h, side, pressed scrolled feather design on shaped crest, button finials on turned stiles, five tapered ring and baluster turned spindles, similar pressed design on shaped lower rail, hip brackets, pressed cane seat, turned legs, turned box stretchers, price for set **525**

Side, 41" h, arched crest rail with pressed compote and fruit decoration, urn form finials on out curved stiles, five curved split arrow spindles, hip brackets, caned trapezoidal seat, turned front legs joined by turned box stretcher **125**

Chifforobe, quarter sawn veneer, rectangular swing mirror with beveled mirror plate on scrolled supports, fall front writing surface, three graduated drawers beside full length closet with paneled door and pullout garment bar, paneled ends, cabriole legs on casters **525**

Chiffonier
28" w, 17" d, 55" h, applied feather decoration on crest of rectangular swing mirror supported by lyre shaped frame, slightly overhanging oblong top, five dovetailed long drawers, paneled ends, square legs **325**

36" w, 19" d, 55" h, shaped crest, slightly overhanging rectangular top, projecting section of two short drawers and paneled hatbox door over four recessed long drawers, dovetailed drawers, incised lines on stiles, paneled ends, shaped apron, brass pulls and escutcheons **385**

Couch, 55" w, 31" d, 34" h, c1890, applied foliate decoration to shaped crest rail, upholstered scrolled arms fold down, overstuffed seat, straight seat rail, carved paw feet **500**

Cupboard
Corner, 45" w, 20" d, 97" h, molded cornice, pair of glass doors, shelved interior, chamfered stiles, pair of recessed paneled cupboard doors, shaped apron **925**

Step Back, 40" w, 19" d, 84" h, two sections: upper section: molded cornice, pair of glass doors, shelved interior, incised lines on stiles, random board back; slightly overhanging rectangular top, two of short drawers over single long drawer over pair of paneled cupboard doors, incised lines on stiles and feet, shaped brackets **700**

Straight Front, 37" w, 16" d, 73" h, molded cornice, pair of glass doors with scalloped top over two short drawers, pair of paneled cupboard doors below, paneled ends, bracket feet **575**

Desk
Child's
Fall Front, 22" w, 11" d, 33" h, arched crest, rectangular top, applied leafy decoration on fall front writing surface, single long drawer with turned wood pulls, recessed base shelf, shaped bootjack ends with cutout tulip decoration **200**

Rolltop, 26" w, 16" d, 37" h, rectangular top, C–curve tambour sliding door, slightly overhanging rectangular writing surface, single long drawer, square legs, stretchers at sides and back, turned wood pulls **225**

Parlor
25" w, 12" d, 42" h, applied decorations, shaped crest, molded edge on rectangular top, applied feather decoration on face of fall front writing surface, single long drawer with turned wood pulls, shaped ends, applied scalloped decoration on shaped apron, recessed base shelf **325**

26" w, 14" d, 48" h, some quarter sawn, shaped crest on edge molded rectangular top, applied C–scroll and gadrooned decorations on face of quarter sawn veneered fall front writing surface, single swelled long drawer with embossed bail handle pulls, cabriole legs, shaped base shelf ... **350**

26" w, 17" d, 38" h, quarter sawn veneer, brass gallery on slightly overhanging edge, molded rectangular top, applied C–scroll decorations on fall front writing surface, single long drawer with brass ring drop pulls, shaped apron, cabriole legs **525**

Rolltop
36" w, 28" d, 44" h, rectangular top, C–curve tambour sliding door, fitted interior, single drawer over bracketed kneehole beside bank of four short drawers surmounted by pullout writing board, paneled ends **750**

50" w, 34" d, 46" h, quarter sawn, rectangular top, S–curve tambour sliding door enclosing fitted interior of central prospect door flanked by small drawers, shelves, and file slots, rectangular overhanging writing surface, center drawer and kneehole flanked by banks of short drawers

surmounted by pullout writing
boards, paneled ends 2,500
55" w, 34" d, 53" h, S–curve tambour sliding door, fitted interior
with twenty–four pigeonholes
and two small drawers, overhanging rectangular writing surface, shaped apron, kneehole
flanked by tambour sliding door,
pullout shelf with cutout handle,
single drawer on left, pullout
writing board over bank of three
drawers over a double fronted
file drawer, inverted fan style
wood drawer handles 2,500
65" w, 36" d, 50" h, quarter sawn,
rectangular top, S–curve tambour sliding door, fitted interior
with small drawers and pigeonholes, molded edge on writing
surface, central kneehole flanked
by banks of four graduated short
drawers with wood inverted fan
pulls, paneled ends 6,500
Divan, 38" w, 23" d, 34" h, incised
carved foliate decoration on shaped
crest rail, fluted stiles continue to
flared rear legs, incised carved design
on two shaped splats frame tufted upholstered back panel, shaped arms,
upholstered seat, straight seat rail, S–
curved arm supports continuing to
cabriole front legs 475

Dresser
23" w, 9" d, 37" h, miniature, Victorian, c1890, swan's neck pediment
on carved swing mirror over three
drawers, leaf carved column sides,
scroll feet, brass bail handles 300
40" w, 20" d, 84" h, very ornate applied scroll, feather, swag, and
wheat sheaf decorations on swing
mirror and frame, shaped crest over
beveled mirror panel, scroll shaped
mirror supports, overhanging serpentine front oblong top over conforming case, two short over two
long drawers with embossed brass
pulls with bail handles, paneled
ends, scalloped apron, cabriole
legs, animal paw feet on casters,
quarter sawn veneer drawer fronts 375
42" w, 20" d, 65" h, princess style,
beveled mirror plate, lyre form mirror support, bow front, conforming
top, three short over single long
drawer, quarter sawn veneer on
center bowed drawer, turned wood
drawer pulls, paneled ends, square
legs on casters 395

Hall Tree
80" h, applied C–scrolled molding on

shaped crest, scrolled finials on rectangular stiles, crest shaped beveled mirror panel above vasiform
splat, straight arms, curved arm
supports, hinged lift lid seat,
shaped scalloped apron, cabriole
legs, four double hat hooks 600
81" h, Victorian, late 19th C, carved,
rose carved standard with six hook
branches, umbrella stand with fitted lens in lower section 400

High Chair
39" h, T–back, hinged bowed front
food tray, square arm supports,
shaped seat, out curved legs with
ring and baluster turnings at top
legs, rectangular footrest, box
stretchers 175
42" h, go cart style, pressed arch, leaf,
and fan decoration on shaped crest,
pressed foliate design on splat,
turned stiles, hinged shaped food
tray, turned arm supports, caned
trapezoidal seat, shaped footrest on
turned posts, ring turned stretchers,
iron spoked wheels 450

Icebox
26" w, 19" d, 48" h, one over one
double paneled hinged doors,
straight apron, paneled ends, zinc
lining 450
28" w, 17" d, 43" h, lift lid ice compartment with raised panels on
front over single raised panel door,
molded base, label reads "Cold
Storage" 450
35" w, 20" d, 48" h, Ramey Refriger-
ator Company, Greenville, Michigan, double paneled full length
door beside pair of two paneled
doors, paneled ends, straight
apron, square feet, label reads
"Lapland Monitor, The Ramey Re-
frigerator Co., Greenville, Mich" . 575

Mirror
Cheval, 20" w, 9" d, 25" h, swing
mirror, tombstone arched frame
holding conforming beveled mirror
plate, scrolled mirror supports, rectangular top, two small drawers
with brass button pulls, flattened
bun feet 175
Hanging
18" sq, hall, hung diagonally, applied beading on outer and inner
edges, beveled mirror plate,
three ornate double hat hooks at
lower corners 225
36" w, 72" h, rectangular, quarter
sawn oak, applied foliate decoration at top, beveled mirror

plate, two double hat hooks at upper corners   275

Pie Safe, 41″ w, 15″ d, 56″ h, slightly overhanging rectangular top, two short drawers, pair of doors with six pierced tin panels, concentric circle and diamond design, paneled ends, French feet   525

Rocker

26″ h, Mission style, straight crest rail, three vertical slats, straight arms with rounded corners, six board seat   165

28″ h, Victorian, c1880, child's, pressed back, large shaped crest with pressed foliate decoration, six rope turned spindles, shaped scrolled arms on turned arm supports, trapezoidal caned seat, turned front legs joined by turned stretcher, box stretchers   215

28″ h, pressed flower between beaded line design on straight crest, bulbous finials on round tapering stiles, seven round spindles, bentwood arms, trapezoidal seat, splayed base with turned legs conjoined by box stretchers   150

35″ h, sewing, shaped crest rail with pressed beaded fan and scroll design on central tablet, turned stiles, seven narrow spindles with ball turned ends, shaped lower rail, hip brackets, trapezoidal pressed cane seat with slightly bowed front, round tapering legs conjoined by two turned, slightly bulbous stretchers   85

38″ h, quadruple pressed back, shaped crest with pressed C–scroll and leafy designs, flattened ball finials on turned stiles, six turned spindles, hip brackets, two lower rails with pressed floral designs, trapezoidal pressed caned seat, pressed floral design on shaped apron, turned front legs, box stretchers   145

38″ h, 22″ w, platform, applied leaf and vine decoration on shaped crest, square stiles, upholstered back panel, scrolled arms, turned vasiform arm supports, overstuffed seat, platform base, rectangular front stretcher with incised lines, casters   200

39″ h, pressed back, shaped crest with pressed Man of the North Wind design, ball finials on ring turned stiles, six vase and ring turned spindles, hip brackets, shaped seat, ring turned front legs, two ring turned

front stretchers, turned stretchers on sides and back   200

Secretary

38″ w, 18″ d, 85″ h, applied scrolled decorations to scrolled pediment, molded cornice, pair of glass doors, shelf interior, fall front writing surface with applied scrolled decoration, fitted interior, three long drawers, paneled ends, shaped apron continuing to bracket feet   1,200

38″ w, 22″ d, 85″ h, applied leafy decorations to shaped pediment, molded cornice, pair of glass doors enclosing shelved interior, cylinder roll flanked by reeded stiles surmounted by dies with concentric ring design, fitted interior, single long drawer over two short drawers beside single cupboard door, paneled ends, applied leafy decorations on shaped apron, scroll feet, embossed brass bail handle drawer pulls   2,000

Sideboard

40″ w, 19″ d, 74″ h, applied decorations, two sections: upper section: applied foliate decoration on shaped crest, rectangular top with scotia edge supported by cabriole shaped columns with applied leafy decoration, rectangular beveled mirror plate in backboard flanked by etagere shaped shelves, molded base on backboard; lower section: rounded corners on slightly overhanging molded rectangular top, two short drawers over single long drawer over two paneled cupboard doors, paneled ends, turned wood pulls on short drawers and doors, bail handled pulls on long drawer, shaped apron continuing to French feet   600

45″ w, 21″ d, 58″ h, shaped crest with applied leafy decoration and central oval beveled mirror plate, molded edge on rectangular top, two bombe shaped short drawers flanked by similarly shaped reeded blocks, pair of recessed cupboard doors centering a bank of two short drawers, brass flowerhead pulls on quarter sawn veneer drawer and door fronts, molded edge on base shelf, applied gadrooning on shaped apron, front cabriole legs, casters   650

46″ w, 20″ d, 40″ h, slightly arching crest, serpentine shaped oblong top, conforming case, one drawer over two shorter drawers, bottle drawer, concave glass door, single recessed long drawer below, shaped apron, bootjack ends, teardrop, oval drop, and bail handled pulls on drawers, turned wood pull and applied foliate decoration on bottle drawer 375

48″ w, 23″ d, 76″ h, applied decoration, two sections: upper section: shaped crest with central fan flanked by applied leafy decoration, dentil molded cornice, turned columns with cabriole legs and paw feet surmounted by brackets with applied leafy decoration, oval beveled mirror plate in backboard flanked by rectangular etagere shelves; lower section: molded edge on serpentine front oblong top, conforming case with bank of three serpentine short drawers flanked by two cupboard doors over single long flat drawer, applied wreath decoration to cupboard doors, quarter sawn veneer short drawer fronts, applied foliate decoration on center of long drawer, egg and dart pattern molded apron, paneled ends, cabriole legs, animal paw feet on casters 1,000

48″ w, 24″ d, 77″ h, quarter sawn, applied decoration, two sections: upper section: central grotesque face flanked by gadrooned ram's horns and leafy decoration, beveled mirror plate flanked by rectangular etagere shelves on shaped backboard, ornate reeded and spiral turned columns; lower section: ovolo edge on overhanging rectangular top, two short drawers over single long drawer over two cupboard doors, carved shell motif on short drawer fronts, inverted wood shell pulls on long drawer, applied conch shell decoration on cupboard doors, applied scroll decoration on top and bottom of stiles, molded base, paneled ends, paw feet on casters 1,750

54″ w, 23″ d, 54″ h, 1920s, quarter sawn veneer, Empire style, two sections: upper section: straight crest, shaped top supported by S–scrolled columns centering a rectangular mirror plate; lower section: overhanging rectangular top, swelled fronts on two short drawers, molded frieze above pair of recessed cupboard· doors, single recessed long drawer, S–scrolled stiles on scroll feet 425

55″ w, 18″ d, 51″ h, Mission style, two sections: upper section: rectangular top supported by shaped brackets centering a rectangular beveled mirror plate flanked by outset etagere shelves; lower section: rectangular top, two short drawers over two short drawers flanked by a pair of hinged doors over single long drawer, square wood pulls on drawers, geometric fretwork on glass paned doors, shaped apron, paneled bootjack ends 395

Stand

Plant

12″ d, 34″ h, circular top, turned and reeded baluster pedestal on circular base, four scroll feet . . . 125

12″ sq, 15″ h, square scalloped top, ornately scrolled cutout apron continuing to scroll feet 100

12″ sq, 19″ h, square top, quarter sawn, keyhole design cutout sides and legs 95

14″ w, 20″ h, hexagonal top, three shaped legs with bootjack feet, hexagonal medial shelf 75

16″ sq, 31″ h, square top, splayed base, ring and baluster turned legs, square medial shelf 80

Smoking, 9″ sq, 27″ h, circular ashtray cutout and metal striker in square top, single drawer frieze, square legs, square medial shelf 45

Stool, 12″ d, 20″ h, piano, adjustable height, circular swivel seat, base with circular top, reeded bulbous pedestal, four splayed reeded bulbous legs joined to center pedestal by turned stretchers, claw and glass ball feet . . 175

Table

Dining, extension

42″ sq, 30″ h, square top, incised lines on straight apron, five reeded ring and ball turned legs, ball feet on casters 425

44″ sq, 29″ h, ovolo edge and rounded corners on square top, straight apron, six reeded bulbous legs continuing to blocks with concentric ring designs conjoined by concave stretchers surmounted by spherules, incised lines on stretchers, reeded bulbous feet on casters 875

45″ d, 30″ h, round top, raised square beading on straight apron, turned pedestal base, four cabriole legs, carved paw feet on casters 850

48″ d, 29″ h, round top, straight apron, octagonal pedestal with molding at base mounted on concave shaped base with scroll feet, two hinged legs drop down from underside of tabletop to provide additional support when table is extended 575

54" d, 30" h, round top with conforming straight apron, square pedestal divides when table is extended, plain squared cabriole legs, casters 750

Dropleaf, 41" l, 22" w, 31" h, oval, 13" drop leaves, round ring turned legs continuing to round tapering feet on casters 325

Library

32" w, 23" d, 30" h, slightly overhanging molded rectangular top, single long drawer frieze, paneled ends, square double tapering reeded legs, rectangular medial shelf, brass bail handle drawer pull, tapered feet on casters 395

34" w, 22" d, 28" h, rectangular

Wardrobe, knock-down, shaped pediment with applied molding, molded cornice, two recessed panel doors divided by center stile, pair of short drawers with bail handles, shaped apron, golden oak finish, 56½" w, 16½" d, 90" h, $800.00.

overhanging top, single overlapping frieze drawer with turned wood pull, shaped medial shelf, rope turned legs above medial shelf, spool turned below, ball feet 225

38" w, 24" d, 30" h, quarter sawn, slightly overhanging oval top, conforming single drawer frieze, two pillar legs mounted on oval shaped lower shelf, four scroll feet 350

45" w, 26" d, 30" h, quarter sawn, rectangular top, bombe apron with single drawer, two turned wood pulls, shaped medial shelf, scrolled lyre shaped legs, carved paw feet 575

50" w, 32" d, 30" h, Imperial Furniture Co, Grand Rapids, Michigan, quarter sawn, rectangular top, two short drawers with triangular copper drawer pulls, square legs, three vertical slats each side, side stretchers, medial shelf, applied tenons on legs and side stretchers 450

Parlor

23" sq, 29" h, square scalloped top, conforming apron, splayed base, spiral, ring, and baluster turned legs joined to scalloped medial shelf with metal brackets, ball feet 175

24" sq, 30" h, quarter sawn, square scalloped top, conforming serpentine apron, S–scrolls continuing to cabriole legs, carved leafy decoration on top of legs and C–scrolled leg brackets, scalloped medial shelf, scroll feet 350

26" w, 29" h, octagonal top, beaded apron, splayed base, slender spiral turned legs continue to ring and baluster turnings terminating in flattened ball feet, scalloped medial shelf 275

30" sq, 30" h, slightly overhanging square top, beaded apron, splayed base, heavy spiral and ring turned legs, beaded edge on shaped medial shelf joined to legs by ring turned stretchers, brass claw and ball feet 425

30" w, 22" d, 29" h, scalloped edge on rectangular overhanging top, incised lines on scalloped apron, ring and rope turned legs, scalloped medial shelf, square splayed feet 150

Work

41" w, 20" d, 32" h, quarter sawn,

straight crest rail, oblong top with slightly bowed center, conforming case, center bowed drawer over enclosed concave shaped shelf flanked by two doors, interior drawers, carved oval sunburst design on doors, shaped brackets, reeded stiles, reeded round legs, tapered feet on casters 375

42" w, 25" d, 30" h, overhanging rectangular top, single drawer frieze, square legs on casters ... 225

Wardrobe

39" w, 16" d, 80" h, spoon carved decoration on arched pediment, molded cornice, pair of double paneled cupboard doors, long drawer in base 750

43" w, 17" d, 83" h, break down, molded cornice, applied scrolled decoration on frieze, pair of paneled cupboard doors over two short drawers in base, scalloped apron, square legs on casters 950

Washstand, serpentine shaped towel bar support with applied molding, serpentine shaped top, two conforming long drawers with bail handles, recessed cupboard doors with applied molding, shaped apron, golden oak finish, $250.00.

Washstand Commode

32" w, 18" d, 28" h, reverse ogee edge on rectangular marble top, slightly projecting upper long drawer over recessed lower long drawer, pair of paneled cupboard doors, incised lines on shaped stiles and drawer fronts, incised leaf decoration on cupboard doors 450

32" w, 19" d, 36" h, spoon carved

decorations, circles and incised lines on shaped backsplash, slightly overhanging rectangular top, single long drawer over paneled cupboard door beside two graduated short drawers, acorn spoon carved designs and incised lines on drawer and door fronts, incised lines on stiles, brass bail handle drawer pulls 350

34" w, 20" d, 53" h, applied feather decorations on lyre shaped towel bar with molded base, serpentine oblong top, conforming long drawer over bank of two flat short drawers beside a raised panel cupboard door, shaped apron, square legs on casters 350

PINE

History: Pine was the favored wood for many vernacular forms throughout the eighteenth and early nineteenth centuries because it was inexpensive and easy to work with. It also served as an important secondary wood in period design furniture.

Unfortunately, pine does not weather well, so most pine furniture was originally painted. During the colonial collecting craze of the 1930s through the 1960s, collectors and dealers preferred the natural grain look. As a result, thousands upon thousands of pine pieces were stripped of their paint. This alone is bad enough; in addition, few individuals wanted their pieces left as natural pine. As a result, stains of all types, especially cherry, mahogany, maple, and walnut, were applied.

Note: This is a good point to place a reminder that one should never, never trust the surface color of a piece to determine what wood is being used. The only true indication is the wood grain. If the applied stain makes it difficult to see the grain clearly, look at the inside or underside of the piece at the unfinished surfaces.

Collectors and dealers now know to preserve the paint on a piece if it is period. However, if the paint is badly destroyed and the piece is not of museum quality, refinishing it to make it usable makes perfectly good sense.

One of the results of the crafts revival of the 1970s and 1980s is the rediscovery of the paints used to decorate pine furniture. Several manufacturers make a high quality milk–base paint. Individuals skilled in nineteenth and early twentieth century painting and graining techniques can recapture the period feel of pieces.

Final Note: "Pine," especially when coupled with "Country," has become a generic term in the trade to refer to: (a) all vernacular furniture forms other than oak and (b) pieces that have been refinished in a "Country" look. Occasionally an oak piece, especially if it's a store cabinet, is included. The Swedberg's *Country Pine Furniture* illustrates pieces made from butternut, cherry, chestnut, maple, oak, poplar, and walnut as well as pine.

References: Constance King, *Country Pine Furniture*, Chartwell Books, 1989; Kathryn McNerney, *Pine Furniture: Our American Heritage*, Collector Books, 1989; Robert and Harriett Swedberg, *Country Pine Furniture*, Wallace–Homestead, 1983.

Bench
 Porch, 92" l, 10½" d, 18½" h, rounded corners on top, bootjack feet, old worn putty colored repaint **175**
 Settle
  54" w, 16½" d, 49" h, paneled back, shaped sides continue to arms, hinged lift seat on paneled storage chest, bracket feet **1,000**
  66½" w, 13" d, 61" h, Vermont, cutout ends form armrests, random board back, plank seat, straight apron, bootjack feet, old refinish **650**
  70" w, 19th C, straight crest rail, high back with winged sides, plank seat, paneled apron **275**
 Water
  44½" w, 15½" d, 35" h, two shelves, bootjack ends, old worn yellow repaint, water damage, shelves slightly warped **450**
  48" w, 17½" d, 27" h, rectangular overhanging top, bootjack ends, rectangular base shelf, one board top, ends, and shelf, square nail construction **150**
  61" w, 13" d, 30¾" h, single shelf,

scalloped apron, block and turned legs, old worn blue and white repaint **520**
Blanket Chest
 Decorated
  38½" w, 17½" d, 18¼" h, six board, edge molding on hinged lid, dovetailed case, till, base molding, black brush stamped polka dots on red ground, lid hinge rail repaired, end piece of base molding replaced, base cut down **220**
  46¾" w, 19¾" d, 19½" h, edge molding on hinged lid, dovetailed case, till, base molding, heart decoration on old red repaint, bracket feet removed flush with bottom board **750**
  48½" w, 19" h, New England, early 19th C, applied edge molding on hinged lid, dovetailed case, painted top, front, and sides, black sponged spots on gray ground **1,430**
 Federal
  45¼" w, 32" h, early 19th C, hinged rectangular molded edged lid, interior well with till, single long thumb molded drawer, molded bracket base, repair to back edge of top and lock **935**
  45½" w, 21¼" d, 25" h, early 19th C, hinged lid, two drawers, peg feet **250**
  48" w, 21" d, 25" h, c1800, hinged rectangular lift lid, interior well, three thumb molded long drawers, oval brass bail handles and escutcheons, bun feet **350**
 Grain Painted
  37¾" w, 18¾" d, 25" h, edge mold-

Bench/Table, painted pine, multiple board top, seat section doubles as chest, trestle feet, castors, possibly made for the trade, $3,300.00. Photograph courtesy of Pettigrew Auction Company.

ing on hinged lid, dovetailed case, till, base molding, turned ball feet, brown and black graining **450**

50¼" w, 23¼" d, 25½" h, applied edge molding on hinged lid, dovetailed case, lidded till, applied base molding, turned feet, red flame graining, black trim and feet **475**

Miniature, 18½" w, edge molding on hinged lid, dovetailed case, lidded till, molded bracket feet, old worn dark patina, some edge damage .. **450**

Painted, 49½" w, 20¾" d, 19" h, edge molding on hinged lid, dovetailed case, till, base molding, wrought iron strap hinges, old green paint over blue **275**

Box

Apple, 11¾" w, slanting sides, original worn green paint **195**

Candle, 11½" w, sliding lid, old green paint, "G.M.D., 1858." in white on front, old touch up to initials and date **150**

Hanging, 9" w, 19" h, cutout crest, four compartments, scalloped bottom, old finish, age crack in backboard **115**

Utility

24¾" w, hinged lid, dovetailed case, base molding, refinished . **250**

26½" w, 17" d, 36" h, butt construction, arched crest, shaped sides, slanted front of well **150**

Candlestand

Primitive, 27" h, 18" w, 17¾" d, gallery edge on two board top, chamfered rectangular standard tapers to point at bottom, four whittled legs originally fastened by early wrought iron rosehead nails, old worn gray paint over earlier green, one gallery edge section replaced, three rosehead nails replaced **350**

Chest

Mule

35¼" h, 36" w, 17½" d, hinged lift lid, two graduated dovetailed overlapping drawers, scrolled cutout apron and feet, old red repaint **2,550**

43½" h, 42" w, 19" d, Queen Anne style, hinged lift lid, three faux drawers over two long dovetailed overlapping drawers, bracket feet, staple hinges, refinished, replaced brass bails, one back foot ended out by 2" **650**

Six Board, 18" h, 29¼" w, 14½" d, eastern Massachusetts, early 19th

Stage Coach Chest, New England, 19th C, three drawer dovetailed chest with period red paint, yellow stencils highlighting the stage stops, replaced hardware, minor imperfections, 32¼" w, 15¼" d, 39¼" h, $1,650.00. Photograph courtesy of Skinner, Inc.

C, hinged lid, nailed construction, cyma shaped cutout feet, painted red **450**

Sugar, 45" w, 20" d, 27" h, rectangular lid, paneled sides, pegged walnut legs, square tapering feet **400**

Chest of Drawers, 33½" h, 37" w, 19½" d, c1875, Victorian, straight front, four molded drawers, brass bail handles, bun feet **350**

Cradle, 28" h, 39" w, 13½" d, New England, c1830, hooded top, shaped sides, scrolled rockers, red, yellow, and green fruit border on brown ground **650**

Crock Stand, 38¾" h, 34½" w, three tier, graduated half round shelves, three part stepped scalloped frame, dark finish **295**

Cupboard

Chimney

24" w, 19½" d, 76" h, stepped cornice, upper and lower molded paneled cupboard doors **450**

26" w, 17¾" d, 64 h, single board construction, board and batten door, traces of red paint, replaced hinges **480**

Corner

34" w, 16" d, 74" h, open, molded cornice, scalloped opening on top, scalloped front edge on two shelves, single recessed panel door with H–form hinges, shaped apron, bracket feet **950**

46″ w, 23″ d, 80″ h, 19th C, flat molded cornice, single glazed lattice door over single paneled door, bracket feet, mahogany stained **1,700**

46½″ w, 83″ h, mid Atlantic, early 19th C, Federal, carved, two sections: upper section: molded cornice, two molded panel doors, three interior shaped shelves, molded and fluted pilasters; lower section: two molded panel doors, single shelf interior, molded base **2,475**

47″ w, 78″ h, c1810, Federal, two sections: upper section: cove molded cornice, single glazed fan vaulted lattice door; lower section: twin paneled doors, bun feet **3,000**

47½″ w, 78½″ h, New England, early 19th C, Federal, molded cornice, pair of upper and lower recessed panel doors, three shelf upper interior, single shelf lower interior, bracket feet restored ... **2,100**

48½″ w, 45½″ d, 82½″ h, Pennsylvania, architectural, two sections: upper section: molded and dentilated cornice, reeded stiles, carved sunbursts surrounding arched door with keystones, three interior shelves, shaped apron over pie shelf; lower section: reeded and molded trim, wide reeded stiles, two dovetailed drawers with applied beading and wooden pulls, two raised panel doors, chip carving on bracket feet, yellow–brown grain painted door panels and drawer fronts, yellow side panels top and bottom, red ground, old repaint, feet replaced, some Victorian era trim added, cornice reworked, replaced hardware **3,600**

Jelly

36″ w, 19″ d, 54″ h, c1800, Federal, shaped splashboard, straight front fitted with two small drawers and pair of paneled doors, turned wood pulls, straight bracket feet **975**

41″ w, 15½″ d, 54½″ h, slightly overhanging rectangular top, single long drawer, pair of recessed panel cupboard doors, pegged doors, plank ends, turned wood pulls **425**

Pewter

43″ w, 14″ d, 72″ h, open, molded rectangular top with scalloped apron, scalloped ends, two shelves, single door in base with two raised panels, shaped apron, bracket feet, H–form hinges ... **1,000**

49″ w, 19½″ d, 78¾″ h, open truncated top, three shelves, single flush panel door in base, old red paint, replaced HL–form hinges, top cut down **725**

Step Back

41″ w, 17″ d, 81″ h, blind, cornice, pair of raised panel cupboard doors, slightly overhanging pie shelf, pair of raised panel cupboard doors in base, one board ends, pegged construction, bracket feet **850**

43″ w, 83½″ h, New England, early 19th C, Federal, two sections: upper section: molded cornice, two raised paneled cupboard doors centering a molded panel, two interior shelves, beveled edges on three small drawers; lower section: two raised paneled hinged cupboard doors centering a molded panel, one interior shelf, shaped apron, bracket feet **3,850**

47″ w, 21″ d, 86″ h, early 19th C, Federal, two sections: upper section: molded cornice over twin paneled doors; lower section: dry sink over twin paneled doors and four graduated drawers **775**

53″ w, 23¾″ d, 89″ h, molded cornice, edge molding on ends, three open shelves, two nailed drawers, two raised panel doors, random board back, dark refinish **1,225**

57″ w, 21¾″ d, 86¼″ h, c1820, Federal, two sections: upper section: flat step molded cornice, twin glazed lattice doors, open shelf; lower section: three drawers over two paneled doors, half ring and block turned column supports **2,100**

Straight Front

17¼″ w, 10″ d, 36½″ h, single board and batten door in beaded frame, reset H–form hinges, old red paint, possibly originally built–in **550**

38″ w, 18″ d, 83¼″ h, three shelves in open top, two doors and two graduated drawers in bottom, one board ends, interior back boards painted red, stripped ex-

terior, altered base door and
drawer arrangement **300**

42" w, 17½" d, 79" h, c1800, flat
molded cornice, single paneled
door, straight bracket feet,
stained **225**

43¼" w, 21½" d, 87" h, 1800–25,
molded cornice, pilasters flanking two glazed hinged cupboard
doors, white painted shelved interior, single raised panel cupboard door in base, painted
green **1,980**

44¼" w, 19¾" d, 71½" h, molded
cornice, dovetailed case, two
butterfly shelves with scalloped
surround, single paneled door,
scalloped apron, old finish,
painted green interior, scalloping
below cornice possible later addition, nailed repair to door stile
corner **725**

51" w, 18½" d, 81" h, New Jersey,
Bergen County, 1800–25, two
sections: upper section: molded
and reeded flat top cornice, two
glazed mullioned doors, two
shelf interior; lower section:
three molded drawers over two
paneled doors, molded panels on
doors and stiles, rectangular feet,
stained **5,500**

58" w, 12¾" d, 58" h, 1800–50,
blind, molded cornice, two
raised panel doors, four shelf interior, doors and panels with
frame molding, cutout feet, rattail hinges, refinished, one shelf
missing **3,080**

Desk
Carpenter's, 43" w, 19" d, 42" h, lift
lid in rectangular top, hinged slant
front, pair of wainscoted cupboard
doors, square feet on casters,
painted red **275**

Clerk's, 40" w, 20¾" d, 43½" h, fixed
slant top, two dovetailed drawers,
beaded edge on curved apron,
square legs, brown simulated oak
grain painting, one escutcheon
missing, repair to bottom edge strip
of writing surface **400**

Schoolmaster's, 36" w, 39" h, New
England, early 19th C, ash secondary wood, two sections: upper section: shaped three–quarter gallery,
slant lid, dovetailed case, interior
well with five pigeonholes and two
small drawers; lower section: single
overlapping long drawer, block and
ring turned legs, rectangular box

stretchers, tapered feet, painted
green **3,300**

Slant Front, 48" w, 24" d, 78" h, two
sections: upper section: arched
pediment, molded cornice, pair of
glazed cupboard doors, single shelf
interior; lower section: hinged slant
lid supported by chains, pair of recessed panel cupboard doors,
shaped apron, bracket feet,
paneled back **1,800**

Dough Box
27½" w, 15" d, 10" h, rectangular lift
lid with cleats, dovetailed box,
slanted sides, molded base **225**

39" w, 19" d, 26½" h, rounded corners on rectangular overhanging lift
lid, slanted sides, splayed base with
straight skirt, square tapering legs . **475**

Drying Rack, 41" w, 54½" h, three mortised horizontal rails, shaped and
chamfered stiles, diagonal braces at
bottom rail, shoe feet, old worn yellow repaint, edge damage on one stile **200**

Dry Sink
36" w, 19" d, 28" h, rectangular well,
pair of recessed panel cupboard
doors, straight base **425**

39" w, 16" d, 51" h, rectangular overhanging top, shaped ends, single
narrow shelf, rectangular well, pair
of one board cupboard doors separated by center stile, straight apron **625**

43" w, 18" d, 37" h, early 19th C,
single drawer, twin paneled doors **800**

44" w, 17¼" d, 57½" h, Pennsylvania,
two sections: upper section:
straight crest, three aligned drawers, horizontal random board back,
shaped ends; lower section: drain
board, single short drawer, open
well, pair of recessed panel cupboard doors, two shelf interior,
scalloped apron, turned wood
pulls, polychrome pineapples and
feathery decoration on red and
green ground, some height loss .. **825**

47" w, 18¼" d, 48½" h, rectangular
overhanging top, single narrow
shelf, rectangular well, pair of
dovetailed short drawers over pair
of recessed panel cupboard doors,
turned wood pulls, straight apron,
bracket feet, one board ends **725**

48" w, 17" d, 48" h, poplar secondary
wood, rectangular top with two
short drawers flanking center shelf,
down curving sides, shallow rectangular well, pair of recessed
panel cupboard doors separated by
center stile, straight apron, bracket
feet **650**

52" w, 22" d, 44" h, single shelf on shaped crest, molded edge on rectangular well, pullout cutting board, pair of molded recessed panel doors separated by center stile, straight apron continuing to bracket feet, wainscoted ends   600

56" w, 25" d, 34" h, straight crest, projected rectangular tin lined well, pair of recessed panel cupboard doors separated by center stile, missing feet   550

59" w, 19" d, 30" h, shallow well, two paneled doors, cast iron latches with brass knobs, cutout feet, worn and scratched old red finish   1,000

Footstool

12½" w, incised edge on aprons, cutout feet, worn old red paint   125

Pie Safe, Southern, refinished yellow pine, high square post feet as extensions of corner posts, raised panel doors, two dovetailed drawers and double top doors with applied moldings at base and cornice, ten punched tin panels with whirligig designs, minor repairs, tins replaced, found in Savanah, GA, 43¾" w, 19½" d, 70¾" h, $2,090.00. Photograph courtesy of Garth's Auctions, Inc., and *Antique Week*.

14¼" w, 6½" d, 8" h, rounded corners on aprons, cutout legs, polychrome decorations of two dogs, loving couple, and lovebirds on top, two dogs on one apron, green ground   180

24" w, 11" d, 14" h, rectangular top with diamond cutout, rounded corners on straight aprons, bootjack ends, painted red   65

Pie Safe

30½" w, 15" d, 44" h, cutout decoration in stepped gallery, rectangular top, two doors with screen panels, three interior shelves, block feet   350

36" w, 19½" d, 34¾" h, Pennsylvania, hanging, two doors, single full length tin panel on each side and door, pierced concentric circle design, pegged construction, mortise and tenon joints, hand planed . . .   725

41" w, 15" d, 54" h, straight crest, single long drawer, pair of doors, three tin panels each door, pierced star and heart design, bootjack ends   425

Potty Chair, child's, shaped crest with cutout handle on high back, shaped sides and arms, scrolled apron, rockers, painted   125

Rocker, 12¾" h seat, 37½" h overall, brace back, shaped crest, vasiform splat, shaped lower rail continuing to scrolled plank seat, turned braces and posts, ring and baluster turned front legs and stretcher, cheese cutter rockers   95

Shelf

One Shelf, 13" h, 24¼" w, 6⅜" d, hanging, dovetailed drawer under shelf, decorative cutout brackets, old red paint   1,100

Two Shelves, 23¾" h, 20" w, hanging, scalloped ends, old refinish   225

Three Shelves, 29" h, 28½" w, 6¾" d, hanging, cutout ends, old yellow repaint   125

Four Shelves, 37" h, 68½" w, 11" d, plate rack, hanging, plate bars on two center shelves, cutout ends, gray repaint   155

Six Shelves, 21¼" h, 9¾" w, 6½" d, 1800–50, upright, rectangular, painted green   715

Sideboard, rounded corners on thumb molded rectangular top, two short drawers with molded edges, pair of recessed panel cupboard doors separated by center stile, scalloped apron, bracket feet, turned walnut drawer pulls   450

Spinning Wheel, 37" h, 19th C, ring turned round splayed legs   110

Stand
    Night, 21" w, 19" d, 28½" h, over-
        hanging rectangular top, two draw-
        ers, ring and baluster turned legs,
        ball feet 225
    Occasional, 19½" sq top, 31" h,
        square two board top, straight mor-
        tised and pinned apron, splayed
        base, ring turned legs, tapering feet,
        old red repaint 450
    Work, 12½" w, 15" d, 29½" h, early
        19th C, Federal, rectangular top,
        two drawers, circular brass pulls,
        ring turned legs, ball feet 55
Table
    Decorated, 29" w, 18¾" d, 29¼" h,
        two board molded edged top, mor-
        tised and pinned apron, pencil post
        legs, heart applied to apron center,
        traces of old blue paint 225
    Harvest, 62½" w, 19¾" d, 28¾" h,
        dropleaf, two board top, rounded
        corners and square butt joints on
        11¾" w leaves, square tapered
        legs, gold graining on yellow, old
        repaint, corners possibly recut ... 1,000
    Hutch, 47" d, 29" h, secondary hard-
        wood, pine seat and two board
        round top, mortised and pinned
        apron, square legs, mortised and
        pinned stretchers, old red paint on
        base, center cleat support added to
        underside of top 3,000
    Sawbuck, 35¾" w, 23¼" d, 27½" h,
        two board top, square nail con-
        struction, old nut brown finish, an-
        imal scratches on legs 250
    Side, 31" w, 19" d, 22" h, 19th C,
        rectangular plank top, block and
        ring turned round supports con-
        joined by stretcher 1,475
    Tavern
        26" d, 27½" h, mid 18th C, round
            top, single drawer, square taper-
            ing legs 385
        28½" w, 24¼" d, 25" h, oval top,
            Queen Anne style, two board
            top, mortised and pinned apron,
            turned legs and feet, mortised
            and pinned stretchers, hardwood
            base, old red repaint on base,
            one inside apron edge repaired,
            brace added to tabletop under-
            side, possible replacement top . 2,300
    Work
        21" w, 15¼" d, 24" h, one board
            top, square legs, base shelf,
            square nail construction, worn
            red paint, loose top 150
        24" w, 15" d, 18¼" h, one board
            top, rounded corners, square ta-

pered legs, cross stretcher, red
paint on base, age crack in top   350
43½" w, 27½" d, 28½" h, Chippen-
    dale style, one board top, single
    dovetailed drawer, hardwood
    base, molded outside corner on
    square legs, traces of old brown–
    red paint on base, edge damage,
    repaired apron   400
54" w, 27" d, 24" h, Chippendale
    style, one board breadboard top,
    single dovetailed drawer, mor-
    tised and pinned apron, square
    legs, hardwood base, worn old
    red finish on base, casters added,
    wear and age cracks on top ...   975
Trunk, 36" w, 19" d, 22" h, rectangular
    hinged lift lid, dovetailed case, bail
    handles, bracket base   175
Wardrobe
    39½" w, 20" d, 74" h, c1800, flat
        molded cornice, single paneled
        door, cylinder hinges, straight
        bracket feet   600
    46" w, 18½" d, 77½" h, break down,
        molded cornice, pair of molded
        paneled doors, single long drawer,
        turned wood pulls, shaped apron,
        bracket feet, pegged construction .   750
Washstand
    14½" sq, 28½" h, gallery with shaped
        sides, bowl cutout in square top,
        straight apron, square tapering legs,
        square medial shelf with single
        drawer frieze, walnut wood pull .   200
    17" w, 14" d, 37½" h, shaped and
        scrolled dovetailed gallery, bowl
        cutout, turned legs and posts, base
        shelf, dovetailed drawer, tapered
        feet, black striping on yellow, gal-
        lery piece missing, old repaint ...   200
    18" w, 15" d, 30¼" h to crest, scal-
        loped edge on shaped crest of
        dovetailed gallery, rectangular top
        with bowl and accessory cutouts,
        straight apron, ring turned posts,
        medial shelf, single dovetailed
        drawer, ring turned vasiform legs,
        ball feet, brown striping and sten-
        ciled and freehand decoration on
        yellow ground, white undercoat,
        worn and flaking paint, wear and
        age cracks   400
    34½" w, 17½" d, 35¼" h, shaped
        crest, slightly overhanging rectan-
        gular top, single long drawer, ring
        and block turned legs, rectangular
        base shelf with straight apron,
        turned feet, turned wood pulls ...   275
Washstand Commode
    30" w, 15" d, 29" h, scalloped splash-
        board, rounded corners on slightly

overhanging rectangular top, single
long drawer, pair of cupboard
doors with tombstone shaped recessed panels, shaped apron,
bracket feet, turned wood pulls on
drawer   325
30½" w, 15" d, 29" h, thumb molded
edge on shaped crest and slightly
overhanging rectangular top, single
long projection drawer, turned
wood pulls, pair of recessed panel
cupboard doors, scalloped apron,
bracket feet   275

PAINTED AND GRAIN PAINTED

History: Painted furniture falls into two distinct
groups: (1) painted period design pieces and (2)
painted vernacular pieces. Although examples of
painted furniture can be traced back to antiquity,
painted furniture became part of the American
furniture vocabulary in the first two decades of
the nineteenth century.

Between 1800 and 1820 the tendency was to
paint the surface a single color. Thomas Sheraton
introduced the concept with chapters on "Of
Painting Chairs" and "Of Drawing Lines on
Chairs" in his *The Cabinet Directory*. For this
reason, high style pieces from this era are known
as Sheraton Fancy pieces.

Beginning in the 1820s grain painting gained
in popularity, especially painting that imitated
rosewood. Graining often was enhanced through
the use of stenciling, freehand gilt painting, and
some polychrome decoration. By the 1840s the
use of painting on design style pieces faded.
From this point forward, the preservation of the
tradition rested in the hands of the vernacular
makers.

The earliest vernacular painted form was the
Windsor chair. Because it was made from a variety of woods, staining it to achieve a uniform
appearance was impossible. Painting solved the
problem. Throughout the nineteenth century,
paint was used to disguise the use of secondary
woods, preserve the piece, and add a note of
gaiety to household decoration.

Painting conveys a sense of individual craftsmanship. However, the truth is that the vast majority of painted pieces are the result of factory
production. Hitchcock chairs are an excellent
example; thousands were made. Graining especially was a factory–oriented skill.

Graining was achieved in a variety of ways,
the most common was through the use of a
feather. Another tool, a metal comb, was used
to imitate the grain of oak and other woods. In
the late nineteenth century a wavy gold graining
on a light yellow ground known as stippling became popular.

The folk art revival of the 1970s called attention to the elaborate graining patterns of individual craftsmen and factories. Emphasis was placed
on the unusual and highly ornate. One positive
result was an appreciation for the painted piece.
No longer were pieces arbitrarily stripped and
stained.

Collectors and dealers of painted and grain
decorated furniture must constantly remind
themselves of two key points. First, the tradition
of painting and decorating furniture continued
throughout the twentieth century. In almost every
locality there was an individual or individuals
who repainted and/or restored older painted
pieces. Second, the craft revival of the 1970s
and 1980s renewed interest in painting and grain
decorating. A new group of highly skilled artisans
arose. Several delighted in their ability to fool
collectors and dealers into thinking that their
work was much older. One such individual includes a hidden signature of a scratched stickman
in the aging characteristics that he adds to his
pieces. Painting and graining that looks new or
too good to be true probably is.

Major Craftsmen: David Alling, New Jersey; Jule
Chalk, Ohio; Hugh and John Finlay, Baltimore,
MD; L. Hitchcock, Hitchcocksville, CT.

Major Manufacturer: Hitchcock Chair Company, Hitchcocksville, CT.

References: William Elder, III (introduction and
commentary), *Baltimore Painted Furniture 1800–
1840*, The Baltimore Museum of Art, 1972; Dean
A. Fales, *American Painted Furniture*, Dutton,
1972.

Bed
    42" h, 52 x 70½" mattress size, can-
        nonball, rope, scrolled headboard,
        shaped footboard, turned posts, red
        and black simulated rosewood
        graining, original side rails, minor
        age cracks   350
    48" h, 54 x 70¾" mattress size, rope,
        hardwood, acorn finials on turned
        posts, scrolled headboard, turned
        blanket rail, smoke grained white
        paint, original side rails, repaired
        split one leg   600
Bench
    Settle
        57" l, eastern Massachusetts or
            New Hampshire, c1820, pine
            and maple, rabbit ear posts, thir-
            teen arrow form spindles, shaped
            and scrolled arm supports,
            bowed front and incised edge on
            plank seat, bamboo turned legs,
            H–form stretchers, green and red
            freehand stylized foliage decora-
            tion on ochre ground   49,500

Dry Sink, Pennsylvania, oak and pine, painted polychrome decoration on red and green ground, $825.00. Photograph courtesy of Skinner, Inc.

81″ l, triple back, shaped three part crest rail, turned half spindle back, shaped arms, plank seat, turned legs and front stretchers, brown and white grain painting **900**

Blanket Chest

22½″ w, 12¾″ d, 15¾″ h, Pennsylvania, Soap Hollow, 1856, miniature, pine and poplar, edge molding on hinged lid, dovetailed case, single dovetailed drawer, porcelain drawer pulls, dovetailed bracket feet, red stain, black trim, yellow striping, gold and red stenciled decoration, old edge damage, repaired feet, minor age crack in lid **13,000**

29″ w, 12½″ d, 24¾″ h, New England, 19th C, miniature, applied edge molding on hinged lid, deep well, two graduated drawers, ends form bootjack feet, red and yellow stylized trees, flower, and houses painted as decoration on front, paint grained ground **3,960**

35″ w, 17¼″ d, 21″ h, poplar, edge molding on hinged lid, picture frame molding around front panel on dovetailed case, till, scrolled bracket feet, blue ground, red and green stenciled foliage decoration and "H.E.B." on white front panel, repaired breaks in back feet, worn lid **1,200**

38½″ w, 17″ d, 16½″ h, pine, hinged lid, dovetailed case and base molding, brown rainbow shaped vinegar graining, light blue trim, lid replaced **170**

39″ w, 18¾″ d, 22¾″ h, New England, 1825–35, six board, hinged lid, bootjack feet, red–brown and yellow vinegar grained seaweed decoration **1,650**

39¾″ w, 16½″ d, 31¾″ h, New England, northern state, early 19th C, molded edge on lift lid, deep interior well, two thumb molded long drawers, straight skirt, bracket feet, red and black fanciful graining, black skirt and feet, oval brasses . **3,025**

40″ w, 16″ d, 15½″ h, Salem, Massachusetts, 1832, pine, edge molding on hinged lid, dovetailed case, lidded till, base molding, black brushed graining, red ground, initials "B.S." in yellow medallion on lid, "South Salem, May 16th 1832" interior inscription, age cracks in lid at hinge rail, varnished interior, repaired split in till lid **500**

40″ w, 16¼″ d, 22¼″ h, New Eng-

Blanket Chest, six-board, Northern New England, 19th century, grain painted, black and red graining simulating rosewood with dark red paint on top, period paint, repairs, 42″ w, 16″ d, 22″ h, $775.00. Photograph courtesy of Skinner, Inc.

land, early 19th C, six board, hinged lid, shaped bootjack feet, yellow ochre and burnt umber graining, minor imperfections **2,475**

40" w, 18" d, 36" h, Vermont, South Shaftsbury, attributed to Thomas Matteson, c1824, pine, hinged lid, single molded drawer, shaped skirt, bootjack feet, red, green, and black graining and stippling on yellow ground **34,100**

41½" w, 16¼" d, 21½" h six board, edge molding on hinged lid, lidded till, base molding, cutout feet, brown simulated mahogany flame graining, inlay decoration **450**

42¼" w, 18¾" d, 31" h, poplar, edge molding on hinged lid, three section paneled front, one board ends, 5" vertical tongue and groove boards on paneled back, cutout feet, paint graining simulates figured wood with burl inlay on front panels **350**

43" w, 17¾" d, 24¾" h, Pennsylvania, Soap Hollow, attributed to Jeremiah H Stahl, poplar, edge molding on hinged lid, dovetailed case, lidded till, dovetailed scrolled bracket feet, red–brown vinegar graining, dark green feet and molding **5,500**

43¾" w, 17½" d, 43¼" h, Vermont, pine and poplar, six board, edged molding on hinged lid, lidded till with secret drawer, scalloped apron, cutout feet, brown graining simulates figured wood with inlay, one reset lid hinge prevents opening of till lid, lid molding replaced one end, back edge of lid damaged **1,700**

44¼" w, 19¼" d, 23¾" h, pine and poplar, edge molding on hinged lid, paneled case, lidded till, base molding, turned legs, stenciled and freehand designs on stiles and rails, green and red, hinge repaired, replaced molding, old repaint **275**

45¼" w, 18¼" d, 30½" h, New England, early 19th C, hinged lid, single drawer, wooden pulls, molding above straight apron, shaped bootjack feet, red and yellow graining **1,500**

51" w, Pennsylvania, c1800, edge molding on hinged lid, green sunburst motif with hearts painted on front and sides **1,200**

52" w, 22¼" d, 21¼" h, 1797, pine, edge molding on hinged lid, well with till, molded base, bracket feet, two rectangular panels enclosing a polychrome vase with tulips, "Jacob Seltzer" inscription both vases,

one dated "1797," feet reduced in height, some restoration to painted ground **4,950**

Box

Bentwood

8½" d, 4" h, New England, c1850, utility, pine, round, fitted lid, compass drawn five pointed star within star decoration on lid, black and dark green on yellow ground, dark blue sides and bottom, inside lid inscribed "James H. Barry" **1,210**

21" w, oval, pine, polychrome floral decoration and striping on sides, orange ground, decoupage print on lid of children in goat cart, minor wear, edge damage, replaced lid seam **750**

Hanging, 9" w, 8" d, 14¼" h, New England, Connecticut River Valley, 1750–1800, hanging, wall mount, pine, pierced crest forms stylized figures, sloping hinged lid, inner well, single drawer below, wooden pull, stylized polychrome pinwheels and stellate devices on dark blue–green ground sides and back **8,500**

Storage, 23" w, 11½" d, 11½" h, 19th C, storage, dome top, tree on sprig like devices decoration, black and gray on salmon ground, paint loss, hinges replaced with leather strap **715**

Utility

5¼" w, 9¾" d, 5" h, New England, 19th C, rectangular, molded edge and bail handle on cotter pin hinged led, interior till, polychrome painted decoration three sides and lid, invected corners on outlined rectangles framing central motifs of four pointed stars on ends and lid and stylized potted flower on front, some wear and paint loss **2,200**

10¼" w, 5⅝" d, 4½" h, 19th C, hinged lid, polychrome decoration, hunter and hound on lid, roses and berries on front, eagle with American shield and compote with fruit on sides, brown ground **250**

21" w, dome top, poplar, yellow stylized foliage decoration, red ground, minor age cracks, one end of interior lid baffle missing **500**

24" w, 9" d, 11½" h, pine and poplar, iron lock and hasp, brass keyhole cover, black and white graining **1,450**

26" w, 14¾" d, 11½" h, New England, late 19th C, iron handles, grain painted, yellow ochre and burnt umber, surface mars **95**

Candlestand, 11¼" d, 29½" h, western Pennsylvania or Ohio, c1830, cherrywood, circular dished top, turned standard, down curving cabriole legs, yellow, green, red, and black stripes painted on top and standard, legs painted black **5,225**

Chair

Set of Six

31½" h, side, shaped crest rail, rabbit ear posts, four turned half spindles, shaped plank seat, turned front legs and stretcher, splayed base, stenciled and freehand fruit and foliage decoration on crest rail, lower rail, and seat and black and gray striping on putty–colored ground, price for set **1,500**

32" h, side, straight crest rail, four

turned spindles, turned posts, legs, and front stretcher, shaped plank seat, red and black grain painting, yellow striping, polychrome tulip decoration on crest, price for set **540**

32¾" h overall, 17½" h seat, Pennsylvania or Ohio, c1840, side, shaped crest rail, vasiform splat, plank seat, rolled seat rail, turned legs, splayed base, green and yellow striping and white leaf decoration on dark brown ground, some paint wear, price for set **825**

Side

34¼" h overall, 16½" h seat, Maine, pair, rabbit ear posts, scrolled crest rail, three arrow shaped spindles, plank seat, bamboo turned legs and stretchers, splayed base, stenciled and freehand vintage decoration on crest rail, green and yellow striping, red and black graining, history attached to underside of seat, age crack in one post, price for pair **700**

35" h overall, 18" h seat, Connecticut, Hitchcocksville, 1829–39, pair, rush seat, simulated rosewood graining, gilt and green striping, price for pair **1,650**

Chest

Apothecary, 36¼" w, 62½" h, New England, 19th C, pine, rectangular gallery, four columns of small graduating drawers, total of thirty–two drawers, shaped bracket feet, faux bird's eye maple drawer fronts, grain painted case **27,500**

Dower, 47" w, 21" d, 22½" h, Pennsylvania, 1826, pine, edge molding on hinged lid, dovetailed case, wrought iron strap hinges, till, dovetailed bracket feet, blue, yellow, black, and white polka dots, stylized potted flowers, eagles, names of couple, and date "September 21, 1826," red ground, faint signature inside lid, till lid and lock missing, feet repaired, lid molding replaced one end, lid decoration very worn, decoration on chest may be old repaint **1,650**

Immigrant's, 50½" w, 23" d, 21" h, 1820, pine, hinged lid, paneled lid and sides, dovetailed case, iron bear trap lock and key, blue ground, red trim, polychrome flowers, name, and date on light blue panels on front, traces of paint on

Cupboard, straight front, Georgia, mid 19th C, ogee molded cornice, single raised panel door, bracket feet, black striping and cream colored compass stars and scrolling on olive green raised panels, Spanish brown ground, $1,320.00. Photograph courtesy of Skinner, Inc.

lid panels, old repairs, turned feet missing, iron strapping added to front and sides **650**

Chest of Drawers, miniature, Empire, pine, shaped crest, two small recessed drawers over one overhanging drawer over two drawers, face turned design in ends, scrolled cutout feet, simulated curly maple paint graining, replaced crest **300**

Cupboard

Corner

42¾" w, 78" h, poplar, two sections: upper section: cove molded cornice and single nine pane glazed door, two interior shelves; lower section: single dovetailed drawer over two paneled doors, cutout feet, red–brown flame graining, originally one section, glass partially replaced, missing piece of molding between sections **3,300**

44½" w, 24" d, 110" h, c1800, one section, swan's neck pediment over arched single glazed lattice door with keystone, reeded stiles, one raised panel door in base, ogival bracket feet, sponge painted **6,500**

57½" w, 76¾" h, poplar, one section, crown molded cornice, two paneled doors top and bottom with beaded frames, base molding, bracket feet, red–brown comb graining, age cracks in two door panels, one end of cornice and back corners of feet cut out **700**

Jelly, 41" w, 14½" d, 54¼" h, poplar, two nailed drawers over double raised panel doors, wooden pulls, cutout feet, brown paint, burl grained door panels and drawer fronts, nailed repair on one door . **400**

Straight Front

43¼" w, 16¾" d, 76¼" h, Georgia, mid 19th C, ogee molded cornice, single raised panel door, five interior shelves, bracket feet, black striping and cream colored compass stars and scrolling on olive green raised panels, Spanish brown ground, script on backboards reads "C. W. Robinson, Salisbury, Mass." **1,325**

49¼" w, 78¼" h, pine and poplar, two sections: upper section: molded cornice, six pane double doors over three beveled front drawers; lower section: double doors with two diamond beveled panels, brown paint graining,

three cracked glass panes, paint touched up, refinished walnut upper doors are replacements .. **300**

Footstool, 13½" w, cherry, shaped aprons, bootjack ends, primitive village landscape on top, sponging, old repaint **225**

High Chair, 24" w seat, 36½" h overall, Pennsylvania or Ohio, rolled crest rail, plank seat, shaped footrest, splayed bamboo turned legs, olive green stencil decoration and black striping on yellow ground **935**

Mirror, 9" w, 17⅜" h, 18th C, Queen Anne style, scrolled crest, white floral sprigs and flourishes on black ground **10,450**

Rocker

26½" h, child's, shaped crest rail, four turned spindles, plank seat, splayed base, red and black grain painting, traces of striping and stenciled decoration **125**

38" h, arm, ladderback, finial posts, three slats, short scrolled arms extend halfway to front of seat, turned arm supports extend to side leg stretchers, splint seat, turned stretchers, dark grain painting, yellow striping, worn floral decoration **400**

38¾" h, shaped crest rail, continuous arm, five spindles, turned uprights and front legs, plank seat, scalloped apron, stretchers, refinished with original freehand foliage decoration on crest rail, two spindles possible replacements **85**

Shelf, 23¾" w, 5½" d, 39" h, hanging, four shelves, cutout ends, grain painting simulates bird's eye maple **850**

Table

Dressing, 31¼" w, 16" d, 39¾" h, pine and hardwood, scrolled crest, shelf with two dovetailed drawers below, single long dovetailed drawer under tabletop, wooden pulls, turned legs, black and gold stenciled fruit and foliage decoration on crest and single drawer front, black and gold striping on crest, drawer fronts, stiles, and turnings, yellow ground, old repaint **200**

Game, 17¼" w, 17¼" d, 30¾" h, northeastern Massachusetts, c1850, painted squares on square chess board mounted above straight apron, lidded medial container holds carved and painted chessmen and rooks, molded edge on chess board, turned and tapering legs and feet, red and black and gilt scrolling and striping on board

Work Table, popular, old (but probably not original) red and black paint, legs are black, apron has red graining, removable top is red, turned legs, two dove-tailed drawers which overlap, the legs have plugged holes from an added and removed shelf, 48″ w, 35¾″ d, 28¼″ h, $1,000.00. Photograph courtesy of Garth's Auctions, Inc. and *Antique Week*.

edges, apron, medial container, and legs **24,200**
Work
    18¼″ w, 19¼″ d, 28″ h, New Hampshire, 1820s, dropleaf, wooden pulls on two drawers, ring turned legs, simulated rosewood graining, red painted base, surface mars on top **715**
    37″ w, 17¼″ d, 28½″ h, poplar, shaped crest, dovetailed drawer, wooden pulls, square posts, base shelf, square tapering feet, smoked graining on yellow ground **1,700**
Trunk
    30½″ w, 15″ d, 14″ h, New England, 19th C, dome top, grain painted, yellow ochre and burnt umber, minor surface mars **140**
    40¾″ w, dome top, dovetailed, iron lock with shield shaped escutcheon, red and yellow grain painting, replaced hasp, edge damage, age cracks **90**

STENCILED

History: Stencil decoration first achieved widespread popularity when applied to Fancy Sheraton pieces. It was part of a much larger decorative movement that saw stenciling used for textile (theorem) and household (floor and wall borders) decoration.

Stencil themes ranged from florals and scrolls to patriotic symbols such as the American eagle. Many motifs were highly realistic, the result of the use of a number of stencil overlays. The art of stenciling at this level was done by a specialized craftsperson.

The stencil decoration of furniture continued throughout the nineteenth and twentieth centuries focusing heavily on chair sets for kitchen use. The wide back splats of Hitchcock and balloon back chairs lent themselves well to this form. Another area where extensive stencil decoration is encountered is on wooden farm equipment.

Stencil motifs and colors reflected current period design styles. Painted cottage furniture from the Victorian era relied on stenciling as a decorative motif. As the nineteenth century progressed many of the images grew more abstract.

Mass–produced stenciled furniture achieved its greatest popularity in New England, the Middle Atlantic states, and the Midwest—the areas of the country settled by 1840. Southern tastes and the Southern clime excluded it from that region.

Many stenciled examples were lost to refinishers between 1930 and the early 1970s. The folk art craze and crafts revival drew attention to the skill of early stencilers and led to a duplication of the motifs that they used.

Reference: John Tarrant Kenney, *The Hitchcock Chair*, C. N. Potter, 1971.

Bed, 72″ l, 30½″ w, 44 x 66″ mattress size, pine, pullout side expands size, red and black striping and foliage decoration on mustard ground, old repaint over earlier red **150**

Bed, rope, old (but not original) red and black graining with red and gold stenciled floral decoration, turned posts, replaced side rails, mattress size approximately 49" x 76", bed 48" h, $412.50. Photograph courtesy of Garth's Auctions, Inc., and *Antique Week*.

Bench
  Settee
    75" l, c1820, Federal, open arm, straight crest rail, triple back splat, plank seat, ring turned round tapering legs, stretcher, yellow, green, and brown stenciled fruit decoration on crest rail   **725**

    77½" l, Empire, wide shaped crest rail, three vasiform splats, scrolled arms, turned uprights, wide S–scroll seat, turned legs, wide flat stretchers, olive green and black stenciled and freehand vintage, foliage, and angel wing decoration and striping on white ground **2,000**
    80" l, flat crest rail, two part back, twenty–two turned spindles, shaped arms, plank seat, turned posts and front legs, three part base, flat stretchers front and back, black and red paint graining, fruit and foliage decorated crest rail, striping **750**
Settle
    72" l, straight crest rail, two part back, sixteen spindles, shaped arms, plank seat, turned posts and front legs, one piece flat stretcher front and back, gold stenciled vintage decoration on crest rail, black ground, old repaint **400**
    73" l, shaped two part crest rail, turned half spindle back, shaped arms, rolled plank seat, turned legs and front stretchers, polychrome stenciled birds and fruit on crest rail, white and yellow striping on arms, seat, and turnings, dark ground, striping may be old repaint **900**
    76½" l, Ohio, Cincinnati, straight

Settle Bench, worn original grayish yellow paint with brown and black striping, angel wing plus fruit and foliage dec, shaped crest, fan vase splats, "S" scroll seat, scrolled arms, turned legs, 80½" l, $1,375.00. Photograph courtesy of Garth's Auctions, Inc. and *Antique Week*.

crest rail, three part back, graduated center and lower rails, twenty—one turned third spindles, shaped arms, turned legs and front stretchers, splayed base, red and black grain painting, yellow striping, stenciled floral decoration on crest rail and center rail, old minor touch up to paint **1,100**

Chair
Arm
34" h, Hitchcock style, straight crest rail and two graduated slats, rabbit ear posts, shaped scrolling arms, shaped rush seat, turned legs and front stretcher with diamond shaped center, button feet on front legs, yellow decoration on crest rail and striping on dark brown ground, alligatored finish, orig worn rush seat **175**
34½" h, Hitchcock style, three turned half spindles, shaped seat, turned posts, front legs, and front stretcher, red and black graining, yellow striping and foliage decoration, repaired split in one arm, age crack in one back post, worn finish **175**
Set of Four, 33¼" h, side, shaped crest rail, vasiform splat, chamfered and turned posts, shaped plank seat, turned legs and front stretcher, red and black grain painting, yellow striping, gold foliage decoration on crest rail and splat, one has crack

in crest rail, three have worn decoration, price for set **260**
Set of Six
31½" h overall, 17" h seat, shaped crest rail, four turned half spindles, shaped plank seat, turned legs and front stretcher, splayed base, polychrome stenciled fruit and foliage decoration on crest rail, lower rail, and seat, two tone yellow striping, red stained ground, repairs, repainted, price for set **870**
32" h, side, straight crest rail, three half spindles, turned posts, shaped plank seat, turned front legs and two front stretchers, splayed base, yellow striping, red and yellow stenciled decoration on crest rail, brown grain painting, price for set **420**
32½" h, Pennsylvania, Lititz, straight crest rail, four arrow shaped spindles, shaped plank seat, turned front legs and stretcher, black and yellow striping and stenciled floral decoration on crest rail, olive green ground, "Samuel Wonder, Lititz, Pa" pencil inscription on bottom, price for set **1,650**
33" h overall, 17½" h seat, Connecticut,   Hitchcocksville, c1835, attributed to Lambert Hitchcock, curved crest rail and horizontal splat, rush seat, ring turned front legs and stretcher,

Side Chairs, New England, c1830, painted, gold accent on ring turnings, applied polychrome stenciled decoration in a swirl and grape leaf motif, set of six, $1,000.00. Photograph courtesy of Skinner, Inc.

gilt stenciled foliage, fruit, and striping on black painted ground, worn stenciling, price for set ...   **825**

34" h overall, 17¾" h seat, New Hampshire, Rochester, c1850, side, Windsor, straight crest rail, rabbit ear posts, five turned spindles, shaped plank seat, splayed base, bamboo turned legs and stretchers, gold stenciling and yellow striping on black painted ground, surface wear to stenciling, price for set **775**

Side

30" h, Maryland, Baltimore, straight crest rail, upholstered slip seat, turned front legs, flat front stretcher, white and gold striping and decoration, urn of fruit and foliage scrolls on crest rail, foliage decoration on front stretcher, black ground, reupholstered, old repaint **245**

33" h, Pennsylvania, Pottstown, pair, arched crest rail, four turned half spindles, plank seat, turned legs and front stretcher, polychrome stenciled bird, vintage, and foliage decoration on crest rail, white and yellow striping, red and black graining, "F.M. Morris...Pottstown, Pa" stenciled label, some wear on seats, price for pair **570**

33½" h, pair, Sheraton, Hitchcock style, turned curving crest rail rail, wide scrolled slat, cross piece, rush seat, turned front legs and stretcher, gilt stenciled fruit and foliage decoration on slat, yellow striping, red and black graining, price for pair **400**

Writing, 34" h, shaped crest rail, vasiform splat, shaped writing surface, turned posts, plank seat, turned front legs and stretcher, splayed base, stenciled foliage decoration on crest rail and splat, striping, black ground, repaired split on arm, old repaint **105**

Rocker

35¾" h, shaped crest rail, four turned spindles, scrolled arms, plank seat, turned legs and front stretcher, gilt stenciled coach with four horses and palm tree decoration on crest rail, yellow and green striping, red and black grain painting, bottom of seat signed, nailed split on seat edge **115**

41" h, shaped crest rail, vasiform splat, shaped arms, turned uprights, front legs, and stretcher, shaped and rolled seat, polychrome stenciled foliage decoration on dark ground, old dark varnish, one arm repaired **110**

42" h, shaped crest rail, vasiform half splat, shaped and scrolled arms, turned uprights and front legs, flat front stretcher, bronze powder stenciled decoration, Lady Justice in laurel wreath on splat, eagle on globe surrounded by laurel wreath, flags, and foliage on crest rail and lower rail, yellow striping, dark ground, minor repairs **105**

44" h, New England, early 19th C, arrow back, comb over crest rail, arrow shaped spindles, turned legs, handpainted landscape on crest rail, gold stenciling and striping on black ground **415**

45" h, 16¼" h seat, 24½" w, Pennsylvania or Ohio, mid 19th C, shaped crest rail, vasiform splat, hinged writing surface on scrolled arms, turned arm supports, shaped plank seat with rolled seat rail, turned legs, front and back stretchers, shaped rockers, gold stenciling and green and gold striping on red–brown grained surface **450**

Dressing Table, Hepplewhite, possibly Maine, c1820, pine, shaped splashboard and top, square tapering legs, grain painted, polychrome floral decoration, $1,000.00. Photograph courtesy of Skinner, Inc.

Table, dressing
  23" w, 15½" d, 34" h, pine, scrolled
  crest, single dovetailed drawer,
  turned legs, tapering feet, red and
  black graining, yellow striping, gilt
  stenciled compote of fruit and flowers on crest, embossed brass pulls,
  minor wear **400**
  39¼" w, 41" h, New England, 1815–
  20, Federal, scrolled shaped gallery
  with two drawers set back above
  one long drawer, ring turned legs,
  ball feet, gilt stenciled decoration
  on black ground **825**

RURAL CRAFTSMEN/ PRIMITIVE

History: Furniture was made on a wide variety
of levels. It does not require a great skill with a
hammer and saw to construct a simple bench.
During the winter season many members of the
rural community constructed furniture for use in
and around the home. The furniture was practical, functional, and basic.

By the end of the nineteenth century, patterns
for most vernacular furniture forms were available from mail order firms or in books. A farm
repair shop could easily be used to build furniture, and many were. Available wood was used,
resulting in a single form being found in a wide
variety of woods. Items were painted to hide the
many woods used in a single piece. Many of the
pieces were not meant to last longer than a lifetime.

In addition to the "amateur" builder, many
rural communities contained a cabinetmaker
who made basic furniture forms, e.g., bee boxes,
benches, blanket chests, chairs, desks, dry sinks,
ladders, jelly cupboards, tables, traps, washstands, etc. The rural cabinetmaker also included
among his wares miniature furniture and games
for children.

A few craftsmen marked their pieces. Most did
not. This listing contains pieces that can be attributed to a specific craftsperson; unmarked
pieces are found in the previous vernacular categories to which they apply.

Beware of confusing this furniture with that
originating in the thousands of home workshops
of the 1920s through the 1960s. Dagwood Bum-
stead, a character in the "Blondie" cartoon strip,
is a good example of the typical basement hob-
byist. The home craftsman was deluged with information about what and how to build. *Popular
Mechanics* and *Popular Homecraft* are just two
of several dozen magazines available by sub-
scription or at the newsstand.

Little study has been done on furniture produced at this level. In many cases these individuals were highly skilled amateurs. They were as
capable of reproducing a period design as they
were of constructing a modern piece. Many of
the present day "period" pieces appear to have
been produced by them.

This category also contains listings of pieces
that are heavily weathered and/or show signs of
heavy use. These are the "primitive" pieces that
held such a strong appeal for Country collectors
in the 1970s. The critical question that needs to
be asked is "Are they really primitive?"

One must look past the current state of these
pieces and attempt to understand how they appeared when they were first made. In doing so,
one often finds that primitive is an incorrect term
to apply. Likewise, if the piece simply was made
poorly, either in construction or design, it is simply a poorly made piece. Nothing is gained by
venerating trash with a name, i.e., primitive.

Few builders start out to make something in a
crude or primitive fashion. Lack of skill or understanding of construction techniques results in
the crudeness. However, one must remember
that the rural concept of "good enough to use"
applies in many of these cases. The initial builders never imagined or intended that their efforts
wind up on a pedestal or as a display piece in
the home of a collector.

Better terms to describe "primitive" furniture
are "charming" and "weathered." Some pieces
have evolved to where the final result is aesthetically pleasing—not many, but a few. A skilled
eye can spot them. The rest of the pieces deserve
to be treated as what they are—crude junk.

Reference: *A Craftsman's Handbook: Henry
Lapp*, reprint by Good Books in cooperation with
the Philadelphia Museum of Art, introduction
and notes by Beatrice B. Garvan.

Bench
  Bucket, 37" w, 14" d, 32" h, Ohio,
    ash, mortised construction, rectan-
    gular top, two shelves, one board
    bootjack ends, old varnish finish .   **250**
  Porch
    24" w, 11" d, 20½" h, pine,
    rounded corners on rectangular
    top, scalloped apron, cutout feet,
    stripped **115**
    39½" w, 12" d, 17½" h, pine, rec-
    tangular top, splayed pencil post
    legs mortised through top, worn
    orange–tan paint, minor worm
    holes **150**
    92" w, 10½" d, 18½" h, pine,
    rounded corners on oblong top,
    bootjack legs, old worn gray re-
    paint **175**
  Settle, 54" w, 13¾" d, 55¼" h, New
    England, early 19th C, pine, curv-
    ing S–shaped ends, horizontal

board back, hinged lift seat, old Spanish brown paint **3,000**

Water

35½" w, 12" d, 36½" h, pine, rectangular top, one board shaped sides with cutout feet, two shelves, groove joint construction, old mellow refinish, age cracks, some edge damage and repairs **525**

36" w, 11¾" d, 29½" h, late 19th C, poplar, rectangular top, straight skirt, bootjack ends, dark brown finish **175**

38½" w, 19½" d, 29¾" h, pine, one board top, one board bootjack ends, two board shelf, support added to shelf **175**

48" w, 13" d, 24½" h, pine, rectangular top, bootjack ends joined by flat stretchers, old worn red paint **350**

48" w, 15" d, 47½" h, poplar, arched crest over rectangular step back shelf with two short dovetailed drawers below, shaped one board ends, open lower shelf over pair of paneled doors separated by center stile, cutout feet, old varnish finish, door latches replace with turn buckles, drawers have old cast iron pulls **1,000**

63¾" w, 11½" d, 43½" h, rectangular top, shaped ends, two graduated shelves with straight back galleries, cutout feet, painted red **150**

Bin

21½" w, 21¼" d, 28½" h, poplar, two board lift lid with breadboard ends, base molding, crude scalloped apron, cutout feet, red repaint, edge damage, age cracks **425**

37" w, 24¾" d, 34" h, poplar, rectangular top with hinged slant lid, nailed construction, interior deep till and divider, turned feet, old red stain **400**

Blanket Chest, 38" w, pine, six board, rectangular hinged lid, lidded till, cutout feet, old red paint with black splotches shows lighter red beneath, some edge damage **375**

Candlestand

14½" w, 11½" d, 24" h, pine, cut corners on rectangular top, chamfered edges on square column, mortised T–shaped foot, old worn patina **325**

18¾" w, 14⅛" d, 32½" h, New England, 18th C, maple, ash, and poplar, ratchet type, rectangular top on

adjustable ratchet stand, tripod base with turned legs, old red paint on stand, top refinished **2,000**

Chair, 33½" h, ladder back, flat circular finials on square tapered stiles, two slightly arched flat slats, split hickory seat, square legs joined by stretchers, old blue paint with some touch up, replaced seat **150**

Chest

Apothecary, 45" w, 11½" d, 71" h, pine, one piece, pair of paneled doors, beaded trim, and interior shelves in step back top above sixteen drawers, one board ends, scrolled apron continuing to bracket feet, finish cleaned down to old blue paint, several drawers have different shade of blue paint, some edge damage, one back foot repaired, surface burns in one end of top **2,600**

Mule, 30" w, 20½" d, 30" h, Hampshire County, Massachusetts, 1710–30, pine, oak, and maple, joined, paneled, cleated single board lid opens to interior well, single long drawer, turned ball feet, original engraved brasses, 20th C green paint, wooden hinge pins missing **6,500**

Crock Stand

29" w, 25¾" h, three tiers, graduated rounded shelves, stepped frame, green repaint over weathered surface, repairs **250**

52" w, 55" h, pine, five tiers, graduated rounded shelves, stepped frame, removable back legs, worn and weathered old green repaint, age cracks, some repairs **200**

Cupboard

Chimney

19¾" w, 14" d, 76" h, poplar, full length raised panel door, interior shelves, old olive green wash over white, incomplete cast iron latch, replaced brass thumb latch **1,000**

32" w, 15½" d, 98" h, poplar, pair of recessed paneled doors over shorter single recessed paneled cupboard door, weathered and flaked old green repaint **400**

Corner, 51" w, 83¼" h, pine and poplar, two sections: upper section: molded cornice, single door with nine panes of old wavy glass, three interior butterfly shelves, molded waist; lower section: pair of recessed panel cupboard doors, old green repaint, replaced wrought iron rattail hinges, height loss to base, feet removed, ends of cornice, waist molding, and bottom and back boards replaced **2,500**

Hanging

13" w, 29½" h, corner, relief carved tulip on one board door, scalloped top and bottom, simple construction, old nut brown finish, minor repairs **375**

23¼" w, 11½" d, 36½" h, poplar, molded cornice, dovetailed, board and batten door, two interior nailed drawers, molded base, original red paint, turnbuckle latch added **1,125**

26" w, 13½" d, 37" h, poplar, open top with beaded surround enclosing two shelves, single dovetailed drawer with brass pulls, old red paint, may be cut down, brass pulls are battered **500**

Jelly, 37¾" w, 13¾" d, 54¼" h, Hudson Valley, New York, pine, simple construction, board and batten door, five interior shelves, turnbuckle latch, blue–green repaint over earlier red, minor nailed repair to door **600**

Kas, 64" w, 21½" d, 76¾" h, pine, break down, molded cornice, pair of paneled doors with beaded frame, one board ends, molded edge base, cast iron hooks inside, original red paint, several hooks broken **1,500**

Pewter, 40¼" w, 18¾" d, 73½" h, hardwood, rectangular top, two open shelves, horizontal boarded back, two cupboard doors separated by center stile, worn layers of old dark paint **1,250**

Step Back

34½" w, 18" d, 80¼" h, New England, early 19th C, open, three shelves, random board back, paneled ends, molded edge above single recessed panel door enclosing single shelved interior, original red surface with pewter green paneled ends, worn finish **1,500**

38" w, 18" d, 83¼" h, pine, three open shelves over base with pair of doors separated by center stile, vertical board back, one board ends, turnbuckle door latches, stripped exterior, interior back boards painted red, top left stile replaced **475**

58½" w, 20" d, 87" h, butternut, two sections: upper section: molded cornice, pair of double paneled cupboard doors enclos-

ing shelved interior, pie shelf; lower section: three dovetailed short drawer over pair of double paneled cupboard doors, paneled ends, cutout feet, turned wood drawer pulls, brass hardware, refinished **3,000**

Straight Front, 39" w, 12" d, 41½" h, rounded front corners, single paneled door, tin lining, iron side handles, brass latch, shoe feet, refinished **135**

Daybed, 76" l, 24¾" w, 16" h, cherry and other hardwoods, shaped side rails slightly elevated at head end, dovetailed frame, shaped cutout feet on casters **100**

Dry Sink

48½" w, 19½" d, 32¾" h, poplar, shaped front edge on well beside short dovetailed drawer, pair of recessed paneled cupboard doors, short cutout feet, worn and weathered old finish, replaced end boards on vertical board back, iron thumb latch badly rusted **650**

52" w, 18¾" d, 33¼" h, pine, molded edge on rectangular well, pair of wainscoted doors separated by center stile, two interior shelves, old worn blue repaint over gray, drain hole cut through top and shelves . **350**

Footstool, 14" l, pine, rectangular top, shaped aprons, splayed bootjack ends, traces of old brown paint **95**

Pie Safe, pine, slightly overhanging rectangular top, two doors each with three punched tin panels, diamond and circles design, three matching panels each end, single nailed long drawer, high square feet, worn bluish–green paint, replaced porcelain knobs, bottom side tins have rust damage **1,100**

Rack

Candle Drying, 32" d, 40 h, pine and hardwood, eight spoked wheel raised on center column, octagonal base, removable hanging disk with wire wick hooks suspended from each spoke, old patina **575**

Drying, 29½" w, 49" h, pine, three square mortised bars on square posts, shoe feet, old green–gray paint **175**

Shelf

Corner, 60" h, five shelves, top three shelves graduated in size with stepped scalloped sides, bottom two shelves same size as third shelf, worn dark red paint, late wire nail construction **750**

Hanging, 22½" w, 7½" d, 24½" h, two shelves, cutout ends, late wire nail construction, old finish **150**

Wall, 10" w, 6" d, 41¼" h, pine and poplar, six shelves, rectangular top, one board ends, scrolled upper edge on front base board, old green and red paint, backboards have age cracks **525**

Stand, lighting, 35" h, walnut with some curl, adjustable candle arm and threaded column, circular turned tripod base with three turned legs, age crack in column, base is an old restoration **350**

Stool, 18" l, 13" w, 16" h, pine, joined, rectangular top, splayed base, chamfered corners on square legs joined by stretchers, traces of old red paint, stretchers worn thin, one foot replaced **200**

Table

Hutch, 65" w, 36" d, 27" h, walnut, two board overhanging rectangular top, cleats, one board ends with cutout feet, rectangular seat with straight apron, gray scrubbed finish, some water damage to feet, slightly warped top has age cracks and has been reattached to cleats **1,500**

Sawbuck

43" w, 21" d, 26½" h, pine, one board top, flat stretchers, square X–form legs, refinished, some stains and scars on top **500**

90" w, 25" d, 29½" h, pine and hardwood, one board breadboard top, horizontal cleats, X–form legs, old mellow refinish, one end of cleat ended out **1,000**

Tavern

27" w, 20" d, 25½" h, New England, 18th C, maple, oval top, straight apron, block and ring turned legs, molded square stretchers above turned feet, remnants of paint on base **3,000**

35½" w, 25¼" d, 28" h, New England, 18th C, maple, ovolo shaped corners on scrubbed rectangular top, straight skirt, turned tapered legs ending in padded cup feet, brown stained base .. **1,500**

Trestle, 30" w, 8½" d, 26½" h, oak, rounded corners on oblong top, wedged trestle base with shoe feet, old patina **75**

Work, 47¼" w, 39½" d, 31¼" h, southern states, yellow pine, two board overhanging rectangular top, single nailed overlapping drawer, turned legs, tapered feet, old worn blue paint **525**

DEPARTMENT STORE MODERN

History: The large urban department store arrived on the scene in the last quarter of the nineteenth century. Even small–town America had its local emporium. The department store quickly became the arbiter of American taste, and everyone wanted a taste of the good life.

The end of the nineteenth century also witnessed the establishment of numerous mail order firms. A few examples are Marshall Field & Company (1881, with portions dating back into the 1850s), Montgomery Ward, May & Malone, Peck & Hills (1896), Sears, Roebuck and Company (1886), and Spear & Company (1893). In 1930 Peck & Hills, a wholesaler of furniture and floor coverings, promised direct shipment from Boston, Jersey City, New York, or Philadelphia. Homeowners looked forward to the arrival of catalogs from these and hundreds of similar firms. They carefully scanned the pages for the "latest" fashions in household furnishings.

Following World War I, mass–produced furniture for sale through department stores assumed its rightful place as the most common vernacular furniture form of the twentieth century. The forms which dominate are the breakfast suite (table with four matching chairs), kitchen cabinets, seating furniture, furniture for the den, and wardrobes. Living room, dining room, and some bedroom suites are generally found in a period design style category, most likely Colonial Revival.

In the 1930s, the breakfast suite might have consisted of a porcelain–top table on an oak frame and legs with a matching set of slat back, solid seat rectangular chairs. By the 1950s the porcelain top became formica and the oak base evolved to a chrome skirt with "V" shaped chrome tubular legs. A typical fifties chair consisted of a box–like chrome frame with a solid color vinyl seat and back rest.

The key to collecting Department Store Modern is to focus first on suites and second to complement suites with pieces in the same design styles. Department Store Modern does not mix and match well. The furniture was designed to work together. Introducing incompatible elements causes a clash.

The bulk of Department Store Modern is traditional. It is the next generation of the oak, pine, and painted furniture from the end of the nineteenth century. However, there is a second side— the introduction of new materials into vernacular furniture. The use of porcelain, formica, chrome, aluminum, and a host of other materials reached the "common man" through the department store. It is this latter group rather than the traditional wood pieces that has captured the interest of modern collectors and dealers.

References: *Furniture Dealer's Reference Book, Zone 3, 1928–1929,* reprinted as *American Manufactured Furniture,* Schiffer Publishing, 1988; Robert and Harriett Swedberg, *Collector's Encyclopedia of American Furniture, Volume 2: Furniture of the Twentieth Century,* Collector Books, 1992; Robert and Harriett Swedberg, *Furniture of the Depression Era: Furniture & Accessories of the 1920's, 1930's, & 1940's,* Collector Books, 1987.

Bed, Table Rock Furniture Company, Morgantown, North Carolina, 1929, burl mahogany veneer on headboard, burl mahogany and bird's eye maple veneer on footboard, gently arched headboard, conforming footboard with applied roundels and veneered band of triangular designs, ring turned posts with acorn finials **200**

Bedroom Suite, Helmers Manufacturing Company, Leavenworth, Kansas, bed, chifforobe, dressing table, ivory painted finish, incised decorative lines; bed: applied decorations on rectangular headboard, reeded posts; chifforobe: applied decorations on shaped back and two cupboard doors, interior with three pullout drawers, two lower drawers; dressing table: applied decorations on drawer fronts and molded cornice over full length mirror, flanked by rectangular movable mirrors above three drawer pedestals, tapered legs; price for three piece suite **580**

Bench, vanity, Broyhill Furniture Factories, Lenoir Furniture Corp, Lenoir, North Carolina, 1940s, bleached and artificially grained mahogany back, birch base, upholstered seat, 24" w, 31" h **50**

Blanket Chest, cedar lined
    Billington Manufacturing Company, Sheboygan, Wisconsin, 1938, waterfall veneers, intricate design on front panel, V–shaped veneers on end, molded base, French bracket feet, original paper label **175**
    Lane Company, Inc, Alta Vista, Virginia, 1930, walnut veneer top and sides, figured walnut veneer front, applied diamond shaped center decoration, applied half spindle columns, bulbous feet **150**

Cabinet, radio, Showers Brothers Company, Bloomfield, Indiana, 1931, designed for Crosley radio, walnut veneer top and sides, pieced burl walnut veneer door panels, bulbous leg turnings, X–stretcher with center carved urn finial, teardrop pulls **50**

Chair
    Corner, Colonial Manufacturing Company, Chippendale style, mahogany, green leather seat, 32½" h .. **450**
    Dining, Stomps–Burkhardt Company, Dayton, Ohio, 1920, oak, shaped crest rail over simple straight back

Dual-Davenport, S. A. Cook & Co., Medina, NY, 1910s, sofa bed, upholstered, triple section, square back, rolled arms, square tapered feet, spring construction, 84" l, $200.00.

slat, leather seat with brass studs, 38" h 70

High, Heywood–Wakefield, 1950, folds down to playset, hard rock maple, kidney shaped tray, 42" h . 120

Office, North Hickory Furniture Company, swivel, open arms, red cordovan leather upholstery, 41½" h . 225

Set of Eight, dining, Old Hickory, Indiana, 1900, spindle back, woven seat, thick legs, marked, price for set of eight 850

Wing

Emerson Leather, Hickory, North Carolina, Chippendale style, matched pair, gray–green leather upholstery, 43" h, price for pair 700

North Hickory Furniture Company Beige and ivory silk brocade upholstery, Queen Anne style, cabriole legs, turned H–stretcher base, 41" h 250

Gray–green leather upholstery, swivel base, minor wear in seat, 44½" h 275

Chest of Drawers, Kindel

Bow Front, Hepplewhite style, mahogany, five dovetailed drawers, French feet, some wear to old finish, 36" w, 21¾" d, 50¼" h 325

Chest on Chest, Chippendale style, mahogany, worn finish, worn edge damage, 41½" w, 21" d, 68¾" h . 700

Chifforobe, Tri–Bond Furniture, Art Deco style, c1940, waterfall veneer, narrow center mirrored section, deep

Chest of Drawers, Bagby Furniture Co., Baltimore, MD, 1914, mahogany, rectangular beveled swivel mirror, scrolled supports, rectangular top, two projecting short drawers, two long drawers, scroll feet, casters, $75.00.

Armchairs, designed by Michael Taylor as part of a three-piece suite, square back and scroll-over arms, upholstered in quilted green floral on ivory ground chintz with fringed valence, price for sofa and two armchairs, $5,250.00. Photograph courtesy of Butterfield & Butterfield.

drawers on one side, cedar lined short wardrobe above drawers on other side 225

Desk

Colby, 1930, Sheraton style, mahogany veneer top and sides, curly maple veneer apron and drawer fronts, ring turned hardwood legs 195

Heywood–Wakefield, 1950, hard rock maple, kneehole, rectangular top, pair of two drawer pedestals, demilune base, 44" l 200

Innes Pearce & Company, Rushville, Indiana, 1920, bird's eye maple veneer table top and drawer front, single long drawer, maple base with slightly scrolled feet, 36" l 90

Kittinger, partner type, mahogany, rectangular top with center long drawer flanked by two smaller drawers, tooled leather inset, two pedestals each with three drawers, worn finish, 60" l, 32" d, 30¼" h . 450

Stand, smoking, Metal Stamping Corp, Streator, Illinois, 1925, shaped square top with outset corners, arched handle, bamboo type side columns, single door in cupboard base, lower shaped shelf, ring turned legs, 10" square, 31" h 40

Table

Coffee

Colonial Manufacturing Company, Zeeland, Michigan, 1930s, cloverleaf shaped top with tooled leather surface, solid mahogany frame, 28" w, 19" h 65

Table, dining, The Bogardus-McDaneil Furniture Co., Warsaw, Kentucky, 1914, extension, quarter sawn oak and veneer, round top, pedestal base, scroll feet, $350.00.

Imperial Furniture Company, 1930s, glass top, hand painted floral design in center, white background, blue trim, beaded apron, reeded tapering legs, 25" w, 18" d, 18" h 100

Console, American Woodcraft Corp, Evansville, Indiana, 1920s, striped mahogany veneer on top and apron, black painted turned legs . 35

Dropleaf, Imperial Furniture Company, Grand Rapids, Michigan, Duncan Phyfe style, black lacquered finish, Oriental design ac-

Department store furniture was available in a wide variety of qualities. In some cases, well–known designers brought their expertise to this largely generic area. Michael Taylor designed this Chesterfield sofa for Grace Paxton's (Mr. Taylor's mother) residence in Santa Rosa, California. Square back and scroll–over arms, upholstered in quilted green floral on ivory ground chintz with fringed valence and cushions, price for sofa and two armchairs, $5,250.00. Photograph courtesy of Butterfield & Butterfield.

cents, gold trim, 8" l leaves, 20" w,
18" d, 27" h **150**
Pembroke, Colonial Art Furniture
Shop, Grand Rapids, Michigan,
1940s, Hepplewhite style, plain cut
mahogany veneer top, drop leaves,
figured mahogany drawer front,
solid mahogany base, 10" l leaves,
15" w, 22" d, 27" h **75**
Side
Heywood–Wakefield, late 1940s,
nesting, set of three, rock maple,
rectangular tops, slightly tapered
legs, largest: 21" w, 15" d, 25" h,
price for three piece set **200**
Mersman, Celina, Ohio, 1920s,
oval walnut veneer top and gallery, lyre base, hardwood base
with carving on knees, 24" w, 18"
d, 26" h **75**

UPHOLSTERED

History: The Restoration design period included
upholstered armchairs, couches, and side chairs.
Few design styles excluded upholstered furniture.
However, it was not until the 1920s and later
that upholstered furniture played a major part in
the vernacular furniture movement.

Upholstered furniture of the 1920s and 1930s
was massive and rectangular in shape. Although
often overstuffed, the frame still was visible on
many pieces. Fabric patterns were floral or solid.
All the pieces in a suite tended to be covered in
the same fabric.

Art Deco introduced block stuffed sectional
furniture, a concept that enjoyed a revival in the
1950s and 1960s. Vernacular furniture quickly
adopted the fully upholstered style, surrounding
the entire frame with fabric. In many cases, suites
were upholstered in the same fabric pattern but
often in a different color, e.g., the sofa (davenport) and one chair in gray and a second identical
chair in burgundy.

By the early 1960s, vernacular overstuffed furniture had lost its appeal. Until the late 1980s
collector and dealer interest was minimal. Most
examples were junked.

Currently there is a growing interest in the
upholstered furniture of the 1920s through the
1960s among collectors and dealers in large urban areas. It is a "trendy" item in the suburbs
surrounding Los Angeles. Prices fluctuate as sellers try to find the "going market price."

Beware of buying a piece with "modernistic"
fabric patterns. These fabric patterns are difficult,
if not impossible, to replace. Manufacturers of
reproduction textiles have not seen enough demand to produce a wide variety of modernistic

fabric designs. As a result, buy only pieces whose
fabric remains in fine or excellent condition.

Major Manufacturers: American Parlor Furniture
Co., Chicago, IL; Delker Brothers Manufacturing
Co., Henderson, KY; Dunbar Furniture Manufac-
turing Co., Berne, IN; Marshall Field & Compa-
ny's Home–Crest line, Chicago, IL; Fullerton Fur-
niture Factories, Fullerton, PA; Furniture City
Upholstery Co., Grand Rapids, MI; Globe Parlor
Furniture Co., High Point, NC; Jamestown
Lounge Company, Jamestown, NY; Jamestown
Upholstery Co., Jamestown, NY; Levin Brothers,
Minneapolis, MN; S. Kappen & Bros., Chicago,
IL; John J. Madden Mfg. Co., Indianapolis, IN;
H. Z. Mallen & Company, Chicago, IL; North-
field Company, Sheboygan, MN; Spencer–Duffy
Company, Grand Rapids, MI; C. F. Streit Mfg.
Company, Cincinnati, OH; and, William Sultan
& Co., Chicago, IL.

Reference: *Furniture Dealer's Reference Book,
Zone 3, 1928–1929,* reprinted as *American Manufactured Furniture,* Schiffer Publishing, 1988.

Bench, Frank S Harden Co, Mc-
Connellsville, NY, rectangular upholstered top, six bulbous turned legs,
shaped double X–form stretchers with
center turned finials, paw feet, velour
upholstery with floral decoration on
top, 43" l, 18" w, 18" h **250**

**Armchair, Coxwell, S. A. Cook & Co.,
Medina, NY, 1910s, mahogany, square
button-tufted back, open arms, padded
armrests, spring seat, padded slipper feet,
floral patterned back and seat, $175.00.**

Box Couch, S Karpen & Brothers, Chicago, IL, 1930s, tufted rectangular spring seat, square box feet on casters, floral upholstery, 76" l **150**

Chair

Arm

Delker Brothers Manufacturing Co, Henderson, KY, 1930s, mahogany frame, tufted square back, rolled arms with exposed scrolled arms, spring seat cushion pierced mahogany apron with central fan decoration flanked by pairs of C–scrolls, fluted flattened ball feet, mohair upholstery **125**

Fullerton Furniture Factory, Fullerton, PA, 1930s, overstuffed, rounded back, rolled arms, spring seat cushion, mahogany cabriole legs, mohair upholstery, 36" w, 23" d, 35" h **125**

Peck & Hills Furniture Co, NY, 1930, square back, rolled arms, spring seat cushions, mahogany square tapered feet, taupe mohair upholstery with reversible cushions upholstered in walnut linen frieze, 35" w, 22" d, 35" h   **85**

Coxwell

Fenske Brothers, Chicago, IL, 1930s, mahogany, high square back, open arms with ball turned handholds, turned arms supports, and padded upholstered armrests, spring seat cushion, bulbous turned feet, baluster turned box stretchers, large floral patterned upholstery on back and seat cushion, black velour piped edges **150**

Peck & Hills Furniture Co, NY, 1930, exposed mahogany frame, rolled square high back, padded armrests, carved arching swan's neck handholds, overstuffed seat, scrolled feet, plum colored mohair upholstery with back and reversible cushion upholstered in floral pattern, down filled cushion, 26" w, 36" d, 37" h **250**

Fireside, Dunbar Furniture Manufacturing Co, Berne, IN, 1930s, arched tufted back, rolled arms, spring seat cushion, carved leaf decoration on exposed arms and apron, webbed bottom, carved knees on cabriole legs, scrolled feet, solid color upholstery with floral upholstered seat cushion, 33" w, 37" d, 38" h **175**

Occasional, Jamestown Lounge Co, Jamestown, NY, 1930s, mahogany, serpentine shaped crest rail on high square upholstered back, carved serpentine shaped arms continue to scrolled arm supports, serpentine front upholstered seat, carved floral decoration on shaped apron, cabriole legs, scrolled feet, large floral patterned mohair upholstery **175**

Slumber, C F Streit Manufacturing Co, Cincinnati, OH, chair and matching footstool, Queen Anne style, mahogany frame, chair: upholstered high back, open arms, shaped armrests, down curving scrolled arm supports, upholstered spring seat, cabriole legs, slipper feet; footstool: rectangular double cushion spring upholstered top, cabriole legs, slipper feet; attached triangular name plate "The Beautiful Streit 'Slumber' Chair," each piece upholstered in jacquard velour with raised floral pattern, price for two pieces **150**

Chaise Lounge, Marshall Field & Co, Chicago, IL, 1930–40, carved mahogany frame, carved floral decoration on crest rail, curved back wraps around to sides, shaped down curving arms, down filled reversible oblong seat cushion with rounded foot, turned tapered fluted legs, large floral design Canterbury fabric upholstery .   **450**

Davenport

Delker Brothers Manufacturing Co, Henderson, KY, 1930s, exposed mahogany frame, carved leaf decoration on crest rail, three section back and seat, spring cushions, webbed bottoms, rolled arms, exposed scrolled arm and triple bowed seat rail, four animal paw front feet centering leaf carved aprons, velour upholstery, 80" l, 32½" d, 36¼" h **325**

Franklin Furniture Co, Columbiana, OH, 1930s, exposed mahogany frame, triple seat bowed back, rolled arms, reversible spring seat cushions, carved exposed scrolled arms and lower rail with central leaf carved tablet, cabriole legs, scrolled feet, rose colored mohair upholstery, attached nameplate, 86" l, 23" d, 37" h **250**

Jamestown Upholstery Co, Inc, Jamestown, NY, Aristocrat, triple seat serpentine shaped back, serpentine shaped rolled arms with loose pillow cushions, rounded sides, three seat cushions, three ogee front feet, mohair upholstery, 98" l **350**

Love Seat

Frank S Harden Co, McConnellsville, NY, 1930s, double seat back, square back, straight sides, two seat cushions, three turned front legs, two flaring square back legs, floral upholstery with solid color piping, 53" l, 32" h **225**

Globe Parlor Furniture Co, High Point, NC, 1930–35, serpentine shaped back, slightly flared arms with exposed mahogany reeded arm rail continuing to arm support and seat rail, down filled reversible seat cushion, carved cabriole legs, padded slipper feet **200**

Rocker, Spear & Co, Pittsburgh, PA, c1920, rounded back wraps around to sides, rolled arms, flaring sides, spring seat, Queen Anne style feet on runners, floral tapestry upholstery .. **185**

Settee, Peck & Hills Furniture Co, 1930s, double seat square back, rolled arms, two spring seat cushions, walnut cup turned feet, Sheraton tapestry upholstery, 55½" l, 22" d seat, 34" h **200**

Parlor Suite

Brandts Furniture Co, Celina, OH, 1930s, three pieces, davenport, club chair, and high back chair, each piece with rounded tufted back, rolled arms, exposed carved scrolled arm and lower rail, slightly bowed seat front, cabriole legs, solid colored mohair upholstery with floral design seat cushions, 81" l, 34" d, 32" h davenport, 32" w, 31" d, 32" h club chair, 32" w, 37" d, 35" h high back chair, price for three piece suite **500**

Furniture City Upholstery Co, Grand Rapids, MI, three pieces, davenport, armchair, and fireside chair, each piece with rolled tufted back, rolled arms with exposed mahogany arms, spring seat cushions, carved seat rail, pierced apron with carved feather decoration, and cabriole legs, scrolled feet, 84" l, 44" d, 35" h davenport, 36" w, 43" d, 35" h armchair, 35" w, 36" d, 46" h fireside chair, price for three piece suite **650**

Peck & Hills Furniture Co, MA, 1930, two pieces, davenport and fireside chair, each piece with square rolled back, rolled arms, padded slipper feet, Jacobean style floral tapestry upholstery, 79" l, 33" d, 33" h triple seat davenport, 33½" w, 35" d, 33" h chair, price for two piece suite . **275**

Davenport, S. A. Cook & Co., Medina, NY, 1910s, exposed mahogany frame, carved floral and scroll decoration on serpentine shaped crest rail, three section spring back and seat, rolled arms, floral and leaf carved arms, serpentine shaped seat rail, padded slipper feet centering scroll carved aprons, velour upholstery, floral patterned seat cushions, 81" l, $300.00.

Peck & Hills Furniture Co, 1930s, two pieces, sofa and armchair, each piece with arched back, rolled arms, loose seat cushions, mahogany bulbous feet, three tone Jacquard upholstery with black velour edging, 76" l, 33" d, 34" h cabriole three seat sofa and 32" w, 34" d, 38" h high back armchair, price for two piece suite   350

Sears, Roebuck & Co, 1936–37, two pieces, davenport and armchair, each piece square back and sides, carved decoration on exposed arm posts, molded block feet, velour upholstery, 77" l, 22" d, 33" h triple seat davenport, 36" w, 22" d, 33" h armchair, price for two piece suite   375

S Karpen & Brothers, Chicago, IL, 1930s, two pieces, sofa and armchair, overstuffed, triple seat sofa with loose back and seat cushions, padded armrests, molded bulbous birch feet, floral upholstery, down cushions, price for two piece suite   250

GARDEN FURNITURE

History: Around the middle of the nineteenth century Americans renewed their interest in the outdoors. American landscape architects turned to the British naturalistic model for their park and garden designs. The need for seating, baskets, statues, and a host of other outdoor ornaments led to a thriving new furniture industry during the latter half of the nineteenth century.

The American Civil War led to a number of technological advances in the cast iron industry. Inexpensive delicate casting was possible for large size pieces. Pieces could be manufactured in parts and assembled on the spot. Outdoor cast iron furniture arrived.

Cast iron furniture burst upon the scene primarily in Rococo Revival design patterns. However, few design styles escaped its influence; patterns were easily and quickly copied. The English as well as Americans were caught up in the craze. Whenever encountering a lack of detail in the casting, collectors immediately suspect a reproduction or copycat.

Early cast iron pieces show a very high aesthetic quality. Later pieces seem forced, box–like, and unnatural. Much of the furniture was painted in order to preserve it. Multiple layers of paint can make a casting look flat and artificial. Double check all painted pieces.

Cast iron furniture experienced a number of revivals. A major one occurred in the late 1920s and 1930s, a time during which many reproductions and copycat pieces based upon mid–nine-

teenth century examples were made. Another revival occurred in the late 1980s.

Collectors and dealers are advised to become familiar with the cast iron examples from Virginia Metalcrafters illustrated in Ruth Webb Lee's *Antique Fakes & Reproductions, Enlarged and Revised* (Lee Publications, 1938, 1950 edition). Many of the "period" examples currently being offered for sale are not "period" at all but from the 1920s/1930s production era.

All forms of garden accessories are collectible—benches, birdbaths, fountains, gates, statuaries, sundials, tables, and urns. Emphasis is on formal pieces. The primitive look is out. Terra cotta and lead pieces currently are commanding premium prices.

Reference: Margaret Lindquist and Judith Wells *The Official Identification and Price Guide to Garden Furniture and Accessories,* House of Collectibles, 1992.

Note: See *Rustic* category in Vernacular Section.

Bench
Cast and Wrought Iron, late 19th C, Gothic and Arabesque type designs on back, slotted rail seat, price for pair **800**
Cast iron, 19th C
Fern back, pierced seat, splayed legs, painted, 48" l **500**
Floral pattern, marked Hinderers Iron Works, N. O. **1,250**
Lacy scrolled back surmounted by intricate crest rail with foliage scrolls, flowers, and center Minerva portrait, front cabriole legs with acanthus decoration at knees and elaborate terminals, splayed rear legs with pierced design, repainted white, 45½" l . .   **1,525**
Renaissance Revival, elaborate crest rail with central urn of flowers above woman's head, flanked by scrolls and circular elements, ornate acanthus and floral cast legs, 40" l, 41" h **900**
Rococo style, repainted, 48" l **1,500**
Scrolling design, three chair back, crest rail with intricate center medallion, gently scrolling arms with curved handholds, pierced apron, nameplate on back: C. Coughlin, Jr; green repaint, 44" l   **500**
Vintage pattern, worn, rusted white repaint, 42" l **500**
Chair
Arm, cast iron
1850, W McHose & Company, Dayton, Ohio, barrel back continuing to form high arms, molded leafy lily of the valley

flowers, scroll pierced seat, apron, and legs with conforming decoration, painted white, 27" l, 33" h **1,650**
1865, rustic branches and foliage **700**
1880, fern pattern, painted **375**
Set of Four, 1875, arm, cast iron, Renaissance Revival, price for set of four **1,700**
Side, 19th C, cast iron
　Racket back, painted **275**
　Vintage pattern, old worn blue repaint, minor rusting **250**
Conservatory Gazebo, rattan, semicircular latticed domed top, four supports, circular base inset with woven rush seat platform **500**
Fountain
　Cast Iron, 1880, Neoclassical style, three circular tiers with egg and dart rim borders, fluted columns, square base. repainted, 30" d, 70" h **5,000**
　Terra Cotta, shallow circular basin, deeply everted lip, molded relief laurel and flowers, putto on one side, naked winged mermaid with crossed arms as baluster, coved circular base, acanthus cast scrolled feet, weathered patina, minor losses, repaired basin, 54" h **4,125**
Porch Glider, attributed to Old Hickory Company, Indiana, 20th century, basket woven reed settee, rustic wooden T–shaped floor frame, held by chains, some breaks to reed, 62" l, 26" d, 35½" h **990**
Settee
　Cast Iron
　　Double balloon back, Kreamer Brothers Mfg, Dayton, Ohio, pierced design of scrolling daisies, vines, and leaves, back

curves around to form arm supports, pierced scrolled seat, straight round front legs, painted white, 40½" l, 30" h **1,100**
D–shaped back, molded grape clusters, oblong reticulated seat, conforming seat rail with grapevine decoration, out scrolled foliate form legs, X–stretcher base, painted white, some rust and wear, 43" l **625**
Fern pattern back, Naturalistic style, 1845–65, pair, arched double chair back, scroll cast seat, splayed legs, fern stretchers, 39½" w, price for pair **2,400**
Tall shaped back, flat crest rail, back with row of diamonds, Gothic quatrefoils and trefoils center, down curved latticework seat, Gothic scrolls, slender legs, dark paint, one rear leg repaired, 56" l **3,520**
Twig back, Naturalistic style, 1865–85, stylized twig pattern back, seat, sides, and arms, dog's head arm supports **1,750**
Cast Metal, 1920, arched back, interlaced floral and foliage pattern, center arch interlaced with two side arches which extend to arms, parrot head arm supports, original paint . **1,250**
Wirework, Victorian
　Curved back, lacy scrollwork design, old white repaint, 55" l ... **225**
　Flat crest rail of heavy wire, interlacing arches of lighter wire, scrolled arms, interlaced ovals form pierced seat, arched bands form legs with twisted bar center bands, flowerhead feet, 82" l .. **12,100**
Suite, 1865–85, Naturalistic style, settee

Suite, c1850, settee 47½" l, $935.00. Photograph courtesy of Neal Auction Company.

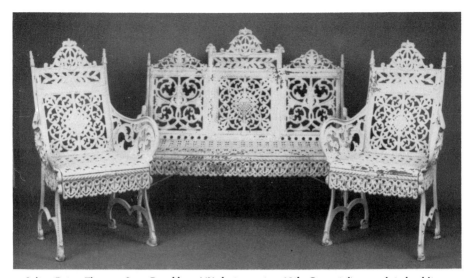

Suite, Peter Timmes Son, Brooklyn, NY, last quarter 19th C, cast iron, painted white, $2,650.00. Photograph courtesy of Skinner, Inc.

and two arm chairs, cast iron, fern pattern, repainted, price for three piece suite **3,000**

Table, 19th C

Cast Iron

Rococo style, round, painted, minor pitting **600**

Scroll pattern, round pierced top, three scroll molded cabriole legs joined by rounded triangular lower shelf, paw feet, painted white **660**

Vintage pattern, circular top, old worn blue repaint, wooden replacement top, 24″ d, 16″ h . . . **175**

Cast Stone, Baroque style, hexagonal top, molded leaf and bead border, triform festooned standard, conforming base, mossy weathered patina **1,200**

Urn

Cast Iron

Kreamer Brothers, Dayton, Ohio, pair, black repaint, 21″ h, price for pair **550**

Unknown maker

Neoclassical style, 1845–65, pair, gadrooned body, flared petal base, square pedestals, stepped form base cast with laurel wreaths on side, peeling original paint, 25″ d, 46″ h, price for pair **2,750**

Neoclassical style, 1865–85, pair, fluted top, egg and dart molded hexagonal base, lion mask handles, repaired crack, repainted, price for pair **3,000**

Renaissance Revival, 1870, griffin handles, round base cast with dolphins and griffins, repainted, 34″ d, 43″ h **5,500**

Lead, Neoclassical style, molded acanthus decoration, frieze of classical figures, circular foot, 20½″ h **600**

Marble, Neoclassical style, pair, campana form, circular foot, square base, rim breaks, price for pair **1,900**

NATURAL MATERIALS

During the middle of the nineteenth century, two vernacular styles evolved—one which preserved and tested the natural characteristics of wood, and the other which sought a substitute for traditional woods. Both represented a significant departure from established design styles. Each was involved with the return to nature phenomenon of the period.

One group experimented with bending wood, exploring the tensile strength of wood as they went. The experiments took place on two fronts—solid wood and laminated woods. The strengthening nature of lamination was known since the eighteenth century. Belter used it to strengthen the portions of his furniture that featured elaborate carvings. Experimentation continued for almost one hundred years, from the 1850s through the 1950s. The era came to an end when new polymer materials became part of the furniture vocabulary.

A second group focused on preserving the natural qualities of wood. Hickory furniture was made with the bark still remaining on many of the elements. When the bark was removed, it was done in a shaved fashion. The rustic furniture movement coincided with Victorian and early twentieth century America's fascination with the forest environment. Furniture was designed to fit into a natural setting. Alas, the only pieces that survive are those whose principal function was indoors.

The need for outdoor furniture that could survive the elements was answered by wicker. Wicker furniture was the rage by the latter third of the nineteenth century; its popularity lasted for close to seventy–five years. Over a hundred major furniture forms can be found in wicker.

One of the difficulties in assessing vernacular furniture is that its designs and forms are not protected by patent. Anyone can manufacture any form, and indeed many did. The result is a wide range of quality in natural material pieces. Collectors and dealers have begun to define the characteristics of a quality piece. The most advanced work has been done in the wicker area. Only recently were the first bentwood and rustic furniture museum exhibitions held.

This section introduces you to three basic areas—bentwood, wicker, and rustic. It is a beginning. Future editions of *Warman's Furniture* will explore bamboo, metal, and synthetics, i.e., plastic and Fiberglas.

BENTWOOD

History: The name that immediately comes to mind when one hears bentwood is Michael Thonet (1796–1871), who founded the Thonet Company in 1849 after experimenting with tying strips of wood together and boiling them in glue. Thonet's glued pieces had problems. They came apart in hot weather. Some furniture elements still had to be carved.

Thonet solved his problems in 1856 when he developed a procedure for steaming and bending wood. The steamed wood was attached to a metal strip by clamps. The metal strip and wood were bent to the desired shape. After a few days, the metal strip and clamps were removed, and the wood held its shape.

In 1853 the firm became Gebruder Thonet when Thonet's five sons joined the firm. In 1856 they opened a factory in Moravia, Austria. Mass–production became a reality. Consecutive production numbers were used as pieces were added to the company's catalogs. This allows for accurate dating of Thonet pieces.

Thonet patented his famous bentwood chair. When the patent expired in 1869, hundreds of firms quickly copied it. Thonet opened its first New York sales room in the 1870s. By 1900, the company had six factories capable of producing 4,000 pieces of furniture daily.

Bentwood furniture attracted the interest of a number of major designers—Marcel Breuer, Charles and Ray Eames, and Joseph Hoffmann in addition to Michael Thonet. Thonet constantly evolved his designs, beginning with Rococo Revival, extending through Art Nouveau, and ending with early modernistic pieces. Hoffmann developed the famous bentwood "tub" chair.

In the 1930s a group of designers led by Gilbert Rhode, Alvar Aalto, Paul R. Goldman, and Gerald Summers experimented with bent plywood. Chairs, desks, and tables were the most popular form. The use of bent laminated plywood in furniture was made possible by several new glue products developed in the late 1920s and early 1930s.

Charles Eames' LCW (Lounge Chair Wood), circa 1946, represented a major breakthrough in plywood furniture. First, it showed that a chair could be permanently molded in two planes instead of one. Second, it was truly a sculptured chair. Bentwood had completed its twentieth century evolution.

Major Manufacturers: Jacob and Joseph Kohn, Vienna, Austria; Gebruder Thonet, Moravia, Austria.

Reference: Derek E. Ostegard (ed.), *Bent Wood and Metal Furniture: 1850–1946*, The American Federation of Arts, 1987.

Chair, Gebruder Thonet, rectangular back panel, surrounded by diamond form panel continuing to form back legs, surrounded by rectangular panel continuing to form front legs, paper label, $425.00. Photograph courtesy of Leslie Hindman Auctioneers.

High Chair, c1890, caned seat, $275.00.

Bed, c1900, scrolled and carved headboard, conforming footboard, full size mattress, 60" h	750
Candlestand, Josef Hoffman, c1905, round top, rim with spheres decoration, 21¼" h	400
Chair	
Arm	
Austria, designed by Siegal, c1900, pair, curved crest rail, shaped upholstered back, curved arms, D–shape upholstered seat, square legs, arched bentwood braces, shaped brass sabots, blue and pale ochre geometric woven upholstery, price for pair	4,400
J & J Kohn, c1930, pair, rectangular bentwood back continuing to open arms, square upholstered seat, cylindrical legs, arched stretchers, price for pair	750

Samuel Gragg, Boston, c1815, Federal style, shaped crest rail, five shaped uprights, scrolling arms, sabre legs, stretchers, painted stylized leafage and peacock feather decoration on crest rail, knees, and seat rail	2,350
Thonet, c1900, scrolled back and arms, cane seat, splayed legs, original label and stamp	300
Thonet, c1935, pine, upholstered back and seat, lacquered, 43" h	400
Child's, open arm, worn red paint	175
Desk, office, c1890, arched crest rail, tightly woven cane back, scrolled bentwood arms, woven cane rounded seat, adjustable pedestal, X–form base	475
Side	
Attributed to Samuel Gragg, Boston, c1815, shaped crest rail, shaped upright stiles, slat seat, shaped legs, turned stretchers, hoof feet	1,850
J & J Kohn, c1900, oak, pressed wood seat insert, branded and paper label, 36" h	125
Josef Hoffman, three horizontal turned slat back, five turned vertical rods, solid seat, straight legs with stencil decoration, paper label, 36" h	300
Chaise Lounge, Austria, c1900, long curved adjustable back and seat, scrolling runners, 66½" l	850

Cradle

Thonet, c1904, suspended type, rectangular cradle, arched fronts, inverted U–shape bands, curved hood, U–shape support, two legs, 41" l, 43" h 275

Unknown Maker, c1900, shaped, oval bentwood basket, extended ornate scrolled support, 52" l, 36" h 750

Hall Tree

Austria, c1900, arched X–form top, two tiers with attached coat hooks, rectangular legs conjoined with circular bands with umbrella holder, brass inset drip pan, pad feet, 31½" w, 74½" h 1,750

Overhead spindle shelf, spindle back with central mirror, bentwood hook on outside rails, spindle containers flank horizontal rack, bentwood frame, natural color, 48½" w, 17" d, 74¼" h 1,320

Magazine Stand, Thonet, Austria, c1900, four sections with arched di-

Cradle, walnut, original finish, some painted decoration, $310.00. Photograph courtesy of Neal Auction Company.

viders, trestle support with intertwined loops form feet, lower platform shelf, 24" w, 17½" d, 43½" h . 2,475

Mirror, attributed to Koloman Moser, c1902, rectangular beveled mirror plate, arched support mounted with three pierced circles, bulbous pierced base enclosing pierced oval, 41½" h 1,750

Rocker

Attributed to Thonet, c1915, caned oblong back, rounded corners, conforming square seat, elaborate bentwood scrolled sides, integral runners 850

Austria, c1900

Arched upholstered back, rectangular upholstered seat, curved arms, scrolling supports and runners, adjustable footrest 3,850

Oval back with inset oval caned center, turned supports, curved arms continue to scrolling support, flaring rectangular caned seat, integral runners 1,450

Child's, rustic construction, curved caned back, scrolled supports, scrolled arms, cane seat, tied joints, 27" h 150

J & J Kohn, c1870, caned back, bentwood loop arms, caned seat, 44½" h 1,320

J & J Kohn, elaborate scrolled base forms arms and sides, caned seat, adjustable back hinged at center, 70" h 1,650

Shaker style, probably Henry Seymour, Troy, New York, curved crest rail, tape back, curved arms,

Chair, Thonet, maple, curved rectangular back on molded plywood supports, saddle seat on molded plywood legs, "Thonet Bent Ply" paper label, $135.00. Photograph courtesy of Leslie Hindman Auctioneers.

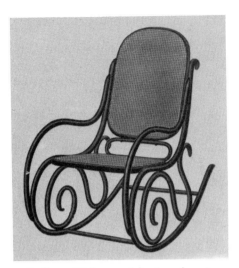

Rocker, c1890, caned back and seat, $350.00.

stripped seat frame, U–shape medial stretcher, box shape stretcher below, back bottom rail repaired, two seat rails replaced, 37" h .... | 75

Thonet, arched twined crest rail, cut velvet fabric upholstered back, armrests, and seat, elaborate scrolling frame, curved runners, 53" l .. | 700

Unknown Maker, early 20th C, arched back with conforming shaped inset caned panel, broad sweeping supports, elongated S–form arms form runners, caned seat with rounded corners .... | 2,200

Screen, Thonet, c1904, Spanish Wand model, three sections, laminated panels with cut geometric designs, green glass insets above .... | 3,000

Settee, J & J Kohn

44" l, c1900, shaped back with scrolling cane lobes, shaped caned seat, turned legs, flaring feet, bentwood box stretcher .... | 550

47" l, three part scrolled cane back, scrolled arms, cane seat, splayed legs .... | 700

54" l, interlaced scrolled back, inward scrolled arms, shaped oval seat, flared cylindrical legs, original paper label "Jacob & Josef Kohn, Vienna" .... | 950

Sofa, Thonet, Model #9752, sleeper type, adjustable backrest, scrolling legs, 70" l .... | 1,250

Stool, Thonet, Austria, c1901, attributed to Marcel Kammerer, beech, square

seat, four legs with U–shape braces forming spandrels, shaped bronze sabot feet, 14¼" sq, 18½" h .... | 1,430

Suite, Jacob & Josef Kohn, c1902, settee, armchair and two side chairs, blue upholstered oval backs, continuous curvilinear arm rails with vertical spindles, blue upholstered seat, tapered legs, spheres on seat rail and legs; settee: 61¼" l; each chair: 39" h, price for four piece suite .... | 20,900

Table, writing, J & J Kohn, c1900, rectangular top, scrolled supports and stretchers, impressed mark "J J Kohn," 37" w, 21" d, 30" h .... | 300

WICKER

History: The origins of wicker furniture date back to ancient civilizations. Wicker was known to the Egyptians, Greeks, and Romans. It was a desirable construction material because its flexibility allowed it to conform to a body's shape, thus providing durable and supple support. It also enjoyed strong popularity in the Orient, the source from which most wicker forms were introduced into the American market in the nineteenth century.

Actually, wicker is a generic term used to describe furniture made from a wide variety of natural fibers among which are cane, rattan, reed, rush, and willow. Cane comes from the bark of the rattan plant and is used primarily in seats, backs, and for wrapping. Rattan, a climbing palm found in Ceylon, China, India, Malaysia, and other countries in Southeast Asia and the Far East, can be bent without breaking and exhibits a natural, high–gloss shine. Its water resistance makes it ideal for outdoor furniture. Reed is the central core of the rattan palm. It takes stain and paint far better than rattan, replacing rattan as the principal form of wicker furniture by the mid–nineteenth century. Rush is a perennial plant, classified as a grass, that is rarely used in wicker furniture. Willow, a plant that grows in wet lowlands through much of the world, is almost indistinguishable from reed. Look for small knots where shoots have been cut off.

Around 1917 Marshall Lloyd invented the Lloyd loom that produced a fiber–reed, consisting of machine–twisted paper fibers surrounding a wire core. A tightly woven product was the loom's trademark. By the 1930s this manmade fiber was used in the production of most "wicker" furniture.

Wicker furniture enjoyed its first period of popularity in the latter half of the nineteenth century. The introduction of the porch as a major architectural element on homes, summer cottages, and hotels, required durable, serviceable outdoor furniture. Wicker fit the bill. Wicker's adaptability and wide variety of forms quickly took it inside as well.

Few forms escaped adaptation in wicker. Babies had wicker carriages, cradles, and cribs. Milady had planters, shelves, and stands for her special needs. Wicker fretwork served as architectural embellishments. Even the Victrola could have a wicker case.

Wicker designs changed to conform to popular tastes. Mid–nineteenth century wicker was highly ornate and light in appearance. By the turn of the century it developed a more practical appearance—tighter weaves, rectangular shapes, and an emphasis on fully–painted pieces. These pieces blended well with furniture from the Arts and Crafts movement.

Wicker's popularity continued in the 1920s and 1930s, then waned in the 1940s and 1950s as emphasis was placed on bent bamboo forms. A revival took place in the late 1960s as collectors discovered the older pieces and others wanted contemporary examples.

Major Manufacturers: J. and C. Berrian, New York, NY; Bielecky Brothers, New York, NY; Chittenden and Eastman Company, Burlington, IA; Dryad Works, England; Ficks Reed Company, Cincinnati, OH; Glendon Iron Wheel Company, Toledo, OH; Heywood Brothers and Company, Gardner, MA; Heywood Brothers and Wakefield Rattan Company (consolidated 1897); Lloyd Manufacturing Company, Menominee, MI; Maple and Company, England, with showrooms in London, Paris, and Buenos Aires; Joseph P. McHugh and Company, New York, NY; Minnet and Company, New York, NY; Prairie Grass Furniture Co., Glendale, NY; Charles Schober Company, Philadelphia, PA; Slocombe and Son, England; Gustav Stickley, Eastwood, NY; Wakefield Rattan Company, Boston, MA; and John Wanamaker Company, Philadelphia, PA.

References: Richard Sanders, *The Official Price Guide To Wicker, Third Edition*, House of Collectibles, 1985; Tim Scott, *Fine Wicker Furniture, 1870–1930*, Schiffer Publishing, 1990; Robert and Harriett Swedberg, *Wicker Furniture: Styles and Prices, Revised Edition with Current Prices*, Wallace–Homestead, 1988.

NATURAL MATERIALS

Bench
  Settee
    35″ w, 31″ h, hooped crest rail flanked by rows of decorative curlicues, spiral wrapped posts and six spindles, oval pressed–in seat, decorative curlicue apron, wrapped cabriole legs joined by X–form stretcher, white **425**
    37″ w, 31″ h, tight weave, arched back with central diamond de-

sign, back wraps partially around to sides, armless, upholstered seat cushions, straight skirt, wrapped legs, machine woven .   **350**
    41″ w, 18″ d, 29″ h, 1910–40, straight crest rail, continuous arms, tightly woven panels above and below open area on back and sides, braided edge on tightly woven lift seat and seat rail, long skirt with central diamond design, white **600**
    41″ w, 20″ d, 39″ h, 1920–30, rectangular double chair back with tight weave over open work, wrapped down curving arms, tightly woven seat and skirt, wrapped legs and X–form stretchers, white **325**
    43″ w, 36″ h, tightly woven rectangular back with inverted triangle decoration, tightly woven arms, rectangular seat with woven diamond herringbone pattern, continuous braided edging from crest to front legs, turned spindle apron . .   **450**
    57″ w, 33″ h, 1950s, hoop back, rolled crest rail continuing to down curving armrests, very ornate open work curlicue heart design in back, sides, and apron, tightly woven oblong seat, cabriole legs, X–form stretcher, white **350**
  Window, 34″ w, 18″ d, 29½″ h, tightly woven rolled arms, curlicue design on sides, rectangular pressed–in seat, wrapped legs, three stretcher front and back with S–scrolled curlicues above and below, natural color **350**
Birdcage Stand, 74″ h, tightly woven quarter moon shaped cage holder raised on wrapped pole standard, tightly woven conical base, white . .   **175**
Bookcase, 19½″ w, 14″ d, 42″ h, ring turned spire type finials on front and back spiral turned posts, arched crest with turned vasiform spindles surmounted by balls, seven spindles with curlicue tops form back, four wood shelves, open sides, ball feet, natural color **350**
Chair
  Arm, 29″ w, 32″ h, barrel shaped, rolled arm, tight weave over open work on back and sides, removable spring cushion seat, braided edge on back and seat, open work skirt, wrapped legs, natural color **235**
  Desk, 36″ h, square back, arched crest rail, central tightly woven panel on open work splat, wrapped

posts and hip brackets, upholstered seat cushion in woven trapezoidal seat, tightly woven seat rail, open work skirt, wrapped legs joined by X–form stretcher, white 175

Funeral Parlor, 36" h, arched crest rail, triangle design in tightly woven upper half of back, open work lower half, wrapped hip brackets, tightly woven trapezoidal seat with braided edge, wrapped legs and X–form stretcher, white 150

Hall, 1885–1900, tall, narrow, peacock fan top, interwoven uprights, stick and ball decoration, repainted 700

Lounge, 33" w, 18¼" d, 26" h, 1920s, child's, square back, tight weave, wrapped crest rail, arms, legs, and arched stretchers, matching similarly woven footrest with slanting top and foot bar with ball finials, 17" w, 20" d, 11" h footrest, white 165

Photographer's, 20" w, 42" h, oval panel with tightly woven radiating design supported by posts and central spindle flanked by curlicues, tightly woven S–scrolled rolled down curving arms continue to long skirt with diamond design over open work and braid, pressed–in round seat, wrapped legs, white .. 435

Reception, 17½" w, 39" h, tightly woven shaped crest rail with radiating weave design and "V" decoration, splat with S– and C–scrolls and curved stick and ball spindles, spiral turned post with balls on each end, pressed–in seat,

wrapped turned ball legs with curlicue apron and X–form stretcher, natural color 275

Side

32" h, 29" w, hoop back, tightly woven crest rail continuing to armrests, very ornate open work heart design in back, curlicue and bead work sides, pressed–in oval seat, open work skirt, wrapped cabriole legs flanked by curlicues, X–form stretcher, white 450

34½" h, 16½" w, 1910–20, square back, cutout blocked diamond design in tightly woven back, upholstered slip seat, braided edges on seat, similar cutout designs in arched skirt on three sides, turned wrapped legs joined by stretchers, white 175

37" h, square back, diamond and X–shaped designs in tightly woven back, wrapped hip brackets, trapezoidal seat with upholstered seat cushion and braided edge, tightly woven skirt, wrapped legs joined by X–form stretcher, white 175

Wing, 33" w, 40" h, braided edges, openwork back, wings, and sides, magazine pockets both sides, hinged lids serve as armrests, tightly woven seat rail, arched open work skirt, tightly woven bulbous feet .. 400

Chaise Lounge

54" l, 33" w, braided edge on tightly woven back with double row of X–

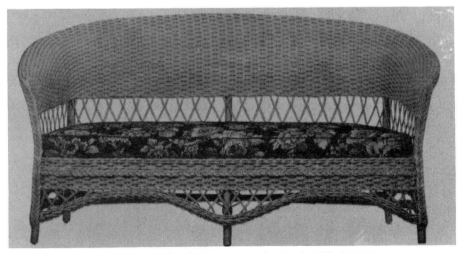

Davenport, tapestry upholstery, seat 60" w, back 19" h, $650.00.

shaped decoration, open work lidded magazine pocket arms, serpentine shaped seat and foot rest, scalloped open work skirt, ball feet,
white 750
58" l, 35" w, 36" h, tightly woven crest
continuing to braced armrests, one
arm shorter, open work back,
tightly woven seat and seat rail, upholstered seat cushion, open work
arched skirt, wrapped tapering legs 875
Daybed, 54" l, 24" d, 36" h, 1910–30,
molded back and half arm, cushioned
back and seat, repainted, minor
breaks to woven wicker panels 725
Desk
28½" w, 18" d, 30" h, tightly woven
arched crest, rounded corners and
braided edge on rectangular wood
top, tightly woven single drawer
frieze, wrapped out curving legs
joined by stretchers, white 300
36" w, 19" d, 34½" h, tightly woven
gallery with two attached letter baskets on kidney shaped wood top,
conformingly shaped tightly woven
single drawer frieze, seven
wrapped round legs braced to skirt,
tightly woven band above ball feet,
white 350
Divan, 34" w, 18" d, 38" h, 1900–05,
tightly woven heart shaped back with
curlicue decoration at top and double
diamond design over a lyre shaped
splat with curlicues and stick and ball
decoration, rolled curved arms with
tightly woven armrests above similar
inverted lyre shaped arm supports,
pressed–in seat, tightly woven cab-

riole legs joined by X–form stretcher,
natural color 575
Fernery
12" sq, 30" h, tightly woven square
well with central diamond design
in side panels, wrapped out curving
legs, wrapped X–form stretcher,
white 125
25½" w, 18½" d, 32" h, tightly woven
rectangular well, front of well
shorter than back, wrapped braced
legs, X–form stretcher, white 100
29" w, 10" d, 63" h, round birdcage
with conical top, tapered sides, and
tray with woven wall suspended
from curved arch with open work
sides, open work rectangular well
and scalloped skirt, wrapped round
legs, box stretcher, white 500
Footstool
14½" w, 12" d, 8" h, upholstered
cushion in recessed rectangular top
with braided edge, tightly woven
sides, out wrapped curving legs
with curlicue brackets, white 125
16" d, 23" h, round, tightly woven
pattern radiates from center top and
continues to skirt with open weave
edge design, four wrapped out
curving ball turned legs with brackets, X–form stretcher, white 200
16" w, 11" d, 21" h, rectangular upholstered top, tightly woven sides,
wrapped legs, white 150
20" w, 12" d, 12½" h, tightly woven
rectangular top with braided edge,
open weave skirt with central open
oval design, bracket feet with curlicues, white 150
20" w, 13" d, 16" h, rectangular top
with upholstered cushion, splayed
base, tightly woven full length skirt
with arched lower edge, braided
edges, white 250
Headboard, 36" w, 50" h, single bed
size, inverted tear drop shape, ornate
heart motif with curlicues and C–
scrolls, white 125
Highchair
13½" w, 38" h, 1875–1900, tightly
woven arched crest rail, intricate
open work back and sides, braided
edge on back, arms, and front legs,
trapezoidal seat with loose cushion, scrolled brackets below seat,
out curving legs, X–form concave
stretchers, natural color 235
16¼" w, 21" d, 32½" h, 1910–15,
barrel shaped, tightly woven,
braided edge on back continuing to
down curving arms, hinged food
tray, wood seat, tightly woven skirt,

Fernery, painted white, $180.00.

wood footrest, wrapped out curving legs, wrapped X–form stretchers, white **225**

16½" w, 40" h, 1910–20, tightly woven square back with braided edge continuing to arms, open work sides and lower back, hinged food tray, tightly woven pressed–in seat, wood footrest, wrapped turned tapered legs and stretchers on splayed base, natural color ... **250**

Parlor Set

Two Piece, armchair and rocker, 33" w, 33" h armchair, 34" w, 31" h rocker, rolled backs and arms, tight weave over open work back and sides with large central diamond design, upholstered seat cushion, and tight weave over open work skirt, Heywood–Wakefield, white, price for set **1,000**

Three Pieces

Armchair, rocker, and sofa, 27" w, 35" h armchair, 27" w, 33" h rocker, 80" l, 35" h sofa, early 1900s, braided edge on tightly woven crest rail continuing to rolled arms, woven seat with re- movable cushions, scalloped skirt with tightly woven panel

Rocker, Ordway Mfg. Co., Bristol, Ten- nessee, c1905, alternating ash splints and wicker, "S" shaped arms and arched rocker base, marked with decal, 21" w, 17" d, 44½" h, $725.00. Photograph courtesy Skinner, Inc.

above open work, Bar Harbor set, Ypsilanti Reed Furniture Co, Ionia, MI, white, price for set .. **1,250**

Armchair, rocker, and table, 27", 34½" h armchair, 27½" w, 30" h rocker, 36" w, 24" d, 29½" h ta- ble, barrel shaped armchair and rocker with diamond design in tightly woven back, open work panels on back and sides, rolled arms, upholstered cushion on woven seat, tightly woven seat rails, and tightly woven rectan- gular panel in open work apron, table with braided edge on oval top, rectangular open work panels on tightly woven skirt, and wrapped legs, X–form stretcher, white, price for set ... **750**

Planter, 31" w, 11" d, 67" h, 1910–30, low center well, sides rising up and over to create hanging area **250**

Porch Swing, 72" l, 24" h, double chair back with splayed posts, tightly woven arched crest rail, open work back, tightly woven lower rail, tightly woven sides with braced rolled arms, tightly woven seat with rectangular upholstered seat cushion, seat rests on full length planks front and back with rings for chain suspension, white ... **450**

Rocker

Arm

31" h, 33" w, barrel shaped, tightly woven, diamond design in sides, upholstered seat cushion, arched skirt, X–form stretcher, white .. **125**

33" h, 32" w, square back, basket weave pattern over open work back, rectangular armrests with wrapped braces, open work sides, braided edge on basket weave seat and skirt, X–form, white **175**

35" h, open work scallop shell de- sign back, down curving arms with hooped supports, round pierced seat, open work cabriole legs, white **375**

37" h, 23½" w, hooped back with tightly woven roll continuing to arms, trapezoidal caned panel surrounded by open work C– and S–scrolls, stick and ball arm sup- ports, round seat with pierced design, S–scrolled cabriole legs, natural color **375**

37½" h, 25" w, ornate fan shaped crest rail with tightly woven rolled border centering a con- formingly shaped open work band with a central tightly woven panel, center back spindle with radiating curlicues, tightly woven rolled armrests with stick and ball supports, round seat, basket weave center band on long arched skirt with suspended curlicues, turned ball leg brackets, white 650

38½" h, 25" w, square back, wrapped ball finials on posts flanking raised tablet and stiles, very ornate open work design on back with star patterned cane insert in central fan design, narrow open work armrests, tightly woven serpentine rolled seat, open work apron and similarly worked panels between side stretchers, white 375

Child's

21" h, 1900–20, barrel shaped, tight weave and open weave work continuing from back to sides, tightly woven seat and skirt, wrapped legs, white 165

22" h, 20" w, 1910–25, barrel shaped, rolled arms, tight weave, upholstered slip cushion, long skirt, white 175

22½" h, 1885–1900, rolled arms, fully woven rolled back with intricate design, natural color 225

24" h, 18" w, 1875–1900, ball finials on splayed posts, alternating tight and open weave designs on back, scroll work arms and arched apron, natural color 150

24" h, 21" w, 18" d, 1910–30, woven simple interlaced banding, repainted 175

24¼" h, 1885–1900, turned arms, base, and uprights, spindle and ball decoration on back, two interwoven wicker strips, interlaced circle arm supports, woven seat, repainted 145

24½" h, 18" w, late 1800s, hooped back with central panel with caned star pattern and surrounded by decorative scrolls, continuous arms with decorative stick and ball supports, tightly woven seat, wrapped legs and front stretcher 135

28" h, 18" w, 1910–25, tightly woven rolled back, arms, and seat, open work area on upper back with a diamond design below 150

Platform, 36" h, 20" w, 27" d, square back with braided crest rail, open work design of diamonds, vertical

stripes, and triangles, down curving arms with hooped arm supports, upholstered trapezoidal seat, open work skirt, inset open work panels in platform base, white 550

Sewing, 22½" w, 33½" h, square back with open work panel between tightly woven panels above and below, wrapped hip brackets, tightly woven trapezoidal seat and rectangular skirt, wrapped legs, demilune pocket with braided rim and open work panel over tightly woven bottom attached to side of seat, white 275

Rocker, No. W59D, Heywood Brothers, c1910, willow, flat crest rail continuing to arms, paper label, 32½" w, 23" d, 38" h, $225.00. Photograph courtesy of Skinner, Inc.

Sofa

41" l, 18" d, 24½" h, 1910–20, cabriole, child's, tight weave, two diamonds design on back, rolled arms, long skirt, wrapped legs 375

58" l, 31¼" h, tightly woven crest with diamond designs continuing to rolled arms, open work double chair back and sides, upholstered seat cushion, braided seat rail, tightly woven scalloped apron, wrapped legs, two X–form stretchers, white 475

84" l, 34" h, arched crest rail, upholstered back, tightly woven arms and armrests, open work sides, spring upholstered seat with three seat cushions, three diamonds dec-

oration on tightly woven scalloped
apron   550
Table
Changing, 36″ w, 19½″ d, 38″ h,
1910–30, three tiers of wooden
shelves, galleried edges, repainted,
loss to leg wrappings   300
Coffee, 48″ l, 16″ d, 18½″ h, 1920–
30, rectangular hardwood top, serpentine ends, scrolled wicker base
and legs, natural finish   375
Game, 36″ sq, 30″ h, overhanging
square wood top, tightly woven
skirt, round wrapped legs, X–form
stretcher, arched X–form braces . .   475
Library, 42″ w, 26″ d, 30″ h, slightly
overhanging rectangular wood top,
tightly woven straight skirt, boxed
legs, and rectangular medial shelf,
wicker painted white   300
Parlor
22″ w, 15″ d, 24″ h, basket weave
pattern on rectangular top, similarly woven V–form magazine
shelf below, wrapped legs, white   145
24″ sq, 29¼″ h, tightly woven,
square top, scalloped apron,
cabriole legs, square medial shelf
with woven gallery, white   400
27½″ d, 30¼″ h, tightly woven
round top, wrapped straight legs
with ring decorated braces,
round medial shelf with cane in-
sert, white   125
30″ d, 30″ h, round wood insert
framed by tightly woven apron,
tightly woven cabriole legs continuing to variation ball feet with
animal paw type design, round
wood medial shelf with braided
edge joined to legs by wrapped
stretchers, white   425
30″ w, 20½″ d, 30″ h, braided edge
on oval wood top, round straight
legs, braided edge on square
wood medial shelf, open work
demilune magazine pockets attached to legs on both sides,
white   250
36″ w, 24″ d, 30″ h, oval wood top,
basket weave design on straight
skirt, wrapped serpentine legs
joined at narrowest point by X–
form stretcher, white   300
Sofa
60″ l, 18″ w, 30″ h, rounded corners
on rectangular wood top, conformingly shaped tightly woven
skirt, wrapped legs joined by H–
stretcher with center bracketed
post, white   250
60″ l, 20″ w, 31″ h, 1910–30,

shaped rectangular hardwood
top, serpentine ends, stretcher
base, repainted   400
Tea Cart
41″ l, 24″ d, 39″ h, Heywood Wakefield, 1900–10, snowball finials,
gallery type lower tray shelf, large
wheels with turned spokes, re-
painted   700
36″ l, 21″ d, 30″ h, rectangular wood
top in wrapped frame, half length
wood medial shelf with gallery, rectangular lower shelf with gallery,
braced shelves, large spoked
wheels, white   525

MANMADE FIBER

Bench, settee, 60″ w, 30″ h, tightly
woven, slightly curved back wraps
around to flared sides, central inverted triangle decoration, woven
symmetrical arch design spans from
back to front on each side, upholstered slip cushion, straight apron
with similar inverted diamond deco-
ration, white   600
Chair, arm, 23″ w, 31″ h, plain tight
weave pattern, barrel shaped,
rounded back continuing to sides,
braided edges, upholstered slip seat
cushion, slightly arched apron,
wrapped feet, unpainted   150
Parlor Set, three pieces
62″ l, 32″ h sofa, 30″ w, 32″ h armchair, 29″ w, 31″ h rocker, wrap
around back, braided crest rail continuing to slightly rolled arms,
tightly woven panel between open
work bands on back and sides, upholstered seat cushions, braided
seat rail, open work arched apron,
and wrapped legs, sofa with three
cushions and double arched apron,
painted white, price for set   1,200
65″ l, 37½″ h sofa, 25″ w, 38″ h arm-
chair, 26″ w, 38″ h rocker, tightly
woven, fan shaped back with basket weave band decoration, rolled
arms, upholstered slip cushion, and
arched apron, painted, price for set   1,275
Rocker
31″ h, 17″ w, square back, tightly
woven back with central diamond
over X–shape design, demi arms,
trapezoidal seat with upholstered
seat cushion, straight skirt front and
sides, X–form stretcher with brack-
ets, white   150
36″ h, 30″ w, arched back, tightly
woven upper back with central flattened diamond design over open

work lower section, similarly woven rolled arms and sides, front arm braces, upholstered slip cushion, arched tightly woven skirt . . .   **250**

RUSTIC

History: American rustic furniture has two roots. The first is England's naturalistic garden movement that began in the eighteenth century. Furniture was designed to complement and closely imitate nature. The second is mid–nineteenth century Victorian America's idyllic notion of the great outdoors—basking in the culture of summer chautauquas and camp meetings, viewing sunsets from a rustic chair on a cabin porch, and wandering through the forest on sylvan paths.

Andrew Jackson Downing, in his *The Architecture of Country Houses*, first published in 1850, wrote: "It is the solitude and freedom of the family home in the country which constantly preserves the purity of the nation, and invigorates its intellectual powers . . . Every winding path throughout the woods, every secluded resting–place in the valley, becomes part of our affections, friendship, joy, and sorrows. Happy is he who lives this life of a cultivated mind in the country!" Downing advocated rustic furnishing to enhance the experience. The craze which began in the 1850s lasted until the mid–1920s.

By the end of the nineteenth century, an area of rural retreat within a half–day's to full–day's travel by railroad was being developed near every major American city. New York City had its Adirondacks; Philadelphia its Poconos. The presidency of Teddy Roosevelt and its emphasis on the preservation of the American wilderness further fueled the desire of urban Americans for a respite in the country.

Hickory was an ideal wood for rustic furniture—supple and pliable. Because of its large stands of hickory, Indiana quickly became the production center for hickory furniture, albeit individual craftspersons and small plants produced hickory furniture throughout the northern and midwest woodlands.

Throughout most of the period, the basic furniture forms and designs remained the same. A 1926 catalog of the Rustic Hickory Furniture Company of La Porte, Indiana, offers 146 designs, ranging from bedroom furniture to an octagonal summer house. In the 1920s subtle refinements were made—such as the move to fewer spindles and the addition of more woven materials.

The Depression ended America's involvement with rustic furniture; Other things seemed more important. In the mid–1970s collectors and dealers rediscovered rustic furniture. Several museum exhibitions were held. The folk art community adopted Adirondack furniture as one of its own.

By the 1990s the craze is over and prices are stable.

Leading Manufacturers: Indiana Willow Products Company, Martinsville, IN; Jasper Hickory Furniture Company, Jasper, IN; Old Hickory Chair Company, Martinsville, IN; The State of Indiana Farm Industries, Putnamville, IN; and Rustic Hickory Furniture Company, La Porte, IN.

References: Ralph Kylloe, *The Collected Works of Indiana Hickory Furniture Makers*, Rustic Publications, 1989; Victor M. Linoff (editor), *Rustic Hickory Furniture Co.: Porch, Lawn and Cottage Furniture: Two Complete Catalogs, ca. 1904 and 1926*, reprint, Dover Publications, 1991.

Bed
  Bunk, set, arched rails and three spindles over fiber woven headboard and footboard, fiber woven side rails, woven diamond designs, casters, detachable ladder, twin mattress size, 39" w, 68" h **495**
  Four Poster, Rustic Hickory Furniture Co, La Porte, IN, 1913, bulbous shaped finials on head and foot posts, spindled headboard and footboard and side rails, varnish finish, 74" l, 54" w, 72" h **375**
Bench
  Corner, unknown maker, c1915, cedar, straight upper rails, three posts, smooth planed thirty–five board seat, diamond shaped braces between upper and lower stretchers .   **235**
  Garden, unknown maker, c1920, bark covered cedar, straight rails, geometric and random twig designed back, twig braces, wide armrests with spindle supports, fourteen board seat **275**
Settee
  Indiana Willow Products Co, Martinsville, IN, 1948, hickory, double chair back, open barrel shaped arms, fiber woven back, sides, and seat with diamond designs, box stretchers, 42" w seat, 18" d **300**
  Old Hickory Chair Co, Martinsville, IN, 1912, hickory, triple chair back, upper and lower rails curve around to sides to form arms, flared arm posts, double woven splint back, armrests, and seat, legs joined by box stretchers, 72" l, 19" d, 36" h **200**
Book Shelf, Jasper Hickory Furniture Co, Jasper, IN, 1930s, spindled gallery and sides, five shelves with back rails, 36" w, 12" d, 54" h **185**

Chair
Arm
Indiana Willow Products Company, Martinsville, IN, 1948, high square fiber woven back with rectangular headrest panel, open barrel shaped arm rails, splayed arm posts, fiber woven seat, box stretchers   250

Old Hickory Furniture Co, Martinsville, IN, 1930s, hickory, continuous arm, woven splint back and seat, orange and black wiped enamel finish, 20″ w seat, 19″ d, 20″ h   350

Unknown Maker, c1910, bark covered cedar, straight rails joined by three spindles, V–shaped arm supports, six board seat, inverted V–shaped braces between upper and lower stretchers   150

Morris, Old Hickory Chair Co, Martinsville, IN, 1912, straight shawl rail, adjustable reclining woven splint back, seven spindle arm supports each side, woven splint seat, box stretchers, 20″ w seat, 21″ d, 48″ h   275

Side
Old Hickory Furniture Co, Martinsville, IN, 1930s, hickory, seven spindle back, woven splint seat, 20″ w, 18″ d, 21″ h   125

Rustic Hickory Furniture Co, La Porte, IN, 1904, hickory, central woven splint panel in square

back, woven splint trapezoidal seat, box stretchers, 17″ w seat, 15″ d, 40″ h   95

Steamer, Old Hickory Furniture Co, Martinsville, IN, 1930s, hickory, woven splint back and seat, writing arm, 12 x 24″ writing surface, spindled base, 48″ l, 22″ w, 30″ h   425

Chest of Drawers
Indiana Willow Products Co, Martinsville, IN, 1948, rectangular overhanging top, five long drawers, paneled ends, square legs on casters, 39″ w, 18″ d, 49″ h   275

Rustic Hickory Furniture Co, La Porte, IN, 1913, oak, hickory trim, 24 x 30″ rectangular swing mirror supported by square posts, spindles rail below, two short drawers over two long drawers, square legs on casters, turned pulls, 40″ w, 20″ d . . .   325

Clothes Tree
Old Hickory Furniture Co, Martinsville, IN, c1935, hickory, six peg hooks, tripod base, arched legs, 68″ h   125

State of Indiana Farm Industries, Putnamville, IN, 1930s, hickory, eight peg hooks, four arched legs joined to column by stretchers, 66″ h . . .   150

Cupboard, corner, Old Hickory Furniture Co, Martinsville, IN, 1930s, oak and hickory, spindled gallery, two glazed doors, interior shelf, two paneled cupboard doors, rounded

Settee, Old Hickory Furniture Co., Martinsville, IN, hickory, double chair back with woven splint panels, flared arm posts, woven splint seat, 42″ w, 19″ d, 22″ h, $225.00.

118

feet, dark oak finish, turned wood pulls, 20" w, 66" h 775

Daybed, Old Hickory Chair Co, Martinsville, IN, 1912, hickory, raised curved backrest supported by braces, six legs, box stretchers, reinforced woven bark top, 72" l, 28" w 350

Desk, Old Hickory Furniture Co, Martinsville, IN, 1930s, hickory and oak, arched spindled gallery, oak top and two medial shelves each side, spindles on curved shelf brackets, single drawer, dark oak finish, 36" w, 24" d, 30¼" h 475

Divan, Old Hickory Furniture Co, Martinsville, IN, 1930s, spindles back, arms, and base, wrapped woven splint rail, arms, and seat, checkered diamond design on cushions, 64" l, 22" d, 18" h 500

Flower Box, unknown maker, 1910s, bark covered cedar, two rows of eight upright logs joined together, cutout rectangular planting area, 33" w, 12" d, 8" deep well 45

Glider, State of Indiana Farm Industries, Putnamville, IN, 1930s, hickory, woven splint back and seat, open arms, trestle based stand, set of four swing chains, 86" w, 18" d seat, 36" h 400

High Chair
  Old Hickory Furniture Co, Martinsville, IN, 1930s, hickory, spindled back, tray with gallery, woven splint seat, splayed base, box stretchers 250
  State of Indiana Farm Industries, Putnamville, IN, 1930s, hickory, four spindle back, rectangular tray on hinged arms, woven splint seat, splayed base, shaped footrest, pair of box stretchers, 13" w seat, 14" d seat, 40" h 275

Porch Swing, Rustic Hickory Furniture Co, La Porte, IN, 1913, hickory, three rectangular woven splint panels back, arms on flared arm posts, rectangular woven splint seat, spindled skirt, four suspension chains, 60" l 275

Rocker
  Old Hickory Chair Co, Martinsville, IN, 1912, hickory, barrel back, rectangular woven splint headrest panel raised above woven splint back and sides, woven splint seat, box stretchers, 17" w seat, 15" d, 47" h 250
  Rustic Hickory Furniture Co, La Porte, IN, 1904, hickory, slightly arched top on woven splint back, down curving arms, woven splint seat,

box stretchers, shaped runners, 17" w seat, 15" d, 40" h 175

State of Indiana Farm Industries, Putnamville, IN, 1930s, hickory, child's, arm, three spindled back, woven splint seat, box stretcher, shaped runners, 14" w seat, 12" d seat, 24" h 135

Unknown Maker, 1910s, bark covered cedar, straight upper and lower rails, five straight spindles, six board seat, double stretchers, 40" h 200

Rocking Settee, Rustic Hickory Furniture Co, La Porte, IN, 1913, hickory, double barrel back, woven splint back curves around to sides, flared arm posts, rectangular woven seat, legs joined by box stretchers, on runners, 40" w seat, 16" d 375

Plant Stand, Old Hickory Furniture Co., Martinsville, IN, hickory, round well, crossed tripod base, X-form stretchers, 11" d, 31" h, $65.00.

Stand
  Plant, Jasper Hickory Furniture Co, Jasper, IN, 1930s, oak and hickory, square oak top, four legs, box stretchers top and bottom joined by vertical spindles, 16" w, 16" d, 21" h 75

Umbrella, Jasper Hickory Furniture Co, Jasper, IN, 1930s, four posts joined by two pairs of box stretchers, spindled rails and sides, square bottom on raised legs, 11" w, 11" d, 42" h **100**

Whatnot, corner, New York, late 19th C, oak and thornwood, stripped bark, six tiers, 55½" h **325**

Stool, Rustic Hickory Furniture Co, La Porte, IN, 1913, saddle type, concave top with woven splint seat, splayed legs joined by box stretchers, 20" l, 12" w, 16" h **75**

Table

Coffee, Indiana Willow Products Co, Martinsville, IN, 1948, oak and hickory, round top, flaring legs joined by X–form stretcher, 30" d, 18" h **175**

Dressing, Jasper Hickory Furniture Co, Jasper, IN, 1930s, oak and hickory, hinged triple panel mirror, rectangular oak top, single long drawer, spindles sides, natural oak finish, 38" w, 21" d **250**

Dropleaf, Rustic Hickory Furniture Co, La Porte, IN, 1926, rectangular golden oak top, rounded corners on 11" wide leaves, splayed base, legs joined by X–form stretcher, 44" w open size, 33" d, 31" h **180**

End, unknown maker, 1910–20, cedar, bark covered frame, smooth planed square top and base shelf, X–form braces between underside of top and stretchers **75**

Gate Leg, unknown maker, NY, c1915, oak and hickory, rounded corners on rectangular oak top, rounded corners on two triangular leaves, thick legs, stretchers and rails joined by twenty–two spindles, two swing–out legs, cast iron hinges, 43½" w, 40" d, 33½" h .. **350**

Lamp, Old Hickory Furniture Co, Martinsville, IN, c1932, octagonal oak top, splayed hickory legs, double box stretchers, dark oak finish, 24" w, 30" h **225**

Occasional, Old Hickory Chair Co, Martinsville, IN, 1912, hickory, circular golden oak top, center column on X–form bracket base, block feet, 30" d, 29" h **200**

Tete–a–tete, unknown maker, 1910s, bark covered cedar, two seats opening to opposite sides, straight rails, four spindles on backs and arms, six board seats, double stretchers front and back **300**

Part III
American Regional
Furniture

AMERICA, DESPITE ITS SURFACE UNITY, is a nation of cultural diversity. Wave after wave of immigrants flocked to its shores; with them came the cultural traditions and preferences of their homelands. Assimilation often takes several generations.

Living with pieces that closely copied their foreign heritage helped America's newest settlers adjust. In most cases, only a few basics accompanied them on their journey. Furniture was expensive to transport and usually left behind. The only furniture piece that made the journey was a traveling chest.

In many cases, cultural communities contained furniture cabinetmakers who were trained abroad. They had the ability to build in the old style long after they came to America. Being customer oriented, they built what the customer wanted.

During the latter half of the twentieth century many of the European cultural enclaves that were so much a part of the urban environment of the nineteenth and early twentieth centuries were broken apart. Financial success and a more mobile population contributed to this development. In a few instances urban renewal destroyed entire ethnic neighborhoods.

Little ethnic furniture survives, in part because those who owned it eventually wanted to cast aside their European baggage and enter the

Regional furniture enjoys strong popularity. Although Adirondack, Canadian, Pennsylvania German, and Shaker are among the best known regional types, other regions, such as Kentucky, developed characteristics that allow specific pieces of furniture to be identified with them. Kentucky sugar press, Taylor Country, KY, c1820, cherry, base features lift lid over three section unit (two drawers flank central section with hinged door), $11,000.00. Photograph courtesy of Green River Antiques Auctions and *Antique Week*. Specific forms enjoyed greater popularity in some regions than in others. In Kentucky, the linen press was a favorite. This cherry linen press found in Boyle County, KY, was heavily restored and refinished in the early part of the 20th C. As a result, it only realized $2,000.00. Photograph courtesy of Green River Antiques Auctions and *Antique Week*.

American mainstream. There is a strong tendency to show one's cultural adaptation by looking exactly like the infamous Joneses.

An Americanization of forms and design elements did occur, brought about by the availability of different types of wood, changes in room size, and simple economic necessity. However, whenever possible, pieces were made in the style of the "old country."

The lack of familiarity of American collectors and dealers with many foreign styles, e.g., Germanic, Scandinavian, or Slavic, means that pieces are all too often treated as vernacular pieces instead of being given their proper ethnic attribution. This is the result of two failings in American furniture literature: the lack of (1) translations of European regional furniture studies and (2) interest by American scholars in areas other than the Pennsylvania Germans and Shakers.

It will surprise some to find Canadian furniture included in this section. Our neighbor to the north closely mirrored American formal and vernacular design styles. Regional differences are perceptible to the practiced eye, but many a "Canadian" piece has been sold to an unsuspecting American dealer and/or collector.

There are several regional styles not covered in this section, e.g., the Scandinavian heritage pieces of Minnesota and Wisconsin and the Spanish styles of the American Southwest. You will find these and more in the next edition of *Warman's Furniture*. Meanwhile, take the time to examine and learn about the four categories of regional furniture that are included. They are the most commonly found forms.

REFERENCE: Lyndon C. Viel, *Antique Ethnic Furniture*, Wallace–Homestead, 1983.

ADIRONDACK

History: In the 1980s the folk art community discovered the painted rustic furniture most commonly found in the mountain lodges, summer cottages, and hotels that comprised the Adirondack Mountain resort area of New York state. Although identified with this region, some of the more common pieces, such as the smoking stand with the log–cabin cigarette box, were sold in five and dime stores, such as Woolworth's.

Local guides made the first Adirondack furniture for their shacks and lean–tos. Wealthy vacationers, charmed by the quaint nature of this makeshift furniture, decided to utilize it in their summer cottages, especially in the living room and porch areas. Caretakers of these summer retreats of the wealthy joined with the guides as manufacturers of Adirondack pieces. Eventually a thriving cottage industry developed. The craze lasted from the 1870s through the 1920s.

Ernest Stove, a builder of camp buildings, is one of the best known makers of Adirondack furniture. Using yellow and white birch he built hundreds, if not thousands, of pieces during roughly a twenty year period, i.e., 1890s through 1911.

The demand for rustic furniture in the Adirondacks during the last quarter of the nineteenth century was extremely strong. Local manufacturers could not meet the demand. Indiana hickory furniture was imported. In many cabins, cottages, and hotels, rustic Adirondack pieces were complemented with Arts and Crafts furniture and Indian decorative arts, e.g., Navajo rugs.

There are two design elements that identify the Adirondack subcategory of rustic furniture. The first is the use of elaborate bent twigs in the design. Twigs were interlaced, looped, and/or twisted. In almost every instance, the bark was left on the wood.

The second element, the one which attracted the folk art collector, was line, scroll, and other painted accents used to highlight the piece. The preferred paint colors were gold and silver, albeit pieces have been found utilizing a wide variety of colors.

As soon as the collecting craze struck in the mid–1980s, modern reproductions, copycats, and fakes hit the market. Some enterprising wholesalers ordered volume copies of some forms, e.g., the smoking stand, from abroad. Others simply put their talents to use stateside. The result is that the market currently is flooded with "questionable" pieces.

Candlestand, round pine top, crooked entwined natural roots and burl flaring pedestal base, black paint traces, 16" d, 29" h	**225**
Chair	
Child's, bent sapling frame, oak slat seat and back, minor damage and wear	**100**
Side, bent rustic branches, rounded back with three slats, solid plank shaped seat, stretcher with six radiating spokes	**50**
Plant Stand	
Original green paint with orange and gold decoration, minor paint wear, 52" w, 14½" d, 39¾" h	**550**
Rectangular top, bentwood twig ovals form sides, long straight legs joined by stretchers, base with corner braces and bentwood S–form and central horseshoe with radiating spokes, original green paint with orange and gold, minor damage, 51" w, 14" d, 39¾" h	**550**
Rustic bentwood twig construction, square top, semi–circular branch apron, tripod support with bentwood twig oval decoration, flared feet, painted green, early 20th C, 15½" w, 29¼" h	**275**

Bench, Pedro Castillo, carved oak, $175.00.

Twig construction, square top, bent
twig form hearts attached to one
side, three legs, box stretcher base   **150**
Rocker
Bent twig construction, five vertical
slat back, bowed looped twigs continuing to double twist scrolling
arms, slat seat, plain apron **360**
Bent rustic twigs and branches, interwoven latticework back, downswept arms, round seat, curlicue
skirt, early 20th C **245**
Child's
Arched bentwood back, seven
curved spindles, wide bentwood
twig arms, twig seat, bent twig
rungs, original black paint with
red and silver, 18" h **160**
Elaborate bent twig work, high
rounded back, red painted finish
with silver and gilt striping decoration, 22½" h **75**
Elaborate bent twig back, arms, and
supports **265**
Smoking Stand
30½" h, twig construction, square top
with fitted box form log cabin
model, rounded bent twig handle
arching from one side to other, tall
splayed twig legs with intertwined
bent twigs forming rungs, old black
paint with silver trim **75**
31¾" h, bent sapling construction,
square top, center log cabin shape
smoker's tray with lift off roof **100**

CANADIAN

History: Canada has a rich furniture tradition,
something American collectors and dealers have
only begun to appreciate recently. The same
wood types grow on both sides of the border;
the same European traditions influenced both
countries. Travel between the two countries, especially after the middle of the nineteenth century, has always been relatively open.

Canadian furniture· consists of three basic
types—imported, rural (primitive), and Canadian
period design pieces. Imported furniture came
largely from England and France. Rural furniture
tended to mimic American vernacular forms.
Formal furniture drew upon Canada's rich supply
of birch, butternut, cherry, maple, and pine. Furniture manufactured was mostly custom–made
until the 1840s.

The folk art revival of the 1970s helped turn
collectors' and dealers' attention to Canada.
Slowly a realization grew that many of the
"American" folk art pieces of painted furniture
were not American at all. They were Canadian.
Dealers were raiding the eastern Canadian

provinces for pieces that had an "American"
feel. Canadians reacted to this invasion by re-
newing their interest in Canadian furniture. The
result was a series of exhibits and books on Canadian furniture along with a rise in price to the
point where it was no longer attractive to buy
Canadian and sell it as American.

Warren Johansson's *Country Furniture and Accessories from Quebec* goes to great lengths to
call attention to construction techniques, design
elements, and forms that differentiate eastern Canadian pieces from American pieces. Every collector of American Country and primitive furniture should read it.

One point is especially worth noting—the unusual size of the furniture forms. Canadian pieces
are big. They overwhelm. American collectors
and dealers are advised to use this "form alarm
bell" as a key to questioning pieces. Although
there are significant regional variations in some
American pieces, the basic form proportions remain the same.

The emphasis placed on folk and "primitive"
pieces should not obscure the fact that Canada
had a very active formal furniture industry.
Jacques & Hay and its successors (R. Hay & Co.
and Charles Rogers & Sons Co.), a Toronto firm,
made furniture in styles ranging from Gothic Revival to Aesthetic during the nineteenth century.

Major Craftsmen: Bellrose Brothers, Trois–Ri-
vieres; DeGant Chair Factory, Nova Scotia;
Thomas Nisbet, Saint John, New Brunswick;
John Warren Moore, St. Stephen, New Brunswick; James Orkney, Quebec; Tulles, Pallister &
McDonald, Halifax, Nova Scotia; James Wad-
dell, Tururo, Nova Scotia.

Major Manufacturers: A. T. Davidson, Lucknow,
Ontario; Gordon & Keith, Halifax, Nova Scotia;
Jacques & Hay (R. Hay & Co./Charles Rogers &
Son Co.), Toronto and New Lowell, Ontario;
Alexander Stephen & Son, Halifax, Nova Scotia.

References: Ruth Cathcart, *Jacques & Hay: 19th
Century Toronto Furniture Makers*, The Boston
Mills Press, 1986; Barbara and Henry Dobson,
*The Early Furniture of Ontario and the Atlantic
Provinces*, M. F. Feheley Publishing, 1974; War-
ren I. Johansson, *Country Furniture and Acces-
sories from Quebec*, Schiffer Publishing, 1990;
Howard Pain, *The Heritage of Upper Canadian
Furniture*, Van Nostrand Reinhold, 1978; Jean
Palardy, *The Early Furniture of French Canada*,
Macmillan of Canada, 1963; Philip Schackleton,
The Furniture of Old Ontario, Macmillan of Can-
ada, 1973; Donald Blake Webster, *English–Ca-
nadian Furniture of the Georgian Period*, Mc-
Graw–Hill Ryerson, 1979.

Armoire
Pine, second quarter 19th C, rectangular flat top with cornice molding,

two doors with six inset panels, faint painted linen fold outline on each door, butt hinges, inset panel sides, shaped apron, short bracket type feet, 41¾" w, 17" d, 68¼" h   **2,450**

White Pine, first quarter 19th C, projected rectangular flat top, single door with four inset panels, iron hinges, molding around bottom, straight apron, bracket feet, 41½" w, 18¼" d, 64" h **1,750**

White Pine, second quarter 19th C, flat rectangular top, front framed with molding, two small drawers above two flush panel doors, star and heart carved on each door, chamfered feet, missing one knob handle **1,550**

Bed

Child's, mid 19th C, pine, shaped headboard, two rails around sides and ends, chamfered posts, mortise and tenon construction, 30" w, 54½" l, 30¾" h **225**

Rope, second quarter 19th C, Empire style, birch frame, shaped pine headboard, four turned posts, blanket roll footboard, 51½" w, 42¾" h   **500**

Bench, late 18th C/early 19th C, pine, plank seat, straight legs, H–form stretcher **1,200**

Blanket Chest, early 19th C, white pine, post and frame construction, rectangular top with incised cleats and iron strap hinges, narrow strip molding around sides forms V on front, iron lock plate, molding on bottom, chamfered feet **550**

Candlestand, second quarter 19th C, white pine, projected top, small drawer frieze, birch tapered legs, 18¾" w, 18½" d, 27" h **250**

Chair

Arm

Early 19th C, maple, shaped crest rail, one slat back, straight sloping arms, woven seat, mortised legs, U–shape medial stretcher, box shape stretcher below, 40¼" h **275**

Late 18th C/early 19th C, birch, paneled back, sloping curved arms, solid seat, mortised legs, two box stretchers, 39¼" h **350**

High, mid 19th C, maple, shaped crest rail with rabbit ears, two closely spaced back slats, slightly curved arms, woven seat, straight legs, box shape stretcher, 12⅝" w, 11½" d, 32¼" h **275**

Set of Four, mid 19th C, flame birch and ash, two slat back with cutout clothespin design, woven seat, straight legs, two U–shape stretchers, 34" h, price for set **1,000**

Side

Early 19th C, maple, slightly shaped crest rail, two closely spaced back slats, rawhide snowshoe woven seat, straight legs, two U–shape stretchers, 34¾" h   **200**

First quarter 19th C, maple, three shaped slats, tapered stiles, woven seat, mortised legs, U–shape medial stretcher, box stretcher below, replaced seat, 35" h **250**

Windsor, late 19th C, comb back, shaped crest rail, ten spindle back, U–shape arm rail, spindle arm supports, graduated spool turned front posts, splayed base with graduated spool turned legs, similar turned H–form stretcher, 44" h **110**

Chest of Drawers, mid 19th C, butternut, rectangular projected top, two deep small drawers flanking two medial small drawers, three long drawers, dovetailed drawers, scalloped apron, bracket feet **950**

Child's Toy Furniture

Armoire, second quarter 19th C, white pine, rectangular projected top, two inset paneled doors, solid ends, shaped apron, splayed legs, 19¾" w, 12½" d, 22⅛" h **625**

Chest of Drawers, mid 19th C, Empire style, white pine, rectangular top, two small drawers flanking two small medial drawers, three long drawers, knob handles, shaped sides, ogee trim apron **200**

Cradle, early 19th C, pine, straight sides and one end, other end shaped with open hand hold, four extended posts with knob finials, shaped runners, old paint, one runner replaced, 18⅜" w, 16⅝" d, 17¾" h **225**

Commode, mid 19th C, pine, shaped gallery, one wide drawer, two paneled doors, towel bar, shaped skirt   **350**

Cradle, early 19th C, pine, shaped headboard, straight sides and footboard, four maple turned posts, ball finials, shaped runners, 31" w, 37" l, 29" h **350**

Cupboard

Quebec, early 19th C, pine, one piece step back, rectangular flat top with cornice molding, frieze with cutout designs, three open shelves, bottom with three small drawers above two inset panel doors, panel arrangement on each side of doors, fluted corners, short block feet, 57¼" w, 23" d, 85½" h **1,450**

St Lawrence Valley, early 19th C, pine, one piece step back, rectangular flat top with cornice molding, two inset panel hinged doors, knob handles, mid molding, two bottom inset panel doors with knob handles, shaped apron, bracket feet, painted, 52" w, 22" d, 86" h **4,500**

South Eastern Township, Quebec, third quarter 19th C, bird's eye maple, step back, two sections: upper section: rectangular flat top with cornice molding, dentil molding below, two inset paneled doors; lower section: one long drawer, two inset paneled doors, base molding, knob handles **1,800**

Wall, 19th C, step back, two sections: upper section: pair of paneled doors, interior with three shelves, two drawers; lower section: pair of paneled doors, interior with two shelves, turned wood knobs, original blue paint, minor imperfections, 53¾" w, 17¾" d, 86½" h .. **6,000**

Desk

School, third quarter 19th C, white pine, hinged slant top, square oak legs, 25¼" w, 20¾" d, 34½" h ... **155**

Table Top, mid 19th C, white pine, step back, rectangular top, twelve pigeonholes, slanted writing surface, two small drawers with knob handles, 32¼" w, 25⅛" d, 21½" h **425**

Dough Box, Montreal District, early 19th C, pine, two board top, plank ends, Empire style legs, refinished, 43½" w, 14¾" d, 30¼" h **250**

Linen Press, walnut or butternut, flat top, two doors with raised shaped panels, iron hinges, short chamfered legs, interior shelf missing, replaced cornice of pine crown molding, 38½" w, 22¾" d, 83" h **300**

Rocker

Child's, 19th C, maple, mortise and tenon crest rail, rabbit ears, two closely spaced back slats, curved arms, woven seat, mortised legs, box shape stretcher, 24¾" h **125**

Maple, mid 19th C, curved back, three shaped slats, sloping arms, woven seat, mortised legs, box shape stretcher, shaped runners .. **185**

Mixed Hardwood, mid 19th C, two slat back, slightly curved arms, woven seat, U–shape medial stretcher, box shape stretcher below, 37" h **225**

Sideboard, Drummondville, Quebec, mid 19th C, butternut, rectangular molded top, dovetailed case, three short dovetailed drawers with framed flat strip molding, three inset panel doors, center door stepped back, knob handles, 68" w, 22¾" d, 36" h **850**

Stool, last half 19th C, birch, round top, splayed legs, decked stretcher, 22¼" h **50**

Table

Dropleaf, second quarter 19th C, white pine, two rectangular drop leaves, plain frieze, Hepplewhite style tapered birch legs, gate leg, 65¾" w extended, 51¾" d, 27½" h **1,500**

Refectory, early 19th C, pine, three board top, tapered legs, two benches, 30" w, 122" l, 29" h **2,250**

Sawbuck, early 19th C, pine, mortised and tenoned top, sawbuck ends joined with stretcher, 126" w, 29" d, 35" h **3,150**

Tavern, early 19th C, white pine, incised dovetailed cleated two board top, small drawer frieze, tapered legs, 46" w, 34¾" d, 27" h **900**

Work

First quarter 19th C, pine, multiple board top, small drawer frieze, tapered legs, H–form stretcher, 65" w, 29" d, 29" h **700**

Third quarter 19th C, ash, three board top, small drawer frieze, butternut chamfered tapered legs, 38" w, 30¼" d, 26½" h ... **450**

Washstand, third quarter 19th C, scrolled backboard with double rolling pin crest, towel bars with shaped supports, small drawer frieze with knob handle, turned legs, 25½" w, 36" h **350**

PENNSYLVANIA GERMAN

History: The first Germanic settlers came to Pennsylvania in 1683, followed by a steady stream that lasted until the late 1740s. The vast majority immigrated from the German speaking principalities situated along the upper reaches of the Rhine River. Three important regions whose cultural traditions serve as historic antecedents for Pennsylvania German pieces are Alsace–Lorraine, Palatinate, and Switzerland.

German immigration to Pennsylvania occurred for many reasons—economic, political, and religious. Far too much emphasis has been placed upon pietistic groups such as the Amish, Mennonites, and Moravians. In truth, the vast majority of Pennsylvania Germans were members of Lutheran and Reformed congregations.

The Pennsylvania German culture was primarily a rural and small town culture. The furniture and decorative arts identified with the group have a strong rural flavor.

The term Pennsylvania German is misleading. The Pennsylvania German community spread south into western Maryland near Hagerstown, down the Shenandoah Valley, and into the pine barrens of the Carolinas. Amish and Mennonite settlements can be found in Ohio, Indiana, and Ontario, Canada.

There are two Pennsylvania German furniture traditions—painted and formal. The public's conception of Pennsylvania German furniture is the paint decorated blanket chest or document box. Elaborately painted decorated chests of drawers from the Mahantango Valley and cupboards and schranks (wardrobes) from Berks and Lancaster County are known. The use of flat milk–base paint on furniture also was common, with red and blue the favored colors.

Less documented, but equally important, are formal pieces where the natural wood grain is emphasized. Blanket chests, chairs, cupboards, schranks, tables, tall case clocks, and a host of other furniture pieces can be found in a natural finish. Many of the pieces exhibit a strong Baroque influence.

Pennsylvania German furniture is massive. It was designed to last generations. One often feels that it is rooted in place. Forms were simple and basic, designed to be used by a rural individual who was likely to use the pieces while dressed in work clothing and boots.

During World War II the Pennsylvania Germans became the Pennsylvania Dutch, a patriotic move that has only served to confuse, since few Pennsylvania Germans trace their ancestry back to the Netherlands. Attempts to drop the Pennsylvania "Dutch" nomenclature have been defeated by the tourist industry.

There have been a number of Pennsylvania German craft revivals—in the 1920s–30s and the 1970s. While a few artisans have blazed new ground by building on the traditions of the past, the vast majority's goal has been to copy the past as exactly as possible. As a result, the Pennsylvania German market is loaded with reproductions, copycats, fantasy items, and fakes.

Compounding the problem is the recent arrival of painted furniture pieces from Norway, the German regions of the Oberlausitz, Saxony, and Schwartzwald (Black Forest), the French regions of Alsace and Lorraine, and northern Switzerland, all close enough in form and decorative motif to American Pennsylvania German pieces to be passed as "American" to novice collectors. American collectors and dealers are simply not familiar with European painted furniture, albeit there are a number of excellent books on the subject in German and other foreign languages. Even if one cannot read them, it is worth studying the pictures.

References: Beatrice B. Garvan, *The Pennsylvania German Collection*, Philadelphia Museum of Art, 1982; Beatrice B. Garvan and Charles F. Hummel, *The Pennsylvania Germans: A Celebration of Their Arts: 1683–1850*, Philadelphia Museum of Art, 1982; Monroe H. Fabian, *The Pennsylvania–German Decorated Chest*, Main Street Press, 1978, also available as Volume 12 of the publications of The Pennsylvania German Society.

Museums: Heritage Center, Lancaster, PA; Philadelphia Museum of Art, Philadelphia, PA; Historical Society of Berks County, Reading, PA; Historical Society of York County, York, PA.

Bench
  Bucket, pine and poplar, 1830–40, overhanging top, two mortised shelves with gallery backs, bootjack ends, worn blue paint **1,900**
  Wash, poplar, 1830–40, mortised one board top, straight aprons, scal-

Blanket Chest, miniature, decorated, 13" l, 7¼" w, 6" h, $400.00.

loped bootjack ends, painted red, minor repairs **725**

Blanket Chest

Curly Walnut, 1790–1800, lift lid, dovetailed case, secret drawer in interior till, two drawers below, dovetailed bracket feet, brass fishtail hinges and crab lock **7,000**

Pine

1773, Berks County, molded hinged lid, well with till, two drawers surrounded by beading, brass bail handles, wrought iron lock, heart strap hinges, lid with two stylized potted flowers in tombstone arched panels, front with central tombstone arched panel with potted tree and two stylized birds below partially legible inscription "Michael...Den 19 Daig/Mertz and 1773," flanked by two adjoining symmetrical panels containing a stylized potted flower, four birds perched on corners of arched panels, stylized tulips on drawer fronts, hearts and flowers on ends, scroll cut dovetailed bracket feet, 55½" w, 22¼" d, 29" h **13,200**

c1830, hinged lid, dovetailed case, interior till, wrought iron strap hinges and bear trap lock with escutcheon and key, two arched white painted panels with pots of stylized flowers in red, blue, green, black, and brown, two white and brown stars on lid, dark blue ground, bracket feet, replaced molding, 50" w, 21¾" d, 21" h **2,800**

c1840, lift lid, deep well over three dovetailed drawers, wrought iron strap hinges, brass escutcheons, traces of grain painting on red ground, stenciled initials "W H G," French feet, 50" w, 23" d, 29¼" h **2,200**

1844, Somerset County, miniature, dovetailed, lid and base edge molding, polychrome painted stylized tulips, floral designs, and initials and date "1844" on front panel, red ground, turned feet, 25" w, 13" d, 17¼" h **5,200**

1850, molded hinged lid, well with till, two lower drawers, strap hinges, stenciled "CHARRIMISH STAHL 1850" inscription on front flanked by stylized stenciled fruit and birds, red ground, gilt stenciled designs on black ground on drawer fronts and base, bracket feet, 48½" w, 20¾" d, 26" h ... **1,320**

Pine and Poplar, edge molding on hinged lid, square corner posts with mortised and pinned single board sides and ends, lidded till with secret drawer, base molding, turned feet, hinges marked "Philada," red–brown flame graining, repair in edge of lid at hinge, some edge damage, casters added, 50¾" w, 21¼" d, 24½" h **250**

Poplar

1775, lift lid, two overlapping drawers, large yellow hearts inscribed "Phillip Dutrer 1775," green ground, dovetailed bracket feet, minor repairs **5,000**

1790, lift lid, three drawers, sponged blue arched panel designs, red and black diamond border, orange and blue base, brown ground, bracket feet **15,000**

1820, hinged lid, deep well, two drawers, black and orange, white trim, twelve pointed stars, hearts, and meandering vine and dots decoration, signed "CS 1820," bracket feet **7,000**

1878, Soap Hollow, dovetailed case, interior lidded till, two dovetailed drawers, reeded trim, white porcelain pulls, black trim, yellow striping, gold stenciled initials and date "J. B. 1878" on red ground, bracket feet, 48" w, 21" d, 26½" h **3,400**

Chair, set of six, side, New Oxford, straight crest rail, vasiform splat, turned posts, shaped plank seat, turned front legs and stretcher, splayed base, brown ground, dark red and yellow striping, polychrome rose decoration on crest rail, one signed "Peter Geisen, New Oxford, Pa" on seat underside, one with minor repairs and reglued, one replaced leg, 33" h, price for set **480**

Chest, dower, pine, 1816, Centre County, attributed to Titus Geesey, dovetailed case, till, wrought iron bear trap lock and strap hinges, diagonal braces on front feet, black, brown, and white eagle, shield, banner, pinwheels, tulips, and compass stars in framed central front panel, "Catarina Klinglibe 1816" on banner, traces of compass decoration on lid and ends, dovetailed bracket feet, escutcheon replaced, minor edge damage, minor touch up to eagle, 51½" w, 22½" d, 27" h **3,500**

Step Back Cupboard, 1835–45, painted red, 53¼" w, 19" d, 87" h, $17,600.00. Photograph courtesy of Skinner, Inc.

Cupboard
Corner
  Cherry, c1815, hanging, molded cornice, carved potted tulip on molded flat paneled door, carved ferns on case, spiral inset corner columns, reeding, scalloped apron, cutout feet, refinished .. **10,000**
Pine
  18th C, thumb molded cornice above stylized flowerhead carved dentil frieze, two arched paneled doors enclosing red painted shelved interior, fluted columnar stiles, pair of cupboard doors in base with single shelf interior, red and black grain painting, 53" w, 96" h **6,600**
  1800–25, two sections: upper section: molded cornice, arched glazed door, plate rails and spoon slots on shelved interior; lower section: projecting base with two drawers over pair of cupboard doors, turnip feet, stippled yellow highlights on red ground, door painted white, 38" w, 90" h **21,000**

19th C, one piece construction, perimeter molding with applied scalloping, pair of glazed doors with eight panes of wavy glass, three interior butterfly scalloped shelves and arched baffle with cutout pinwheels, horizontal midsection panel with reeding and relief carving, single paneled door flanked by vertical rectangular panels, finish cleaned down to traces of old blue paint, 54½" w, 89¼" h **6,500**
Pine and Poplar, c1840, two sections: upper section: pair of triple pane glazed doors, shelved interior; lower section: single long drawer, two paneled doors, cutout feet, orange and red geometric stripe design **6,500**
Poplar, c1840, two sections: upper section: double molded cornice, twelve pane glazed door, shelved interior; lower section: three nailed drawers in waist, shaped apron, cutout feet, simulated tiger maple and rosewood graining in yellow, red, and black **17,000**
Dutch
  Butternut and Cherry, c1850, Soap Hollow, two sections: upper section: molded cornice, pair of six pane glazed doors, shelved interior; lower section: two short drawers in waist, turned quarter columns, raised panel cupboard doors, applied bracket feet, refinished **3,800**
  Cherry, c1830, two sections: upper section: molded cornice, pair of six pane glazed doors, scalloped opening around pie shelf; lower section: three short overlapping in waist, chamfered corners, paneled cupboard doors, paneled ends, turned feet, refinished **7,800**
Pine and Poplar
  c1830, two sections: upper section: molded cornice, pair of six pane glazed doors, four spice drawers; lower section: three short drawers in waist, raised panel cupboard doors, turned feet, refinished **4,500**
  c1835, two sections: upper section: molded cornice, single nine pane glazed door, shelved interior; lower section: two short drawers in waist, paneled cupboard doors,

turned feet, old red finish, interior painted white, 42" w .. **4,200**

c1850, two sections: upper section: molded cornice, two paneled doors, shelved interior; lower section: two short drawers in waist, two paneled cupboard doors below, cutout feet, turned wood pulls, mustard grained **1,800**

Jelly

Pine, c1830, molded cornice, two double raised panel doors, chamfered corners on stiles, turned feet, brown grained **2,400**

Pine and Poplar, c1830, molded cornice, dovetailed case, pair of paneled cupboard door, open bucket bench below, cutout tapered legs, painted red **5,000**

Stepback

Pine

c1810, two sections: upper section: large stepped cornice, open shelves; lower section: molded waist, raised panel cupboard doors, tall scalloped bracket base, painted red **11,000**

c1830, pine, molded cornice, pair of glazed doors with six panes, spoon holder shelf, three waist drawers over two paneled cupboard doors, refinished, replaced pulls, 44¼" w, 78½" h **1,500**

Poplar

c1800, blind, two sections: upper section: molded cornice, pair of raised panel doors, shelved interior; lower section: one small drawer flanked by two long overlapping drawers in molded waist, raised panel cupboard doors, grain painted, missing feet and part of cornice **7,500**

c1830, two sections: upper section: molded cornice, pair of glazed doors with sixteen glass panes, shelved interior; lower section: five overlapping short drawers in waist, four paneled cupboard doors, scalloped apron, cutout feet, grain painted, 48" w, 84" h **4,200**

Straight Front

Pine, blind, pair of cupboard doors with arched panels, four small drawers over two longer drawers, paneled lower cupboard doors flanked by turned columns, refinished with traces of original paint, two drawer pulls missing,

replaced hinges, 53" w, 18½" d, 85½" h **2,300**

Pine and Poplar, early 19th C, blind, molded flaring cornice, pair of paneled doors, shelved interior, three small drawers in molded waist, pair of paneled cupboard base doors, paneled ends, old refinishing, traces of old red paint, molding loss, 83" h **3,000**

Cradle

Pine and Poplar, c1825, post and panel construction, mushroom finials, heart cutouts on scrolled headboard and shaped footboard, shaped runners, black panels on orange–red frame **6,000**

Walnut, c1830, heart cutout on headboard and footboard, scrolled headboard, arched footboard, dovetailed case, shaped runners .. **650**

Dry Sink

Pine and Poplar

c1820, dovetailed gallery, two drawers, two flat paneled doors, paneled ends, turned feet, yellow and brown stippled panels **4,200**

c1850, and poplar, high back with two small drawers flanking an open shelf, pair of paneled cupboard doors in base, cutout feet, original salmon colored paint decoration **4,000**

c1850, molded cornice, pair of raised panel cupboard doors in top, paneled back board, shaped ends, bank of three graduated overlapping drawers flanking two raised panel doors in base, cutout feet, grown grain painting .. **2,800**

c1860, scalloped crest, overhanging top, and three drawers in high back, raised panel cupboard doors below, cutout feet, yellow grain painting **1,800**

Poplar, pine secondary wood, open well, single dovetailed drawer, two paneled doors, shaped bracket feet, wooden pulls, red vinegar graining on yellow ground, sunbursts, fans, and "X" decorations, 42" w, 19¼" d, 31¾" h **11,500**

Pie Safe, pine and poplar

c1835, single door with three tin panels flanked by three tin panels on each side, two tin panels on ends, punched star design, square legs, brown finish **5,500**

c1840, hanging, single door, four tin panels with punched diamond and floral design, refinished **1,400**

Schrank

Pine and Poplar

c1780, large blocked cornice, two split raised panel doors, fluted pilasters, two overlapping drawers in base, overpainted, missing ball feet **2,000**

c1790, stepped cornice, raised panel doors, front, and ends, waist molding, three overlapping drawers, applied bracket feet, case painted red, black feet **37,000**

Walnut, c1795

Inlaid pilasters below cornice, two shaped recessed paneled doors flanked by recessed paneled stiles, fluted quarter columns top and bottom, three short drawers over two short drawers in base, overlapping drawers, applied French bracket feet, H–form hinges, refinished **11,000**

Molded cornice above dentil molding and fluting, two double molded raised panel doors, fluted quarter columns, three short drawers over two short drawers in base, overlapping drawers, chamfered corners, ogee bracket feet, H–form hinges, refinished **18,000**

SHAKER

History: The Shakers, so named because of a dance used in worship, are one of the oldest communal organizations in the United States. This religious group, the United Society of Believers in Christ's Second Appearing, was founded by Mother Anne Lee who emigrated from England and established the first Shaker community near Albany, New York, in 1784. The Shakers reached their peak in 1850 with 6,000 members.

Shakers lived celibate and self–sufficient lives. Their philosophy stressed cleanliness, order, simplicity, and economy—concepts clearly seen in their furniture. Highly inventive and motivated, the Shakers created many utilitarian household forms and objects. Their furniture reflected a striving for quality and purity in design.

Shakers constructed most of their furniture for use in their dormitories and workshops. The community lifestyle meant that more than one person might be using a piece of furniture at one time. Sewing stands had drawers on both sides; desks featured a double set of drawers and shelves. Large pieces, e.g., tables and chests, were made. Multi–purpose pieces also played a role. Benches doubled as tables; low tables had cupboards attached to hold required utensils.

By the middle of the nineteenth century the Shakers had developed an active commercial trade with the outside world. Chairs and stools were manufactured at Mount Lebanon, New York, the center of the Shaker community in the East. Furniture sold to the general public was marked with a decal, many of which have been destroyed through refinishing.

Shaker furniture emphasizes practicality. Walls of drawers were built into rooms. Beds had wheels so that they could be moved easily. Early Shaker furniture was painted; but, by the mid–nineteenth century, emphasis was placed on the natural wood grain as pieces were stained, shellacked, or varnished. A wide variety of woods were used depending on the task—butternut, cherry, chestnut, hickory, maple, oak, pear, and walnut.

There were subtle differences in furniture motifs between the various communities. Look for the number and design of slats, finials, and whether or not reed, straw, or tape was used for seats. Pieces made for internal use were not marked.

In every endeavor and enterprise, the members followed Mother Ann's advice: "Put your hands to work and give your heart to God."

Because the Shakers utilized traditional vernacular forms, it is not surprising that many pseudo–Shaker pieces exist. Further, the popularity of Shaker forms attracted individual cabinetmakers and commercial manufacturers. By the end of the nineteenth century, Shaker furniture was being copied.

The craft revivals of 1920s–30s and 1970s–80s witnessed a large number of Shaker imitators. Working from detailed measurements, many of these artisans made exact copies of Shaker pieces. All too often their efforts went unsigned.

For this reason, provenance is a very important consideration when paying a premium for any piece because it is Shaker. Ask the dealer for detailed documentation tracing the piece back to a specific Shaker community. "Looks like Shaker" is not good enough. Without proof positive, the only safe assumption is that the piece is a copy.

Shaker communities include: KY—Pleasant Hill, South Union; MA—Hancock, Harvard, Shirley, Tyringham; ME—Alfred; NH—Canterbury, Enfield; NY—Mount Lebanon, Watervliet; OH—North Union, Union Village, White Water.

References: Michael Horsham, *The Art of the Shakers*, The Apple Press, 1989; Charles R. Muller and Timothy D. Rieman, *The Shaker Chair*, Canal Press, 1984; Don and Carol Raycraft, *Shaker, A Collector's Source Book II*, Wallace–Homestead, 1985; June Sprigg and David Larkin, *Shaker Life, Work, and Art*, Stewart, Tabon & Chang, 1987.

Periodical: *The Shaker Messenger*, PO Box 1645, Holland, MI 49422.

Museums: Hancock Shaker Village, Pittsfield, MA; Shaker Museum Foundation, Old Catham, NY; Shaker Historical Museum, Shaker Heights, OH.

Apothecary Chest, Alfred, Maine, pine, dovetail construction, twelve drawers, old red and black paint, 40¼" w, 11½" d, 16" h **800**

Bed

    Rope, mid 19th C, maple, shaped headboard, square tapered legs, wooden wheel casters, painted green, 35½" w, 74" l **1,400**

    Walnut, two slat headboard, shaped top slat, one slat footboard, plain side rails, turned legs, 34" w, 76" l, 32" h **1,300**

Bench

    Pine, Canterbury, New Hampshire, c1830, painted green, 84" l, 25¾" d, 7½" h **750**

    Pine, Enfield, Connecticut, water, oblong top, lead lined drain, straight sides with bootjack feet, original brown stain finish, 49" w, 17½" d, 33" h **850**

    Cherry, c1850, carved, plank seat, rectangular top, bootjack feet, 96" l, 10" d **2,500**

Blanket Chest

    Enfield, New Hampshire, poplar and pine, oblong lift top, deep well, panel inset sides, square tapered legs, original red paint, 43" w, 18½" d, 23" h **925**

    New York, c1830, lift top, four slightly graduated drawers, original ochre washed finish, high arched dovetailed base, original wood pulls **40,000**

Box

    Bentwood, Massachusetts, oval, Harvard type, single finger construction, iron tacks, lid interior marked "Made in Tanton Bristol Co, Mass," original worn varnish, 6" l **175**

    Storage, pine and hardwood, oval, finger construction, copper tacks, scrubbed patina, worn, lid damage, 11⅛" l **250**

    Utility, Canterbury, New Hampshire, butternut, dovetailed, hinged lid, 12" w, 4" d, 3" h **150**

Candlestand

    Enfield, New Hampshire, birch, round top, turned tapered standard, downswept tripod, pad feet, original finish, 14½" d, 26" h **4,100**

New Lebanon, New York, early 19th C, cherry, round top, turned tapered standard, downswept tripod, elongated pad feet, 15¼" d, 24" h   **11,250**

New Lebanon, New York, mid 19th C, cherry, rectangular top, original finish, 18¼" w, 19" l, 26" h **14,000**

South Union, Kentucky, cherry, round top, baluster turned standard, downswept tripod, snake feet, original finish, 17" d, 25¾" h **1,500**

Chair, ladderback, hardwood, woven splint seat, sgd "Sick, 1840," $1,200.00.

Chair

    Arm

        Sabbath Day Lake, Maine, 1938, ladder back, turned finials, woven splint seat, old worn finish, replaced seat **400**

        Watervliet, New York, early 19th C, four hickory back slats, top slat mortised through uprights, maple uprights, flat scrolling cherrywood arms, original yellow woven tape seat **2,500**

    Child's

        Arm, No. 1, red and black woven tape back, turned uprights, flame finials, burlap seat, worn original finish, original label **550**

        Side, Harvard, Massachusetts, two shaped slat back, turned uprights, flame finials, cane seat, natural finish **1,500**

    Side

        Canterbury, New Hampshire, c1830, pair, yellow birch and maple, shaped pine plank seat, varnish finish, 25" h, price for pair **5,000**

Mt. Lebanon, New York, three slat back, turned uprights, shaped finials, woven tape seat, rear legs with tilting device, box stretcher, original finish **1,500**

Chest of Drawers

Pine, tall, projected molding top, eight drawers, turned wood pulls, dark stained case, natural finish drawers, 33" w, 20" d, 64½" h ... **1,650**

Poplar, Connecticut, projected rectangular top, one deep bonnet type drawer, three graduated long drawers, tapered legs, yellow washed finish, 45" w, 44" h **2,500**

Sugar Chest, found in the Mercer-Boyle counties area, Kentucky, triple compartment interior, lift lid, recessed panel sides, full horizontal drawer on bottom, thick tapered legs that begin with ring and spool turnings and end in a small ball, $3,100.00. Photograph courtesy of Green River Antiques Auctions and *Antique Week*.

Clothes Rack, New England, late 19th C, three horizontal bars, top bar mounted on each side with three hooks, rectangular uprights continuing to form arched feet, painted red, 36½" w, 72" h **2,500**

Cradle, cherry, coffered hood, shaped sides, pierced handholds, shaped rockers **800**

Cupboard

Chimney, Watervliet, New York, pine, flat top, one board back and sides, two paneled doors on front, bootjack feet, natural finish, 21" w, 16" d, 80" h **3,000**

Hanging, pine, molded cornice top, paneled door, knob handle, 24½" w, 14½" d, 31½" h **1,045**

Jelly, Union Village, Ohio, pine and poplar, plain top, one drawer over one door, paint removed down to original red paint **650**

Wall, walnut, molded cornice top, doors with raised panels, door interior stamped Congregational Church, cutout feet, 49½" w, 89½" h **1,900**

Desk

Enfield, New Hampshire, c1825, hinged slant lid, fitted interior, three drawers, pair double paneled doors, drawer and shelf interior, original brown paint, 38½" w, 18½" d, 53½" h **1,650**

Mt. Lebanon, New York, poplar, slant top with back rail, three graduated drawers, turned wood pulls, square tapered legs, 31" w, 21½" d, 32" h **1,500**

Ohio, slant lid, low gallery lifting to fitted interior, one drawer, turned and tapered legs **850**

Dry Sink, hardwood, oblong hinged top, well interior, pair paneled doors, painted finish **1,425**

Linen Press, Mt. Lebanon, New York, cherrywood and pine, simple cornice top, pair paneled doors, two medial drawers, two doors below, bracket feet, original red paint, 41" w, 16" d, 81½" h **3,100**

Rocker

Attributed to Mt. Lebanon Community, second half 19th C, maple, tapered stiles with pointed finials centering three arched slats, lower slat stencil "Shaker's 4 trademark Mt. Lebanon New York," rush seat, turned legs joined by turned stretchers, appears to retain original varnish finish **550**

Mt. Lebanon, New York, 1880–1920, child's, No. 1, slat back, red and olive tape seat, original dark finish, imprinted on reverse of slat "Shakers No 1 Mt. Lebanon, NY", 29¾" h **1,500**

Mt. Lebanon, New York, No. 3, armless, woven splint back and seat, turned finials, old red varnish finish, stenciled label on one runner "Shaker's Trade Mark, No . 3, Mt. Lebanon, NY," worn finish, seat damage, 34" h **275**

Mt. Lebanon, New York, Model No. 4, late 19th/early 20th C, maple, three shaped splats, turned tapering stiles, trapezoidal webbed seat,

Rocker, Mt. Lebanon, NY, 20th C, refinished, web–back in new olive and blue taping, 34″ h, seat height 14″, $225.00. Photograph courtesy of Skinner, Inc.

turned legs, turned stretchers on runners **480**

New Lebanon, New York, c1880, No. 3, armless, original tape seat, acorn finials, original finish **600**

New Lebanon, New York, c1850, maple, four shaped splat back, stiles with rail on top, shaped arms, upholstered splint seat, medial stretcher above box stretcher, old surface, 15″ h seat, 44¾″ h overall **10,450**

Secretary, Harvard Community, Massachusetts, c1855, pine, two sections: upper section: molded cornice over two eight pane glazed doors, inlaid ivory keyholes, paneled drop front writing surface, interior short drawers and large pigeonholes; lower section: three rows of two drawers, 59″ w, 87½″ h **7,750**

Settee, Enfield, New Hampshire, birch and pine, nineteen spindle back, varnished finish, 58″ l, 38″ h **5,000**

Sewing Desk

Enfield, New Hampshire, pine, top with shaped sides, ten small drawers, slide out work surface, case with paneled sides and four small drawers, turned legs, original red finish, 38¾″ w, 26¾″ d, 35½″ h . **27,500**

Sewing Table, probably from Harvard, Massachusetts, first half of 19th C, painted butternut and pine, period red wash, varnished, period pulls, minor imperfections, 21″ w, 23½″ d, 35¼″ h, $3,000.00. Photograph courtesy of Skinner, Inc.

Harvard, Massachusetts, 1860–80, pine, galleried top with four small drawers, slide out work surface with breadboard end and porcelain knob, case with two long drawers, one drawer with metal escutcheon and lock, other drawer with ruler with original varnish stain and incised 1845, tapered legs, old varnish stain refinish, one replaced drawer pull, one leg reglued, 25½" w working surface, 40½" h **10,250**

Stool

Desk, birch, adjustable leather upholstered seat, turned and tapered legs, stretchers, 33" h **1,850**

Foot, pine, upholstered top, bootjack ends, old blue paint, 12" w, 12" d, 10" h **125**

Step, New Lebanon, New York, c1850, butternut, two steps, dovetailed, pegged stretcher, high arch base, natural finish **850**

Utility, New Lebanon, New York, first quarter 20th C, maple, basket weave splint seat, original mahogany stained finish, decal on leg, 15¼" w, 15⅛" d, 16" h **785**

Weaver's, Alfred, Maine, two slat short back, woven tape seat, turned legs, yellow paint **2,250**

Table

Dropleaf, birch base, pine top, oblong top, oblong drop leaves, birch apron, turned legs, tapering feet, refinished, early red stain showing through, 45" w, 17½" d, 11¼" drop leaves, 28½" h **425**

Sewing, Canterbury, New Hampshire, maple, tiger stripe maple top, open front, divided shelf, turned legs, 27" w, 18" d, 27" h **900**

Side, walnut, two board top, single drawer frieze with turned knob handle, square tapered legs, old refinishing, 30" w, 28¼" d, 28½" h . **525**

Trestle, Enfield, New Hampshire, birch, painted yellow, 32¼" w, 72" l, 25½" h **4,500**

Work

Canterbury, New Hampshire,

Work Table, projecting top, single drawer, square tapered legs, $3,750.00.

cherrywood, oblong projected top, single drawer frieze, turned legs, natural finish, 26¼" w, 43½" l, 27" h **1,450**

Mt. Lebanon Community, first half 19th C, pine, rectangular top, single drawer frieze, square tapered legs, 30¼" h, 60¼" w, 34½" d **5,225**

New Lebanon Community, New York, early 19th C, birchwood and pine, rectangular top with splashboard, single molded drawer frieze, circular tapered legs, original red paint, 37½" w, 23" d, 25½" h **9,000**

Wardrobe

Mt. Lebanon, New York, pine and poplar, pair double paneled doors, pegboard interior, drawer in base, red washed stain, 47¾" w, 18" d, 71¼" h **2,125**

Union village, Ohio, walnut and butternut, plain design, one door, 75½" h **525**

Part IV
European Furniture

THE PREJUDICE of American collectors and dealers for things American has led them to virtually ignore the study of European furniture. All know a few generalities, albeit many of these are highly inaccurate. Totally ignored is the cross influences within European design styles.

Americans tend to think of European furniture in American terms, i.e., they base their assumptions about European design styles on American pieces that they assume are direct copies of European examples. Nothing could be further from the truth. European furniture design styles differed significantly from the American pieces of the same period. One need only look at the examples in a survey book about English or French furniture to realize that this is the case.

Further, Americans have little understanding of furniture construction techniques and wood selection, two means of differentiating American from European examples. Available literature is of little help. Museum collections with documented European pieces are largely unavailable for detailed study.

Many examples of European furniture that do exist in America are so heavily repaired, rebuilt, restored, or completely fabricated from old wood or parts—hardly a group worth studying as an example of "how things should be." These are the pieces that are most frequently sold through the auction circuit, all too often cataloged as correct.

Europeans generally follow the principal that for something to be antique, it has to be one hundred or more years old. This approach is being attacked by a number of modern writers. Philip and Walkling's *Field Guide to Antique Furniture* contains the following: "Until about 1870, the word 'antique' was used to describe things appertaining to ancient Greece and Rome—now what we call antiquities—while what we term antiques were known then as curios or curiosities. From then until about 1980, an antique came to mean any artifact over 100 years old, though purists have set earlier, arbitrary datelines, such as the long–revered 1830.

"Since 1980, the unofficial trend has been towards defining an antique as anything made before the outbreak of the Second World War. The pre–war world was in many ways very different from the one we live in today, and in taking 1940 as the cut–off point, this book recognizes that there is now a serious collectors' market in early 20thC furniture."

HISTORY: One of the major problems involved in talking about European furniture design is the modern nation states. One must continually remember that modern borders did not exist in the eighteenth and nineteenth centuries. France occupied sections of the Netherlands, Germany, and Italy. Germany itself was a fragmented group of principalities and city states. Modern Germany did not evolve until the late nineteenth century.

By far the greatest Italian influence on French and English furniture was the Rococo style. This mid-18th C Italian settee has a triple chair arched padded back, conforming seat, scalloped apron, cabriole legs ending in pointed pad feet, is painted white with parcel gilt, measures 63" l, and realized $2,420.00. Photograph courtesy of William Doyle Galleries.

Rather than focus on nation states, one must look to the dominant cities of the eighteenth and nineteenth centuries for leadership in furniture design styles. The two most important centers are Paris and London. Provincial cities ranging from Glasgow to Naples provided their input as well.

The key word is *French;* the key city, *Paris.* Although the Americans and British do not like to admit it, French taste was the design style leader from the seventeenth through the early twentieth centuries. The French court and later the French aristocracy and bourgeoisie of the nineteenth century greatly determined the direction for "high style" furniture design.

The French, in turn, were often influenced by design from Italy and other Mediterranean areas. The Italians blended design elements from Roman, Byzantine, and Sacracenic origins. The Italian Renaissance, Baroque, and Rococo periods laid the foundations for several French and English design styles. Many of these design styles worked their way to France and England through the movement of Italian craftsmen.

The Classical Revival of the late eighteenth century was fostered by the excavations at Pompeii and Herculaneum. However, the Italian re-

The Italian influence was strongly felt in France and England. This late 17th or early 18th century walnut commode marries the concept of a chest of drawers with the traditional blanket chest form. The pieces measures 57½" w, 23" d, 37½" h and realized $6,050.00. Photograph courtesy of William Doyle Galleries.

Collecting prejudices prevent most American collectors from fully understanding the depth and breadth of European furniture development. Mirror, 17th C, carved and gilded, from Spanish art collection of Madame Francisca Reyes, NY and Granada, Spain, one of a matched pair sold in December 1930 at an auction by E. A. Hasseman Galleries, NYC, 24 x 38", $1,650.00. Photograph courtesy of Pettigrew Auction Company.

sponse borrowed heavily upon English and French interpretations. A reverse flow of design style was taking place. Not until the Memphis period of the 1970s did Italian design take center stage.

Most of the histories of European furniture focus on handcrafted examples. Aesthetically pleasing pieces executed by the most skilled craftsmen enjoy the greatest favors. While eighteenth century furniture is largely handcrafted, nineteenth century furniture is divided between handcrafted and industrially manufactured pieces. By the middle of the nineteenth century, factory produced furniture occurred throughout Europe. Only recently have European furniture scholars become interested in mass produced furniture aimed at the growing urban middle class. Much remains to be learned.

With the twentieth century came a major shift of furniture design capitals. The Deutsche Werkstatten and Deutscher Werkbund in Dresden, Dessau Bauhaus, and Gerrit Rietveld's workshop in the Netherlands laid the foundation for the Modernist movement. The distribution of these designs, through magazines and the movement of the designers themselves, made furniture design truly international.

The late 1840s and early 1850s in Europe witnessed a renewal of interest in Europe in folk furniture, due in part to the rising nationalism that swept the continent. Once rediscovered, interest in folk furniture continued. Many major studies have been done on regional painted furniture. When examining pieces, be continually mindful of the nineteenth century revival—many of the pieces date from this rather than earlier periods.

REFERENCES: Joseph Aronson, *The New Encyclopedia of Furniture*, Crown Publishers, 1967; Peter Philip and Gillian Walkling, *Field Guide to Antique Furniture*, Houghton Mifflin, 1992.

LIBRARY: The Furniture Library (1009 North Main Street, High Point, NC 27262) issues a book list each fall of furniture books offered for sale in its bookshop. The list contains a large number of titles relating to European furniture. Titles can be very deceptive. It pays first to check a book that you are considering purchasing at your local library or have your library obtain a copy through inter–library loan before making the actual purchase.

ENGLISH

History: America's furniture roots are clearly planted in England. Yet, American collectors too often make the false assumption that the American pieces are exact copies of British examples. Nothing could be further from the truth. American furniture designers and manufacturers adapted.

British design period furniture differed significantly in size, form, and design from American pieces. American collectors and dealers are encouraged to obtain and read carefully the reference books listed below. In addition, a trip to England to visit major depositories of English furniture, such as London's Victoria and Albert Museum, is advised.

Just as America responded to English tastes, England responded to French tastes. This remained true throughout all of the seventeenth, eighteenth, and nineteenth centuries. British furniture design did innovate in respect to design vocabulary and form. However, the main stylistic impetus was French.

British furniture design of the eighteenth and nineteen centuries relied heavily on design style books. Only those of Chippendale, Hepplewhite, and Sheraton are well known in America, and these books barely scratch the surface. Over fifty major design style books were printed in England between 1750 and 1900. Serious collectors of British furniture are encouraged to seek out and review copies of those books covering the periods in which they collect.

British furniture design moved to eclecticism much earlier than American furniture design. Throughout the seventeenth and eighteenth centuries a multiplicity of design styles enjoyed popularity at the same time. This was due to the strongly stratified nature of British society. Different social groups supported different tastes. Furniture design advances often rested on the willingness of one individual, e.g., Horace Walpole, to build in a new design style.

The English furniture which most closely mirrors American pieces is that made in the provincial centers, such as Bristol and Norwich. London furniture was simply too high style for the American market. The principal method for separating English pieces from American pieces is by examining the secondary woods and furniture construction techniques.

Further, keep in mind that England exported large amounts of British-made furniture in the American taste to America beginning in the late eighteenth century. Much of this furniture now carries an American provenance. Little has been written about these English exports. Once again, examine the secondary woods and construction techniques very closely.

American collectors need to keep three very important points in mind when examining English furniture that has found its way into the American market. First, England experienced a large number of eighteenth century and early nineteenth century design style revivals in the late nineteenth and early twentieth centuries. Much of the English furniture in the design styles of Chippendale, Hepplewhite, Sheraton, and others sold as initial design period examples is actually from these later revivals.

Second, British collectors and dealers willingly accept much greater restoration and repairs to pieces than American collectors. They restore, repair, refinish, replace, and replate with impunity. Further, they make every attempt to hide the work that has been done.

Finally, England has long been the center for furniture reproductions, copycats, and fakes. "Period" design pieces are continually being made from old wood, fresh, or from altered late nineteenth century or early twentieth century forms. W. Crawley's *Is It Genuine?: A Guide to the Identification of Eighteenth–Century English Furniture* (Hart Publishing Company, 1972) is a must read. The book was written by an individual who made his living faking furniture. In addition to England, a number of former British colonies, most notably India, also play important roles in the making of reproductions, copycats, and fakes. A period example is sent there, and is returned with a boatload of copies. The English phrase is that the piece "had puppies."

This first edition of *Warman's Furniture* contains only a few listings of English vernacular furniture. English Windsor furniture and Welsh cupboards are sold primarily to collectors of American Country. The pieces are relatively easy to identify since they differ significantly from American examples in respect to design components and woods. They sell in the range of thirty to fifty percent of the value of their American equivalents.

References: Joseph Aronson, *The New Encyclopedia of Furniture*, Crown Publishers, 1967; Ralph Fastnedge, *English Furniture Styles from 1500–1830*, London, 1962; Rachael Feild, *Macdonald Guide to Buying Antique Furniture*, Wallace–Homestead, 1986; Philippe Garner, *Twentieth–Century Furniture*, Van Nostrand Reinhold, 1980; E. Lucie–Smith, *Furniture: A Concise History*, London, 1981; L. G. G. Ramsey (editor), *The Connoisseur New Guide to Antique English Furniture*, E. P. Dutton & Company, 1961.

EARLY GEORGIAN (1714–1760)

History: During the early Georgian period in England, the Whigs enjoyed political power. Their commercial and financial policies led to increased prosperity, especially for the merchant and landowning class. Merchants as well as urban and rural aristocracy invested heavily in new homes and furnishings as a means of touting their economic success.

In the villages, cottage and farmhouse furniture was made by the homeowner or joiner. In provincial centers such as Bristol and Norwich, capable craftsmen supplied the lesser gentry and middle class with well–made furniture reflecting London tastes. The jewel in the crown remained London which attracted the best craftsmen of the period.

Many London cabinet shops were quite large, almost small factories. The "master" served primarily as a salesperson. Specialization by furniture form was also developing. Several furniture districts developed, e.g., St. Paul's Churchyard and St. Martin's Lane and Long Acre, the latter two areas home to Chippendale, Goodison, Hallett, and Vile and Cobb.

The principal furniture designer during the first part of the Early Georgian period was William Kent (1685–1748), an English architect who viewed furniture as an intregal part of his interior designs. His designs favored the Baroque producing bold, massive furniture with large, elaborately carved festoons, moldings and masks that were often gilted. The Langley Brothers produced less expensive furniture of similar style, thus al lowing the rising middle class to enjoy furniture in the Kent taste.

By the 1740s, a reaction to the Baroque designs took place. Rococo, Chinese, and Gothic influences began to dominate. English furniture became lighter in feel and design. English designers looked to the French designers such as Pierre Lepautre, J. A. Meissonier, and Nicholas Pineau for inspiration. Asymmetrical decoration in the form of intricate curves and "C" scrolls began to appear. Carving was delicately done. The design books of Matthias Lock introduced the new French Rococo designs to England.

The Chinese taste dominated the 1750s. Chinese motifs such a pagodas, long–necked birds, latticework, and open and applied frets appeared on many furniture forms. Japanned furniture experienced a revival. By the mid–1760s the Chinese influence declined, but did not disappear completely.

Horace Walpole's Strawberry Hill led the Gothic Revival. Medieval Gothic motifs were tempered by the Rococo influence. Although the Gothic influence occurred primarily in the first part of the decade of the 1750s, several pieces in this style appeared in the third edition of the *Director*.

The principal wood of the era was mahogany, imported into England in great quantities after the abolition of import duties in 1721. San Domingo mahogany, hard dense wood with little figure, was used first. By 1750, Cuban mahogany with its dark rich color and fine figures was used. Baltic yellow deal was used for veneers early in the period to be replaced by North American red deal by 1750. Oak was used for drawer linings. Beech was a common wood for less expensive furniture. In the countryside, ash, beech, birch, elm, fruit woods, and oak were popular.

Style Books: Thomas Chippendale, *The Gentleman and Cabinet–Maker's Director*, 1754; Matthias Darly, *New Book of Chinese, Gothic and Modern Chairs*, 1750–51; Batty and Thomas Langley, *City and Country Builders' and Workman's Treasury of Designs*, 1740; Matthias Lock and Henry Copland, *A New Book of Ornaments*, 1752; William and John Halfpenny, *Rural Architecture in the Chinese Taste*, 1750–55.

Major Craftsmen: Thomas Chippendale; Benjamin Goodison; Giles Grendey; John Gumley and James Moore; William Hallett; William Vile and John Cobb.

Reference: Ralph Edwards and L. G. G. Ramsey (editors), *The Early Georgian Period, 1714–1760*, London: The Connoisseur, 1963.

PERIOD

Bed, tester, 1760, mahogany, arched canopy lined with pleated blue silk, posts carved below capital with Gothic trefoil arcading, ovulo band ornament on mid section, and baluster form lower section with carved relief Gothic arcading enclosing acanthus leaves on stippled ground in pointed arched panels, blue tasseled green velvet valance around bottom, flowered blue cotton coverlet, 61½" w, 79" l, 101" h **4,250**
Bench, settle, early 18th C, oak, straight crest rail, five panel back splat, open arms, cabriole legs, pad feet, 70" l . **1,045**
Cabinet on Chest, burl walnut, two sections: upper section: double flat molded dome shape cornice with three urn shape finials, pair of arched

Armchair, George I, first quarter 18th C, walnut, racking back, outset wings, scrolled arms, slightly bowed seat, molded square cabriole front supports ending in square feet, back upholstered in petit–point with a pair of courtly figures in 16th C dress against a landscape, seat cushion embroidered with a bouquet of flowers, both panels surrounded by floral gross–point on a dark brown ground, $8,800.00. Photograph courtesy of Butterfield & Butterfield.

and mirrored doors, shelf interior, mid molding; lower section: conforming case, four long drawers, shaped apron, bracket feet, 45" w, 21" d, 90" h **16,500**
Chair
  Arm
    Mahogany, possibly Dutch, mid 18th C, slightly dipped crest rail, S–curved stiles, upholstered back panel, scrolling arms, balloon shape seat with green damask upholstery, cabriole legs, pad feet **3,740**
    Walnut, pair
      1730, walnut, out scrolled solid vasiform splat, tapered uprights with looped finials and scrolled ends, drop–in balloon

Armchair, George II, c1730, gross and petit point upholstered, $80,000.00.

seat, scalloped apron, C–scroll carved and hocked molded cabriole legs, oval pad feet, price for pair **1,760**
1725–55, upholstered rectangular back, out scrolled upholstered arms, flared rectangular seat, cabriole legs joined by stretchers, pad feet, price for pair **3,300**
Desk, mid 18th C, mahogany, yoke form crest rail, two baluster form splats, turned reeded supports, upholstered seat with bold projected center section, front cabriole legs with carved lion mask, claw and ball feet, plain turned tapered back legs with pad feet, turned X–form stretcher **2,970**
Side
English
Early to mid 18th C, pair, high rectangular back, square seat, cabriole legs, pad feet, 41¾" h, price for pair **2,530**
Mid 18th C, pair, carved mahogany, serpentine crest rail carved with leafage and flowerheads over pierced and carved baluster form splat, molded stiles, drop in seat above gadrooned seat rail, acanthus carved cabriole legs ending in claw and ball feet, price for pair **3,575**
Irish, mid 18th C, carved walnut, shaped crest rail, interlaced scrolled splat, flared seat, cabriole legs carved C–scrolls on sides, carved knees with foliate scrolls, foliate carved pad feet, restorations **1,200**
Wing
Mahogany, second quarter 18th C, slightly arched back flanked by scrolled wings, out scrolled arms, bowed seat, shell carved cabriole legs, pad feet **1,980**
Walnut, first quarter 18th C, high arched back, out scrolled arms, bowed seat, needlepoint upholstery, cabriole legs, pointed feet, 48¾" h **4,400**
Chest of Drawers
Burl Walnut, second quarter 18th C, rectangular top with molded edge, notched front corners over two short drawers flanked by deep drawers, three long drawers flanked by canted stiles, bracket feet, minor restorations, 32" w, 34½" h **6,200**
Walnut, crossbanded rectangular top

Chest of Drawers, George II Style, japanned, serpentine top above five conforming drawers, claw and ball feet, gilt chinoiserie dec with figures in landscape, 34" w, 20" d, 35" h, $4,750.00. Photograph courtesy of Leslie Hindman Auctioneers.

with canted corners, two short and three graduated long drawers, stop–fluted pilasters, crossbanded sides, later shaped bracket feet, restorations, 39½" w, 41½" h **3,200**
Chest on Chest, walnut, two sections: upper section: flat ogee molded cornice with chamfered corners, three small frieze drawers, three long molded line inlaid drawers, mid molding; lower section: conforming case, three long drawers, bracket feet, 39" w, 21" d, 70¼" h **6,050**
Clock, tall case, arched hood with molded Gothic style mounting with ball finials, Roman hours and Arabic minutes, waisted case with arched panel with Neo–classical figures and decoration, molded base with urn decoration and molding on bottom, annular ring, date aperture and second hand, engraved plaque "Edmd Bayley London," 19" w, 11" d, 96" h   **4,400**
Cupboard, corner, hanging, early 18th C, oak, flat cornice top, single paneled door, three shaped shelves interior, 40" h **475**
Desk, kneehole, burl walnut, oblong molded and crossbanded top, frieze drawer, two sets of three drawers centering knee well, recessed cupboard

door, bracket feet, 31" w, 17" d, 32"
h **9,350**
Footstool
Oak, mid 18th C, square upholstered
seat, shaped apron, cabriole legs,
pad feet, 17" l, 16" h **660**
Walnut, early 18th C, square uphol-
stered drop–in seat, shaped apron,
cabriole legs, pad feet, 15½" h,
19½" l **1,870**
Mirror
Giltwood and Gesso, second quarter
18th C, pair, crest with flower filled
urn center and floral sprig scrolls,
rectangular mirror plate within
molded and carved C–scrolls and
floral sprigs frame, tied ribbon on
bottom, 21½" w, 42¼" h, price for
pair **7,700**
Walnut and Parcel Gilt, mid 18th C,
foliate carved swan's neck crest
centered by carved cartouche, rectangular mirror plate, re–entrant
upper corners, border of stylized
leaf tips, large shell below, sides
with fruit pendants, regilded,
losses, 28" w, 48" h **3,100**

Spinning Wheel, 18th C, mixed wood,
ring turned round splayed legs, 36" h   **120**
Table
Card, Irish, second quarter 18th C,
carved walnut, concertina–action,
banded top with outset rounded
corners, baise lined playing surface, back legs extending to reveal
drawer, cabriole legs headed by
oak leaf and foliate scroll carving,
hairy paw feet, 37¾" w, 29" h . . .   **13,200**
Dining, mahogany, rectangular top,
two vasiform standards, carved
cabriole legs, scroll decoration on
pad feet, three additional leaves,
44" w, 102" l extended, 30½" h . .   **575**
Dressing, second quarter 18th C, burl
walnut, rectangular top with
molded edge, notched front corners, two short and one long
drawer, flanked by fluted and
canted stiles, scalloped apron, cabriole legs, pad feet, minor restora-
tions, 31½" w, 27¾" h **4,400**
Reading, second quarter 18th C, ma-
hogany, rectangular top with three
wells with sliding panels, single

**Pedestal Desk, Early Georgian Style, 20th C, red lacquer and chinoiserie dec, well-painted
top depicting orientals in a traditional setting above a long drawer set between a series of
three drawers with pull out writing slide, all in gilt floral decoration, raised on square legs,
48" w, 23¾" d, 29¾" h, $825.00. Photograph courtesy of Neal Auction Company.**

drop leaf with crescent form cutout, plain frieze, turned tapered legs with lappet collars, pad feet, 35" w, 14½" d, 29" h **2,200**

Side

Mahogany, mid 18th C, rectangular walnut top, egg and dart carved frieze with center shell, fitted end drawers, acanthus carved cabriole legs, hairy paw feet, caster, restoration, 54" l, 18" d, 32" h . **4,125**

Oak, early 18th C, rectangular molded top, frieze drawer, cylindrical tapered legs, pad feet, 29" w, 15" d, 29" h **385**

Walnut, rectangular top, egg and dart and vitruvian scroll frieze with center scallop shell surrounded by pierced and carved C–scrolls and acanthus, acanthus carved cabriole legs, claw and ball feet, missing top and one leg, restoration, 54½" w, 18½" d, 31" h **1,980**

Tea, tilt top, second quarter 18th C, mahogany, circular top, ring turned swelling cylindrical standard, three foliate pierced cabriole legs with carved shells on knees, pad feet, repairs on two legs, 35¾" d, 28" h **2,000**

STYLE

Cabinet, bedside, mahogany, oblong top with shaped and slightly everted border, conforming case, four short drawers, one long drawer, slender turned tapered legs, pad feet, 20" w, 13" d, 26½" h **880**

Chair

Set of Six, 19th C, carved walnut, raking square back, flared square seat, petit and gros point upholstery, brown ground with brightly colored flowering plants and bowls of flowers, each back with different figures at various pursuits in landscape settings in cartouche border, shell carved molded front supports with scrolled volutes, swept and blocked turned rear supports, H–form stretcher, restoration to upholstery, price for set **12,100**

Side, pair, tall raking back, flared square seat, back and seat with blue and ivory striped woven linen upholstery, hocked molded cabriole front legs, swept and blocked turned rear legs, conforming H–form stretcher, price for pair **1,540**

Desk, 19th C, walnut, rectangular top, tooled leather writing surface within

molded border, shaped apron, corresponding recessed shelf flanked by banks of three serpentine front short drawers, cabriole legs, cartouche carved knees, pad feet, 46½" w, 30½" h **5,000**

Stool, walnut, crimson satin drop–in seat, ribbon and flower carved apron, acanthus and flowerhead carved square cabriole legs, scrolled feet, 21¼" l **1,045**

Table

Breakfast, third quarter 18th C, red walnut and mahogany, figured hinged rectangular two piece top, tapered turned cylindrical standard, tripod legs, pointed dolphin feet, 48" l, 28½" h **1,650**

Center, second half 19th C, square top with molded edge, plain paneled frieze, acanthus carved molded cabriole legs, claw and ball feet, 36½" h **825**

Console

Giltwood, rectangular verde antico marble top, leaf carved frieze, plinth with eagle form support, 41" w, 32½" h **2,475**

Mahogany, rectangular veined gray marble top with molded edge, Vitruvian scroll carved frieze, scalloped apron carved with foliage scrolls and shells, acanthus carved cabriole legs, claw and ball feet, repair to marble, 52" w, 35¼" h **2,475**

Parcel Gilt and Mahogany, pair, rectangular salmon marble top within parcel gilt and floral carved border, frieze centered by carved putto, gilt spread wing eagle support, standing on white painted cloud over mahogany plinth, carved and gilded borders, 48" w, 39" h, price for pair **6,600**

Side, mahogany, rectangular top, central fitted drawer with brass bail handle, square tapered legs, splayed feet, 22½" w, 30" h **660**

LATE GEORGIAN (1760–1811)

History: The Golden Age of English furniture took place between 1760 and 1800; a working harmony between architect and furniture maker existed, resulting in an extremely high level of skilled craftsmanship. The English rivalled the French in setting popular taste and in their workmanship.

Although woodworking machinery was patented as early as the 1790s, handcraftsmanship dominated. Specialization continued: a cabinet shop would have carvers, inlayers, chairmakers, upholsters, etc., in addition to those making the furniture frame. Retail furniture shops developed, selling the wares of cabinetmakers working in small shops or assembling parts supplied by a variety of craftsmen.

London remained the center for English furniture. By 1810, its population exceeded a million. Manchester, its closest rival, had a population of 130,000. The level of craftsmanship in the provincial towns continued to grow, albeit all makers looked to London for the latest in taste and fashion. In London Covent Garden, Old and New Bond Street, Oxford Street, and Tottenham Court joined St. Paul's Churchyard, St. Martin's Lane and Long Acre as principal furniture producing centers.

English furniture was made for export as well as home consumption. Many foreign cabinet makers ordered British examples in order to copy them. Export was not limited to English colonies; traffic was truly worldwide.

The third quarter of the eighteenth century was dominated by furniture designs of Robert Adams (1728–92). Adams introduced England to the neo–classical style, often creating furniture to match the exterior and interior architecture of the homes he designed. Classical motifs such as festoons of florals, husks, paterae, ram's heads, urns, and vases appeared as decorative motifs. The Adams neo-classical style overshadowed, but did not completely remove Chinese, Gothic, and Rococo influences. Furniture in the French taste also continued its appeal among the aristocracy.

Henry Holland (1745–1806) led the attack on the Adams neo–classical style. Unlike many other leading architects of his era, he did not make a trip to tour the classical sites of the Mediterranean. Instead, Holland associated himself with the Prince of Wales, the Regent. When he worked in the neo–classical form, Holland stressed a close adaptation of Greco–Roman forms. He took the French "Directoire" design and gave it an English interpretation, setting the stage of the Regency design style. Holland produced pieces encompassing a wide range of design components, e.g., rosewood ornamented with ormolu mounts, gilted and fluted pillars, and Egyptian motifs.

With Holland's death, furniture design closely followed a narrow archaeological focus, with forms resembling pieces found in Egyptian, Greek, and Roman excavations. The leader of this design style movement was Thomas Hope (1769–1831).

During the Late Georgian period, English cabinetmakers had their choice of the finest wood available. The favored wood was mahogany from the West Indies and Central America. Cuban mahogany was eventually replaced by Honduras

mahogany. As the century ended, satinwood and rosewood began to be used extensively. A group of exotic woods such as calamander, coromandel, thuya, kingwood, and zebra wood were also incorporated into furniture inlays. Red cedar from North and Central America was used for boxes and drawer linings; North American red deal replaced yellow deal for carcass work. Native English woods used by the leading cabinet makers included chestnut, birch, and sycamore.

In summary, Late Georgian furniture demonstrates: (1) the tendency for a multiplicity of furniture design styles to enjoy popularity at the same time and (2) the continued survival and popularity of previous design styles.

Style Books: Alice (George) Hepplewhite, *Cabinet–Maker and Upholsterer's Guide*, 1788; Thomas Hope, *Household Furniture and Interior Design*, 1807; William Ince and Mayhew, *Universal System of Household Furniture And Decoration*, 1759–63; Matthias Lock, *New Book of Pier Frames*, 1769; Matthias Lock, *New Book of Foliage*, 1769; Robert Manwaring, *The Cabinet and Chair Maker's Real Friend and Companion*, 1765; Thomas Shearer, *Designs for Household Furniture*, 1788; Thomas Sheraton, *Cabinet Directory*, 1803; Thomas Sheraton, *Cabinet Maker's and Upholsterer's Drawing Book*, published in parts between 1791–94; George Smith, *A Collection of Designs for Household Furniture and Interior Decoration*, 1808.

Major Craftsmen: Thomas Chippendale the younger; William Gates and John Linnell; Gillow; Ince and Mayhew; William Marsh; George Oakley; Seddon; George Smith, Thomas Tatham; William Vile and John Cobb.

Reference: Ralph Edwards and L. G. G. Ramsey (editors), *The Late Georgian Period, 1760–1810*, London: The Connoisseur, 1961.

PERIOD

Breakfront, 1790, inlaid mahogany, two sections: upper section: thumb molded cornice above fluted frieze, flanked and centered by carved flowerhead roundels, central out stepped section with two glazed doors with Gothic mullions, interior shelves, corresponding recessed doors; lower section: bead and chain carved edge over four paneled cupboard doors, doors with foliate scroll and flowerhead inlaid spandrels, molded plinth base, 106" l, 102" h **33,000**

Cabinet

    Bedside, third quarter 18th C, mahogany, galleried rectangular top, tam-

Display Cabinet, George III, inlaid mahogany and japanned, pagoda top, glazed door and sides, inset lacquer panels, columns, and fretwork, later ebonized stand, electrified, 32″ w, 13¼″ d, 64″ h, $3,575.00. Photograph courtesy of Skinner, Inc.

Bookcase, George III, 19th C, mahogany, broken arch pediment centered over a dentillated cornice topping two glazed doors, sitting atop a chest of four drawers, bracket feet, 50″ w, 24″ d, 88½″ h, $1,045.00. Photograph courtesy of Neal Auction Company.

bour slide, drawer, square molded
legs, 19″ w, 16½″ d, 31″ h **990**
Display, 19th C, mahogany, inlay,
and japanned work, pagoda top
above glazed door and sides, inset
lacquer panels, columns, and fretwork, later ebonized stand, electrified, 32″ w, 13¼″ d, 64″ h **3,575**
Liquor, 1830, mahogany, inlaid, brass
banded corners, 18″ w **450**
Vitrine, last quarter 18th C, satinwood, rectangular recessed glazed
top, crossbanded reserve opening
to red velvet lined interior, painted
on either side with oval reserve enclosing a scene depicting Venus
holding a mirror while reclining on
spouting dolphin, other sides with
calyx and foliate scrolls, tapering
square legs decorated with classical
vases and pen work husks, legs reduced in height, top possibly re-

placed, spandrels of a later date,
34½″ w, 30¾″ h **3,300**
Candle Shield, 1775, mahogany, adjustable screen, easel on ratchet, pair
of silvered brass candleholders, cabriole legs, 54″ h **800**
Cellarette, third quarter 18th C, mahogany, stepped hexagonal hinged top
opens to well, conforming paneled
case, fluted stand, molded square legs
with C–scroll knee brackets, casters,
slight losses, locked, 18″ w, 30½″ h **3,850**
Chair
Arm
Late 18th C, walnut, serpentine
yoke, pierced splat, out scrolled
armrests, drop–in seat with worn
upholstery, square legs joined by
stretcher, worm damage to
frame, restorations **935**
First quarter 19th C, probably Nottinhampshire, elmwood, arched
bowed back, pierced splat
flanked by spindles, turned legs,
concave stretcher, 47½″ h **1,100**
Library, arm, mahogany, arched rectangular upholstered back, upholstered arms on downswept supports, rectangular seat, square legs
joined by stretchers, block feet, restoration and repairs **1,000**

Pair of Arm Chairs, George III, late 18th C, painted beechwood, concave crest above arcaded splat, curving arms centering cane seat, turned legs, surfaces painted black and ornamented with classical figures and trailing foliage, price for pair, $6,050.00. Photograph courtesy of William Doyle Galleries.

Set of Seven, dining, mahogany, shield back, sheaf of wheat center, bowed upholstered seat, square tapered legs, H–form stretcher, distressed green leather upholstery, 36" h, price for set of seven   3,300

Side, early 19th C, pair, oak, scroll carved crest rail ending with volutes, banister back, plank seat, block and ring turned round legs, shaped stretcher, price for pair . . .   2,090

Wing, third quarter 18th C, mahogany, arched back, curved wings, out scrolled arms, bowed seat with loose cushion, carved chamfered legs, straight stretchers, gros- and petit point upholstery, restoration, 46" h   3,300

Chest of Drawers

1765, mahogany, rectangular molded top, slide and four graduated drawers, bracket feet, restoration, 31½" w, 19¼" d, 32½" h   1,210

1790, mahogany, straight front, two small and two long cockbeaded drawers, brass ring pulls, French bracket feet, 41" w, 20" d, 35" h .   625

1800, mahogany, rectangular top, two short and four graduated long drawers, shaped valance, flared feet, minor restorations, 40¾" w, 46" h   1,550

1810, mahogany, bow front, two short and three graduated line inlaid drawers, scalloped apron, outswept bracket feet, repaired front feet, replaced handles, 44¾" w, 41" h   3,025

1815, oak and mahogany, crossbanded rectangular top, thumb

Chest on Chest, George III, projecting molded cornice above a pair of short drawers over three long drawers and chamfered corners detailed with blind fretwork above a lower case fitted with three graduated drawers, raised on purced machet (bracket) feet, restorations, 47" w, 23" d, 68" h, $2,860.00. Photograph courtesy of Neal Auction Company.

molded edge, seven variegated crossbanded drawers, ogee molded bracket feet, 74½″ w, 37½″ h **2,750**

Chests, Other

Bachelor, 1760, mahogany, crossbanded rectangular top with canted corners and molded edge, slide, four graduated long drawers flanked by fluted pilasters on molded base, ogee bracket feet, repairs to feet, 32½″ w, 30½″ h **4,400**

Chest on Chest

1800, mahogany, two sections: upper section: molded cornice, cockbeaded divided top drawer, three similar long drawers, lowest drawer fitted as a secretary with drawers and pigeonholes; lower section: three long drawers, shaped bracket feet, restoration to feet and cornice, 43½″ w, 77″ h **2,475**

1880, mahogany, two sections: upper section: thumb molded denticulated top, two short and two long drawers, canted and fluted stiles; lower section: brushing slide, three long drawers, later bracket feet, minor restorations, 40″ w, 70″ h **4,400**

Mule, 19th C, oak, hinged rectangular top, two aligned faux drawers over one long drawer, two aligned drawers, bracket feet, 68″ w, 23″ d, 41½″ h **1,500**

Commode, late 18th C, oak, rectangular top opens to shallow interior, deep scalloped apron, chamfered square legs, 18¾″ w, 18¼″ h **275**

Desk

Kneehole, third quarter 18th C, mahogany, shaped top, conforming case, center drawer with cupboard door underneath, four graduated drawers on each side, molded bracket feet, 42″ w, 24″ d, 34½″ h **9,900**

Slant Front

Late 18th or early 19th C, burl elm, rectangular top, hinged slant front lid, fitted interior, three graduated drawers, bracket feet, worn, restoration, 38″ w, 40″ h **2,475**

Mahogany, rectangular top, interior with central prospect door flanked by small drawers, divided drawer, three similar long drawers, flanked by fluted quarter columns, later ogee bracket feet, 49½″ w, 43″ h **3,100**

Mahogany, rectangular top, interior with central prospect door flanked by valanced pigeonholes and small drawers, green baize lined writing surface, four graduated long drawers, bracket feet, 37½″ w, 41¾″ h **1,750**

Highboy, Welsh, 19th C, oak, two sections, upper section: projected molded cornice top, four shelves; lower section: central cockbeaded drawer flanked by two bands of two cockbeaded drawers, turned legs joined by tier, turned feet, 84″ w, 92″ h **3,850**

Desk, George III, third quarter of 18th C, mahogany, oblong molded top, re-entrant corners, three cock beaded frieze drawers, twin banks of two drawers centering knee well and two recessed drawers, bracket feet, 39½″ w, 32″ d, 30¼″ h, $3,740.00. Photograph courtesy of William Doyle Galleries.

Desk, George III, early 19th C, double pedestal desk, mahogany, oblong molded top inset with gilt tooled black leather writing surface, three cock beaded frieze drawers resting on twin banks containing on alternate sides drawers or cupboards, plinth bases, 59½" w, 37½" d, 29½" h, $8,800.00. Photograph courtesy of William Doyle Galleries.

Knife Box, pair with matching smaller box, mahogany, serpentine sloped front, inlaid chevron pattern, fitted interior, circular brass locks, 12" and 13½" h, price for set of three boxes .   3,600

Linen Press, early 19th C, two sections: upper section: projected molded cornice, two crossbanded paneled cupboard doors, shelved interior;

Mirror, George II style, early 19th C, giltwood, rectangular two section plate, molded C-scroll borders and pilasters, pierced framework of waves, foliage, and flowerheads, everted foliage crest, 61" h, $8,500.00. Photograph courtesy of William Doyle Galleries.

lower section: four crossbanded cockbeaded drawers above two banks of three graduated drawers, bracket feet, restored, 85½" w, 91½" h   3,025

Mirror
1760, gilt–gesso, rectangular mirror plate within pierced ruffled and scroll carved frame, opposed C-scroll cresting surmounted by spread–winged phoenix, sides with fruit and floral vine pendants, minor repairs, 20" w, 45" h   4,950

1765, giltwood, anthemion crest flanked by urns, divided rectangular beveled mirror plate, conforming pierced frame with carved C-scrolls, husks, and rocaille, 46" w, 100" h   37,400

1780, parcel gilt and carved mahogany, rectangular mirror plate within molded frame, arched foliate cresting centered by gilt phoenix perched on a branch flanked by ruffled C–scrolls, sides with floral vine pendants, scroll carved and incised base below, replaced mirror, regilded, 22" w, 47" h   3,300

1785, giltwood, oval mirror plate, conforming pierced frame with leafy C–scrolls, minor repairs, 33½" h   825

Secretary
Third quarter 18th C, mahogany, two sections: upper section: broken arch pediment with dentil molding, two mullioned glass doors with shelf interior; lower section: hinged slant desk opens to fitted interior with compartments, four graduated drawers below, bracket feet, 39½" w, 23" d, 87½" h   4,950

Late 18th C, mahogany, two sections: upper section: fret carved rectangular cornice, pair of glazed doors, interior shelves over small drawers and pigeonholes; lower section: slant front with patera inlaid prospect door flanked by valanced pigeonholes and drawers, four graduated cockbeaded long drawers, bracket feet, 42" w, 85" h 6,600

Sideboard, 1790, mahogany, demilune form, one drawer flanked by two wide drawers, two cabinet doors, circular brass bail handles and escutcheons, square tapered legs, spade feet, 61" w, 30" d, 33" h 1,050

Stand

Kettle, late 18th or early 19th C, mahogany and fruitwood, dished circular top, plain cylindrical column on arched tripod feet, one foot replaced, 11½" d, 25¾" h 525

Music, early 19th C, mahogany, rectangular top, adjustable support with two swing candle holders, columnar form standard, three cabriole legs, snake feet, 24" w, 43" h 1,430

Work, 1820, mahogany, rectangular flip top opens to compartment, one drawer, two cabinet doors, bamboo turned legs, 25" w, 32" h 275

Table

Breakfast, first quarter 19th C, mahogany, rosewood crossbanded oval tilt top, reeded edge, tapering ring turned waisted cylindrical standard, four downswept legs, brass feet and casters, 60" w, 29" h 5,000

Card

1790, pair, satinwood, crossbanded D–shaped top, felt lined playing surface, crossbanded frieze and borders, bead carved lower edge, tapering cylindrical ring turned and fluted legs, gilding of later date, cracking and losses to veneer, losses to moldings, 36" w, 28½" h, price for pair 13,200

1825, mahogany, hinged rectangular top, rounded corners, gilt tooled red leather playing surface, frieze with bead carved rectangular reserves, corresponding lower edge, turned baluster form support, gadrooned base, coved rectangular platform carved at corners with scrolls, four downswept legs, brass foliate toes, casters, minor repairs to feet, 36" w, 28¾" h 12,000

Center, Irish, mahogany, rectangular top, egg and dart molded frieze, cabriole legs with acanthus carved knees, scrolled feet, 33½" w, 17¾" d, 32" h 3,025

Console, 1810, painted satinwood, D–shaped top, wide crossbanded reserve painted en grisaille in manner of Angelica Kauffmann with foliate scrolls centered and flanked by three seated cherubs within a light and dark banded border, frieze of breakfront outline within dark

Sideboard, demilune, late George III, c1800, mahogany, boxwood strung and satinwood banded top centered at rear border by a semicircular satinwood panel, surmounted by a later arched brass gallery with urn-form finials, similarly inlaid and strung frieze fitted with a central drawer raised on line-inlaid square tapering supports ending in satinwood veneered splayed feet, restored, 66" w, 56¼" h to top of gallery, $3,850.00. Photograph courtesy of Butterfield & Butterfield.

banded reserves, ring turned tapering reeded leg, minor losses to veneer, 48" w, 35" h **60,500**

Dining, late 18th or early 19th C, rectangular top, two rectangular drop leaves, chamfered legs, 54½" l extended, 27½" h **770**

Drum, second quarter 19th C, mahogany, crossbanded circular revolving top, frieze fitted with alternating drawers and faux drawers, ring turned baluster standard, four downswept reeded legs, brass toes, casters, 44" d, 31" h **3,650**

Game, mahogany, demilune hinged top, felt lined playing surface with molded edge, veneered apron with pierced carved brackets, square tapered legs with molded fronts, 35" w, 29" h **1,250**

Library, mahogany, circular tooled leather top, four drawers and four faux drawers, ring turned single pedestal, tripod splayed legs, brass caster feet, 45" d, 20" h **1,700**

Pembroke

1780, mahogany, bowed rectangular top, D–shape leaves, frieze drawer opposed by faux drawer, square tapered legs, 33½" l, 18½" w, 28¼" h **935**

1800, rectangular hinged top, single frieze drawer opposed by faux drawer, square tapered legs, 34" l, 19" d, 27" h **550**

1810, satinwood, rosewood, and tulipwood, rectangular top, shaped flaps, frieze drawer opposed by faux drawer, square tapering legs, brass feet and casters, 33" l, 30" w extended, 26¾" h **3,575**

Serving, third quarter 18th C, mahogany, serpentine top, plain serpentine frieze with canted corners, molded chamfered legs, 53¾" l, 26" d, 33½" h **2,090**

Tea, 1750, mahogany, circular tilt top, vasiform standard, tripod cabriole legs, pad feet, 32½" d, 29" h **500**

Breakfront, George II Style, 20th C, mahogany, scrolled pediment centered over a dentillated cornice topping four doors, the whole sitting atop a center drop front secretary drawer over cupboard doors, flanked by four small drawers, 74″ w, 17″ d, 94″ h, $2,420.00. Photograph courtesy of Neal Auction Company.

Wash Stand, 1820, mahogany, rectangular top and splashboard, includes fitted blue and white transfer decorated porcelain basin and pitcher, two doors, pullout porcelain chamber pot, ring turned round legs, casters, 26" w, 20½" d, 38½" h   880

STYLE

Breakfront, late 19th C, mahogany, two sections. Upper section: slightly projecting dentil carved frieze, four glazed doors with arabesque mullions flanked at ends with arched doors; lower section: acorn pendant carved frieze over six paneled cupboard doors, plinth base, minor losses, 135½" l, 100" h   9,900
Cabinet, liquor, late 19th C, mahogany, dentil molded corners over bottle rack over rectangular top, straight front, two drawers, two cabinet doors, oval brass bail handles, straight bracket feet, 36½" w, 18½" d, 76" h   900

Armchair, George III, c1789, giltwood, in the French style, channel molded frame, cartouche panel back, center-pad arms, bowed seat, fluted seat rail, stop-fluted turned tapered supports headed by rectangular floral paterae, figured cut green velvet upholsteries, $2,000.00. Photograph courtesy of Butterfield & Butterfield.

Canterbury, late 19th C, mahogany, rectangular form with vertical dividers, cockbeaded drawer, turned legs, 20½" l, 20" h   1,430
Chair
Set of Four, rectangular olive green leather upholstered backrest, straight armrests, olive green leather upholstered seat, square straight legs, price for set of four   .   1,980
Set of Twelve, dining, stained mahogany, foliate carved crest rail, center cartouche, elaborately pierced ribbon and foliate scroll carved interlaced splat, shaped seat over rail carved with foliage centered by cartouche, cabriole legs with acanthus and ruffled carving, scrolled feet, design known as "ribband back chair" illustrated in Thomas Chippendale's *The Gentleman & Cabinet–maker's Director*, Plate XV, price for set of twelve   8,000
Side, mahogany, scrolling yoke pierced carved splat, leather upholstered drop–in seat, cabriole legs, claw and ball feet   935
Chest of Drawers, 19th C, mahogany, rectangular top, straight front with two small over three long cockbeaded drawers, oval brass bail handles and escutcheons, French bracket feet, 41" w, 20" d, 41" h   700
Commode, late 19th C, mahogany, square galleried top with handles above tambour and two long drawers, square chamfered legs, 20" w, 29½" h   990
Desk
Partner's, mid 19th C, mahogany, rectangular molded leather inset top, three drawers, pedestals with graduated drawers opposed by cabinet doors, plinth base, 60" w, 41" d, 22" h   2,420
Partner's, walnut, rectangular top with three blind gold tooled green leather panels and molded edge, frieze with three drawers, sides with triple fronted drawers opposing simulated frieze drawer, other side with doors faced to simulate drawers, plinth base, 55¼" w, 31½" h   3,575
Writing, 19th C, walnut, hinged lid opens to fitted interior with ivory pulls, straight front with four graduated drawers, oval brass bail handles and escutcheons, straight bracket feet, 36" w, 16" d, 42" h   .   2,600
Lowboy, 19th C, mahogany, rectangular top, straight front with one drawer,

Settee, George II Style, Late 19th C, stepped camelback, outward flaring side arms, cabriole feet with ornately carved oval cartouche and foliage on knee, hairy paw feet, 81″ l, 37″ h, $950.00.

cabriole legs, claw and ball feet, 30½″ w, 17½″ d, 25″ h 750

Mirror, last quarter 18th C, mahogany, rectangular mirror plate, ogee molded border, scrolled mahogany frame, mirror plate replaced, restoration to one ear, 14½″ w, 24″ h 350

Settee, 19th C, mahogany, rectangular molded backrest, arms form eagle's head, fret carved seat rail, cabriole legs, claw and ball feet, 66″ l, 28″ d, 37¼″ h 1,320

Sideboard, pedestal
    Mid 19th C, mahogany, serpentine edged top, three frieze drawers, one pedestal with cupboard door enclosing slides and shelves, other with shelf and drawer, plinth base, minor cracks and chips to veneer, 73″ l, 38″ h 2,750
    Third quarter 19th C, inlaid mahogany, rectangular top, outset ends, concaved splashboard, frieze fitted with two drawers, pedestal cupboards, doors inlaid with large classical urn, bottle drawers and shelves, plinth base, stamped "James Winter, 101 Wardour St," (James Winter listed as furniture broker, appraiser, and undertaker in London, 1823–40), minor losses and repairs to veneer, 90″ l, 44¾″ h 3,300

Sofa, mahogany, serpentine upholstered backrest, scrolled armrests, loose cushion seat, straight square legs, salmon watered silk upholstery, 80″ l 1,100

Table
    Card, early 19th C, mahogany, hinged rectangular top with flowerhead carved rounded edge, green baize lined playing surface, molded square legs, 32″ w, 27″ h 715
    Dining, mahogany, rectangular top, two demilune drop leaves, straight square legs, 56″ l extended, 28″ h 715
    Drum, 19th C, mahogany, circular gold tooled red leather top, straight frieze with drawers, ring turned standard, four downswept legs with casters, faded leather, 38½″ d, 29″ h 1,320
    Handkerchief, c1900, inlaid satinwood, square top, four triangular flaps inlaid with acanthus filled urns and anthemion, felt lined playing surface with wells, crossbanded frieze fitted with drawer, tapering square legs, spade feet, minor losses to veneer, 22″ w, 28¼″ h .. 2,750
Sofa, mahogany, rectangular drop leaf top, two drawers and two faux drawers, two supports joined by stretcher, flaring legs, brass caster feet, 25″ d, 31″ h 1,100

REGENCY (1812–1830)

History: The Regency period is marked by two major developments in England: the first was a series of prolonged wars with France; the second was a growth in the middle class whose wealth was based on industry, not land. This led to an era when furniture taste was no longer established by the upper class.

Industrially produced furniture was introduced during the Regency period. Carving and inlay were largely abandoned. Arbiters of taste decried the development.

The Regency period actually begins in 1811 when the Prince of Wales became Regent. Close reproduction of antiquarian designs are a hallmark of Regency furniture. However, there was resistance to slavish imitation. Antiquarian forms may have inspirated them, but final products were tempered by discrimination.

Despite the wars with France, French tastes still strongly influenced English furniture design styles. The English especially admired the work of Charles Percier and Pierre Fontaine and the French Directoire and French Empire designs. Henry Holland and Thomas Hope adapted French designs to the English tastes.

Characteristics of Regency furniture include extreme simplicity of outline, large uninterrupted horizontal and vertical surfaces, a very minor role for ornamentation, and a strong sense of solidity. Metal inlay and reeding were the favored decorative elements.

Tastes changed rapidly during the Regency period. In his 1826 guide, Smith noted that the styles of his 1808 guide were obsolete. Chinese, Gothic, and Egyptian revivals occurred at the end of the period. Chinese furniture made use of dragons, pagodas, and other oriental motifs. Bamboo imitations were used on chairs and small tables. Romantic literature inspired the Gothic revival which was divided into two segments—Tudor and Elizabethan. The Egyptian

revival resulted from the reports associated with Napoleon's Egyptian campaign.

During the period, dark, glossy woods such as mahogany and rosewood found favor. Woods such as amboyna, calamander, and zebra wood with boldly striped figures also were utilized. Woods came from around the world—rosewood from Brazil and the East Indies; calamander from India, Ceylon, and the East Indies. Around 1815 French polish was introduced.

Style Books: R. Ackermann, *The Repository of the Arts*, published monthly between 1809 and 1828; Richard Brown, *The Rudiments of Drawing Cabinet and Upholstery Furniture*, 1820; Peter and Michael Angelo Nicholson, *The Practical Cabinet Maker, Upholsterer and Complete Decorator*, 1826; George Smith, *The Cabinet Maker's and Upholsterer's Guide, Drawing Book and Repository*, 1826.

Reference: Ralph Edwards and L. G. G. Ramsey (editors), *The Regency Period, 1810–1830*, London: The Connoisseur, 1962.

PERIOD

Bench, first quarter 19th C, mahogany, oblong upholstered top, curule supports, turned stretcher, later green velvet upholstery, 34" l **1,800**
Chair
  Arm, pair, rosewood, arched back with everted border and red leather upholstery, turned columnar arm supports, turned legs, price for pair **6,600**
  Library, early 19th C, mahogany,

Side Chairs, second quarter 19th C, ebonzied walnut, rope twist crest rail above gilt double arched splat, slip seat, sabre legs, pair, $2,100.00. Photograph courtesy of Leslie Hindman Auctioneers.

Pier Table, rosewood, marble top, $2,420.00. Photograph courtesy of William Doyle Galleries.

molded rectilinear frame, caned back, arm panels, and seat, green leather loose cushion, straight legs, brass caster feet   4,950
Set
Set of Six, first quarter 19th C, side, rosewood, klismos form, concave crest rail, concave splat with scrolling floral brass boulle work, caned seat with loose cushion, sabre legs, price for set   2,750
Set of Seven, early 19th C, mahogany, rope turned crest rail, upholstered splat, scrolling stiles, drop–in seat, sabre legs, price for set   4,950
Set of Ten, dining, eight side and two arm, first quarter 19th C, carved mahogany, slightly concave rectangular crest rail with incised scroll carving, applied rosettes at ends, ring turned tapering concave splat, flared drop–in seat, sabre legs, repairs to seat rail on two chairs, repairs to one arm, price for set   6,600
Commode, tulipwood, oblong molded and shaped sepia marble top, serpentine front, conforming bombe case, two frieze drawers, two shaped parquetry paneled drawers within kingwood border, angled scrolling knife edge corners, bronze chutes and sabots, 50½" w, 23¼" d, 34½" h   8,800
Daybed, c1815, ormolu mounted, grain painted, scrolled sides, three–quarter

upholstered back, supports mounted with ormolu plumes and foliate scrolls, out scrolled legs with lobe carving, foliate brass feet, casters, painted overall in red and brown to simulate rosewood, repairs to feet, 76" l   4,125
Desk, early 19th C, mahogany, rectangular top with D–form recess, adjustable leather lined writing surface, series of small cockbeaded drawers over three large drawers, turned tapered legs, stiff leaf feet, upper right hand

Book Stand, second quarter 19th C, inlaid mahogany, adjustable stand above two shelves, lower drawer on ring turned supports, turned tapering legs ending in brass casters, 20" w, 14" d, 44" h, $1,900.00. Photograh courtesy of Leslie Hindman Auctioneers.

drawer lock plate stamped "E S P & Co Secure Two Lever Lock London" 57" w, 31½" d, 34½" h **7,975**

Mirror

Pine, stripped, arched crest, beveled mirror plate, subsidiary mirrored borders interspersed with pine foliate medallions and rosettes, outer edge with bead and chain carved border, arched foliate scroll carved cresting suspending floral sprigs, minor chips, 39½" w, 79" h **4,500**

Giltwood, first quarter 19th C, circular mirror plate, cavetto molded frame with applied spherules, gilt losses, 17" d **660**

Secretary, early 19th C, mahogany, two sections: upper section: flat with molded Greek Key cornice, two glazed mullioned doors, shelf interior; lower section: one short drawer over three long drawers, bracket feet, 44½" w, 22½" d, 89" h **2,860**

Stand, early 19th C, yew wood, octagonal top with crossbanded radiant parquetry panels, conforming frieze with drawer, tapered paneled standard, conforming octagonal base, compressed bun feet, 23½" d, 30" h **1,760**

Music Stand, adjustable lyre form rest, columnar support, tripod base, 54" h, $1,100.00. Photograph courtesy of William Doyle Galleries.

Stool

Foot, early 19th C, pair, oak, circular needlepoint panel, ogee frame, brass paw feet, 11" d, price for pair **550**

Piano, early 19th C, mahogany, concave crest rail, concave splat centers bronze lyre, reeded stiles, circular upholstered seat, spiral turned standard, reeded downswept tripod base, brass paw feet **1,980**

Card Table, rosewood, satinwood inlay, fold over top, $2,640.00. Photograph courtesy of William Doyle Galleries.

Table

Console, first quarter 18th C, oak, carved, rectangular mottled and figured brown and gray marble top with molded edge, frieze with center pierced shell and scroll carved cartouche, diapered spandrels, pierced scroll and shell carved cabriole legs, molded and scroll carved undulating X–form stretcher, center octagonal platform with relief carved flowerhead, raised hoof feet, minor restorations, 47½" w, 29¾" h **15,400**

Drum, early 19th C, mahogany, circular top with inset tooled black leather surface, frieze drawer, urn form standard, downswept reeded quatrepod, brass caster feet, 48" d, 29½" h **4,400**

Pedestal, inlaid calamander, burlwood banded circular top, plain frieze, molded gilt metal edge, outward flaring octagonal pedestal applied with out stepped burlwood banding above stylized leaf and scroll inlaid band, four downswept

Game Table, mahogany and ebony inlaid, flip top, leather-lined backgammon board, downswept legs, brass paw feet on casters, 34¾" w, 17" d, 28½" h, $2,000.00. Photograph courtesy of Skinner, Inc.

tapered legs, cast claw feet, casters, 36" d, 29" h **5,500**
Sewing, rosewood, rectangular thumb molded top with rounded corners, two cockbeaded drawers, polychrome silk lined basket drawer, two opposing faux drawers, floral carved standard incurved plinth, paw feet, 22" w, 28½" l extended, 29¾" h **950**
Sofa, mahogany, oblong top, two D–shape drop leaves with broad band of rosewood, conforming frieze with two drawers, trestle support, downswept reeded legs, brass caster paw feet, 35" w, 25" d, 29" h **3,575**
Work, c1810, hexagonal hinged top with painted classical scene, fitted interior with basket, pen work decorated frieze, square tapered legs, concave stretchers, 20¼" l, 15½" d, 28½" h **2,640**

STYLE

Bookcase, breakfront, japanned, black, rectangular molded cornice, outset ends, two glazed mullioned doors flanked by two similar doors, conforming plinth, overall oriental court scenes decoration, 86" w, 19½" d, 88" h **3,500**
Cabinet, pair, pale mahogany, rectangular top with outset front rounded corners, side locking, faux front drawers with brass medallion, reeded columns, paw feet, 23" w, 23" d, 37½" h, price for pair **1,300**
Chair, library, mahogany, flat shaped crest rail, oval caned tablet, horseshoe form arms, circular seat, turned legs **550**
Credenza, mahogany, oblong top, conforming frieze with drawer within gilded torus molding, pair of doors with wirework grills resting on plinth, 34" w, 14" d, 36½" h **1,210**
Stand, reading, rosewood, adjustable rectangular support with inlaid central brass and faux tortoiseshell medallion, circular flaring standard with carved gilt water leaves, quatrefoil form plinth, paw feet, 19" w, 31½" h   **2,200**
Steps, library, mahogany, brass rails, ball casters **800**
Table
Breakfast, late 19th C, mahogany, rectangular top, two rectangular drop leaves, ring turned standard, four downswept legs, brass paw feet and casters, worn top, 72" l extended, 29" h **1,320**
Center, rosewood, circular crossbanded top with star center, frieze with rope turned border, gilded standard, incurvate triangular stand with carved whales, ball feet, 48" d, 30" h **2,420**
Dining, satinwood and mahogany, extension, rectangular crossbanded top with rounded corners, two

Console Tables, pair, Regency Style, pine, rectangular marble top, Greek key design frieze, eagle-form support resting on a plinth, restoration to marble, 55" w, 37" h, $5,000.00. Photograph courtesy of Butterfield & Butterfield.

turned column pedestal standards,
fluted downswept legs, brass paw
feet, two leaves, 47" w, 141" l extended, 30" h **2,100**
Drum, second half 19th C, mahogany, circular crossbanded top,
frieze with alternating drawers and
faux drawers, slightly tapering ring
turned and waisted pedestal supported on X–form base, animal paw
feet carved with large scrolls and
rosettes, 45½" d, 29" h **3,575**

WILLIAM IV OR LATE REGENCY (1830–1837)

History: Conservative best describes the furniture
produced during the Late Regency period. Very
little change is noted from the Regency design
styles. A principal reason was the desire of the
nouveau riche to adopt accepted design styles as
an acknowledgment of their good aesthetic
tastes.

The Late Regency period continued the trend
to popularize design styles through mass produced furniture. Many manufacturers did not
employ designers. Instead they repeatedly produced pieces based upon stock design styles.

The Late Regency period witnessed the introduction of two revivals that lead into the Victorian era—Louis XIV and Elizabethan. Louis XIV
marked the return of the Baroque and Rococo
forms of the *ancien regime*. The style was resisted
by established architects and designers such as
George Smith. Despite this opposition, "old
French" gained strong acceptance among the
middle class.

C. J. Richardson lead the Elizabethan revival
movement. Initially old wood was used to make
pseudo–Elizabethan forms such as cupboards.
The movement was touted as pro–British in contrast to the growing acceptance of "old French."

The Late Regency period continued the growing eclecticism of furniture design styles that
reached its zenith during the Victorian era.
Homes started to mix styles—Gothic in the hall
and Louis XIV in the drawing room. A new age
of furniture design styles was dawning.

Style Books: T. F. Hunt, *Exemplers of Tudor
Architectur and Furniture*, 1829–30; Thomas
King, *Designs for Carving and Gilding*, 1834;
Thomas King, *The Modern Style of Cabinet Work
Exemplified*, 1829; J. C. Loudon, *Encyclopedia
of Cottage, Farm, and Villa Architecture*, 1833;
Henry Shaw, *Specimens of Ancient Furniture*,
1832–36.

Reference: Ralph Edwards and L. G. G. Ramsey
(editors), *The Early Victorian Period, 1830–1860*,
London: The Connoisseur, 1962.

Cabinet, second quarter 19th C, mahogany, rectangular top, pair of frieze drawers, two cupboard doors with arched
panels, plinth base, 38" w, 15½" d, 37" h,
$2,000.00. Photograph courtesy of Leslie
Hindman Auctioneers.

Bookcase, mahogany, two sections: upper section: pair of glazed doors,
shelved interior; lower section: pair
of glazed doors, plinth base, 35" w,
75" h **1,800**
Breakfront, first half 19th C, mahogany,
oblong molded cornice top, four
doors with brass grills, adjustable
shelf interior, conforming projected
lower base, four paneled doors,
plinth, 90" w, 23" d, 98½" h **8,250**
Canterbury, burled walnut, tortoise
shape, scalloped apron, Louis XIV Revival feet, brass casters **2,200**
Cellarette
  1830–40, mahogany, carved, sarco-
  phagus form, paneled and beaded
  edge top, frieze with two graduated
  bands of beading, geometrical
  paneled front and sides divided by
  reeded stiles, tapered turned circular feet with casters, 27" w, 21" h   **2,475**
  1835, oak, hinged angled top,
  paneled slanted sides, lead lined interior, base molding, lock signed
  "Aubin," 34" w, 23" d, 23" h **2,500**
  Second quarter 19th C, carved mahogany, coved rectangular top,
  canted corners, metal lined interior,
  tapering rectangular case, shell and
  scroll carved handles, carved animal paw feet, 26" w, 18½" h **2,200**
Chair
  Library, arm, mahogany, carved,

slightly curved upholstered back continues to form seat, open scrolled arm, curved legs, front paw feet, casters on back, back legs branded "J Tooker" **900**

Side, c1840, mahogany, curved crest rail, overstuffed seat, ring turned legs **180**

Clock, tall case, 1830–40, brass framed glazed flat top hood, silvered brass openwork dial with concentric ring inset with Zodiac sign engraved panels, gilt bronze framework with elaborate cast and pierced scrolling foliage and C–scroll decoration enclosing flowers and icicles beneath plumed cresting, massive tapered case, double fielded panel door, ovolo carved borders, angled stiles, paneled base with carved foliate buttress bracket angles, angled ogee bracket feet, quarter striking, plays sixteen nested bells, crown wheel escapement, wheel count, skeletonized three train movement, 32½" w, 103" h **19,800**

Footstool, pair, rectangular upholstered top, gadrooned and waterleaf carved apron, reeded melon feet, 20½" l, price for pair **1,760**

Knife Box, pair, satinwood, incurved square hooded lifting top, finial, fitted interior, gilt metal paw feet, 29½" h, price for pair **1,200**

Mirror, 1830, pair, giltwood and gesso, oval, ribbed deep cavetto border, subsidiary inner and outer molded borders of stiff leaves, cable molding and guilloche, 31" w, 35" h, price for pair **4,125**

Secretary, c1840, mahogany, two sections: upper section: projected dentil molded cornice, mullion glazed doors; lower section: burl inlaid drawer opens to writing surface and fitted interior, pair of doors with oval inlay, bracket feet, 48" w, 22" d, 92" h **6,500**

Sideboard, second quarter 19th C, mahogany, pedestal, bowed crossbanded rectangular top, arched splashboard centered by foliate pierced brass panel, frieze drawers centered by brass inlaid panel, pedestals with coved hinged tops and cupboard doors, interior shelves and drawers, carved claw feet, minor cracking to splashboard, 97½" w, 52" h **2,750**

Stand

Book, 19th C, mahogany, table top, spindle galleries, 9½" h **150**

Reading, mid 19th C, rectangular adjustable top with reeded edge, compartmentalized drawer, adjustable ring turned standard, three downswept supports, ball feet, restorations, missing one shelf support and ball foot, 22" w, 29" h **550**

Table

Breakfast, c1840, mahogany, D–shaped drop leaves, drawer, bold turned legs, brass casters, 48" l ... **380**

Card, mahogany, fold–over top, flattened baluster shaped support, four part base **600**

Dressing, mahogany, rectangular stepped backsplash, marble top, two long drawers, one small drawer, fluted sides, four turned tapered legs, two legs with casters, 26" w, 22" d, 33¾" h **425**

Drop Leaf, mid 19th C, mahogany, rectangular top, two leaves with curved corners, line inlaid apron, turned tapered legs, 42" w, 23½" l leaves, 29" h **550**

Game, early 19th, rosewood, rectangular hinged top, scroll carved frieze, chamfered standard on plinth base, ball feet, 36" w, 29½" h **990**

Occasional, 1830, carved rosewood, top covered in crocodile skin, molded and carved border of S–scrolls interspersed with foliage, tapering circular shaft carved with foliage, shaped triform base, scrolled supports, 25¾" w, 28" h **5,000**

Side, c1830, giltwood, tan violet veined marble top, conforming apron with central applied medallion flanked by paterae, boldly turned and reeded legs, 43¾" w, 24" d, 31¾" h **900**

Tea, c1840, walnut, oval tilt top, baluster pedestal, four splayed reeded legs, bronze lion paw feet, 40" w, 35" d, 30" h **800**

Work, second quarter 19th C, rosewood, rectangular top with retractable fire screen, single frieze drawer, leather lined writing slope, pen drawer on right side, raised columns, shaped base, 22¾" w, 17"d, 33¾" h **1,980**

Teapoy, c1838, carved rosewood, coved rectangular lid, carved at corners with lobes, interior storage area, petal carved baluster form pedestal, coved square base, scrolled feet, inscribed with graphite "George Allievwell, August 1838," 17" w, 32" h **1,650**

VICTORIAN (1837–1901)

History: The age of revivals that began with the Louis XIV and Elizabethan revivals of the Late Regency period continued during the reign of Queen Victoria. The theme which unified all the revivals was the reliance on historical precedent. The mid–century Victorians looked backward, not forward.

Another theme which united Victorian eclecticism was comfort. Upholstered furniture, often featuring large amounts of padding, became fashionable, partly due to the development of cheap worsted covering material made on the Yorkshire power weaving looms. Stylistic consideration often assumed secondary importance. In the last quarter of the nineteenth century, the importance shifted back to stylistic mannerisms.

During the early part of Victoria's reign, architectural elements of furniture tended to blend into a unified whole. Individual ornamentation such as inlay, marquetry, gilding, and ormolu lost favor, not to be revived until the late 1850s. In the 1860s, the use of inset porcelain medallions and embossed leather panels can be found in some furniture forms. The use of exotic woods decreased. Mahogany, rosewood, walnut, and oak regained their importance. In the 1840s, the use of Italian marble for chiffoniers, sideboards, and washstands enjoyed great popularity.

Although patent carving machines were available at the beginning of the Victorian era, their acceptance was slow. Labor was still relatively inexpensive and the division of labor system introduced in earlier decades worked exceptionally well. However, by the 1850s, the use of such machines was common. It was during this time that Sandy and Powell introduced a fret–cutting machine.

The Victorian era witnessed the introduction of material other than wood into the furniture vocabulary. Metal furniture appeared as cast iron garden and hall furniture, very much in vogue during the 1845 to 1855 period. Brass beds were first introduced in the mid–1820s, reaching broad popular acceptance by the mid–1840s. Another popular material was papier mâché, with the premier pieces manufactured by Jennens and Bettridge.

Although furniture introduced at the beginning of the Victorian era favored curved surfaces, there was a return to straight, box lines in the 1860s and 1870s. The Louis XIV revival is a good example.

Another important trend, little understood in America, was the reproduction of eighteenth century pieces. Gillows of London, a mass production manufacturer popular with the middle class, made large amounts of furniture based upon the designs of Thomas Chippendale and Thomas Hope. In addition, there was a strong Hepplewhite and Sheraton revival. As the century ended, it was considered more fashionable to have excellently made reproductions than to live with heavily used originals. Many of these nineteenth century reproductions are passed off today as design period examples.

During the nineteenth century, Great Britain was the leader in the mass marketing of furniture. An expanding population and growing urbanization created a large market. The department store and specialist shop replaced the craftsman's showroom. Buying on credit was introduced and the furniture industry responded by manufacturing large quantities of furniture in a variety of quality grades.

The introduction of vast quantities of mass production furniture and the popularization of styles caused a reaction among English furniture designers. They objected to the excessive naturalism and eclectic historicism. Forward looking designers such as E. W. Godwin, Grimson, Mackintosh, William Morris, John Ruskin, and Voysey laid the foundation and implemented the British Arts and Crafts movement. Arthur Lazenby Liberty's Liberty & Co. help lead the expansion of British taste on the popular level.

English Victorian revivals provided the prototypes from which the American Victorian revivals were copied. Revivals included Greco–Roman, neo–classical; Regency, neo–Gothic, French Empire, Queen Anne, Jacobean, mock Tudor, etc. When Victoria became Empress of India, English furniture featured mother–of–pearl inlays, japanning, and other designs from India and the Orient.

Rather than repeat all those styles and their characteristics, readers are advised to turn back and read the introductions to the Victorian revival pieces in the American Furniture section. The most important thing to remember is that Victoria reigned for such a long period of time that Aesthetic, Art Nouveau, and Arts and Crafts furniture are as much a part of the furniture design legacy of her reign as the Louis XIV and Elizabethan styles that introduced it.

Style Books: Charles Locke Eastlake, *Hints on Household Taste*, London; *Art Furniture Designed by Edward W. Godwin, F.S.A. and Others, with Hints and Suggestions on Domestic Furniture and Decoration by William Watt*, London; Henry Whitaker, *Practical Cabinet–Maker*, 1847.

References: Pauline Agius, *British Furniture, 1880–1915*, Woodbridge, Suffolk, England: Baron Publishing for the Antique Collectors' Club, 1978; Antique Collectors' Club, *Pictorial Directory of British 19th Century Furniture Design*, Woodbridge, Suffolk, England: Baron Publishing for the Antiques Collector's Club, 1977; Elizabeth Aslin, *The Aesthetic Movement, Prelude to Art Nouveau*, New York: Frederick A. Praeger: 1969; Elizabeth Aslin, *E. W. Godwin: Furniture and Interior Decoration*, Long: John

Murray: 1986; Ralph Edwards and L. G. G. Ramsey (editors), *The Early Victorian Period, 1830–1860*, London: The Connoisseur, 1962.

Bird Cage, 19th C, parcel gilt and turned walnut, domed rectangular cage, ring turned columns at corners, suspended within ring turned and molded arched frame surmounted by turned finials, baluster turned standard, shaped molded legs, rubbing to gilt, 25" w, 72" h **1,650**

Bookcase
- 1840, mahogany, projecting molded cornice above inlaid frieze, pair of glazed doors flanked by quarter column stiles, three shelf interior, molded waist above inlaid frieze, pair of paneled cupboard doors with applied molding decoration flanked by quarter column stiles, plinth base, 54" w **3,850**
- 1845, mahogany, projecting molded cornice, pair of two–paned glazed doors, rounded corners on glass panels, molded waist, pair of similarly shaped recessed paneled cupboard doors, flattened bun feet, 75" w **2,000**
- 1850, mahogany, projecting ogee molded cornice above cavetto molded frieze, pair of glazed doors, adjustable shelved interior, scalloped apron, bun feet, 55" w, 87" h **715**
- 1860, mahogany, crenellated cavetto molded cornice, two pairs of Gothic shaped glazed doors and

cupboard doors, two small drawers, long center drawer, 90" w ... **2,000**
- 1860, mahogany, shaped pediment with applied C–scroll molding, projecting molded cornice, pair of arched glazed doors, three shelf interior, molded waist, molded inlaid frieze, pair of arched paneled cupboard doors flanked by half columns surmounted by reeded capitals, molded base, 45½" w, 90" h **2,225**

Breakfront
- 1850, oak, dwarf, molded cornice above frieze with inlaid Greek key design, three line inlaid glazed doors, two interior shelves each section, molded base, 60" w **925**
- Mid 19th C, oak, molded cornice, two pairs of Gothic style glazed doors, shelved interior, molded waist, two pairs of paneled cupboard doors, molded base, 92" w, 93" h **5,100**
- Late 19th C, oak, molded stepped cornice, two pairs of glazed doors, shelved interior, molded waist, two pairs of raised panel cupboard doors, molded base, 88" w **2,175**

Buffet, mahogany, three rectangular tiers with three quarter galleries, acorn finials on ring, block, and baluster turned posts, tapered feet, brass caps and casters, 42" w **600**

Butler's Tray
- 1840, mahogany, rectangular top, hinged D–shaped flaps with cutout handles, X–form base with slender square flaring legs, ring and baluster turned stretchers, 36" h **1,575**

Breakfast Table, carved burl walnut and satinwood inlaid, four column base on downswept legs, $2,420.00. Photograph courtesy of William Doyle Galleries.

1850, mahogany, rectangular top with thumb molded edge and spindled three quarter gallery, ball finials raised on back posts, X–form base with turned reeded tapered legs, sausage turned stretchers, turned tapered feet, 34″ h **450**

Cabinet

Display, mid 19th C, gilt bronze, rectangular, beveled glazed sides surmounted by bow, rectangular plinth with egg and dart edge on paw feet, 22½″ w, 26″ h **1,450**

Folio, 1860, walnut, "J & W Vokins, Makers" label, molded rectangular top, molded paneled ends with handles, glazed front, carved cabriole legs, casters, 33″ h **1,200**

Music, 1870, Gillows, walnut and amboyna, projecting rectangular top with three quarter gallery raised on turned and fluted columns, single paneled door decorated with a porcelain roundel, fluted flattened bun feet, 38″ h **5,000**

Side

1850, mahogany, shaped splashboard with carved center fan and C–scrolled edge, narrow shelf supported by carved half columns centering oval recessed panels, breakfront base, four molded arched recessed paneled cupboard doors separated by half columns with fluted capitals and plinth bases, molded base, 71″ w   **2,125**

1855, walnut and mahogany, inlaid, blocked front, floral inlays, central paneled door with floral spray inlay flanked by two glazed doors, shelved interior, shaped apron, 73″ w **3,000**

1860, walnut, gilt mounts, satinwood inlay, D–shaped top, conforming case with central glazed door flanked by two convex glazed doors, conforming shelf interior, bun feet, 60″ w **1,750**

1890, marquetry, mahogany and satinwood, Sheraton style inlay, rectangular top, two doors with urn in oval inlay surrounded by bowknots and swags, molded base, spade feet, 37½″ w **6,000**

Candlestand

1870, black lacquered and gilt, circular tilt top, painted floral arrangement on keystone, turned shaft, tripod legs, 16″ d, 29″ h **750**

Late 19th C, painted wood, circular tilt top, abalone inlay, gilt highlights, turned standard, circular

base, three upturned feet, 17″ d, 27″ h **250**

Canterbury

1820, music, walnut, rectangular top with three quarter gallery raised on ring turned tapered columns, three section case with pierced ornately scrolled sides, apron drawer, turned tapered feet, casters, 24″ w   **1,500**

1850, rosewood, four dividers with serpentine shaped top edge and ornately scrolled pierced design, rectangular base with apron drawer, bulbous turned tapered legs, casters, 20″ w **1,200**

Chair

Arm, 1850, rosewood, carved, serpentine shaped crest rail, tufted upholstered back, open arms with padded armrests, down curving arm posts, upholstered serpentine shaped seat, carved flowerhead on exposed seat rail, cabriole legs, scroll feet **1,250**

Library, arm, 1850, mahogany, curved crest rail, rolled arms, scrolled arm posts, serpentine shaped seat, cabriole front legs ending in scroll feet, flaring back legs, tufted leather upholstery **6,100**

Set

Set of six, 1850, walnut, oval back, upholstered seat with serpentine shaped front, flaring back legs, cabriole front legs, padded feet, price for set **2,400**

Set of twelve, 1870, dining, side, mahogany, balloon back, upholstered seat, flaring back legs, cabriole front legs, padded feet, price for set **6,200**

Side

1860, papier mâché, gilt decoration, black ground, barley twist support, inlaid mother–of–pearl floral design on oval splat, cane seat, cabriole legs **340**

1865, lacquered, rosette carved crest, open back, upholstered seat, downswept legs **180**

Chaise Lounge, mahogany, scroll end, carved lion's mask on crest rail and front post, fluted bulbous legs, casters, 75″ w **1,200**

Chest of Drawers, late 19th C, pine and inlaid mahogany, arched galleried shelf over five aligned drawers, rectangular top over three aligned drawers, pair of paneled cupboard doors, molded base, 48″ w, 19″ d, 66″ h . .   **800**

Chiffonier, 1840, rosewood, shaped splashboard with narrow shelf supported by turned tapered columns, rectangular top, two short drawers, pair of cupboard doors with arched recessed panels, molded base, 54¾" h **1,350**

Clock, tall case, mid 19th C

Richardson, Kilbirnie, Scotland, mahogany, swan necked hood, spiral twisted columns, line inlaid trunk door, with center oval panel of perching bird, flanked by fluted quarter round stiles, plinth base, eight day time and half hour strike, 14" painted arched dial, subsidiary seconds and date dials, maker's label attached to reverse of dial, seconds hand missing, repairs to hood, 84" h **1,100**

Simpson, Glasgow, Scotland, mahogany, circular hood, square tapering trunk, cushion paneled door, paneled plinth, 13" d signed dial, white enamel chapter ring, Roman numerals, 72" h **1,000**

Commode, bedside, 1850

Mahogany, rectangular marble top, fitted drawer over pair of mock hinged drawers over two drawers, plinth base, 16½" w, 16½" d, 33" h **425**

Walnut, rectangular marble top, single drawer, cupboard door, 16¾" w, 12¾" d, 31½" h **300**

Credenza

1850, walnut, gilt metal mounted decoration, scalloped top, central foliage marquetry paneled cupboard door, flanked by glazed doors, plinth base, restoration, 74" l, 44" h **1,875**

1860, walnut, gilt metal mounted decorations, D–form top, conforming case, inlaid frieze, central paneled door with marquetry flowers in oval panel, flanked by two convex glazed doors, shaped apron, 70" w **5,225**

Crib, late 19th C, tubular brass, rectangular form, projecting canopy, casters, pink satin bedding, 49" l, 65" h **850**

Cupboard, straight front, 1860, incised and ebonized rosewood marquetry, gilt bronze mounts, column front, concave sides, 59" w, 41" h **2,250**

Desk

Cylinder, mahogany, rectangular projecting top with gallery, cylinder roll, fitted interior, reeded stiles, two pedestals with three graduated drawers, molded base, 46½" w .. **1,250**

Davenport

1850, burl walnut, slant front, fitted

interior, bank of four drawers, scroll carved supports, restoration, losses to gallery, 24" w, 36" h **1,650**

1850, walnut, slant front, rectangular top with three quarter gallery, slanted writing surface raised on ring turned columns, bank of four graduated drawers, real and faux drawers, conforming base, 22" w **925**

1860, rosewood, slant front, pierced scrolled three quarter gallery with corner finials on plinths, slanted writing surface with serpentine shaped front and conforming single drawer frieze raised on serpentine shaped columns with scroll feet, bank of four drawers, conforming base, flattened bun feet, 36" h **1,050**

1860, walnut and amboyna banded, slant front, brass galleried stationery compartment, slanted writing surface with fitted interior raised on scrolled half columns, recessed paneled ends, molded base, casters, 21½" w . **3,000**

Kneehole, satinwood and kingwood banded, rectangular top, three drawer frieze, kneehole flanked by banks of three cockbeaded drawers, bail handle pulls, square tapered legs, casters, 48" w **1,750**

Partner's

1850, mahogany, gold tooled orange leather inset top, three frieze drawers, three graduated drawers on each side, reverse with eight short drawers arranged in two tiers, plinth base, replaced handles, 60½" w, 32" h **6,050**

1865, mahogany, gold tooled green leather writing surface, ovolo molded edge and writing slides, paneled frieze drawer, two banks of four paneled drawers with similar opposing arrangement flanked by fluted angles, plinth base, 51½" w, 30½" h **1,950**

1880, mahogany, rectangular top with rounded corners and molded edge, single drawer over kneehole flanked by two pedestals with four cockbeaded graduated drawers, molded base, 65" h **4,500**

Pedestal

1880, oak, molded rectangular top, three recessed paneled doors separated by turned half columns, center door with raised quatrefoil design, molded edge on rectangular projecting writing surface, center drawer with pierced brackets over kneehole, two pedestals with recessed paneled doors with raised quatrefoil design, molded base, 49" h   **1,000**

1887, walnut, rectangular top, one long drawer flanked by two short drawers, two banks of drawers, plinth base, 70½" w, 31" h **2,200**

Etagere, 1845, rosewood, three rectangular tiers, top tier with pierced scroll cut gallery, single drawer below base tier, pierced scroll cut end splats flanked by tapered ring turned posts, turned tapered feet, casters **1,500**

Hall Tree, late 19th C, mahogany, shaped mirror surrounded by pierced back and pegs, lower shelf and drawer flanked by stick wells, shaped base, 48" w, 12" d, 92" h **600**

Meridiennes (fainting couch), 1870, carved oak, upholstered in brown wool fabric by Knoll, 75" l **600**

Mirror
1850

Dressing, walnut, arched rectangular swing mirror flanked by barley twist supports, serpentine base, bun feet, 21" w, 9" d, 23" h **110**

Wall, beech, simulated bamboo decoration, 18½" w, 29½" h ...   **225**

1865, giltwood, foliate and lyre crest, arched rectangular mirror surrounded by fern border, 47" w, 86" h **1,000**

1875, dressing, mahogany, arched rectangular mirror flanked by turned columns with ball turned finials, rectangular base with center drawer, 22" w, 13" d, 30" h **150**

1900, composition, gilt, oval plate, cushion molded foliate and ribbon carved border, subsidiary border, foliate, pierced, and carved decoration, loss and restoration, 31" w, 68" h **1,100**

Screen
Floor

Mid 19th C, three panels, walnut and polychrome decoupage, rectangular panels with scene of human figures at various stages of age and history, molded frame, two white porcelain handles, restorations, each panel 22½" w, 62" h **950**

Late 19th C, four panels, paint decorated leather, street scenes, each panel 21" w, 72¼" h **1,540**

Pole, pair, rosewood, urn shaped finial on tapered pole with ring turned bulbous base, adjustable height circular needlepoint panel with horse and rider design, circular base, scroll feet, 60" h, price for pair **500**

Secretary

1880, secretaire, walnut, projecting molded cornice, pair of molded glazed doors, three shelf interior, molded waist, single cockbeaded long drawer, pair of molded paneled cupboard doors with central carved floral decoration, molded base, 50" w, 89½" h **1,500**

Late 19th C, mahogany, demilune pediment, mullion glazed doors, slant front, fitted interior with writing surface and pigeon holes, three drawers, bracket feet, 36" w, 21" d, 81" h **900**

Server

1860, mahogany, three rectangular thumb molded tiers, trestle type construction, flat rectangular graduated ends, ring turned stretcher, scroll feet, casters, 51" w **4,200**

19th C, mahogany, rectangular top, three quarter gallery on medial shelf with baluster turned and block supports, two paneled cupboard doors below, turned feet and casters, 30" w, 48" h **1,650**

Sideboard

Mahogany, shaped splashboard with ornate scroll carving, rectangular projecting top, molded frieze, double pedestal base with two cupboard doors flanked by turned half columns, plinth base, 82" w **1,000**

Oak, castellated Gothic arched panel, back with plumed finials flanking central shield surmounted by coronet, two aligned drawers, stamped: A. J. Owen & Co. New Bond Street **900**

Satinwood and Mahogany, 1870, inlaid, Wright and Mansfield, two sections: upper section: convex cupboard doors, painted neoclassical panels, distressed flanking shelves; lower section: three frieze drawers above single long drawer, arched recess flanked by cupboards and shelves, leaf carved toupic feet, 95" w, 65" h **5,000**

Walnut and Rosewood, serpentine top, four drawers, pair of cupboard doors, bun feet, 55" w, 22" d, 35" h **650**

Sofa

1850, carved rosewood, exposed serpentine shaped crest rail continues to shaped arms with padded armrests, knuckle handholds, tufted upholstered back and sides, carved down curving arm posts, slightly concave seat rail with center carved floral decoration, conforming upholstered seat, cabriole legs, scroll feet, casters, 63" w **3,750**

1860, walnut, ornately carved and scrolled crest rail, high center back with curving wrap around arms, tufted upholstered back, slightly bowed upholstered seat, exposed carved arm posts, cabriole front legs ending in scroll feet, flaring back legs **850**

Stand

Dinner Wagon, mahogany, three tiers, center rectangular shelf, adjustable upper and lower shelves, arched bracket feet, 45" w, 22" d, 41" h **750**

Folio, 1845, rosewood, trestle base with turned stretcher, carved cabriole legs, scroll feet, casters **3,750**

Shaving, c1855, papier mâché, gilt decoration, mother–of–pearl inlay, black ground, ornate frame, S–scroll supports tilting mirror, scalloped base, losses to inlay **240**

Side, carved walnut, circular top, carved tree form standard, two putti, circular plinth, paw feet, 18" d, 43" h **990**

Stool

Foot

1840, walnut, rectangular needlework and beadwork upholstered top, scrolled supports, 45½" l, 7" h **550**

1850, rosewood curule, rectangular, needlepoint upholstered seat, lotus petal carved frame, X–form legs joined by ring turned stretcher, inward scrolling feet, minor repairs, upholstery distressed **1,650**

1850, walnut, carved, rectangular upholstered needlepoint top, ornately scrolled X–form trestle base with two ring turned stretchers, scroll feet, 28" w **850**

1860, rosewood, carved, upholstered rectangular top, carved cabriole legs, padded feet **500**

1865, carved mahogany, circular green figured satin cushion, molded surround, shallow scrolled feet, 15" d, price for pair   **450**

Gout, 1850, mahogany, adjustable, stamped Holland & Sons, London, 16" w, 28" d, 16" h **850**

Piano, carved mahogany, circular upholstered seat, acanthus carved baluster form standard, trifid plinth, bun feet, 18" d, 17½" h **600**

Suite

1860, drawing room suite, one armchair, five side chairs, walnut, upholstered oval back, scrolled hip brackets, upholstered seat with exposed serpentine seat rail, flaring back legs, carved inverted cup front leg ending in scroll feet, price for six piece suite **2,500**

Late 19th C, sofa, two arm chairs, and four side chairs, mahogany, foliate and C–scroll carved crest rail continuing to form out scrolling upholstered armrests, downswept supports centering upholstered back and seat, foliate carved apron, short cabriole legs, foliate velvet upholstery, restorations, 105" l sofa, price for seven piece suite **4,950**

Table

Breakfast, 1875, carved walnut, oval tilt top, turned center pedestal, four carved scrolled legs, 51½" w, 38" d, 29" h **400**

Card

1850

Mahogany, hinged rectangular top with rounded corners, shaped apron with ornate C– and S–scrolls, fluted bulbous vasiform standard, four carved cabriole legs, scroll feet, casters, 36½" w **1,100**

Rosewood, hinged rectangular top with rounded corners, shaped apron, bulbous turned standard, four carved cabriole legs, scroll feet, casters, 36" w   **1,750**

1860, walnut, hinged serpentine shaped top, conforming apron, bulbous ring turned standard, four cabriole legs with scrolled knees and feet, casters, 36" w ..   **1,275**

Center

1845, marquetry and mahogany, six sided top veneered with concentric panels of different woods, waisted elongated turned tapering pedestal standard, tripod base, 17" d, 27½" h **725**

1860, burr walnut, oval top, straight apron, four turned down curving legs joined to center at spire turned finial and pendant drop, scroll feet, casters, 51" w ... **1,300**

Dining

1840, mahogany, rectangular top with rounded corners, straight apron, ring turned tapered legs, turned tapered feet, casters, two leaves, 95" l extended **1,925**

1860, mahogany, double thumb molded edge on rectangular top with rounded corners, straight apron, six fluted bulbous turned legs, ring turned tapered feet, casters, three leaves, 180" l extended **5,500**

1890, burr oak, oval top with thumb molded edge, conforming apron, carved reeded bulbous turned tapered legs, turned tapered feet, casters, one leaf, 85" l extended **2,500**

Dressing, 19th c, mahogany, hinged rectangular top opening to dressing mirror and marble top over four drawers, molded base, casters, 31" w, 19" d, 38" h **500**

Game, 1840, inlaid rosewood, rectangular top, rounded corners, center sliding panel inlaid on one side with checkerboard, slides to reveal backgammon playing surface, trestle supports joined by stretchers, spade feet, 42" w, 28¾" h **1,750**

Game and Work Combination, rosewood, serpentine shaped chessboard inlaid top, single drawer frieze with ring turned pendant drops at corners, fabric well, ring turned vasiform standard, circular fluted base, scroll feet, casters, 22½" w **900**

Library, 1840, satinwood, stamped "Gillows," rectangular top with fluted thumb molded edge, straight apron, trestle base with two ring turned and carved vasiform standards on arched legs, scroll feet, 48" w **4,500**

Occasional

1850, walnut marquetry and mahogany, octagonal top, center sunburst with radiating panels, multiple banded borders over scalloped apron, slender baluster and ring turned shaft, scroll tripod supports, stamped: G. Larrett, 16¼" w, 29¾" h **800**

1870, eight sided top with cavetto molded edge, inlaid colored seagliola, marbles, and hardstone forming wreath of roses, fuchsia, forget–me–nots, convol-

vulous, lily of the valley, and other English flower sprays, gilt copper clad Rococo style base formed as three kneeling putti, faux verde antico marble triform shaped base, 27¼" w, 18" h ... **4,500**

1900, rosewood and satinwood, molded edge on square top, ring and block turned legs, square medial shelf with spindled gallery and arched brackets, turned tapered feet, casters, 29½" sq .. **625**

Sutherland

1850, satinwood, thumb molded rectangular top, pair of long D–shaped drop leaves with banded border, turned standard with flattened ball pendant, four cabriole legs, scroll feet, casters, 47" w . **1,500**

1860, walnut, thumb molded rectangular top, pair of D-shaped drop leaves with thumb molded edges, trestle base with baluster turned standards and ring and baluster turned stretcher, arched legs, scroll feet, casters, 28½" h **1,250**

Tea, tilt top

1845, japanned, dished oval top, scalloped edge, figural gilt decorated landscape scene, foliate gilt decorated ring turned and knopped standard, three down scrolling supports, losses and wear, 52" w, 29½" h **11,000**

1850, papier mâché, mother–of–pearl inlay, central medallion with floral decoration, black ground, scalloped edge, baluster standard, circular scalloped base with gilt decoration **550**

1865, papier mâché, mother–of–pearl inlay, oval top, minor damage at edges, 20" w, 27½" h ... **715**

Tripod, G. Barrett, mid 19th C, mahogany and walnut marquetry, octagonal, center sunburst within radiating panels, multiple banded borders, scalloped apron, slender baluster and ring turned shaft, scrolled tripod supports, maker's name stamped on top, 16¼" w, 29¾" h **550**

Work

1850, walnut, octagonal floral marquetry lift top, central bird marquetry medallion, molded edge, light blue silk interior, cushion molded crossbanded frieze, quatrefoil and marquetry panels, foliate and scroll carved base with casters, 19½" d, 32" h **990**

1860, walnut, oval lift top, molded

edge, fabric well, trestle base with ring and baluster turned standards ending in ball turned pendants, ring turned stretcher, cabriole legs, scroll feet, casters, 28½" h **975**

Writing

1840, rosewood, rectangular top, ogee molded frieze, open ends with pairs of columns with carved capitals and scrolled feet mounted on plinth bases raised on carved animal paw feet, rectangular base shelf, 48½" w ... **5,750**

1850, mahogany, rectangular top, gold tooled faded brown leather writing surface, three frieze drawers on both sides, ring turned tapering supports, 60" w, 32" h **2,850**

1875, rectangular top, red leather inset writing surface, egg and dart carved border, profiled end standards, leaf carved scroll feet, gilt chinoiseries decoration on black japanned ground, 50" w, 28¼" h **1,650**

Whatnot

1840

Mahogany, arched crest with C– and S–scroll molding, ring and block turned posts surmounted by acorn finials, four rectangular tiers with three quarter galleries, turned tapered feet, casters, 49½" h **2,500**

Walnut, pierced carved gallery, ring and baluster turned posts surmounted by urn finials, three tiers with serpentine shaped front edges, turned tapered feet, casters, 40" h **650**

1870, oak and fruitwood, rectangular thumb molded top tier raised on ring and block turned posts, medial and base tiers with three quarter galleries, single drawer below base tier, bulbous turned feet, brass casters, 40" h **1,775**

EDWARDIAN (1901–1910)

History: The Edwardian period is marked by extreme contrasts in the quality of furniture produced during this time. Large amounts of furniture featuring inferior carcass wood, thin veneer, machine–cut inlay, and painted decoration were produced. In contrast, the very best pieces of Edwardian era furniture exceed those of the Victorian period in quality of manufacture and design.

It was during this period that the Hepplewhite and Sheraton revivals enjoyed their greatest popularity. F. Litchfield's *How to Collect Old Furniture*, one of the first books devoted to furnishing one's home in antiques, was published in 1906. Much of the reproduction and drawing room furniture was designed more to be admired and only occasionally used.

While much of the Edwardian population was enamored by a traditional, conservative attitude toward furniture design, the Modernistic movement was taking root in England. The leading influence was Modernistic architecture. Furniture design largely responded to architectural advances. Emphasis was placed on rectilinear rather than curvilinear design elements.

English furniture designers had difficulty breaking away from the dominance of Arts and Crafts ideas. Charles Rennie Mackintosh of Glasgow was an important exception. His clients were limited due in part to his radical designs. He utilized the space around pieces and light passing through design elements as part of the overall expression of a piece's integrity. Other British designers who followed Mackintosh's lead were G. M. Ellwood and Charles Annesley Voysey.

Reference: Philippe Garner, *Twentieth–Century Furniture*, Van Nostrand Reinhold Company, 1980.

Bench, 1910, lacquered wood, double chair back, scroll crest, vasiform splat, chinoiserie decoration, silk upholstered slip seat, cabriole legs, pad feet, 44" l **550**

Bookcase, 1910, mahogany, ogee cornice top, inlaid frieze, two lattice glazed cabinet doors, square tapered legs, 66" h **1,020**

Breakfront, 1900, mahogany, molded cornice inlaid with leafage and flowers, shelved interior, seven cupboard doors with oval inset panels, 163" w, 91" h **4,750**

Cabinet

Corner, mahogany, serpentine front, inlaid detail cornice, glazed doors, shelved interior, pair of satinwood banded cupboard doors, out scrolled feet, 32" w **1,500**

Display, Sheraton influence, satinwood, bow front, rosewood crossbands, painted panels of cherubs, glazed door and shaped sides, 42" w **1,850**

Hanging, 1900, pair, satinwood, bone and ebony inlaid arched crest, single door, arched apron, 32" h, price for pair **1,870**

Music, mahogany, six drawers, squatty cabriole legs, 21" w **225**

Side, Sheraton influence, satinwood, tambour center flanked by pair of cupboard doors with architectural style cornice and urn finials, shaped rectangular top, single frieze drawer, tapering fluted legs, later caster feet, 36" w **4,250**

Vitrine, hexagonal glass inset top, square tapered legs, X–form stretcher, 27" w, 16½" d, 30" h .. **1,100**

Chair, side, ladderback, shaped upholstered seat, turned legs **75**

Chest of Drawers, walnut, scalloped backsplash, rectangular top mounted with two glove drawers, four graduated drawers, bracket feet, 38" w, 18" d, 45" h **150**

Cupboard, oak, wreath carved crest, two glazed doors above shaped marble top, three drawers and three cupboard doors, 51" w, 22" d, 29" h ... **550**

Desk
1900
Mahogany, tambour cylinder front, inlaid with satinwood and other woods, fitted interior, writing slide, 36½" w **2,000**

Mahogany and marquetry, kneehole, rectangular crossbanded top, central oval medallion and canted front corners, long frieze drawer, two banks of three drawers centering cupboard door, foliate marquetry decoration, 37½" w, 31" h **750**

1905, oak, rectangular top, two long and two small drawers, scrolled legs joined by shaped stretcher on casters, 60" w, 36" d, 31" h **1,100**

Magazine Rack, carved walnut, three slots separated by carved and pierced dividers, frieze drawer, turned legs, 14" w, 20" d, 19" h **375**

Screen, 1900, two panels, carved mahogany and painted paper, each leaf painted with sailing ships, putti on shells and seaweed, coral ground, scroll bead carved cresting, 44¾" w, 55" h **600**

Sideboard
Burl Walnut, rectangular backsplash and top, three aligned drawers, three cupboard doors, scroll feet, 65" w, 24" d, 49" h **400**

Mahogany, satinwood crossbanding and stringing, scrolled crested paneled backsplash, rectangular molded top, two small drawers, long center drawer, two cupboard doors, molded plinth base, 76" l . **1,200**

Stand, plant, marquetry, octagonal galleried top, central shell inlay, square tapering angled supports, 11" d, 26" h **900**

Table
Center, 1900, satinwood, circular inlaid top, square tapered legs, spade feet, 34" d, 35" h **1,650**

Nesting, 1900, set, inlaid mahogany, rectangular foliate marquetry top, crossbanded edge, three crossbanded tables, smallest with frieze drawer, square tapering supports, spade feet, 28" w, 28½" h, price for set of four **725**

Side, inlaid mahogany, circular, narrow banded border, square tapering supports, 36" d, 28" h **350**

Smoker's, stained beech, shield shaped top supporting five graduated urns, cigar cutter, ringed standard raised on three scrolled supports, 33" h **625**

POST WORLD WAR I

History: The Art Deco style, with its static forms, highly colorful appearance, innovative use of new materials, and introduction of a number of new furniture forms, enjoyed a modest following in England. The principal influence was French; in fact, the importation of French pieces is responsible for much of the Art Deco furniture found in England. Eileen Gray, who studied at London's Slade School, is the leading Art Deco designer of English origin, albeit she did all her work in Paris.

The British also resisted the trends to Modernism until the beginnings of the 1930s. Designers such as Gordon Russell and Ambrose Heal were the principal furniture designers of the 1920s. The situation changed with the arrival of Serge Chermayeff, who married into the conservative furniture firm of Waring and Gillow. Marcel Breuer carried the Modernism message to England, working there from 1935 to 1937. Walter Gropius also lived briefly in England from 1934 to 1937. In 1937, Breuer and Gropius both left for teaching positions in America. Isokon, a leading design firm, was founded in 1931 by Jack and Molly Pritchard, Graham Maw, Robert Spicer, and Wells Coates.

British designers continued to innovate during the 1930s. Oliver Hill introduced the use of glass. Denham Maclaren incorporated glass, marble, and tubular metal in some of his pieces. Gerald Summers created a number of innovative designs utilizing plywood.

Despite these trends, Philippe Garner notes: "The most lasting image of British furniture in the thirties, however, is surely the image of large–scaled dining and bedroom suites veneered in high polished figured woods. Vast dining tables

with sets of tub–backed chairs, heavy sideboards, and, of course, the ubiquitous cocktail
cabinet epitomize the era. Indeed, the cocktail
cabinets, lined in mirror–glass or sycamore, cap-
ture the flavour of the thirties more than any other
item of furniture." The influence behind most of
this furniture is French, a country's influence
from which England seemed never to escape.

In the 1940s and 1950s, British furniture design stressed utility, due in part to restrictions of
wood use during World War II. The Utility Furniture Program of the government ended in 1952.
As in America, popular taste stressed a return to
the traditional styles of the eighteenth and early
nineteenth centuries. Designers such as Howard
Keith and Ernest Race incorporated these concerns in their contemporary designs. Designer
Robin Day led the movement to functional pieces
based upon current technological advances in
the furniture manufacturing industry.

1950s contemporary furniture was influenced
by American and Scandinavian designs. In 1956
the Design Center in London's Haymarket was
opened to showcase British goods. Furniture designed by Robin Day, R. Y. Gooden, Brian
O'Roke, and R. D. Russell was featured. British
furniture from the 1950s featured long, low,
straight lines softened at the corners by rounding.
Wood enjoyed a revival, only to be replaced by
metal as the decade ended.

British designers did take part in Neo–Moder-
ism, Pop, and other contemporary furniture design advances of the post–1960 period. In the
1970s a craft revival occurred, led by individuals
such as John Makepeace and Rupert Williamson.
The 1980s is marked by the growth of what is
currently termed the Industrial style. Innovative
work is being done by O.M.K., organized by a
team of designers in 1966.

Reference: Philippe Garner, *Twentieth–Century
Furniture*, Van Nostrand Reinhold Company,
1980.

Bed, 1930–40, Practical Equipment Ltd
  B3, chromed tubular steel, double
  peak head and footboards, single
  bed size, 36¼" w **875**
  B4, chromed tubular steel, double
  hoop headboard, single bed size,
  35½" w **525**
Bookcase, 1913, Sidney Barnsley, re-
  volving, square top, long shelves on
  two opposite sides, short shelves
  other two sides, square base with pro-
  truding shoe feet **450**
Book Cupboard, 1905, Mackay Hugh
  Baillie Scott, inlaid oak, rectangular
  top, long shelf over a short shelf flanking a cupboard door with pewter and
  colored wood inlaid stylized flowerhead decoration, checkered banding   **450**

Sideboard, 1910, oak, two sections. Upper section: Mirror flanked by two carved
wood panels depicting flowers; lower
section: Two drawers above two cupboard doors with copper and brass pulls
and escutcheons, 60″ w, 23″ d, 80″ h,
$550.00. Photograph courtesy of William
Doyle Galleries.

Book Stand, 1930–40, Isokon, white
  painted natural wood, sloping book
  compartments both sides, 15¾" h . .   **400**
Cabinet
  Display
    1905–10, mahogany, stepped corn-
    ice, pair of glazed doors with
    geometric and heart shaped
    muntins, pair of recessed
    paneled cupboard doors with in-
    laid floral design with mother–
    of–pearl details, open base shelf
    with decorative columns, shaped
    apron, square feet, 72" h **1,500**
    1930–40, Ambrose Heal, London,
    limed oak, circular display area
    with glass doors over two cup-
    board doors, block feet **500**
  Side, pair, 1931, Betty Joel, stepped
    stacked cube design, six cubicles,
    square feet, 31½" w, 29½" h, price
    for pair **575**
Chair
  Arm
    1905–10, Charles Annesley Voy-
    sey, oak, slightly arched crest

rail, splayed square stiles, branded monogram on leather upholstered rectangular splat, shaped armrests, square arm posts, leather upholstered seat, shaped apron, square legs joined by box stretchers   450

1925, pair, Art Deco, tub chair, upholstered, reeded bulbous feet, 29" h, price for pair   875

1934, Gerald Summers, Simple Furniture Ltd, London, bent plywood, rolled crest rail, curved rectangular splat, S–form arms continue to legs, open sides, rolled seat rail   300

1935, Ernest Gimson, pair, ash, ladderback, five arched slats, shaped arms, rush seat, turned tapered legs and stretchers, 45" h, price for pair   550

Side, pair, 1905, Glasgow School, stained beechwood, high back, arched crest rail with central gesso roundel, shaped splat, square upholstered slip seat, green velvet upholstery with formalized floral design, square legs with box stretchers at floor form cubic base, 53½" h, price for pair   1,000

Chaise Lounge
1930–40, Ambrose Heal, London, laminated wood and plywood, upholstered, bentwood arms, 55⅛" h   1,850

1936, Marcel Breuer, Isokon, laminated wood and plywood, open arms   1,200

Cocktail Bar Trolley, Art Deco, double cylinder shape, bar handle flanked by two inset clear and satin glass panels by Lalique, 34¾" w   10,000

Desk
1925, Ambrose Heal, London
Kneehole, sycamore, rectangular top with semi–circular end, door in semi–circular end of kneehole, five graduated drawer pedestal, 52½" w   750

Writing, oak, three stepped recessed small drawers on rectangular writing surface with single long drawer, flanked by pair of square file drawers raised on trestle type base, 60" w   4,000

1930, Gerald Summers, white painted plywood, kneehole, rectangular top, left hand pedestal with four small drawers, 46¼" w, 28¾" h   500

1930–40, Practical Equipment Ltd, kneehole, rectangular wood top, tubular steel frame, three drawer

pedestal with wood drawers, 44¾" w   475

Dressing Chest, pair, 1930, Betty Joel, oak, hinged rectangular top with faux drawer front, rectangular mirror plate on top underside, six drawers, price for pair   3,200

Fire Screen, 1900–10, embroidered panel decorated with roses and wild flowers set in arched frame, square tapered posts, flaring pyramid shaped feet, 33¾" h   425

Linen Chest, 1920–30, paneled lid with strap hinges, paneled front and ends with crenellated friezes, square legs, 23½" h   950

Mirror, cheval, 1930–40, Practical Equipment Ltd, rectangular mirror plate, electroplated tubular steel frame with arched legs, casters, 63½" h   325

Secretaire, 1930, Heal & Son Ltd, oak, pair of glazed doors on bookcase top, slant front writing surface, fitted interior, pullout slides, four graduated long drawers, square legs, original label, 68½" h   750

Sideboard, 1900–10, Charles Annesley Voysey, oak, slightly arched crest rail, vertical board back, square stiles surmounted by stepped capitals, open ends, three open set back shelves, rectangular waist shelf, two drawers over four recessed panel cupboard doors, quarter sawn oak drawer and door fronts, paneled ends, fretted brass strap hinges, brass heart shaped escutcheons, shaped apron, square feet   4,500

Stool, bathroom, 1930–40, Practical Equipment Ltd, square cork top, tubular steel base, 17½" sq   175

Suite
Bedroom, 1935, Betty Joel, chest of drawers and two night stands, rectangular, chest of drawers with three short over three graduated long drawers, night stands with three graduated drawers, price for three piece suite   350

Dining Room
1930–40, Ray Hille, burr sycamore, dining table, eight chairs, small and large sideboards, table with oblong top with rounded corners and double rectangular pedestal base; chairs with curved backs, upholstered seats, and square tapered legs; matching sideboards, 102½" l table, price for eleven piece suite   3,750

1935, Art Deco, dining table and

ten chairs, burl walnut, twelve sided oblong table top with banded edge, eight sided oblong molded pedestal base, 91" l table, price for eleven piece suite ... **4,500**

1945, Gordon Russell, dining table and six armchairs, table with circular top and slender D–form legs; armchairs with curved square backs, caned back and seat, shaped arms, and square legs, metal labels with facsimile signature, 36⅝" h chair, price for seven piece suite **750**

Living Room, 1930–40, Art Deco, sofa, two armchairs, and kidney shaped pouffe, tanned leather upholstery, sofa with triple chair back with raised center panel, rounded stepped sides, block feet, 33¾" h, price for four piece suite **2,000**

Table

Dressing

1900–10, Liberty & Co, oak, inlaid pewter designs on mirror support crest rail, adjustable rectangular swing mirror, rectangular top flanked by drop leaves, two drawers with peg handles, splayed legs, 52¼" w extended **800**

1910–20, Peter van der Waals, walnut, rectangular cheval mirror, double pedestals with three graduated drawers each pedestal, 45¾" w **950**

1930, burl walnut, large circular mirror rests on U–shaped stand with small shelves at upper ends, two center small drawers, inverted U–shaped base, 58" h .. **3,500**

Side

1930–40, Practical Equipment Ltd, rectangular laminated dark wood top, four double tubular steel legs **275**

1934, Gerald Summers, The Makers of Simple Furniture, London, laminated beechwood, circular, two tiers supported by three flat rectangular legs, 28¾" d **2,750**

Wardrobe, 1930–40, Gordon Russell, oak, paneled door and ends, octagonal uprights, straight apron, octagonal legs, 75⅝" h **650**

FRENCH

History: It was the French, not the English, who provided stylistic leadership in the area of furniture design throughout the eighteenth, nineteenth, and early twentieth centuries. Just as Americans have always looked with envy toward their British counterparts in respect to quality of taste and manufacturer, so did the English look to the French.

The reasons American collectors have a minimum understanding of French furniture design styles is several fold. First, high style French furniture was highly urban in nature; it never worked its way into the countryside. As a result of the Country craze, Americans are more familiar with French provincial furniture than with the formal pieces. Second, French furniture carries the stigma of aristocracy. In America it was a style enjoyed by the select urban and pretentious rural rich. Third, French furniture is not particularly comfortable; its design, as interpreted by American manufacturers, is stiff and formal. Simply put, it is not inviting. Finally, high–quality French period design pieces are rare in the American antiques market. The leading New York and regional auction houses do offer pieces for sale several times a year; bidding is brisk for the premier examples. Most of the bidders are urban based. Little notice of the sales appear in the trade literature.

Americans tend to simplify French design styles and lump them together. There are major differences between Restauration, Louis Philippe, and Second Empire pieces. Americans also are much more familiar with the French design style revivals of the middle– to late–nineteenth century and tend to accept these forms as exact copies of period pieces, which they are not.

As with British furniture, French furniture periods are defined by monarchs and empires. This is a dangerous approach since styles could and did change significantly during several of the periods, e.g., Louis XV and the Second Empire. Likewise this approach tends to suggest a single, unified style for each period when, in fact, a multiplicity of styles often occurred simultaneously.

Actually, to suggest that most eighteenth and nineteenth century design styles originated in France is false. In many instances France looked to Italy, Greece, and other parts of the Mediterranean for inspiration. Occasionally Germanic influences were felt.

France's leadership in furniture design changed significantly at the end of the nineteenth century. French designers concentrated on the development of Art Nouveau and Art Deco, two movements which had minimum impact in the furniture area. True, both movements enjoyed major success in the area of decorative accessories, a fact well known, documented, and appreciated by collectors. However, many individuals have assumed that success in the decorative accessory area carried over to furniture. This is not the case.

While France was concentrating on Art Nouveau and Art Deco design styles, England, Germany, and the United States were involved in the Aesthetic, Arts and Crafts, and Modernism movements. These major furniture movements led to contemporary design. Immediately following World War I, Germany and Austria took over furniture design leadership on the Continent. This is not to say that France was totally isolated. A number of French designers made the transition from Art Deco to Modernism and International Modernism.

One final point worth making: France in the eighteenth and nineteenth centuries was a very different country than France in 1993. Geographic boundaries were different; spheres of influence in the Netherlands, Germany, and along the Mediterranean coupled with marriages among royal families gave French influence a dominance over a much broader area than France itself. Remember, the principal language of foreign diplomacy through World War II was French.

French influence was never dominant in America in the eighteenth, nineteenth, and early twentieth centuries. Americans never forgot their English roots; however, it is a major mistake to assume that what is true in America is true worldwide. Throughout the rest of the civilized world, including England, French taste and styles were dominant. It is time that American collectors and dealers learned more about them.

LOUIS XV (1723–1774)

History: Louis XV, Louis Quinze, reigned as King of France from 1715 to 1774. The Rococo–influenced furniture designs produced during this period are considered by many to be the ultimate in French decorative furniture. Actually, Rococo designs gained favor as early as the first decade of the eighteenth century and remained dominant until the early 1760s when neo–classical styles challenged their influence.

The Baroque styles, influenced by Italian Jesuit architecture, dominated during much of the reign of Louis XIV (1643–1715). Furniture was massive, lavish in detail, and symmetrical. The straight line predominated. When used, curves were restrained. Carving was rich and varied, ranging from satyrs to musical instruments. The use of marquetry was highly developed. Gilding was used extensively. As the seventeenth century drew to a close, a fascination with Chinese motifs occurred.

Louis XIV died in 1715. From 1715 to 1723, France was governed by the regency of Philippe d'Orleans. During the regency period the harsh styles of Louis XIV softened. Furniture design began to flow. The cabriole leg assumed its present day shape. Carvings often featured birds, flowers, rocks, or shells. A strong sense of symmetry was maintained.

The French Rococo design style's flowing lines replaced the straight line, doing everything possible to avoid a rectangular appearance. Asymmetrical decorations appeared. Flowers, musical instruments, pastoral objects, and shells were among the favorite motifs for carving. Marquetry and inlay achieved even greater importance than in the furniture of Louis XIV.

Mahogany was used extensively, albeit cherry and plum, both native fruitwoods, also were popular. Large pieces of amaranth, rosewood, satinwood, and tulipwood served as veneers. Painted furniture, often in contrasting colors, e.g., gold on black, came in vogue. The Brothers Martin developed a varnish that closely imitated Oriental lacquer.

The use of metal appliqués was universal. Marble in a variety of colors was used for commode tops. Small pieces can be found with alabaster or onyx tops. Occasionally small ceramic plaques were inlaid in pieces of furniture.

Major Craftsmen—Regency: Berain, Boulle, Robert De Cotte, Charles Cressent, Mansart, and Jean and Daniel Marot.

Major Craftsmen—Rococo: Philippe Caffieri, Meissonier, Jean Francois Oeben, Oppenord, and Oudry.

Cabinet, provincial Louis XV, fruitwood, inlaid, wire door, 55" w, 18" d, 73" h, $1,450.00. Photograph courtesy of William Doyle Galleries.

PERIOD

Armoire, mid 18th C, oak, molded cornice top, foliate vine carved frieze, two grilled doors with center reserve carved with scrolling tendrils issuing foliage and flowerheads, shelf interior, scroll carved apron, scrolled feet, cornice losses, later feet, 57½" w, 96" h   3,025

Cabinet, bedside, mid 18th C, kingwood parquetry, oblong galleried top, dressing slide, cupboard, bombe case, slender cabriole legs, 17½" w, 11½" d, 32" h   2,100

Chair
  Arm, walnut
    1775, pair, carved, molded crest rail with center carved floral sprig, padded back and armrests, volute supports, padded seat with serpentine front, cabriole legs, price for pair   2,750
    Third quarter 18th C, molded and

arched shell carved crest rail, molded stiles, upholstered back, scrolled padded arms, upholstered sides, shaped seat rail with loose upholstered cushion, scroll carved cabriole legs   1,650
Set of Four
  Arm, fruitwood, pastel flame stitch upholstery, price for set   1,250
  Side, mid 18th C, walnut, crest rail with carved flowers, arched cartouche form back, serpentine seat, reupholstered with orange roller embossed mohair velvet, cabriole legs, price for set   4,500

Chest of Drawers
  Fruitwood, third quarter 18th C, shaped rectangular top, serpentine front with three drawers, rounded stiles, scrolled feet, restorations, 52" w, 35½" h   3,300
  Walnut, rectangular molded top, conforming case, three short drawers, two long drawers, fluted sides, cabriole legs, restored, 44" w, 20¼" d, 33" h   1,650

Tall Case Clock, Louis XV style, late 19th C, dial surrounded by cavorting cupids, tapering rectangular pedestal with elaborate gilt bronze mounts and lion's paw feet, shaped rectangular base with toupie feet, 97" h, $7,750.00. Photograph courtesy of William Doyle Galleries.

Clock, tall case, Benois Girand, Paris, kingwood, hood mounted with gilt bronze figural Father Time, glazed cartouche with figural sunburst pendulum, signed white enamel face with Roman numerals, marquetry inlaid body with gilt bronze musical instruments, foliage scrolls, plinth base, 28" w, 15" d, 106" h **8,000**

Commode

Kingwood and Tulipwood, c1780, variegated shaped marble top with step molded edge, bombe shape case, two drawers with *sans traverse* inlay, diapered basket with scrolling foliage and flowerhead stems within irregular outline reserve, similar inlay sides centering foliate and scroll cast cartouche, shaped apron with cast mount, cabriole legs with foliate scroll cast knees, cast feet, stamped "W Thomas, JME, c1780," crack in marble, minor repairs, 39½" w, 33½" h **14,300**

Tulipwood, third quarter 18th C, rectangular top with molded edge, three bow front drawers, scalloped apron, cabriole legs, replaced top, 48½" w, 39" h **3,575**

Walnut, mid 18th C, shaped top with inlaid central star, serpentine front with three short and two long drawers, scroll carved tapered stiles, claw and ball feet, distressed, 45" w, 37¾" h **7,150**

Cupboard, c1760, hanging, corner, kingwood, graduated scalloped sides with three graduated serpentine front shelves, base with two inlaid quarter veneered and crossbanded doors, bracket feet, feet restorations, 17½" w, 34" h **1,100**

Sideboard, mid 18th C, oak, shaped rectangular molded top, conforming case, three central drawers, two paneled doors, shelved interior, scrolled feet, 79" l, 22¼" d, 39½" h **1,375**

Sofa, walnut, arched crest rail flanked by shaped wings, out scrolled padded arms with foliate scroll carved terminals, foliate scroll carved serpentine front seat rail, leather upholstery, cabriole legs with carved floral sprigs at knees, foliate carved feet **4,675**

Stool, choir, pair, oak, molded D–shape top, square legs, stretchers, 25¼" h, price for pair **450**

Table

Console, mid 18th C, giltwood, oblong sepia and liver molded marble top, serpentine front, conforming

frieze, pierced foliage decoration, S–shape legs, pierced and shaped silhouette upswept stretcher, 44" w, 22" d, 33½" h **8,700**

Game, mid 18th C, fruitwood, lift–off rectangular top with leather inset, tric trac playing surface with later needlepoint, shaped apron with fitted drawer on each side, cabriole legs, restorations, 36" w, 27½" h . **4,950**

Library, shaped rectangular top with gilt tooled leather inset within banded reserve with applied gadroon cast edge, foliate and scroll cast cap applied corners, shaped small drawer with parquetry reserve within gilt banded border flanked by two larger shaped drawers with banded parquetry reserves, other side with sham drawers and parquetry ends, cabriole legs with term and scroll cast decoration, foliate and scroll cast feet, 60" w, 32" h . **2,750**

Side, mid 18th C, walnut, oblong dished top, recessed frieze with two end drawers, shaped apron, cabriole legs, whorled feet, 15" w, 23½" d, 26½" h **3,200**

Vitrine, ormolu mounted amaranth marble top, glass shelf interior, stamped on back "BOUDIN," capital, intertwined script "ME," 37½" w, 15" d . **3,750**

Folding Dressing Screen, Louis XV Style, late 19th C, three panels, giltwood, beveled glass shaped panels atop lower fabric panels, 60½" w, 63" h, $850.00. Photograph courtesy of Neal Auction Company.

STYLE

Bench, window, fruitwood, scrolled voluted arms, pale gray and dusty rose striped silk upholstery, cabriole legs, 41½" l **250**

Bookcase, late 19th C, oak, thumb molded cornice, central grilled door, opposing foliate scroll carved frame on top and mid–section, grilled panels, plinth base, 60" w, 87" h . . .   **3,300**

Cabinet

Pair, third quarter 19th C, mottled pink marble top, two cupboard doors with inlaid ribbon–tied floral sprigs within gilt bronze foliate scroll borders, shaped crossbanded legs, cast hoof form feet, stamped "Nogaret a Lyon, Third Quarter 19th Century," one marble top cracked, minor chips and losses, 28½" w, 36" h, price for pair **1,870**

Pair, c1900, tulipwood and marquetry, ormolu mounted, vernis martin, marble top, conforming bombe case, door polychromed with couple in landscape scene, price for pair **15,950**

Side, c1900, mahogany, brown and white veined marble top with molded edge, cupboard door mounted with canvas panel with painted 18th C couple, sheep, and pastoral setting within gilt bronze foliate border, angled stiles with gilt bronze foliate decoration, ruffled foliate feet, 36" w, 44¼" h **3,575**

Chair, arm

Pair, mid 19th C, molded crest rail, upholstered back, padded armrests, volute supports and upholstered sides, shaped seat rail with upholstered loose cushion, cabriole legs, scrolled feet, serrated beige and puce striped floral sprig needlepoint upholstery, paint flaking, price for pair **4,400**

Walnut, shaped crest rail, bird, figural, and floral petit–point and needlepoint upholstered back and seat, matching upholstered loose cushions, shell carved apron, cabriole legs, 35" l **2,000**

Chaise Lounge, pair, walnut, floral carved crest rail, yellow and ivory stripe upholstered back and seat, shell carved seat rail, cabriole legs, price for pair **385**

Chest of Drawers, black lacquer, ormolu mounted, overall oriental court scene decoration, stamped "Millet A Paris, Bronzes & Meubles D'Art" **5,500**

Commode

Burled Fruitwood, c1900, shaped white marble top, two sans traverse drawers, bottom drawer shaped to form apron, cabriole legs with gilt bronze mask decoration, animal paw feet, 48½" w, 33½" h **2,750**

Kingwood and Mahogany, late 19th

Commode, Louis XV Style, late 19th C, tulipwood and kingwood, oblong gray and liver marble top with shaped sides, serpentine front, conforming bombe case of two frieze drawers and one full drawer ornamented with compressed oval parquetry panels, shaped apron within S-curved knife edge corners enriched by gilt bronze chutes and sabots, 44½" w, 13½" d, 35" h, $4,400.00. Photograph courtesy of William Doyle Galleries.

C, serpentine breche dalep marble top with molded edge, two long drawers with gilt metal elaborate handles and lock plates, scalloped apron with gilt metal mounted decoration center, shaped legs with gilt metal mounted female term angles, gilt metal paw feet, veneer loss to front, restorations, restorations and losses to marble, 52″ w, 35″ h ... **4,125**

Tulipwood, Kingwood, and Parquetry, c1900, serpentine marble top, conforming case, three drawers, shaped apron, sabot feet, scrolling metal mounts on side corners, apron, and feet, 47″ w, 24″ d, 35″ h **6,325**

Curio Cabinet, walnut, single serpentine glazed cabinet door with painted armorial panel, mounted ormolu decoration, 26″ w, 14″ d, 59⅝″ h **465**

Desk, lady's, parquetry burl walnut, polychrome decoration, cabriole legs, 35½″ w, 18¾″ d, 49″ h **1,600**

Mirror
Mantle
Composition, gilt grapes and C–scroll crest, arched rectangular mirror plate with gilt cushion molded surround applied with foliate swags, scratches to plate, gilt loss, 57″ w, 82″ h **1,100**

Giltwood, rectangular beveled mirror plate with foliate and ribbon carved surround hung with foliate swags surmounted with

quiver and torch, minor gilt loss, 43½″ w, 74″ h **2,200**

Pair, 19th C, giltwood and gesso, carved floral crest surrounded by sectioned inner mirrors, rectangular carved frame, raised outer edge, mirrored oval reserves, 66″ w, 86″ h, price for pair **26,500**

Pier, walnut, foliate pierced carved crest, scalloped beveled rectangular mirror plate surrounded with molded carved foliate decoration, 34″ w, 92″ h **2,750**

Suite
Canape and Four Fauteuils, second half 19th C, giltwood, foliate tapestry upholstery, each piece stamped "Lexcellant, Paris," price for five piece set **12,100**

Settee, two armchairs, and two side chairs, second half 19th C, giltwood, slightly arched crest rail with asymmetrically carved rocaille cartouche center, upholstered back, scroll carved stiles, scrolled padded arms above scrolled supports, upholstered seat, serpentine seat rail with center shell and scroll carved cartouche, cabriole legs, scroll carved feet, 63½″ l settee, price for five piece set **4,950**

Settee, 19th C, walnut, carved rectangular back with rocaille carved crest rail, inward swept stiles with acanthus carved armrests, caned scalloped seat, rocaille carved

Commode, Louis XV Style, Provincial, late 19th C, walnut, rectangular top with chamfered corners above two *rocaille* carved drawers, scalloped apron flanked by chamfered stiles continuing to form acanthus-carved cabriole supports, 45″ w, 32″ h, $2,250.00. Photograph courtesy of Butterfield & Butterfield.

Desk, Louis XV Style, kingwood, slant front, shaped skirt, simple cabriole legs, $1,650.00. Photograph courtesy of William Doyle Galleries.

apron, cabriole legs, damage to cane seat, 65" l 1,210

Sofa, walnut, serpentine crest rail with carved center floral sprigs, back with tapestry upholstered blue, green, and brown exotic birds perched on branches and marsh scene, scrolled sides, padded armrests, volute supports, floral carved serpentine seat rail with loose cushion with continued upholstery design, cabriole legs, scrolled feet, 18th C tapestry, c1900 frame, 74" l 4,125

Table

Center, late 19th C, kingwood, shaped foliate marquetry top with gilt metal edge, scalloped apron with one drawer, cabriole legs with gilt metal female term chutes, gilt metal scroll feet, missing three feet, 41" l, 30½" h 1,100

Console, pair, marble top, painted white, price for pair 2,600

Dressing, 19th C, marquetry and parquetry, top with center mirrored lift lid and two lift lid compartments, straight front with fitted slide and two drawers, cabriole legs, 31½" w, 19" d, 29½" h 700

Game, oak, square top, red leather inset surface with gilt decoration, shallow gallery, scalloped apron, cabriole legs, 32¼" w, 28¾" h ... 2,000

Library, late 19th C, rectangular top with gilt tooled leather writing surface, central ribbon inlaid frieze drawer, two parquetry inlaid

shaped drawers, reverse side with faux drawers, slight cabriole legs with foliate cast gilt bronze knees and feet, scuffed leather, minor losses and repairs, 59" w, 29½" h   4,950

Dressing Vanity, Louis XV Style, c 1900, carved and parquetry inlaid walnut, triple beveled glass mirrors, part of suite but sold separately, $1,650.00. Photograph courtesy of Neal Auction Company.

Vitrine

Kingwood, projected molded cornice with gilt metal cartouche center and mounted angles on corners, two glazed doors with gilt metal square panel decoration, adjustable shelved interior, scalloped apron with gilt metal decoration center, cabriole legs with gilt metal decoration on knees, gilt metal scroll feet, 56" w, 102" h 5,500

Marquetry, demilune form, mirror back, one glazed cabinet door, two glass shelves interior, sabre legs, 28" w, 58" h 1,300

LOUIS XVI (1774–1793)

History: In much of French furniture design, developments associated with a specific king usually began during the final decades of the preceding monarch. Such is the case with the neo–classic revival of Louis XVI, i.e., Louis Seize. As with English neo–classicism, the inspiration for this form were the many excavations in Greece and Italy.

The excavations at Pompeii and Herculaneum sparked the neo–classical revival of the post–1760 period. Furniture design returned to simpler and straighter forms. Legs were true vertical supporting structures, enhanced by fluting, reeding, and architectural capitals. Ornamentation was lessened but, when used, it was symmetrical, classic in its motifs, and delicate.

Mahogany remained the favorite wood. Geometric marquetry in the shape of diamonds and lozenges was often made from rosewood and tulipwood. Contrasting black and gold lacquer and ebony appeared on many furniture forms. Occasionally Sevres china plaques were incorporated as a decorative motif.

New furniture forms include the curule chair, rollback sofas, and vitrine (curio cabinet). Beds were small, continuing a trend that began under Louis XV.

Major Craftsmen: Etienne Avril, Aubert, Beneman, Martin Carlin, Georges Jacob, Lalonde, Leleu, Levasseur, Montigny, Jean Francois Riesner, David Roentgen, Saunier, Severin, Schwerdfeger, and Weisweiler.

PERIOD

Armoire, 18th C, flat molded cornice, two carved glass panel doors, glass paneled sides, reeded tapered legs, 59" w, 22" d, 90" h **2,600**
Bed, c1785, mahogany, paneled headboard and footboard, stop fluted pillars, pomegranate finials, stamped "G Jacob," 45" w, 77" l **3,100**

Cabinet, late 18th C, mahogany, rectangular white marble top, bronze gallery with three–quarter fret, conforming case, three drawers, tapered turned fluted legs joined by basal shelf, 19" w, 13½" d, 28½" h **1,250**
Chair
Arm, late 18th C, pair
  Arched molded back, pierced fanned baluster form splat with carved pearl bands and patera, delicate curved upholstered cap arms, saddle seat with green damask upholstery, straight tapered turned legs with chandelle decoration, price for pair **8,800**
  Molded frame, upholstered back, upholstered cap arms, upholstered serpentine seat, coral upholstery, straight tapered fluted legs, toupie feet, price for pair . **1,210**
  Molded frame with carved entwined ribbon design surmounted with bowknot, upholstered back, cap arms, and loose cushion seat, molded arm supports, carved seat rail, straight tapered turned fluted legs, painted gray, price for pair **5,225**
  Molded giltwood frame, arched crest rail, upholstered back, upholstered cap arms, curved arm supports with carved leaf tips, guilloche, and acanthus leaf decoration, Aubusson tapestry upholstery, straight tapered fluted legs, price for pair **3,850**
Set of Four, late 18th C, arm, molded frame, rounded upholstered back surmounted with two flowerhead knots and leaves, upholstered cap

Chairs, bergeres, Louis XVI Style, painted gray, price for the pair, $2,640.00. Photograph courtesy of William Doyle Galleries.

Chairs, pair, late 18th C, carved gesso and gilt wood, wreath carved crest rails above padded medallion shaped backs, padded arms, bow front seats, upholstered in pink and green striped watered silk, fluted legs, price for pair, $2,640.00. Photograph courtesy of Freeman/Fine Arts of Philadelphia.

arms, serpentine upholstered seat, striped brocade upholstery, straight tapered turned fluted legs with carved chandelle decoration, toupie feet, price for set **9,350**

Slipper, third quarter 18th C, beechwood, molded frame, oval back, serpentine seat with red corduroy upholstery, turned tapered fluted legs with carved chandelle decoration, front rail stamped "P Laroque JME" **880**

Chest of Drawers

Satinwood, late 18th C, rectangular top with fitted tooled red leather, two side slides, three front drawers, three back faux drawers, reeded inlaid tapered legs, 52" w, 27" d, 29½" h **6,750**

Walnut, 18th C, rectangular top with rounded corners and molded edge, three drawers, foliate carved scrolled stiles continuing to form bracket feet, 50" w, 33" h **6,600**

Chiffonier, tulipwood, parquetry, oval top with quartered veneer squares held in trellis with cast and pierced three quarter bronze border, conforming case, three drawers, slender curved legs joined by basal shelf, gilt bronze sabot feet, 18¼" w, 13" d, 30" h **4,400**

Commode

Mahogany, 18th C, marble top, three graduated paneled drawers, front fluted column stiles, rear pilaster stiles, paneled sides, toupie feet, 45½" w, 33¾" h **4,125**

Mahogany and Tulipwood, rectangu-

lar marble top, raised pierced bronze border, conforming case, two drawers, with *sans traverse* decoration, straight tapered turned legs joined by basal shelf, 19" w, 13" d, 29" h **6,050**

Walnut, rectangular thumb molded top, three drawers, square legs, 43" w, 21" d, 33½" h **2,900**

Mirror

21½" w, 42" h, first quarter 19th C, giltwood, scrolled crest with fruit and foliate filled vase center, rectangular mirror plate within subsidiary mirrored borders, intertwined fruiting vines on sides **880**

28" w, 45" h, Continental, giltwood, pierced scrolling foliate crest, rectangular mirror plate, conforming beaded frame, shaped side brackets   **1,875**

32" w, 49" h, late 18th C, giltwood, fluted plinth crest with molded oval reserve center surrounded with opposing carved scrolls, rectangular mirror plate with leaf tip and bead carved molded frame, foliate pendants on sides, minor losses and restorations **2,200**

Shelf, hanging, late 18th C, three graduated serpentine molded shelves, pierced stiles, conforming cabinet below with two doors, mustard ground, chinois and landscape decoration, 17" w, 7" d, 32½" h **825**

Sofa, late 18th C, slightly curved arched molded crest rail with three carved flower knots, upholstered back, upholstered loose cushion seat, cream striped satin upholstery, molded skirt

Fauteils, part of a parlor, suite, Louis XVI Style, giltwood, third quarter 19th C, acanthus carved crest, Aubusson tapestry upholstered back, arms, and seat, turned fluted legs with rosette carved knees, price for four fauteils and setee, $7,500.00. Photograph courtesy of Leslie Hindman Auctioneers.

with carved floral sprays, turned tapered fluted legs with chandelle decoration, toupie feet, 84" l **2,420**

Table

Console, late 18th C, oak, semi–oval marble top with molded edge, carved apron with swag pendants, tapered fluted legs, D–shape platform base, 34½" w, 24" h **1,650**

Dining, late 18th C, mahogany

Oblong top with brass border, two demilune drop leaves, recessed rectangular frieze, turned tapered legs with gilt bronze molded capitals, cup casters, 44¼" w, 109" l extended, 28½" h **19,800**

Oval top, two drop leaves, recessed frieze, straight tapered legs, octagonal cross stretcher, brass casters, four 19½" w leaves, 55½" w, 62" l, 28" h **8,250**

Dressing, fruitwood, oblong molded top with chevron bands tambour surface, opens to cosmetic well centering mirror, straight tapered turned fluted legs, 23" w, 16" d, 29½" h **1,650**

Library, walnut, carved and gilted, shaped top with inset white leather, leaf carved corner blocks, single drawer frieze, reeded tapered legs joined by stretcher, 53" w, 30" d, 30" h **450**

Side, late 18th C, fruitwood, square top, single frieze drawer, square tapered legs, shaped platform stretcher, 28½" h, 25½" w **1,045**

Writing, mahogany

Malachite, rectangular top with rounded outset corners, frieze with gilt bronze foliate swags and drawer with gilt bronze mask medallion centered by sphinxes and drapery swag panels on either side, gilt bronze female shape (from waist up) forms top part of leg, leg tapers to square, interlaced stretcher outlined in gilt bronze centered with pierced basket, spiral carved tapered cylindrical feet with gilt bronze ends, 33½" l, 31" h **9,900**

Gilt tooled tan leather top with molded edge, paneled sides, five projecting paneled drawers, brass inset fluted stiles, square tapering legs, block feet, 63" l, 31½" h **5,500**

Vitrine

Gilt bronze mounts, single door, ebonized legs, 50" h **2,200**

Mahogany, projected molded cornice, gilt metal dentil frieze, two glazed doors, foliate gilt metal mounted apron, toupie feet, 48" w, 74½" h **4,125**

STYLE

Candlestand, mahogany, circular top with pierced brass border, paneled standard, shaped tripod base, 14½" d, 26½" h **1,210**

Clock, tall case, late 19th C, gilt bronze amorini on clouds and holding floral garlands, mounted square tapered pedestal section with elaborate gilt bronze floral mounts, lion's paw feet,

Commode, Louis XVI Style, c1890, gilt bronze mounted mahogany, brown and white marble top, rectangular case with three long drawers inset with fleur de peche marble panels, sides similarly inset, 50" w, 22½" d, 35½" h, $8,250.00. Photograph courtesy of William Doyle Galleries.

Secretary, Louis XVI Style, c1890, gilt bronze mounted mahogany, later fleur de peche marble panels and gilt bronze enrichments, 38" w, 16½" d, 56" h, $4,124.00. Photograph courtesy of William Doyle Galleries.

shaped plinth, four gilt bronze cast acanthus feet, 90½" h **13,500**

Commode, late 19th C, rouge marble top with inset rounded corners, three drawers, top drawer with intertwined ormolu foliate scrolls, other two drawers with *sans traverse* with central mahogany diamond within pen work leaf tip, rosewood and fruitwood borders, and mounted with foliate scroll pulls, intertwined ormolu foliate scroll above fleur–de–lis sides, tapered cylindrical legs headed by ormolu foliage, leaf tip cast ormolu collar feet, stamped twice "Beurdeley Paris," repaired marble, 35¾" l, 34" h **12,100**

Console, mahogany, rectangular mirror plate with downswept sides and gilt bronze framework, green marble top with rounded ends, frieze with one long drawer with gilt bronze decoration and rounded ends with drawers, two marble lined shelves with rounded ends and pierced gilt bronze galleries, toupie feet, 93½" w, 60" h   **5,500**

Footstool, walnut, petit–point upholstered top, 4" h **200**

Mirror

Cheval, 1889, mahogany, swiveling rectangular frame, inset oval mirror plate, gilt bronze spandrels, floral sprays, and winged griffins, square pilasters, candle arms and flame finials on each side, shaped cabriole legs, gilt bronze sabots, stamped "Wararian," 48" w, 84" h **11,000**

Settee, part of a parlor suite, Louis XVI Style, giltwood, third quarter 19th C, acanthus carved crest over Aubusson tapestry upholstered back, sides, and seat, turned fluted legs with rosette carved knees, 51″ l, price for setee and four fauteils, $7,500.00. Photograph courtesy of Leslie Hindman Auctioneers.

Giltwood, late 19th C, laurel and wreath entwined lyre crest, rectangular mirror plate, beaded and leaf tip carved molded frame, 30″ w, 51″ h **2,200**

Pair, giltwood, floral filled basket crest, rectangular mirror plate with conforming frame, 24½″ w, 54″ h, price for pair **1,760**

Sideboard, late 19th C, variegated mustard marble top, two drawers, two panel doors, two mirror back marble top open shelves, reeded tapered legs, painted green, 76″ w, 39″ h ... **1,050**

Table

Bouilotte, 19th C, brass mounted mahogany, circular galleried marble top, molded frieze, stop fluted legs, pierced stretcher, 30½″ d, 31″ h .. **1,870**

Console, rectangular marble top with floral inlay, guilloche carved edge, frieze with putto on center front, rosettes on sides, fluted trumpet legs, 59″ w, 28″ h **3,750**

Dining, mahogany, circular top with brass banding, straight tapered legs, brass toe caps, 54″ w, 82″ l extended, 27½″ h **1,500**

Writing, mahogany, rectangular parquetry top, frieze with two leather inset slides and two faux drawers, fluted tapered legs, casters, 29″ w, 28½″ h **425**

Vitrine, shaped curved molded top with swag decoration, bow front, glazed sides and door, pale lime silk lined shelf interior, fluted tapered legs, 30¼″ w, 17″ d, 60″ h **1,900**

DIRECTOIRE (1793–1799)

History: The French Revolution began in 1789. France entered a period of chaos. Louis XVI was executed in 1793. The Directoire assumed control in 1795.

The Directoire design style essentially was a simplification of the design style of Louis XVI. Craftsmen were instructed by the Directoire to eliminate the trappings of royalty by reducing scale, eliminating ornate and exotic materials, and stressing the pure neo-classical forms.

Ornamentation focused on the symbols of revolution—arrows, clasped hands, Phrygian caps, triangles, wreaths, etc. The lyre, star, and swan supplemented these motifs. Native fruitwoods, oak, and walnut gained favor over mahogany.

While short–lived in France, the Directoire design style survived in England as Early Regency; in America through the work of Duncan Phyfe; in a capricious style in Italy; and as a sober classicism in Scandinavia. In November 1799, Napoleon ended the Directoire and created the Consulate.

Major Craftsmen: Beneman, Georges Jacob, Percier and Fontaine, Jean Francois Riesener, and David Roentgen.

PERIOD

Cabinet, 1800–30, double level, Greek pediment with inlay, hanging bin for bread storage, intricate turnings, 36″ w, 19″ d, 34″ h **4,000**

Chair, arm

Last quarter 18th C, beechwood, molded upholstered back, bowed upholstered seat, circular tapering legs with patera carving, restorations, 36½" h **1,100**

Late 18th C

Beechwood, molded rectilinear frame, concave crest rail, columnar stiles enclosing padded back, cap upholstered arms, loose cushion seat, fluted urn form arm supports continuing to turned tapering legs, reupholstered in rose watered silk **950**

Painted, concave molded crest rail, padded back, cap arms, bowed seat, straight tapering legs, painted gray, covered in later green fabric **1,250**

First half 19th C, fruitwood, shaped crest rail above pierced and intertwined scroll form horizontal splat, scrolled arms over flared leather upholstered seat, tapering square legs, flared feet **850**

Chest of Drawers, 1800, Stumpff, variegated green and pink breche marble top, three triple fronted crossbanded and checkerbanded drawers flanked by rounded simulated inlaid fluted stiles, two sides painted with banded borders, turned tapering supports, beaded gilt brass collars, incised tapering brass sabots, stamped maker's mark, 49¾" w, 33¼" h **3,515**

Commode, late 18th C

Mahogany, oblong white veined molded marble top with outset corners, conforming case with three frieze and two full drawers, quarter round brass moldings, fluted corner columns continuing to top form feet, 50" w, 23⅕" d, 34½" h **3,960**

Moucheter, mahogany, oblong black fossilized marble top with outset corners, conforming case with three long drawers, each with sunken panel bordered by brass torus moldings, fluted stiles continue to top form feet, 54½" w, 24" d, 34½" h **6,600**

Walnut, oblong top with outset corners, conforming case with three full sunken panel drawers, fluted stiles, ebonized turned legs, 48" w, 23" d, 35½" h **2,860**

Desk

18th C, Bonheur du Jour, cherry, rectangular fold over writing surface, recessed cabinet back with two glazed doors, two frieze drawers, carrara marble surface enclosed by pierced three quarter bronze border, two apron drawers, turned tapering legs, 26½" w, 15" d, 45" h **2,100**

Late 18th C, mahogany, oblong brass bordered top inset with tooled green leather writing surface, frieze of three drawers and apron, knee well flanked by two small drawers, turned fluted legs, brass capitals, toupie feet, 43½" w, 23½" d, 29½" h **5,250**

Late 18th C or early 19th C, mahogany, oblong brass bordered top inset with tooled green leather writing surface, conforming case, two side slides, central frieze drawer within

Desk, mahogany, oblong brass bordered top inset with tooled green leather writing surface, frieze of three drawers, apron containing one long drawer over knee well and two small drawers, turned fluted legs, brass capitals, toupie feet, 43½" w, 23½" d, 29½" h, $5,250.00. Photograph courtesy of William Doyle Galleries.

double depth ink drawer, two small drawers, raised on turned tapering fluted legs, toupie feet, 45" w, 24" d, 28½" h 5,775

Secretary

Early 19th C, fruitwood, oblong top, conforming frieze with full drawer, sunken panel fall front writing surface, three full basal drawers, 36" w, 14½" d, 58¼" h 1,320

First half 19th C, walnut, oblong top, frieze drawer, fall front with writing surface, fitted interior, three full basal drawers, fluted corner columns, 37" w, 15" d, 56½" h 6,875

Settee, 18th C, fruitwood, triple chair back, rectangular crest rail, pierced swan lyre splats, loose cushion seat, square tapering legs, 52" l 4,000

Sofa, French, 1800–30, cherry, molded, bowed vertical slats on three sides, splayed tapered legs, replaced seat frame, reglued, cleaned, and reupholstered, 68" l, 22" d, 32" h 3,200

Table

Console, late 18th C, mahogany, oblong molded carrara marble top, conforming frieze with full drawer, ribbed corner blocks, straight tapered line inlaid legs joined by basal shelf, brass toe caps, 32" w, 14½" d, 32" h 1,760

Dressing, late 18th C, walnut and mahogany, hinged rectangular molded lift top, interior mirrored panel, paneled dressing surface, conforming frieze of three drawers, turned tapering legs, 31½" w, 18¼" d, 29" h 990

Game, 1800–30, mahogany, backgammon, reversible leather baize top, storage wells, brass line inlays, brass mounted legs with later casters, old repairs, 47" w, 23½" d, 29" h 16,000

Library, 19th C, in the manner of Riesener, satinwood and tulipwood parquetry, rectangular glazed lid with rounded ends, gilt bronze surrounds, lattice parquetry interior, conforming straight frieze, lyre form supports, under tier pierced gallery, downswept feet, 28" w, 30½" h 6,600

STYLE

Cabinet, bedside, late 19th C, mahogany, oblong white veined dark gray marble top, three quarter pierced bronze border, two full drawers with sunken panels, quarter round brass

moldings, fluted stiles, straight tapered legs, basal shelf, brass toe caps, 18½" w, 9¾" d, 29" h 990

Chair, arm, late 19th C, pair, parcel–gilt and carved walnut, concave outward flaring crest rail with applied gilt flowerhead with foliate trailings, downswept arms, urn form supports, bowed seat rail, tapering square legs, price for pair 2,750

Commode, 19th C, mahogany, oblong carrara marble top, pierced three quarter bronze gallery, conforming case with two frieze and two full drawers, quarter round moldings, sunken panels, fluted corner columns, top form feet, 35½" w, 18" d, 36" h 2,420

Desk, late 19th C, walnut, rectangular top with gilt tooled leather inset writing surface, central frieze drawer flanked by band of two drawers, reverse with faux drawers, tapering square legs ending in brass sabots, 51¾" w, 29½" h 1,100

Table, center, base second half 19th C, painted iron, orange variegated faux marble top with beveled edge, black painted frame, shaped X–form end standards, centered and headed by applied lion masks, 48" l, 28½" h .. 700

EMPIRE (1799–1815)

History: The Napoleonic Consulate (1799–1804) set the stage for the First French Empire (1804–1815). Napoleon's edicts dominated French life. He imposed his will and taste on all levels of the arts, including furniture. David Roentgen headed a committee of artists who developed a design style based upon the Imperial forms of ancient Egypt, Greece, and Rome. This style stressed copying archaeological forms in a grand manner.

During this time, furniture size increased; proportions were large, heavy, and solid. Furniture became architectural with a single geometric shape, usually cubic or rectangular, often dominating the appearance and motif of a single piece. Strict treatment formulas were developed and followed. Many furniture pieces resembled miniature buildings.

Many surfaces were completely free of molding or paneling. Wood grain was emphasized— the more sumptuous and rich the grain, the better. Much of the furniture's block–like simplicity was offset by brass or gilt mounts.

Ornamentation usually was limited to applied bronze or flat gilt appliqués often featuring strong military motifs, e.g., arrows and wreaths or shields and swords, or static and precise archaeological motifs, e.g., winged figures. Napoleon himself contributed a few design motifs, such as the bee and the letter "N." The only places carving appeared were on arms and posts of chairs and on table legs.

Mahogany regained its position as the most favored wood. Rosewood and ebony continued their revival. Marble tops are found on many of the tables.

Style Book: Charles Percier and Pierre F. L. Fontaine, *Recuil de decorations interieures*, 1801, revised edition in 1812.

PERIOD

Bed
  1815
    Burl Elm, lit en bateau, curved headboard and footboard, sides inlaid with stylized floral cornucopia decoration, bottom with mid molding and inlaid stylized floral cornucopia decoration, plain club feet, 59" w, 79½" l, 48" h **7,500**
    Mahogany, straight headboard and footboard with inlaid brass musical trophies decoration, shaped sides, square feet, 43¾" w **1,560**
  1820, mahogany, gently scrolling headboard and footboard, later anthemion and wreath plaques, later canopy and matching curtains, 35" w, 71½" l **4,500**
  1825, mahogany, lit en bateau, straight headboard and footboard, sides with circle and floral decoration, block feet with casters, includes box spring and mattress, 48" w, 86" l **4,680**
Bench, early 19th C, fruitwood, square padded saddle seat, taupe velvet upholstery, splayed legs joined by molded H– form stretcher, ebonized paw feet, 19" l **935**
Bookcase, 1810, mahogany, rectangular rouge marble top, ormolu scroll mounted frieze decoration, 20½" h . **1,990**
Bureau, mahogany, rectangular white marble top with pierced brass gallery, cylinder front, interior with six small drawers, mid molding, two long drawers **1,700**
Cabinet
  Corner, 19th C, mahogany, two sections: upper section: projecting molded cornice with pierced gallery over straight frieze, Gothic arched glazed cupboard doors, flanked by female terminals; lower section: two paneled doors, straight

apron, straight stiles, square tapering supports, 35" w, 97" h **3,025**
  Music, mahogany, gilt bronze mounted decoration, two doors, fitted interior, 27½" w, 15½" d, 40" h **1,650**
Pier, 1810, ormolu mounted mahogany, rectangular black marble top raised on female terminals fronting mirror plate, ormolu mounted long drawer, two cupboard doors with central female mask ormolu medallions, plinth and ebonized paw feet, losses and wear, back feet missing, 33" w, 53½" h **6,000**
Chair
  Arm
    1800, mahogany, plain rounded crest rail, upholstered red and gold back pad, curved arms with carved leaf stiles, lotus leaf knuckle, armrest with carved relief anthemion, upholstered red and gold seat, saber legs **4,290**
    1810–15, pair, mahogany, rectangular slightly concave upholstered back, dolphin carved armrests, loose cushion, saber legs, price for pair **5,170**
    1815, tub form, mahogany and parcel gilt, molded crest carved with laurel leaves, C–scroll arms supported by massive birds with scrolling wings, monopodial feet **3,025**
  Side, 1810–20, in the manner of Jacob–Desmalter, mahogany, gilt metal mounted decorations, upholstered half paneled raking back flanked by stiff leaf carved terminals, ringed cylindrical crest rail with center gilt metal pierced plaque of leaves and flowers, crest rail ends terminating in acanthus carved ram's horn finials, elongated flaring seat, saber rear supports, straight cylindrical front supports, gilt metal flowerhead finials, ringed circular feet, later casters, mustard linen upholstery, old repair to seat rail **1,980**
Chest of Drawers
  First quarter 19th C, mahogany, rectangular top over frieze drawer, three bowed and recessed drawers flanked by gilt gesso Egyptian caryatid form stiles, rectangular base fitted with drawer, bracket feet, 36½" w, 41" h **2,750**
  1810, bronze mounted fruitwood, rectangular black marble top with stepped frieze over bureau drawer enclosing row of three drawers, gold tooled leather writing surface

above two long drawers flanked by gilt bronze mounted female terminals, square tapering angles, animal paw feet, 40″ w, 38½″ h **4,000**

Clock, 1800–20, Meuble D'Entre Deux D'Horloge, in the manner of Jacob Desmalter, ormolu mounted mahogany, clock: 6½″ d white enamel dial with black Roman numerals, movement striking on the hour and half hour, encircled by twelve zodiac signs flanked by foliate festoons, acanthus balusters surmounted by warrior profiles, one with Pegasus, the other with dragon, sides with military motifs above large festoons, three sided frieze of honeysuckle below; single cupboard door centered with maenad within lozenge form cartouche, flanked by female terms above foliate devices, lion's paw feet with anthemion pendants, sides with musical trophies and lozenge form encadrements, bun feet, 35½″ w, 65½″ h **16,500**

Commode, early 19th C, walnut, D–form black fossilized marble top, conforming case, four full drawers of quartered veneer, turned tapering legs, 25″ w, 12″ d, 31¼″ h **2,420**

Credenza, painted, D–form, shaped white veined black marble top, conforming frieze of rosette filled entrelac, Egyptian canephorae, two open shelves, 42″ w, 14″ d, 34½″ h **5,500**

Desk, early 19th C
Bonheu du Jour, ormolu mounted mahogany, rectangular black marble top with frieze drawer, mirrored fall front flanked by female terminal angles, plinth, minor losses and restoration, 30″ w, 50″ h **3,780**
Cylinder
Mahogany, rectangular verde antico marble top, three small drawers below, cylinder front with ormolu mounted decoration, fitted interior, two drawers, square tapered legs, ormolu mounted feet, 49″ w **2,800**
Part ebonized walnut, rectangular top, three drawers, interior drawers and shelf over pullout writing surface, two drawers below flanked by free standing ebonized columns, block feet, 52″ w, 45¾″ h **4,400**

Fire Screen, mahogany, straight crest with ears, screen frame flanked by pillars, trestle base with arched feet, worn silk screen, 24″ w **500**

Meridiennes, 1837, in the manner of Jacob Desmalter, mahogany, ormolu mounted, scrolled ends terminating in gilded wood swan's head finials, side rails with leaf tip cast applied borders, plaque of winged deity in chariot in clouds and drawn by butterflies, flanked by stars and fern leaves, snarling winged lion's head *Monopodaie*, gold and green moquette trellis work and flowerhead upholstery, incised date, crowned initials: M. L.; painted monogram: J. P. T.; 67″ l **15,000**

Mirror, mantel, gesso and giltwood, projecting molded cornice, half column decorations divide mirror into three sections, 41″ w, 18″ h **500**

Stand
Basin, early 19th C, mahogany, circular white marble slab with pierced brass gallery, three Doric style colonettes, triangular incurvate base, 12½″ d, 36½″ h **740**
Gueridon, 19th C, mahogany, circular marble top, rope form gilt bronze mounted decoration on apron, three curved supports joined by gilt bronze mounted decoration on front, tripartite base, 17″ d, 26″ h **1,800**

Stool, 1800–30, mahogany, curule form, turned stretcher, hairy paw feet, needlework cover, worm damage, reglued, 18″ w, 15″ d, 18″ h **2,400**

Table
Center, mahogany, gilt bronze mounted decoration, round top, conforming apron, square tapering legs with caryatid mounts, joined by stretcher, round tapering feet, 33″ d, 27½″ h **2,200**
Console, mahogany, white marble rectangular top, straight frieze with gilt metal decoration, incurved front supports attached to straight square back legs, paw feet, 44″ w **2,025**

STYLE

Cabinet, side, mahogany, oblong black and white fossilized marble top, conforming cabinet with frieze drawer, two cabinet doors, caryatid colonettes, paw feet, 27¾″ w, 15¼″ d, 31″ h **990**

Chair
Arm, pair, mahogany, gilt bronze mounted decoration, scrolling back continuing to flat arms supported by winged sphinxes, winged lion legs, lion's paw feet, price for pair **3,300**
Set of Four, two arm and two side, mahogany, gilt bronze mounted

maiden, stepped square base, paw feet, 12" w, 37¼" h, price for pair .. **6,500**

Secretary, mahogany, ormolu mounted, rectangular top above fall front drawer, fitted interior, three graduated drawers, bracket feet **600**

Settee, mahogany, gilt bronze mounted decoration, scrolling back, two flat arms supported by winged sphinxes, winged lion legs, lion's paw feet, 51" l **935**

Table

Center, 19th C

Fruitwood, circular tilt top, center column, tripartite base, 32" d, 25" h **1,500**

Mahogany, circular gray variegated marble top, four ormolu mounted columnar supports, platform base, 32" d, 27¼" h .. **1,980**

Console, 19th C, walnut, rectangular top with rounded corners over two frieze drawers, columnar supports with brass capitals and bases, plinth base, 50" w, 32" h **825**

Dining, carved mahogany, oval top, thumb molded edge, gilt metal mounted straight frieze, circular tapering supports with swan carving, 73" l extended, 30" h **1,250**

Arm Chair, Empire Style, gilt bronze mounted mahogany, scrolling back continuing to flat arms supported by winged sphinxes, legs in form of winged lions ending in lion's paw feet, price for pair, $3,300.00. Photograph courtesy of William Doyle Galleries.

decoration, rectangular crest rail, Neoclassical figures, slip seat, saber legs, price for set of four **2,600**

Chaise Lounge, carved and gilt wood, eagle form terminals, reupholstered, 84" l **1,650**

Commode, pair, fruitwood, cylindrical, gray mottled marble top, one door, circular base, 20½" d, 42" h, price for pair **850**

Desk

Mid 19th C, mahogany, rectangular top, inset leather writing surface, single frieze drawer, tapering fluted round legs, matching caned seat chair, 43" w, 25" d, 30" h, price for two pieces **1,430**

Late 19th C, mahogany, gilt bronze mounted decoration, marble top, pierced brass gallery with three drawers below, center section with cylinder opening, three drawers and pullout writing surface, single long drawer, two short drawers, tapering fluted legs, 50" w, 26" d, 45" h **3,850**

Pedestal, pair, malachite veneer, square, gilt metal mounted decoration of applied plaque of classically draped

RESTAURATION (1815–1830)

History: The fall of Napoleon led to the restoration of the Bourbon family to the throne. Louis XVIII reigned from 1815 to 1824 and Charles X from 1824 to 1830. Both were brothers of Louis XVI.

Much of the furniture retained the strong geometric Empire forms. Ornamentation was minimal. The overall appearance was one of plainness.

Native woods challenged the dominance of mahogany, rosewood, and exotic woods. Light woods (*bois clair* or pale wood) gained favor due in part to the ability of new industrial machinery to cut smooth, regular veneers. Contrast was achieved by the use of ebony and similar inlays and brass and pewter appliqués as opposed to the bronze and gilted appliqués of the Empire period.

A Gothic Revival occurred. Furniture was embellished with Gothic tracery (*a la cathedrale*). The French movement into Algeria, and numerous essays about the Orient created a romanticism that was reflected in some furniture design.

Style Books: Pattern book of Michel Jansen, 1835; Augustus W. N. Pugin, *Gothic Furniture in the Style of the 15th Century*, 1835; Augustus

W. N. Pugin, *The True Principle of Pointed or Christian Architecture*, 1841.

Bed, first quarter 19th C, pine, carved and painted ochre and orange, paneled scrolled ends, sides of headboard carved in relief with recumbent leopard–headed sphinx with upswept wings and scaly winding tail, front rail with conforming decoration and palmettes, ball feet overhung by frieze of carved pendant stiff leaves, black line borders, ends painted dark green, 67½" l, 44" h   2,750

Bureau, mahogany, projected rectangular marble top, frieze with gilt bronze mount, paneled cupboard doors flanked by round columns with gilt bronze mounts, plain apron, front short rounded tapered feet, square back feet, 56" h   4,000

Chair

Arm

1815, mahogany, scrolled tablet crest rail, upholstered back rest, downscrolled dolphin armrests, straight seat rail with upholstered seat, square tapered scrolled support, brown leather upholstery .   1,430

Arm Chair, Charles X, fruitwood, $2,860.00. Photograph courtesy of William Doyle Galleries.

1820, pair, inlaid and carved mahogany, bergere form, broad arched line inlaid crest rail, bowed back, continuing to downswept arms carved in upper corners with organic reeded foliage terminating in lobed circular flowerhead finials, outlined in fruitwood stringing caught up in loops with fleur–de–lis crestings, slightly bowed seat rail outlined in stringing and supporting inswept C–scroll arm supports, lappet carved slightly shaped legs with scroll finials, ending in bronze cappings and pad feet, brown suede and watered brown silk upholstery, nail head trim, price for pair   3,850

1825, mahogany, parcel gilt, gilt metal mounted decorations, upholstered square paneled back, cresting with center plaque of two hippocampi, molded arms with fern leaf finials, gilded and reeded sections above carved scrolled terminals, fluted and gilded square uprights, bowed upholstered seat with shaped seat rail, slightly outswept shaped molded front supports, carved gilded leaf beneath rosette, casters, ivory medallion embroidered satin upholstery   3,300

1830, pair, ashwood, curved crest rail, upholstered back, curved arms ending with scroll, straight seat rail with upholstered seat, front carved cabriole legs, straight square back legs, price for pair   1,975

Side

1820, carved mahogany, square upholstered back, bowed upholstered seat, saber legs, green velvet upholstery, old repairs to back   660

1830, broad bowed semi–circular crest rail with four inlaid lines of stringing ending with relief carved S–scroll terminals, four outscrolled rectangular splats centering inlaid lyre splat, striped satin circular upholstered seat, reeded edge on seat rail, turned legs   825

Chiffonier, 1825, cherrywood, projected rectangular top with edge molding, five long drawers, rounded stiles, base molding, 62½" h   1,075

Commode

1820, mahogany, rectangular gray

marble top, plain frieze with square ends, three long drawers flanked by round columns with gilt metal mounts, plain straight apron, columns form front feet, square back feet, 51" w **2,560**

1825, George Jacob Desmalter, mahogany, rectangular marble top, plain frieze, three long drawers flanked by turned columns with ormolu mounting, columns form front feet, 52" w **19,800**

Daybed, mahogany, slightly bowed rectangular upholstered back, upholstered seat, turned tapered legs, ball feet, crimson silk upholstery **525**

Mirror, 1815, gilt and gesso, rectangular mirror plate, leaf molded corners and trailing flower heads and foliage, plain reserves centering molded flower heads on each side, recessed leaf molded edge, 47½" w, 58" h ... **935**

Settee
  1810, mahogany and parcel gilt, upholstered, carved sphinx heads, tapering supports, claw feet **800**
  Walnut, channel molded frame, slightly arched back rail continuing to downswept sides, out scrolled knuckled terminals, inswept uprights, undulating seat rail, four sharply tapering paneled square legs headed by rectangular dies, two flaring back legs, sea green velvet upholstery, 56" l **3,200**

Sofa, mahogany, asymmetrical shape, rolled ends, loose cushion seat, plain straight apron, turned legs, bell shape feet, 66" l **750**

Table
  Center
    1815, walnut, circular top, veneered in radiating sections of Circassian walnut, plain deep frieze, single drawer, applied molded brass lower border, three inswept square supports, shaped triform stretcher, shallow block feet, 27½" d, 28¾" h **2,500**
    1820
      Gilt bronze, tray type top with later verde antico marble, three cabriole legs with scrolled supports, tripod base, 32" h **17,710**
      Mahogany, gray and black round marble top, three round supports, tripod base, flattened ball feet **3,750**
    Second quarter 19th C, mahogany
      Oval top with beaded edge, urn shape carved standard, flared legs, paw feet **2,310**
      Round tilt top, carved standard, tripod base, paw feet, 60" d . **11,000**
  Console, c1830, pair, mahogany, rectangular top, two drawers in frieze, six turned legs joined by two shelves, mirrored back panels, 48" w, price for pair **17,600**
  Dressing, c1830, mahogany, swivel mirror, gray marble top, frieze with drawer, four round legs joined by shelf, 53" h **1,300**

Commode, Charles X, burl walnut veneer, marble top, four drawers, plinth base, $4,400.00. Photograph courtesy of William Doyle Galleries.

Occasional, mahogany, round marble top, three lion supports, triangular base, 29¼" h **15,530**

Pier, 1835, mahogany, black marble top, frieze drawer with center ormolu mount, monopodial supports, plinth base, 42" w, 16" d, 36" h .. **1,700**

Sewing, second quarter 19th C, mahogany, square lift lid top, interior with fourteen compartments, turned standard with scrolled supports, square carved base, four scrolled feet, 29¼" h **1,760**

LOUIS PHILIPPE (1830–1848)

History: Louis Philippe reigned as King of France from 1830 to 1848. The era had three distinct characteristics that influenced furniture design: a strong romanticism inspired by renewed interest in the Orient; increased economic wealth among the bourgeoise; and the maturing of the French Industrial Revolution.

The last vestiges of the Empire design style gave way to furniture that incorporated Rococo and Renaissance design elements. Much of the design was anonymous. In addition, reliance on industrial production meant that design interpretation occurred over a wide quality range.

Louis Philippe abidicated in 1848, leading to the formation of the Second Empire.

Armoire, 1850
Burl Elm, double doors, straight grained uprights and cross members, carved apron, stylized paw feet, shrinkage gaps in panels, 44" w, 24" d, 80" h **6,500**

Pine, projecting molded cornice, two paneled doors, painted interior with shelves over two aligned drawers and two paneled cupboard doors, bracket feet, 52" w, 20" d, 98" h **1,600**

Chair, arm, pair, walnut, carved crest rail over upholstered back and seat, scrolled arms, round tapering saber legs, price for pair **2,800**

Commode
1830–45, bombe, black marble top, three drawers, satinwood geometric parquet panels, walnut banding, bronze mountings, marble top repaired, 45" w, 20" d, 33½" h **5,900**

1875, mahogany, shaped marble top, fluted cylindrical body, 14" d, 31" h **1,600**

Desk
Burl walnut and ebonized wood, gilt metal mounted decorations, Sevres porcelain portrait and floral plaques, mirrored niche flanked by two doors, rectangular top with three frieze drawers, leather pull-out writing surface, shelf stretcher and mirrored back, 53" w, 21½" d, 59" h **5,225**

Burl walnut and marquetry, lady's, mirrored center section flanked by three short drawers, lower section

Secretaire, pine, rectangular top, paneled apron with one drawer, tapering reeded legs, 54½" w, 27½" d, 28" h, $1,900.00. Photograph courtesy of Leslie Hindman Auctioneers.

Secretaire Abattant, 19th C, walnut, projecting cornice, single drawer over a fall front writing surface, three drawers, turned feet, 40″ w, 20″ d, 65″ h, $1,450.00. Photograph courtesy of Leslie Hindman Auctioneers.

with one drawer, cabriole legs, gilt bronze sabots, 36″ w, 23″ d, 48″ h	2,310
Secretary	
1830, mahogany, serpentine top, foliate gilt metal mounted edge, bombe form door, sides with landscape marquetry, single door, fitted interior, valanced niche with oval mirror, two banks of foliate marquetry drawers, three short drawers, angled cabriole legs with rocaille decoration, acanthus sabots, 26″ w, 55″ h	6,000
1840, walnut, projecting cornice, single drawer, fall front writing surface, three drawers, turned feet, 40″ w, 20″ d, 65″ h	1,300
Stand, music, mid 19th C, mahogany, adjustable candleholders and height, tripod formed as human legs, 50″ h extended	2,860
Table	
Center, late 19th C, ebonized wood, gilt bronze mounted decorations, shaped rectangular top with inset	

engraved brass central floral medallion, single frieze drawer, cabriole legs, 52″ w, 30″ d, 30″ h ...	1,320
Dressing, mid 19th C, Boulle, shaped brass and lacquer inlaid hinged top, dressing mirror, fitted interior over two drawers, cabriole legs, gilt bronze chutes and sabots, signed "R. Caster," 28″ w, 19″ d, 29″ h ..	2,200
Writing	
Gilt and ebonized wood, shaped rectangular top, three frieze drawers, cabriole legs, 51″ w, 26″ d, 30″ h	825
Pine, rectangular top, paneled apron, tapering reeded legs, 54½″ w, 27½″ d, 28″ h	1,700

SECOND EMPIRE (1848–1870)

History: Louis Philippe became president of the Second Empire in 1848; in 1852 he was made Emporer, reigning as Napoleon III. Interest in Renaissance and Rococo design elements continued. France's prosperity is reflected in furniture that is opulent and often blends a variety of design elements from different historical periods.

France became a leader in the arts during the period of the Second Empire. The principal interpreter was the Ecole des Beaux–Arts.

The Second Empire in France corresponds closely with the Late Biedermeier period in Germany. As in America, it was an eclectic period, dominated by numerous romantic revivals. The typical bourgeois home of the period featured over–stuffed seating and ornately carved woodwork.

Leading Designer: Viollet le Duc.

Note: During this period skilled French craftsmen began copying eighteenth century pieces, utilizing many of the same tools and techniques of their historic counterparts. The work of these craftsmen is easily confused with similar pieces made over a hundred years earlier.

Armoire, 1860, walnut, deeply molded projecting cornice, long recessed paneled door, chamfered and paneled sides, shaped block feet, 36″ w, 22″ d, 90″ h	900
Bed, pair, brass and gilt bronze, arched crest, center foliate medallion above spindles, twin size, 52″ w, price for pair of headboards	1,300
Cabinet	
Boulle, ebonized, rectangular marble top with outset corners, two doors, elaborate brass design, 46″ w, 17″ d, 43″ h	1,980
Walnut and parcel gilt, foliate scrolling decoration, pair of mirrored	

Side Cabinet, late 19th C, rectangular inset black marble top above two doors each mounted with a classical figure in high relief, various gilt bronze ormolu dec motifs, raised on short block feet, 49¾" w, 14½" d, 38" h, $4,250.00. Photograph courtesy of Leslie Hindman Auctioneers.

Cabinet on Stand, walnut and parcel gilt, glass doors, third quarter 19th C, 43" w, 24½" d, 94½" h, $3,400.00. Photograph courtesy of Skinner, Inc.

shaped doors, conforming marble top stand, 43" w, 24½" d, 94½" h	3,400
Chair, 19th C, arm, mahogany, scrolled tablet crest rail, upholstered backrest, down scrolled dolphin armrests, straight seat rail with upholstered seat, square tapered scrolled support, brown leather upholstery	1,430
Chest of Drawers, mahogany, sliding and telescopic coffered top, fitted interior, four drawers, molded plinth base, teardrop pulls, 31" w	1,650
Commode	
Painted, variegated marble top, serpentine front, bombe base, two drawers with painted vines and flowers, ormolu pulls and mountings, stamped with seal and "V. B.," 35¾" w	2,860
Walnut, rectangular marble top, single drawer, single cupboard door faced with faux drawers, 15" w, 12" d, 33½" h	200
Desk, burl walnut, shaped paneled fall front, leather lined writing surface bordered by tulipwood, inlaid brass lines, 55" w	2,450
Floor Screen, late 19th C, five panels, giltwood, painted scenes by Georges Antoine Rochegrosse, each panel 27½" w, 100" h	22,000
Mirror, pier, gesso and giltwood, scrolled and mask crest, arched mirror plate with molded frame, 29" w, 70" h	900
Secretary	
Boulle, serpentine marble top, con-	

Canape, beechwood and parcel gilt, shaped crest above curved arms, bowed seat above shaped apron, cabriole legs, 71″ l, $450.00. Photograph courtesy of Leslie Hindman Auctioneers.

Writing Desk, gilt bronze mounted burl walnut, ebonized, Sevrés porcelain portrait and floral plaques, upper section with mirrored niche flanked by two doors, rectangular top with three frieze drawers, central section with leather pull out writing surface, lower section with shelf stretcher and mirrored back, 53″ w, 21½″ d, 59″ h, $5,225.00. Photograph courtesy of William Doyle Galleries.

forming case, fall front writing surface, interior standish and two drawers, four drawers, bracket feet, 21½″ w, 13″ d, 49″ h	**2,600**
Fruitwood, burl maple, kingwood, and ebony marquetry, gilt metal mounted decorations, rectangular white marble top, serpentine front, long frieze drawer, fall front with central urn marquetry medallion, flanked by disengaged fluted and gilt metal mounted columns above plinth, interior valanced cubbyhole and rectangular velvet writing surface, three long drawers with foliate and trophy marquetry, toupie feet, 33″ w, 56½″ h	**3,575**
Settee, beechwood and parcel gilt, shaped crest, curved arms, bowed seat, shaped apron, cabriole legs, 71″ l	**400**
Table, writing, third quarter 19th C, kingwood and parquetry, shaped rectangular top, frieze drawer, tapering saber legs, sabot feet, 29½″ l, 17″ d, 26½″ h	**2,310**

THIRD EMPIRE (1870–1940)

History: The furniture design traditions that dominated the Second Empire remained strong during the first three decades of the Third Empire. In fact, these late nineteenth century revival designs continued to be popular with large segments of the bourgeois throughout the Third Empire. New design styles such as Art Nouveau and Art Deco did occur, but never achieved the popularity of the more traditional nineteenth century pieces.

Art Nouveau marked a return to nature as an inspiration for design form. Graceful, flowing curves dominated. The movement showed its greatest strength in France in the cities of Paris and Nancy. In Paris, Samuel Bing's Maison de L'Art Nouveau introduced the work of some of France's most talented designers, e.g., Georges de Feure, Edward Colonna, and Eugene Gaillard. In 1898 Julius Meier–Graefe opened his La Maison Moderne, introducing Paris to the work of Abel Landry, Paul Follot, and Maurice Dufrene. This latter group provided the inspiration for the transition to the Art Deco period.

Nancy's claim to fame rests with the work of Emile Galle, better known for his ceramic and glass designs than for his furniture. The extensive use of marquetry decoration marked many of his pieces. In 1901 Galle founded the Ecole de Nancy, training ground for designers such as Louis Majorelle, Eugene Vallin and Jacques Gruber.

The Arts and Crafts movement appears to have had little effect in France. While the seeds of modernism were being sown in Austria, England, Germany, the Netherlands, and the United States, France turned its attention to the Art Deco movement. After a lengthy transition, made even longer by the intervention of World War I, the style reached its zenith at the 1925 Paris Exposition Internationale des Arts Decoratifs et Industriels Modernes. Its more disciplined, restrained, and classical style provided a sharp contrast to Art Nouveau. It also marked France's answer to the growing modernism movement outside its borders.

French Art Deco exhibits a strong feminine image of luxury and refinement. As such, it achieved its finest expression in furniture designed for the salon and boudoir. Exotic materials, ranging from novel veneers to lacquer, were utilized.

The transition from Art Nouveau to Art Deco was lead by Follot, Dufrene and Francis Jourdain. Leading designers include Emile–Jacques Ruhlmann, Louis Sue and Andre Mare (Compagnie des Arts Francais), Andre Groult, and Clement Mere. Ruhlmann clearly dominated the era. Several key design groups include Decoration Inerieure Moderne (DIM), Dominique, and Salon des Artistes–Decorateurs. Among the foreign craftsmen who came to Paris was Jean Dunand, who did much to revive the use of Oriental lacquers.

The United States' Wall Street crash of 1929 brought an end to the Art Deco movement. Modernism came to France through the work of Le Corbusier, the Union Des Artistes Modernes (U.A.M.), and Eileen Gray. A turning point piece was Le Courbsier and Charlotte Perriand's 1928–29 chaise lounge. In 1930, Helene Henry, Rene Herbst, Francis Jourdain, Robert Mallet–Stevens, and Raymond Templier founded U.A.M. The group emphasized the practical over the decorative. Regular exhibitions of their work were held. The end result was the acceptance of International Modernism as a major design style.

France experienced a series of design revivals during the later half of the 19th C. All earlier design styles were copied. Liege Rococo vitrine, walnut, arched projecting *rocaille* carved cornice above an arched glazed door and sides above a rectangular glazed door and cartouche carved apron, raised on scroll feet, 57" w, 81" h, $1,320.00. Photograph courtesy of Butterfield & Butterfield.

Bed, carved and gilded wood, massive scrolled headboard and footboard, shaped scrolled sides with strapwork molding, 77" w, 89" l **9,000**
Bibliotheque, c1900, mahogany, breakfront outline, cornice molded shaped top, frieze with elaborate gilt bronze

classical maidens decoration, two glazed doors flanked by cupboard doors with gilt bronze wreaths, plinth base, 78" w, 67" h **3,850**

Desk, Bonheur du Jour, 1900, tulipwood and parquetry, bowed rectangular top, gold tooled brown leather writing surface, arched superstructure incorporating clock with white enamel face, spring released cupboards with faux book spines, three drawers, scalloped apron with drawer, cabriole legs ending in gilt metal cartouche sabots, 27" w, 41½" h **2,200**

Stand, pedestal, gilt metal mounted kingwood and tulipwood marquetry, square marble top with molded serpentine sides, bombe form standard, crossbanded sides with central ribbon tied foliate marquetry, flanked by gilt metal mounted foliate and C–scroll casting, acanthus scroll feet, 13½" d, 51" h **3,000**

Table
 Center
  Gilt bronze mounted Sevres porcelain circular top, painted with half length portrait of Louis XVI, bleu du roi ground, foliate and floral chased broad gilt border inset with oval porcelain plaques of court beauties, ring turned ebonized standard supported by openwork scrolled brackets, tri-

form base, restored, 29¼" d, 31½" h **6,000**

Mahogany, early 20th C, oval white marble top, pierced gilt metal mounted edge, four square tapered legs with gilt metal mounted female heads, X–form stretcher with urn shape finial center, gilt metal paw feet, 34" w   **1,750**

Console, 1910–20, pair, Art Deco influence, wrought iron, scalloped shape outline surmounted by shaped St. Anne marble top, swelling frieze, center open tendrils, openwork slender tapering columns headed by ball finials, ball feet, later painted green, 38¾" l, 30½" h, price for pair **3,575**

Library, 1900, Regency influence, kingwood, gilt metal mounts, rectangular brown simulated leather writing surface, kingwood surrounds, gilt metal edge with rocaille clasps, single long drawer flanked by two short drawers, cabriole legs headed with espagnolettes ending in scroll acanthus sabots, 63" l, 31" h **5,500**

Pedestal, late 19th C, mahogany, circular gray and white mottled marble top, molded border, lobed baluster form standard, three acanthus carved cabriole legs, animal paw feet, 38¼" d, 29½" h **1,760**

GERMAN

History: "Germanic Speaking" would be a more accurate title for this section. The furniture and design style movements in this section cover a wide geographic region that encompasses modern day Germany, Austria, and parts of Poland, France, and Switzerland.

Germany as a nation state did not exist in the eighteenth century and during much of the nineteenth century. The region consisted of numerous independent principalities, city states, and fiefdoms controlled by foreign governments. Complicating matters was religious division, Catholicism versus Protestantism, and distinct geographic differences between the northern and southern regions. Alliances shifted on a regular basis. A strong sense of competition existed between all parties.

Competing rulers and ruling families expressed their individuality by looking to different sources for leadership in taste and style. In the eighteenth century, the principal design influences were French and Italian. English influences gained favor as the eighteenth century came to a close.

High design styles from England, France, and Italy were constantly tempered by the Germanic love of the Gothic and Baroque, and a rich rural tradition, based in part upon Scandinavian influences in the northern region and Roman influences in the southern region.

Italian furniture design had a strong influence on German furniture design. These Italian Rococo mid-18th C encoignures exhibit a design conservatism that hallmarks German furniture from the late 18th through the late 19th C. These walnut wall cabinets have a triangular cross section, molded serpentine front, full paneled cupboard door, later cabriole legs, measure 25″ w, 18″ d, 37″ h, and realized $2,860.00 for the pair. Photograph courtesy of William Doyle Galleries.

Massiveness is the one characteristic, more than any other, which dominated all German furniture, regardless of period. German pieces are solid, built to last for several generations. When decorative elements, e.g., moldings, are used, they are emphasized. Rectilinear forms are preferred. Finally, Germans loved wood and wood grain. The best pieces exhibit a harmony between grain and form.

The period of greatest German influence in furniture design occurred between 1890 and 1935. The Art Nouveau *Jugendstil* movement coupled with a strong interest in the British Arts and Crafts movement set the stage for Modernism whose design principles have shaped most contemporary furniture design. Vienna (Wein), Dresden, and Weimar were the principal design centers. Bauhaus is the name best known to American collectors and dealers, but the movement was broad and included a number of key architect and designer groups. Berlin remained a bastion for the more traditional Biedermeier designs.

The rise of National Socialism brought an end to the Bauhaus and other "modernistic" design schools. Many of the teachers and students worked their way to England and the United States. As a result, Germanic furniture design became truly international in scope.

Following World War II, Germany failed to regain the leadership role in furniture design that it held during the first third of the twentieth century. The division of Germany was partially responsible.

ROCOCO (1730–1790)

History: Eighteenth century German cabinet-makers were strongly influenced by the Rococo styles of Louis XV that spread to Germany through Belgium and Lorraine. Leading architects Francois de Cuvilles and Georg Knobelsdorff introduced the style in Bavaria. The French manner dominated. In fact, the importation of French-made pieces was quite common during this period.

German Rococo is identified by unrestrained fantasy. The term excessive can be applied to many of the pieces. Carvings became sculptural

as pieces were embellished with birds, flowers, fruits, garden tools, and musical instruments. Much of the carving was elaborately gilded.

The divided nature of Germany encouraged competition between the residents of palaces in the north, the south, and along the Rhine. Some of the best work originated in Wurzburg and Mainz. Brightly painted carved furniture is indicative of Bavaria and Austria.

Although the Rococo influence lasted until the end of the eighteenth century, its influence was challenged as early as the 1760s by the neo–classic revival.

Bureau Bookcase, attributed to Peter Schuss, c1763, walnut, fruitwood marquetry, and parcel gilt, ormolu, brass, and gilt metal mounted decorations, slant front, $500,000.00.

PERIOD

Armoire, South German, 18th C, walnut, massive arched molded cornice, pair of doors with beveled and crossbanded raised panels within ogee molded frame, molded plinth, 70" w, 28" d, 90" h **3,190**

Cabinet

Fruitwood, mid 18th C, rectangular top with fielded parquetry panels, pair of doors with parquetry birds decoration within scrolling inlay borders, fitted interior, 16½" w, 11¼" d, 13½" h **825**

Walnut, 18th C, scrolling heavy molded open pediment, gilded bronze cartouche plate center, pair of arched doors with fielded panels, marquetry court ladies' figures,

basal molded and conforming stand, shaped apron, cabriole legs, 46" w, 19½" d, 71½" h **4,500**

Chest of Drawers, South German, first half 18th C, walnut, parquetry, rectangular top, S–curved canted lid, interior with stepped drawer centering well and slide, three banks of drawers with crossbow outline, bracket feet, 43½" w, 26½" d, 48" h **3,100**

Commode

First half 18th C, South German, walnut, oblong molded top, reverse serpentine front, conforming case, three long drawers, broadly crossbanded, quarter and chevron veneered panels, bun feet, 49" w, 27½" d, 32½" h **5,225**

Mid 18th C, South German, walnut, oblong molded top, reverse serpentine front, conforming case, three long drawers with chevron parquetry panels, molded base, bun feet, 49½" w, 27" d, 34" h **4,950**

1770, walnut and parquetry, serpentine top, conforming case, three drawers, cabriole legs, 51" w, 23½" d, 34½" h **23,100**

Desk, mid 18th C, walnut, oblong molded top with three quarter gallery, canted lid with marquetry roses panel, stepped drawer interior, full serpentine frieze drawer, cabriole legs, 46½" w, 23" d, 41½" h **2,200**

Table

Card, third quarter 18th C, carved mahogany, hinged top with serpentine edge, green baize lined playing surface, serpentine apron, cabriole legs **2,000**

Console

Pine, mid 18th C, rectangular top, pierced and acanthus carved bowed frieze with drop pierced pendant, carved cabriole legs ending with waterfall, square ovolo carved block feet, missing top, 31" w, 18" d, 32" h **3,300**

Giltwood, rectangular top, shaped foliate pierced apron with carved acanthus leaves, C–scrolls, and rocaille, carved cabriole legs, scrolled feet on shaped supports, missing top, 42" w, 28" d, 34" h **7,700**

Tea, early 18th C, shaped top with molded edge, overall chinoiserie figures on pale yellow ground, tilt top, pierced baluster form standard carved with acanthus and husk swags, scrolled feet joined by platform stretcher with center pineapple finial, 38" w, 32" h **4,950**

STYLE

Canterbury, carved mahogany, scrolling
brass trim, hinged lid on seat **1,200**
Chair, set of ten, two arm, eight side,
slightly arched back, square seat,
scroll and shell carved seat rails,
molded foliate carved cabriole legs,
wavy cruciform stretchers, yellow floral upholstery on back and seat, price
for set **3,850**
Mirror, mantel, giltwood, pierced
carved cartouche, shaped rectangular
mirror plate, scroll carved frame, gilt
losses, 53" l, 42" h **770**
Settee, walnut, upholstered serpentine
back, out scrolling arms, loose upholstered cushion seat, scalloped
apron, cabriole legs, scroll feet,
cream silk upholstery, 72" l **990**
Sideboard, carved, marble top, marquetry and parquetry panels, 77½" l ... **1,600**
Table
　Center, late 19th C, serpentine top
　with central foliate marquetry med-
　allion and gilt metal gadrooned
　edge, scalloped frieze with drawer,
　cabriole legs, 41" l, 30½" h **1,980**
　Dining, scalloped rectangular faux
　verde antico marble top, molded
　edge, rocaille carved scalloped
　frieze, cabriole legs with car-
　touche, scroll feet, includes five
　leaves, 183" l extended, 30½" h . **2,200**
　Game, late 19th C, burl walnut, ser-
　pentine swivel top with thumb
　molded edge, foliate marquetry
　borders, green baize playing sur-
　face, four baluster turned supports,
　down scrolled legs, 38" l, 29" h .. **1,210**
　Writing, mid 19th C, walnut, serpen-
　tine edged rectangular top, outset
　rounded corners, frieze fitted with
　long drawer, cabriole legs, scrolled
　feet, 58" w, 30" h **2,475**

GERMAN NEO-CLASSICISM (circa 1760–1800) and EMPIRE (circa 1800–1815)

History: The English and French design styles of
the late eighteenth century introduced the classic
influence to Germany. German pieces most
closely copied the proportions and austerity of
the French with one major exception—a greater
use of ornamentation.
　The style was largely urban. In the countryside,
Rococo continued to dominate. Once English
Hepplewhite and Sheraton influences entered the

German furniture vocabulary, classic design
pieces gained some popular acceptance.
　During the Napoleonic era, German furniture
follows the classic forms in a very light, graceful
manner. Furniture forms exhibit a livable, human
quality. Excessive ornamentation is avoided.
Smooth veneer surfaces of light mahogany, ash,
cherry, pear, and poplar are popular. In certain
sections, painted furniture enjoyed a revival.

Major Craftsman: David Roentgen.

PERIOD

Chair
　Set
　　Set of Four, 1825, burled walnut,
　　upholstered backs cresting in leaf
　　carved volutes, terminating in
　　scrolls, highly figured seat rail,
　　saber legs, 36" h, price for set of
　　four **600**
　　Set of Six, side, late 18th C, walnut,
　　slightly curved rectangular back,
　　leaf tip carved frame, crest cen-
　　tered by carved acanthus, slightly
　　bowed seat raised on acanthus
　　carved stop–fluted tapering cy-
　　lindrical legs, price for set of six **5,000**
　Side, late 18th C
　　Satinwood, inlaid, reticulated rec-
　　tangular crest rail above rectan-
　　gular splat pierced with arch and
　　diamond panels, flared seat, ta-
　　pering square legs, inlaid overall
　　with pen work masks, husk pen-
　　dants, and foliate scrolls, minor
　　restoration **900**
Daybed, Italian, late 18th C, walnut,
deep paneled sides with channel
molded frieze supporting turned and
tapering ebonized leaf carved column
at front, square fluted back pilaster,
turned finial with stamped brass knop,
inverted turned vasiform feet joined
by channel–molded rails, 76" w, 66"
h **3,200**
Mantel, Italian, last quarter 18th C, parcel–gilt and painted, rectangular out
stepped white faux marble shelf over
faux Sienna marble frieze, carved gilt
foliate vine centered by mask, tapering jambs headed by rams' heads,
molded plinth base, paint of later
date, 100½" w, 53" h **16,500**
Mirror
　Pier, mid 19th C, painted and parcel
　gilt, rectangular molded cornice
　over applied lion mask, foliate dec-
　oration above rectangular mirror
　plate, flanked by pair of pilasters,
　33" w, 75½"h **2,200**

Chairs, side, early 19th C, bowed crest rail with stepped rounded terminals and gilt stenciled with scrolling foliage, cross-rail composed of interlaced pointed ovals with gilt-line dec, flared slightly serpentine seat, sharply tapering square supports with gilt-line dec, repainted, price for set of eight, $5,000.00. Photograph courtesy of Butterfield & Butterfield.

Wall, giltwood, rectangular frame, eagle crest, 23½" w, 41" h 715

Stand, Italian, 19th C, pair, painted, square faux marble top and out stepped yellow painted cornice above square shaft, grisalle cartouche within black painted diamond reserve on yellow painted ground above molded and out stepped faux marble base, yellow paint of a later date, losses and rubbing to paint, 13¼" w, 28½" h, price for pair 1,500

Table

Center, inlaid walnut, rectangular top, inlaid central scrolled cartouche within banded reserves, apron inlaid with octagonal medallions flanked by foliate swags and Greek key borders, tapering square legs of a later date, 57¼" w, 31½" h 4,400

Console, painted green and gold, oblong molded rose marble top, conforming frieze carved with panel of laurel leaves within dies, straight tapered fluted legs, 39½" w, 19½" d, 32½" h 1,500

Dressing, 1840, mahogany, rectangular white marble top, surmounted by oval mirror raised on swan's neck supports, 59" h 1,200

Serving, early 19th C, rosewood, oblong white marble top, gilt bronze Greek key fretwork border, recessed shelf, conforming base, door with mounted porcelain Roman riverscape roundel, Neo–Egyptian term figures, turned legs,

gilt bronze fretted border, 24½" w, 13" d, 44½" h 30,000

STYLE

Bench, painted ivory, oval cushioned top, fluted frieze, collared fluted square tapering supports, tapered feet, 18" l 350

Cabinet, side, 19th C, pair, walnut and parcel gilt, rectangular cornice of conjoined octagons, molded frieze, conforming case with full sunken panel door of cast brass musical putto, ebonized colonettes, splayed legs, 31½" w, 14½" d, 35" h, price for pair 3,100

Chair

Arm, 19th C, pair, parcel–gilt and cream painted, arched crest rail above pierced foliate splat centered by oval portrait medallion, rectangular arms, caned seat, tapering square legs, repairs, price for pair 2,750

Side, pair, painted and gilt carved wood, lyre shaped back, price for pair 1,100

Mirror, reverse painted, vertical mirror plate, pastel Grecian figures on pedestals, overhanging tree, plant filled garden with center fountain, unframed, chip to upper left hand corner, 53" w, 56" h 800

Table

Console and matching mirror, table: rectangular faux marble top, foliate scroll carved frieze, central mask flanked by patera, square tapering supports; mirror: rectangular mirror plate set within green painted and parcel gilt surround, flanked by masks and leaf tip subsidiary border; table: 45½" w, 34½" h; mirror: 29" w, 52" h; price for two mirrors and two matching tables **1,950**

Side, 1900, pair, carved silver giltwood, glazed floral fabric inset top, rosette and acanthus carved frieze, fluted baluster supports, arching stretchers, ball feet, 14" d, 18¼" h, price for pair **1,000**

BIEDERMEIER (1800–1880)

History: During the first third of the nineteenth century, German furniture closely followed the forms of French Empire. It found its strongest admirers among the lesser nobility and growing bourgeois.

Furniture from this era takes its name from Papa Biedermeier, a comic paper character identified for his homeliness and *Gemutlichkeit*. This middle class idol expressed his political and other views in *Fliegende Blatter*.

The ability of the Germans to copy and adapt French designs varied greatly. Local materials and skills resulted in sophisticated pieces as often as those with naive proportions and techniques. Classical flora occasionally resembles more familiar vegetable forms. Elaborately carved details are captured in paint.

Favored woods included ash, beech, birch, fruitwood such as apple and pear, maple, and walnut, albeit a large amount of furniture was made of mahogany or utilized mahogany veneer. Seating furniture often featured large amounts of upholstery in horsehair, clico, and rep.

Although some Gothic elements appeared on German furniture during the 1840s, the country escaped the influence of the Gothic revival. It did yield to the Renaissance and Rococo revivals. In fact, by the 1870s, German furniture was every bit as eclectic as that in England, France, and the United States.

As the nineteenth century neared its end, Biedermeier furniture was viewed as the "old fashioned" look, a design style with which the vast majority of the populace felt comfortable.

Reference: Dominic R. Stone, *The Art of Biedermeier Viennese Art and Design, 1815 to 1845,* Chartwell Books, 1990.

Armoire, 1830–45, Scandinavia, burl ash, pine secondary wood, two doors over two drawers, ebony escutcheons, square feet, minor cove molding replacements, 66" w, 24" d, 85" h   **12,000**

Box, sewing, musical, 1830, walnut, ebony and fruitwood inlay, rectangu-

Secretaire Abattant, 19th C, mahogany, ormolu mounted columns, fall front, lid opens to reveal an arched interior with columns, fitted with five drawers and two secret drawers, the lower case with a pair of cupboard doors fitted with a drawer, 37" w, 16" d, 54½" h, $1,760.00. Photograph courtesy of Neal Auction Company.

lar form, crossbanding and central decoration of man and woman in landscape, hinged lid, mirrored interior with arched colonnade and brick design, inlaid covered sewing compartments and implements, two musical mechanisms, 13¾" w, 10½" d, 5" h **1,900**

Cabinet, display, c1820, fruitwood and parcel ebony, top with fretwork gallery of interlacing pointed arches, pair of multi–panel glazed and paneled doors, shallow raised stiles, splayed shaped legs, 37½" w, 75" h **3,300**

Chair

Arm, second quarter 19th C, broad bowed crest rail, lyre shaped splat, slightly curved arms, machine tapestry upholstered seat, splayed square legs **465**

Set of Four

1820–30, fruitwood, rounded and reticulated key shape back, flaring straight front loose seat, tapered square legs, price for set .   **4,125**

Secretary Bookcase, drop front, Biedermeier Style, fruitwood, shaped and molded cornice above mirrored double doors, hinged rectangular drop front reveals drawers and cubby holes, two aligned drawers over double cabinet doors on bracket feet, 42″ w, 22″ d, 80″ h, $1,000.00. Photograph courtesy of Leslie Hindman Auctioneers.

Second quarter 19th C, walnut, curved back, pierced splat, upholstered seat, square tapered legs, 33½″ h, price for set **1,980**

Side, second quarter 19th C
Burl maple, shaped rectangular back, turned legs **200**
Burl walnut, minor losses, restoration, 38¾″ h **425**

Chest of Drawers, 1830, mahogany, tablet top above projecting beveled edge, three long drawers of unequal depth, block feet, 39½″ w, 32½″ h . **1,450**

Commode
1820, walnut and parcel ebony, rectangular top with beveled ebonized edge, projected frieze with drawer, two long drawers below flanked by ebonized and parcel gilt monopo-

dial pilasters with female Egyptian heads, splayed short legs, 45¾″ w, 32¼″ h **6,050**
1830, highly figured walnut, rectangular marble top, top with single drawer, base with three drawers, shield shaped escutcheons, straight apron, short bracket feet **1,800**
1840, North German or Scandinavian, pearwood, three drawers, shaped apron and feet, 35″ w, 20″ d, 31″ h **1,800**
Second quarter 19th C, mahogany, serpentine tablet top, three drawers, square scrolled legs, 26½″ w, 32″ h **770**

Desk
1825, fruitwood, cylinder top surmounted by three quarter gallery fretwork of interlacing pointed arches, two drawers flanking recess and pullout writing slide and three canted drawers on each side of interior, two long drawers, shaped square legs, ebonized feet, 45¾″ w, 49″ h **4,125**
1830, fruitwood and ebony, rectangular top, cylinder front opening, three compartments and drawers, sliding tooled leather writing surface over two long drawers, square tapering legs, 44¾″ w, 24¼″ d, 45″ h **8,500**

Mirror
1820, fruitwood and parcel ebony, crest with glazed gilded bas relief of classical sacrificial scene, cavetto molded ebonized upper and lower border, vertical mirror plate, glazed gilded panel of foliage spray, issuing from medallion on bottom, worn ebony on lower border, 14¾″ w, 56″ h **1,320**
1820, walnut and parcel gilt, projected triangular pediment, paneled entablature below with applied gilt metal foliage sprays and flowers, shallow pilasters with gilded foliate capitals below, two section vertical mirror plate, block ends on bottom with gilt flower medallions, 29¼″ w, 60″ h **2,090**
1825, mahogany, architectural pediment with center jasperware floral medallion, rectangular mirror plate, 23″ w, 66″ h **715**
1830, mahogany, vertical two section plate beneath a panel frieze and cavetto molded cornice, slightly projecting apron, rolled molded base, 24″ w, 60″ h **875**
1875, fruitwood, arched pediment,

Secretary, second quarter 19th C, fall front, ebonized and parcel gilt mahogany, ormolu mounted decorations, $50,000.00.

rectangular panel and mirror plate, 15" w, 28" h 375

Secretary

Mid 19th C, walnut, two sections: upper section: shallow triangular pediment, pair paneled doors; lower section: sloping fall front, plain fitted interior, three long drawers, square block feet, 39½" w, 81¾" h ... 1,870

Second quarter 19th C, mahogany, one piece construction, rectangular tablet top, drop front, maple veneered interior with drawers and pigeonholes, two long drawers, ebonized half rounded column stiles over cavetto molded ebonized plinth, projected arcaded base drawer, shallow block feet, 46" w, 48½" h 3,025

Settee

1830, fruitwood, ebonized string line inlaid back, scrolled ends above convex molded seat rail, profile scroll supports, floral design machine tapestry upholstery, 78" l ... 2,750

Second quarter 19th C, walnut, molded crest rail, upholstered back and seat, open arms, straight legs, 40" l 2,250

Sideboard, second quarter 19th C, ebonized and fruitwood, rectangular slate top, two aligned drawers, ring turned supports, two shaped shelves, turned feet, 53" w, 27½" d, 38" h .. 3,000

Suite, probably Scandinavian, c1830, sofa and two arm chairs, straight broad crest rail, curved ends, straight arms with scroll finials, square tapered legs, ivory and green striped satin upholstery, reinforced rear legs, 57½" l sofa, price for three piece set 9,350

Table

Center

1830, birch and parcel ebony, circular top with ebonized edge, plain frieze, three inswept S–scroll legs joined by circular medial shelf, triform platform base, ebonized shallow block feet, losses and repairs to veneer, 34½" d, 27¾" h 2,750

1830, oval top inset with variegated black marble slab, four inswept molded supports, lotus leaf feet, shaped cruciform platform base, later Sienna finish, 31" l, 27½" h 850

Second quarter 19th C, fruitwood, rectangular top, frieze with fitted long drawer, trestle support, plain stretcher, 62" l, 26½" d, 30¾" h 1,430

Console, 19th C, fruitwood, center backboard, rectangular deep frieze with drawer, canted base, scroll supports, 21" w, 12½" d, 33" h .. 600

Occasional, probably Scandinavian, 1820–30, figured maple, veneered oval top, central drawer, square tapered inswept splayed legs joined by oval medial shelf, one foot repaired, reinforced legs, 32¾" w, 24¾" h 2,475

Side, fruitwood, walnut, and parcel ebony, paneled rectangular top, drawer with ebonized borders, square tapered legs, splits and veneer losses to top and sides, 22" w, 29" h 825

Writing, second quarter 19th C, cherry, rectangular top, deep frieze

Settee, second quarter 19th C, walnut, molded crest, upholstered back, open arms, and seat, straight legs, 40" l, $2,250.00. Photograph courtesy of Leslie Hindman Auctioneers.

with drawer, angled molded S–scrolled tapered legs 37¼" w, 30" h **1,650**

Vitrine

1830, fruitwood, tablet top surmounted by serpentine front structure with fitted drawer, glazed panel door, shelf interior, projected roll molded stiles, conforming sides, apron with line inlaid drawer, shallow turned feet, minor losses to veneers, frieze molding cracks, 36" w, 82" h **4,400**

Early 19th C, fruitwood and ebony, stepped projecting cornice, four glazed panel doors, disengaged columns raised on paneled plinth, block feet, veneer losses, 66" h, 24" w **2,475**

Second quarter 19th C, mahogany, stepped cornice with projecting gadrooned surrounds, line inlaid frieze, arched glazed door flanked by columns with Corinthian capitals, four–shelf interior, drawer, circular feet, 32" w, 64" h **2,200**

REVIVALE (circa 1830–1880)

History: Modern furniture historians now separate the Biedermeier movement into two periods-an early period when French Empire design styles dominated, and a later period when romantic and other revivals held sway. However, much of the furniture literature separates the second period from the first and calls it Revivale.

The Revivale period is marked by the same revivals that influenced English and American design. A multiplicity of design styles occurred simultaneously. Since many developed at the whim of a particular designer, manufacturer, or patron, it is extremely difficult to assign specific beginning and ending dates. The safest approach is to view the latter half of the nineteenth century as a period of eclecticism.

As elsewhere, much of the furniture was mass produced. Wide differences can be found in aesthetics of design and quality of manufacture.

Many of the revivals were limited geographically. Throughout the period, the furniture of the middle class retained the design elements associated with the French Empire and Restauration periods.

Armoire, 19th C, oak, rectangular top with molded cornice, two molded paneled doors and sides, base molding, ball feet, 69" w **2,435**

Chest, walnut and elmwood, rectangular, hinged top, conforming case, architecturally carved front, bun feet, restored, 46½" w, 21½" d, 19" h . . . **1,430**

Cupboard, court, incorporating period and later elements, carved oak, two sections: upper section: projecting scroll carved cushion molded cornice, two elaborately carved cupboard doors centered by similarly carved panel, two long foliate carved drawers, center mask carved panel; lower section: arched open shelf flanked by spiral reeded disengaged columns, four foliate carved panels, plinth base, 56" w, 66" h **2,250**

Sideboard, Renaissance Revival with Neo-Classical themes, c1880, oak, rectangular top inset with black, green, and white striated marble, carved with neoclassical motifs including dolphin and female heads, 75" w, 27¼" d, 47¾" h, $3,000.00. Photograph courtesy of Neal Auction Company.

Rocker, c1850, walnut, upholstered back with brass tack trim surmounted by carved mythological animals, shaped arms, upholstered seat, carved mythological animals between arms and runners, two spindle turned stretchers 2,350

Secretary, 19th C, walnut, rectangular molded top, fall front writing surface, three valanced pigeonholes and small

Bookcase, Rococo Revival, c1870, ebonized oak, upper section with a carved cornice above an egg and dart molding over a frieze with applied floral and leaf molding, two large beveled glass doors flanked by carved columns and curved glass sides, lower section with wreath carved edge and a central double door cupboard carved with musical instruments, curved sides with applied carving in form of basket of fruit and flowers surrounded by branches and a ribbon wreath, 95" w, 21½" d, 110½" h, $6,600.00. Photograph courtesy of Neal Auction Company.

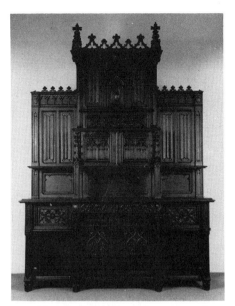

Sideboard, Gothic Revival, c1850, oak, central cornice dec with trefoils and crockets, back with linen fold carving with a central double door cupboard, base with two frieze drawers over two cupboard doors flanked by two hinged compartments, Gothic arch and trefoil ornaments above all doors, 82" w, 22" d, 116" h, $3,500.00. Photograph courtesy of Neal Auction Company.

drawers interior, two long drawers, square feet, 41½" w **1,400**

Table, library, 19th C, mahogany, circular gray St. Anne marble top enclosed by pierced bronze border, conforming frieze with Mercury masks, straight supports enriched by bronze caducei, incurvate triangular base, 31½" d, 28½" h **1,200**

Vitrine, mid 19th C, walnut and burl walnut, arched door, fitted interior with shelves, 35" w, 15¼" d, 74" h . **525**

JUGENDSTIL/MODERNISM (circa 1880–1920)

History: French– and Belgium–influenced Art Nouveau's exuberant curvilinear styles did not gain wide acceptance in Germany and Austria where designers favored a more rational, rectilinear approach. The elements of the modernistic movement were in place by the end of the nineteenth century.

The German and Austria design movements of the late nineteenth and early twentieth centuries are cries for reform in furniture design and a resistance to increased mechanization in the furniture industry. The contemporary emphasis on Modernism tends to overshadow the German Art Nouveau movement.

An Art Nouveau style did gain favor with a number of Munich designers including August Endell, Hermann Obrist, Bernhard Pankok and Richard Riemerschmid. The furniture of Endell and Orbist had joints resembling human bones. In Berlin Van de Velde's interiors for the Haby Barbershop and Havana Company Cigar Store mark the epitome of Art Nouveau design.

German Art Nouveau designs reached others through the publication of journals such as *Deutsche Kunst und Dekoration, Dekorative Kunst, Jugend,* and *Pan.* Jugendstil, named for *Jugend,* is another term for German Art Nouveau.

Hermann Muthesius, a German architect and civil servant, published a survey of the British Arts and Crafts movement that laid the groundwork for the development of Modernism. Muthesius objected to the craft emphasis as much as he did to the eclecticism and historicism of German furniture manufacturers. He wanted pure design to dominate. In 1907 he helped establish the Deutscher Werkbund.

German architects and designers quickly formed schools and cooperatives. Three leading institutions are the Vereinigte Deutsche Werkstatten in Munich, the Deutscher Werkbund in Dresden, and the Kunstgewerbeschule in Weimer. The latter group became the Bauhaus in 1919. Membership in the Deutscher Werkbund was by invitation and included among its participants Behrens, Walter Gropius, Josef Hoffmann, Bernard Pankok, Bruno Paul, Richard Riemerschmid, Henry Van de Velde, and Otto Wagner. The group's principal role was to create an active interchange between designers and manufacturers.

Another key center in the evolution to Modernism was Vienna. The Wiener Secession which became the Wiener Werkstatte brought together the talents of Josef Hoffmann, Koloman Moser, and Joseph Olbrich. The group stressed the rectilinear, strongly influenced by Mackintosh. The group was a fertile source for furniture design. In addition to working on designs for luxury furniture, the group worked closely with industrialized furniture manufacturers. Otto Wagner and Adolf Loos also contributed in this area.

World War I temporarily halted the growth in German architectural and furniture design. When the war ended, Walter Gropius became director of the Bauhaus, an institution that brought together in one place the architect, craftsman, designer, painter, and sculptor. Cooperation was the order of the day: a building or a piece of furniture required the joint efforts of all; unity of purpose was critical. The Bauhaus survived from 1919 until 1933.

The Bauhaus produced a number of legendary designers among whom are Josef Albers, Marcel Breuer, Gropius, and Mies van der Rohe. The movement of these individuals from Germany to England to the United States gave Modernism its true international form.

Cabinet
  1899, Henry Van de Velde, folio, rectangular top with lift lid center section, two small paneled cupboard doors above two larger paneled cupboard doors flanked by vertical divided open shelf, carved shaped front bracket feet, square back feet   **3,600**
  1903, W Von Beckerath, Munich, rectilinear style, rectangular projected top, two long cupboard

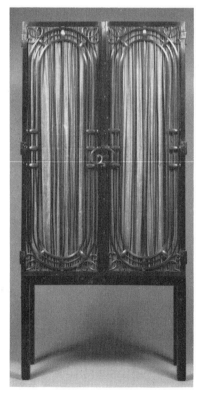

Cabinet, Art Deco, brass and copper, rectangular case having two brass doors with oval borders and scroll pattern corners, faux tortoise shell dec case, straight block legs, 35½″ w, 13″ d, 74″ h, $675.00. Photograph courtesy of Leslie Hindman Auctioneers.

doors on right side, left side with two open shelves above two cupboard doors, top shelf with drapery closure, short square feet   **2,550**
  1910–14, Joseph Hoffmann, stylized graduated stepped form, front faced with mother–of–pearl and ebony inlay, five rows of drawers above two cupboard doors   **1,450**
Chair
  Arm
    1902, Adolf Loos, dining, slightly rounded shaped crest rail continues to arms, slightly curved stiles, solid seat with leather upholstered center with brass tack trim, round tapered legs, H–form stretcher, metal mushroom shape feet   **650**
    1904
      Koloman Moser, straight solid back with figured wood veneer and mother–of–pearl inlay design on back, straight arms with figured wood veneer decoration on ends, solid seat with upholstered center section, straight legs, H–form stretcher, bronze square feet   **1,250**
      Otto Wagner, rounded crest rail continues to arms, decorative metal strip on arms, two slat back, pierced seat, straight front legs, flaring back legs, medial box stretcher, metal pillar type cap feet   **850**
    Reclining, 1905, Josef Hoffmann, straight crest rail with curved ends, square pierced back splat, straight arms terminating in ball pendants, straight arm supports continuing to curved back, pierced section between arm supports, pullout footrest   **1,500**
    Set of Six, Wiener Werkstatte, black stained limed oak, straight crest rail, oval padded back, slightly shaped arms, upholstered seat, square legs, U–shape stretcher base, price for set   **25,340**
    Tub, 1901, Josef Hoffmann, beechwood, mahogany, and aluminum, solid rounded back continuing to sides, molded edge, line of circular devices decoration around back, upholstered seat   **1,750**
Desk, 1904–06, designed by Otto Wager, executed by Gebruder Thonet, stained beechwood and aluminum, rectangular top, beige felt inset writing surface, mounted shelf on back, two short drawers in apron,

round straight legs, side stretchers, front legs with alumunim studs, back panel with row of aluminum studs, 42½" w, 26⅜" d, 43" h **22,000**

Stand, plant, rectangular standard, block legs, 31" w, 11" d, 34" h **200**

Table

Dining

1902, Adolf Loos, rectangular top with edge molding, straight frieze, round tapered legs, X–form stretcher, metal mushroom shape feet **1,650**

Wiener Werkstatte, black stained limed oak, rectangular top, dec-

orated frieze, decorated square legs, H–form stretcher, 88½" l . **2,280**

Occasional, 1903, Josef Hoffmann, oak, square top, four square supports attached to block base, platform base **550**

Vitrine, 1900–10, carved mahogany, center shaped rectangular beveled glass door flanked by rectangular platforms with outset rounded corners, two interior shelves, leafy tendril supports over two glazed cupboard doors, inverted floriform feet, 42" w, 63" h **6,600**

SCANDINAVIAN

History: Beginning in the eighteenth century, Scandinavian nobility copied the design styles of England and Germany. These design elements were blended with the strong native traditions of this largely rural area. Especially favored were the design motives of Louis XV and Rococo England. Painting and carving appeared on many flat areas.

As new styles evolved, the Scandinavian countries adopted and adapted them. Empire, due largely to the patronage of the Bernadotte family, lasted well into the twentieth century.

Knowledge of Scandinavian style in America rests primarily on the twentieth century revivals of its rural furniture. Rural Scandinavian forms blended well with the Arts and Crafts and Modernism movements. Emphasis was placed on craftsmanship, a love of wood, restrained forms, and comfort.

The Scandinavian Arts and Crafts movement stressed the democratization of functional design. Natural woodgrain was emphasized. Furniture was decidedly human in scale. Throughout Scandinavia the furniture industry copied the organizational patterns of the British Arts and Crafts Guilds. In Sweden, the Svenska Slojdsforeningen, and in Norway the Brukskunst, (Applied Arts Association) provided stylistic leadership. Kaare Klint, a Danish designer, exercised great influence during the first third of the twentieth century. The principles of the Scandinavian Arts and Crafts movement remained dominant through the 1920s.

Alvar Aalto, a Finnish architect designer, substituted bent laminated wood in place of tubular metal as a element of modern design. His 1930 laminated birchwood chair for the Paimio Sanatorium project won international acclaim. Aalto and other Scandinavian designers provided a tempering element to the coldness of Bauhaus tubular furniture.

A golden age in Scandinavian design occurred in the 1950s when traditional Scandinavian design forms were mellowed by the addition of discreet luxury features. Carl Malmstem is the father of modern Scandinavian furniture. His goal was to harmonize the demands of function with those of the visual. Bruno Mathsson, who experimented extensively with laminated wood seating furniture, shared his philosophy.

Scandinavian furniture design became increasingly sophisticated during the 1950s. A series of international exhibitions promoted the design.

In Denmark, the firm of Johannes Hansen reproduced the designs of Hans Wegner. Borge Mogensen, who worked for Boligen Byggeskabe, stressed sculptural forms. Finn Juhl utilized sensuous curves for his seating furniture. Hansen produced Arne Jacobsen's "Swan" and "Egg" chairs. Poul Kjaerholm's designs were manufactured by E. Kold Christiensen of Copenhagen as well as Knoll International.

Leading Finnish manufacturers include Artek and Asko Finnternational. Aalto founded Artek in 1935 to manufacture his laminated wood furniture. Finnish manufacturers stressed mass production, occasionally at the expense of the craft tradition. Ilmari Tapiovaara and Antti Nurmesniemi are two leading Finnish contemporary designers. Both design metal furniture for commercial mass production.

Cabinet on Chest, 19th C, Dutch, Baroque, walnut and fruitwood, carved arched pediment, two glazed cupboard doors, bombe case, four graduated drawers, floral inlay, paw feet, 38" w, 22" d, 67" h 4,800

Chair
Arm, pair, late 19th C, Baroque style, upholstered with 17th C Flemish tapestry, 53" h, price for pair 2,750
Set of Six, dining, second quarter 19th C, Neoclassical, birch, bow tie shaped crest rail, beaded horizontal backrest, striped upholstered slip seats, block and ring turned front legs, 34¼" h, price for set of six .. 2,200
Side, pair, Dutch, mid 19th C, walnut marquetry, arched crest rail continuing to form inward scrolled stiles, center baluster form splat, serpentine tapestry upholstered seat and straight apron, slight cabriole legs, price for pair 2,650

Chest of Drawers, c1800, Dutch, Rococo style, mahogany, bombe, rectangular crossbanded top, serpentine molded edge, three short and two long cockbeaded drawers, cavetto molded plinth, shaped bracket feet,

restorations, originally cupboard base, 70" w, 35" h 2,400

Clock, tall case, Dutch
18th C, Johannes Witkamp, Amsterdam, Baroque, walnut, arched glazed door, conforming hooded case, stepped superstructure, waisted case with arched door, paneled base, silvered chapter ring with Roman hours, Arabic minutes, subsidiary date, month, and day of the week aperture, second dial, moon phase, 18¼" w, 9" d, 111" h   4,400
Third quarter 18th C, C Voorhelm, Haarlem, walnut, eight day clock, arched hood centered by carved acanthus cresting over attached half columns, trunk door centered by oval lenticule, crossbanded base above cavetto molded plinth on bun feet, Dutch striking on two bells and alarm, 12¼" square engraved brass dial with silver engine turned arch with moon phases, 117" h 6,600

Dry Sink, pine, shaped crest, rectangular overhanging well, single square door with raised center panel and three concentric molded squares,

Center Table, mahogany marquetry, ivory inlaid, rectangular molded top, frieze drawer, spiral turned legs, X-form stretcher, 37½" w, 25" d, 30¼" h, $4,950.00. Photograph courtesy of Skinner, Inc.

scrolled apron, 27¾" w, 15¾" d, 43" h 475

Kas, mid 17th C, Flemish, Baroque, ebonized and rosewood, projecting ogee molded cornice, cornered and central lion carved mask, pair of raised paneled cupboard doors, paneled long drawer, flaring plinth base, bun feet, restorations, 81" w, 77½" h 4,500

Mirror, Neoclassical, gilt foil and verre eglomise, rectangular, floral urns and columns, minor loss, 24" h 330

Secretary, Dutch, Rococo style, walnut, floral and scrolling marquetry, masks, double dome top, conforming glazed mirrored doors, two candle slides, concave fall front writing surface, richly fitted interior of drawers and pigeonholes, bombe front, three drawers, angled buttress stiles, double banded borders, 76½" h 4,500

Settee
Neoclassical, early 19th C, painted cream, parcel gilt decoration, 70" l, 23" d, 35" h 1,100
Queen Anne, Dutch, 18th C, beechwood, quadruple molded chair back, vasiform splats, serpentine seat, pad feet joined by stretchers, aubusson tapestry upholstery, 73½" l, 38¼" h 1,760

Stand, serving, Dutch, Rococo style, composed of antique elements, molded rectangular lift top, folding two tier shelf, fitted interior, bombe apron with frieze drawer, two slides,

cabriole legs joined by shelf stretcher and drawer with lower slides, interior distressed, 33" w, 32" h 600

Table
Center, Dutch, Baroque style, mahogany, marquetry and ivory inlaid, rectangular molded top, frieze drawer, spiral turned legs joined by shaped stretcher, 37½" w, 25" d, 30¼" h 4,950
Dressing, Dutch, Baroque style, mahogany, marquetry inlaid, oval mirror, shaped rectangular top inlaid with flowering vase and scrolling foliage over shell carved and inlaid recessed drawer, flanked by two banks of small drawers, cabriole legs, claw and ball feet, casters, 31½" w, 19" d, 60" h 1,700
Game, Dutch
19th C, fruitwood marquetry, hinged triangular top inlaid with chessboard and game pieces, floral inlaid square legs, 43" w, 29" d, 29½" h 1,000
Composed of antique elements, Rococo style, carved mahogany, scalloped folding top, fitted interior, undulating apron with frieze drawer, cabriole legs, C–scroll carved knees, claw and ball feet, 28½" w, 29½" h 750
Work, 19th C, Neoclassical, grain painted, rectangular beveled top, canted corners, two frieze drawers, square tapering legs, 32½" w, 29½" h 575

EUROPEAN FOLK FURNITURE

History: Throughout the eighteenth and nineteenth centuries, regionalism played an important role in European geography, politics, religion, and social structure. The evolution of the modern national state in the mid–nineteenth century subdued regionalism, but never destroyed it. In many areas, it remains a strong challenge to the central government.

It is difficult for many Americans to understand the fierce regional loyalty of the Europeans. Those in New England and the South have some sense, but lack the communal unity that typifies European regionalism. In the United States, you are an American first and resident of your state second. In many parts of Europe, you are a resident of your locale first and a citizen of the nation second.

It makes sense to divide European folk furniture into two main groups: rural and village furniture, i.e., generic furniture; and furniture that exhibits strong regional characteristics in its carved or painted decoration. It is the second group that is best known by American collectors. Painted furniture from the Scandinavian countries, Alsace, Bavaria, Saxony and the Oberlautiz, Schwarzwald, and Czechoslovakia, was often confused with and passed as Pennsylvania German pieces by unscrupulous dealers. It is collected in the 1990s in its own right.

A limited amount of European generic furniture is found in the American market. Its primitive forms and construction have little appeal. Collectors tend to collect the furniture of the wealthy, not of the peasant and petit bourgeois.

Because of the lack of examples of European generic furniture in the United States, Americans have little understanding or appreciation that many of these forms are prototypes for American pieces. A number of seminal studies have been published abroad, e.g., Bernard D. Cottons's *The English Regional Chair* (Antique Collectors' Club, 1990). Alas, they receive little circulation or attention in the United States.

American Country has introduced some aspects of middle and high–end generic furniture to Americans. English, French, and Mediterranean provincial furniture all enjoyed Country crazes in the 1980s and 1990s. Unfortunately, many of the pieces sent to the American market were made from old parts or were entirely new fabrications; authentic pieces tended to remain in their country of origin.

Although folklorists include generic furniture with the folk art tradition, the vast majority of collectors view folk art furniture as decorated furniture, usually painted, showing regional design characteristics. Once again, a knowledge of European history is required because the European folk furniture of 1810 is vastly different from European folk furniture of 1910.

On the Continent, royal families ruled much of the geographic territory during the eighteenth and nineteenth centuries. Little national loyalty was felt on the local level, perhaps explaining in part why regionalism was so strong. The revolutions at the end of the eighteenth century, in the years immediately before and after 1848, and again in the 1870s, led to a revival of interest in native folk traditions. Especially noteworthy is the Revolution of 1848.

As the modern European nation state evolved, individuals looked to the past for traditions and customs they could use to promote national unity. The final results were highly interpretative. Craft revivals occurred everywhere. Rarely were older pieces and decorations copied exactly. Instead, the end products reflected the taste of the era in which they were created and that era's interpretation of what it felt the past was like.

One must be extremely careful of painted pieces with dates. Many of these pieces were manufactured during these cultural craft revivals and decorated with dates from a much earlier period. Always look closely at construction details and paint tones. Folk furniture always was meant for use. A piece two hundred years old should have the wear and aging characteristics of a piece two hundred years old.

The tradition of painted folk furniture extends throughout Europe, from Norway to Italy. Regional differences are well documented. However, Americans tend to simply lump all this furniture under a single heading, much as I am doing in this book. Until American buyers become more sophisticated and discriminating, this is the approach that will be used in this book.

Reference: Lyndon C. Viel, *Antique Ethnic Furniture*, Wallace-Homestead, 1983.

Bench, chorister's, Continental, carved oak, rectangular plank seat flanked by arched and figural carved trestle supports, chamfered plinth base joined by flat rectangular stretcher, restorations, 42" w, 49" h **825**

Blanket Chest, Continental, 1817, pine, decorated, molded edge on lift lid, dovetailed case, interior till, molded base, polychrome floral panels, inscription and date on blue ground, wrought iron lock, hinges, and side handles, broken hinges, worm holes, edge damage, one end of lid molding missing, 46" w, 24" d, 20" h **500**

Chair, kubbestol, Norwegian, c1900, carved from hollow log, grain painted, rounded curved back, oval wedged seat **625**

Cupboard, corner, hanging, Finnish, c1850, barrel front style, conforming open shelves, shaped opening, pegged construction **625**

Mirror, courting, Northern Europe, 18th

Bench, late 19th C, carved standing bears supporting rectangular seat, 54″ w, 39″ h, $6,600.00. Photograph courtesy of William Doyle Galleries.

C, gabled crest on rectangular frame, polychrome eglomise liner, boxed, 11½″ w, 17½″ h 600

Shelf, hanging, pine, scalloped crest, shaped ends, mortar and pestle holder on single shelf with scalloped apron, towel bar below, old worn finish, age cracks, edge damage, worm holes, 26½″ w, 20½″ h 100

Table
  Cricket, English, pine, circular top, shaped skirt, triangular base with three square tapered legs, refinished, 35″ d, 30¼″ h 275
  Tavern, Alpine, baroque, carved pine and walnut, rectangular cleated triple plank top, geometrically carved frieze on step molded plinth, carved lunette shaped trestle supports, sleigh feet, two straight stretchers, worm holes, restorations, 46″ w, 29″ h 5,000
Truhe, northwest German, gothic, wrought iron mounted oak, rectangular strap hinged top, strap metal decorated top and straight sides, stiles continuing to form supports, extensive wear, restorations, 67½″ w, 32″ h 30,800
Trunk
  Finnish, 1798, humped back, lid underside painted with stylized flower and vegetable decorations, signature and date, interior till, iron straps and hardware 525
  German, humped back, decorated, iron strapwork and lock plate, red and white flowers on blue ground 450
Woodbox, southern Germany, shaped crown headpiece, two upper shelves, horizontal backboards, shaped ends, open box base, molded bottom edge 750

Index to Craftsmen and Manufacturers

Index to Design Styles and Periods